LAST MISSION TO TOKYO

* * *

The Extraordinary Story

of the

Doolittle Raiders

and Their Final Fight

for Justice

MICHEL PARADIS

SIMON & SCHUSTER

New York   London   Toronto   Sydney   New Delhi

Simon & Schuster
1230 Avenue of the Americas
New York, NY 10020

First Simon & Schuster hardcover edition July 2020

SIMON & SCHUSTER and colophon are registered
trademarks of Simon & Schuster, Inc.

For information about special discounts for bulk purchases,
please contact Simon & Schuster Special Sales at 1-866-506-1949
or business@simonandschuster.com.

The Simon & Schuster Speakers Bureau can bring authors to
your live event. For more information or to book an event,
contact the Simon & Schuster Speakers Bureau at 1-866-248-3049
or visit our website at www.simonspeakers.com.

Interior design by Lewelin Polanco

Manufactured in the United States of America

1   3   5   7   9   10   8   6   4   2

Library of Congress Cataloging-in-Publication Data is available.

ISBN 978-1-5011-0471-8
ISBN 978-1-5011-0474-9 (ebook)

To Zelda XIV

THE MURDER

* * *

How do you tell a man that he will be killed tomorrow? Sotojiro Tatsuta confronted this question on the evening of Wednesday, October 14, 1942. He had just gotten off the phone with his boss in Nanking. As the warden of the Jiangwan Military Prison, the Japanese Army's brig on the outskirts of Shanghai, this execution would be his responsibility.

Tatsuta gathered the three American prisoners who would soon hear this news together. Higher-ups had spared his five other Americans, who were still back in their cells. Only these three men would be shot through the head the next morning. Tatsuta's job was to organize it all, and at this moment, his job was to tell them.

A skinny man with a gold tooth that tended to flash when he talked, Tatsuta was conflicted. Yes, these men were his enemies—or at least the enemies of Japan. Yes, they had been duly convicted of atrocities against his people. And yes, only these three men would have to die tomorrow, instead of all eight, thanks to the mercy of Emperor Hirohito. But these kinds of rationalizations, all perfectly good and reasonable, were hard to keep at the front of his mind as he looked at the still living, breathing, blinking young men—barely more than boys, really—whose every hope, dream, fear, ambition, and debt would be soon rendered moot. A single bullet was scheduled to break through their foreheads, scramble their brains, and leave nothing but paperwork. Tatsuta would inventory their belongings, and see to it that their bodies made it to the crematorium, and they would be gone.

Standing before them with his translator at his side, Tatsuta stalled with small talk. He showed some snapshots of his wife and kids back in Japan and they shared their own family photos. None was married, but William Farrow, who stood nearly a foot taller than Tatsuta, showed him the picture of a girl named Lib Sims. A lean six foot three with blond hair and a square jaw, Farrow had an all-American look that fit his earnestness. Lib, he said, was going to be his wife when he got back home.

The war had been raging for nearly a year. Japan was still on top, though its victory looked less certain than it had back in April, when these Americans had supposedly bombed Tokyo. They were his enemies. He was theirs. But sitting face-to-face, looking at the picture of a girl who would have to find someone else to marry, made the war rather remote.

When the eight Americans had been brought to Jiangwan two months earlier, Tatsuta had been told that they had attacked schools, temples, and hospitals in Japan, killing many civilians. To look at them, though, it was hard to believe. Something about the youngest of them, a nineteen-year-old sergeant by the name of Harold A. Spatz, couldn't help but remind Tatsuta of his oldest son, who was just twenty-one years old and off fighting with the Japanese Army somewhere.

After chatting for a bit, all Tatsuta could bring himself to say was that "something might happen" tomorrow, and he gave the three of them some blank sheets of paper to write out their wills. He promised that if anything did happen, he would personally make sure that they were forwarded to the Red Cross. And he suggested that they also take the chance to write some letters home. He left for the night and, on his way out, told one of his men to give the three Americans some of the food he had bought in Shanghai so they could have a nice last meal.

Tatsuta's translator, Caesar dos Remedios, stayed behind and, once Tatsuta was gone, put things more bluntly: the three of them, were being executed as war criminals. The letters home would be their last and it would be a good idea to give a little "top hat" to the Japanese about how good their treatment had been. Saying something nice would be seen as a good gesture and would help make things better for the other five Americans after they were gone.

Before Remedios left them to their final thoughts, Billy Farrow stopped him. Farrow emptied his pockets and gave the handful to Remedios. It was not much: a Social Security card, a Red Cross card, $110 in Bank of America traveler's checks, and his photo of Lib. "I hope you might make use of them," Farrow said.

The next morning, Tatsuta went out to the old Chinese cemetery, just outside the redbrick walls of the headquarters of Japan's 13th Army, the "Noboru Unit," where the overgrown grass was littered with lost golf balls from the links next door. Japanese military tradition called for a rope to be laid around the execution site to purify it. As his men planted three wooden crosses in a line, whose crossbars were about waist high, and placed straw mats at the foot of each cross, Tatsuta set up a small table for incense and flowers.

Once everything was ready, Tatsuta ordered his men to bring the three condemned Americans out to the cemetery, and before long a crowd gathered at the execution grounds. All sorts of people from the 13th Army came. Major Itsuro Hata, the prosecutor who had won the death sentences against the three men, was there to serve as the official witness, along with his clerk, a medical officer, and an interpreter. Senior officers from Japan's secret police, the Kempeitai, had even driven the hour from Shanghai to attend. Everyone knew that this was a historic moment. These Americans were the first foreigners ever to succeed in attacking Japan. Everyone was there to see that Japan had not let them get away with it.

It was early evening, but still light out. The three young Americans were helped off the truck. The medical officer examined each man and pronounced him "physically sound" for execution. They were then led in a procession to the crosses that had been planted over the straw mats. Major Hata read the judgment against the three men aloud: William Farrow, Dean Hallmark, and Harold Spatz, enemy airmen, all found guilty of atrocities against civilians; sentenced to death. He then added a few consoling words and bowed deeply to them as a sign of respect.

A firing squad—three riflemen, three alternates, and three men to stand guard—assembled stiffly about thirty feet away. There was one bullet for each man. Tatsuta and his men then made Farrow, Hallmark, and Spatz kneel on the straw mats and tied each man by his forearms to the crossbar behind him. They knotted white handkerchiefs around their faces and painted a black mark on the point between each man's eyes where the bullet was to go.

The commander of the firing squad called out, "Attention!"

The squad snapped to attention.

"Face the target!"

The squad turned crisply toward the three crosses.

The commander raised his arm.

"Prepare!"

The squad took up a squatting position and took aim at their targets. A moment passed.

The commander brought down his arm.

"Fire!"

The squad's rifles let out a near-simultaneous crack that echoed in the air. Farrow, Hallmark, and Spatz slumped by their elbows.

The medical officer stepped forward to inspect each body and confirmed that two were dead. The third, though, still had a slight pulse.

The crowd waited awkwardly as the medical officer peeled fragments of sticky handkerchief from each man's forehead and his assistants got to work cleaning their wounds, occasionally rechecking the one with the lingering pulse as they dabbed away the blood. After five minutes or so, the medical officer confirmed that the third man's pulse was gone and pronounced them all dead.

Tatsuta instructed his men to untie the bodies from the crosses and load them into coffins. The bodies in the coffins were laid side by side and, amidst the streams of incense smoke, the assembled crowd gave a final salute before scattering for the evening.

Tatsuta got into his truck and drove back to his prison, leaving his men to cart the coffins to the crematorium. He went into the storeroom and ordered the clerk to bring him Farrow, Hallmark, and Spatz's belongings. As he sorted through them, he picked up one of the bomber jackets and inspected the name tag: "D E HALLMARK." It was a fine jacket, the famous A-2 flight jacket: good horsehide on the outside, insulated with cotton on the inside, and with a metal zipper all the way up the front with a flap to keep the draft out. A jacket like that was hard to come by, and Tatsuta thought it might make a good fishing jacket. It was too big for his slight frame, so he gave it to Caesar dos Remedios and told him to take it into Shanghai to have it tailored down. Tatsuta also wanted the name tag taken off.

Tatsuta's thoughts turned to his remaining five American prisoners. Earlier that day, they had been informed that their lives had been spared thanks to the mercy of the emperor and that their sentences had been commuted to life imprisonment with "special treatment." Winter was coming, and Tatsuta was considering letting them bunk together. He had kept them in solitary cells since their transfer to Jiangwan that August. That was according to the rules. But the raised wooden floors could get frigid and the ceilings were also quite high, which made the cells hard to keep warm. Tatsuta could also tell that the isolation was hard on them, and if the emperor had seen fit to show them a little mercy, why not do the same? They caused him no trouble. They were friendly, even. And they were, after all, Japan's prisoners for life.

THE WITNESS

* * *

ONE

Chase Jay Nielsen joined the US Army Air Corps as a flying cadet in 1939. For a twenty-two-year-old, it was a steady paycheck with a bit of glamour. Nielsen also had a head for numbers; he was always ready to impress a room with his ability to add large digits together without a paper and pencil. Being a flight navigator suited his natural talents, and the only real risks were the inevitable dangers that came with hurtling through the air in a machine whose basic concept had been perfected only thirty years earlier.

Now, though, there was a war on. Japan's surprise attack on Pearl Harbor on December 7, 1941, had made Nielsen's life more complicated, and not just because his dark hair, dark eyebrows, and swarthy complexion made it easy at first glance to mistake him for Japanese. Nielsen was engaged to marry a good Mormon girl by the name of Thora Ricks that December. Stationed with the Seventeenth Bomb Group in Pendleton, Oregon, the start of the war meant that Nielsen was stuck doing patrols along the Pacific Coast for enemy submarines at the very time he was supposed to be getting married. Undeterred, Thora made the trek all the way to Oregon to elope, which Nielsen could relish as a sign of her love and devotion despite the thousand miles between them. But it also made Nielsen a relative rarity for the flyboys of his generation. He was a husband.

In February, Nielsen and the rest of the Seventeenth Bomb Group received an enigmatic request: "Volunteers for a dangerous mission." The request was worded perfectly to seduce restless men of a certain age, who in every generation are convinced that theirs is the first for whom the laws of mortality do not apply. Such men ruled the ranks of the Seventeenth Bomb Group, and Nielsen, though now a family man, was as unable to resist as the others. It was a difficult choice. Once married, Nielsen knew that a Mormon man's first responsibility was always to his family, so he broke the news to Thora as gently as he could: he had a special assignment, and she might not hear from him for a while.

Nielsen soon found himself stationed at Eglin Field, near Pensacola, Florida, with more than 120 other flyboys from around the country who had been just as seduced by the prospect of such an enigmatic risk. No details were provided to explain the strange training regimen they were all being put through. But Nielsen could take comfort in knowing that any risks he would be asked to take were finely calculated ones. The man requesting volunteers was Jimmy Doolittle.

* * *

Short, balding, and bubbling over with energy, James H. Doolittle embodied the popular conception of the flyboy—lunatics with no sense of mortality who rode airplanes like unbroken horses—but he had somehow always survived. A lieutenant colonel in the US Army Air Force, Doolittle had been a junior officer at the end of the First World War in what was then called the Army Air Service. By the time he had his wings, it was too late to take part in the Hell's Angels era of sky jousting, when pilots' mortality rate was one in five in combat and nearly half if accidents were included. But that fateful lack of action allowed Doolittle to become something of a celebrity stunt pilot in what soon became the era of aviation. And he did it by always making the numbers add up.

Doolittle was famous for getting both air traffic tickets for "unlawful aerial acrobatics" and a doctorate in aeronautical engineering at MIT. He developed cockpit navigation instrumentation that ensured that piloting decisions were made based on data, not the gut. And throughout his career, the very stunts that made him look insanely fearless were, in truth, proofs of scientific concepts. In 1928, he even went so far as to blackout the windshield of his airplane before taking off from Mitchel Field on Long Island, flying fifteen miles overhead, and landing smoothly without ever being able to see a foot in front of him. It was proof that he could calculate his way out of any risk. He could even fly blind.

As war had begun to loom the summer before, Doolittle had left a lucrative job with the Shell Oil Company to mobilize again and became a close advisor to General Henry "Hap" Arnold, the commanding general of the US Army Air Forces. He was a week away from his forty-fifth birthday when Japan attacked Pearl Harbor. President Franklin D. Roosevelt was impatient for a counterattack, but when Special Aviation Project No. 1 was proposed, there was no technology in the US arsenal that could reliably drop a bomb on Japan. Arnold asked Doolittle to make the numbers add up.

Doolittle's solution was to get an aircraft carrier as close to the Japanese mainland as possible, launch a squadron of modified B-25B "Billy Mitchell" Army bombers on a one-way raid over Japan, and then fly them on to a landing strip in China that—hopefully—Chiang Kai-shek, the leader of the US-allied Kuomintang, would set up. That was the only way the brute arithmetic of weight, fuel, and time would add up, and just barely at that. Doolittle had to replace every unnecessary ounce of his B-25Bs with fuel tanks, which meant fewer guns, fewer defenses, and fewer provisions for contingencies. The tail guns were even replaced by broomsticks.

Once assembled in Florida, Nielsen and the rest of Doolittle's volunteers trained for weeks on the magic number: five-hundred feet. They had to get off the ground in five-hundred feet, not the near half-mile of runway that the B-25B had been designed to take off from. Early on, the best the crews could manage was six hundred feet, so Doolittle kept drilling them, looking for any extra piece of unnecessary equipment to dump to save weight or any extra bit of finesse that could get the wheels off the ground a few feet sooner.

By the end of March, it was time to go and Doolittle led them all in a test flight of their flying gas cans across the country to Alameda, California. He chose to fly the lead plane himself, and selected seventy-nine men to join him, the happy few to crew the sixteen planes that could be loaded by crane onto the deck of the USS *Hornet*, one of the few aircraft carriers that was mission ready in the US fleet.

Nielsen was tapped to be the navigator on the sixth plane off the deck, which he and the crew nicknamed the *Green Hornet*. Nielsen's crewmates were a cross section of a remote America he would have never known had the war not brought them all together. There was the pilot, Dean "Jungle Jim" Hallmark, a thick-necked Texan Baptist who had played football for Auburn. A flyboy if ever there was one, Hallmark had a loud laugh and a flush that never left his cheeks, which gave the impression that his blood vessels couldn't contain some fire that was coursing through him. His copilot, Robert Meder, was a study in contrasts. Meder had a basketball player's lanky frame, a subtle wit, and a heavy brow that gave the impression he was always thinking ahead of everyone. The son of Austrian immigrants, Meder was from Cleveland, which to men like Nielsen and Hallmark made him seem as urbane as the most Boston Brahmin. Then there was their bombardier, William Dieter, who came from a town as small as Vail, Iowa, and their gunner, Donald "Fitz" Fitzmaurice, who came from a city as big as Lincoln, Nebraska. The two became fast friends as the *Green Hornet*'s pair of good Catholic boys.

On April 1, 1942, they all boarded the *Hornet* with the flyboy's nonchalance about the dangerous mission for which they had volunteered and disembarked the following day from San Francisco Bay into a dense fog. No one, except for Doolittle and a few other high-ranking officers, knew the precise nature of their mission, and the sailors of America's Navy were less than pleased to share their beautiful new aircraft carrier with a hoard of flyboys, who were rowdy, dressed in all manner of wrinkled shirts, jackets, and trousers, and strutted about in unpolished shoes as if they were on a leisure cruise. But resentments faded away two days into the voyage, when the *Hornet*'s loudspeaker broke in: "This force is bound for Tokyo."

It was official. After the surprise attack on Pearl Harbor and the humiliating defeats the Allies had suffered in the Pacific from Shanghai to the Philippines, the United States was finally taking the fight to Japan. And Doolittle and his men, eighty men who would forever be celebrated as the "Doolittle Raiders," were going to be the ones to do it.

* * *

Doolittle had scheduled his raid for the evening of April 18, 1942. It would be a Saturday, and they would be protected by the cover of darkness as they made their bombing runs across Japan. Doolittle organized a series of briefings with the help of a naval intelligence officer, Stephen Jurika, who had been stationed in the US Embassy in Tokyo before the war and had even been awarded the Order of the Rising Sun by Emperor Hirohito, a medal Jurika asked Doolittle to return to the emperor on the nose of one of his bombs.

Doolittle handed out the target list and let the pilots select which targets they wanted to bomb. The pilots had drawn cards to see who got to bomb the Imperial Palace, but Doolittle disappointed them with the news that it was off limits. Doolittle had contemplated bombing the palace but had decided against it after reflecting on the German Blitz on London. The Germans had attacked the city for weeks, destroying docks, supplies, factories, and houses, and had put a slow but sure drain on public morale. The public's mood had changed, though, when the Germans had hit Buckingham Palace. Public sentiment rallied around the idea that "if the king can take it, we can take it," and Doolittle did not want to give the Japanese a reason to rally around the emperor.

Hallmark chose some steel mills in downtown Tokyo, and Nielsen was handed two-and-a-half-square-foot target maps of Japan to study. Each map covered only a small area and showed the highways, railroad tracks, and other geographical details around each target. Doolittle had instructed them to conduct low-level bombing to frustrate Japan's air defenses. But that created a large trade-off in terms of accuracy and navigation. At a normal bombing altitude of 10,000 or 20,000 feet, Nielsen could easily track their position. Navigating at only a few hundred feet off the ground, though, was like trying to find an address in a new city while speeding at 150 miles per hour.

To help, Jurika marked off Tokyo's major buildings. "The Diet Building," he said, "was something that you could fly over, go a very short distance, and be in Kawasaki, perhaps three or four minutes, no more than that, on a bombing run, and the first major point under you would be the Tamagawa River, and just beyond that would be a major petro-chemical works. You don't have to estimate, you don't have to use a stopwatch. You have these major physical points to look at."

Nielsen studied the aerial photographs and maps, trying to prepare the approach they would make and the landmarks they would see on the ground before their targets came up. "Fly over these and go on an absolute course," Jurika explained. "You then pass over a river and the next big complex that you see, with chimneys belching yellow smoke, that's where to lay your eggs."

There was less ability to prepare for when they got to China. Chiang Kai-shek had supposedly set up on a landing strip in Quzhou that they could locate by sending out a call—"57"—on a special radio frequency. But if they did not make it that far, Jurika was pessimistic. "If captured dropping bombs on Japan, the chances of survival would be awfully slim;

very, very, slim." They should expect he said to be "paraded through the streets as Exhibit A, and then tried by some sort of a kangaroo court and probably publicly beheaded."

Still, Jurika offered some tips for staying alive. He taught them Chinese phrases such as *Lusau hoo metwa fugi* ("I'm an American") and explained that they could tell Chinese soldiers apart from Japanese soldiers based upon their footwear, since the Japanese wore socks that separated the big toe from the rest of the toes.

The day before the raid, Nielsen sent Thora a letter. "Tomorrow is the big day," he wrote, hinting that he was about to go on a dangerous but very important mission. "Keep your chin up and don't worry," he assured her. "I have a feeling I'll be coming back."

*   *   *

At 3:10 a.m. on April 18, 1942, the *Hornet* made radar contact with a Japanese picket boat, the *Nitto Maru*. They were still seven hundred nautical miles from Japan; too far to get deep enough into China. Doolittle fought for more time to get just a few more nautical miles closer, but Admiral William "Bull" Halsey, Jr., the commander responsible for the well-being of the USS *Hornet*, was unwilling to take any more risks with one of the few operational aircraft carriers the Navy still had, not to mention the lives of the sailors on board. With the sun about to rise over the horizon behind them, Halsey gave the order to launch.

By daybreak, the sea was rough and the wind blew across the deck at 40 knots, causing the *Hornet* to pitch so violently that it kept taking water over the bow. Doolittle took the lead and, at 8:21 a.m., sped his B-25B down the slippery deck and up into the clouds in just 467 feet. Minutes later, it was the *Green Hornet*'s turn, and when the flagman gave the signal, Hallmark got up in just about 500 feet.

As they made their way to Japan, the weather cleared. Nielsen navigated the *Green Hornet* to their targets in downtown Tokyo with a northern approach over Japanese farmland. A bit of flak fired up from some antiaircraft gunners on the ground, but nothing caused them any trouble. All the anxieties that had quietly built up over months swelled into giddiness as they realized how easy it all was turning out to be. As Dieter dropped their incendiary clusters over Tokyo's suburbs, Hallmark led them all in a chorus of the song "I Don't Want to Set the World on Fire." In the ballad's slow, swaying rhythm, they all crooned:

I don't want to set the world . . . on . . . fire
I just want to start . . . a flame in your heart.

But as they escaped toward China, flying low over the water, the weather turned again. The clouds and rain came in and the sun began to set in front of them. Nielsen kept track of their position and began to doubt that the *Green Hornet* had enough fuel to get over land, much less to the rendezvous site Chiang Kai-shek had supposedly set up for them in Quzhou.

Hallmark made the call. It was time to strap on their "Mae Wests," life preservers that wrapped around the neck and inflated two large balloons at the top of their chests. As soon as land was in sight, they would make a water landing and paddle to shore on the emergency raft.

By the time land was visible, it was nearly dark. Hallmark slowly edged the *Green Hornet's* belly closer and then closer still to the blackening surface of the East China Sea. The altimeter wound down like the hands of a clock going back in time. When it reached midnight, the *Green Hornet* would be at sea level. The attitude indicator, the circle on the left side of the instrument panel whose top half was sky blue and whose bottom half was ground green, wobbled as Hallmark adjusted the yoke by inches to keep the wings level. The hands on the altimeter wound down to midnight, and Hallmark lined up the belly of the plane to skid across the tips of the waves as smoothly as a big fat B-25B Billy Mitchell could.

But then, with only a few seconds left, the engines started kicking out. The propellers sputtered, first on the left and then on the right, a delay that made the shaky attitude indicator spasm. The *Green Hornet's* left wing clipped the waves. At the speed they were going, the water was only just softer than concrete and the impact tore the wing clean off, whipped the fuselage onto its side, and slammed its glass nose into the blackness of the water.

Nielsen smacked his head and came to waist deep in sea water that was flooding into the navigator compartment. The *Green Hornet* was sinking with him inside, so he pulled himself out through the cockpit. Once on the surface, he saw Fitz, the gunner, floating limply with a deep hole in his head that was draining blood. Dieter had been seated in the plane's glass nose, which had crushed him inside before spitting him out to the surface. Now he was floating by the life preserver around his neck, telling Nielsen "I'm hurt all over."

Nielsen tried to regroup with Hallmark and Meder on the sinking fuselage. Meder pulled out the emergency raft and yanked its cord to inflate it. But a combination of Meder's anxious strength and shoddy manufacturing ripped the cord clean off. Then, as Meder scrambled to fill the raft with the hand pump, a wave washed over them.

Nielsen bobbed to the surface. He could tell that Hallmark and Meder were still alive and floating nearby. Whether Fitz and Dieter were was less clear. But soon the tide scattered the five of them into the cold darkness. And before long, Nielsen could no longer hear anyone's cries but his own over the drumming of the rain.

The next morning, Nielsen found himself in Juexi, a seaside town on the Xiangshan Peninsula, south of Shanghai. Nielsen, Hallmark, and Meder had all been rescued by some locals who had seen the crash the night before. The bodies of Fitz and Dieter had just been found washed up on the shore.

Juexi's mayor, Shimiao Yang, was welcoming and seemingly sympathetic to all they had endured. He had coffins made so that Nielsen, Hallmark, and Meder could give Fitz and Dieter a proper funeral. At a scenic spot on a hill that overlooked the coast, they packed sawdust around the bodies, lowered the coffins into the ground, and said a prayer.

Yang had assured them that he was trying to find a way for the three of them to get to safety, but it wasn't long before some Chinese guerrillas came around. Nielsen could never figure out who had tipped them off. And soon the guerrillas were joined by a cadre of Japanese regulars, whose interpreter greeted Nielsen, Hallmark, and Meder with surprising cordiality.

"You now Japanese prisoner," Nielsen heard him say. "You no worry. We treat you fine."

TWO

The Japanese soldiers marched Nielsen, Hallmark, and Meder in a caravan through the hilly Chinese countryside and then to a dock in the coastal city of Ningbo, where they stayed the night before boarding a ship north. All along the way, the Japanese Army kept its promise to treat them fine, giving the three of them as much to eat and drink as they could stomach.

Two days later, they were in Shanghai. It was early afternoon, and as soon as Nielsen stepped off the boat, he sensed that things had changed. He was blindfolded, separated from Hallmark and Meder, and driven somewhere in the back seat of a car. He could hear the commotion of Shanghai all around him but had little sense of it before it faded.

An hour later, the car stopped, and Nielsen listened carefully. From the sounds of things, he guessed he was at an airport.

Yanked out of the car, Nielsen was rushed down corridors, through doorways, and past men shouting over noise. Things were happening quickly, and suddenly he found himself pushed into a chair. His blindfold was taken off, and as he looked about, he saw that he was seated before a table in a small room. A little frosted window in the corner refracted the afternoon sunlight and cast shadows on the faces of what seemed like a dozen Japanese soldiers, who were all intently looking at him.

The pace of the questioning that followed was intense. Why was Nielsen in China? How had he gotten there? Where were the others? Nielsen answered with his name, rank, and serial number.

"We have methods of making you talk" Nielsen remembered the

translator saying. One of the guards gave him a kick to the shin with the edge of his hobnailed boot. It drew blood, and the pain was sharp.

"You understand, nobody in your country know you live. We have torture you to death your people think you missing in action. You want to talk now?"

Nielsen resisted the best he could that afternoon, as one well-practiced method of making him talk followed another. As the interrogator asked and reasked his questions, his goons went to work.

At one point, they forced Nielsen to kneel on the floor, fixed a bamboo pole behind his knees, and pushed him back until his hamstrings pressed into his calves. The pole strained against his ligaments, and soon it felt as if his kneecaps were just floating between his bones. Nielsen could barely breathe, let alone scream, as the goons started storming on his thighs. Boot-stomp, boot-stomp, boot-stomp, mashing down on his thighs and sending bolts of pain through every part of him until he went numb, even to the bamboo pole, and became seized by the thought that they were going to pull him apart. The only thing that kept him sane was the little frosted window in the corner where he could see sunlight still coming through. "If I could just get outside," he thought, "I might have a chance to make a break for it."

But that chance never came. Instead, grosser forms of brutality yielded to subtler tortures that were even harder to withstand. Legs still numb, Nielsen was plopped back into the chair, and his interrogator drew out a few thin sticks that looked like skinny pencils. Nielsen suddenly realized his wrist had been pinned to the table, and the interrogator slid the tips of those skinny pencils clean through the webbing between Nielsen's fingers and down into his nerves.

The goon pinning his wrist to the table then squeezed Nielsen's fingers together as the interrogator slid and twisted the sticks in and out, side to side, and in circles as each question came. The more he twisted, the more blood squeezed up between Nielsen's knuckles and the more deafening the pain radiating through his nerves became.

When the interrogator ran out of questions, he left Nielsen to hang for the night by his hands. The hook was so high on the wall that Nielsen was barely able to scratch the floor with his toes. His arms pulled, first at the shoulder, then at the elbow, and then at the wrist, as he dangled. The more he twisted, the sharper the pain became. It was hard to breathe. Nielsen shouted for help, but was just left to dangle there until the next morning.

The same Japanese goons who had strung him up dragged him out and reunited him with Dean Hallmark and Robert Meder, as they were all packed up to be flown to Tokyo. A no-talking rule was strictly enforced, but Hallmark flashed Nielsen a thumbs-up all the same.

* * *

The two months Nielsen spent in Tokyo went by quickly. The questioning was constant, but things seemed professional. The main interrogator was a Japanese lawyer, who looked to be about sixty and sported a potbelly. He never gave his name, but he claimed to have gone to Stanford and to like America, particularly American girls. He was chatty, friendly even and, if nothing else, talking to him broke up the monotony of sitting alone in a cell all day.

It was in Tokyo that Nielsen learned that the crew of William Farrow's *Bat Out of Hell* had also been captured. Farrow's crew was just as much a sampling of 1940s America as Hallmark's had been. In addition to Harold Spatz, Farrow's gunner and the baby of the group, there was his copilot, Robert Hite, a tall man with a rather birdlike face that made him look ten years older than he was. The most that could be said of Hite's internal life was that he strongly identified the plains of central Texas with home. George Barr, Farrow's navigator, was a six-foot-two orphan from Brooklyn whose shock of red hair made him something of a freak of nature to the Japanese. Opposite Barr and Hite in seemingly every way was Jacob DeShazer, their bombardier, who stood five foot eight in shoes and was as mild-mannered as anyone from Madras, Oregon, would be expected to be. Farrow's crew had bailed out over China but had all been captured within a day.

The first time the eight lost Doolittle Raiders were together was on June 20, 1942, when the guards took them all out into a courtyard. It was the first time any of them had seen the sun in two months. The Japanese had decided to ship them back to China as a group, and after a three-day voyage, they found themselves in Shanghai.

From the city's docks, they were driven through the gray stone outer walls that surrounded Bridge House, an apartment building that the Kempeitai had repurposed into its Shanghai headquarters. Bridge House's ground floor had been converted from servants' quarters into a dungeon of twenty-six makeshift cells that measured no more than ten by twenty feet. The windows had even been painted over to enhance the feeling that one was entering a salty pit lit by incessant electric lights that only went out when the power failed.

The eight of them were led to Cell 5, a ten-by-fifteen-foot wooden cell already packed with fifteen other men and women. The overcrowding throughout Bridge House was rampant. As many two dozen men and women were packed into nearly every cell.

To Nielsen's relief, their cellmates were led out after a few days, leaving the eight of them to themselves. The extra room meant that they could all lie down to rest at the same time. But they never dared to. At night, they had to take turns playing guard duty against the rats, who thought nothing of taking a bite out of a sleeping prisoner. And when laying his head down to sleep, Nielsen had to block out the sound of the big mamma rat who had birthed a litter that now squirmed under the wooden floorboards.

Everything inside Bridge House seemed to be made out of wood. The cells had wooden walls, wooden bars around the perimeter, and a raised wooden floor with a wooden bucket in the corner for a toilet. In the summer heat, the humidity caused the wooden walls, which leaked when it rained, to sweat as mosquitoes, flies, and centipedes invaded between the boards and Nielsen's hands and face soon swelled from all manner of festering bites.

Even more than the filth, Bridge House was notorious for its guards. Just boys mostly, barely peasants back home in Japan, they found themselves with unaccountable power over hundreds of men and women whose language they could not understand and, by virtue of being Japan's enemies, whose humanity seemed at best alien and diminished.

Nielsen was spared much of the brutality that was inflicted, seemingly at random, on the others. The guards once responded to Robert Hite's implacability by chopping a chunk out of his scalp with a scabbard. Hallmark and Meder were taken up to the infamous fifth floor, where the Kempeitai did its torture-enhanced "interrogations" in which inmates were routinely waterboarded, pulled into stress positions, or hung from the ceiling. Both came back limp.

Then there was the starvation. Breakfast every day was a small cup of congee, a starchy rice water that had no flavor and was the consistency of snot. It was the only food until 5:30 p.m., when dinner was served; four ounces of dried bread or rice and a sip from a common cup of tea. All eight of them lost weight fast, even after they realized in early August that the guards could be bribed to bring more food with the American dollars they still had in their pockets.

Hallmark had become obsessed by thoughts of food. He dreamed of the dinners he would be having back home of smothered steaks and fried potatoes with banana pudding and blackberry cobbler and a big old slice of syrup pie and some apricot pie and then, after a good night's sleep, biscuits and cream gravy with bacon and eggs and stewed apricots on the side.

Hallmark succeeded in bribing one of Bridge House's guards to smuggle him a slab of beefsteak, but it hit his stomach the wrong way. Before long, he was bursting his bowels into the wooden shit bucket they all shared a few times every hour. The stink and filth became overwhelming, but the guards did nothing until the day he collapsed. A doctor rushed in, gave him some kind of injection, and put him on a strict diet of apple cider and a horrid vegetable soup. Hallmark was forbidden to drink water, but the cider was bitter and he would defiantly sneak a sip of water whenever it came around. As the weeks went by, Hallmark's weight dropped from 200 pounds to a listless 140.

As hard as it all was, they still had one another. During the day, they passed the time by playing games such as "To Tell the Truth" or "Password" or shaking out their blankets in the middle of the floor and competing to see who could catch the most black fleas and white lice that crawled out. A louse was worth five points, and though a flea only earned one point, Nielsen developed a strategy for racking up points with fleas by wetting his fingers before going in for the catch. Meder even came up with a mealtime game, in which they would trade their cups of soup and bowls of rice back and forth in a duck-duck-goose lottery, so that someone might end up with two bowls of rice or two cups of soup. They even scratched their names onto the wall with the note, "We crashed!"

The solidarity gave them the comfort with one another to compare notes on what they had been through. They commiserated about the Japanese methods of trying to make them talk. Three of them had been subjected to the notorious waterboard, Hallmark and Meder when they had been taken up to Bridge House's fifth floor and George Barr soon after he had been captured. And they all remembered the potbellied interrogator from Tokyo, whom they nicknamed "Well-Well" for his verbal tic of saying "well, well" as he looked for the right English words to say what he wanted to say.

*   *   *

At the end of August, they were all told to go and get themselves cleaned up. Ordinarily, the most they had was the rare chance to rinse themselves with the water pump in Bridge House's courtyard. But this time they were led up to the fourth-floor bathtub, where there was hot running water. They all enjoyed it, but Hite luxuriated long enough to go through one and a half bars of soap. When he was done, he said, he could not "remember a kinder feeling than the soothing wet warmth of that tub."

Once they all had gotten themselves cleaned up, the Kempeitai loaded them onto an open truck and drove them to the Japanese 13th Army's headquarters in Jiangwan. The hour's drive north up Tazang Motor Road in the fresh air was the first truly pleasant moment Nielsen had enjoyed since leaving the deck of the *Hornet*. The landscape north of Shanghai was a patchwork of green fields punctuated by the occasional picturesque cottage. Washed by the summer air, it was a sight to see how beautiful China could be outside the walls of Bridge House.

Soon the truck pulled up to the gates of a brick garrison, which abutted a golf course and was marked with a sign that read, "Headquarters Japanese 13th Army, Shanghai Area." Through the gates were large modern buildings, some with pagoda tile roofs in the Chinese neoclassical style, surrounded by meticulously manicured gardens with vegetables, assorted flowers, and a meditation pond, complete with a stone lantern that cast reflections from the center. The odd Japanese soldier could be seen milling about half naked outside a bathhouse, the exterior wall lined with brushes each of which was on a designated hook in precise rows.

The eight of them hopped off the truck, except for Dean Hallmark, who had to be carried off on a stretcher. They were all then ushered into a crowded L-shaped courtroom with seven or eight Japanese officers arrayed along a judge's bench. People talked back in forth in Japanese.

The interpreter was a chubby lieutenant whose English was surprisingly good, though he was oddly dressed in tweed and golf socks that seemed to match his British accent. He was nice enough, but he struggled to give them the gist of what was being said. All the while, Hallmark stayed lying on his stretcher as flies buzzed around him, and the rest of them did their best to stay on their feet. At one point, George Barr almost collapsed in the August heat, but an alert Japanese soldier jumped in to catch him and saw to it that he got a chair.

The officer in the middle of the judge's bench spoke at them in Japanese, and at one point, it was clear to Nielsen that he was being asked a question. The interpreter leaned in and told him to give his life history since high school. Nielsen complied, as did all the others, including Hallmark, who stayed lying down while he talked.

After a bit more talking back and forth, it was all over. They were taken outside the courtroom to pose for pictures. A Japanese officer took a few solo shots of William Farrow in his bomber jacket and then lined the rest of the men up as a group. Hallmark was then loaded back onto the truck, while Nielsen and the rest were led into Jiangwan's brig.

The brig was little more than a kennel. The cells had high ceilings that made them feel even narrower than they already were, and a light bulb dangled above a small window eight feet above the latrine hatch. A Japanese guard led them each to a separate cell and made a show of telling them the rules. Nielsen could not understand a word of what he said, but the guard seemed content in having done his job and left them alone.

Then, on a foggy morning in the middle of October, Nielsen was taken back into the crowded L-shaped courtroom by guards dressed in ceremonial uniforms. Meder, Hite, DeShazer, and Barr were also there, but Hallmark, Farrow, and Spatz were missing, and when asked where they were, all Nielsen could get were rumors that the three of them had been taken to another prison camp. There was no telling what the truth was, though, because when the hearing started, the courtroom interpreter nervously stepped forward to read from a document that made the blood run cold.

"For bombing and strafing school areas you have been sentenced to death," he said as a wave of unease spread through the room. "But, through the gracious majesty of the Emperor, you have been spared to life imprisonment with special treatment." The five of them were then ushered out of the courtroom as quickly as they had been brought in and taken back to the prison, where Nielsen returned to the routine of spending day after day alone in his cell with the light bulb hanging above.

Things got better in early December, when the warden allowed them to live together in one big cell. But then that spring, on the one-year anniversary of their raid as it happened, they were moved around again. Nielsen was shackled, blindfolded, and flown with Meder, Hite, DeShazer, and Barr to what looked like a new prison in Nanking, which one of the guards said had been built especially for the five of them.

*   *   *

Nanking Prison was located in the northeast of the city whose very name had become synonymous with Japanese brutality. The walls were high and built of concrete and brick, and Nielsen was deposited into a nine-by-twelve-foot cell that had a small window seven feet from the floor.

The cell's thick wooden door had a small porthole that would snap open and closed each time a guard checked on him or handed him some food, which was better than it had been at Jiangwan but was terribly monotonous. Three times a day, through the porthole, Nielsen was handed the same half pint of soup, pint of rice, and half pint of cool tea.

On the bright side, the meals brought the "tin cup news" broadcast. After the porthole closed, Nielsen would peek under his teacup to see if there were any updates that someone somewhere had etched onto the bottom with the edge of a button. The cups invariably made their way all around the prison, so over time it was possible to get a sense of who else was being held. One time the cup reported "Connie G. Battles, United States Marines." Another time, Nielsen got a lift when he read "Russians on German border."

As everywhere else, the guards in Nanking Prison were a mixed bag. Some were nice—one even sneaked them some extra food now and again—but others thought nothing of throwing a shove or a sharp whack with a baton. The only real power the five of them had was the fact that the guards didn't understand a word of English. That allowed them to increase their collective resistance by calling the guards nicknames they came up with during the few brief minutes they got each day to exercise together. Meder was always the best at nailing the perfect nickname for a guard. There were "Big Ugly" and "Little Ugly," "Goon," "Mule," "Goofy," and "Cyclops," named for his enormous Coke-bottle glasses. The nice guard was honored with the nickname "Sportsman."

Meder was always looking for ways to keep up their morale. He developed a system of Morse code so they could send each other messages through the walls: tap for a dot, scratch for a dash. It was a tedious way to have a conversation, but it gave them all the chance to learn more about each other, to share their dreams, and to bitch about the indignities of daily life in a way that made them feel less alone.

As summer turned to fall, however, Nielsen could tell that something wasn't right. Meder was finding it increasingly hard to hold eye contact and was moving awkwardly. He couldn't keep down food, and when he did, it went right through him two or three times a day in a sticky, muddy mess. By the middle of October, Meder's legs started to swell. The prison doctor tried giving him some vitamin B shots and glucose in addition to pills and yeast packets that the nurse started bringing around every few days. But he just got thinner and weaker.

Even as he wasted away, Meder kept his daily appointment with the rest of them in the exercise yard. He would work his arms a bit or stretch and keep up his end of the conversation as best he could. He never let on how hard it was on him.

Then, on the afternoon of December 1, 1943, Barr had been asked to help with food delivery. He knocked on Meder's door, but got no answer. When the guards opened the door, Meder was motionless. The medical staff rushed in, tried mouth-to-mouth resuscitation, and even gave Meder an adrenaline shot in the heart. But he was too far gone.

Two days later, the prison warden gave Nielsen, Hite, DeShazer, and Barr a chance to pay their final respects. When Nielsen entered Meder's cell, he found Meder lying in an open casket, his face distorted from the wads of cotton stuffed into his nose and mouth. There were a few chrysanthemums on his chest, and his eyes were closed. His body had withered down to a skeleton. Nielsen said a prayer and his goodbyes, not just to the loss of a friend, but to the comradery that Meder had relentlessly kindled, no matter how hopeless and terrified they all had every reason to be.

As a Mormon, Nielsen could take solace from the holy scriptures, which brimmed with heroes from Daniel in the lion's den to Alma and Amulek in captivity, all of whom had endured injustice through faith. Joseph Smith, the founding prophet of the Church of Jesus Christ of Latter-Day Saints, had himself been imprisoned during the persecution the Mormon community suffered in Missouri in 1838. Cramped in a frigid dungeon beneath the city jail in Liberty and told that the rotten meat he was fed was the flesh of his murdered followers, Smith had pleaded desperately, "O God, where art thou?" And God had answered him, "My son, peace be unto thy soul; thine adversity and thine afflictions shall be but a small moment; And then, if thou endure it well, God shall exalt thee on high; thou shalt triumph over all thy foes. Thy friends do stand by thee, and they shall hail thee again with warm hearts and friendly hands."

Nielsen did all he could to endure it well and to keep his mind alive in the solitude. He added the biggest numbers he could think of together in his head. And the more time he spent alone, the better he got at it.

He also took flights in his mind to the future. His biggest project was building his homestead in Utah, where he and his wife, Thora, could raise some children. They had ten brothers and sisters between them. Thora had been the youngest of six and Nielsen the middle of six. Five years younger than Nielsen, Thora was still in her early twenties. Her mother had been in her early thirties before she had had Thora's oldest brother, Gordon, and had still managed to have four more before giving birth to Thora in her midforties. Who knew how many children they might have?

Nielsen imagined every detail of their future home. He traced the roll of the property across his mind, keeping an eye out for all the landscaping that needed doing. He picked out the color scheme and tried out different plumbing fixtures for the bathroom. He built their home hundreds of times, feeling the weight of each shovel full of dirt as he dug out the basement, the splinters of each beam as he assembled the frame, the grit of each brick he placed in each wall and of every shingle he nailed into its place. But there was only so much building he could do. Eventually the house would disappear. Thora would disappear. And every flight of imagination landed him back in the same place: sitting alone in his cell.

* * *

Nielsen spent more than two years in Nanking Prison. And then, at 6:30 in the morning on June 12, 1945, he was wrested from his lonely cell, hooded, bound, and packed into a train with Hite, DeShazer, and Barr, and taken to Fengtai, a prisoner of war camp on the outskirts of Beijing. The trip took two days and the heat was suffocating, though Nielsen took some solace in the fact that he had it no worse than the Japanese soldiers, who all looked as ragged, undernourished, and sweltering as he felt. It was peculiar. The Japanese had loomed so large in his mind for years. They had all the power. But on this train and in this car, they were just as miserable.

Fengtai Prison Camp was situated in a disused rail depot that the Japanese had ringed with electrified barbed wire. There was no plumbing, and, nurtured by the summer heat, the flies swarmed by the millions.

The four of them were taken to Fengtai's brig, and Nielsen soon found himself once again in a small prison cell by himself. It was not the best he'd seen. It was also not the worst. There were no electric lights, which kept things pretty dim, but there was not much to look at in any event. The cell was a little smaller and sparer than his cell in Nanking had been. But it had a little window near the ceiling, and if he pulled himself up to the sill, he could look up into the sky or out into the yard, where Japanese soldiers drilled each morning. There was a little less food, but there was also more to drink, which was nice in the summer. The guards were about average in their cruelty. For the first full week, they hovered over him and made him sit on the floor, facing the wall all day. But gradually, everyone got used to everyone else, and Nielsen was left alone to do what he would in the solitude of his eighty-eight square feet.

Things stayed the same until the evening of August 20, 1945, 1,220 days and 11 hours after the *Green Hornet* took off from the USS *Hornet*. It was a Monday, and the previous Thursday morning, Nielsen had listened and then looked for the Japanese soldiers in the yard doing their morning drills. It was a routine that happened every day without fail. But that morning, there was not a soldier to be seen.

When the soldiers finally did come out, they were in trucks brimming with paper of all kinds—maps, ledgers, photographs, reports—that they then dumped into an enormous firepit. All weekend, truck after truck, the Japanese seemed intent on destroying every trace of what had been done in Fengtai.

Nielsen called over to Hite and DeShazer, who were alone in their own cells, to take a look. A guard scolded Nielsen for talking, but he and the rest of the guards seemed less directed than they had been just days before. Nielsen heard one say something about a powerful new weapon that Japan had developed that was many times more powerful than a normal bomb. But if the Japanese were on the cusp of victory, why would they be destroying all their records?

Nielsen then heard single-engine fighter planes buzzing overhead. He pulled himself up by the sill of his window to look for them in the sky, but he couldn't see anything that would tell him whose planes they were or why they were there.

Then, on Monday evening, a guard called him out of his cell and told him to go get cleaned up. Nielsen had every reason to worry, but he compliantly went to the prison barber, who buzzed his black hair down to his scalp. The barber then took out a straight razor, splashed him with some cold water, and shaved his face so close that it seemed as if he were trying to peel the skin off a potato. It smarted, but when it was over, Nielsen's face felt clean and bright for the first time in a while.

Robert Hite and Jacob DeShazer were also brought in for a shave and a haircut, and all three men were given soap and tubs in which to take a long-overdue bath. The only one missing was George Barr. They could tell that Barr had been getting sicker—there had been less and less sign of him in the sparse calls they made to one another through their cell windows—but they had no idea where he was or if they would have been told if he had died.

Their worries about Barr aside, their cause for anxiety deepened when a guard interrupted their baths, barking at them in Japanese to hurry. Were they going back before some Japanese court? Had the emperor's commutation of their death sentences been revoked? Would they be the next fuel for another massive firepit burning in the yard?

The three of them did as they were told, hurried up, and got dressed. The impatient soldier then led them out to the front of the Fengtai compound, where smartly dressed Japanese soldiers were already gathered, including a number of very-high-ranking officers; the kind of crowd that would assemble for an execution.

Nielsen had promised Thora that he would be back. However far away she and their homestead in Utah were, they had given him hope. He had made them as real as any memory as he languished alone in his small cell. And now he had gotten himself cleaned up only to be surrounded by what looked like an execution party that could snuff out him and all his memories, real and imagined, with a single bullet through his forehead.

But then Nielsen saw that some of the soldiers were dressed in US Army uniforms. Ragged and with a few days of beard growth over their sun-leathered skin, they didn't look beaten or submissive the way prisoners typically had to act around the Japanese. In fact, they were all armed to the teeth. Then one of them, a middle-aged major by the name of Ray Nichols, came over to Nielsen.

"Well, son," Nichols said in a midwestern accent. "The war is over. Now let's go home."

THREE

The assignment that brought Ray Nichols to Fengtai had come together on August 10, 1945. A welder by trade, Nichols had been in the
service for nearly a decade after signing up with the Wisconsin National
Guard and was now a commando team leader in the Office of Strategic
Services, the "OSS." His team's mission was to drop into enemy-occupied
territory to find prisoners of war and prevent evidence of war crimes—
documents and human—from being destroyed.

Under the name Operation Magpie, his team's target was Fengtai,
about which intelligence was thin. All they knew was that three months
earlier, a report had come in identifying the camp as the location of Colonel James Devereux, who had commanded the marines at the Battle of
Wake Island and was still believed to be alive in Japanese custody.

On August 17, 1945, Nichols loaded his team onto an overstuffed
B-24 with food, blankets, supplies, and leaflets to drop over Beijing. The
leaflets proclaimed that the war was over and promised favorable treatment to anyone who helped safely locate prisoners of war. Of the seven
men on Nichols's team, only one, the medic, had been trained as a para-
trooper.

As the B-24 flew over Beijing, a young Japanese American staff sergeant
by the name of Richard "Dick" Hamada stood over the jump hole with the
tightly wrapped package of leaflets in one hand. Born in Hawaii, Hamada
had seen the Pearl Harbor attack as it happened and made a point of being
one of the first Japanese Americans to sign up for the 442nd Regimental

Combat Team, the all-Nisei army unit established in 1943. Hamada, who was a crack shot, got tapped to join the OSS and spent the last year of the war doing covert actions deep inside the Burmese jungle, where, he later joked, he had been more afraid of the tigers than the Japanese.

Now Nichols watched as Hamada slashed the wrapper of the leaflet packet open, oblivious to the wind rushing up from the jump hole. The packet burst in Hamada's face, and the leaflets sprayed like startled bats around the belly of the B-24. Hamada flailed about, swatting the papers out of the air, but Nichols was not amused.

The leaflets were now unlikely to do any good, if they ever had been, and Nichols could see that they were quickly approaching the jump site outside Fengtai. The emperor had announced Japan's surrender only two days earlier, so there was no guarantee that word had traveled this far.

Nichols and his team poised themselves. The jumpmaster wished them all "good luck and good hunting." The red jump light flashed, and its buzzer crowded out any second thoughts. "Go! Go! Go!"

Nichols's team scattered in an open meadow about a thousand feet from Fengtai. The B-24 circled back around to drop their gear and then disappeared into the sky. It was quarter after five in the evening. The feeling of isolation was intense, and the danger was obvious.

Nichols was in the middle of Japanese-occupied China, getting ready to walk up to a prison defended by hundreds, if not thousands, of Japanese regulars. The only thing preventing him and his team from becoming prisoners themselves was the United States' two-day-old truce with Japan, agreed to after four years in which the countries' citizens had slaughtered each other by the hundreds of thousands. If push came to shove, Nichols was not equipped to put up much of a fight. Each of his men was armed with only three pistols, a few thousand dollars in cash, a carton of Lucky Strikes, and a letter—written in English—from General Albert C. Wedemeyer, the commander of US forces in China.

Each man kept a tactical distance from the others as they walked through a meadow toward the camp's fence line. Then, from the direction of Fengtai, came some pops.

Nichols hit the ground as fast as he could as bullets buzzed past in a swarm. Man by man, each member of his team gave a shout confirming that he had not been hit. Nichols gave the order to freeze in place, and the team stayed still in the tall grass as Nichols watched a truck drive toward them from the camp. As it got closer, a white flag came into view. The truck then sped toward where the team's medic was holed up and off-loaded three Japanese soldiers, who quickly surrounded him with rifles, bayonets fixed.

An angry Japanese lieutenant stepped out of the truck, making a show of the fact that he was in charge. The medic pointed the few hundred feet to Nichols. The lieutenant drew his sword and marched Nichols' way. "What is the meaning of this parachute jump?"

Hamada quickly ran over to intervene. "Did you not see the leaflets we dropped," Hamada asked in Japanese, "before jump?"

"What leaflets?" The angry lieutenant snapped.

Hamada took a crumpled leaflet from his pocket, and the lieutenant looked it over. "The war is not over," he snorted as he looked back up. "So get in the truck."

Each American was placed between two Japanese soldiers, who seemed to have no idea what to make of the men who had just dropped out of the sky. The ride was tense, but the lieutenant made no effort to disarm Nichols or his team.

The truck lurched over a bump and one of the Japanese soldiers fell toward Nichols, nicking him in the chest with a bayonet. It was just a scratch and clearly an accident, but blood started wicking through the fibers of Nichols' shirt. The pistols he and his team were carrying could make quick work of these soldiers in the close quarters of the truck. All Nichols had to do was give the signal.

Hamada broke in to diffuse the situation. "You have just earned your purple heart," he joked, "if we get out of here alive." Nichols had a reputation for being one of the most humorless Americans in the Pacific, but he let the scowl he had long ago etched into his face crack into a brief smile and gave a nod.

With the situation defused, Hamada asked the lieutenant to send out some soldiers to round up the supplies the B-24 had dropped into the meadow.

"Japanese soldiers do not work for the Americans."

"What about coolies?" Hamada asked, using the not entirely complimentary slang for Chinese peasant laborers.

"Perhaps you can get some at headquarters."

When they pulled up to what looked like an administrative building inside Fengtai, they were cordially greeted by a Japanese major, who welcomed them in. Nichols demanded to see the prisoners as Hamada translated his speech regarding the humanitarian nature of their mission.

The major asked them to be patient. Lieutenant General Gaku Takahashi, the Japanese general in charge of this part of northern China, was on his way. Hamada asked again for help in collecting their supplies. The major readily agreed and ordered the lieutenant to do the job.

While they waited, the major ordered up some tea. Nichols sipped along uncomfortably with everyone else as curious Japanese soldiers sneaked peeks through the windows or the break in the doorway. The soldiers were intrigued by Hamada; seeing a young Japanese soldier in a US Army uniform was as exotic to them as seeing Nichols in a kimono would have been to the Americans.

At about 6:30 p.m., General Takahashi arrived and the room clicked to attention. After the perfunctory introductions, Nichols repeated his demands.

Takahashi asked Nichols to be patient; he would need approval from Nanking.

"How long?" Nichols snapped.

"About two or three days," Takahashi suggested.

Takahashi gave the impression of wanting to help and joined them for tea. He propped his head lazily on his sword and made small talk, even mentioning a trip he had taken to New York before the war.

After the mood had relaxed some, Takahashi remarked on what a dangerous thing they all had just done. Had they landed even a few hours later, they would likely have gotten themselves killed. The Japanese soldiers who had picked them up did not know that the war was over. If the guards on night duty saw some Americans charging the camp, they would have just gunned them all down. Only the officers knew of the peace negotiations. Nichols and his men, Takahashi explained, were in "extreme danger."

Nichols made a show of being unmoved. Considering the pieces of leverage at his disposal, he opted to lead with his letter from General Wedemeyer. After giving Takahashi a moment to look it over, Nichols made clear to him that if anything happened to him or his men, it was he—Takahashi—who would be in "extreme danger."

Takahashi remained genial and invited Nichols to join him for dinner. Nichols appreciated the gesture but "regretfully" declined. He was there to accomplish his mission.

Takahashi was understanding and told Nichols that if he and his team wanted to get around Beijing safely, they would need a better letter than the one from Wedemeyer. Takahashi wrote one letter for each man—in Japanese—under his own signature. They would be their passports in China. He then offered to put them all up in Beijing's Grand Hôtel des Wagons-Lits, a brand-new hotel that originally been a geisha house. Takahashi made it clear that although there were no restrictions, it would be dangerous to wander around alone in Beijing. In addition to his handmade passports, Takahashi assigned two plainclothes officers from the Kempeitai to serve as their personal bodyguards.

Takahashi's eagerness to be cooperative was surprising for someone who had, just a few days before, been a sworn enemy, but he had good reason to want to make friends. The Soviets, Japan's longest-standing enemy, were continuing their advance south despite the armistice. Atrocities were rampant, and Japanese forces and civilians alike were being rounded up by the hundreds of thousands and deported into the Russian interior as slave labor. Takahashi knew it was only a matter of time before he would be surrounded and had even sent a cable to General Wedemeyer asking for Allied intervention to prevent the Soviets from crossing the Great Wall of China. Mending the relationship with the United States was not just the least worst option, it was a necessity.

*   *   *

Within three days of his arrival and with the help of the Swiss consul in Beijing, Nichols negotiated the release of more than three hundred prisoners of war. Nearly all were provided rooms at the Grand Hôtel des Wagons-Lits. Operation Magpie was a success.

When the first group of liberated prisoners of war arrived at the hotel, the Japanese concierge warmly welcomed them, though his hospitality soon faded as the filthy horde of liberated American soldiers and other prisoners piled into his lobby. The hotel had brand-new tatami floors, and the concierge nearly provoked a riot when he demanded that his newest guests take off their shoes before coming inside.

The newly liberated men celebrated the end of the war and the return to victorious freedom, pilfering the hotel's sake, beer, and food as booty. Then, after the long-awaited victory party was well under way, a rumor made its way to Nichols that four of the Doolittle Raiders had been among the prisoners at Fengtai.

Nichols confronted Fengtai's warden, a heavyset bureaucrat with bushy eyebrows and a graying handlebar mustache. None of the guests of the Grand Hôtel des Wagons-Lits was a Doolittle Raider. When the warden pretended not to know what Nichols was talking about, Nichols got into his face.

"You're a damned liar!" he shouted. "I know that you saw these men last Tuesday at five thirty, and I want them."

An investigation was promised, and later that evening, three freshly groomed young men were brought out of Fengtai's brig. All three were dramatically emaciated, festering with sweat rash, and a bit bewildered. The swarthy-looking one with close-clipped black hair introduced himself as Chase Nielsen, Doolittle Raider.

"You better watch out for this guy," Nichols said, turning to his men with a tone that made it hard to tell if he was joking. "He's off his rocker." But it was true. Nichols had found the lost Doolittle Raiders.

*   *   *

It was hard for anyone to believe. When the press had first reported that eight of the Doolittle Raiders had been captured in the fall of 1942, everyone had assumed the worst. Then, on the one-year anniversary of the raid, President Roosevelt had revealed their tragic fate and the worst was confirmed on front-page banner headlines across the country.

Hap Arnold had written an open letter to the Army Air Forces. "In violation of every rule of military procedure and of every concept of human decency, the Japanese have executed several of your brave comrades who took part in the first Tokyo raid," he lamented. "These men died as heroes. We must not rest—we must redouble our efforts—until the inhuman warlords who committed this crime have been utterly destroyed. Remember those comrades when you get a Zero in your sights—have their sacrifice before you when you line up your bombsights on a Japanese base."

As recently as the previous March, there had been reliable reports from informants inside China that the lost Doolittle Raiders had been publicly beheaded. No one, save perhaps their families, held out any hope that any of them were still alive.

But now here they were. Chase Nielsen, Robert Hite, and Jacob De-Shazer were alive and in Fengtai, of all places. It was miraculous, and Nichols saw to it that the three were booked in as the newest honored guests of the Grand Hôtel des Wagons-Lits, where they spent the next three days talking and singing into the night, eating themselves fat on Irish stew and ice cream, and pocketing the leftovers from the dinner table.

But where was the fourth? Nichols wanted to know, and when the warden claimed that the fourth man was dead, Nichols demanded to see the body.

The warden dutifully fetched the ninety-seven-pound body of George Barr. His feet were the only parts of him where skin was not over bone, and that was only because they had plumped up so morbidly from beri-beri. When Nichols got close to him though, he could tell that Barr was still breathing faintly. He ordered the team's medic over. It did not look as though much could be done, but Nichols ordered the medic to do whatever was possible. The man was a Doolittle Raider.

FOUR

After three days at the Grand Hôtel des Wagons-Lits, Nichols's team took Nielsen, along with Hite and DeShazer, to an airfield outside Beijing. Barr remained comatose and unsafe to move.

Nielsen found it all hard to believe. There had been so many tricks and false hopes. The rescue, the hotel, the food—it all was just so hard to believe. But there it was on the tarmac: a C-47 "Gooney Bird" with the name *Lady Jean* painted on its side. It was waiting just for them. They were finally going home.

The first stop on their journey halfway around the world was the Seven Dragons Airport and the US Army's headquarters in Chongqing, China. As Nielsen stepped unsteadily down the gangplank, he was unaware of what celebrities they had become. But it became clear as reporters and gawkers clamored the moment they set foot on the tarmac.

Nielsen had barely stepped onto solid ground when he was handed a telegram. It was from Thora, the woman who had filled his lonely dreams, welcoming him home. The news that Nielsen was alive, she said, was "the most wonderful news I ever heard in my life."

It was a hero's welcome that surpassed even the revelry of the Grand Hôtel des Wagons-Lits. Instead of the barracks, Nielsen, Hite, and De-Shazer were invited to stay in the prime minister's mansion, where they were feted with a feast of roast pork, tomato soup, lemon pie, and cold beer, a beverage Nielsen discretely declined. And to the great envy of every other soldier, sailor, airman, and marine in Chongqing, each of them was given a pass to stay out past the Army's 11:00 p.m. curfew for a government-sanctioned taste of the nightlife.

It was a lot for Nielsen to take in all at once, even if it was intended with affection. Seeing as much, a colonel from Texas, whose son had been taken prisoner in Italy and had spent nearly a month in solitary confinement, made a point of giving Nielsen some advice. Tell your story as many times as you can, he told him. "That's the only way to forget."

By the time the feast was over, Nielsen had told his story so many times, his throat had gone sore. He had not spoken more than a few words above a whisper in more than three years. Now the conversation kept coming. All those years alone in his cell, he had been waiting to talk someone's ear off. But after a while, before an audience that hung on his every hiccup, he found it hard to say anything at all. And so, with his belly full, he collapsed into a freshly made bed in the prime minister's mansion at 10:30 p.m., half an hour before his highly coveted curfew pass could have done him any good.

The next morning, he was given a brand-new, freshly pressed airman's uniform. No matter how deeply he tucked his new shirt into his new pants or how tightly he cinched his belt, the fresh khaki cloth billowed around his skin and bones. As he made his way back out into the crowd, the awkwardness of his oversized uniform only enhanced his heroic image in the eyes of all those who wanted to get their own look at him. He looked like who he was: a man who had suffered for his country.

* * *

From the moment he navigated the *Green Hornet* over Tokyo, Nielsen had known that he had done something extraordinary. But he had had no idea that he had become a legend. While he had been whiling the years away alone in a small Japanese prison cell, the world had become captivated by the story of the Doolittle Raid, and the Doolittle Raiders had become some of the most celebrated Americans of the 1940s.

From its inception, the Doolittle Raid had been a test of impossibility. Japan had existed as an independent nation, seemingly unconquerable, for more than two thousand years. Kublai Khan had been the last foreign invader to get close to putting a hostile foot on its soil. Yet, despite his vastly superior numbers and modern weaponry, including gunpowder, Kublai's attempted invasion had been foiled in 1281 after his fleet was destroyed by a typhoon that ripped through the Sea of Japan. That freakish weather event was written into Japanese lore as the *kamikaze*, or "divine wind." To the militarists who came to dominate Japan's politics in the 1930s, Japan was divinely ordained to be invulnerable. An attack on the mainland was impossible.

Japan's hegemony was not simply a national myth. Starting with its expansion into China throughout the late 1930s and its stunning series of victories after Pearl Harbor, which had ousted the United States, Great Britain, France, and the Netherlands from their most prized Asian colonies, the country had ruthlessly spread its defensive perimeter across the continent of Asia to the west and down the archipelagoes to the south. The Soviet Union, to the north, maintained strict neutrality, faced as it was with mounting a counteroffensive against Nazi Germany following Operation Barbarossa, and to the east, the vast Pacific Ocean was a moat that made Japan unreachable. The Japanese did not need to rely upon divine intervention. The brute arithmetic of weight, fuel, and time made them untouchable. But then Jimmy Doolittle shocked the world by making all the numbers add up.

The day of the raid, April 18, 1942, was a Saturday, and within a few hours, news reached President Roosevelt at his home in Hyde Park where he was drafting a fireside chat about wartime inflation. Upon hearing that Japan was burning, Roosevelt giddily called his press secretary, Stephen Early, back in Washington. Mum was the word, Roosevelt instructed him. If any reporter asked, Roosevelt told Early, he should speculate that Japan had been attacked by "Shangri-La," the Himalayan utopia in *Lost Horizon*. Early did his part, prompting one reporter to run with the headline "Early Knows 'Nothing.'"

The news that Japan was burning did not stay secret for long. Before the sun had risen on Hyde Park, Japanese radio broadcasts about an attack on Tokyo had made their way around the world and onto the front pages. On April 19, the *New York Times* ran a multipage spread under the headline "United States Bombers Take the War to the Japanese."

Everyone wanted to know how the mission had been pulled off. Fueled in part by German broadcasts, which erroneously claimed that the Japanese Navy had sunk a US carrier in the hours around the attack, media analysts speculated that new top secret bombers could take off from aircraft carriers in

the Pacific. Others speculated that the attack had been launched from the Soviet Union, which was desperate to maintain its neutrality with Japan and vehemently denied having had anything to do with the raid. Others speculated
about the existence of secret air bases hidden inside China or the Philippines.

Roosevelt held his first press conference after the raid on the afternoon
of Tuesday, April 21, 1942. When the questions came, he relished the opportunity to tease the reporters with all he knew they knew he knew but
would not say.

"Mr. President," Fred Perkins of the Scripps-Howard News Service
asked, "is there any comment you can make on the—on the recent developments in the Southwest Pacific?"

"No," Roosevelt replied, "I don't think so, except I can suggest that
people shouldn't believe what they read in certain papers."

"How about the—the—the—the story about the bombing of Tokyo?"

"Well, you know occasionally I have a few people in to dinner, and
generally in the middle of dinner some 'sweet young thing' says, 'Mr. President, couldn't you tell us about so-and-so?'

"Well the other night this 'sweet young thing' in the middle of supper
said, 'Mr. President couldn't you tell us about that bombing? Where did
those planes started from and go to?' "

Roosevelt paused and said with a cheeky flourish, "And I said, 'Yes, I
think the time has now come to tell you. They came from our new secret
base at Shangri-La!' "

The press corps erupted into laughter, most of it genuine. "And she
believed it!" Roosevelt said enjoying himself.

"Mr. President," Perkins asked, "is this the same young lady you talked
about—" The press corps again erupted into a squall of laughter.

"No. This is a generic term," Roosevelt interrupted playfully, feigning
his indignation. "It happens to be a woman." As much as the press corps
exercised discretion in what they wrote, they were not beyond ribbing the
President for his rakishness.

"Is it always feminine?" May Craig, a reporter from Gannet, interjected, roiling the laughter even louder.

"Now May, why did you ask me that?" May was one of the few female
political reporters in Washington and a friend of his wife, the First Lady.

"I wondered."

"I call it a 'sweet young thing,'" Roosevelt teased her. "Now when I talk about manpower that includes the women, and when I talk about a 'sweet young thing,' that includes young men . . ."

"Would you care to go so far, Mr. President," Fred Perkins jumped back in, "as to admit that this Japanese . . ."

"Wait a minute—wait a minute," Roosevelt interrupted. "'The President Admits'—there's the headline." He was not going to say anything and the press corps' willingness to laugh at each deflection demonstrated its willingness to stay in on the joke. "Go ahead now," Roosevelt permitted him.

"Would you care to go so far as to confirm the truth of the Japanese reports that Tokyo was bombed?"

"No. I couldn't even do that. I am depending on Japanese reports very largely." The laughter continued.

The reporters filed out, and Steve Early, the Press Secretary, bid them all goodbye, "Sweet little things!"

"Steve," one called out from the departing laughter, "does he mean to imply that Fred Perkins is a sweet little thing?"

When Roosevelt delivered his fireside chat a few days later, he continued to play the fool. After praising the resistance to Nazi and Japanese occupation around the world, he deadpanned, "It is even reported from Japan that somebody has dropped bombs on Tokyo, and on other principal centers of Japanese war industries." Then, with more feigned disbelief, he said with a chuckle, "If this be true, it is the first time in history that Japan has suffered such indignities."

Roosevelt's early unwillingness to tout the raid was, in part, a demonstration of his canny political skills. By withholding information and winking as he pretended it was a secret, he whipped the media into a frenzy. The coverage lasted for weeks. As each detail emerged, the column space devoted to the story of the still mysterious attack from Shangri-La came at the expense of the near-daily setbacks the Allies were experiencing: the Bataan Death March, the establishment of Vichy France, the loss of Burma and the Philippines.

Inside the government, the first word from Jimmy Doolittle came a week later. He was holed up in Quzhou, China, and sent a message through Chiang Kai-shek's forces: "Bombing mission to Tokyo carried out as planned. Owing to bad weather conditions in China, it is suspected all planes have probably been destroyed or damaged. So far 5 pilots are definitely known to be safe."

It was miraculous. Unbeknownst to Doolittle or his men, Chiang Kai-shek had refused to set up the promised airstrip. But Doolittle had somehow pulled it off anyway. On the spot, Roosevelt nominated Doolittle for promotion to brigadier general, leaping the rank of full-bird colonel altogether.

Over the next three weeks, Doolittle stayed in China as the rest of the Doolittle Raiders gradually joined him in a cave in Quzhou that he had turned into their rallying point. There was only one confirmed fatality, a sergeant by the name of Leland D. Faktor, who fell into some rocks as he jumped from his plane over China. The crews of the *Green Hornet* and the *Bat Out of Hell*, however, remained missing, and it had become increasingly difficult to get reliable intelligence about what had happened to them.

Soon after the raid, Chinese guerrilla forces loyal to Chiang Kai-shek reported that the Japanese had captured the crew of an American airplane that had crashed in occupied territory. Then another intelligence report surfaced, saying that another American airplane had crashed into the ocean seventy-five miles south of Shanghai. The last names of the three captured airmen from that plane—Hallmark, Meder, and Nielsen—were confirmed. But there was no word on the other two crewmen. There was also a rumor that one of them, possibly Nielsen, had been bayoneted while trying to escape.

Doolittle and General Joseph W. Stilwell, the United States' top commander in China, tried for months to work back channels to ransom Nielsen and the other captured Raiders. But there was no stomach for a deal from anyone in a position to make one. These were the highest-value detainees in Japan's already vast system of wartime detention, and by early June, it had become clear that no one was willing to take the risks associated with selling them.

* * *

At the end of May 1942, Doolittle returned safely to Washington, and the first official details of what soon came to be known as the Doolittle Raid were revealed on the front page of every major newspaper, next to a picture of Roosevelt pinning the Congressional Medal of Honor to Doolittle's chest. Doolittle became a household name. The hit radio comedian

Red Skelton composed the tribute "Not So Dipsy Doolittle." Warner Bros. optioned the rights to "The Life and Exploits of Jimmy Doolittle." The author James Hilton, enjoying the sudden uptick in interest in *Lost Horizon*, told reporters that he wanted to meet Doolittle: "He's the only fellow who could really tell me what my Shangri-La is like."

Roosevelt saw to it that all of Doolittle's men were awarded the Distinguished Service Cross, and newspapers and radio broadcasts around the country breathlessly reported the biographies of any local hero who could claim the mantle of Doolittle Raider.

Nielsen's family got the news at the same time as everyone else did. Reporters were eager for reactions, and Nielsen's father beamed, "We're not surprised that Chase was with the first squadron to raid Japan. And I'll bet he's awful happy. He always liked to do things first." Nielsen was the only Doolittle Raider to come from Utah, and the local papers took particular pride in that fact, in no small part because being from Utah was code for being a Mormon.

The War Department publicly claimed that all of Doolittle's planes had made it to their destinations in China. But soon after the raid made news, Doolittle sent Nielsen's family a confidential letter, letting them know that Nielsen had fallen into enemy hands. Doolittle impressed upon them that he was doing everything in his power to get Nielsen out safely, but they had to keep mum because the information was a classified secret.

For Nielsen's wife, Thora, the stress of that summer was a lot to bear. She fell ill and stayed bedridden well into the fall. Then, in late October 1942, Japanese radio broadcasts released the names of four of the captured Doolittle Raiders, including Nielsen.

The public was shocked to learn that two of Doolittle's crews had, in the War Department's bureaucratic euphemism, "gone missing." The War Department defended itself by claiming that secrecy had been "highly desirable in the hope of saving the lives and securing the freedom of certain crew members who crash landed in areas controlled by the enemy."

Though it was a relief to have the truth publicly known, for Thora, the news was still grim. Nielsen's name was only now coming to light because the Japanese Army's Information Department had mentioned him in a press release announcing that "the American aircrews who attacked Japan proper on 18 April last and who were captured have been severely punished owing to military law, the results of the investigation showed that they disregarded humanitarian laws."

The outpouring of community support was overwhelming. Utah's Governor wrote Nielsen's family a personal note of support, and a few weeks later, Thora accepted her husband's medals on his behalf in a massive full-dress ceremony organized at Salt Lake City's air base. She did not know if he was alive or dead but said she was proud of him for being where he had needed to be.

All hope seemed lost on the first anniversary of the Doolittle Raid, when Roosevelt publicly announced that at least some of the Raiders had been executed after being tortured into falsely confessing to war crimes. Thora first heard the news while riding a bus home from her job at the Ogden Quartermaster Depot. All around her, strangers chatted about her husband, her family, her future, and how he had been tortured and executed as if it were just the news of the day. The front pages of all the local papers ran thinly veiled obituaries that began, as every obit does, with the place and date on which the deceased was born. "One of the prisoners presumed to have been put to death," one read, "was Lieut. Chase J. Nielsen of Hyrum, Utah."

Of the ten missing Doolittle Raiders, Nielsen was the only married man, and his grieving widow offered a human interest angle that reporters used to froth the coverage. Newspapers around the country ran any photo of Thora they could find, but Thora didn't want to talk to reporters. She stopped going to her job at the depot and went out of town to stay at her mother's house. Nielsen's mother was the only one willing to give the reporters quotes. She refused to believe the news and said as much to anyone who called.

As the years went by, the reporters went elsewhere, but Nielsen's legacy as a Doolittle Raider became etched in marble. North American Aviation, the company Doolittle had contracted to build his modified bombers, named a B-25 after him. And 20th Century–Fox adapted what little information was known into a sensational courtroom drama in which the torture and execution of the captured Raiders were luridly imagined on the silver screen.

The Purple Heart, released in 1944 along with advertisements for war bonds, opens with Dana Andrews as the fictional pilot Captain Harvey Ross being led with his men into a grand courtroom in Tokyo. Ross demands counsel of choice but is given a feckless Japanese lawyer, who proudly boasts of having gone to Princeton. Ross's lieutenant snorts back that he went to the City University of New York and breaks into a lengthy argument about the Geneva Conventions. But the presiding Japanese judge, dressed like a character out of the Fu Manchu movies, dismisses their arguments and tells Ross that they have been charged with atrocities.

As Ross and his men protest furiously, the villain of the film appears: General Ito Mitsubi. A smugly grinning salamander of a human being, costumed in Japanese Army khakis and a pencil thin mustache, Mitsubi recounts how the Raiders had taken off from an aircraft carrier in the Pacific and then falsely accuses the Raiders of committing atrocities against Japanese civilians. Mitsubi calls a Chinese collaborator to the stand to fraudulently testify that "They laughed as they told me how they machine-gunned children at play in a schoolyard."

A controversy erupts, though, when the fictional commander of the Japanese Imperial Fleet objects to General Mitsubi's version of events. The Imperial Navy, he insists, would never have let an aircraft carrier so close to Japan.

The question of where the Doolittle Raiders had begun their mission becomes the central controversy of the trial, and to prove his case, General Mitsubi subjects one Raider after another to crippling torture. But each man stays mum, refusing to betray the details of the mission. Mitsubi then offers Captain Ross a deal: if he will admit to having taken off from an aircraft carrier, Mitsubi will have the charges dismissed, spare Ross's men's lives, and send them all to a prisoner of war camp.

Ross leaves the decision to a secret ballot of his fellow Raiders. Grabbing an oriental vase, he tells them each to drop in his wings. To reject the deal, they are to drop the wings in whole; to take the deal, they are to drop the wings in broken. "If there is one pair of broken wings in this vase," Ross assures them, "we'll tell them what they want to know." One man after another, physically and mentally shattered, approaches the vase and makes his choice.

Not knowing what his men have decided, Ross delivers the vase to the Japanese judge, who plucks the wings out one by one. Not a single pair is broken. The deal rejected, Ross is asked for his final words.

"You can kill us," he proclaims. "But if you think that's going to put the fear of God into the United States of America and stop them from sending other fliers to bomb you, you're wrong. Dead wrong. They'll come by night, they'll come by day. Thousands of them. They'll blacken your skies and burn your cities to the ground and make you get down on your knees and beg for mercy."

Humiliated, General Mitsubi commits suicide in the courtroom by shooting himself in the chest, and the judge sentences the Raiders to death. Ross and his men march in lockstep from the courtroom to the gallows, heads held high, as the Army Air Forces anthem plays behind them. The credits roll as the anthem reaches the final couplet of its first stanza:

> *We live in fame or go down in flame. Hey!*
> *Nothing can stop the Army Air Corps!*

The Purple Heart played in Ogden along with newsreels about the war and the romantic comedy *What a Woman!*, starring Rosalind Russell, in the summer of 1944. For Thora, its message was clear: Nielsen was never coming home. He was a martyr to the hated Japanese.

But then that immutable fact changed at the end of August 1945 as dramatically as anything could, and the reporters returned, eager to write the story of long-lost love reunited. Asked for her reaction, Thora gushed, "We have never given up hope that he was all right."

* * *

Now, very much alive and preparing to leave Chongqing for his long-awaited reunion with Thora, Nielsen agreed to sit, along with Robert Hite and Jacob DeShazer, for a press conference. Dressed in new, albeit oversized uniforms, the three of them sat around a wooden table and greeted the assembled press corps, who gawked as if Lazarus had come back from the dead. Every newspaper in the country featured the story.

The reporters asked a barrage of questions: Did their reality live up to the movies? How did they endure all that torture? Why were their lives spared? What was the best thing about being free? Nielsen, hunching forward in his seat with Hite and DeShazer on either side of him, fielded most of the questions with a clarity of mind and a wry sense of humor that was startling under the circumstances.

"Our life rafts, it seemed, were made in Japan," Nielsen joked as he described crashing off the Chinese coast. "Because they didn't work."

Asked about the show trial that had been at the center of *The Purple Heart*, Nielsen replied, "Our charge and sentence was for bombing non-military objectives and schools and strafing innocent children." He chortled, then boasted scornfully, lest there be any doubt, "Our targets were bulls'-eyes; we hit oil tanks and factories and I saw them in flames."

Nielsen got emotional only when asked how he felt now that he was on his way home. The reporters had gotten word of Thora's telegram and wanted to know what was going through his mind.

"I feel," he said in a trembling voice that had grown hoarse, "that I'm an American again."

The only questions Nielsen said he could not answer were the reporters' questions about the "special treatment" they had received at the hands of the Japanese. He hinted that the gory imaginings washing about in the reporters' minds were all true but he had been instructed not to disclose the details for security reasons. If he could, he would. He had a story to tell, a story he had been waiting to tell. But the details were now the subject of a war crimes investigation.

FIVE

Nielsen had thought a lot about his revenge. Under torture in Shanghai, only days after his capture, he had imagined getting his hands on a gun and killing every last one of the bastards, regardless of whether he made it out alive or not. George Barr had had the sand to brawl with what seemed like a dozen guards in Nanking, his flaming red hair making him look like a war mad Cúchulainn in full manly fury. The revenge Nielsen always imagined came at the end of a fist or a gun. What he could not have imagined was that when it would be finally offered for real, it would be by a rather professorial lawyer in his late forties who introduced himself as Colonel Young.

* * *

Colonel Edward "Ham" Young had grown up in Wisconsin with a lifelong desire to attend the US Naval Academy but had been rejected for being flat-footed. That left him to go to West Point instead, which turned out to be a boon for the Army. Taking the opportunity to get his law degree from New York University, he had become a career military lawyer in the Army's Judge Advocate General's Corps, or "JAG Corps," and had devoted much of his life to making JAGs a respectable part of the legal profession.

One of Young's greatest achievements had been setting up a new military law school, the Judge Advocate General's School or "JAG School." Housed for most of the war on the campus of the University of Michigan in Ann Arbor, Young supervised the education of the thousands of new

JAGs who entered the ranks after Pearl Harbor and saw to it that lawyers who graduated from the nation's top law schools, many of whom had been drafted into the Army, were put onto the faculty.

In December 1944, Young was selected to be the top lawyer for General Albert Wedemeyer, who had just been ordered to Chongqing to replace General Joseph Stilwell as the US commander in the China theater. Stilwell's relationship with Chiang Kai-shek had become unremittingly bitter. To Chiang, Stilwell was a hotheaded, entitled American. Stilwell would, in turn, describe Chiang as "a vacillating, tricky, undependable, old scoundrel who never keeps his word."

Other than the professional cachet a career officer earns from a wartime deployment, the transfer to Chongqing was not an obvious step up for someone with Young's background and ambitions. He was an intellectual, having authored two books on constitutional law, including *Constitutional Powers and Limitations*, the official textbook at West Point. His leadership of the JAG School had earned him a Legion of Merit and an honorary doctorate from the University of Miami Law School in recognition of his work to bring academic respectability to military law.

Though the position in Chongqing was a deployment, working for Wedemeyer did not offer any real wartime action in which to display valor. After being bombed in the first few years of the war, Chongqing was largely quiet by the time Young got there and had become a tediously political city. Wedemeyer's primary mission, like Stilwell's before him, was to engage in endless negotiations over force deployments with Chiang Kai-shek, who resented his dependence on his US allies and was preoccupied with staving off Mao Zedong's People's Liberation Army, his long-term rival for control of China.

Still, Young saw a unique opportunity. In February 1945, barely two months into his tour, he worked to establish the China Theater's War Crimes Office as a partner organization of the War Department's War Crimes Office in Washington, DC, which had itself been established the previous fall. With China home to some of the most established US Army headquarters in all of Asia, Young's War Crimes Office had a real chance to be at the center of the Allied war crimes prosecutions in the Pacific.

From the war's earliest days, there had been talk about prosecuting Axis war criminals, and the Japanese treatment of the Doolittle Raiders was a major driver of public opinion in favor of doing so. After word first surfaced in October 1942 that they somehow had been "punished," Roosevelt had sent diplomatic inquiries through the Swiss Legation to find out exactly what that meant.

Japan's Foreign Ministry had responded with a formal communiqué in February 1943 that was full of platitudes about Japan's obligation to "limit the tragedies of war to a minimum" and claims that the Doolittle Raiders had confessed to bombing with "malice." Japan, it said, sentenced these "enemies of humanity" to death. However, as a matter of grace, "the sentence of death was applied only to certain accused," though the Japanese refused to give the names.

In response, the State Department had sent Japan a formal diplomatic protest whose public release was timed to correspond with the one-year anniversary of the Doolittle Raid. "Instructions to American armed forces have always ordered those forces to direct their attacks upon military objectives," it had insisted. "The American forces participating in the attack on Japan had such instructions and it is known that they did not deviate therefrom."

"There are numerous known instances," the diplomatic protest had continued, "in which Japanese official agencies have employed brutal and bestial methods in extorting alleged confessions from persons in their power. It is customary for those agencies to use statements obtained under torture, or alleged statements, in proceedings against the victims." In closing, it demanded that Japan restore the Raiders to "the full rights to which they are entitled under the Prisoners of War Convention."

The revelation of the Doolittle Raiders' fate stoked the public mood for revenge against Japan to a burning intensity unseen since Pearl Harbor. The press used every epithet possible to dismiss Japan's "ridiculous and monstrous" claim that the Doolittle Raiders had committed atrocities. Congressmen called for the Roosevelt administration to "show no mercy" and promised that "we won't take many prisoners after that."

Yet Roosevelt resisted the lusty calls to spill the blood of all Japanese. The Undersecretary of War publicly denounced indiscriminate violence against Japanese prisoners in retaliation. "We have faithfully lived up to our commitments under the Geneva Convention," he reminded the public. "Reprisals for this act directed against Japanese soldiers who have fallen into our hands would lower us to the level of our enemy without touching the evil individuals who alone are responsible. We shall have our reprisals, but they will be directed against the officials of the Japanese government who instigated these crimes."

When War Department censors had reviewed the script for *The Purple Heart*, their main objection had been that the film did not sufficiently show that it had been Japan's militarists, not its people, who had been responsible for the torture and murder of the Doolittle Raiders. And Roosevelt assured the public not that Japan would be annihilated in fire and fury but that "the American Government will hold personally and officially responsible for these diabolical crimes all of those of the Japanese Government who have participated therein and will in due course bring those officers to justice."

In the early days of the war, war crimes prosecutions were primarily of academic interest to legal scholars, who advocated "peace through law." At the time the Doolittle Raiders' fate was announced, the only actual prosecution the Roosevelt administration had attempted was the trial of some Nazi saboteurs, who had been captured inside the United States and tried before a secret military commission. Though approved by the US Supreme Court, the proceedings had been highly controversial and were not soon repeated.

But as Allied victory seemed more certain in the final year of the war, the rather grandiose notion of actually holding "Tojo and his gang" accountable through war crimes prosecutions seemed increasingly possible. The Allied Translator and Interpreter Section for the South West Pacific Area began cataloging Japanese war crimes and consolidating captured Japanese documents and statements by liberated prisoners of war into lurid accounts of murder, cannibalism, rape, and perfidy.

With the Potsdam Declaration in July 1945, the United States made it known that one of the consequences of Japan's unconditional surrender would be the prosecution of those who had mistreated prisoners of war. By the following month, the US Army in the Pacific had compiled massive lists of suspected war criminals and potential witnesses. Thousands upon thousands of names were tied to war crimes big and small.

Now, with his own War Crimes Office up and running, Ham Young initiated a public education campaign about war crimes to help build Chinese public support and formulated a plan to send teams of his lawyers and investigators out to Hong Kong, Shanghai, Mukden, and Beijing to build cases, real cases that could be brought to trial in public. But before he put those plans into action, his first big opportunity stepped off a C-47 "Gooney Bird" for a brief stopover in Chongqing.

*   *   *

Nielsen, Hite, and DeShazer sat across from Young and his staff from the War Crimes Office and told their story. Hite and DeShazer explained how they had been on the *Bat Out of Hell*, the last plane to take off from the USS *Hornet*, which they had thought would make for good luck, since it gave them the most runway. Things were still tense, though. The wind was blowing so hard that everything was vibrating and a minute or so before takeoff, a sailor had slipped in front of their right propeller and gotten his arm clipped. Hite had a clear image in his mind of the poor wretch squirming on the deck, the blood from his arm perfusing into pink puddles of sea spray.

Despite their shaky start, the takeoff from the *Hornet* and the bombing run over Japan had gone as smoothly as any of them could have hoped. It had been cloudless open flying all the way to their targets in Nagoya, and the Japanese had put up almost no air defense. Hite had even goaded DeShazer into taking a few shots from the .30-caliber nose gun at some fishing junks around Ise Bay as they made their escape.

The weather got choppier, though, as they approached the Chinese coast. Billy Farrow pulled above the cloud cover as Hite searched for the homing beacon that Chiang Kai-shek had supposedly set up on a landing strip in Quzhou. Hite repeatedly sent out the call—"57"—on the frequency they had been given. But they were met with radio silence.

It did not take long for the fuel tanks to dry up. The navigator, George Barr, estimated that they were about six hundred miles inside China, over Nanchang, a city the Japanese Army had occupied since 1939. They might as well have been in the suburbs of Tokyo, but when the fuel light came on, they were out of options. Farrow gave the order to jump for it.

Hite landed at the edge of a rice paddy, spraining his ankle when he hit the ground. The only light for miles was the fire the *Bat Out of Hell* had started when it had crashed on the banks of a lake in the distance. Hite thought to himself that he was "10,000 miles away from home and in the rain." It was the quietest quiet he had ever heard and he tried to comfort himself with the Jimmie Rodgers song "Waiting for a Train" as he wandered through a maze of rice patties in search of safety.

The next morning, he stumbled upon a peasant farmer who seemed happy to help and eventually led him to some kind of "coolie hut," where Hite was greeted by what seemed like a dozen Japanese soldiers, who came running out with rifles, bayonets fixed. The Japanese soldiers unceremoniously relieved Hite of his .45, loaded him onto a 1938 Ford pickup, and drove him to a schoolhouse that the Kempeitai had requisitioned as its headquarters in Nanchang. The fact that it was a Ford still galled him.

DeShazer was picked up by a Japanese patrol around daybreak, and man by man, the *Bat Out of Hell*'s five crewmen—William Farrow, Robert Hite, George Barr, Jacob DeShazer, and Harold Spatz—were rounded up and taken to the schoolhouse in Nanchang by morning.

The whole atmosphere in Nanchang was rather festive. Under questioning, DeShazer admitted firing off a few rounds over Japan, but no one seemed to take it all too seriously. Things got dangerous only the next day, when the five of them were loaded onto a cargo plane and taken to the Japanese Army headquarters in Nanking. Each man was bound, blindfolded, and dragged into a different interrogation room, where the questions came impatiently. Where were they from? Who was their leader? What is a "hornet"? Hite was slapped around quite a bit but was macho about it. It was nothing he couldn't take.

George Barr, the *Bat Out of Hell*'s navigator, always got the worst of the abuse. Growing up an orphan in Brooklyn had taught him that the best way to handle a schoolyard bully was to punch him in the nose. But Nanking was no schoolyard. Barr had apparently held out during questioning, even as four or five Japanese soldiers had taken turns having a swing at him. Then Barr's Brooklyn-born fuck-you cool had provoked the bastards to waterboard him.

* * *

Young asked Nielsen, Hite, and DeShazer where the rest of the Doolittle Raiders were now, and the honest answer was that they didn't know. Fitz and Dieter, Nielsen explained, died in the crash. Meder, they explained, had died back in Nanking of beriberi right before Christmas 1943. But as for Hallmark, Farrow, and Spatz, they weren't sure. DeShazer said he thought they had been taken to a prisoner of war camp in Mukden, China. But Nielsen and Hite were not so sure. The last time they had seen any of them had been back in October 1942, at the headquarters of Japan's 13th Army in Jiangwan, a place everyone called the Civic Center. That was where the trial had taken place.

For Young, the mention of a trial raised several questions. In *The Purple Heart*, the Japanese trial of the Doolittle Raiders was a spectacle that spanned days and was witnessed by reporters from across the Axis alliance in one of the grandest courtrooms in Tokyo. But that was just the movies. Young wanted to know what had happened at the real trial. What had been the evidence? Why had it been conducted in Shanghai? And, most important, who had been the mastermind behind it all? Who was the real General Ito Mitsubi?

Again, the truth was that Nielsen, Hite, and DeShazer didn't know. Everything was a blur. Back in Tokyo, they explained, the Japanese had collected a lot of intelligence about them before shipping them all to Bridge House and then to Jiangwan for their trial. There was one detail that stuck out, though.

Before they all left Tokyo, the Japanese lawyer they all called Well-Well had given them each a little booklet to sign. Nielsen remembered it having been written all in Japanese and Well-Well explaining that it was just a transcript of their interviews. Perhaps those booklets had been used at the trial, but Nielsen was not sure. The trial itself had lasted maybe half an hour, and once it was done, everyone had been sequestered away into cells in the Jiangwan Military Prison, except for Hallmark, who had been sent back to Bridge House.

Things stayed quiet after that until the morning of October 15, 1942, when they had been taken before a second trial, as Nielsen described it, except, unlike in the first trial, Hallmark, Farrow, and Spatz had been missing. There had been some commotion the night before in the prison hallway, cell doors opening and closing. But no one had ever seen them again after that, and no one had ever told them where they had gone.

* * *

Nielsen gave Ham Young and his assistants as many details as he could. Pressed for names, Nielsen, Hite, and DeShazer could come up with only a few. The higher-ups had never gotten their hands dirty, and the guards had all seemed to go by nicknames or numbers. At Bridge House, the most physically abusive had been known as "the Big Bad Wolf." He would randomly scream at prisoners or beat them whenever he felt the inclination. Then there had been the interpreters, such as "Well-Well" in Tokyo. At Bridge House, the interpreter had been "Guard Number 56," who was a sleazy son of a bitch.

As far as real names were concerned, there was a young guy at Jiangwan the Raiders all remembered as going by the name "Remedios." Remedios had always been close at hand, and he had always been good for information. Nielsen thought he could probably fill in some of the missing details, since as far as he knew, Remedios still lived in Shanghai. The one name De-Shazer remembered for sure was "Tatsuda." He had been the prison warden at Jiangwan and had been, DeShazer said, "good to the fliers."

When it came to mistreatment, they all agreed that some places had been worse than others. At Jiangwan, they said, they had been more or less ignored, and to Young's surprise, they considered their treatment "far superior to that meted out to most Chinese and some Japanese soldiers themselves."

Hite thought their treatment had been the worst in Tokyo. It had not been as violent as in Nanking. Well-Well had never abused them physically. But he and the other interrogators in Tokyo had known how to get into their heads. They would keep them up for days, questioning them over and over again. There had been no control over anything. Sometimes, Hite said, he had been tied to a chair. Sometimes blindfolded. When he had forgotten something, as inevitably he did, a guard might give him a whack with a belt or a bamboo stick. It had not been hard; just enough to remind him that he was not in control.

Nielsen disagreed. For Nielsen and the other surviving crew of the *Green Hornet*, Tokyo had been an improvement over what they had experienced that day in the airport in Shanghai. Nielsen lifted his pant leg to show Ham Young the scar that remained across his shin from where the Japanese soldiers had kicked him with their hobnailed boots. He recounted the bamboo pole they had put behind his knees to pull him apart and showed Young the scars in the webbing between his fingers where thin sticks had been jabbed into his nerves.

At Nanking, where they had spent most of the war, the hardest thing had been the isolation and neglect. The prison guards would occasionally be rough with them. But there had been no torture there the way there had been in the first few months after they were captured. The only exception had been the time the guards in Nanking had put George Barr into a straitjacket.

When Young asked for details, Nielsen, Hite, and DeShazer explained that it had been the winter after Meder had died. The four of them had all been out in the yard for daily exercise. The guards had always given them flimsy slippers to wear outside, but it had been hard to run in them, so they had typically just ran barefoot, despite the cold. The bit of snow made the ground muddy, and when Barr came in from the yard, one of the guards had told him to wash his feet off so as not to track dirt inside. Barr had pointed to the faucet inside the gate, but the guard had stopped him and told him to use the snow instead. When Barr made a move toward the faucet, the guard had grabbed him. Barr took a swing and had gotten the son of a bitch right in the nose.

That, of course, had set the rest of the guards onto Barr, who took a few more swings before being wrestled to the ground. Furious, the guards had dragged Barr back out into the yard and tied him up in a straitjacket. They had pulled the straps as hard as they collectively could to squeeze the air right out of him and then dropped him like a sack of bricks onto the same snowy mud that had caused the problem in the first place.

It had been horrible. Barr gasped for breath by the mouthful and yaulped like a dying animal with the little air he had. After about half an hour, the guards had undone the buckles and let him catch his breath. But as soon as Barr had come to his senses, they grabbed him and did it again, yanking the straps as tight as they could. Another half hour had gone by before they had let him out and dragged him back to his cell. Barr was different after that.

As they recounted all this to Ham Young, no one was sure if Barr was still alive. To Nielsen, Barr was yet another one of his brothers in arms who had likely been murdered by the Japanese. In prior wars, there would have been little that could be done to avenge his or any of the other Raiders' deaths. They would all have just been the tragic costs of victory against a vicious enemy. But Young offered Nielsen something new. Murdering prisoners was a war crime under international law. If they could find the men responsible, Nielsen could have justice; he could see the bastards hanged by the neck.

THE PROSECUTION

* * *

SIX

Ham Young chose a few dozen of the military lawyers available to him in China to work for his War Crimes Office. Some worked full-time, others only part-time. Young, though, had not asked Captain Robert E. Dwyer, which was a conspicuous oversight.

Dwyer had served under Young on the faculty of the JAG School in Ann Arbor. A graduate of Harvard Law School, Dwyer had an intellectual bent that suited Young's broader ambition of making military law respectable and would have had obvious value given how complicated the war crimes prosecutions were expected to be.

The truth, though, was that Dwyer had a reputation as a bit of a hothead, a brashness that fit his out-of-shape boxer's build and his massive Irish head. Dwyer looked, drank, and had the temperament of a beat cop, the kind of Paddy who hunted down bar fights to break up in the hopes of getting a few good swings in himself. And brash was not Young's style.

Dwyer worked in the legal office for the Fourteenth Air Force, the storied "Flying Tigers." His boss, Lieutenant Colonel John Hendren, Jr., was his opposite in every noticeable way. Though three years younger, Hendren outranked Dwyer twice over. Dwyer came from a family of New York Republicans; Hendren was a New Deal Democrat from Missouri. Dwyer was voluble; Hendren seemed to polish every word before he allowed his mouth to open. Dwyer was balding, paunchy, and a bit of a slob; Hendren was coiffed, square jawed, and always dressed impeccably.

Dwyer and Hendren shared office space on the eleventh floor of the

Development Building, a ten-year-old art deco tower on Fuzhou Road in downtown Shanghai. The Development Building had been home to the US Consulate before the war, and the US Army had reclaimed a few of its floors in the middle of October 1945, when General Wedemeyer had relocated his headquarters from Chongqing to Shanghai.

A modern city, famous for its *chao nao*, its noisy and unceasing assault on the senses, Shanghai had been a foreign city even to the Chinese in the century after the Opium War, when it had been carved into colonial enclaves by the British, French, Americans, and later the Japanese. It had come out of the war largely unscathed, and for someone like Dwyer in the fall of 1945, it was an easy place to get comfortable.

Each morning, Dwyer awoke in his bachelor pad in Broadway Mansions, the city's twenty-two story landmark hotel. It had opened in 1934 just north of where the photo-ready Garden Bridge crossed the Suzhou Creek, connecting Shanghai's landscaped riverfront to the south, which locals called "the Bund," to the northern part of the city known as Japan Town. Depending on his mood, Dwyer could sit for a finely prepared meal in Broadway Mansion's fifth-floor dining room, which spanned the full length of the building's southern exposure and was lavishly appointed in gold with brown leather upholstery. Or he could go down to the first floor and sip a drink in the officers' club, "East Meets West," under its enormous mural of reclining naked beauty.

Passing through Broadway Mansions' red-and-gold art deco lobby, Dwyer could expect to be greeted cordially by Chinese bellmen or warmed by the sight of one of the girls at the concierge desk. There was Elsa (a blond German), Minnela (a petite Portuguese), and Elizaveta (a coy Russian). Elizaveta's sweaters fit so pleasingly to leering American eyes that she came to be universally known as "Sweater Girl."

Dwyer was ostentatious in his affection for Sweater Girl. The ubiquitous Russian women in Shanghai, nicknamed "Petrushkas," were synonymous with the sex trade and it was said that every Russian girl was on the prowl to catch an American husband. The editor of the Shanghai *Stars and Stripes* even printed a bawdy poem entitled, "Three Little Girls," whose opening verse was:

There were three little girls on Bubbling Well,
Olga and Sonya and Tanya.
They did many things and they did them all well.

The poem was quickly adapted into a hit song in the cabarets, where Dwyer and his brothers in arms could rollick along with a flesh-and-blood Olga, Sonja, or Tonya right beside them. Sweater Girl, however, always deflected Dwyer's boisterous charms, though somehow with a warmth that kept him returning time and again with flattery and even the occasional gift.

Broadway Mansions offered a mere taste of the city that greeted Dwyer as he stepped out its front doors. "Wine, women and song," the guidebooks advertised. "Whoopee! Let's go places and do things! When the sun goes in and the lights come out Shanghai becomes another city, the city of blazing night, a nightlife Haroun Al-Raschid never knew, with tales Scheherazade never told the uxoricidal Sultan Shahryar."

Shanghai seduced those keen for a taste of the exotic and erotic at a reasonable price. There were discreet parlors hosted by Chinese courtesans dressed in elegant *qipao*s and loud nightclubs such as the Black Cat, whose Korean "hostesses" sported just-visible black cat tattoos on their buttocks. There was the Red Rose, which offered Russian women and Gypsy music. In Japan Town, there were geisha houses and restaurants that featured Cantonese women, who strolled about barefoot and sang fishing ballads. Walking the streets were countless "jeep girls," a class of available young women the Chinese called "pheasants," and at any nightclub, a few dollars could be given to a "taxi dancer," who would sway in a GIs arms as his one and only for the length of a song.

The fruits of the Orient were all there, candied for easy consumption so that every man who returned to his predictable, moral, and most of all quiet hometown was sodden with memories of Xanadu. General Joseph Stilwell, Wedemeyer's predecessor in China, had visited Shanghai before the war and mused that "this town would ruin anybody in no time. The babes that twitch around the hotels need attention so badly that it is hard not to give it to them."

It was an extraordinary time to be an American in Shanghai. Everyone knew it. All around Dwyer were Americans of every rank and service chewing gum, catcalling pretty girls, and providing a regular source of work for the military police. Making his way to his office in the Development Building, which was only two blocks west of the Bund, Dwyer could look up at bespoke American flags flying from buildings that looked as if they had been lifted brick by brick from London, Paris, and New York and built anew on the other side of the world. Those hand-sewn flags might have any random number of stars and stripes, but they left no doubt that the war had yielded a victor and a vanquished. There were a right and a wrong, and those on the winning side could look out at the world unencumbered by doubt, flush with the means to pay, and convinced—not without good reason—that they had landed on the right side of history. The Americans who had arrived in Shanghai in October 1945 were ready to do big things. And Dwyer was with them.

That Dwyer had the chance to stroll down those streets at all was something of a fluke. He was thirty-seven when he was drafted into the Army, a bit old to become a soldier, and had his number not come up, he would probably have still been back in Rochester. His father, E. J. Dwyer, had been a New York State assemblyman and prominent lawyer, which had given Dwyer a certain local notoriety and the expectation that his personal accomplishments and goings on would be regularly featured in Rochester's gossip columns. His graduation from Harvard Law School in 1930 portended an even brighter future and perhaps a political career on the national stage.

In 1934, Dwyer tried to prove as much by running for his father's old Assembly seat on the Republican ticket—and lost. He took the defeat hard, though he continued to enjoy being a big fish in a small pond. He built a law practice and remained active in the city's civic life, even taking a few acting roles in community theater, and remained on Rochester's most eligible bachelors list even after his physique began to soften.

When he was drafted in August 1942, Dwyer got fitted out for a uniform and served his country along with millions of other young men of his generation, whose coming of age in the Great Depression had made it seem as if living a life smaller than your father's was just the way things were now going to be. For some of those young men, the happy few, the war offered the chance to be a hero in the most epic drama in human history. Dwyer, though, was not one of those heroic happy few.

Dwyer served the first year of the war in Oakland as a weather observer, before getting himself into Ham Young's new JAG School in Ann Arbor. For a draftee, becoming an officer and then a law professor was an assignment with an air of prestige, but it meant that Dwyer's role in the most epic drama in human history was serving on the front lines of a college town, where the deadliest enemy was a winter not all that different from the one back in Rochester.

In December 1944, Dwyer followed Young to China, but the work turned out to be pretty mundane. If airmen got into trouble, Dwyer and Hendren would oversee the court-martial. If a soldier needed a will or wanted to marry a foreign girl, Dwyer and Hendren would help make sure that the desk trolls approved all the necessary paperwork. Like most of the 7 million men who served in World War II, Dwyer's war stories would have to be borrowed or embellished to be interesting over drinks back in Rochester.

* * *

Things changed the day Hendren was asked to take a look at a file containing the evidence the War Crimes Office had collected on what had happened to the lost Doolittle Raiders. Ham Young wanted to know if Hendren thought there was enough there to bring a case to trial and, if so, if he wanted to take it on as the prosecutor. The trial would be conducted before a military commission, a special kind of military tribunal that was like a court-martial, but with rules designed to prosecute war criminals.

The file contained lurid allegations far beyond anything Hollywood had dreamed, and it took little imagination to see that the lawyers who prosecuted Tojo and his gang for that barbarism would be Doolittle Raiders by association. They would see their names written into history as the men who had fulfilled Roosevelt's personal promise that justice be done.

Young's choosing Hendren, rather than Dwyer, for such a plum assignment made some sense given how high profile the trial was expected to be. A courtroom defines each person's role in space by means of overpolished wood. To the left is the defense table. To the right is the prosecution table. To the front is the judge's bench. To one side is the witness stand. To the other side is the jury box. From the public gallery, separated always by a railing of overpolished wood, all of these distinct roles are dramatized architecturally, and every gap between them where someone might rest their eyes away from the players on this stage, is decorated with ornamentations of authority, prudence, and received wisdom. Tall and graceful, his trousers creased sharp as a blade, Hendren was built from overpolished wood, and if the voice of reason sounded like that of any single man, it was John Hendren's.

Hendren had been an assistant attorney general back in Missouri and had made something of a name for himself by going after corporate tax cheats. It was the perfect kind of battle on behalf of the public good against corporate greed to help a New Deal Democrat get noticed.

During the war, Hendren had served as an officer in the JAG Corps, mostly in Washington with his wife, Wilmoth, at his side. Wilmoth was a savvy political operator in her own right back in Jefferson City. In 1936, the newspapers had cooed about Wilmoth, the "youngest delegate to the Democratic National Convention—and by all odds the prettiest," when she made a splash at the convention's beauty pageant. Wilmoth knew how to politic for her equally photo-ready husband, making sure their goings-on were always in the local society pages. She was an ideal companion in the nation's wartime capital, which had become engorged by billions of dollars in military spending and a million other itinerant newcomers, all vying for their piece of the action in a company town that lacked New York's glitz but was obviously where the big things were happening.

Hendren was deployed to China in the same wave of turnover that had taken both Dwyer and Young there the year before, and it did not take long for him to make international news. In January 1945, a B-25 crashed during takeoff in Kunming and flipped into a culvert along the runway. By the time rescue crews got to the crash site, they found the twenty-year-old tail gunner desperately trying to pull himself out of the rear turret. His legs had been crushed by the crumpled metal of the fuselage, which had been ignited by the unused fuel. Six men tried to wrest him free, but it was useless. With the flames getting hotter, the caustic black fuel smoke getting thicker, and the tail gunner's wails getting more desperate, a lieutenant colonel on the scene drew his sidearm and put two into the poor kid's head.

Hendren was given the task of representing the lieutenant colonel on murder charges. Strictly on the law and on the facts, Hendren faced an open-and-shut loser; maybe he could avoid the death penalty on the grounds that it had been a mercy killing, but the defendant's guilt was indisputable. No matter how noble the reason, shooting a defenseless man twice in the head is always a crime. The absolute best Hendren could have hoped for was to get the charge reduced to manslaughter on the ground that the lieutenant colonel had been so distraught at the sight of the poor dying wretch that he hadn't been in full control of himself when he pulled the trigger.

Undeterred, Hendren ran with the case. Nearly a dozen witnesses testified at the court-martial, including medical experts whom Hendren called to cast doubt over whether the real cause of death had been the injuries the tail gunner had suffered in the crash or the two slugs of lead the lieutenant colonel had put into his brain.

On its face, it was a preposterous defense. It would have been just as plausible to claim that the poor tail gunner had been born with a congenital heart defect that just by coincidence had killed him in the split second between when the lieutenant colonel had drawn his sidearm and when he had pulled the trigger. But coming out of John Hendren's mouth, doubts about the cause of death just somehow sounded more reasonable. The court-martial wasn't looking to nail the lieutenant colonel to the wall. Who could blame him? Hendren won a full acquittal.

The Doolittle case, though, wasn't some splashy court-martial or the rolling up of some Missouri tax cheats. This was applying international law like a criminal code to the highest-ranking members of a foreign enemy government. Every step Hendren took, including all the missteps, would have the rapt attention of the nation, if not the world. Hendren knew he needed a first-rate legal mind with the bullheaded grit to put it all together. So he handed Ham Young's file to Robert Dwyer to see what he thought.

* * *

The file itself was a bit thin. There were no obvious suspects for the worst of what had happened to the Doolittle Raiders. Those known to have had a direct role in the murders of Dean Hallmark, William Farrow, and Harold Spatz were all low-level grunts and functionaries, and, save for Emperor Hirohito, whom no one reasonably expected to be shipped off to Shanghai to stand trial, there was no clear legal theory for charging anyone higher up the chain of command.

The starting point of the investigation had been the three Doolittle Raiders the OSS had rescued the previous summer from Fengtai. Ham Young had written an eight-page report summarizing his interview with Chase Nielsen, Robert Hite, and Jacob DeShazer, and it was grisly stuff. Though the Doolittle Raid was of marquee quality, there was no glamour in the needless suffering those boys had endured. There was nothing Hollywood about dying alone of neglect in some prison cell in Nanking. There was no romance to the waterboard. It was just blunt human cruelty.

The rest of the file was mostly reports complied by Captain Jason Bailey, an investigator Young had sent to Shanghai back in September. Bailey had been an FBI agent in San Francisco before the war and seemed to do everything he could to look the part of a G-man. There was no significant American presence in Shanghai, except for the B-29s dropping food and relief supplies onto nearby internment camps, meaning that Bailey had to work out of a storage room in the Shanghai YMCA and was at the mercy of anyone who was willing to lend him a jeep.

Bailey's biggest find had been the urns containing the cremated remains of Hallmark, Farrow, and Spatz. For there to be a murder case at all, Bailey had needed to find the *corpus delicti*—literally the "body of the crime"—he needed definitive proof that the crime actually occurred.

Bailey had spent a frustrating month going down numerous dead ends until he had gotten a tip from a Japanese soldier at the 13th Army headquarters in Jiangwan, which had led him to International Funeral Directors in downtown Shanghai. In its storeroom, he had found twenty-three urns marked as having come from Jiangwan, but only twenty corresponded to the Japanese Army's records. The remaining three urns were numbered 170, 104, and 103, respectively, and each was marked with the same date: October 15, 1942, the day Hallmark, Farrow, and Spatz had disappeared.

Bailey's other major discovery was a document dated August 28, 1942, whose last page read "Noboru Unit Military Tribunal." Only four pages long, it was the official judgment against the lost Doolittle Raiders.

The Noboru Unit Judgment said that the Raiders had been charged "with the article of war which concerns enemy pilots and crew by judiciary Major Itsuro Hata." It traced the basic facts of the Doolittle Raid in detail and said that all eight had been convicted under Article II, sections 1 and 2, of something called the "Military Law Concerning the Punishment of Enemy Airmen," or the Enemy Airmen's Law for short. They were all sentenced to death, but attached to the Noboru Unit judgment was a follow-up report, which said that on October 14, 1942, the emperor had decided to commute the sentences of five of the prisoners; Hallmark, Farrow, and Spatz, though, were shot the next day.

It had been sheer luck that any of these documents made it into Bailey's hands. A young Japanese Army lawyer by the name of Lieutenant Tadahiro Hayama had come forward while Bailey was at Jiangwan and confessed that the Japanese Army had been busy burning documents over the previous summer. Most of the records about the Doolittle Raiders had been destroyed, but Hayama had secreted away copies of the few documents he could, including the Noboru Unit judgment, which provided the real names of several key witnesses. There was the prosecutor: Major Itsuro Hata. There were three military judges: Lieutenant Colonel Toyama Nakajo, Lieutenant Yusei Wako, and Lieutenant Ryuhei Okada. And it had all been done under the authority of the Japanese general in charge of occupied Shanghai: Lieutenant General Shigeru Sawada, whose signature stamp, or "chop," had been pressed onto the original Noboru Unit judgment to make it official.

With those documents and the urns he had found in International Funeral Directors' storeroom, Bailey had excitedly cabled back to Young with the message INVESTIGATION DOOLITTLE CASE COMPLETE. Young, in turn, told him to call a press conference to share the news.

Bailey had promptly gathered the press to the Cathay Hotel, one of Shanghai's central landmarks, and performed true to his G-man form. No matter how harrowing the details he described, he was just delivering the facts. The Doolittle Raiders had taken off from the *Hornet*, had attacked Tokyo heroically, and then had crash-landed in China after they had run out of fuel. Eight men had been captured by the Japanese and taken to Tokyo. Bailey had a habit of saying the full date as a kind of bullet point:

> On June 20, 1942, the Japanese had taken the fliers back to Shanghai and then held in the infamous Bridge House.

> On August 28, 1942, they had been tried before a Japanese court-martial. The proceedings had lasted half an hour.

> On October 15, 1942, Lieutenant Hallmark, Lieutenant Farrow, and Sergeant Spatz had been taken to Jiangwan Cemetery, which was near the golf course and used

regularly by the Japanese as an execution ground, and there shot.

"Robert Meder died in Nanking December 1, 1943," Bailey continued without the faintest inflection of emotion. "He had been suffering from dysentery and beriberi for 90 days. He had had no medical attendance until 10 days preceding his death, and then only a few pills and injections."

"Will you repeat that please, sir?" one of the reporters interjected.

Bailey plodded along without even so much as acknowledging the question. "The five who were spared were kept in Jiangwan until April 7, 1943. Meder died in December, 1943, with no more medical attention than I stated earlier. The others were held in Nanking until June, 1945. Then the Japs took them to Fengtai prison near Beijing. The recovery teams got them out in August—that was last month."

Bailey made a particular show of his copy of the Noboru Unit judgment. The proceedings, he explained, had been conducted entirely in Japanese. He then read aloud from his translation, making a point to speak the full names of the Doolittle Raiders as if it were a memorial service and clearly enunciating the names of the Japanese involved. "Army prosecutor, Major Itsuro Hata," he read, "participating." Never had the word "participating" sounded so culpable.

*   *   *

Having gone through Ham Young's file, Dwyer and Hendren outlined their case. They had the ashes from the funeral parlor in Shanghai as well as Meder's ashes from Nanking, which Bailey had also recovered. They had the Raiders' account of their captivity and a list of twelve potential witnesses, some of whom were already in custody in China and Japan.

There was still a lot of work to be done, including coming up with a clear theory of how and why it all fit together. Torture was clearly a war crime, as was the murder of prisoners of war. But it was not clear who the torturers or murderers were. They could not very well bring charges against "Well-Well" and "the Big Bad Wolf."

Dwyer and Hendren also knew that there would be no room for mistakes. The case would be a media spectacle, particularly when, as Dwyer expected, General Jimmy Doolittle came to Shanghai to testify. The first

American war crimes prosecution was already under way in Manila—General Tomoyuki Yamashita was accused of overseeing the perpetration of mass atrocities in the Philippines—and from what Dwyer could see in the papers, the trial was a circus. The public scrutiny of the Doolittle Trial was likely to be orders of magnitude greater.

Hendren sent the outline to Young along with a request for what he needed to get the job done, including translators, a dedicated military police officer to make arrests, an ethnographer to help them understand Japanese culture, and a public relations officer to manage the reporters. He also asked to have General Wedemeyer sign an order giving the prosecution of the Doolittle case top priority. That would provide him and his team with unlimited use of the Army's resources, as well as final say on all questions of trial strategy.

Dwyer also made sure that Hendren put in a by-name request for Captain Robert Dwyer. Young was unlikely to agree to put additional lawyers on the case this early, not least Dwyer, but Hendren needed someone to put the case together. So they framed the request as Dwyer's being assigned as Hendren's "investigator."

Hendren then closed the memo with a thinly veiled threat: "If the above minimum authority and assistance cannot be given the undersigned and his assistant respectfully request to be relieved of this assignment."

That threat might have been a bluff, but it did not matter. In short order, Young put Hendren in charge of the prosecution, assigned Dwyer as his investigator, and secured a top priority order from General Wedemeyer that gave them the "full cooperation and priority in all requests for transportation, either ground or air to any point, reporter and interpreter service and in all matters in connection with the above named case so that their mission may be accomplished with the least delay."

Dwyer had what he wanted, at least for now. Hendren was not in a position to start interviewing witnesses, hunting down suspects, and crafting a theory of the case under international law, but if Dwyer did those things, he would make himself indispensable and Hendren would have no choice but to insist that Young give him a seat at the prosecution table. Dwyer was in Shanghai to do big things, and this was something big. Now all he had to do was pull it off.

SEVEN

Before the ink on their top priority order had time to dry, Ham Young announced that war crimes trials in Shanghai would begin before the new year and that the Doolittle Trial would be the main feature.

Part of Young's reason for haste was China's rapidly escalating civil war. Mao Zedong's People's Liberation Army had already amassed half a million men in the territory around Shanghai. A spokesman for Chiang Kai-shek played down the threat, claiming that Mao's numbers were exaggerated, but Chiang's grip on China was tenuous and there was no telling how long American war crimes trials in China would even remain a possibility.

Young was also striking for the public's attention while the iron was hot. By November, war crimes trials against the former Axis powers were all the rage. In Nuremberg, Germany, the Allies were getting ready to begin the trial of major Nazis, and Tomoyuki Yamashita's trial was making front-page headlines almost every day.

That left Dwyer a month to build a blockbuster case that could actually go to trial in the real world. He needed to find a villain big enough to satisfy the public's expectations and to collect enough evidence to prove that villain guilty of real crimes beyond a reasonable doubt.

Dwyer turned to a stack of about a dozen photographs that he had been given. They were mostly posed shots of the captured Doolittle Raiders, taken by the Japanese in the summer of 1942; some also featured random Japanese soldiers standing around like a hunting party. Any one of the faces in those pictures could be Dwyer's villain. In one pair of photos labeled "No. 7," one of the Raiders was shown blindfolded, his mouth slightly agape in seeming terror as he was frog-marched by Japanese soldiers at each arm. The guard on the right, a slight snarl seeming to break at the sides of his mouth, could be the torturer Dwyer was searching for.

But maybe the Raider's mouth was open in a cough. Maybe it was a yawn. And the Japanese soldier on his right, maybe his snarling grin revealed the heart of a sadist, eager to drag his prey to the waterboard. But maybe his mouth had just been caught in midsentence, saying the Japanese equivalent of "Watch your step." Maybe he was just nervously mugging for the cameraman, who would have been as obvious to him as he was necessarily invisible in the photo.

Roosevelt had promised that the United States would hold "personally and officially responsible" anyone in the Japanese government who had "participated" in the Raiders' mistreatment and executions. Surely any one of the nameless Japanese faces in Dwyer's stack of photographs had "participated" in some way. Simply being close enough to get caught on film proved that; but were they actually responsible? And for what, exactly?

The only thing those photos told Dwyer for sure was that a given person had been there with those other people at the moment the photographer had opened the camera's shutter. Dwyer couldn't build a case that put on trial every Japanese guard who had crossed paths with the Doolittle Raiders over the course of their three and a half years in prison. That would be dozens, maybe even hundreds, of men. Dwyer needed to tie the Raiders' mistreatment and executions to the criminal acts of specific people. If the Doolittle Trial was going to be the most celebrated war crimes trial of the war, Dwyer needed a villain worthy of the crime. He needed a mastermind.

* * *

The first and most likely candidate was Sotojiro Tatsuta. The record of execution named Tatsuta as the "executioner," and during the Raiders' interview with Ham Young the previous summer, Tatsuta's had been one of the few names they could recall, along with that of Tatsuta's translator in Jiangwan, Caesar dos Remedios.

In Shanghai, Bailey had located Remedios, who had helped him track down Tatsuta in Hangkou. Tatsuta was now incarcerated in Shanghai's

Ward Road Jail, a massive stone complex adjacent to the city's Jewish ghetto that Young had persuaded the Chinese to let him use as a detention facility for suspected war criminals.

Remedios had lived his whole life in Shanghai as the son of a Japanese mother and a father who was a Portuguese citizen, a distinct ethnic group known as the Macanese. The British had treated the Macanese, due to their skills as translators, as a special case in the otherwise rigid caste system that ranked Asians and dogs as roughly equivalent.

Remedios fit the Macanese stereotype perfectly. Retreating and unremarkable, he spoke half a dozen languages, and his small role in the Doolittle Raiders' saga had been the result of his own imprisonment by the Japanese and a deal he had taken to get out early by serving as an interpreter at Jiangwan. Now, with the war over, he was happy to put his skills to use for the US Army. Dwyer found Remedios ready and willing to serve as his translator and general fixer around Shanghai as he tried to put the case together as quickly as possible.

Dwyer and Remedios passed through the Ward Road Jail's twenty-foot stone walls into a concrete central hall from which long corridors spoked out in all four directions. Tatsuta would be Dwyer's first major interview, and more than anyone, he seemed to have the Raiders' literal blood on his hands. His arrest had been kept out of the papers, and he had not yet been questioned by war crimes investigators. Dwyer had read up on him as much as he could, but nothing quite prepares for the moment of sitting face-to-face with someone in a holding cell for the first time.

When Dwyer saw Tatsuta, he saw a gawky man in his early fifties with a head the shape of a cantaloupe and a gold tooth that flashed under his mustache when he talked. "Mastermind" was not an apt description.

Tatsuta claimed to have liked the Raiders on a human level. Though he did not speak English, he recounted how he and Remedios had chatted with them in the exercise yard about "whether they were married, about their families, what food they eat, etc. This is the conversation I had had with them." They had been young boys, and Tatsuta had made a point of saying that one of them had reminded him of his own son, who was about the same age and serving in the Japanese Army. He said he could not remember any of the Raiders' names but said he would probably recognize them if he saw them.

Seeing an opening, Dwyer pulled out his stack of photographs and asked Tatsuta to identify anyone he recognized. Tatsuta looked closely but couldn't be sure.

"I will show you a picture marked No. 10," Dwyer said, "and ask you if that is one of the executed fliers." It was a picture of Harold Spatz.

Tatsuta looked closely. "It might have been one of them."

"Isn't that the one who reminded you of your son?" Dwyer asked.

"All the young people that were taken in by the Japanese military police always reminded me of my son," Tatsuta answered.

Dwyer asked if Tatsuta recognized any of the Japanese soldiers in the photos. Again Tatsuta pleaded ignorance, but when it came to his own involvement in the Raiders' executions, he was unguarded to the point of being blasé. The only time he seemed to get nervous was when Dwyer brought up Dean Hallmark's bomber jacket.

"Did you take one of the field jackets of one of the fliers," Dwyer asked him, "and have it tailored or altered to fit you?"

"I received one leather flying jacket from the prosecutor," Tatsuta tried to explain, adding "as a remembrance of one of the Doolittle fliers."

It was a dubious excuse for looting a dead body and came with a deflection of responsibility to "the prosecutor." It was a constant refrain from Tatsuta, who always deflected to "the prosecutor." When the execution grounds had been ready, Tatsuta had reported it to the prosecutor. When the bodies had been cremated, they had been delivered to the prosecutor. The prosecutor had reported the results of the trial and execution to the commanding general. When Dwyer asked Tatsuta why the Raiders had been put into his brig at all, Tatsuta answered, "The prosecutor have to make a warrant to keep them in jail and the man who brought the warrant told me that these fliers bombed schools, churches, and killed many civilians."

Dwyer tried to dig into who was ultimately responsible above Tatsuta in the chain of command. Tatsuta, though, always gave some loopy "so-and-so reported to so-and-so" answer. For a military organization, the lines of authority were a mess.

The prosecutor, to whom Tatsuta reported, worked for the Noboru Unit, which was just another name for the 13th Army. Tatsuta's actual supervisor had been Captain Tikojiro Oka, the warden of the Nanking

Prison, which had put Tatsuta under an entirely separate chain of command from the prosecutor, who had reported to General Shigeru Sawada. That meant that the 13th Army was technically responsible for the Doolittle Raiders' trial but that Nanking Prison was technically responsible for their execution. And even that was not precisely accurate in the special case of the Doolittle Raiders, because as far as Tatsuta knew, the orders for everything had come directly from Tokyo.

"Who," Dwyer demanded, desperate for a simple answer, "had charge of the execution?"

"I would like to explain the details of the execution?" Tatsuta told Remedios, sensing Dwyer's frustration.

"Go ahead," Dwyer said, his exhaustion mounting.

"The order to put the three men to death came from the Japanese Army headquarters in Tokyo to Commander Lieutenant General Sawada of the 13th Army," Tatsuta explained. "Lieutenant General Sawada then reissues the order for execution to the prosecutor to proceed with the execution. The prosecutor has to carry out the order by sending out the papers to Captain Oka, the Governor of the Nanking Japanese Military Prison, whose branch is in Shanghai. I, at the time a sergeant, acted for Captain Oka because he was not present."

To Dwyer, it was bureaucratic word soup, and the more time he spent trying to pin it all down, the more complicated it became. No one, it seemed, had been making any of the key decisions. They had simply been reporting up the chain of command or reissuing orders, whose origin was some faceless system at Tokyo headquarters.

"Do you know what Army Officer or Officers at Headquarters approved this case?" Dwyer asked.

Tatsuta's response was maddening: "I don't know the Officer."

* * *

Convicting Tatsuta wouldn't take much. He had admitted to executing three innocent men and then pillaging their clothes for good measure. But it was clear to anyone who spent more than a minute with him that Tatsuta was no mastermind. Back in Japan, he had been a farmer and was looking forward to returning to his farm once it was all over. He was a simple man who was overeager to please and possibly the stupidest Japanese soldier

Dwyer had ever met. Hendren could make the case against Tatsuta all by himself.

Dwyer needed to go up the chain of command. And so, a few days after interviewing Tatsuta, Dwyer and Remedios made a trip out to Jiangwan.

The date on the calendar—November 20, 1945—was auspicious. Later that day, on the other side of the world, the Nuremberg Trials would begin. The presiding judges came from the four major European allies—the United States, Great Britain, the Soviet Union, and France—with Francis Biddle, Roosevelt's former attorney general, taking the bench for the Americans in what the *New York Times* celebrated as an event that would set "the first precedents for a common law of nations."

As Dwyer tried to put together his own precedent-setting case in Shanghai, he encountered more and more difficulties. Chief among them was a lack of physical evidence. Japan's 13th Army had done an exemplary job at burning its records after the war. In the dozen or so interviews he conducted in Jiangwan, man after man spoke of records, records, and more records. Dwyer would ask, "Do you know where the records are?" And the response was always some variation on "On the capitulation of Japan, the records were burnt." Given the jungle of paperwork Dwyer was learning about, the bonfires must have darkened the skies for days.

Most of the men still in Jiangwan who had anything to offer Dwyer were low-level guards and grunts. Many of them had witnessed the Raiders' execution personally, and whatever else they did or didn't know, it had clearly been one of the few truly historic moments of their lives. Dwyer asked one guard if the Americans had been known as the "Doolittle fliers."

"I do not know the Doolittle fliers," the guard replied, "but I knew they were the first airmen who bombed Tokyo."

Each man described the day of the execution with the same broad strokes, though the details varied wildly. One man recalled the firing squad as standing fifteen meters away. One said twenty. Another said fifty. One recalled the execution as taking place in the early morning. Another remembered lunchtime. Tatsuta had said sundown. Most remembered one Raider whose pulse had lingered as he dangled limply, bleeding from his forehead, but where Tatsuta said the pulse had held on for five minutes, others said it lingered for ten.

Some even seemed to remember Tatsuta giving the order to fire, which was an intriguing lead if true. If Tatsuta had given the order to fire, he could be shown to have orchestrated a murder from beginning to end. The guns might not have been literally in his hands, but they had been at his command. It would not be difficult to convince the Army colonels who would be sitting as the judges and jury in the Doolittle Trial that this Japanese soldier, who had turned a scrubby lawn next to a golf course into the Doolittle Raiders' Golgotha, should be convicted as a war criminal and hanged by the neck until dead.

Getting that same kind of clear evidence against anyone higher up in the chain of command, however, remained elusive. Every time Dwyer broke out his stack of photographs, the answers were the same: no one knew a thing. The Japanese faces remained as nameless as the American ones.

"Do you remember which flier you handled?" Dwyer asked a guard who had admitted to personally tying one of the Raiders to a cross.

"I cannot remember," he replied.

Dwyer showed him the stack of photographs, asking which of the Americans he had seen in the last moments of his life. Was it Harold Spatz, the young one? Was it William Farrow, the tall one? Or was it Dean Hallmark, the sick one?

"I do not remember the face," the guard said plaintively. It was the same refrain each time. "I cannot recall anyone," another guard said. "They all looked alike."

One of the only men to admit recognizing any of the photos was Lieutenant Tadahiro Hayama, the 13th Army's military lawyer, who had come forward the previous September and given Jason Bailey the only known copy of the Noboru Unit judgment from August 1942. Fearing that innocent people might be wrongly held responsible, Hayama had secreted away copies of whatever he could as soon as word of Japan's surrender spread.

Looking through Dwyer's stack of photographs, Hayama stopped at the photos labeled "No. 7." "Pictures No. 7," he said, "were printed in the Tokyo Papers." It had been in late October 1942. The photos had been on the front page of nearly every Japanese newspaper under headlines proclaiming "American Pilots Confess Wanton Attack on Tokyo School,

Hospital Civilians." The first was the picture of the blindfolded Raider being marched out of an airplane with a Japanese soldier at each arm.

The second was a lively group shot of the crew of *Bat Out of Hell* taken outside the Kempeitai's headquarters in Nanchang, China, the day after the raid. The scene showed Robert Hite glowering at the photographer as William Farrow and George Barr cracked a joke next to him. The diminutive Jacob DeShazer slouched in front next to Harold Spatz, whose long hair was spiked up with bed head and who posed with the cool of James Cagney, bomber jacket unzipped and cigarette dangling between his fingers. The very casualness of their pose both corroborated and amplified the outrage the accompanying story sought to inspire as it recounted the "craven attitude of the Raiders" as they confessed to bombing and machine-gunning "innocent, unarmed civilians, school children and non-military objectives, such as hospitals, during the air raid on Tokyo April 18."

Hayama did not know anyone in the photographs personally, neither the Japanese nor the Americans. The Doolittle Raid and its immediate aftermath had all taken place before he had been drafted into the Japanese Army in 1943. He was from a good family, had graduated from the prestigious Tokyo Imperial University in 1939, and had won a coveted appointment as a judge. As a result, Hayama was not eager to be shipped off to serve, but, like Dwyer, he had been drafted and ultimately was stationed in the 13th Army's Legal Department in Shanghai in the summer of 1944. By that point, almost anyone who had participated in the case was long gone, but Hayama's professional curiosity had led him to read the Japanese case file on the Doolittle Raiders.

Hayama remembered the case file being about an inch and a half thick, running easily to two hundred pages. Most of it was made up of various transcripts and cables between different Japanese commands. It had been a year since Hayama had read it, but he was certain he had seen a cable from Lieutenant General Shigeru Sawada to Tokyo headquarters asking to execute the Doolittle Raiders. Tokyo's response, so far as Hayama remembered, was that three could be executed but the other five had been granted clemency by the emperor. It was unusual for reports to be sent directly to Tokyo, Hayama explained, but he was sure of what he had seen. "The Doolittle fliers case was specially sent to Tokyo."

"Was the sentence of death for the other three fliers approved by the Emperor?" Dwyer asked, wanting to be sure.

"It was from the order of Lieutenant General Sawada," Hayama explained, "13th Japanese Army Commander."

"Was he the officer approved the death sentence for the three fliers?" Hayama was certain. "Yes."

Shigeru Sawada's name was high on Dwyer's list of potential suspects. Dwyer knew that he had been the Japanese general in charge of Shanghai in the summer of 1942 and Bailey had asked General MacArthur's men in Tokyo to hunt him down. MacArthur's announcement of Sawada's arrest had made international news with breathless headlines such as "Jap Killer Arrested," but concrete information about him had proven elusive. Few, if any, Americans had ever heard of Sawada.

Sawada's chop, which was stamped onto the Noboru Unit judgment, was certainly incriminating, but his actual role in the mistreatment and execution of the Doolittle Raiders, beyond being in command of the 13th Army, was hardly obvious. Having now spent years inside the US Army's bureaucracy, Dwyer knew that a commanding general's name could find its way onto nearly anything without his knowing it. Hayama, however, provided the first hint that Sawada was the man Dwyer had been searching for; he had knowingly and personally participated in, if not directed, the executions of the Doolittle Raiders.

Dwyer needed to get his hands on the Japanese case file, but Hayama was not sure if it still existed. "If the records are not burnt, they must be in Tokyo," he said, trying to be helpful. He remembered that a Japanese major had come from Tokyo earlier that year to fetch a copy, saying that he wanted to write a textbook on the Japanese law of trying war criminals. It was certainly possible that the major still had it.

If Sawada was sending cables to Tokyo, personally seeking permission to execute the Raiders, then Dwyer could prove he was the criminal mastermind behind it all and Dwyer's seat at the prosecution table would be all but assured. Dwyer needed that case file.

"Where is the case file now?" Dwyer pressed Hayama. "Do you know?" Hayama could only guess. "It must be in Tokyo."

EIGHT

The week after Thanksgiving, Dwyer flew into the once mysterious capital of the Empire of Japan and saw a city largely reduced to a field of ashes. For miles, nothing stood taller than man's height except for occasional brick or stone ruins that jutted up like stalks inadvertently left unscythed after the harvest.

Airmen trained in the lead-up to the war had been taught that the deliberate bombing of civilians was "repugnant to our humanitarian principles, and certainly it is a method of warfare that we would adopt only with great reluctance and regret." Following Germany's blitz on Poland, Roosevelt appealed to the world to "in no event, and under no circumstances, undertake the bombardment from the air of civilian populations." Official US military doctrine was that bombers could only target the enemy's "bottlenecks," the key pathways of the enemy's economy, in order to prevent them from producing the means to wage war. Doolittle had sternly instructed his men to "avoid nonmilitary targets" during his now famous raid, and in its diplomatic protest over Japan's execution of the captured Raiders, the State Department was adamant: "The Government of the United States brands as false the charge that American aviators intentionally have attacked noncombatants anywhere."

By March 1945, however, there were no longer many bottlenecks left to be bombed in Japan, and the commander of US air operations, Major General Curtis E. LeMay, was under tremendous pressure to end the war from the air to forestall a land invasion of Japan that was expected to cost a million lives.

Chemists at Harvard University had developed a new kind of incendiary chemical called napalm. With a runny jelly consistency that stuck to nearly anything, it burned unceasingly once ignited, quickly consuming all available oxygen. Never a believer in the bottleneck theory to begin with, LeMay decided to arm his B-29 bomber fleet with what came to be called "goop bombs" and "block burners," which sprayed sticky fire 180 feet in every direction after striking the ground.

On March 9, 1945, squadrons of B-29s took off from island bases in the Pacific for a night bombing raid. The first planes over Tokyo were instructed to fly across four aiming points, dropping enough incendiaries along the way to paint the city with a giant flaming X. Behind them were more than three hundred B-29s with instructions to drop their block burners on any area within the X that was not yet on fire.

The resulting firestorms blew Tokyo's pagodas, street stalls, and wooden town houses with their tatami floors and sliding paper walls into clouds of ash. In that one night, more than one hundred thousand residents of Tokyo were immolated, asphyxiated, or crushed as the wooden beams of their homes collapsed and LeMay's B-29s returned to base with their chrome underbellies blackened by the columns of soot that had been the imperial capital when the sun had set that evening.

Over the next ten days, LeMay incinerated the urban map of Japan. Two days after Tokyo came Nagoya. Then came Osaka. Then Kobe. Then Nagoya again. In late May, LeMay leveled another nineteen square miles of Tokyo. With Japan's major industrial and urban centers destroyed, the targets turned to smaller cities, towns, and suburbs throughout the spring and early summer. At the end of July, LeMay agreed to drop warning leaflets onto targeted cities the night before each attack. Over the following two weeks, LeMay duly dropped leaflets on a handful of industrial towns and then on Hiroshima and Nagasaki. Before more leaflets could be dropped, the Soviets invaded Manchuria—the final straw prompting Emperor Hirohito's surrender on August 15, 1945.

By the time Dwyer arrived, sixty-two square miles of Tokyo had been razed. Its Japanese population had fallen to half its prewar level, and those who remained lived mostly in shantytowns made up of 100-square-foot bungalows. The only area still in any recognizable shape was the city's downtown, which was home to the Imperial Palace and had been resettled as "Little America" by the quarter-million US service members now living there under the command of General Douglas MacArthur, the Supreme Commander for the Allied Powers, or "SCAP."

Little America was the Emerald City, and MacArthur's headquarters in the Dai-ichi Seimei Building was the wizard's palace at its heart. Army jeeps, rickshaws, and imported American cars jammed the grid of streets that had been renamed "Avenue A" and "MacArthur Blvd.," leaving no doubt that the Americans had reestablished Edo as Japan's capital and MacArthur was now its shogun.

Dwyer made his way to SCAP's Legal Section in the Meiji Building, eight stories of granite built in 1934 with towering ornamental pillars that made it indistinguishable from the dozens of government office buildings erected in Washington, DC, during the New Deal. It was just around the corner from MacArthur's headquarters, and machine-sewn American flags cut, colored, and stitched to US federal government specifications flew above Dwyer's head from nearly every building.

With a staff of two hundred men, SCAP's Legal Section was a far vaster enterprise than anything Dwyer had experienced back in China. MacArthur was undertaking a radical effort to remake postwar Japan in the American image, what was called the "democratic revolution from above." That revolution required a lot of lawyers, and many of Dwyer's former colleagues from the JAG School in Ann Arbor were now in charge of everything from rewriting the Japanese constitution to redistributing the wealth of Japan's former oligarchs. It was an enviable opportunity for the ambitious, especially compared to the humdrum legal work Dwyer would otherwise be doing in Shanghai had he not gotten his role on the Doolittle case.

War crimes prosecutions were where all the glamour was. President Truman had just appointed Joseph B. Keenan, the former head of the Justice Department's Criminal Division, to lead SCAP's International Prosecution Section, whose singular mission was to try Japan's so-called Class A war criminals, such as the former prime minister, Hideki Tojo. Every component of SCAP's Legal Section was eager to do its part to help Dwyer make his case, from the Criminal Registry Division, which was doing SCAP's manhunts, to the Investigation Division.

Though far less swashbuckling than arresting Japanese war criminals, the work of the Investigation Division was arguably far more important to the nuts and bolts of building the case Dwyer needed to make. If a bureaucracy is a machine, the exhaust it belches is the stream of paper on which words are written by people who are paid to write what others are paid to read: records, memos, receipts, inventories, requisition forms, cables, minutes, letters, orders, and even the occasional photograph. Japan was one of the world's most bureaucratic of bureaucracies, and despite fire's almost unique affinity for paper, the Investigation Division had raked up millions of documents just in case the needles in those haystacks turned out to be crucial pieces of evidence.

A trove of such paper had been compiled and translated for Dwyer, anything and everything that remotely seemed as though it might be related to the Doolittle case. Some of the documents in the trove were interesting. Most were not. And most frustrating, the key document that Dwyer needed—the inch-and-a-half-thick Japanese case file on the Doolittle Raiders—was not among them. Tadahiro Hayama had convinced Dwyer that the case file would prove his case against Shigeru Sawada beyond a reasonable doubt, but despite the Investigation Division's extraordinary progress in tracing the old empire's paper trail, that needle had not yet turned up.

Some cables from the Ministry of War in Tokyo about the case had been found. They showed a level of direct involvement at the highest levels of Japan's wartime bureaucracy that everyone had suspected but could now be proven. Still, none of them was addressed to Sawada personally or even to the 13th Army in Shanghai directly. Based on Hayama's description of what was in the Japanese case file, Sawada had not only participated but had taken the initiative. But all Dwyer could show for the moment was that Sawada had been in command.

*　*　*

Before returning to Shanghai, Dwyer caught an early afternoon flight to Manila. Back in Shanghai, as part of the endless victory party, the Army was throwing a girlfriend derby, in which America's fighting men were scheduled to race one another with their Chinese, Russian, and occasionally American girlfriends riding them as jockeys. "Pretty girls all are over town," the Shanghai *Stars and Stripes* crowed. "Just yours for the asking." Dwyer, though, spent the day sitting for eleven hours in what seemed like

1945's slowest airplanes as they island-hopped, repeatedly refueling along the two-thousand-mile journey south. By the time Dwyer landed, it was midnight, and though it was December, he stepped off the plane into a sweaty, bug-ridden heat.

Manila was nothing like Tokyo in terms of the totality of the destruction Dwyer had seen, but the scars of war were everywhere in the pockmarked facades and blownout windows of the buildings that were still standing. Manila had been at the center of some of the most dramatic episodes of the Pacific War; MacArthur had made his infamous retreat from Corregidor Island in Manila Bay in March 1942, relinquishing the Philippines to Japanese occupation. The Philippines had been the United States' largest colony for more than forty years, and its loss, along with the capture of more than a hundred thousand Americans across the Philippine archipelago, was the greatest humiliation of the war. Three years later, MacArthur had made good on his promise to return and wiped out the Japanese forces in the Battle of Manila. Now Manila was again on the front page every day and around the world as the site of the trial of General Yamashita.

Yamashita had been the most celebrated Japanese general of his generation, leading the stunning invasion of Malaya and the capture of Singapore, a crown jewel of the United Kingdom's Asian empire, at the outset of the war. The jungles of the Malay Peninsula were dense and difficult to navigate, and, knowing that time was on the defenders' side, Yamashita had decided to pare down his force to 36,000 men and equip his forward infantry with 18,000 bicycles so that they could quietly ride down the network of roads the British had laid all the way to the heart of Singapore.

The lightning-fast advance down the peninsula had bewildered the British, who found themselves consistently surrounded and seemingly outnumbered. In just seventy-three days and with the loss of only 3,000 of his own men, Yamashita had taken Singapore and the rest of Malaya from a British force of 130,000. It had been a stunning victory for the Japanese and had marked the beginning of the end for the centuries-old British Empire. Around the world, Yamashita earned immediate celebrity under the nom de guerre, "the Tiger of Malaya."

A political rival of Prime Minister Tojo, Yamashita's reward for that success was to spend most of the war far from the action, lest he earn more fame on the battlefield and challenge Tojo's control over Imperial Japan's war cabinet. But by October 1944, Tojo had been ousted and Yamashita was brought back to command Japan's Army in the Philippine archipelago just days before General MacArthur's forces waded onto the eastern shores of Leyte Gulf.

Yamashita found his position more desperate than he could have imagined. His forces were thinly dispersed over dozens of islands, poorly disciplined, and plagued by guerrilla attacks. He knew it was only a matter of time before the Americans would take the sword from his hand.

By early February 1945, MacArthur had nearly encircled Manila, and Filipino guerrilla activity against the Japanese became irrepressible. The Japanese response was brutal. In his diary, a Japanese soldier chronicled near daily massacres against suspected guerillas. "150 guerillas were disposed of tonight," he wrote on February 7, 1945. "I personally stabbed and killed 10." Two days later, "Burned 1,000 guerillas to death tonight." Four days after that, "I am now on guard duty at Guerrilla Internment Camp. While I was on duty, approx. 10 guerillas tried to escape. They were stabbed to death. At 1600 all guerillas were burned to death."

Yamashita retreated with his army northward into the mountains and ordered all Japanese forces in Manila to evacuate. Despite the order, approximately 20,000 Japanese Army soldiers and Navy sailors stayed behind. The results were catastrophic.

As they had done in caves throughout the jungle islands of the Pacific, the Japanese fought to the death or committed suicide attacks instead of submitting to capture. Massive shelling left the city in ruins. The fighting ceased only on March 3, 1945, when every Japanese soldier and sailor in the city was dead, along with 30,000 to 40,000 Filipinos.

Yamashita waited until the formal Japanese surrender on September 2, 1945, to come down from the mountains and relinquish his sword. At MacArthur's war crimes conference two weeks later, the decision was made to make an example of him, and from the Yamashita trial's first session on October 29, 1945, newspapers around the world offered a daily chronicle of horrors: priests killed in churches; patients killed in hospitals; babies bayoneted in their mother's arms; sex slaves mutilated by having their breasts cut off. For the Japanese soldiers and sailors who had stayed behind in Manila, it had been the end of the world. None had expected to—or did—survive.

*   *   *

From the moment Dwyer had taken on the Doolittle case, he had wanted to get a firsthand look at the Yamashita trial. The Fourteenth Air Force's legal department was one thing; he had seen plenty of courts-martial. But prosecuting the Japanese for war crimes in a military commission was something else altogether. There were so few precedents, and it was not wholly obvious how to put a man on trial for violating international law.

The morning after his arrival, Dwyer made his way to Manila's T & C Building, which had been repurposed as the offices of SCAP's Legal Section in Manila. It was a Sunday and Yamashita's trial was in recess, but Captain William Yard was in the office. Another former colleague of Dwyer's from the JAG school, Yard was now in charge of the nuts and bolts of running the Army's war crimes prosecutions in the Philippines.

For someone in such a plum spot, Yard was rather cynical about the whole enterprise. General MacArthur wanted Yamashita convicted and fast, but he refused to understand that the prosecution was moving its case along as fast as it could. The generals they had gotten assigned to serve as the military commission's judges and jurors, called "the members" in military legal jargon, weren't the problem, either—they had picked five career "desk generals" for the job, who weren't lawyers and had gotten to where they were by knowing how to give the chain of command what it wanted.

The obstacle to getting the trial wrapped up quickly were the JAGs at the defense table. They were all Army officers, many of whom Dwyer had known in Ann Arbor. But Ham Young, it seemed, had trained them all a little too well on how to be lawyers of military law rather than military lawyers—and there was a difference. They fought every point they could find and always kept going back to the rules in the *Manual for Courts-Martial*, but those weren't the rules here. As Yard repeatedly explained, these were not courts-martial, these were military commissions, and a military commission had only one rule of evidence: Did the evidence have "probative value"? No one really knew what "probative value" meant, so it should have been an easy standard to meet, but the lawyers at the defense table would not let it go and pressed the prosecution on every stupid point.

Captain A. Frank Reel, in particular, had been a pain in the ass from the beginning. Dwyer knew Reel well. He had gone to Harvard about the same time as Dwyer, and they had spent most of the war together back in Ann Arbor, where Reel had directed a graduation day skit in which Dwyer got a chance for a star turn.

Like Dwyer, Reel did not cut an impressive figure as an officer. Balding and not in particularly good shape, his enormous glasses accentuated the roundedness of his thick lips and his khaki uniform tended to sag like laundry in Manila's humidity, which was not helped by Reel's habit of buckling his wristwatch into the button of his shirt pocket.

In a courtroom, though, Reel was relentless. Assigned to defend Yamashita and unwilling to accept that this trial was not about law, his command of legal procedure was better than anyone else's and he was physically incapable of concealing his contempt for how indifferent, ignorant, or both the desk generals who presided over the trial. If the prosecution was questioning a witness on the stand, Reel seemed to object every time he took a breath.

"Objection," Reel would call out from the defense table.

"Objection not sustained," the presiding judge would reply as habitually as if saying "God bless you" to a sneeze. At one point, one of Yamashita's Japanese advisers asked, "Who is this Mr. Jackson that Captain Reel is always talking about?" When the question elicited puzzled faces, he attempted to clarify: "He always jumps up and says: Jackson. Is Jackson's last name, Notsustained?"

Reel and the rest of Yamashita's defense team had even gone to the Philippine Supreme Court and filed a lawsuit against the Army arguing that Yamashita's whole trial was illegal. MacArthur had been furious when he had found out and had sent orders down to Yard's office to ignore it all, including any rulings or paperwork that came from the Filipino courts. That, in turn, had led to a ridiculous chase around Manila when Yamashita's lawyers attempted to personally serve process on MacArthur's deputy in the Philippines, Lieutenant General Wilhelm D. Styer, the commanding general for the Western Pacific. The Philippine Supreme Court had dismissed the case out of hand, but now Reel was trying to get the US Supreme Court involved.

To Yard, all of this was a nuisance. If there was a piece of advice Yard wanted Dwyer to take away for the Doolittle Trial, it was to keep the number of oversmart lawyers to a minimum. That went for the military commission judges, who ideally would not be lawyers at all. But that went doubly for the lawyers the Army assigned to the defense team.

*   *   *

Dwyer got his chance to take in the spectacle of the Yamashita trial the following day. The proceedings were entering their final week, and Yamashita himself was due to take the stand.

The drama unfolded in the ballroom of Mansion House, a whitewashed palacio surrounded by landscaped gardens and palm leaves that had been the center of the United States' colonial government in the Philippines. Yard drove Dwyer up the gravel driveway to the gate, where four smartly dressed military police searched them and handed them their passes to enter the courtroom. All around the grounds, tents and temporary huts had been put up to service the trials inside, making the mansion look like a castle within a miniature village. Military police were everywhere and made conspicuous by their white pith helmets stamped with the letters "MP" in place of the usual round white helmets.

Once inside, Dwyer was in awe of the production values. The ballroom turned courtroom with its large windows overlooking scenic Manila Bay was not simply a courtroom; it was a Hollywood set. Cables snaked along the floors, and tripods positioned stage lights and speakers around the judge's bench, the lawyers' podium, and the witness stand to make sure the cameramen could get the cleanest shots. More cameramen were positioned in the ballroom's balcony to shoot B-reel footage that could be worked into newsreels to dramatize the trial.

Waiting for the proceedings to begin, Dwyer counted more than forty reporters from every newspaper, radio, or magazine he could think of: *Life, Time, Fortune, Newsweek*, the *New York Times*, the *Chicago Sun*. Even *Reader's Digest* had sent a correspondent. The lawyers for both sides had grown comfortable to the point of casual with the assembled press corps as they milled about waiting for the court to be called to order. Dwyer knew many of the JAGs from back in Ann Arbor, and it was quite a sight to see them all, relatively junior Army lawyers, chatting like movie stars with reporters from *Life* and the *New York Times*.

Dwyer even recognized one of the Japanese soldiers sitting beside Yamashita who was acting as his interpreter. It had been well over a decade, but there was Masakatsu Hamamoto, who had been at Harvard at the same time as Dwyer and Reel. Hamamoto had always stood out to Reel as "an earnest oriental," regularly spotted dashing through Harvard Yard outfitted in tennis whites. He had returned to Japan after attending Harvard and through the many bizarre twists of wartime fate had become Yamashita's personal secretary.

A pith-helmeted MP called the room to attention and announced the rules of court, and the military commission judges then took their seats behind the bench, and the presiding judge had the kindly face of a basset hound, which—though he was not actually a lawyer—gave him the gravitas of a county judge.

Yamashita himself was big for a Japanese man of his era, standing five feet, seven inches, with a thick build and a neck nearly the width of his head. As he took the stand for the final testimony of the trial, he sat with a martial posture, hands gripping but not clenching the arms of the wooden witness chair. His words came out crisply and his head stayed stiff as he spoke, except for a taut nod he would occasionally make for emphasis. No matter the topic, Yamashita had the patient dispassion of a man dictating to a slow secretary, which in this case was a table of courtroom translators who relayed his answers sentence by sentence into a chrome radio microphone.

As horrific as the Battle of Manila had been, the links between it and Yamashita were tenuous. There was no clear evidence that he had ordered his men to fight to the death or to commit the necrophiliac orgy that had so shocked the world. In fact, he had ordered his men out of the city before the fighting had even started. Those who had participated in the Battle of Manila had, for whatever reason, stayed behind when Yamashita had made his tactical retreat into the mountains—how could he be held criminally responsible for what his subordinates had done after he was gone?

The answer, Dwyer discovered, was found through clever lawyering. Prosecutors could not prove that Yamashita had ordered his men to commit atrocities in Manila, but Yamashita had not stopped them, either. Ordinarily, that wouldn't be enough. A person minding his own business has no legal duty to stop a crime in progress. But that rule was no longer as ironclad as it had once been. A simple-seeming case from New Jersey of all places had set a precedent that would turn out to change history.

Benjamin Harrison had been hired to man the gate where the tracks of the Erie Railroad crossed over Rutgers Street in the town of Belleville, New Jersey. His job was as simple as it was dull. When a train approached, an electric mechanism would trip a signal bell telling him to lower the gate to stop the traffic along Rutgers Street from crossing. When the train passed, he was to raise the gate back up. However simple and dull a job it was, Benjamin Harrison had been trusted to do it. And he ordinarily did, except for one summer night in 1929, when he let one too many cars pass under the gate after the electric mechanism had tripped the signal bell. He had done nothing when it was his job to do something. And for that he was found guilty of homicide.

Yamashita, the prosecutors had figured, was Benjamin Harrison. The dogs of war are a rabid pack, and by world-historical standards, what Yamashita's men had done to Manila was as inevitable as what the Roman legions had done to Carthage. But the previous half century had sought to change all that. In 1907, the major world powers, including Japan, had accepted the Hague Convention, which had radically transformed the standards for how civilized nations went to war against one another. Rape and pillage were banned. The protection of the sick and wounded was required. Even the definition of a true soldier was changed. A civilized army was no longer permitted to be a savage mob; it had to operate under a responsible chain of command. The dogs of war had to be kept on a leash.

When Yamashita had fled Manila, he had done nothing when his job had been to do something. It had been his command responsibility to protect the people of Manila from what the men under his command might do. If he could not carry out that responsibility, it was his duty to surrender because he was no longer in command of a real army. An army without a commander is a mindless steel beast, and Yamashita had failed to lower the gate.

Making commanders responsible for war crimes perpetrated by their subordinates was a powerful legal theory that solved the single biggest problem war crimes prosecutors faced. As Dwyer had discovered in his hunt for the missing Japanese case file, evidence was easily lost in the fog of war. The theory of command responsibility being used in the Yamashita case offered a shortcut around that by making it unnecessary to prove what had actually been going on in a military commander's mind. If a commander's subordinates committed war crimes and he did nothing to stop them, he was responsible. That was it.

Still, as useful as it was, the theory of command responsibility was novel. Novelty is not normally associated with legality; in criminal cases nothing is less legal than an ex post facto law. There were a handful of older military cases in which commanding officers had been prosecuted for letting subordinates abuse prisoners, but there had been nothing like the "brother's keeper" theory that the prosecutors in the Yamashita case were pushing. For the more rule of law minded, such as Frank Reel, command responsibility smacked of victor's justice, of prosecuting a man simply for having been the enemy because the prosecutors didn't have the evidence to show that he had done something criminal himself. Making a military commander personally responsible for what someone at the bottom link of his chain of command did was also not a rule that the higher-ups in the US Army were eager to apply to themselves.

It had not been clear if the military commission judges would accept the idea or convict Yamashita based upon it, and it remained even less clear that the US Supreme Court would go along if Reel persuaded it to take up Yamashita's case. But when it came time to announce the verdict at the end of Yamashita's trial, the theory worked.

"It is absurd," the presiding judge explained through his basset hound jowls, "to consider a commander a murder or rapist because one of his soldiers commits a murder or rape. Nevertheless, where murder and rape and vicious, revengeful actions are widespread offences, and there is no effective attempt by a commander to discover and control the criminal acts, such commander may be held responsible, even criminally liable, for the lawless acts of his troops, depending upon their nature and the circumstances surrounding them." The judge then concluded by addressing Yamashita directly, "during the period in question you failed to provide effective control of your troops as was required by the circumstances. Accordingly upon secret written ballot, two-thirds or more of the members concurring, the Commission finds you guilty as charged and sentences you to death by hanging."

Yamashita, as ever, was unfazed. He nodded and was escorted back to his cell. It was December 7, 1945, four years to the day after the attack on Pearl Harbor. MacArthur had gotten his man. And Dwyer had his legal theory.

NINE

It was bitter cold when Dwyer got back to Shanghai. Coal for the boilers was in short supply, but Dwyer had come back from Manila with a head of steam.

He had not yet turned up the Japanese case file that would prove that Sawada had been the mastermind of the Doolittle Raiders' torture and execution, but Dwyer had not yet given up hope that it would materialize in time. The Investigation Division was gathering and translating reams of new Japanese documents every day, and Dwyer had seen to it that an arrest warrant was issued for the Japanese major who had taken a copy of the case file from Tadahiro Hayama the year before. Just days after Dwyer left Tokyo, SCAP's manhunters found the major and hauled him off to Sugamo Prison. If that case file still existed, Dwyer was happy to let the major cool his heels in jail until he coughed it up.

But if the case file remained lost in the fog of war, Yamashita's case had given Dwyer a backup plan: to base the charges on command responsibility. The legalities took a fair bit of explaining—the kind of explaining Dwyer had practiced throughout his time as a law professor in Ann Arbor. If Shigeru Sawada had been in command of the 13th Army when Sotojiro Tatsuta had led his execution party out to the old Chinese cemetery, Dwyer could prove that Sawada had been responsible for the murders of Dean Hallmark, William Farrow, and Harold Spatz. And he could prove that Sawada, by virtue of being Japan's commander in Shanghai, had been responsible for everything that had happened while the Raiders were there, from their arrival at Shanghai airport to their time in Bridge House.

Dwyer spent an inordinate amount of time looking for people who had been held in Bridge House at the same time as the Doolittle Raiders. He wanted to show that the horrors Sawada had allowed to be visited upon the inmates of that notorious dungeon were just as vicious as those Yamashita had allowed to be visited upon the city of Manila.

Dwyer's most promising lead was a Soviet by the name of Alexander Hindrava. A Georgian by birth, Hindrava's story was that he had moved to Shanghai in the late 1930s and worked as a broker until the Kempeitai had come knocking in the fall of 1942. He had been accused of espionage, and the Kempeitai had hauled him off to a crowded cell in Bridge House along with eighteen Chinese, a Russian, and an American, who turned out to be Dean Hallmark.

Hindrava remembered how sick Hallmark had been, spending his days delirious on the floor. The only time Hallmark had ever tried to pick himself up, Hindrava recalled, was when he needed to use the shit bucket. Hallmark had been too weak to do even that most of the time, and so Hindrava and the other cellmates would pitch in to help him up.

Hindrava remembered Hallmark's health turning for the better after he was sent upstairs to Bridge House's clinic in early October. It had taken only a few days, and soon Hallmark had been sharing stories and complaining about the food with the rest of them. When one of the guards had come by in the middle of October to tell Hallmark that he was being transferred to what all had assumed was a prisoner of war camp, everyone had been happy for him.

Dwyer asked about Hindrava's own experiences at Bridge House, but the former prisoner was reluctant to talk about them. "Were you ever harmed physically during your time there?" Dwyer asked him.

"Yes." Hindrava said, volunteering nothing further.

"Please describe what happened?" Dwyer pressed him.

"I received water treatment," Hindrava said in his thick Georgian accent. "Through the nose."

"How many times?"

"Four nights."

"All night long?"

"All night about every half an hour."

"Did they strike you?"

"Yes."

"How many times?"

"So many times that I cannot remember."

"With what?"

"Sometimes with the hands and sometimes with the fencing sword made of bamboo. They also burnt some parts of my body with the cigarettes."

Hindrava offered no more details, but Dwyer persisted. "In the groin?" he asked.

"Yes."

"How long did that happen?"

"Four nights also. When I would lose consciousness by the water they would revive me with the cigarette burns."

Hindrava had no names to give, not even Shigeru Sawada's, but Dwyer did not need to figure out who they were any more than Yamashita's prosecutors needed to put names to the Japanese soldiers who had bayoneted babies in their mother's arms. Sawada had been in command of Shanghai. Bridge House was in Shanghai.

*   *   *

Dwyer appeared to have cracked the case; the legal theory of command responsibility put Sawada into an airtight legal box. If the missing case file turned up in Tokyo, the evidence would only be that much more damning, and even if it didn't, Dwyer could call Hayama to the stand to testify that he had read the missing case file and seen the cables with Tokyo headquarters that showed Sawada masterminding the torture and execution of the Doolittle Raiders. Relying upon what someone says they read that someone else had said to someone else a year earlier is not ordinarily accepted as a reliable way to send a man to the gallows. But these were military commissions and Hayama's testimony certainly had probative value.

By being at the top, Sawada was guilty of everything that happened below him. And even though Sotojiro Tatsuta had not technically been under Sawada's command, the connection was clear. From top to bottom, Dwyer had done it. He had built a plausible case, a compelling case, that was ready to go to trial. Neither John Hendren nor Ham Young could doubt that he had earned his place at the prosecution table in what promised to be the most celebrated war crimes trial of the Pacific war, possibly the whole war. All that was left was to bring Sawada from Sugamo Prison to Shanghai, and Hendren had already scheduled a trip to Tokyo just after the New Year, when he would do just that.

But then word came from Washington, DC. Frank Reel's long-shot effort to get the Yamashita case in front of the US Supreme Court had worked. Five days before Christmas, the Supreme Court issued an order setting the case for argument on January 7, 1946. Everything was now thrown into doubt. Young told reporters that it would likely now be a month before the trials could get going, and soon afterward, the Department of War sent a cable to General Wedemeyer putting a moratorium on further trials pending bureaucratic review.

* * *

Hendren decided to make his trip to Tokyo all the same. He had been happy to let Dwyer do the hard and often frustrating work of putting the Doolittle case together. As a colonel, though still short of the full bird, Hendren had earned the privilege of being a supervisor for whom most things fell below his pay grade. His job was to lead and inspire and to save himself for the tasks where his leadership was called for and most especially where it would be rewarded with the perquisites of a mission accomplished.

"Japs to Face Brilliant Prosecutor" was the headline of one newspaper profile written in anticipation of the trial. When big, important things were happening, the statuesque Hendren knew how to look as though he belonged. It was as if life had trained him to know that being handsome made everyone assume that he was also intelligent and deserving of credit. The real danger was upending that assumption by saying the wrong thing.

By the time Hendren boarded the C-47 "Gooney Bird" for Tokyo, the case Dwyer had built against Sawada was seemingly perfect and had only a few loose ends left. Hendren could tie those right up if he could be the one to recover the missing case file.

Like Dwyer before him, Hendren made his tour through the Emerald City of Tokyo as the celebrity lead prosecutor of the Doolittle case. SCAP's Investigation Division was happy to help him and had compiled a thick dossier of documents for him to collect upon his arrival. But the Japanese case file he wanted so badly remained missing.

Hendren went to Sugamo Prison to question the Japanese major whom Hayama said had taken it, but the major made it clear to Hendren that he had nothing to offer. In fact, he seemed to take pleasure in the fact that Hendren had come all that way for nothing. The case file, he said, had been "burned in a severe air raid on May 25, 1945, with other important documents in the Legal Division building." In other words, the case file had been blown into a cloud of ash by Curtis LeMay.

Hendren was undeterred, however. Sawada was also in Sugamo Prison, and Hendren figured he could sit down with him and bluff him into confessing all he had done.

Sure enough, the questioning started off well. With very little prompting Sawada assumed responsibility. He claimed to have been away from Shanghai directing operations in the Chinese countryside the summer of 1942 and so was unsure about the fine details, but he did remember that a new law had been passed by the Japanese Army and that the Raiders had been tried and sentenced to death under it.

"What was required of you," Hendren asked him, "under the new law that was passed?"

"If they were found guilty of bombing objectives other than military objectives, such as schools and churches, and other buildings," Sawada replied, "they were subject to execution."

"What evidence did you have," Hendren pressed him, "that they had bombed schools and churches?"

"We made a survey of the bombing and we based our evidence on the survey," Sawada explained. "These fliers were supposedly oriented as to where they were supposed to have bombed, but due to difficulty in finding their objective, they dropped bombs on other places. To my knowledge," he then added, almost offhandedly, "I know that these Doolittle fliers actually killed civilians."

"How do you know that?" Hendren snapped in an unusual display of temper. To Hendren's ears, Sawada was aping Japanese propaganda to justify himself.

"I read the confession," Sawada replied confidently, "that the Kempeitai obtained from the fliers." He seemed convinced that that was all the justification he had needed. If the Doolittle Raiders had confessed to the Kempeitai, what else was necessary? Who would confess to something like that if it wasn't true?

Sawada was, of course, overlooking the fact that that was what Kempeitai agents did: they got people to confess, and they were good at it. It was the only situation in which their studied practice in the art of torture worked reliably. To be effective, a torturer has to know when the victim has finally cracked. And to know when the victim has cracked, the torturer must know what the victim will say at that magic moment. If the torturer doesn't know the answer he is supposed to get, how is he supposed to know when to stop torturing?

Hendren pushed Sawada on whether he'd done any investigation himself or whether he had just taken the propaganda about the Raiders and the so-called confessions from the Kempeitai without a second thought. Had he even read the case file to see whether all the so-called evidence fit together?

Sawada admitted that he hadn't; that kind of thing was below his pay grade. His men had investigated and had conducted the trial according to the rules. They had known what they were doing. Why would he have thought that anything more was necessary?

"Your failure to make an investigation," Hendren scolded him, "has caused the death of three American boys who were not guilty. Do you know that?"

Sawada seemed unfazed by Hendren's belief that he'd walked into a confession of total indifference. Yamashita had at least tried to order his men to evacuate. Sawada had been happy to let the Kempeitai torture men into confessing and to order their executions without a second thought.

When asked the crucial question, how he had so negligently exercised the responsibilities of his command, how he had ordered Dean Hallmark, William Farrow, and Harold Spatz to be taken out to the old Chinese cemetery and shot through the forehead, Sawada caught Hendren up short.

"At that time," Sawada said, "I was relieved of my duties as commanding general of the 13th Army and was back in Tokyo."

What? Sawada had been relieved of command? Relieved by whom? When? Why? Why hadn't Dwyer discovered this?

"Who," Hendren asked, "was the commanding general of the 13th Army in October 1942?"

"Shimomura," Sawada said, as if it were obvious.

"Did General Shimomura order the execution of the fliers?"

"Under the results of the trial," Sawada confirmed, "Shimomura issued the orders to execute these prisoners."

Just like that, the whole theory of the case Dwyer had built, the theory that Sawada could be convicted no matter what because he had been in command the day the Doolittle Raiders had been murdered, was burned to ash.

How could that be? Tadahiro Hayama had told Dwyer in no uncertain terms that Sawada had been the mastermind. The case file proved that to a mathematical certainty. Weren't there cables from Sawada to Tokyo headquarters asking to execute the Doolittle Raiders? Wasn't it possible that Sawada was lying? He had to know the stakes. He had every incentive to pass off his responsibility to some mysterious new general.

Hendren, though, soon confirmed that Sawada's story was true. Before leaving Tokyo, Hendren spoke to Yasuo Karakawa, who had been the 13th Army's chief of staff throughout 1942, and to Shoshin Ito, the head of the 13th Army's Legal Department at the time. Both were in a position to know, and neither had any incentive to protect Sawada; if anything, they both had an incentive to give Hendren what he wanted. But it was true: Sawada had been relieved of his command sometime in early October 1942. Lieutenant General Sadamu Shimomura had issued the orders to execute the Doolittle Raiders after he had taken command. Shimomura was responsible.

In puzzling all this out, Hendren discovered that Shoshin Ito was a gold mine of information and, surprisingly, a man he could relate to. Like Hendren, Ito had been ambitious, spoke seemingly every word he said with the utmost of patience and precision, and had known the unique stresses that came with being the top lawyer for one of his country's storied military organizations: Ito for the 13th Army and Hendren for the Fourteenth Air Force. Hendren and Ito spent two days together in Tokyo during which Ito tried to be as helpful as he could, even giving Hendren a dossier of sensitive Japanese government documents about the Doolittle Raid that none of SCAP's paper-sifters had turned up.

Ito had known Shimomura well. After little more than a year in command in Shanghai, Shimomura had been promoted to command the Western District Army in Fukuoka, Japan, and had asked Ito to head its legal department. Ito had been happy for the promotion, but now that the war was over, Ito appeared to have no interest in protecting Shimomura.

"Who was the Commanding General of the 13th Army," Hendren asked him, "at the time the fliers were executed?"

"Lieutenant General Shimomura," Ito replied.

"Did Lieutenant General Shimomura order the execution of the fliers?"

"Yes," he confirmed.

Hendren then repeated the question, just to be sure: "Was this execution carried out on orders of General Shimomura?"

"Yes, it was."

Who was this mysterious General Shimomura? And where was he? Hendren had asked Sawada the same question.

"In all probability," Sawada had answered with slight bemusement, "he is in Tokyo right now."

* * *

Sadamu Shimomura had been Japan's final War Minister, a seat previously held by Hideki Tojo himself and one that he had occupied until shortly before Hendren arrived in Tokyo. SCAP had just disbanded the War Ministry as part of its "democratic revolution from above," which meant that all throughout Dwyer's time in the Emerald City, ex–War Minister Shimomura, the commander responsible for the execution of Hallmark, Farrow, and Spatz, had likely been a five-minute drive away, sitting at a desk in an office building in the Ichigaya neighborhood.

Shimomura was unquestionably one of the highest-profile Japanese generals to survive the war. Hendren could see it all clearly. If John Hendren sent Sadamu Shimomura to the gallows, he would be the man who made Japan's last War Minister face righteous, history-making justice for his crimes against the Doolittle Raiders, the first great heroes of the war.

Hendren ran to SCAP's Apprehension Section and insisted that Shimomura be taken into custody at once, but the officer in charge told Hendren that he would need to take the matter up with Joseph Keenan's office. Keenan was in charge of the Tokyo Tribunal and would have to sign off, so Hendren made his case to Keenan. Without Shimomura, he argued, "it will appear to the military commission and the public that we are attempting to hold junior officers for offenses which they were ordered to commit on command of higher authority." He even suggested that Hideki Tojo should be tried in Shanghai for his role in authorizing the Doolittle Raiders' executions.

The suggestion of prosecuting Tojo in Shanghai was preposterous, of course, but Keenan appreciated Hendren's desire to shoot the moon. Plus, he didn't think that Shimomura would be of much value to him at the Tokyo Tribunal. Keenan was focusing on the attack on Pearl Harbor and the early years of the war. The only thing Keenan asked was that Shimomura not be executed until his team in Tokyo figured out whether he would be needed as a witness. Other than that, Hendren was free to put Shimomura's name up on his marquee in Shanghai.

With Keenan's approval, Hendren filled out the rest of the bureaucratic paperwork to have Shimomura arrested, locked up in Sugamo Prison, and shipped off to Ward Road Jail. The request had to be personally approved by General Albert Wedemeyer once Hendren got back to Shanghai. But once it was, Hendren would have Sadamu Shimomura.

* * *

For Dwyer, missing Shimomura was an embarrassment that was soon compounded by the discovery that Sawada had not actually been in command of all of Shanghai. The Kempeitai turned out to have operated under a chain of command all its own.

Long a dumping ground for delinquent soldiers from throughout the Japanese Army, the Kempeitai was also, by accident of bureaucratic history, answerable only to itself in occupied foreign cities such as Shanghai. That meant that being in the Kempeitai was a license to torture, kill, and steal. A report from the Swiss consul complained in the strongest possible diplomatic euphemisms that the group, "being directly responsible to the Emperor, are all-powerful and do not stop at consideration of international custom." Though it numbered only one thousand officers at its peak, the Kempeitai's reign of terror in Shanghai was such that even the Japanese despised it and Sawada was no more in command of it—or of Bridge House—than he was of the US Army.

Dwyer's case against Sawada was falling apart along with any claim he might have to sit alongside Hendren at the prosecution table, and the timing could not have been worse. The Doolittle Trial was starting to receive the full glare of the international limelight. Only a few days after Hendren returned to Shanghai, so did Chase Nielsen.

TEN

John Hendren stood next to Chase Nielsen before the assembled press corps in his crisply pressed Army khakis, smartly tucked in and buttoned over his athletic frame. Hendren looked every bit the righteous avenger. Nielsen, he explained, was going to be the star witness in the upcoming Doolittle Trial. Though it was still only mid-January, the prime suspects were in custody and the trial would begin right there in Shanghai sometime in February, where the public would see two high-ranking Japanese generals sitting in the dock.

Asked how long the trial would last, Hendren was optimistic. "It shouldn't take long to try these Japs," he said. "We believe we have open and shut cases against every one of them. We have eyewitnesses who can testify to everything the Japs did to the Americans from the time they crashed on the China coast after the Tokyo raid on April 18, 1942."

Nielsen wore his airman's "pinks and greens," khakis under a double pocketed forest green jacket with the Army Air Forces' insignia on the shoulder, wings above the breast, and—in Nielsen's case—seven gold service stripes sewn onto the cuff. His body and face had filled out since the previous August, when he had been so emaciated that it seemed as if his head might tumble right off his neck, but he was still lean, and the lines of his jaw etched a smooth curve from his ears to his chin.

Nielsen's face was lively, his thick black hair had grown to a length where it could be fashionably parted, and his black eyebrows formed sharp peaks that somehow made him look stern, thoughtful, and playful all at the same time. Articulate, apt, and quick with a good quote, he embodied the press's off-the-shelf imaginings of how an American war hero would look, sound, and act. The day of his homecoming in Utah, his hometown paper had filled three front-page columns under the headline "Hero Reunited with Family" with a two-column photo spread of Chase and Thora Nielsen, reunited at last.

Dwyer and Hendren had known early on that they would need to bring at least one of the Doolittle Raiders back to Shanghai to testify. The press as much as the military commission's judges needed to hear firsthand what the Japanese had done. But that was easier said. The very thing that made the four surviving Raiders so compelling as potential witnesses was the very thing that kept them as far away from Shanghai as possible.

George Barr, in the face of all the odds, had turned up alive in an Iowa mental hospital. His testimony about everything from the waterboard to the straitjacket would have been gripping, but he was having a tough time getting his mind, let alone his life, back together; there was no telling what returning to Shanghai might trigger in him or how he would hold up on the stand. Barr would not only have to relive his experiences before the glare of the public, he would have to submit to cross-examination. Given Shimomura's high profile, Dwyer and Hendren had to expect that the case would attract some Clarence Darrow type who would try to hog the limelight by being so aggressive that Frank Reel would look like a good little soldier boy by comparison.

Robert Hite, meanwhile, had always worn his macho sense of humor as a suit of armor. His unshakable place within the community of Earth, Texas, had always given him the confidence to endure anything life threw at him, and when news of Hite's liberation had reached home, the entire town celebrated. His mother had told a reporter, "We're all rejoicing and they'll be plenty more rejoicing when he gets back."

But once the euphoria of liberation dissipated, it became clear that Hite had changed. He now found nearly everything irritating; even the idea of talking to people made him anxious. Those feelings confused him, but spending so much time alone in a cell, he lost the ordinary habits of being around other people. It was all too common. Strangers had become strange, and talking to people provoked a kind of stage fright. As with Barr, it was not at all clear that Hite could—or should—be put through the psychological test of being put on the witness stand.

Jacob DeShazer, for his part, appeared to be acclimating better to life back home. Before the war and throughout much of his captivity, he had been an avowed agnostic on all questions of religion, a point of irritation for guys such as Dean Hallmark, Robert Hite, and William Farrow, who came from parts of the country where the question wasn't whether you were a Baptist but which Baptist church you attended. But in his final month in Fengtai, DeShazer had had a religious epiphany of the enthusiastic sort. He had come to believe that God would see him through, as long as he devoted the rest of his life to being a Christian missionary to the Japanese.

By New Year's 1946, DeShazer was already making good on his vow. He was out of the Army and immersed in studying to be a minister. His newfound love of all humanity, and the lost souls of the Japanese in particular, meant there was no telling what he would say, and the last thing Dwyer or Hendren wanted was a born-again Christian preaching the virtue of forgiveness on the witness stand.

Nielsen, however, was different.

* * *

Because Nielsen was still in the Army, he could have simply been ordered back to Shanghai to testify. But Hendren did him the courtesy of sending a personal telegram asking him to come, and Nielsen was more than happy to oblige. "When Washington asked me to come out here to testify in the trial," Nielsen told the phalanx of reporters Hendren had assembled, "I told them I would do so—even if I had to come out on a stretcher."

The Shanghai of January 1946 was a far different place than it had been the last time Nielsen had been there. Three years earlier, he had narrowly escaped execution as a convicted war criminal. Now he was the newest celebrity guest at Broadway Mansions, where on any given day he would be welcomed by Elsa the German, Minnela the Portuguese, or, of course, Sweater Girl the Russian, and he was free to go where he pleased in a city that had been transformed from a bastion of British and then Japanese colonialism into an American Army town, right down to the locals dressed in standard-issue boots as they trudged through the snow or any other random piece of a uniform they had picked up on the gray market.

The self-serious tea salons had been replaced with fast-food joints, such as the "U.S. Navy Hamburger Stand" in front of the stately Cathay Hotel. Going to the dog races at the Canidrome had been replaced by going to football games, and, walking down the street, Nielsen was likely to hear Chinese street musicians fiddling "Oh! Susanna" on their erhus. Even the traffic pattern had been changed, such that the American jeeps that clogged the streets now drove on the right, instead of the British left.

Hendren naturally chose Broadway Mansions as the venue in which to reintroduce Nielsen to the world. The Foreign Correspondents' Club of China leased the six upper floors, and reporters could always be relied upon to be lurking about, not the least because the seventeenth floor housed one of the best bars in all of Shanghai.

Nielsen, standing before them with his Purple Heart particularly noticeable among his other military decorations, did not disappoint. Though the patient softness of his southwestern accent could come off as monotone, Nielsen was a natural storyteller with an eye for vivid details, and by that point, he had become something of a professional at telling his story.

For the first few weeks after Nielsen had gotten back to the United States, he had stayed in the Walter Reed Army Medical Center for observation and had spent most of that time looking back over the past three years. He thought about his capture by the Japanese and the three-day trek they had taken up the Chinese coast from Juexi to Shanghai. He remembered being taken along the way to a wreckage site about twenty miles south of Ningbo, where some of the other Doolittle Raiders had evidently crashed off the coast. The wreckage, Nielsen remembered, was from the *Ruptured Duck*, which had taken off from the *Hornet* right after Nielsen's plane did.

During the years Nielsen had spent alone in a Japanese cell, the pilot of the *Ruptured Duck*, Ted W. Lawson, had become an international celebrity. Though he ultimately had to have one of his legs amputated due to injuries he suffered in the crash, Lawson and his men had made it out to safety, following a harrowing odyssey through the Chinese countryside. As Nielsen was being interrogated by the Kempeitai in Tokyo, Lawson was being reunited with his wife, Ellen.

Lawson wrote of his saga for *Collier's* magazine in 1943 to correspond with the first anniversary of the Doolittle Raid. The article was a sensation, and Lawson expanded it into a book that became the immediate bestseller

Thirty Seconds over Tokyo, which he dedicated to "William Farrow, Dean Hallmark, and the rest of the captured Doolittle Raiders." "They didn't get back," he wrote, "God help them."

Of all the books written about the war to that point, *Thirty Seconds over Tokyo* was praised as the "most stirring story of individual heroism that it has so far produced." The following year, a few months after *The Purple Heart*'s theatrical release, MGM released a blockbuster adaptation of *Thirty Seconds over Tokyo*, starring Spencer Tracy as Jimmy Doolittle and Van Johnson as Ted Lawson, to just as rave reviews. Together, the book and film earned millions of dollars and made Ted Lawson a household name.

It had been so random. Lawson and Nielsen had taken off within minutes of each other and had crashed only minutes apart into the same ocean off the same Chinese coast. Yet the courses of their lives had been so different. Lawson had come up heads, Nielsen tails.

Nielsen decided to write his own story from his bed in Walter Reed with Hite and DeShazer. He called it "Saga of Living Death," and it had all the lurid detail Nielsen had given back in August to Ham Young's investigators in Chongqing and then some.

The public took a gawker's delight in tales of torture. Waterboarding, in particular, was a source of peculiar fascination. It was demonstrated at public events as a horrifying spectacle. The "water cure," the "water torture," the waterboard seemed to fit the American sense of the insidious cruelty of the Orientals, a torture applied by the weak on the helpless. It came to be that a torture story only counted as a true torture story if it included descriptions of waterboarding, and Nielsen did not disappoint.

Nielsen recounted how his interrogator had snapped his fingers in frustration at Nielsen's bull-like refusal to talk. That snap of the fingers prompted three Japanese goons to pin him to the ground; one on each leg and a third gripping him by his still handcuffed arms. "The fourth put a towel over my face," he wrote, "arranging it in a cup-like fashion over my mouth and nose. It was like a barber getting ready with a hot towel. Then he began to pour tepid water into my mouth and nostrils. This is the famous Japanese water torture and it is brutal. A man has to breathe and every breath I took I sucked water into my lungs. I twisted my head once and got a mouthful of air, but the guard twisted it back again. I tried to move my legs and arms, but the guards were too strong."

Nielsen wrote about how he had writhed on the floor, trying to catch a breath, choking on the water. He had known he was dying, he wrote, but had refused to talk no matter what brutalities the Japanese sadists contrived, even when they had put him before a mock execution squad.

"Well, if you insist on not telling us anything we might as well finish the job right away," Nielsen recounted the interrogator as saying. "You will face the firing squad for execution immediately." Nielsen then described being blindfolded, dragged outside, and frog-marched down a gravel path, a man on each side, each step taking him closer to death until they came to a sharp stop. He described hearing the men behind him drawing up their rifles in unison. The next command had come in unintelligible Japanese. But he hadn't heard a shot. Instead, his Japanese inquisitor had laughed. "Well, well, well. We are all Knights of the Bushido of the Rising Sun and we don't execute men at sundown. It is now sundown, so your execution will take place in the morning. We will shoot you then unless you decide to talk in the meantime."

The International News Special Service paid $2,250 to run "Saga of Living Death" as a newspaper serial starting in the middle of September 1945. No book deal had been forthcoming by the time Nielsen arrived in Shanghai, but if the reporters' reaction at Broadway Mansions was any indication, one was sure to come along. No matter how jaded, no one could help but hang on Nielsen's every word.

The Japanese had accused the Doolittle Raiders of bombing schools and strafing civilians. "But this is absolutely untrue," Nielsen said indignantly to the assembled reporters. "We bombed military objectives only. Our targets were steel mills and factories at the northeast edge of Tokyo Bay and an oilfield in the Nagoya area. We didn't use our machine guns at all."

* * *

Bill Newton, who wrote for the Scripps Howard News Service, had unsuccessfully lobbied Ham Young since November for the opportunity to interview some of the war crimes suspects being held at Ward Road Jail. Now Hendren invited the assembled reporters and photographers to witness the first dramatic confrontation between Nielsen and his former jailer Sotojiro Tatsuta who was being held in a cell on the second floor.

When they arrived at Ward Road Jail, Tatsuta was dressed in a pressed

Japanese Army uniform with well-polished riding boots. He extended "the best Japanese etiquette to bow and hiss to me," wrote one reporter. Another asked Tatsuta if he recognized Nielsen.

"Yes," Tatsuta admitted ruefully.

Asked if he recognized Tatsuta, Nielsen let his nostrils flare. "I'd know that thing anyplace," referring to the quivering Tatsuta. "You ought to know what is going on in my mind right now."

Tatsuta was eager to please and posed for whatever pictures the cameramen requested. In one, he bowed timidly at the waist as Nielsen glowered down at him. In another, he poked his face through the bars of his cell like a mope. Tatsuta told reporters that he felt nothing but kindness and sympathy toward the Doolittle Raiders and claimed that they had all "made friends and the fliers showed me pictures of their sweethearts." Before they were executed, he claimed, he had consoled the men, saying "You are dying a heroic death and your names will be outstanding in American history."

The *New York Times* ran a photo spread recounting how the Japanese had "avenged the Doolittle attack on Tokyo" with Tatsuta as the star, looking pathetic behind the bars of his cell door. Dwyer and Hendren were also featured, reenacting the moment of the Raiders' execution in a tableau of Japanese soldiers made to kneel with their hands spread apart on the grounds of Jiangwan, as if tied to a cross.

* * *

The following Saturday, Dwyer took Remedios and Nielsen back out to Ward Road Jail for a private confrontation. It was very much in Dwyer's interest to give Nielsen everything he wanted and just as important for Nielsen to know that Robert Dwyer was in his corner. If Dwyer was going to secure his place at the prosecution table, he needed Nielsen to want him there.

Dwyer sat Tatsuta down and put on his best bad-cop performance. "Captain Nielsen," he said menacingly, "has talked to me about the trial and told me numerous things about it. I want to ask you about the trial. I want you to tell me the truth."

"I understand," Tatsuta agreed.

Nielsen was adamant that he had never signed any confession, in Japanese or otherwise. That refusal made him all the more admirable, but it also created a gap in Dwyer's evidence. Everyone Dwyer interviewed had said there were confessions individually signed by each of the Doolittle Raiders, including Tadahiro Hayama, who was unwavering in his memory of having seen signed confessions from all eight men. Hayama's credibility would be key in proving the case against Sawada, and Dwyer needed to account for the discrepancy. He could not have his star witnesses contradicting each other. How had Hayama seen a confession signed by Chase Nielsen that Nielsen insisted he had never signed?

In trying to puzzle out an answer, Dwyer's mind returned to something small but suspicious that Tatsuta had said back in November. The night before Hallmark, Farrow, and Spatz had been executed, Tatsuta admitted having given them blank pieces of paper to sign after each had written his last letters home. Tatsuta explained away the peculiar request by saying that he wanted to make receipts for the three men's belongings and that he had given the signed blank papers to a sergeant named Suzuki to fill in with the inventory. But that made no sense. Why would Tatsuta need a signed receipt for the belongings of three dead men? Wasn't it at least possible that those papers were part of a frame-up of the Raiders?

"When was it," Dwyer demanded, "that you had the Doolittle fliers sign some blank pieces of paper which you turned over to Sergeant Suzuki?"

"It was given to Sergeant Suzuki," Tatsuta explained, "to write out their personal belongings on the papers."

"Tell me when it was that he had the fliers sign blank pieces of paper," Dwyer barked at Remedios to translate. "When it was with relation to the trial?"

"It is the truth I'm saying," Tatsuta claimed. "The fliers signed the papers and it was given to Sergeant Suzuki to get their personal belongings on and if the prosecutor's office wanted any papers to be signed by the fliers I do not know because they took care of that special investigation."

"You had the fliers sign blank papers, didn't you?" Dwyer accused him as Nielsen glowered down at him from under his sharply peaked eyebrows.

"Yes," Tatsuta confessed. "Every time people are to be executed they have to sign before the execution, or after the trial, they have to sign pieces of paper."

"Did all the fliers sign?" Dwyer asked, making clear that the only acceptable answer was an unequivocal yes.

"Only three."

"Captain Nielsen says he signed one," Dwyer said almost daring him to call Nielsen a liar.

"Yes," Tatsuta attempted to agree. "Nielsen signed one."

"Who else signed?" Dwyer asked, seeing that he had finally broken Tatsuta's resistance.

"It must have been a mistake about Nielsen signing," Tatsuta tried to backpedal, "because only three signed."

"Isn't it a fact," Dwyer bellowed, "that you had each of the fliers sign a blank piece of paper?"

"No," Tatsuta answered meekly.

Dwyer then started asking him about the show trial in August 1942, where the fraudulent confessions had supposedly been used. Who had been there, who had been responsible, and how long had it taken? Dwyer's questions were meant less to discover information than to twist the skinny little bastard into telling Dwyer what he wanted to hear. So when Tatsuta claimed that he had only popped in to watch the trial for a few minutes, Dwyer lunged at him. "Captain Nielsen says you were in the court during the trial."

"Nielsen must have been mistaken," Tatsuta pleaded.

"Nielsen is not mistaken!" Dwyer scolded him. "Did you think they were guilty?"

"Yes, I thought they were guilty," Tatsuta admitted.

"You wanted them to die, didn't you?"

"No, I thought they would be sentenced to ten or fifteen years."

"Did you have some special love for these men?"

"Yes, I love the fliers."

"Did you love Nielsen?"

"Yes."

"Nielsen says you hated every one of them!" Dwyer thundered. "You hated all these men like you hated all Americans!"

"No, I had the feeling of neighborly love," Tatsuta chirped.

"We will question you again," Dwyer warned him. "Think it over. You're lying about loving the Americans, lying about the number and names of who were at the execution, lying when you said you were only ten minutes in the courtroom, and lying when you said you did all these things for the fliers!"

"Please," Tatsuta implored, "do me the favor of meeting the guards of the prison and I can talk to them and get these things straightened out. Please tell the guards of the prison to think well and give the right answers because I giving the right answers."

"Request is denied," Dwyer snorted.

Dwyer's performance, bellowed with the full thickness of his chest and jowls, was over. Maybe he couldn't get Tatsuta to fess up, to admit that he had had the Raiders sign blank pieces of paper as part of an overall plot to frame them, but he showed Nielsen that he could sure make the pathetic little bastard shake.

* * *

However useful it was for Dwyer to emotionally bludgeon Tatsuta for Nielsen's enjoyment, there was something unsatisfying about it. Dwyer knew it. Nielsen knew it. It was easy to bully someone as pathetic as Tatsuta, and the honest truth was that it wasn't wholly fair. Tatsuta had been comparatively kind to Nielsen and the rest of the Raiders when they had been his prisoners in Jiangwan. They had admitted as much to Ham Young back in August 1945, and the fact that he was now having to stand in for the many other Japanese soldiers who had genuinely mistreated Nielsen, the fact that he was now being inflated into "the Big Bad Wolf," exposed a serious gap in the case that Dwyer was hoping to take to trial.

Dwyer and Hendren had focused intensely on figuring out who could be held responsible for the murders of Hallmark, Farrow, and Spatz. Roosevelt had promised justice for their murders, and, short of persuading Joseph Keenan to send Tojo and Emperor Hirohito to Shanghai, Dwyer and Hendren had gotten as close as anyone could to fulfilling that promise. They had Sawada; Tadahiro Hayama would testify that Sawada had personally masterminded their executions in cables with Tokyo headquarters. They had Shimomura; Yusei Wako would testify that Shimomura had personally issued the order to carry out their executions. And they had Tatsuta; his former underlings would testify that Tatsuta had orchestrated the executions down to giving the order to fire. It was an airtight case, and any holes that remained in the evidence could be pasted over with the theory of command responsibility that Dwyer had brought back from Manila. It was perfect, but only because it left something out: Chase Nielsen.

Nielsen and the rest of the Doolittle Raiders had suffered at least as much as Hallmark, Farrow, and Spatz. Robert Meder would have been lucky to die of a clean rifle shot to his forehead rather than suffer to death all alone in some barren Japanese prison cell. Nielsen was more than a star witness; he was a victim, too. All the Doolittle Raiders were.

But getting justice for Nielsen—or for Meder, Barr, Hite, and De-Shazer—forced Dwyer to solve the same seemingly insolvable problem he had confronted the first time he had leafed through Ham Young's case file: There were hundreds if not thousands of people who had had roles in Nielsen's saga from the shores of Juexi through his rescue at Fengtai. Dwyer had stacks of photographs, piles of documents, lists of names and aliases. But who could actually be held responsible?

Perhaps Dwyer could build a case against Captain Oka, the prison warden in Nanking or his henchmen, "Big Ugly," "Little Ugly," "Goon," and "Mule," or perhaps he could draft charges against General Takahashi, the commanding officer responsible for Fengtai, or perhaps he could dig further into Bridge House and pin down the real name of of the "Big Bad Wolf." There were many possibilities, but the inescapable fact was that he did not have enough time.

Dwyer agonized over how to get justice for Nielsen and everything he and the other Doolittle Raiders suffered, and then he realized that the solution had been in front of him the whole time. Right there in Ham Young's case file, the starting point of Dwyer's whole investigation, was a single document that was the axis around which everything that had happened to the Raiders turned: the Noboru Unit judgment from August 1942.

The Noboru Unit judgment had laundered everything that had been done and would be done to the Doolittle Raiders. All the torture they had suffered—the bamboo pole, the sleep deprivation, the stress positions, the waterboard—could be rationalized away because the Noboru Unit judgment had labeled them "war criminals." In Japan's vast and bureaucratic prison system, the label on a prisoner's file determined everything and the "war criminal" label meant that Hallmark, Farrow, and Spatz could be shot through the head, Meder could die of starvation, Barr could suffocate inside a straitjacket, and Nielsen, Hite, and DeShazer could be left to go mad in isolation. When Sawada had put his chop on the Noboru Unit judgment, the default logic of the Japanese bureaucracy had made the rest inevitable.

Sawada, though, had not acted alone. Written on the very first page of the Noboru Unit judgment, as if penned by the ghost of Franklin Roosevelt himself, there it was in black and white: "Army prosecutor, Major Itsuro Hata, participating." Then, on its last page, next to the death sentences that had been imposed on all of them as war criminals, there were the names of the judges: Toyama Nakajo, Yusei Wako, and Ryuhei Okada.

The officious listing of names, perfectly routine in any official record of a court proceeding, inspired a radical new idea: the lawyers and judges were responsible.

To Dwyer, the son of a lawyer, whose main life achievement had been getting a law degree from the nation's oldest law school and who still retained his Catholic boy's reverence for the law as a moral force in the world, these men had committed the most serious crime of all. They had perverted justice.

The Noboru Unit judgment said the Raiders had violated the Enemy Airmen's Law of 1942. Dwyer had gotten his hands on a copy of that so-called law, and it was no law at all. It had not even been promulgated until August 13, 1942, four months after the Raiders had been captured. It made no secret about what it really was. "This law," it said, "is applicable to the conduct committed before the effective date." It was a naked ex post facto law, a violation of basic fairness forbidden by every civilized legal system in the world since before Julius Caesar up through and including the Japanese criminal code.

The Enemy Airmen's Law was a perversion of everything that the law was supposed to be about. It had been written after the fact for the purpose of trumping up charges against the Doolittle Raiders. It had also been written so that it could only ever be used to prosecute non-Japanese. By treating Japan's enemies differently than the Japanese were willing to be treated, it denied the Raiders equal justice under law. It violated something as basic as the Golden Rule.

Hendren, for his part, liked the idea of prosecuting the Japanese lawyers and judges for participating in the Doolittle Raiders' show trial. It would afford justice to Nielsen and all the others who had suffered as a result. There were problems, though, the most obvious being that neither the Hague nor the Geneva Conventions listed the perversion of justice as a war crime.

Dwyer was untroubled by this. He had seen in Manila that legal precedents had to start somewhere. There had been no precedent for the theory of command responsibility before the Yamashita trial, but army prosecutors had been able to draw guidance from the trial of a lazy gatekeeper in New Jersey to make the Hague Conventions' requirement that soldiers behave in a disciplined fashion meaningful.

Framing innocent people had been a crime for hundreds of years, as fraud if nothing else. Hendren's home state of Missouri even allowed people to sue prosecutors for charging them based upon "false or fraudulent" evidence. It made no sense for international law to protect prisoners from being abused and killed if that protection could be stripped away whenever their captors cynically went through the motions of a fraudulent trial. Punishing those who perverted justice was the only way to make the Hague and Geneva Conventions' protections meaningful.

Proving their case against the prosecutor, Itsuro Hata, would be straightforward. Tatsuta had said that the prosecutor had been at the center of everything, up to and including his looting of Dean Hallmark's bomber jacket. They also knew who he was. Hata was in a Tokyo hospital undergoing treatment for stomach ulcers.

Less clear was how they would prove that the three Japanese judges had perverted justice. If they planned on drawing guidance from the personal injury law of Missouri, Dwyer and Hendren would have to show that the three judges had convicted the Raiders on false and fraudulent charges based upon evidence that they knew was false and fraudulent. What if the prosecutor had simply done a good job defrauding the judges?

During his trip in Tokyo, Hendren had interviewed one of the judges, Yusei Wako, who had been a detainee in Sugamo since October. Hendren had found Wako odd and a bit compulsive. Small even for a Japanese man, Wako had the weathered skin of someone who smoked a lot, and his eyes were set so widely apart that they seemed to look in slightly different directions. He had been rather helpful as Hendren worked to bolster his case against Sawada and Shimomura, but Wako refused to admit that he had personally done anything wrong.

"Did you get specific instructions to find the fliers guilty?" Hendren had asked him.

"I had no specific instructions," Wako had responded matter-of-factly.

"Isn't it a fact," Hendren had pressed him, "that you had your mind made up that you're going to find them guilty prior to trial?"

"I had not made up my mind," Wako had replied just as flatly.

To Dwyer, though, that was all bullshit. Over the course of his investigation, he had discovered that the Raiders' saga from Bridge House to Jiangwan was not unique. Alexander Hindrava, who had suffered plenty in his own right at Bridge House, had also been sent to Jiangwan and put before a show trial as an accused spy based upon the confessions the Kempeitai had wrung out of him. The same thing had happened to Caesar dos Remedios. It all fit a pattern: the Kempeitai extorted confessions at Bridge House, and the 13th Army in Jiangwan used those confessions to fabricate convictions.

Sawada and the lawyers working for him were prostituting Japan's military justice system to launder the Kempeitai's dirty work. The only thing unique about the Doolittle case was that this particular time, the victims were some of the most famous American airmen in the world.

Dwyer's quick temper ignited incandescently at the farce that the Raiders' trial had been. They had had no lawyers, no witnesses, no opportunity to defend themselves. Dean Hallmark could not even stand. How could any man sit in judgment of another man who lay prostrate on the floor, flies buzzing about his face? How could so-called judges ignore the clear evidence of torture that tainted the whole case? If they had been defrauded by the prosecutor, they had all been happy to let themselves be defrauded. They had denied the prisoners justice, and for that Robert Dwyer would see to it that they faced justice themselves, right there in Shanghai.

Yusei Wako was still detained in Sugamo and could be brought to Shanghai right alongside Hata, Sawada, and Shimomura. The other two judges, though, were proving to be elusive. SCAP had searched its files and claimed to have no record of anyone by the name Toyama Nakajo. They also could find no one by the name of Ryuhei Okada, who had been deployed with Japan's 13th Army in the summer of 1942. There was no record of either man ever returning to Japan.

That meant that both men could still be in China, which was by no means a guarantee that Dwyer and Hendren would be able to find them before the trial was due to begin in February. The Japanese population in China, not including Manchuria and Taiwan, numbered nearly 1.5 million. There were 80,000 Japanese civilians still in Shanghai alone. Nakajo and Okada could be right around the corner in Japan Town, hiding in plain sight.

ELEVEN

Frustrated by SCAP's lack of progress, Dwyer flew with Remedios to Nanking to search for himself. Nanking had been the headquarters of Japan's army in China, the China Expeditionary Army, and was the most obvious place to find the whereabouts of a Japanese soldier deployed to China during the war.

Nanking, though, turned out to be a far stranger place than Dwyer had expected. Chiang Kai-shek had reclaimed the city as his capital in September 1945, but everywhere Dwyer looked, Japanese soldiers were out and about as if the war had never ended.

With Mao Zedong's People's Liberation Army stretching Kuomintang forces beyond their capacity, Chiang had enlisted the Japanese to help. He euphemistically told his American patrons that the Japanese had been hired simply to serve as his "technicians," leaving unstated the fact that their only real technical expertise was in fighting the People's Liberation Army. Like every other American who thought the United States had just won a war against the Japanese, Dwyer found it unnerving every time a group of those "technicians" walked past him on the streets of Nanking, fully armed and on patrol.

Dwyer's feelings of unease deepened when he reached the Japanese garrison and was confronted with how much more the Japanese knew about China than he did. The Japanese officers he spoke to had already known that he was coming. They knew who he was and why he was there. They were all up on the latest news about the war crimes prosecutions down in

Shanghai and told him that they could offer no help in finding Toyama Nakajo; he had been redeployed from China years earlier. But they did know where Ryuhei Okada was or at least should be: he was in Shanghai, still stationed with the 13th Army in Jiangwan.

It hardly seemed possible. Dwyer had interviewed dozens of people at Jiangwan over the past few months, and none of them had bothered to mention that a judge at the Raiders' trial had been there all along. Dwyer had scoured hundreds of square miles of China. Cable after cable had been sent to SCAP's manhunters in Tokyo. Man after man had sat across from him during hours of questioning. And the whole time, the bastard had been hiding in plain sight.

Dwyer rushed to catch the next plane back to Shanghai. If Okada had been able to hide that long, people might be trying to protect him, and if the Japanese in Nanking knew that Dwyer was coming, word was likely to travel fast. If Okada could slip out of Jiangwan and into Shanghai's Japan Town, it did not matter if he was right around the corner; Dwyer could lose him for good.

The good news was that the 13th Army's headquarters was right near the airport. Dwyer and Remedios were due to land in the early afternoon and could have Okada in custody before dinner.

The bad news was that Ham Young had asked Dwyer to escort a few other Japanese prisoners back from Nanking to Ward Road Jail, which meant an hour's drive back to Shanghai, god-knows-how-long getting the prisoners processed, and then another hour's drive back to Jiangwan. Every minute counted. But Dwyer was not in a position to say anything other than "Yes, sir, right away, sir."

Before taking off, though, Dwyer got the idea to call ahead to Shanghai and ordered the military police to send a few MPs to meet him at the airport. He could pass off Young's prisoners, hop into a jeep with Remedios, and arrest Okada before he had a chance to slip away.

But as soon as Dwyer touched down in Shanghai, he discovered that the MPs he had ordered were otherwise occupied. While they had been waiting for him, they had been given a new mission by one of the many, many officers in Shanghai who were above Dwyer in the chain of command, meaning that Dwyer would have to shuttle Ham Young's prisoners back to Ward Road Jail himself.

Dwyer wasted no time, but it was getting dark and by the time he off-loaded Young's prisoners, hours of precious time had slipped away. Even under the best of circumstances, arresting war crime suspects could be a time-consuming and diplomatically delicate business.

Chiang Kai-shek was touchy about China's sovereignty and resistant to the idea that more than one police force could make arrests inside China. Protocol demanded that if Dwyer wanted to arrest someone, he first get a warrant from Colonel Jensen Wu, the head of the Department of Investigation for Foreign Affairs of the Chinese National Army in Shanghai, which had taken over the Kempeitai's offices at Bridge House. That was only a few minutes' drive from Ward Road Jail, but by the time Dwyer had gotten rid of Young's prisoners, Wu had left for the day.

Strictly speaking, the warrant from Colonel Wu was not *required*. Ham Young, more than anyone, knew what a pain in the ass Chiang and his people could be. They always dragged their feet, and Young's investigators had repeatedly encountered roadblocks to making arrests of any kind.

Young had deliberately avoided entering into any formal agreement with the Chinese on how Americans could go about arresting Japanese. Instead, he let his people know that they should do their best to get a warrant from Colonel Wu, but if it happened that they could not get in touch with him, Young would have their back if they just went ahead and made the arrests themselves.

Every minute wasted made it more likely that Okada would disappear. He had every incentive to run and, given his elusiveness over the past few months, every ability to hide. Dwyer therefore decided to hell with protocol and drove the hour back out to Jiangwan. If he couldn't get permission, he would pray for forgiveness later.

* * *

It was well past dark by the time Dwyer and Remedios pulled up to Jiangwan's gate. It was a chilly January night, and the electric lights outside refracted through Remedios' breath as he asked the guard on duty to see the commanding general. After they had stood in the cold a few minutes, Major General Funtaro Kawamoto came out dressed rather incongruously in a tweed suit. At his side was his second in command, a lieutenant colonel named Mori, who was also dressed in tweeds. Together, the two looked like a pair of English gentlemen weekending at their country house.

Dwyer didn't waste time. He demanded to know if there was a captain by the name of Ryuhei Okada presently serving with the 13th Army.

Kawamoto replied that there was.

Dwyer demanded that Kawamoto bring Okada forward immediately. Dwyer was being rude, deliberately so.

Kawamoto, however, remained self-possessed and gave no indication that he had been tipped off that anyone was coming for Okada. He also gave no explanation for why it had taken until now to disclose Okada's whereabouts. Instead, he calmly instructed one of his men to fetch Okada and bring him to the gate.

After a few more awkward minutes spent standing in the cold, a man in his early forties strolled to the gate. He had a soft chin, a thick mane of black hair that was shaved on the sides, and the posture of someone who had reached middle age mostly sitting at a desk. His upward-tilting eyebrows gave him the look of a quiet man unsure of why he was suddenly the center of attention.

Using Remedios to translate, Dwyer asked the man if he was Captain Ryuhei Okada.

He was.

Had Okada served as a judge before Japan's military commissions?

He had, at least for a time.

Had Okada presided over the trial of the Americans who bombed Japan in 1942?

He had.

With that, Dwyer told Okada he was under arrest.

"What for?" General Kawamoto interjected.

"We are taking the captain into Shanghai to question him," Dwyer said, "upon the authority of Commanding General Wedemeyer."

Kawamoto replied in a stream of mellifluous Japanese, a language that readily lent itself to the maintenance of a calm patter in even the tensest of moments. Remedios turned to Dwyer and explained that the general was unwilling to turn Okada over. "He only recognizes the authority of the Chinese." Where was Dwyer's warrant from Colonel Wu?

"Do you refuse," Dwyer bellowed, his already short fuse singed down by the day's frustrations, "to turn Captain Okada over for questioning under the authority of Commanding General Wedemeyer?"

"I refuse to release him," Kawamoto replied coolly.

Dwyer panned the scene around him. His increasingly loud altercation with Kawamoto had drawn attention. It was dark, but Dwyer guessed that there were about two hundred Japanese soldiers within earshot, and he could see that twenty-five or so were now brandishing their arms.

Dwyer blinked and stepped back from the gate. He told Remedios to tell Kawamoto that he would "return in the morning to pick up the captain under the authority of the Chinese" and warned that if Okada was not "present for any reason, that General Kawamoto and Lieutenant Colonel Mori would be personally held responsible to the court-martial jurisdiction of the United States."

Kawamoto replied that he understood and bade Dwyer a polite good night.

By the time he got back to Shanghai, Dwyer had worked himself into a lather of rage and frustration. It had been a long day. He had spent his morning loading himself and some useless prisoners onto an overlong flight from Nanking. He had been jerked around by the MPs at the airport. He had been humiliated by some Japanese general. And so he vented the magma from the molten core of his gut to Ham Young and demanded to have Kawamoto arrested. The humiliation of it. The smugness of it. Kawamoto was obstructing justice.

Young, who by that point had known Dwyer for years, told him to put the request into writing. Dwyer duly complied and Young duly filed it in a drawer.

* * *

The next morning, Dwyer went to Bridge House to fetch his warrant from Colonel Wu, who agreed to join him for the trip out to Jiangwan along with two guards and his own interpreter in case there were any more problems.

When they arrived, the tweeds were gone. Kawamoto was waiting for Dwyer inside the gate in full martial glory with five hundred of his men assembled behind him. The air was just as tense in the wintery daylight as it had been under the electric lights the night before. But true to his word, Kawamoto had Okada next to him.

Dwyer walked through the gate and presented his warrant. Kawamoto's assistant, Lieutenant Colonel Mori, tried to step in front of Dwyer. The issue of Okada's arrest, Mori attempted to explain, needed to be discussed further.

Dwyer ignored Mori and ordered Colonel Wu to have his men seize Okada and take him to the jeep outside. Wu complied, and his two men—armed but absurdly outgunned—took Okada by the arms.

Kawamoto looked on as his five hundred men stood behind him, poised to carry out any order he might give. Okada was led out, and Dwyer followed him. Once the engine of the jeep started up, it was done. Okada was under arrest.

* * *

Dwyer got Okada to Ward Road Jail around noon and then went for lunch to decompress. When he returned, he found Okada reluctant to cooperate, answering questions evasively and in short, unhelpful bursts. Dwyer, though, kept at him for more than four and a half hours.

One of the first questions out of his mouth was whether Okada was a lawyer.

"I studied philosophy," Okada replied.

"Any law?"

"No." Okada had been in the 13th Army's Special Services Section, dealing mostly with diplomatic and public relations matters.

Well, in that case, Dwyer insisted, he must have known about the Doolittle Raid.

"I read it in the newspaper," Okada admitted.

"When did you first see any of these Doolittle fliers?"

"I met them in a courtroom."

"Hadn't you met them before in connection with your press bureau job?" Dwyer asked. It seemed impossible that a public relations officer would not have been involved when Hallmark, Nielsen, and Meder had first been taken to Shanghai back in April 1942. Okada's face was not in Dwyer's stack of photographs, but it stood to reason that he could have been with the cameraman.

"I never met them before," Okada insisted.

Okada's recollection was sketchy, but he did remember the trial and that one of Americans was lying down, though he had not been sure why.

All three of the judges, Okada admitted, had voted to convict, and from his standpoint, it was an open-and-shut case.

"When you voted the death penalty you wanted to see those fliers die, didn't you?" Dwyer snapped.

"I did not have that feeling," Okada objected, somewhat puzzled by the accusation.

"Did you want them to live?"

This question struck Okada as even stranger. So he simply replied, "Yes," as if asking a question himself.

"You loved them very much," Dwyer snarked, "didn't you?"

"No," Okada said hesitatingly.

"You hated them, didn't you?"

"Because they were our enemy," Okada said matter-of-factly. It wasn't personal. Okada had been told to be a judge, and so he had acted as a judge.

"So you really wanted to see them die, didn't you?" Dwyer barked.

"I cannot answer that question," Okada told Remedios. He was having trouble following Dwyer's questioning, or at least Remedios's translation of it, and was increasingly worried that he was going to incriminate himself accidentally.

"How do you explain," Dwyer pushed him, "the beating of the American prisoners and other prisoners by Japanese guards, the failure to give them water, making them sit up in a squat position facing the wall for long periods, giving them the water cure, and all that, how do you explain that?"

"The equipment for the water cure, the string up, and electricity shocks, and all those different things approved by the higher-ups," Okada said, unaware that he was now incriminating himself, "and equipment are there so they are used by the guards."

Despite being one of the few clear answers Okada had given on any topic, the response caught Dwyer up short. It was a clear admission, an unequivocal admission, of the use of torture by the Japanese Army by a Japanese officer.

None of the other men Dwyer or Hendren had questioned had ever dared say such a thing. They had all dismissed the suggestion that the Japanese Army used torture as a legend. But here was Okada, undoubtedly under some stress as Dwyer badgered him, confirming it shamelessly.

By admitting to the Japanese Army's use of torture, Okada was breaking a profound taboo. Japanese interrogation manuals euphemized torture as "skillful methods" interrogation as part of a broader policy of denial and secrecy. A secret memorandum on interrogations prepared during the war had admonished, "Nobody must know about the application of torture except the persons concerned with this. Under no circumstances must other prisoners know about it. It is very important to take measures to prevent shrieks from being heard."

This need for secrecy was to be inculcated into the torture victims by persuading them "out of a sense of pride, sense of honor, etc., not to speak of it afterwards." And if prisoners were visibly wounded or could not be expected to remain silent about their treatment, the memorandum ominously instructed that "measures must be taken" to keep them silent.

The imperative for secrecy was a vestige of the self-image Japan had created for itself over the previous century as among the world's most modern and liberal societies. It had struggled for decades to shed its reputation as a backward hermit state, which it had been for centuries under its period of military dictatorship. To become a respected world power, a peer of the Western colonial powers, Japan had radically reformed its legal system, abolishing the old rules under which the death penalty was applied profligately and torture was routine. In 1879, Japan's parliament had abolished all state-sanctioned torture, and in 1882, it had adopted a reformed criminal code that had made it a crime for any judge, prosecutor, policeman, or other official to abuse or be complicit in the abuse of a criminal suspect.

The abolition of torture was a singular point of national pride, marking the moment that Japan reentered the world after the dark ages of military dictatorship. During the war, it was conventional wisdom among the Japanese public that the torture of prisoners was something that the ruthless Allies did, not the Imperial Japanese Army. To the extent the public believed any allegation of atrocities committed by Japanese forces, responsibility for such "blood carnivals" was ascribed to the "Young Officers," a fascist clique that operated secretly within the army. If atrocities such as torture occurred, the public comforted its conscience with the belief that they were the work of bad apples.

The banality of Okada's explanation, as much as the shock of his admission, was disturbing. There was a taboo against torture, sure, but taboos regulate what is said more strongly than what is done. Secrecy afforded permission, and torture had simply become part of the climate at places such as Bridge House. There was nothing more to it than that.

For Dwyer's purposes, Okada had unwittingly confessed to being a war criminal. If he knew that much, he must have known—or at least suspected—what had happened to the Doolittle Raiders. Yet he had looked the other way.

All the frustrations and humiliations Dwyer had endured to put Okada where he was at that moment were now worth it. This was not just some legal technicality. This was not just some handy analogy to the personal injury law of Missouri or the law of homicide in New Jersey. This was evil.

Dwyer wanted to reveal the corrupt moral obscenity of it all before the world, and if he got a seat at the prosecution table, he could be the one to do it. Finding Okada and getting this confession was just the kind of thing to make up for his failing to have found Shimomura earlier. But then everything was thrown into doubt again; a cable had just come in from Tokyo, and Dwyer had an urgent flight to catch.

TWELVE

There were plenty of better things Dwyer could be doing than sitting for half a day on the never-comfortable bench seat of a dimly lit C-47 "Gooney Bird." He had intended to leave Shanghai on Monday, but due to bad weather, the flight had been pushed back until Wednesday afternoon. Now, since he was going to be getting into Tokyo around dinnertime, he couldn't even try to get things fixed until Thursday morning.

It should have been simple enough; it was just paperwork. With Ryuhei Okada and Sotojiro Tatsuta already in Shanghai, the only suspect still missing was Toyama Nakajo. That was not ideal, but Dwyer knew they could go to trial without him if necessary, as long as they had the rest.

All SCAP's people had to do was fill out the paperwork to have Sadamu Shimomura, Shigeru Sawada, Itsuro Hata, and Yusei Wako transferred from Sugamo Prison in Tokyo, hand them over to some MPs, and sit their sore asses on the bench seats of a Gooney Bird for half a day, so that Dwyer could then welcome them all to their new home in Ward Road Jail.

Hendren had submitted all the necessary requests with all the necessary approvals, but weeks had gone by without any word. He fired off a cable asking for an update, impressing upon SCAP that the failure to transfer the suspects to Shanghai was delaying the start of the Doolittle Trial. But nothing came back over the wire.

It was the Monday of the last full week in January before SCAP finally sent its response. The cable confirmed that Sawada and Wako were both in Sugamo and that Hata remained in the hospital. But with respect to Toyama Nakajo, there was some confusion; according to SCAP's records, Toyama was already in custody in Shanghai. As far as Ryuhei Okada was concerned, the cable explained that there was no one in the Japanese Army by that name. It then concluded by saying "Request that you arrange escort to return Sawada and Wako for trial."

What the hell? According to SCAP, Toyama was in custody in Shanghai, when he was, in reality, missing. Okada did not exist, when he was, in reality, in custody in Shanghai. And they had completely failed to mention Shimomura or the prosecutor, Itsuro Hata. But before Dwyer and Hendren could respond, another cable arrived, clarifying that Hata, the prosecutor, who had been perhaps the most responsible for the Doolittle Raiders' corrupt show trial, was no longer in custody; he had been released from the hospital in Tokyo.

Furious, Hendren shot back a cable demanding that the SCAP's Apprehension Section arrest Hata and prepare him for transfer to Shanghai. He also demanded to know the status of Sadamu Shimomura. As soon as they told him, Hendren promised, SCAP would need to do nothing more. Hendren would arrange for his own escorts to fly to Tokyo and bring the four of them back.

Almost a week went by before a response: "It is impracticable at this time to accede to your suggestion for unilateral action by your area in the case of General Shimomura, which is now under investigation and consideration from an international standpoint. MacArthur."

What the hell did that mean? What was an "international standpoint"? Hendren took the cable to Ham Young, who wasn't sure what to make of it, either. Hendren had gotten the personal approval to arrest Shimomura from Joseph Keenan, the man in charge of the Tokyo Tribunal. If there was an "international" standpoint, it was his standpoint. It made no sense. And what was with the signature? "MacArthur." That kind of thing was well below the Shogun of Tokyo's pay grade; it was probably just some desk troll a million rungs down the chain of command trying to bluster. But still, they had wasted precious weeks waiting for SCAP and hoping that its bureaucratic legions would do their jobs. They were only a few weeks out from when Hendren had promised that the trial would begin, and they did not even have their prime suspects in Shanghai.

Hendren persuaded Young to let Dwyer go back to Tokyo. Dwyer knew most of the people working in SCAP's Legal Section from the JAG School and could try to pull personal connections to get things done. And so, the following Thursday morning, Dwyer got to work.

Dwyer made his way to the Meiji Building and checked in on Colonel Alva C. Carpenter, an old friend from Ann Arbor who headed SCAP's Legal Section. Where was Itsuro Hata? Where was Sadamu Shimomura? And what the hell was an "international standpoint"?

Carpenter wasn't sure. It was all news to him. As far as he knew, Hendren had gotten all the paperwork in order. Both the Legal Section and the International Prosecution Section were completely on board with sending Shimomura and the rest to Shanghai. Carpenter suggested Dwyer head upstairs to see Joseph Keenan's people on the seventh floor.

Dwyer asked if Carpenter would come with him as backup, since Carpenter was a full-bird colonel and Dwyer was still just a captain. To Dwyer's annoyance, Carpenter declined to do him this favor, but he did agree to let Dwyer set up shop in the Legal Section's offices while he figured things out in Tokyo.

Dwyer went up to the International Prosecution Section's offices and asked to see Joseph Keenan. Keenan, he was told, was out, but his deputy, Abraham M. Goff, was there.

Good enough, Dwyer decided, and he asked Goff what "international standpoint" was so important that it was holding up the start of the Doolittle Trial. He then launched into a prepared, but not yet practiced, soliloquy on how essential Shimomura was and how the Doolittle Trial, which was the personal legacy of Franklin D. Roosevelt, would be the most important war crimes trial in the Pacific Theater—after the Tokyo Trial, of course.

Dwyer knew he was out of his depth. Here he was telling Abe Goff, Joseph Keenan's deputy, what was what when it came to the prosecution of Japanese war criminals in the Pacific. Goff, though, needed no convincing. He remembered Hendren, and both he and Keenan were entirely behind what the two of them were trying to do in Shanghai; Keenan was hoping to see a few death sentences come out of it. It would put the wind at their back as the Tokyo Tribunal got going and, if nothing else, give the Japanese more reason to cooperate.

Whoever's "international standpoint" was giving them a problem, it wasn't the International Prosecution Section's. Goff suggested that Dwyer head over to the Counter-Intelligence Section to see if that was the source of the holdup. It sometimes played a role in approving arrests, and maybe it had an issue.

Dwyer thanked Goff for the support and made his way out. But then, as Dwyer was stepping out the door, Goff stopped him. He told Dwyer to come back after he had checked in with Counter-Intelligence. Keenan was interested in the Shanghai trials and wanted to chat while he was still in town. Would he be free for dinner Friday night?

With the confidence of a man who had just secured a Friday dinner invitation from Joseph Keenan, Dwyer made his way to the Counter-Intelligence Section's offices in the Yusen Building, a ten-minute walk through the cold.

The head of the Counter-Intelligence Section was out, but his deputy, a captain like Dwyer, was there. Dwyer again launched into his explanation of how prosecuting Shimomura in Shanghai was the only way to honor the legacy of FDR. The captain, though, needed no convincing and assured Dwyer that Counter-Intelligence had signed off on Shimomura's arrest. He wasn't sure what the holdup was. Had Dwyer checked with the Chief of Staff's office?

Of course Dwyer hadn't. No one had mentioned the Chief of Staff's office to him before. And so Dwyer made his way through a labyrinth of office hallways and meandering Tokyo streets, remarked in English but still confusing all the same, to the imposing Dai-ichi Seimei Building, the Wizard's Palace at the heart of the Emerald City, Douglas MacArthur's general headquarters. Almost immediately upon his unannounced arrival, he was intercepted by the Chief of Staff's assistant, a full-bird colonel by the name of Laurence E. Bunker.

Dwyer delivered his prepared and now twice-practiced soliloquy on the importance of prosecuting Shimomura in Shanghai. FDR had promised justice at the war's end, and Dwyer was there to deliver that justice. Without Shimomura, the trial would not live up to the expectations that had been built up in the press. He was, Dwyer said, the "top level man upon whom the responsibility for this war crime may be placed without going to the level of the Class A war criminals, such as Emperor Hirohito or Prime Minister Tojo."

What Colonel Bunker knew (and Dwyer did not) was that MacArthur had just sent a secret cable back to Washington absolving Emperor Hirohito of all criminal responsibility to preserve social stability in occupied Japan. Priorities were shifting. Shimomura, Bunker explained, had been the War Minister in Japan's postwar cabinet. He had succeeded in peacefully demobilizing 2.3 million Japanese soldiers over the course of little more than a few months, earning the personal praise of MacArthur, who had remarked, "I know of no demobilization in history, either in war or peace, by our own or any other country, that has been accomplished so rapidly and so frictionlessly." SCAP was still in the process of repatriating millions of Japanese from around the Pacific. From the standpoint of the postwar occupation, arresting Shimomura and shipping him off to some Army trial in Shanghai was ludicrous. "This matter," Bunker told Dwyer bluntly, "raises a flat conflict of interest between war crimes and occupation."

Dwyer demanded to talk to the Chief of Staff personally, but Colonel Bunker made it clear that Captain Dwyer was not going to be given such an opportunity. What Dwyer needed to do, Bunker told him, was put everything he had just said into a formal memorandum. The Chief of Staff would consider that.

Dwyer asked if he should sign the memo himself or sign it "for the commanding general," brandishing the fact that Wedemeyer had given him top priority.

Bunker told him that he should sign it for himself.

Dwyer sprinted back to the Meiji Building and up to the Legal Section's offices. For the fourth time that day, he recited his prepared and now well-practiced soliloquy to Alva Carpenter's secretary, who furiously transcribed every word.

Any defense lawyer worth his salt, Dwyer explained, would use Shimomura's absence to limit "the severity of the penalty to be imposed," and the failure to get the death penalty in the Doolittle Trial would be a spectacular disaster.

"The press in China," he explained, "has given a vast amount of coverage to this case. It has transmitted copy to the United States through all of the worldwide news services. A considerable amount of space is being given to the fact that President Roosevelt personally released a statement 21 April 1943 that the United States government will hold personally and officially responsible for these diabolical crimes all of the officers of the Japanese government who participated therein and will in due course bring these officers to justice. This statement was made relative to the execution of the Doolittle fliers immediately upon the news thereof having been given the world."

Dwyer then ran back to the Dai-ichi Seimei Building and up to Bunker's office to present his memo. Bunker looked it over and scowled at Dwyer's final paragraph, which threatened the failure of the United States' war crimes mission if Captain Dwyer did not prosecute General Sadamu Shimomura in Shanghai. Bunker took out a pen, struck it through, and added some language of his own. He would pass on the memo, as revised, to the Chief of Staff. He then told Dwyer to come back the following morning for his answer.

Dwyer returned at 10:00 a.m. the next day. As it happened, Bunker was talking to a reporter from United Press. Dwyer pressed the issue, and with a reporter in the room, Bunker made a show of being more sympathetic to Dwyer than he had been the day before.

Dwyer had to understand that what he was asking for was a big deal. Shimomura was, Bunker explained, "vital to the occupation program." There were a lot of considerations in play. "When dealing with important Japanese," he pointed out, "it is not good policy to accept their services in the occupation program and then proceed to hang them for war crimes." He told Dwyer to come back that afternoon. SCAP's decision would be ready by then.

Dwyer went around the corner to the Meiji Building. As he sat in Carpenter's office fuming at being stymied and trying to figure out how to navigate SCAP's labyrinth, a reporter from the Associated Press came in and introduced himself. Was it true, he asked, that Dwyer was in Tokyo to arrest Shimomura?

Dwyer conspicuously declined to offer a denial. Instead, he played coy and stated that he was not authorized to talk to the press.

The reporter persisted. Dwyer was one of the prosecutors preparing the Doolittle Trial, though, wasn't he?

Again Dwyer explained with false humility that he wasn't free to comment on such matters. The reporter thanked him for the scoop and headed out.

When 4:00 p.m. rolled around, Dwyer made his way back to Bunker's office. There was still no word, and without a reporter in the room, Bunker was less inclined to fake sympathy. He told Dwyer to come back again the following morning.

*　*　*

That night, Dwyer had dinner with Joseph Keenan. Keenan's assignment as chief prosecutor had been the result of a dispute between MacArthur and the War Department over how to try Hideki Tojo, the former prime minister and war minister, who had led Japan into war back in 1941.

MacArthur wanted to try Tojo individually, the way he had tried Yamashita in Manila. It was faster and cleaner than what was being done in Nuremberg. The War Department had concluded otherwise, however, and had told MacArthur to put Keenan in charge of the prosecution of Tojo along with the rest of Japan's war cabinet. And so Keenan had gone to Tokyo and, despite the prestige of the job, found himself working at the behest of the imperious MacArthur, who made it publicly known that he did not want him there in the first place.

Keenan was nearing sixty and shared Dwyer's love of copious eating and drinking, a fact that was self-evident from the ruddiness of his cheeks and his alcoholic's nose. He had been sober for more than a year before his arrival in Tokyo, but after a few months, the loneliness and stress of the job had caught up with him. Keenan and Dwyer were two Irish Catholic lawyers with short tempers and a firm conviction in the justness of their cause, a conviction that inevitably got firmer with each glass they tossed back.

Keenan had graduated from Harvard Law School a generation before Dwyer and fancied himself a theorist of natural law. These war crimes trials were, in his mind, "manifestations of an intellectual and moral revolution which will have a profound and far-reaching influence upon the future of world society."

Keenan's strategy for the Tokyo Trial was to treat the Japanese militarists like members of a gang, and he had brought in a recently retired assistant director of the FBI, whom he lauded as having cracked some of

"America's most baffling cases," including the Lindbergh baby kidnapping. He wanted to interrogate the suspects relentlessly until they started confessing or turning on one another.

Keenan was frustrated, though, by his staff. All of the Allies were allowed to put their own lawyers on his staff: the Netherlands, Australia, France, Russia, Canada, the Philippines, New Zealand, China, and Great Britain. None of them could appreciate the pressures Keenan was under.

Keenan empathized with Dwyer's frustration in getting SCAP to turn over Shimomura. Emperor Hirohito had been Keenan's marquee suspect, but MacArthur had let him off the hook just the week before. Keenan and the lawyers working for him were furious, and his staff continued to investigate Emperor Hirohito despite MacArthur's absolution. Keenan assured Dwyer that it wasn't his people who were getting in the way of putting Shimomura or anyone else on trial.

*   *   *

The next morning, Dwyer got himself together and headed back to Bunker's office. Bunker was waiting for him. Dwyer's mucking about had caught the attention of the press and the press had caught the attention of MacArthur, which was never a good thing. MacArthur had sent Wedemeyer a personal cable asking whether he had authorized some captain to travel to Tokyo and make problems for the occupation by arresting the former war minister. Dwyer asked for a copy, but Bunker either did not have one or did not want to give it to him.

As far as SCAP was concerned, Bunker explained, the whole business about arresting Shimomura was suspended. He told Dwyer to stand down but to remain in Tokyo until the precise nature of his authority was cleared up. In the meantime, Bunker ordered Dwyer to report to his office each morning and afternoon. He wasn't about to let Dwyer go running about Tokyo making any more trouble with muckraking reporters.

*   *   *

The storm Dwyer had started in Tokyo quickly blew into Shanghai. MacArthur was unhappy. And if MacArthur was unhappy, Wedemeyer was unhappy. And if Wedemeyer was unhappy, Ham Young was unhappy. Young called Hendren into his office.

Hendren took full responsibility for Dwyer but protested that Shimomura was the "key general" in the Doolittle Trial. As things stood, their case had already taken two enormous hits that week.

Another cable had come in from Tokyo: Hata had died of stomach ulcers. SCAP's earlier cable saying that Itsuro Hata had "left the hospital" had forgotten to mention the reason why: he was dead.

And then, the very day Dwyer had kicked up his little press storm over Shimomura, more bad news had come in: the US-British liaison in Singapore had found Toyama Nakajo, the senior most military judge to preside over the Doolittle Raiders show trial, dead on the island of Rempang. "Much regret failure to catch him alive," the cable lamented.

In just that week, the seven-defendant, two-general war crimes trial of the century that Dwyer and Hendren had spent months preparing was whittled down to five defendants. Losing General Shimomura would be a disaster. "Without Shimomura," Hendren protested, "we are trying only the 'lesser lights' in this case, and as you know all of the accused will contend at the trial that Shimomura had the final authority, and that he actually ordered the sentences into execution." If Shimomura was not in the dock, they might not even get a death sentence out of the trial.

Young heard Hendren out but made it clear that for now Shimomura was off limits. Perhaps he could be tried later, after things cooled down.

To Hendren, who was due to return to the United States after the trial was over, that was totally unacceptable. If Shimomura's prosecution had to wait months, Hendren would not get to try the case; he would be stuck with the trial of the "lesser lights," and some other prosecutor would get to reap the glory.

Young remained unmoved. Hendren, he said, needed to accept that Shimomura was not coming to Shanghai anytime soon. He still had a great case with four dead American heroes. How could he not get the death penalty? The wind was at his back, but he was going to have to let Shimomura go or risk everything.

* * *

On Monday morning, Dwyer got word that regular flights between Tokyo and Shanghai were about to be discontinued. That meant the last flight for sure out of Tokyo would be that evening. Dwyer told Bunker that time was running out. They needed to arrest Shimomora immediately.

Bunker, for his part, let Dwyer know that he would be well advised to be on that flight. He could still take Shigeru Sawada and Yusei Wako back to Shanghai with him, but he had worn out his welcome in Tokyo.

Dwyer sprinted back to the Meiji Building and up to the Legal Section's office to fetch the necessary paperwork to transfer Sawada and Wako from Sugamo Prison. Dwyer had asked for it to be done the previous Thursday, but the desk trolls had either lost it or forgotten to do it, so Dwyer again dashed from office to office among the Meiji, Yusen, and Dai-ichi Seimei Buildings, all around Little America, getting every stamp, signature, and carbon copy necessary to check his two prisoners out of Sugamo and onto the 8:00 p.m. flight.

By the time Dwyer touched down in Shanghai, the press was waiting for him. He had traveled through the night and the photographers snapped a shot of him, haggard, eyes open extra wide in order to keep them open at all, marching Sawada and Wako in for booking into Ward Road Jail.

In the stories that ran in the following days, the deaths of Itsuro Hata and Toyama Nakajo were lamented and Sadamu Shimomura was revealed as a prime suspect. And to complete the humiliation, the *Shanghai Herald* coupled its photo of Dwyer marching Sawada and Wako with a story headlined "Arrest of Shimomura Is Ordered." Almost as soon as the C-47 had lifted Dwyer and his two prisoners into the night sky over Tokyo, SCAP had issued orders for Shimomura to be arrested and taken to Sugamo Prison so that SCAP could investigate his possible involvement in the case of the Doolittle Raiders.

It was an insult laid on top of all the setbacks Dwyer had endured that week, but any pall it might have cast was soon lifted. Within days of his return to Shanghai, the US Supreme Court issued its decision in Yamashita's case. It was a long and complicated legal opinion, and it took the Court a while to get to the point, but the outcome was clear from the first page: "Throughout the proceedings which followed, including those before this Court," Chief Justice Harlan Fiske Stone wrote, "defense counsel have demonstrated their professional skill and resourcefulness and their proper zeal for the defense with which they were charged." It was a nice thing to see said about Dwyer's old friend from Ann Arbor, Frank Reel. But no court ever praises a criminal defense lawyer unless what follows is the conclusion that his client, who had been so ably defended, is about to be hanged by the neck until dead.

Yamashita's trial and the Court's decision were controversial. Frank Reel had tirelessly sought to present Yamashita in a softer light in the press, and the fact that MacArthur had seen to it that Yamashita was sentenced to death on the four-year anniversary of Pearl Harbor certainly did not make the trial appear any less politicized. But whatever the controversy, the Supreme Court had given its blessing to the legal theory of command responsibility, which Dwyer had brought back from Manila, and removed the last legal obstacle to the Doolittle Trial.

With the trial set to begin in less than two weeks, Dwyer had earned his seat at the prosecution table. He had risen from being Hendren's investigator to being his cocounsel, a full-blown prosecutor, a banner carrier for the legacy of FDR and the Doolittle Raiders.

Buoyed, he went out to Ward Road Jail to confront Shigeru Sawada, taking Chase Nielsen along for the show.

"This guy is Nielsen," Dwyer told Sawada as if the word "Nielsen" were synonymous with "venomous pit viper." "And he was about to kill you."

Sawada looked back implacably at the what-do-you-think-about-that expression on Dwyer's face.

"As the prosecutor," Dwyer emphasized in the face of Sawada's silence, "I'm going to demand the death penalty for you." All Dwyer needed Sawada to admit was that he had been in command, so he asked him flat out, "Did you exercise court-martial jurisdiction over the Shanghai area in 1942?"

"Yes," Sawada answered, "they must have my 'chop.' From May 7, 1942, up till September 17, 1942, between this time I was at the front, so my assistant had my 'chop' and did the work for me."

Dwyer realized that the legal term "jurisdiction" had gotten lost in translation and tried to clarify. "Do you feel you were responsible because you were commanding general?"

"Yes."

"Do you assume *responsibility* for the death sentences imposed on the Doolittle fliers?" Dwyer asked carefully, working through the precise legal language the Supreme Court had used to uphold Yamashita's conviction.

But Sawada again responded with a circuitous answer, and Dwyer couldn't be sure if Sawada was being evasive or just confused. So Dwyer pressed him for specifics: "The court was appointed by your Headquarters, wasn't it?"

"Yes."

"The sentence of death imposed by the court was approved by your Headquarters?"

"The commanding general of the 13th Army had no power to change the court sentence," Sawada attempted to explain by way of mitigation.

"You approved the sentence," Dwyer pinned him down, "didn't you?"

"Yes."

It was hardly the clear acknowledgment of guilt Dwyer had hoped for, but it was a "yes." Sawada admitted that he had been in command, took responsibility, and confirmed that he had approved the sentence of death for eight innocent men, framed as war criminals with "evidence" that had been tortured out of them. That was more than enough to ensure that Sawada would follow Yamashita to the gallows.

After that, Dwyer did a few cleanup interviews. He questioned Yusei Wako and went back again to Sotojiro Tatsuta, trying unsuccessfully to get them to corroborate Chase Nielsen's claim that he and the rest of the Raiders had been forced to sign blank pieces of paper that had then been used to forge false confessions. There were a few outstanding leads and rabbit holes Dwyer could go down, but with Sawada and the rest now in custody, the case was ready for trial.

In an ordinary military case, the charges were levied in the name of some investigator or lawyer who had helped put the case together. But for Shigeru Sawada, Yusei Wako, Ryuhei Okada, and Sotojiro Tatsuta, the honor went to Chase Nielsen.

Nielsen signed the charges against his former captors: Sawada, by virtue of his command, for "knowingly, unlawfully and wilfully" murdering the Raiders by having had them tried "on false and fraudulent charges"; Okada and Wako for "knowingly, unlawfully and willfully" convicting the Raiders and sentencing them to death "without a fair trial"; and Tatsuta for "knowingly, unlawfully and wilfully" denying the Raiders their rightful status as prisoners of war and for commanding "Japanese soldiers to fire upon and kill the said Lieutenant Dean E. Hallmark, Lieutenant William G. Farrow, and Sergeant Harold A. Spatz."

The release of the charges coincided with Dwyer finally getting his long-overdue promotion to major; no longer would he be a lowly captain. Victory in Shanghai would undoubtedly lead to even bigger and better things, maybe even a return to the Emerald City to work on the Tokyo Tribunal. With Shimomura in Sugamo, who better to build the case against him and the rest of the Class A war criminals?

Almost single-handedly, Dwyer had grown a thin file into a precedent-setting case. Ham Young knew what he had accomplished. He was even on friendly terms with Joseph Keenan. However lackluster his war stories had been up until now, he was preparing to take the stage in the closing act of the epic saga of the Doolittle Raiders. All those months spent freezing in the Ann Arbor winter were about to pay off: Major Robert Dwyer was the one doing the big things.

THE DEFENSE

* * *

THIRTEEN

Elizaveta Snigursky went by the last name of her ex-husband, who had died nearly a decade before in Harbin, China. She had been born Sadovskaya, a name still used by her mother, Paraeskeva (or "Pasha"), and brother, Pytor, with whom she shared a fourth-floor apartment at 672 Avenue Joffre in Shanghai's former French Concession. To the erotically adolescent Americans at Broadway Mansions, where she also had a room, her name was "Sweater Girl." But to Edmund J. Bodine, she was "Lailia."

Elizaveta had put Bodine off at first. Though Elizaveta had gone on dates with a few Americans since the US Army horde had sacked Broadway Mansions back in October 1945, they had left her unimpressed. They were preferable to the Russians, Chinese, and Japanese guests, who had regarded her as barely more than a talking dog to whom commands needed to be sternly barked, never mind that she spoke all of their languages and could offer the latest thinking on Pushkin or Palestine, or plutonium. To them, she was just their girl-get: "Girl, get me this. Girl, get me that." And she would be expected to respond:

к вашим услугам
乐意效劳
私はあなたを助けることができてうれしいです

—or now a familiar "At your service."

The Americans were friendly, but they were not manly. They could often be good-looking enough, but there was nothing sexy about them.

They were schoolboys, and she was the teacher on whom they had a crush, all toothy smiles, chewing gum, and googly eyes, clumsy drunks, insisting that anyone and everyone know that they were having a good time.

They seemed to think that when she was at the concierge desk, she was really sitting at a bar next to an open stool waiting for them to buy her a drink. And when they made their move, she could never understand how they had come to believe that the best way to snag a date with a girl whom they had never met was to present her with a stack of family photos and a lengthy recitation of the biographical details of people who lived thousands of miles away, whom she would never meet and often included a wife and children.

No, Elizaveta wanted a man with class who knew his Pushkin, who had opinions about Stravinsky. She wanted a man who knew or wanted to know something about the world—or at least one who could correctly identify her as a Russian. One time, she had accepted a dance from an American officer who had asked her, foolishly, "Are you a German?" To Elizaveta it was a laughable, even insulting, question.

Elizaveta did not resent the uxorious Americans. If wearing a tight sweater made them eager to please her, then her job was a lot easier. They made Broadway Mansions more fun than it had been during the war. Her colleagues at the concierge desk, Elsa the German and Minnela the Portuguese, also had their share of American fawns, and they enjoyed the chance to compare notes on the laughable men.

Edmund Bodine had been one of them. He was tall, athletic, and square-jawed—it was no surprise that he had been a spokesmodel for Ford back in New York. He was known all around Broadway Mansions for his prowess at baseball, having almost gone pro, and possessed the warm, happy-to-be-liked-by-everyone confidence that being a good-looking jock affords a man. He had the effortless charm of the broad-shouldered nice guy who instinctively welcomed everyone along for a good time.

Elizaveta could not have cared less about baseball. Being good at an American child's game was the opposite of debonair, and to make matters worse, Bodine was a redhead. Elizaveta found that even less appealing than baseball. And so, when Bodine first asked her out, the answer was self-evidently no.

It was Christmas Eve, and everyone—Elizaveta included—was going to make a night out of the dances being thrown all around Shanghai. She had been working a shift at the concierge desk and, needing to run upstairs, crossed the lobby's art deco floor to one of the elevators as its doors closed. There was Bodine, standing tall, much taller than she, and looking nervous.

Bodine wasn't a total stranger; she had gone out with one of his best friends, Cullen "Cab" Brannon, with whom Bodine worked in the Plans Office of the Army Advisory Group's Operations Division. Still, she hadn't thought much about him, so when Bodine began to speak, her main thought was of how she had to crane her neck to look up at him in the tight confines of a Broadway Mansion elevator. But then the questions started coming.

Did she have a date for the dances that night?

No, she answered honestly.

Would she be his date?

No, she answered just as honestly. She was not cruel about it, but the answer came out without hesitation, deliberation, or room for negotiation. When the elevator door opened, she ejected herself with the relief of an airman vaulting through the escape hatch of a plane crashing to the earth in flames.

It was only a little while later, though, that she sent Elsa the German to see Bodine, who was still licking the wounds to his pride. Elsa had always been much more persuaded by Bodine's charms, even though the previous Christmas, flirting with each other would have been treasonous, as their countrymen were in the midst of a mutual slaughter. Elizaveta had sent her with a message: "Tell that redheaded major I will go out with him."

Bodine picked Elizaveta up that night decked out in his freshly pressed "pinks and greens," looking as sharp as Dwight D. Eisenhower. And despite herself and despite Bodine's lack of opinions about Pushkin or Stravinsky, Elizaveta had a good time.

Bodine was very American. Everyone called him "Ed." Sometimes people called him "Red," a nickname he had picked up back at Georgetown University because of his hair. Elizaveta, unhappy with either name, called him "Edmund." When Bodine inevitably broke out the photos of his family, his very big family, from Douglaston, Long Island, she wondered which of the women was his wife. He had so many "sisters." But she held her tongue.

Elizaveta normally resisted laughing, that is not what Russian aristocrats did, but she would occasionally flash Bodine a sly grin that accentuated her cheekbones. And when she did break a smile or start to laugh despite herself, her face lit up with pure joy.

They talked for hours that night, and she found a depth beneath Bodine's too-quick American smile. Bodine's father had died when he was still at Georgetown, so he had become the patriarch of his rather large family much earlier than he had expected or desired. His mother, Alma, adored him and tried to keep him and everyone else in the family close, but he was restless. And though it made Alma unhappy, Bodine was delighted to be in China. He wanted to see the wider world.

The band struck up the song "Time on My Hands (You in My Arms)," and Bodine asked Elizaveta to dance. This time, her first and only answer was "Yes." It was a slow song with corny words:

> *Time on my hands, you in my arms*
> *Nothing but love in view*
> *Then if you fall, once and for all*
> *I'll see my dreams come true*
> *Moments to spare*
> *With someone you care for*
> *One love affair for two*
> *And so with time on my hands*
> *And you in my arms*
> *And love in my heart all for you.*

As they danced, Bodine said, "You're the kind of girl a guy could marry." He made sure to phrase it as an observation, not a question. But she knew what he was asking—many men in Shanghai made similar observations in the hopes that girls would offer the perks of marriage without all of the paperwork.

"What about your wife?" she asked, undoubtedly feeling clever as she continued to sway in his arms.

"I'm not married," Bodine stiffly insisted.

"Sure you're not," she said. Sweater Girl was not stupid. She had already given in to him once that day, and there was nothing he could say to change her mind a second time. But then he did.

"We can call my mother," Bodine protested. And he meant it. They would go to the nearest phone and call Alma Bodine back in Douglaston, Long Island. It was morning there, and she would be home getting the house ready for family Christmas.

The absurd earnestness of Bodine's insistence broke Elizaveta into another laugh. Calling Alma Bodine, she assured him, would not be necessary. She would believe him.

*   *   *

Bodine enjoyed the Christmas Day feast in the Broadway Mansions dining room, overlooking Shanghai's Bund, of roast pork, chicken, plum pudding, ice cream, and cocoa. It was his first Christmas away from Alma and the rest of the clan back in Douglaston, but the food was so good that he saved the menu. He was an American officer in Shanghai. The world had been born anew. And he was in love. The catch, and Bodine knew it, was that he was on the other side of the world from where he belonged.

Bodine had been deployed to China the previous winter to fly liaison flights in the closing months of the war. And he loved being a pilot. The airplane was the most romantic invention in the still unrivaled technological revolution that had defined the turn of the twentieth century. Sure, the electric light, chemical fertilizer, and the internal combustion engine had made it so that Bodine's life expectancy at birth was double what it would have been a generation earlier. But it was the sight of a man, a human man, taking to the air not as a bird or an angel but in a loud, heavy steel machine that preyed on his yearning for the heroic.

Bodine was no different from the farm boys Jimmy Doolittle had taken on his famous raid, even though Bodine had grown up as a relatively affluent Republican in New York City. His father, an accountant for the IRS, had had a gambling habit—a habit Bodine had inherited despite his mother's scolding—but also a lucky break. One day, he had won $60,000 at the track (the equivalent of nearly a million dollars today). Overnight, the Bodines had gone from being another large Catholic family struggling to stay middle class into the kind of people with real estate holdings and enough passive income to make the family comfortable during the Depression.

As a young man, Bodine had had the luxury of focusing his energies on being a well-rounded athlete on the varsity baseball, football, and basketball teams at Xavier high school in New York, and at Georgetown, from which he graduated with gentleman's C's. After college, he had played a bit of minor-league baseball and taken various jobs, including as a policeman in Long Island, a teacher back at Xavier, and a pitchman for Ford. But despite the worldliness that urban affluence afforded him, Bodine was still seduced by the air.

At twenty-seven, Bodine was frustrated to learn that he was just too old to enroll in the Army's regular flight school, where he could learn to fly the newest fighters or bombers. But he was still eligible to fly noncombat aircraft, which were generally called liaison aircraft. He took the chance to get his wings, though those wings were stamped with a conspicuous *L* to set him apart from the regular pilots. When he got to China in early 1945, the Army put him into the L-5 Sentinel, one of the so-called L-Birds, which were more truly and widely called "flying jeeps."

L-Birds had a single 65-horsepower engine mounted on the nose, two very cozy seats behind the windshield, and a flat truck bed in the back that was only big enough to hold one man and his gear. Though L-Bird pilots did not have the swagger or prestige of the Army Air Forces' fighter jocks and bomber crews, L-Birds were deployed all over the messy and vast terrain of the Pacific Theater. They could take off and land with virtually no runway and could fly low enough to drop some smoke onto a target, rescue the stranded, or resupply some commandos behind enemy lines—and they did all of it unarmed.

There had been guns in the Air Force arsenal that could have been rigged up without weighing down the L-Birds too drastically. Early in the war, the Air Force had equipped many of their flight crews with a .30-caliber machine gun. It weighed only thirty-odd pounds and did not need to be mounted, but it bounced around so hard it could crack the glass of the plane's nose, meaning it was inaccurate on top of not being very powerful. So back in August 1942, the Army Air Forces phased it out and standardized all their planes and ammunition around the mounted .50-caliber machine guns, steel beasts that weighed more than a hundred pounds.

The L-Bird's maximum load was less than five hundred pounds, including the pilot. But rather than revive the .30-caliber, the Air Force sent the L-Birds out over enemy territory armed only with prayers. To those who truly appreciated them, L-Bird pilots were "air commandos," and the Air Force even obliged the sentiment late in the war by creating three so-called Air Commando Groups, where pilots of the L-Bird and the Army's other light aircraft got a title befitting the dangers.

Bodine had distinguished himself during the war and was awarded the Bronze Star for heroism in combat. As a major, he outranked the vast majority of other L-Bird pilots and had received some choice assignments as a result. But when the war ended, he had been dropped into the Plans Office with not much to do.

The only flying that needed doing was the occasional Gooney Bird trip, shuttling from one Chinese city to another, and the Army had little incentive to continue to subsidize Bodine's stay in Shanghai. Hundreds of men were being sent back to the United States each week. For most, the downsizing offered a long-wished-for return to home, hearth, and a good American steak. But for Bodine, it meant leaving Lailia.

One part of the Army, though, appeared intent on staying in China for a while. The exploits of Ham Young's War Crimes Office were in the newspapers almost every day, and Young needed people badly.

Bodine was not especially well qualified to work in the War Crimes Office. He had done a little night school at Fordham Law School while working odd jobs after college but had gotten so little out of it that he dropped out to become an Army pilot in 1940. When the recruiter asked for his educational background, Bodine mentioned the three years he had spent at Fordham, which the recruiter assumed had been enough to graduate, meaning that as far as his Army records were concerned, Bodine had a law degree from Fordham Law School.

As it happened, Young's deputy, Lieutenant Colonel Jeremiah J. O'Connor, had been two years ahead of Bodine at Georgetown. They knew each other from the basketball team and had picked up a friendship in the Broadway Mansions social scene. Whether he knew the truth about Bodine's lack of legal credentials or not, O'Connor was happy to vouch for Bodine, who soon found himself appointed as the defense counsel for the Japanese.

For Young, Bodine and his strong desire to stay in Shanghai solved one of his biggest problems. No one was willing to defend the Japanese at the Doolittle Trial except for Captain Charles Fellows, a young-looking thirty-two-year-old captain who did yet not have enough points in the Army's bureaucratic redeployment system to be entitled to a ticket home. Fellows was junior enough that he could be told to take the job and smart enough to understand that doing so without complaining would be the quickest path back to his wife and son in Oklahoma.

Still, Young couldn't make Fellows the lead defense lawyer. John Hendren was a lieutenant colonel, and Robert Dwyer was now a major. Fellows, with his light blond hair, a habit of fastidiousness, and a quick smile that accentuated the bit of chub left in his cheeks, looked like an Eagle Scout. Despite his penchant for chain-smoking, he looked barely old enough to have joined the Army. Young could not very well try the Japanese for conducting an unfair trial and then assign the most junior officer in the room as their lawyer.

Bodine, by contrast, looked the part. Though only a year older than Fellows, his hairline was receding a bit and he already had some manly lines in his face. He also had a sterling military record, was up for promotion to lieutenant colonel, and had gone to a prestigious law school. And, most important, he was strongly motivated to stay in Shanghai.

Bodine was no more excited by the prospect of being forever known as the defense lawyer for the Japanese who had murdered the Doolittle Raiders than Charles Fellows was. But based on the press coverage, the outcome looked as obvious as it had in the Yamashita trial. His clients were sure to be found guilty and hanged by the neck until dead whatever he did. It was not a job he had to take all that seriously. His assignment was to be a tall, handsome, smartly uniformed prop, and as unsavory as it was to be associated with a bunch of Japanese war criminals, the means-and-ends calculation led him to take the job, so that he could be right where he wanted to be: 672 Avenue Joffre.

*   *   *

The first time Bodine made his way to 672 Avenue Joffre was to meet Elizaveta's mother, Pasha, and her brother, Pytor. Bodine had known few Russians in his life, but the image of the Russian bear had convinced him that the best way to make an entrance was with fresh game in hand. He had heard somewhere that it was pheasant season, and he told Elizaveta that he was going hunting so that they could all enjoy fresh bird for dinner.

The problem was that Bodine did not particularly like hunting and certainly was not any good at it. And so, on his way to 672 Avenue Joffre, he stopped by one of the Chinese markets, where unplucked birds could be bought for a few dollars.

The old French Concession was an odd place. Vichy France had given up its share of Shanghai in 1943, technically making it part of China again, but it remained very much the French Concession. Unlike the redolence one endured in other parts of the city, the crisp winter air of Avenue Joffre had the scent of the caramelizing butter and sugar that wafted from its many bakeries. French colonial subjects from Indochina directed traffic in their conical *nón lá* hats, and the jingling tram cars stopped abruptly once they reached Avenue Foch, the border with the British part of town, where passengers had to switch to double-decker buses and traffic directed by turbaned Sikhs.

Passing Haussmann-style building after building, with their bubbly cornices and lacy iron railings over petite Juliet balconies, it was enough to convince any stranger that he had arrived in the uncanny Paris of a dream. And as if that were not enough to disorient a new-in-town like Bodine, the painted signs that hung above the bakeries and seemingly everything else were in Russian.

If the French were content to be absentee landlords in their chunk of Shanghai, exiled Russians made do with a particular kind of life in what everyone came to call "Little Moscow." Russian couples had Russian children who went to Russian schools and fell in love and evaded the watchful eyes of their Russian mothers. They mourned the dead with Russian prayers in the Orthodox Cathedrals on Rue Paul Henri and Rue Corneille. On June 8 each year, they celebrated Pushkin's birthday. They staged Russian ballets and plays and organized Russian cultural societies, the most prestigious of which was a collective of local artists, writers, painters, and musicians whose acronym celebrated the unrivaled tradition of Russian sarcasm by spelling out the word "хлам," or "junk." With a literacy rate for Shanghai's Russians that exceeded 98 percent, hundreds of bookstores, radio stations, newspapers, and publishers thrived, all with their own signs out front and all indecipherable to Bodine as he made his way to a particular Russian home at 672 Avenue Joffre.

Bodine climbed the stairs to Elizaveta's fourth-floor apartment with pheasants in hand and proudly brandished the day's kill as he was welcomed in. Pasha, only fifteen years older than Bodine, had ice blue eyes that pierced through him with an intensity befitting a tsarist aristocrat. Pasha liked him immediately and gave the birds to the cook, a Chinese woman the family employed, who took them back into the kitchen to ready dinner.

Elizaveta's brother, Pytor, also welcomed Bodine warmly but was nothing like what Bodine imagined. He was rather slim and unassuming. There was no Russian bear in this apartment, just a close family trying to get a read on the American that Elizaveta had talked so much about.

Pasha had married Elizaveta's father, Ivan, when she was fifteen and he was an officer in the Tsar's army. Seeing the turn against White Russians such as herself, Pasha had braved the Siberian winter and crossed the frozen Lake Baikal into China on a dogsled with her young children bundled into blankets while Ivan was off fighting the civil war against the Bolsheviks. It was only a matter of time after their exile before Pasha got word of Ivan's death at the front.

The family settled in Harbin, which had been a fine place for Pytor and Elizaveta to grow up. Near, but not too near, the Russian border, it had been flooded by tens of thousands of Russian refugees. But then, after the Second World War started, the city became dangerous. Ukrainian gangs started kidnapping young Russian women for ransom and only occasionally returned them alive after getting paid. Shanghai was safer but still difficult in its own ways. Through it all, though, Pasha had kept the family together. They were the unbreakable *troika*.

While Bodine and the troika chatted, the Chinese cook barged in, complaining to Elizaveta, who was the only one who could speak the language. Elizaveta politely excused herself, and though she was gone only for a moment, her absence left an awkward silence. Neither Pasha nor Pytor spoke English any better than Bodine spoke Russian. Without Elizaveta to translate, all the three could do was trade awkward smiles until she returned.

The warmth of a family dinner was something that Bodine had not enjoyed in quite some time, though it was different from what he had grown accustomed to back in Douglaston, Long Island. Pasha clearly enjoyed the dinner of pheasant, personally shot by a handsome American lawyer her daughter seemed to love, and her aristocratic posture and delicate movements with the cutlery left no doubt where Elizaveta had gotten her impeccable table manners. The troika's close intimacy was nothing like dinnertime with the sprawling Bodine clan, but it was family.

Elizaveta, for her part, was glad she could bring Bodine into this part of her life. Her family was everything to her. Nothing could ever be allowed to come between them. Bodine, therefore, needed to pass the family test if he was to remain her Edmund, and thankfully he did, even if she now saw through his little ploy with the pheasant.

For when she had gone back into the kitchen, the Chinese cook had indignantly revealed a mess of tightly packed rocks and straw stuffed inside the bird that the young man had so proudly scored while "hunting." Eager not to embarrass Bodine during his first test flight before the troika, Elizaveta slipped the cook a bit of cash to discreetly fetch the missing ingredient that was to be the centerpiece of their dinner. And so as Bodine, Pasha, and Pytor enjoyed their pheasant in happy ignorance, Elizaveta amused herself with the knowledge that her beloved Edmund was as good a negotiator in the markets of Shanghai as he was a small-game hunter. It was among the best meals she had ever had.

FOURTEEN

Being the defense lawyer for Japanese war criminals gave Bodine an excuse to stay in Shanghai with Elizaveta, but it had also put him into a tricky spot. Bodine could see it when he picked up the Shanghai *Stars and Stripes*. In a letter to the editor, one US soldier complained that affording people like Yamashita lawyers meant they were "able to take advantage of every legal opportunity that exists under present American laws." It was galling, he wrote, because, as the treatment of the Doolittle Raiders had shown, "such conditions would not prevail if the situation were reversed. Let's make up our minds whether war criminals are to be tried for the vicious crimes they've committed in an efficient manner, or if they are to be nursed along at the expense and time of our government and its people."

Bodine was a pilot. He admired his fellow pilots, for whom the Doolittle Raiders were sainted brethren. He knew whose side he was on. But he soon found that the case was following him everywhere he went. Elizaveta was encouraging and proudly showed him that the case made the front page of a local Russian paper, though when asked what the massive banner headline said, her answer was less encouraging, "The Doolittle Raiders Murderers Face Trial."

Bodine and Elizaveta became fixtures on the Broadway Mansions social scene, which meant making regular appearances at East Meets West, where everyone had thoughts about the upcoming Doolittle Trial. Bodine's broad smiling athlete's charm made it hard for anyone to hold his new role against him. But the only appreciation, if any, he could expect was a begrudging "Somebody's got to do it."

On one occasion, the case came up while he was trying to chat up Colonel Gabriel Disosway, who was in Shanghai leading the Army Air Forces' part in the United States' broader effort to keep the Chinese Civil War from escalating or at least turning against Chiang Kai-shek. During the war, Disosway had been a fighter pilot in Italy and then in China, where he had been shot down over Japanese-controlled territory. Only thirty-five, he was already a legend. He was the gleaming chrome future of the Air Force, and if Bodine wanted a career as a military pilot, Gabe Disosway would be a good friend to have.

Disosway had a wry sense of humor and gave no indication that he held Bodine's new clients against him. But the only question in his mind was how they would be executed. Would they be hanged like Yamashita? Would they be sent to the electric chair, as Roosevelt had done with some of the Nazis? Or would they be shot as the Doolittle Raiders had been?

If Bodine wanted to get ahead as an Air Force pilot, he had to yuck-yuck-yuck right along. Hatred of a common enemy ranks up there with sports and the admiration of pretty girls as the currency of comradery in man-to-man conversation, and Bodine already had ground to make up in the minds of the real fighter jocks, such as Gabe Disosway, for whom the unarmed L-Birds were just little "cubs" or "grasshoppers."

It was not just career anxiety, though. Bodine just identified more with the pilots than with the lawyers, and nothing forced him to search his soul more over his excuse for staying in Shanghai than when Chase Nielsen had agreed to make dinner plans. It was in the same sumptuous Broadway Mansions dining room where Bodine had enjoyed a Christmas feast in the afterglow of new love. If Bodine felt a bit chapped when men like Gabe Disosway ribbed him, sitting across the table from Nielsen squeezed Bodine by the guts, knowing that there but for the grace of God went he.

Nielsen was a gifted storyteller, and his descriptions of things such as the waterboard were enough to make Bodine feel the fear, agony, and hate right down into the base of his windpipe. Nielsen's smarts, his ability to discipline his mind, had clearly kept him alive. But after just a few minutes over a meal, Bodine could see that Nielsen was much more fragile than he played at being for the reporters. Nielsen was holding on tight, and no matter how quick his wits or smooth his words, Bodine got the sense that he might just unravel with one wrong pull.

The truth was that Nielsen's life had fallen apart. The newspapers had gorged themselves on the storyline of Chase and Thora Nielsen reunited, and Thora had dutifully played the role of the lovelorn wife finally living happily ever after. But after the reporters lost interest, Thora had broken the news: She no longer loved him. She had met someone else. There would be no picking up where they had left off. After everyone but Nielsen's mother had presumed him dead, she had started dating again and had made no secret of it. Out arm in arm with other men at nightclubs and restaurants, she had made no secret of the fact that she had given up hope.

As it happened, Nielsen had been back in Utah finalizing their divorce when he had gotten the telegram from John Hendren asking if he would come to Shanghai for the trial. At that point, what did he have to lose? The Cache County District Court had awarded him their only marital asset, a 1941 Chevy coupe.

For Bodine, Nielsen's presence was a stark reminder of what was at stake. Nielsen had enlisted as a flying cadet in 1939, just a year before Bodine had decided to get serious about a military career. Had Bodine made the leap just a bit earlier, he would not have been too old for the regular flight school and he could just as easily have found himself on a B-25B bomber taking off from the USS *Hornet*. Had Bodine simply not tried to stick it out in law school for one more year, it could have been him who was locked away in Bridge House, shot through the head in Jiangwan's Chinese Cemetery, or left to die alone in Nanking Prison. It could have been him, instead of Nielsen, sitting across from some so-called lawyer whose job was to stand in the way of his just revenge.

* * *

If Edmund Bodine was a pilot uncomfortably tasked with looking the part of a lawyer, Charles Fellows was a lawyer uncomfortably biding his time as a soldier. Fellows had no intention of pursuing a career as an officer, not the least as a pilot, and the truth was that he had not particularly wanted to join the Army in the first place.

When the war had started, some of his friends back in Oklahoma had seen what was coming and taken an early opportunity to sign up with the JAG Corps. With the prospect of a draft imminent, getting a commission as a military lawyer ensured that your assignments would usually not be all that dangerous. Fellows passed on the chance, though, only to find himself drafted in 1942 and inducted as a private. It had taken a bit of bureaucratic magic over the next couple of years, but he had ultimately gotten himself into the JAG Corps, which had led to his current deployment in China.

Without question, being assigned to the Doolittle case, even on the side of the Japanese, was the most interesting thing Fellows had done during the war. It was the most interesting thing he had ever done as a lawyer. He had not gone to Harvard or Fordham or any of the other elite East Coast law schools; he had gone to the University of Oklahoma in the midst of the Great Depression for the practical purpose of being an oil lawyer in Tulsa with his father, who couldn't have been happier to rebrand his firm as Fellows & Fellows. But the work of a Tulsa oil lawyer was not glamorous and was not that interesting as legal work went. Fellows spent most days proofreading for rich people, making sure the contracts got the oil going in one direction and the money going in the other. It was the kind of law practiced on the golf course, not in a courtroom.

The Doolittle case seemed to have it all. It was a high-profile murder case, a war crimes trial that was all over the papers. To his fellow members of the bar back in Tulsa, it would give Fellows a credential as a lawyer's lawyer, even if he never set foot in a courtroom again. It was also fascinating work in its own right. Here was a criminal trial being conducted by the US Army in Shanghai, China, under international law, something an oil lawyer from Tulsa would normally never have had the chance to think about, let alone argue in court.

The more he studied up, the more Fellows thought he and Bodine had a real case, despite what the papers said. He came up with all sorts of legal arguments and identified what seemed like major problems with the charges that Dwyer and Hendren had drawn up.

To be a war crimes trial, the charges had to allege actual war crimes, actual violations of international law. Some of the things that had happened to the Raiders, not the least the torture, did violate international law. But Dwyer and Hendren's effort to make Sawada responsible for everything that had happened looked like a stretch.

What had Sawada personally done to violate international law? The charges said that Sawada "did appoint a military tribunal to try United States Army personnel who are entitled to the honorable status of Prisoners of War". But what was wrong with appointing a military tribunal? Wasn't that precisely what the US Army was now doing to Sawada? Neither he nor the other Japanese on trial were being held as prisoners of war. They were being held in Ward Road Jail as suspected war criminals, just as the Raiders had been in Jiangwan. It was hypocrisy in the extreme to send a defeated Japanese general to the gallows for doing precisely what the US Army was now doing to him.

The charges against Sotojiro Tatsuta seemed even stranger. How could a prison warden be charged with running a prison and carrying out the sentences handed down by a duly constituted military court? It made no sense. It was not as if Tatsuta were being charged with the Raiders' torture. In fact, none of the four defendants were.

So far as the charges revealed, the closest Dwyer and Hendren had come to charging anyone with mistreating the Raiders was the charge against Yusei Wako and Ryuhei Okada, but the crux of that charge was that they had presided over an unfair trial. How could that be considered a "violation of the laws and customs of war"? There was no international law on what a fair trial required. Sure, the Japanese did not have the same rules of Americans were accustomed to. But was being a military judge in Japan a war crime akin to the mass slaughter of civilians that Yamashita had presided over during the Battle of Manila?

Fellows also turned up legal arguments for why the Army's decision to conduct a trial at all was illegal. The most obvious among them was that the US Army had no business conducting trials in China in the first place. Unlike the Philippines, where Yamashita had been tried, Shanghai was not US territory. China was a sovereign country, and the Army was not occupying it the way it was occupying Germany and Japan. Congress had passed no law authorizing the Army to set up its own court system in China.

The Chinese were also perfectly capable of conducting their own war crimes trials. They were in the midst of doing so, including one high-profile case against Chen Kung-po, Wang Jingwei's successor as leader of the Republic of China, for allying with the Japanese during the war. The trials were even taking place in Ward Road Jail in a special courtroom the Chinese had called the Shanghai High Court.

If Sawada and the rest were going to be put on trial for crimes they alleged had been committed in China, why not insist that the Chinese be the ones to try them? It was a technical legal argument, to be sure. But there was something to it. It was precisely the kind of argument about jurisdiction and international law that could get the case in front of the US Supreme Court.

One problem with the argument, though, at least from the perspective of the Japanese whose lives were at stake, was that it seemed like asking to be dumped from the frying pan into the fire. At their first meeting, Bodine had put the question squarely to Sawada: "Would you rather be tried by the Americans or by the Chinese? If you wish we will try to transfer you to the Chinese."

Sawada did not hesitate before giving his answer: "This has nothing to do with the Chinese. I would prefer to be tried by the Americans."

* * *

Meeting with Sawada, Bodine felt conflicted. It was one thing to yuck-yuck-yuck along as men he respected mused about how a stranger could be driven from this earth. It was quite another to look at that stranger in the flesh after exchanging a cordial greeting. And it was another still to introduce himself as that stranger's lawyer, knowing full well it meant that Bodine was asking him to trust him with his life.

Bodine had been there. Back in 1930, when still in high school, Bodine had had his own run-in with the law. He knew the feeling of being under arrest, of not being able to leave, not knowing what was in store. He knew the unstable mixture of terror and relief seeing a lawyer walk into the room for the first time; terror over the prognosis but relief that someone was there at all.

Luckily, Bodine did not have to face Sawada alone. He had Fellows, who had at least some experience self-identifying as a lawyer. And he had Elizaveta. He had asked Elizaveta to marry him a few weeks earlier, and she had answered him with the same lack of hesitation she had displayed when turning him down for a date in the elevator on Christmas Eve. But this time, she had said yes, and now they were spending their first Valentine's Day together in a prison.

Dwyer and Hendren had just formally issued the charges in the Doolittle case, which meant that Sawada was now permitted to consult with his lawyers. Neither Bodine nor Fellows spoke a word of Japanese, and Sawada spoke only slightly more English. Given the nature of their assignment, Elizaveta was one of the few people willing to help, and she was also one of the only people Bodine and Fellows could trust.

Bodine, Fellows, and Elizaveta became their own odd troika. Bodine was to be in charge by virtue of his rank, despite the fact that he had only the barest of qualifications; Fellows was to make sense of the law; and Elizaveta was to make sense of everything else. The odds against them were astronomical. Assuming that Fellows's legal arguments did not save the day, there was not much standing between Sawada and the gallows. But perhaps if they could persuade Sawada to be contrite, to show remorse, and to throw himself on the mercy of the court, they could at least save his life. And so, presented with a task that was intended to be impossible and about which they were at best ambivalent, the three spent Valentine's Day together in Ward Road Jail with the man accused of being the most notorious Japanese war criminal in Shanghai.

Sawada was noticeably tall for a Japanese man. He had a longish face, a bald dome of a head, and the hair he still had was trimmed close. He wore the small, round spectacles that were fashionable at the time; perched as they were on his protruding ears, he looked more like a weary accountant than a fearsome general.

Born in Kochi, Japan, the third son of a farmer, Sawada was like many of the rural men of his generation. A military career was the way to both financial security and respectability, so he attended the Imperial Japanese Army Academy in Hiroshima, graduating in 1905, and then began a successful career ascending the ranks of the Japanese Army. He took command of the 13th Army in Shanghai in December 1940 and largely retired to civilian life—or more accurately was retired—soon after returning to Tokyo from Shanghai in early October 1942.

Sawada did not have the look of a war criminal mastermind, whatever that was. Now nearing sixty, he was losing his eyesight, which accentuated a certain frailty about him. He was unfailingly polite to his new US legal team, though he had difficulty hiding the fact that all three of them were young enough to be his children. Though he made it clear that he was grateful to them for being there, he asked them, if possible, to find a Japanese lawyer, ideally one with a lot of experience.

When it came to the charges against him, Sawada was defiant. Once past the pleasantries, he vaulted into a lengthy defense of himself. "During the forty years I was in the Army, I never did anything wrong," he insisted. "All I had to do was because it was ordered by the Emperor and it is not my fault what happened. I feel very sorry for what I had to do but it was because it was the order of the Army with the order of the Emperor. I did nothing in my own will."

Bodine tried to interrupt him with a question. "If you refused to carry out the order," he asked, "what would've happened?"

"There is no question of not obeying orders," Sawada replied. "I was in the Army."

"We are soldiers, we understand," Bodine tried to explain, "but if you had refused to obey what would've happened? Would you have been relieved of your command or be court-martialed?"

"I would've been punished," Sawada said without hesitation. He then added, in what seemed like overselling, "I might have been executed."

Bodine tried to reassure Sawada that he did not have to sell them on anything. They were not there to judge him. They were his lawyers. They needed to know the truth if they were going to have any chance of doing anything for him. "If you are asked a question," Bodine tried to assure him, "the truth is the answer you should give."

"I understand," Sawada replied before continuing to rattle off the thoughts that had been on his mind since he first found himself under arrest the previous October. "The situation of the time was different to now," he insisted. "The first time they bombed Japan it was a great surprise for the population and the authorities had to do something to prove to the people that it would not happen again in the future but later on, many places were bombed and destroyed. But the first time they never expected there would be bombs they had to make an example and show the people that if they were bombed again the fliers would be punished—"

"You are free to talk," Bodine tried to interrupt him again, "because no one will know what you say except your defense counsel."

The dam, though, was broken. "The way the fliers bombed," Sawada said, dismayed, "destroyed many houses and many people wounded and injured. In one place there was machine-gun many people were killed and injured. The population was very angry because of how they bombed."

After the attack on Pearl Harbor, Sawada had anticipated that the war with the United States would be a "clean war," but the reports he had read about the Doolittle Raiders were shocking: hospitals attacked; children gunned down in schools. What kind of soldier would kill innocent children? That was when, he claimed, he had known this was going to be a "dirty war."

Bodine stopped him curtly. They did not have a lot of time and even less for Japanese propaganda. What they needed were basic facts. They were going to get at most a week or two to investigate in Japan, and what they found there was going to make or break their case. If Sawada or the others were going to have any chance of avoiding the death penalty, Bodine, Fellows, and Elizaveta needed to know who would vouch for Sawada and argue that his life should be spared.

Sawada seemed to get the picture and promised to write out a list for them. Sawada also tried to explain how things had been back in 1942, who had been in charge of what, and what he had been doing that summer.

In the days after the Doolittle Raid, Sawada had received orders from the Japanese headquarters in Nanking to suspend the 13th Army's current plans and stand by for further instructions. As it happened, Sawada had just gotten a report from the field that his men had captured three Americans south of Ningbo. Sawada had relayed all that to headquarters, which in turn had ordered him to send the Americans to Tokyo.

About a week after the raid, General Shunroku Hata, Japan's top commander in China and Sawada's direct superior, had received instructions from Tokyo to mobilize Japan's forces in China for the en masse destruction of Chinese airfields. Though dubious of the military value of the operation, Hata duly complied and had his chief of staff cable back to Tokyo.

"We cannot allow the American Air Force, after inhumanely blind bombing at the time of air raids of the mainland, to escape to the Chinese continent," he wrote. "We want positively to destroy such enemies and we intend to punish such actions severely as grave offenses of war." The proverbial gloves were being taken off.

Sawada had departed for the front on May 7, 1942, with orders to destroy every Chinese airfield in Quzhou, Lishui, and Yushan as the rest of the Japanese armies under General Hata's command scorched their way through the Chinese provinces that had helped the Raiders escape. The rampage became known as "China's Lidice," after the Czech village that Hitler had annihilated when local insurgents had assassinated the Germans' colonial governor. There were reports of as many as 25,000 Chinese killed.

It was the largest operation Sawada would ever oversee. Over the course of the summer, communications had become more and more difficult, depending upon unreliable wireless radios or the hand delivery of messages by airplane, which itself had been made increasingly difficult by the fact that any airfield Sawada's forces came upon was to be destroyed. The operation had stretched into the rainy season, and flooding made many parts of the countryside traversable only by boat. Complicating matters further, Chinese guerrillas had started demolishing train tracks, roads, and communication wires, making travel times double what they ordinarily were.

As a consequence, the whole issue about the captured Doolittle Raiders had largely been resolved in Sawada's absence. "When I first came back on September 17th," he explained, "I got a report that an order was made for the American prisoners to be executed." He claimed that that had been the first time he had heard anything about their having been returned to China. The head of the 13th Army's Legal Department, Colonel Shoshin Ito, had taken care of all the details.

Still, Sawada wanted one thing to be clear. "I am responsible for this," he said with matter-of-fact defiance. As far as he was concerned, "We lost the war, and whatever the verdict, I must willingly assent." He wanted Bodine, Fellows, and Elizaveta to know that what was at stake for him in this trial was not his life. "I don't care what kind of penalty will be given to me," he insisted. "But I want you to make it clear that I acted as a military commander in accordance with the rules of the Japanese Army and haven't done anything illegal. Please persuade them that the Japanese Army behaved rightly."

Elizaveta understood Sawada's stubbornness. She had gotten to know the Japanese well during the war and had been friends with some of Japan's expats in Shanghai, who called her "Eli-san." One had even attempted to entrust her with a string of pearls after the armistice had been declared, confident that it would be only a matter of time before things would be back to normal.

Tradition-minded Japanese people like Sawada just had a much stronger sense of community than the individualistic Americans did. Americans worried about guilt; the Japanese worried about shame. Someone like Sawada not only was willing to take responsibility, he wanted to. When he used the Japanese word for "responsible" (責任, pronounced "sekinin"), he did not mean that he had done anything wrong. He was not even making any claim about who had caused what effect. He was saying "I embrace responsibility." It was an act of martyrdom to prove that he and his community had no reason to be ashamed.

Bodine, though, was frustrated. Sawada wanted him to mount the single defense that was certain to lose at trial and leave Sawada hanging by the neck until dead. No US Army officer in 1946 was going to think that either Japan or the Japanese general accused of presiding over the torture and murder of the Doolittle Raiders had "behaved rightly." There was not a single officer in the US Army who would go on the record to spare Sawada's life for that reason or, for that matter, to salvage Bodine's military career after he dared to suggest it.

Fellows decided to go back to talk with Sawada the next day, not to persuade him to change his mind, but because there had been a few things in Sawada's description of who had been doing what that Fellows wanted to pin down. Bodine decided to not to go. He figured there was better uses of his time, particularly given the news that was about to break: General Wedemeyer had given the go ahead to start the trial.

FIFTEEN

On February 27, 1946, the trial *United States v. Sawada, et al.* commenced as every trial does with an arraignment. Shigeru Sawada, Yusei Wako, Ryuhei Okada, and Sotojiro Tatsuta were to stand in front of the public for the first time and enter their pleas—guilty or not guilty—to the charge of being war criminals.

To attend the day's session, members of the public had to walk down Ward Road Jail's seemingly endless maze of corridors, passing one locked door after another, until they reached the sixth floor, where the cell block had been remodeled into a courtroom. From there they would be led to the public gallery, which was separated from the well by a polished wooden railing. The judges' bench was elevated and had enough room to sit six across with an enormous American flag pinned to the wall behind them. On the left was the defense table and on the right, the prosecution table. One radio microphone was propped up between the two tables, and another was situated to the right of the judge's bench, where a sturdy wooden chair sat atop a small platform to be used as the witness stand. Along the far-right wall were rows of desks for the media to chronicle the goings-on. The far-left wall was where the accused were expected to sit in rows of simple wooden chairs.

The air was so frigid that space heaters cluttered the floor, but the courtroom was packed with spectators. Scattered about were military police, with the stenciled "MP" on the front of their helmets to let everyone know that law, order, and decorum would be maintained. Waiting for the proceedings to begin, the room bubbled with conversation and mingling; the sentiments about war crimes prosecutions ranged from "Why don't they hang them now?" to "Why all this waste of money?"

The hubbub ceased when the MPs escorted Sawada, Okada, Wako, and Tatsuta into the courtroom. The gallery collectively craned its neck to get a my-own-eyes look at the four men. Few are assessed as scrupulously as notorious criminals brought before the fresh eyes of courtroom specta-tors, who are thrilled to be in such close proximity to infamy as they seek out some feature of the face, some tilt of the gait, some subtle mannerism, some physical trait to explain all that has brought them there.

Three of the four defendants wore wrinkled business suits that looked a size too small. Only Ryuhei Okada wore his Japanese Army khakis, though, as it had been stripped of its epaulets and decorations, it looked a bit as though he had strolled in wearing pajamas. The four sat stiffly on their wooden chairs, not shackled but clearly nervous and having every reason to be.

That weekend, the trapdoor below Yamashita's feet had swung open, snapping the noose around his bull-like neck. Sawada had known Yamashita well. They had been classmates at the military academy and had remained friends ever since. In issuing the final order of execution, MacArthur had praised Yamashita's military prowess but condemned him for failing to up-hold his principal duty: "The soldier, be he friend or foe, is charged with the protection of the weak and unarmed. It is the very essence and reason of his being. When he violates this sacred trust, he not only profanes his entire cult but threatens the very fabric of international society."

* * *

Sawada had asked Bodine, Fellows, and Elizaveta to find an experienced Japanese lawyer to help him avoid Yamashita's fate. And in the two weeks they had to prepare before the arraignment, they had succeeded, at least somewhat. They had found one Japanese lawyer who was younger than even they were and they had found an experienced Japanese banker who was happy to play the part of a lawyer.

The banker, Moritada Kumashiro, had just stopped by their office one afternoon. His long black hair was pulled back into a tight pony tail that made him vaguely look like a samurai, but his fashionable spectacles and impeccable three-piece suit would have allowed him to blend in as just another part of Shanghai's executive set had it not been for the white armband that he was required to wear as a not-yet-repatriated Japanese.

Like the rest of his countrymen, Kumashiro was confined by military order to Japan Town. Situated right above Suzhou Creek, it was a neighborhood whose locals walked freely about in kimonos to sukiyaki stalls, to homes with sliding paper walls, or to the many Japanese movie theaters.

Kumashiro and his wife, Kiyoko, had first moved to Shanghai in 1940 and lived in a modest but comfortable house on Cherry Terrance Lane. During the war, the city had become the business hub of what the Japanese government would call the "Greater East Asia Co-Prosperity Sphere," an ambitious, albeit often cynical, program to economically modernize Asia and put the patina of decolonization on Japan's military adventures. It enticed many Japanese idealists, who earnestly—if naively—believed that the Co-Prosperity Sphere was a force for good in a part of the world that had been riven by corruption, inequality, and colonial exploitation.

Kumashiro was one of the idealists. His English was excellent, and that had made him indispensable at the Bank of Taiwan, which prior to Pearl Harbor had remained under British control. There were about a hundred thousand Japanese expatriates living in Shanghai, and, like the British and French before them, Kumashiro's generation had quickly learned that the colonial life could be the good life. It was also a precarious life. When Japan had surrendered in August 1945, Kumashiro had been purged from his job after the bank had come under the control of Chiang Kai-shek's Kuomintang.

Repatriation to Japan was tightly regulated, and, because Kumashiro and Kiyoko had no children, they were not high on the priority list. But Kumashiro was also not in a hurry to return. He liked Japan Town and enjoyed the view of the wider world it gave him. Shanghai was a city of many newspapers, and with few commitments to fill his days, Kumashiro had gotten into the habit of reading the news in every language he could read. And that was what had brought him to Bodine, Fellows, and Elizaveta.

Leafing through the Saturday edition of the *Shanghai Herald*, Kumashiro had come across an article titled "Japanese Officer Wanted by USAF Is Caught in Camp." A Japanese officer named Okada, it said, had been arrested in Jiangwan as a suspected war criminal. Okada was a relatively common name, but it had caught Kumashiro up short. Could it be Ryuhei Okada?

Okada was a few years older and had been Kumashiro's mentor in high school, when Kumashiro had the nickname "Gochu," or "Hot Pepper," which was just a silly pun on the Kanji spelling of his name, but also seemed to fit his spirited personality. They had been on the tennis team together and had even won a championship. Over time they had lost touch, but when Okada was stationed in Shanghai during the war, the two had picked up their friendship.

Before being drafted, Okada had taught German and philosophy at a high school in Tokyo. Thirty-seven years old, he had not expected to be drafted, but in 1940, he was and, given his level of education, was inducted into the officer corps. The Imperial Army had assigned him to its Special Services Section in Shanghai, where he wrote for its newsletter, *Nippon*. Nearly a generation older than his fellow lieutenants in the 13th Army and not particularly well disposed to military life, he made the most of his time in Shanghai, taking special care to protect its schools and its YMCA from the more bloody minded of his compatriots who assumed nothing in China was worth preserving. The reunion with his old friend Gochu in Shanghai had been a welcome surprise for them both.

Kumashiro had not seen Okada since the surrender in the summer of 1945, but it was hard for him to imagine that the Okada he knew had been implicated in atrocities. Kumashiro called the Special Services Section, and after he was passed around a bit, a soldier who knew Okada picked up the phone. Yes, he told Kumashiro, Ryuhei Okada had been arrested by the Americans.

Kumashiro typed a petition in English, personally addressed to General Wedemeyer, asking to meet with Okada. He then walked to Wedemeyer's office to present his petition in person, and, to his great surprise, was allowed to walk right in to meet the general as he sat behind his desk. Wedemeyer looked it over and shot a slightly suspicious glance up at Kumashiro but then politely referred him to Ham Young's office, who sent him along to Bodine's.

Upon his arrival, Kumashiro was greeted warmly by a chatty Army captain, who looked like a boy, smoked like a chimney, and introduced himself with startling conviviality. "I was appointed to be defense counsel on the case by the Army," Fellows said. "I'm happy to talk to you, but I have to quickly eat lunch, so I can get to the prison by 1300. Want to join me for lunch?" Fellows poured two cups of coffee and put one in front of Kumashiro. "Cream and sugar?"

As Kumashiro sipped his coffee, Fellows munched away on his boxed lunch of fried chicken. Kumashiro explained who he was and felt a combination of delighted surprise and growing suspicion by how readily Fellows agreed to his request to see Okada.

"You know, it would be great to see Okada," Kumashiro asked warily, "but where is the prison?"

"It's an ex–Chinese prison," Fellows said blithely, "near the Yangpu district."

Kumashiro knew that was Ward Road Jail. It was not as notorious as Bridge House, but it had been Shanghai Municipal Council's jail before the war and had become a holding center for political prisoners in addition to its eight thousand ordinary criminals. Kumashiro began to worry that he was walking into a trap. "I want to see Okada with you," he said anxiously. "But will I be able to go home afterwards?"

Fellows laughed as if it were the funniest thing he had heard that day. "Don't you worry about it," he assured Kumashiro. "We'll go together and you'll leave with me."

Fellows finished up his boxed lunch and walked Kumashiro downstairs to a jeep, the singular symbol of the American presence in Shanghai as they shoved their way between rickshaws and pedicabs by the tens of thousands. Kumashiro had never ridden in one, and before he knew it, there he was, speeding north across Suzhou Creek.

Fellows tried to bring Kumashiro up to date. "This trial here in Shanghai is going to be the precedent for the Tokyo trials," he explained. "The chief prosecutor, the American, and the judges are going to visit Shanghai to see how well this trial goes. As a consequence, everything about this trial is extremely important. We have this immense responsibility."

Fellows pulled up to Ward Road Jail's high stone walls and escorted Kumashiro through its gates. "Sure, I'm in the Army now, but I'm used to being a lawyer." The only time Fellows had fired a shot in anger was at China's formidable rats. "I want to get to the bottom of this," he told Kumashiro earnestly. "I want to make sure this is a fair trial."

The guards brought them to Okada, who stayed silent, not recognizing

Kumashiro at first. But on second look, Okada's face lit up. "Gochu?" he exclaimed with a combination of confusion and surprise. "Why are you here?"

Kumashiro asked Okada the same question.

"Basically, I'm OK here," Okada assured his old friend as Fellows left them alone to chat. "The Americans don't treat us too badly." But there was one thing that was hard to endure: "I want to eat rice. They force me to eat bread with butter and cheese. I'm sure it is nutritious, but—" Okada started to laugh.

Okada had grown to like Fellows, who he thought was "really kind and attentive." He had not expected that from the Americans. "He tries to cheer me up and even gives me cigarettes every so often," Okada said. The only American he had a problem with so far was Robert Dwyer. "He is a little scary, but as long as I tell him the truth he stays in a good mood and doesn't give me any problems."

Okada, though, was terrified. He couldn't make himself understood. The translators were terrible. Dwyer would ask questions, and when the answers were confusing, Dwyer would get frustrated. "He tells us that we really should have studied English more. Maybe Americans should have studied Japanese more. I understand that the translators are doing their best, but it is shameful that they don't understand me, especially when I'm talking about very sensitive matters."

When time was up, Kumashiro and Okada said their good-byes, not knowing when they would see each other again. But as Fellows escorted Kumashiro out of Ward Road Jail—as promised—he pitched the banker on joining the legal team.

"We don't have a trial date yet," Fellows said. "But there are orders for this trial to happen as soon as possible. Ultimately it is up to MacArthur's headquarters. They want this trial to be done before the Tokyo Trial for the Class A war criminals, like Tojo, takes place. They want to get the kinks out for the Tokyo Trial."

Kumashiro promised to help as much as he could, not the least with finding them an experienced lawyer. As far as joining the team himself, he hesitated. But Fellows persuaded him to agree as long as the bureaucratic paperwork could be worked out and General Wedemeyer approved.

There was one more thing, though: "I also like to bring some Japanese food the next time I visit Okada for him and the others."

"No problem," Fellows assured him.

From then on, Kumashiro made a point of visiting Ward Road Jail nearly every day. Whatever his initial misgivings, he relished his new job. Bodine had gotten him his own jeep from the car pool, along with a personal driver, an enlisted man by the name of Jackson, who delighted Kumashiro with how American he was and regaled him with funny stories or songs sung at the top of his voice as their jeep menaced Shanghai's carts, rickshaws, and pedestrians.

Kumashiro quickly gained notoriety around Japan Town for the work he was doing, but none of the Japanese lawyers still in Shanghai wanted anything to do with accused war criminals. They just wanted to get back to Japan. The only candidate Kumashiro could find was a young Japanese lieutenant who was already familiar with the case: Tadahiro Hayama.

Hayama had helped the Americans make their case and had done so for all the right reasons. He didn't want innocent people to be blamed or—worse—executed, when he had the documents naming those truly responsible. But now, he was wracked with guilt and after hearing about the work Kumashiro was doing, Hayama paid him a visit to unburden his conscience.

Kumashiro liked Hayama immediately. He was an earnest and easygoing young man with impressive credentials. He did not have any more real legal experience than Fellows did, but Kumashiro could see the incredible opportunity that had presented itself. Dwyer and Hendren could not very well make Hayama their star witness if he was now a lawyer at the defense table.

Hayama had mixed feelings about the case. Back in Tokyo, he had been a judge. Japan's legal profession had staked out a fiercely guarded independence that, as a matter of Japan's own constitution, was rivaled only by the independence of the military, even through the darkest days of the war. When Tojo publicly attacked the judiciary for not cooperating with the military, the Chief Judge of the Court of Appeals publicly counterattacked Tojo for questioning the judiciary's independence. Fairness in trials was a constitutional duty that real Japanese lawyers internalized as a point of professional pride and, to Hayama, the way the Japanese Army had handled the Doolittle Raiders' trial was disturbing. What kind of murder trial only lasted an hour?

Kumashiro welcomed Hayama into his home on Cherry Terrace Lane, which was far more comfortable than the barracks in Jiangwan, and the two talked over the case for days, sometimes well into the night. Soon, Hayama grew convinced. Joining Kumashiro on the defense team was the surest way to vindicate Japan, to vindicate himself.

Whatever Sawada, Okada, Wako, and Tatsuta may have done, they were victims too. They, like the Raiders, like the rest of Japan, were victims of the militarists, who had left millions dead for nothing. By joining Kumashiro in the courtroom, Hayama could show the world how fair, how sophisticated, real Japanese lawyers were. Hayama was a young man. He was Japan's future. He could put all of that, all of his education and skill, on display for the world.

* * *

The morning of the arraignment, Bodine and Fellows waited for the judges to arrive with Kumashiro and Hayama next to them at the defense table; Elizaveta was made to sit in the row of seats behind the defense table, behind the wooden railing everyone called, "the bar," where Kiyoko Kumashiro was also sitting and happily playing the part of dutiful wife. It was, of course, grossly insulting. Elizaveta had done as much to prepare the case as any of the men at the table, but only lawyers were allowed to sit in front of the bar (Bodine and Kumashiro notwithstanding).

At 10:00 a.m. sharp, the proceedings came to order with a crisp "Attention!" The murmured conversations startled into a silence broken only by wooden chair legs scraping back across the floor as everyone stood in place and turned toward the American flag hung behind the bench.

There was a script for how the morning was to proceed, and that script had been duly distributed to all concerned. According to script, the six judges, called the "members of the military commission" to highlight their mixed role as judges and jurors, marched toward their seats behind the bench in a line. They were all Army colonels and lieutenant colonels, dressed not in robes but their well-decorated dress uniforms, and none was a lawyer. At the back of the line was the lowest-ranking officer, Lieutenant Colonel William Berry. At the front was the most recognizable, Colonel Gabriel Disosway, the gleaming chrome future of the Air Force, whom General Wedemeyer had assigned as the alternate.

Technically, only the five full judges would be determining the final verdicts and sentences, and, at least technically, the presiding member, Colonel Edwin McReynolds, would direct the trial proceedings and the judges' deliberations. But to say that Disosway's presence did not matter because he was technically only an alternate required a willful suspension of disbelief. Though the judges would be making decisions about law, the fine parsing of legal doctrines and theories would carry a lot less weight than their commonsense balancing of mercy and revenge, and Disosway, Bodine knew, had some opinions he was willing to share. His only uncertainty was how the Army should go about killing the four men sitting nervously on the wooden chairs to his right.

Disosway's name had been on the script that was circulated ahead of time. Bodine, Fellows, and Elizaveta knew he would be sitting up there. But what could they do about it?

The risks, particularly for Bodine, of challenging Disosway were obvious. Raising the issue at all would turn Disosway's private musings over how Sawada would be executed, which might have been nothing more than a joke over drinks in the officers' club, into a public spectacle. There was not even a rule allowing lawyers to challenge the judges. If Bodine asked to disqualify Disosway and lost, not only would he have embarrassed and probably made an enemy out of the best friend he could possibly have in the Air Force, he could turn the whole bench of judges against him. And for what? It was not as if Disosway's attitude toward the Japanese was rare or unexpected. Did McReynolds, whose career had also been as a pilot, think any differently?

Fellows thought nothing of challenging Disosway. American lawyers asked to disqualify judges all the time. It wasn't an attack on Disosway's character to argue that he had formed the opinions he had. They could call Disosway to the witness stand, and he would probably admit what he had said proudly. Whatever biases McReynolds or anyone else might be harboring, Disosway had said his out loud. It was an understandable opinion, given who he was, so what was the big deal?

Elizaveta agreed with Fellows. Bodine was always telling her how America was different, how it had a rule of law, that it cared about fairness. What kind of trial would this be if the judges had made up their minds before it even began? Wasn't that what the Americans were accusing the Japanese of having done?

The moment to do or not do something came quickly. Everything had proceeded according to the script, all the way down to the "I do," from the court reporters as they were sworn in. McReynolds made a show of announcing the rights of the accused, reminding them that they had the right to know the charges against them, to be represented by counsel, to present evidence and cross-examine witnesses, and to have the proceedings translated into a language they understood. This routine formality took on a special poignancy, with one reporter noting the "striking contrast between American Justice and the Japanese court-martial that decreed death for Lieutenant William G. Farrow, Lieutenant Dean E. Hallmark and Sergeant Robert Spatz."

Everything was going according to the script until Bodine stood up unbidden. "At this time," he interjected, "I'd like to challenge a member of the court."

The courtroom stirred. Whispers were traded. Kumashiro and Hayama, who had not been part of the discussions about Disosway, were aghast. And McReynolds was caught up short, having no provision for this in the script in front of him.

"If the court please," Hendren objected, "there is no provision made in the regulations appointing this court for challenge."

"In any trial the United States has," Bodine retorted, "the basic function of it is to have justice. Therefore, if one member of the court has expressed an opinion before the case is gone to trial I think it should be heard."

Doing his best to keep the proceedings in some semblance of order, McReynolds turned to Bodine and said, "State the circumstances under which you base your objection or challenge."

"If the commission desires," Bodine continued, "I would like to put the member that I would challenge on the witness stand and have him testify under oath."

With the reporters now paying close attention, Hendren could see that the trial was about to turn into a circus before it even began. He could not have the newspapers running photos of one of the judges, a judge handpicked by General Wedemeyer, sitting in the witness chair and testifying about his ability to be fair or not. So Hendren asked McReynolds to close the courtroom so the judges could deliberate among themselves.

"If any member of the commission feels he should not serve because he is biased or prejudiced because he has formed an opinion as to the guilt or innocence of the accused," Hendren begrudgingly conceded, "the commission should have to excuse the member."

McReynolds took Hendren's suggestion and ordered the court into recess. Twenty minutes later, they were back in session, and McReynolds announced that there was "no precedent for a motion to challenge for cause." They had been at this for only an hour, and already they were in unprecedented territory. Nevertheless, the judges had discussed the matter and discovered that Disosway was, in fact, "prejudiced regarding the accused. Accordingly, the Commission has decided to relieve Colonel Disosway as an alternate to this Commission. Will Colonel Disosway please retire."

Disosway stood up crisply. He collected his things from the bench and walked out of the courtroom without uttering a word to Bodine or anyone else.

Eager to move on, McReynolds returned to the script and invited the prosecution and the defense to make legal motions. Over the course of the next two hours, all of the arguments Fellows had devised, challenging the basic legality of the charges and the trial itself under international law, were given their day in court. And after each argument was made, McReynolds said the same thing, as if a mantra had been added to his copy of the script: "Subject to objection by any member, the motion is denied."

Each of the accused was then asked to plead: guilty or not guilty. All four stood up, one at a time, and Kumashiro relayed their responses into English.

Sawada spoke first, and Kumashiro said, "He is convinced he is innocent." Then Okada: "He is also convinced he is innocent." Then Wako: "He is convinced also he is innocent."

Finally it was Tatsuta's turn. "He is deeply convinced himself to be innocent," Kumashiro said as Tatsuta bowed dramatically from the waist toward McReynolds. The gesture was so awkwardly obsequious that the otherwise stern-faced McReynolds had to suppress a wry smile as he wrapped up the proceedings.

"There being no additional matters to be considered at this time, the Commission will now recess and will be reconvened at 11 March 1946 at 0900 hours at Ward Road Jail, Shanghai, China," he concluded.

With that, they had gotten through the first day. Dwyer and Hendren would present their first witness in two weeks. And, weather permitting, Bodine and Fellows would board a Gooney Bird for Tokyo the next morning.

SIXTEEN

Elizaveta went out to the Jiangwan Airfield to see Bodine and Fellows off on their big trip to Tokyo. As the team's Japan expert, at least before Kumashiro and Hayama had come along, she was disappointed that she was not allowed to go. Being stateless meant that she had no passport, making foreign travel against the rules (though the Army always seemed to find a way around its rules when it really wanted to).

Elizaveta's knowledge of the Japanese had always come through the peculiar lens of Shanghai, a place that the culturally fastidious Japanese viewed in equal turns as noxious and seductive. During the war, her mother had rented out rooms in the family apartment on Avenue Joffre to visiting Japanese students, and Elizaveta could always make a little extra cash by giving them lessons in English, Russian, and French. The Japanese she had gotten to know in Shanghai all shared a certain worldliness that seemed at odds with the rigid chauvinism Japan had projected throughout the war.

Elizaveta's disappointment in being left behind was made all the worse by the realization that, despite herself, she had become lovesick. It was the first time that she and her Edmund had been apart since Christmas Eve. They had been dating for less than a month when he had proposed. She had opened the door of her room on the second floor of Broadway Mansions, and there he was, breathless, dressed in his Eisenhower jacket and at least as nervous as he had been when he had gawkily asked her out in the elevator. He had apparently been spurred to pop the question by a fit of jealousy after a dentist, whose office happened to be down the hall from her room, had told Bodine that he was going to ask Sweater Girl to marry him.

Bodine's jealousy was the harmless kind that could be as endearing as the folded-up schoolboy love notes he would drop as he passed by the concierge desk. Once he had seen a new bottle of her favorite French perfume on her dresser. Asked where she had gotten it, she shrugged it off as just another gift from Dwyer, but almost as soon as her back was turned, Bodine "accidentally" knocked the bottle onto the floor. Elizaveta had soaked up what she could between the broken glass with one of her furs and held nothing back in letting Bodine know how furious she was. It had been a jerk thing to do. Though seeing him jealous did offer a gratifying thrill.

Now, though, Elizaveta was the jealous one. She was jealous that Bodine would be going to Japan, when she could not, and she was jealous of all she imagined he might find there.

A front-page article in the New Year's Day edition of the Shanghai *Stars and Stripes* had advertised "Geishas for Tokyo GIs." To draw the Americans away from Japan's respectable women, the Japanese government had put fifteen hundred dancing girls and six hundred geisha on the public payroll. MacArthur had officially banned this government-subsidized prostitution in January after 90 percent of the the geisha had tested positive for venereal disease, but that still left Tokyo's infamous "panpan girls," Japanese women of marriageable age who had thrown off the wartime yolk of martial piety for loud colors, heavy makeup, and "Panglish," a Japanese-English argot of free love that was fueled by black-market Coca-Cola. Rumors abounded about the "temporary wives" of Tokyo, such that one Army sergeant bragged to *The Stars and Stripes*, "I've promised many girls but have married none. You can get married for a night for a chocolate bar. When I am overseas, my motto is send me crates of candy."

All Elizaveta could think about was her Edmund drinking, talking, laughing, and dancing with some lithe Japanese . . . *babenka* was the Russian word for it. He had promised to marry her and only her, and she worried that he might be getting cold feet. When she had gone to see him off at the airfield, he had forgotten to kiss her good-bye. She had waited for her kiss as he and Fellows were about to board, but he had just smiled and promised to write from Tokyo.

The Army had given them permission to marry a few days earlier. Because she was not a US citizen, she and the rest of her family had had to submit to a full US Army background investigation. They could have gotten married before he left for Tokyo, but Bodine was all of a sudden stalling, and Elizaveta knew he was not just preoccupied with the trial; he was as, if not more, anxious about breaking the news to his mother, Alma Bodine.

Bodine had passed up plenty of opportunities to tell his mother about his new fiancée. They had already been engaged when Bodine had gotten his promotion to lieutenant colonel. He had sent news of that great fact back to Douglaston, Long Island, with alacrity, but had not once mentioned his Russian bride-to-be. Alma Bodine, for her part, had beamed back her pride with such dispatch that it seemed unbelievable a letter could have traveled halfway around the world so quickly. "You seem to get everything you go after," she wrote. "I am very proud of you. Love from all home and all my love. Lovingly, Mother." She always signed off "Lovingly, Mother."

Alma had strong opinions about her children's romantic choices. Bodine's sister Claire had also just gotten engaged to a young man named Bob Krugbaum. "Krugbaum?" Alma had scoffed. "What a terrible name to carry through life." She only decided that she approved of Krugbaum after he agreed with her that his name was terrible and explained that the only reason he did not change it was his father's threat to disinherit him. Alma wrote to Bodine that Krugbaum was "a very fine young man. A very serious type and we all like him very much. I think he will take good care of Claire and will be a good provider."

Alma was less pleased with Bodine's younger brother, Byron, and his recent change of fiancées. Byron had been stationed in Europe but back in Douglaston, Long Island, was engaged to a girl named Delva. Alma adored Delva and had been furious when Byron left her for a French girl, whom Alma refused to mention by name. "The French girl could never live up to Delva no matter what she looked like," Alma fumed. "Those damn foreigners. They want to get to this country and no matter what method they use they get what they want."

With Bodine in Tokyo, Elizaveta tried to distract herself from thinking about whether she was just another "damned foreigner" and what Bodine might be getting up to. She went out to nightclubs with their usual friends and tried to cool her longing with Russian cynicism, wondering aloud to Ham Young if her Edmund was in "someplace of amusement, in any of Tokyo's nightclubs," while she was left lonely in Shanghai.

Young laughed her off. Her Edmund was probably in bed thinking of her with a heart full of longing, Young consoled her. "When a man is in love, he never looks for anything else."

"My sweet boy! My love!" Elizaveta wrote to Bodine in an ever-growing diary of her heartache. "Now when you are not here, I can see what you mean to me!" She wrote about her worries and how Young had tried to re-assure her that her Edmund would not stray for any of Tokyo's temporary wives and panpan girls. "I want to be sure about that!!!" she wrote before effusing "The time is so slow! The mood is so blue—and all because you!!!" She wrote to him sometimes every hour. "I wish I can see you right now! My love hurt me so much, I want to cry! Please be faithful to me! I can't stop myself I still worry so much!"

Bodine and Fellows were supposed to have been in Tokyo for only five days, but that quickly turned into another five days and then another. All the while, there were no letters, no postcards, no word from Tokyo except secondhand reports, sometimes delivered slyly by none other than Robert Dwyer, breaking the news that Bodine and Fellows had extended their trip by a few more days.

John Hendren even teased Elizaveta that the Army might decide to send her Edmund back to the United States directly from Japan. Elizaveta was sure Hendren was kidding, but even the thought pained her. No mat-ter how many days passed, it somehow was always five more days. "Five days more!" she wrote in anguish. "Five days more without you!"

*　*　*

The two weeks Bodine spent in Tokyo coincided with the public release of the new draft constitution of Japan. A model of New Deal idealism, it protected the rights of labor and guaranteed equality before the law. It enshrined the right to a public trial before an impartial tribunal along with the right to obtain witnesses and to have the assistance of counsel. Torture was prohibited. Confessions could not serve as evidence if taken under "compulsion, torture or threat, or after prolonged arrest or detention," and no one could be punished for crimes decreed after the fact. It was, in short, a document designed to prohibit exactly what his clients were accused of having done to the Doolittle Raiders.

The authors of that document were Army lawyers working in the Meiji Building, right in downtown Little America, where Bodine dutifully checked in upon their arrival with Dwyer's old friend Colonel Alva Carpenter, the head of SCAP's Legal Section, and with Joseph Keenan on the seventh floor.

Keenan was contemplating a trip to Shanghai to sit at the prosecution table with Dwyer and Hendren. Bodine and Fellows's arrival gave him the opportunity to size up the two young officers who would be seated across the aisle.

Bodine's little stunt with Gabe Disosway had not gone unnoticed and had echoes of all the troublemaking MacArthur had unhappily endured— and was still enduring—from the Yamashita case. Supreme Court Justice Frank Murphy had accused MacArthur of making Yamashita's trial the beginning of "a procession of judicial lynchings without due process of law," and Keenan had been forced to leap to MacArthur's defense, telling reporters "The American people can rest assured that a 'procession of judicial lynchings' will not occur in the prosecution of any Japanese war criminals. The mere suggestion that such a procedure can follow or that 'revengeful blood purges' be permitted when Americans are charged with the prosecution and judgment is offensive to say the least."

Bodine had no intention of talking to reporters the way Yamashita's lawyers had or making any kind of public splash in Japan. Their main reason for having made the trip was to track down character witnesses for Shigeru Sawada, and Keenan was happy to let the boys do what they could to smooth the edges off the mastermind of the torture and murder of the Doolittle Raiders. Keenan was even willing to be helpful and gave them free rein to build whatever case they could muster now that they were in Tokyo.

*   *   *

Japan's fallen capital was nothing like what Bodine, Fellows, or Elizaveta could have imagined. Outside Little America, Tokyo resembled the surface of the moon. The scale of the devastation inspired a certain morbid awe, particularly given the fact that between the Doolittle Raid in April 1942 and LeMay's firebombing in March 1945, the US Army Air Forces had left Tokyo entirely unmolested.

Roosevelt had wanted the city attacked earlier. In 1944, he had written to the Air Forces' commander in China, Major General Claire L. Chennault, saying that "as a matter perhaps of sentimentality, I have a hope that we could get at least one bombing expedition against Tokyo before the second anniversary of Doolittle's flight. I really believe that the morale effect would help!" The plans never came together, though, meaning that all the devastation, which seemed to spread as far as the horizon in every direction, had been achieved in only five months and, truly, on only two nights.

With the city still in the grip of winter, shelter remained scarce, and Bodine and Fellows encountered thousands of locals huddled together in what remained of the city's train stations or prefab American-made micro huts that rented out for 35 yen a month. MacArthur was trying to distribute blankets that had been stockpiled during the war by the Japanese military, and although the famine everyone feared was averted, food remained so scarce that one in ten residents showed signs of severe malnutrition, a rate that jumped to one in five Tokyo women.

Yet somehow Tokyo was orderly and clean. Even the rubble was neatly piled up, and despite American-occupied Tokyo's reputation as an erotic lion's den of temporary wives and panpan girls, it had none of Shanghai's rampant carnality, none of its *chao nao*.

That all suited Fellows just fine. He had never liked Shanghai, partly because being there meant being away from his wife and young son, but it went deeper than that. Fellows's father had been a perfectly good schoolteacher in Missouri until he had been seduced by the oil boom of the 1920s, moved to Tulsa to become a lawyer, and started running around with his secretary. His mother had filed for divorce, which meant that the *chao nao* of nightclubs and nightclub girls—be it in Shanghai or Tulsa—had little appeal for a boy raised during the Depression by a single mother who hated everything to do with Oklahoma.

For Fellows, who preferred to keep his shirt and tie on when mowing the lawn, Shanghai was a rampage of seedy chaos. In Tokyo, though, even the black markets had a certain curated discipline. In the Ginza, the storied shopping district where the Army had located its massive PX, "beautiful goods" from leather shoes to chewing gum were advertised for sale in meticulous rows of well-kept stalls.

In Shanghai, the Chinese—who supposedly had been the United States' wartime allies—had come to despise the US Army presence. By March 1946, the afterglow of postwar victory had yielded to incessant anti-American street protests and general strikes. The friendliest locals Fellows typically encountered were street hustlers shouting "Shoeshine, Joe" or shaking him down for a "cumshaw," a bastardization of the Chinese expression "Grateful, thank you," that became slang for a bribe. "Cumshaw, thankayou, seeuh, seeuh nee. Cumshaw, thankayou." "American chocolate candy for me." "Camel cigarettes." "You want Russian money very good souvenir." "Thankayou, cumshaw, thankayou." "You want a nice girl very cheap?" "Buy genyouwine Samurai sword, very pretty." "Cumshaw." "Shoeshine, Joe."

The Japanese, by contrast, to whose capital Fellows's countrymen had laid such magnificent waste, were unremittingly polite. At Tokyo's Imperial Hotel, beautiful Japanese women, dressed in smartly tied kimonos, instantaneously refilled nearly every sip taken from a cup of coffee or a glass of water or sake. When Fellows forgot his briefcase on a city bus, not only was he able to track down the bus as it kept to its schedule, but his briefcase was exactly where he had left it, undisturbed, by the time he found it hours later.

The Japanese, he found, were also eager to help, particularly when they discovered why he was there. Fellows wanted to put together the best possible case for the men whose lives were now in his hands. Everything from the language barrier to the sense that the fix was in to the mundane burdens of trying to get anything done in Shanghai had made it a thankless, frustrating task. In Tokyo, though, as soon as Bodine and Fellows met up with Taosa Kubota, every door seemed to be open, and respect, even admiration, for what they were trying to do followed.

Kubota was Sawada's closest friend. The retired governor of Japan's Fukui Prefecture, he spoke impeccable English and served as their trusted guide and fixer. Sawada had wanted a qualified Japanese lawyer, and so Kubota introduced them Lieutenant General Ayao Oyama, who had been the War Ministry's top lawyer since 1933.

Upon hearing that Sawada wanted an experienced Japanese lawyer, Oyama coordinated with the Foreign Ministry to send Shinji Somiya, a prolific and highly respected law professor, to Shanghai. Asked what he knew about the Doolittle Raid, Oyama handed them a copy of the Kempeitai's investigation file. Fellows asked if the file had been presented at the Doolittle Raiders' trial in 1942. Oyama could not be sure, but no other Americans had seen it, including Dwyer and Hendren, which was a boon, because after learning what was inside, Fellows began to develop a very different picture of the defense's case and the former enemy general they were representing.

Sawada had given Bodine and Fellows a list of witnesses to interview, which was nothing if not ambitious: Prime Minister Hideki Tojo; War Minister Sadamu Shimomura; the commander of Japan's Army in China, General Shunroku Hata. With Kubota's help, though, Bodine soon found himself across from the man who had so deftly eluded Robert Dwyer: Sadamu Shimomura.

* * *

Dwyer's conspicuous visit to Tokyo the month before had made the fate of Shimomura a political issue. With the press clamoring for Shimomura's head, MacArthur had had him locked up in Sugamo Prison. But Shimomura did not seem the least bit concerned. Wiry and energetic, he was happy to talk to Bodine about Sawada and all that had happened around the time of the Doolittle Raiders' executions.

Shimomura liked Sawada. Back in 1942, Shimomura had been the commandant of the Army Staff College in Tokyo, and the reassignment to Shanghai had been both sudden and something of a step down, since he would no longer have a direct line of communication to the headquarters in Tokyo. But the order to replace him had come directly from General Hajime Sugiyama, the Chief of Staff of the Imperial Army.

Barrel chested and jowly with a barely discernible neck, Hajime Sugiyama had been one of the hardest of the hard-line militarists, and the Doolittle Raid had been the greatest humiliation of his career. The brazenness of the attack and the ability of nearly all the Raiders to escape had betrayed Japan's vulnerability in a way that few could have imagined. Everyone knew that if anyone in the government was responsible, it was Sugiyama, who had been one of the loudest advocates of the war and who had personally assured the emperor that victory would be secured in a matter of three months.

Shimomura had no idea why Sawada had been relieved of command, but the raid was still clearly on Sugiyama's mind as he briefed Shimomura on his new assignment. "The trial of the American fliers who bombed our homeland in April of this year has been conducted by military court-martial of the 13th Army," Sugiyama had explained. "As a result of review-ing the report from the 13th Army in regards to this trial, the Imperial Headquarters in Tokyo made a final decision that from among the fliers, three were to be executed. The orders for this final decision will probably be issued to the 13th Army from Nanking before you reach Shanghai for duty. So you can expect that."

Shimomura, of course, knew about the Americans from the newspa-pers, the newsreels, and the occasional army gossip, but he had not known anything about their being taken back to China for trial and expressed some concerns to Sugiyama.

"This affair has been thoroughly investigated and the final decision has been made in Tokyo," Sugiyama assured him. "As a result, there is nothing that Shanghai or Nanking can do about this decision except carried out."

To Shimomura, it seemed as if there had been a lack of faith that Sawada would carry out the executions as ordered; he had a reputation for being a bit soft.

Hearing that about Sawada, the genteel but defiant old general Bodine and Fellows had come to know, a man who would accept death before he would admit that he or the Empire of Japan had done anything wrong, was unexpected. The accused mastermind of the torture and murder of the Doolittle Raiders was "soft"?

Yet, as strange as it sounded, it seemed to be the opinion of everyone who knew Sawada. Kubota said the same thing. Sawada, he said was "very soft minded," hesitating to make it clear that he did not mean that Sawada was foolish or stupid. It was just that Sawada was unlike the other army officers Kubota had known over his career.

Sawada cared about the rest of the world in a way that was almost politically incorrect for an army officer. He had held a number of quasi-diplomatic posts, including in Russia before the Revolution and in Turkey right after the First World War. He had spent time in Poland and Manchu-ria and made frequent trips to France and Switzerland, even to the United States and England. Had Sawada been born into the right family instead of some farm town in the middle of nowhere, Kubota said, he would probably have been a diplomat.

When Bodine and Fellows interviewed Yasuo Karakawa, who had been Sawada's chief of staff back in Shanghai, he said the same thing. A city like Shanghai, with its political crosscurrents from all over the world, was perfect for Sawada, and he had proven that the day the Great Pacific War had begun.

As Japanese Zeroes were dive-bombing Pearl Harbor, Sawada instructed his forces that "The key to complete success in the movement into the Shanghai settlement, is absolute protection against bombs and destruction by fire and strict enforcement of discipline and calmness. Of particular importance is the prevention of any acts of violence or unnecessary hardships against enemy nationals and neutral nationals residing within the settlement."

When the time had come to attack that night, Sawada's men strolled calmly across the Garden Bridge, which connected Japan Town to the British district along the Bund. By sunrise, the Japanese had lowered the Stars and Stripes that had flown over the American Club and replaced it with the Rising Sun.

Sawada's troops had succeeded in putting Shanghai under total Japanese control in a single night and did it nearly bloodlessly. Businesses had opened as usual, and Sawada notified the residents of Shanghai that the Japanese Army would "respect the life and property of the general public, even in the case of nationals of the enemy countries, unless either they act against the interests of the Japanese forces or their property is liable to hostile usage." The British-controlled Shanghai Municipal Council responded the very same day with a resolution stating that it had "unanimously decided to comply with the wishes of the Japanese authorities." Over the months that followed, the city's British residents became models of collaboration, to the international embarrassment and apoplexy of Winston Churchill's floundering wartime government.

As Karakawa explained it, Sawada wasn't soft, he was strategic. He had always insisted on what he called the principle of "construction," or counterinsurgency. Sawada understood that the occupation of China would succeed only if the population came to believe that the Japanese were more legitimate than the notoriously corrupt and brutal Chiang Kai-shek. Otherwise, the Japanese Army would always be more hated than the Kuomintang, if for no other reason than that they were foreigners.

Once, when Sawada had received reports that his subordinates were mutilating the corpses of Chinese guerrillas, he issued a general order directing that "the enemy dead must not be abandoned but given a burial with due ceremony and we must mourn for their souls." When reporting the results of the battle, the 13th Army was no longer to report "number of enemy dead abandoned" but "number of enemy dead buried by our troops."

Karakawa had resented Sawada's unceremonious dismissal as the commander of the 13th Army. Sawada's "construction" strategy had given Japan unrivaled control over what was arguably the single most significant trading port in Asia. Those who fought alongside Sawada in China respected him and what he had achieved. Yet, because he had done it with minimal bloodshed, his rivals in the Japanese Army said he was "soft."

Karakawa could not be sure, but Sawada's sudden replacement by Shimomura had certainly looked as though it had something to do with the Doolittle Raiders. He confirmed that Sawada had been at the front during August 1942 and had learned about it all in September during a briefing by the head of the 13th Army's Legal Department, Shoshin Ito. Sawada had scolded Ito for only telling him about it after the fact, since the trial of such famous Americans was a sensitive diplomatic matter. Sawada, Karakawa said, had even sent a telegram to Tokyo objecting to the imposition of the death penalty.

He did what? Sawada tried to stop the executions? Sawada had never mentioned doing anything like that, and it was difficult for Bodine and Fellows to believe.

When pressed, though, Karakawa said he was sure of it. Sawada had sent a message to Tokyo asking that the death penalty not be imposed. A few weeks after that, he had been fired. It was only after Sawada had been relieved of command that Sugiyama had sent the order to carry out the sentences of death against Hallmark, Farrow, and Spatz.

Karakawa's revelation was extraordinary. When Bodine and Fellows had made all of their well-thought-out but nevertheless doomed to fail legal arguments at the arraignment, the only time McReynolds had perked up was when they had argued that Sawada could not be convicted as a war criminal for simply failing to nullify the results of the Doolittle Raiders trial back in the summer of 1942.

"Are you there contending," McReynolds had asked Hendren in an unusual flash of skepticism, "that because General Sawada did not commute the sentences that he did not properly act upon the records? Are you asking us to review the record to determine what he should've done?"

"I think so," Hendren had replied hesitantly. "If you have the authority to remit the sentence, and should have commuted or omitted the sentence which we think we can show, then he has caused the death of these men unlawfully, which is a war crime."

It was an awkward answer, but McReynold's questioning brought out the fact that it was also an awkward charge. Could a general really be put to death for failing to grant clemency to men who had been tried and found guilty as war criminals? Hendren's answer had been that because the Doolittle Raiders had been wrongfully accused, it had been up to Sawada to save their lives. "They were captured prisoners," he had insisted. "They had no right to be tried by anyone. They did no wrong."

Now here was Karakawa saying that Sawada had actually tried to do exactly what he was charged with having failed to do. If Sawada had not only been away at the front when the trial had taken place, not only relieved of command at the time Hallmark, Farrow, and Spatz had been executed, but had also sacrificed his military career in an effort to stop the executions altogether, Bodine and Fellows might just have found a way not only to spare Sawada from the gallows but for him to be acquitted outright.

Karakawa, though, was not enthusiastic about flying to Shanghai to testify. He was still a free man in Japan. So far, his name had, happily for him, stayed off the lists of senior Japanese officers now designated as suspected as war criminals, and as the 13th Army's Chief of Staff, he had reason to worry. Per the chain of command, Karakawa had been the acting commander of the 13th Army between the time Sawada was fired on October 8 and when Shimomura arrived on October 14. Sure, the executions had not been carried out until October 15, but Karakawa had been the one to actually receive Sugiyama's execution order and to relay it to Colonel Ito in the Legal Department for action. If he admitted all of that on the stand in Shanghai, there was a good chance that he could find himself reclassified from a visitor to an inmate of Ward Road Jail.

Bodine and Fellows asked if he would at least be willing to write a statement. The rules of evidence in the military commissions were flexible, and Dwyer was planning on submitting statements from all sorts of people, including Jimmy Doolittle, as evidence. If Karakawa wrote out what he knew, it would not carry as much weight as testifying in person would, but it would be something. And he could stay put in the relative safety of Tokyo.

Karakawa agreed. "As Commanding General, Sawada was well versed in international questions," he wrote. "He regarded the problem of the fliers' punishment as of great importance and assumed a careful attitude toward it. Namely his telegram to Tokyo on the finding of the trial was that he wished 'the authorities in Tokyo to reflect and take a more sympathetic dealing at' the finding of the death penalty for the fliers." Karakawa signed his name, and Bodine and Fellows made a point of both signing their names as witnesses.

SEVENTEEN

Everyone kept saying that the Doolittle Raiders case had been directed "from Tokyo." Everything had come "from Tokyo." "Tokyo" had been responsible. But what did that mean? It seemed to ensure no one was responsible for anything. Dwyer and Hendren were intent on proving that Lieutenant General Shigeru Sawada, born on March 29, 1887, in the village of Kamobe in the prefecture of Kochi, Japan, the third son of Einosuke Sawada, should take his place on the gallows. Blaming "Tokyo" might have been sufficient to assuage individual consciences, but Bodine and Fellows could not shelter a real man under abstractions.

When people said "Tokyo," what they really meant was that the treatment of the Doolittle Raiders, or the "enemy airmen," as the Japanese called them, had been handled by Japan's war cabinet. And because the issue of the enemy airmen fell under the authority of the Army, two cabinet members, in particular, embodied "Tokyo."

The first was the Army Chief of Staff, the jowly and irascible Hajime Sugiyama. If Shimomura was to be believed, Sugiyama had been the man most at the center of things. He had relieved Sawada of his command and sent Shimomura to Shanghai just in time to carry out the executions. He had also directed the Japanese Army to take vengeance across the Chinese countryside in the months after the Doolittle Raid. If there was any man who knew why "Tokyo" had done what it did after the Doolittle Raid, it was Sugiyama. Sugiyama, though, was dead; he had shot himself the previous September after Japan's formal surrender on the deck of the USS *Missouri*.

That left the minister of war, Hideki Tojo, the most infamous Japanese general of them all. Tojo was still alive and in Sugamo Prison, awaiting his own trial before Joseph Keenan's Tokyo Tribunal and near-certain execution as a war criminal.

*   *   *

Bodine drove out of Tokyo's city center and through a gate under a large hand-painted sign that read "Sugamo Prison/A.P.O. 500." A large modern prison in Tokyo's northwest, Sugamo was a compound of six parallel cell blocks, all gray concrete and three stories high. Inside, the cells ran along the walls with wide corridors in between that were divided down the middle by a skylight.

All the major Japanese war crimes suspects were in Sugamo, but to visit Tojo, SCAP's desk trolls informed Bodine that he needed the personal permission of "God" himself: General Douglas MacArthur. For whatever his reasons, God had granted Bodine this dispensation and soon Bodine found himself sitting across from *the* Hideki Tojo.

The United States' enemies had had three faces during World War II: Adolf Hitler, Benito Mussolini, and Hideki Tojo. When Mussolini was overthrown, President Roosevelt had reminded the nation that "we still have to knock out Hitler and his gang and Tojo and his gang," the latter being the people Roosevelt blamed for the torture and murder of the Doolittle Raiders.

Tojo's bald, long mango of a head, his trademark circle-framed glasses, his close-cropped mustache, which looked enough like Hitler's that it seemed to have explanatory power, was on all the posters for war bonds. "JAPS EXECUTE DOOLITTLE MEN" read one banner above a caricature of Tojo, apelike and vampire fanged, being strangled by Uncle Sam. "WE'LL PAY YOU BACK TOJO if it takes our last dime! Buy more war bonds."

Bodine had seen that face countless times in newspaper photographs and newsreels. Every American had. But there was something uncanny about it, now that the real Tojo was sitting across from him.

Tojo did not have the charisma that had led Hitler and Mussolini to be the world-historic figures they had become. In fact, he was rather meek, even clerklike, in the way he talked. Nor was he physically impressive. Bodine hulked over his five feet, four inches, and accentuating his feebleness, he was still recovering from an embarrassing suicide attempt.

On September 11, 1945, three days after MacArthur's arrival in Tokyo,

US military police had surrounded Tojo's home in the city's western suburbs. Throngs of reporters and gawkers had crowded around. After a brief standoff, Tojo sent his wife out of the house, drew a .32-caliber Colt pistol, pointed it at his heart, and fired.

The MPs had found Tojo slumped over his desk, bleeding from the chest. "I would not like to be judged before a conqueror's court," he told them. "I wait for the righteous judgment of history."

But that wish had gone unfulfilled, and in a surreal pantomime of Japan's postwar humiliation, the MPs had propped Tojo up back into his chair and put his pistol back into his hand, not so that he could finish the job, but so that photographers could snap a few trophies for the newspapers. As if that were not bad enough, the doctors had then saved Tojo's life with a transfusion of blood donated by American soldiers, and the fact that he now had some *baijo* serum in his veins led his countrymen to joke that Tojo was now of "mixed blood."

For Bodine, seeing this instantly recognizable man so humbled by his surroundings, the question was irrepressible: *You?* You are *the* Tojo?

Bodine introduced himself as the defense lawyer for General Shigeru Sawada. Tojo returned the pleasantries and said that Sawada was a "very dear and old friend of mine."

At the end of 1939, Sawada had come to Tokyo to serve as the Army's Deputy Chief of Staff. It was a tumultuous time politically, not the least because of the unending guerrilla war in China that no one ever called a war but merely an "incident." In the summer of 1940, the cabinet had been dissolved for the fifth time since the "China incident" had started three years earlier, and Sawada had been instrumental in pushing Tojo's name forward as the new war minister.

Tojo told Bodine that he had been waiting for someone to ask him about Sawada and had made some notes that he wanted Bodine to have. "Colonel," he then added, "what you are doing for the Japanese military prisoners is an honorable and glorious duty for which you will be ever proud during your life." Given the decidedly mixed opinions of his current task that Bodine was used to enduring over cocktails at Broadway Mansions, it was an oddly comforting sentiment.

* * *

Tojo knew what "Tokyo" had known back in 1942; he had been "Tokyo," at least as much as any one man could ever be. In 1941, he had gotten himself appointed both prime minister and war minister, consolidating unprecedented power over Japan's national security bureaucracy. In a country like Japan, though, that did not mean as much as it might have seemed.

Under Japan's constitution, each branch of government was accountable solely to the emperor, which in practice meant that each branch was independent of the others, the way the US Constitution makes the president, congress, and the courts independent of one another. Complicating matters, however, the Army and Navy were also their own branches of government. That meant that as prime minister, Tojo was the head of the civilian government. As war minister, he could control the Army's budget and generally set policy, but Army Chief of Staff Sugiyama had no real legal obligation to do or not do anything Tojo told him to do. From the decision to attack Pearl Harbor up through the decision to surrender, divisions within the cabinet had made every military and political choice the compromised product of a fraught consensus. And almost nothing had surfaced the personal and professional resentments between the civilian and military leadership as much as the Doolittle Raid had.

The Army and Navy had both failed spectacularly, but to Sugiyama's disgrace, the Navy had at least done something. It had been the Navy's picket boat, the *Nitto Maru*, that had spotted the USS *Hornet*. Vice Admiral Matome Ugaki, the Chief of Staff of the Combined Fleet, had promptly relayed a warning of a potential attack. Prince Naruhiko Higashikuni, Emperor Hirohito's uncle, who was in charge of the General Defense Command, had sent the alert far and wide within Japan's civil defense system. Ugaki had rapidly scrambled the Navy's forces en masse out into the Pacific, though they had failed to catch up to the USS *Hornet*. Ugaki had written two haikus to vent his frustration over the failure to intercept the Americans:

> Spring is departing
> while the long snakes slithers to the east,
> the planes flew to the west.
> Yamabuki petals
> have fluttered down,
> and the bomb craters remain.

The Army had failed totally. Sugiyama knew it. Everyone knew it. The warning had come early enough; even schoolteachers had received it. But the Army's lookouts on the eastern shore of Tokyo Bay had been caught completely off guard. As the Americans flew unmolested over the Japanese mainland beneath a crystal-clear blue sky, the Army's lookouts had missed them because they had turned their telescopes inland and down toward the adjacent mustard fields so they could ogle the sundressed farm girls.

The Army's fighter aircraft had been patrolling at 20,000 feet, which made them useless against Doolittle's bombers, which had flown in low over the city. The Army's radiomen had been stunned speechless by the surprise of it all, unable to compose themselves enough to relay basic information about the position or direction of the enemy planes, let alone to convey orders efficiently down the chain of command. When the artillerymen finally started blasting away on the antiaircraft guns, they had done more damage to Tokyo than to any of the American planes overhead. The attack had been so brazen. It had been done in broad daylight over the nation's capital. Tojo was not the only one to wonder, What was the Army doing?

Even the newspapers could not resist criticizing the Army, albeit with allegories that could slip past the censors. One celebrated the tale of Mrs. Aoki, a housewife who had just sat down to lunch with her children when an incendiary bomb had broken through her ceiling. The quick-thinking Mrs. Aoki had used her rice pot to smother the canister, preventing it from starting a fire that would have engulfed her home, if not the rest of her city block. The "housewife who captured the incendiary bomb," the story implied, was more effective than the Army.

Within the cabinet, the raid had set off a bitter round of recriminations. Sugiyama had nearly come to blows with Prince Higashikuni after learning that he had reported to Emperor Hirohito on the Army's failures. Higashikuni had been a skeptic of Japan's decision to attack Pearl Harbor and was now pressing the emperor to sue for peace since Japan's early victories in the Pacific had given it the upper hand.

For Japan's militarists, such as Sugiyama, political legitimacy had depended on a mythology of unerring military victory and the country's self-image as being ruthlessly organized and disciplined. They had promised to return Japan to the greatness of an imagined past, secure that the nation's millennial permanency would continue to protect it against any blowback from its foreign adventures. The raid had been the first inkling that Japan was not as invulnerable as it thought.

The press, of course, could be relied upon to reassure the public that the raid had been nothing for a country like Japan. It had been a mere bug bite. "There is no country which has been defeated only by air raids, regardless of how many it sustained," one Japanese newspaper explained. "Moreover, our country will not be reduced to ashes by incendiary bombs."

In a private meeting soon after the raid, however, Prince Higashikuni had asked Prince Fumimaro Konoe for his thoughts. Konoe had been Tojo's predecessor as prime minister and had resigned after failing to keep Japan's militarists, Sugiyama in particular, under control. He had lobbied Emperor Hirohito to appoint Higashikuni as his replacement, and as a member of the royal family, Konoe remained the emperor's confidant.

"The Japanese are, although they do not say anything outwardly," Konoe had said, "extremely dissatisfied on the inside with how the military is meddling in government, foreign affairs, and the economy, and acting extremely forcefully. In the future, many more large enemy air raids will shake Japanese public opinion and threaten domestic stability."

Sugiyama had looked genuinely vulnerable. But then the damage reports started coming in.

* * *

It hadn't taken long for the Japanese press to get the party line: the Doolittle Raid had been a wild-eyed exercise in terror bombing. At 2:45 p.m., when the Raiders would have just reached the Sea of Japan in their escape toward China, Japanese radio had already been broadcasting:

> A large fleet of enemy bombers appeared over Tokyo this noon and caused much damage to nonmilitary objectives and some damage to factories. The known death toll is between three and four thousand so far.

Accounts of injuries to civilians, the more lurid the better, had washed over the papers, newsreels, and radio broadcasts. In Osaka, where a clothing factory had been bombed, the bodies of the factory workers had been strewn among shattered glass and broken sewing machines on a floor flooded with blood. The Tokyo suburbs had been firebombed, as had a schoolyard, where sixth graders had been forced to form a bucket brigade to save their school. A humble telephone company employee, Keizaburo Nakanishi, who had dutifully rushed to work when the raid started, had returned home to find his wife and son dead, his home a rubble-filled crater, and his only surviving son with a face mutilated by the blast. Hospitals had been hit. Defenseless fishing boats had been strafed, with one fisherman killed and at least two others wounded, including an old woman who had been collecting shells along the beach. A young boy had died after a bullet had ripped through his belly in a classroom.

An article in *Photo Weekly Magazine* had brooked no doubt that the Americans had "focused their attack on innocent people and ordinary city streets, then dropped incendiaries and other bombs." "The fact," it had continued, "that the enemy has gone so far as to strafe our schools and fire upon helpless children particularly reveals his true but diabolical character." These "guerrilla-type air raids," it said, were acts of cowardice, especially when compared to the heroic effectiveness of Japan's firefighters, who had defended the "front behind the lines."

The raid had been the first real moment of national insecurity in at least two generations. But the press's ability to focus attention on the Americans as the newest Mongol horde, drunk on the blood of innocent Japanese schoolchildren, had steeled public opinion.

On April 30, the day of the parliamentary elections, voter turnout was 83 percent of the eligible population. Right-wing candidates had routed the opposition in a landslide, taking 82 percent of the seats. The public mood was for revenge, and as long as that remained the only politically correct response a patriotic Japanese citizen could have to the Doolittle Raid, it could not very well be the opportunity to criticize Sugiyama's management of the Army.

When word had gotten back to Tokyo that eight of the Americans had been taken into custody in China, the excitement was palpable. And there had been no doubt what Sugiyama wanted: they should all be executed as publicly and spectacularly as possible. The issue, though, was more complicated.

Foreign Minister Shigenori Togo had been adamant that the government comply with international law when dealing with prisoners of war. Togo had little political credibility within the cabinet, having been against the war from the outset, but he had the ear of Emperor Hirohito, who had let it be known that his inclination was to respect international law, particularly when dealing with the Doolittle Raiders. There had even been rumors that the emperor privately chastised Sugiyama for openly advocating summary execution.

Emperor Hirohito had been concerned about all the Japanese being held by the Allied powers. There were still tens of thousands of people of Japanese ancestry living in the United States, most of whom were now facing internment in concentration camps. Cruelty toward such high-value detainees as the Doolittle Raiders could provoke reprisals. The emperor did not want to give the Allies an excuse for abuses.

The debate over what to do with the Raiders tore the scabs off a debate that had roiled Japan's cabinet since July 27, 1929, when Japan had been one of the first countries to sign the Geneva Convention Relative to the Treatment of Prisoners of War. Japan's militarists, politically on the rise throughout the 1930s, had successfully blocked its ratification, and one of their principal objections had been that the Geneva Convention made it harder to deter bombing Japan. Given developments in technology, it was clear that Japan could no longer count on its surrounding seas to serve as an effective moat. Airpower had become too sophisticated. Article I of the 1929 Geneva Convention guaranteed humane treatment to any airman captured in the course of an air attack.

To the militarists, promising good treatment to enemy airmen created a perverse incentive: enemy bombers could conduct air raids against Japan without having to worry what would happen if they were captured. That would, in effect, double the flying range of enemy bombers because aircrews would know they did not need to return home to be safe. They could just burden Japan's resources further by being taken prisoner. Treating the Raiders as prisoners of war would defeat the whole purpose of not having ratified the Geneva Convention in the first place.

But after Pearl Harbor, Foreign Minister Togo succeeded in pushing Japan toward respecting the Geneva Convention. Vice Minister of War Heitaro Kimura generally handled questions of international law that affected the Army and was initially unmoved by Togo's concerns that Japan was becoming a rogue state. In light of the emperor's refusal to ratify the Geneva Convention, Kimura said, "we can hardly announce her observance of the same." But Kimura agreed to a compromise: to the extent the Allies were concerned about ensuring that their prisoners had food and clothing, Kimura had no problem with Togo assuring the Allies that their prisoners would be treated humanely. "It would be safe to notify the world," Kimura told Togo, that Japan would act consistently with the "principles" of the Convention, though not conceding that it was bound by their letter.

That, in turn, allowed Togo to deliver a diplomatic communiqué to the Allies in January 1942 that finessed the issue. Japan had "not yet ratified the Convention relating to the treatment of prisoners of war," Togo reminded them, and as a consequence was "not bound by the said Convention." Nevertheless, Japan would "apply *mutatis mutandis* the provisions of the Convention to American prisoners of war in its power."

Mutatis mutandis was a slippery phrase that had come from lawyers in the Foreign Ministry's Treaty Bureau. As legal jargon it meant "all things being equal," and Togo understood it to convey the idea that in the absence of "serious hindrances the convention would be applied." Kimura, for his part, assumed that it put Japan under no obligation to do or not do anything in particular. The capture of the eight Doolittle Raiders, however, forced the issue.

Prime Minister Tojo needed to placate Sugiyama. Tojo was losing support from within the Army's rank and file, which was a notoriously dangerous position for a Japanese prime minister be in. In the weeks after the raid, a protest had been lodged by the Army Staff to the fact that Tojo was simultaneously holding the offices of prime minister and war minister, a first step to a broader push of no confidence. But it was the emperor, not the Army, who had the ultimate say over Tojo's political future, so Tojo echoed the emperor's views as his own: He wanted to respect international law. He was open to treating the Raiders as prisoners of war, but he wanted to explore all the options.

* * *

For the short term, Tojo directed Colonel Kenshichi Masuoka, the head of the Tokyo Kempeitai, to keep the Raiders in Tokyo and under constant surveillance for intelligence. Masuoka was to do whatever was necessary to keep them safely and securely detained. If one of them got sick, nursing him back to health was given top priority. There would be no escapes, no suicides, no "accidents."

For the long term, Tojo searched for another legal compromise. Wasn't there some legal way of executing the Raiders? The War Ministry Legal Department set to work researching the question, but the straightforward answer they returned was no. "They should be treated as prisoners of war," the lawyers concluded. "An execution was illegal." There was no Japanese law criminalizing what they had done. To punish the Americans, the government would have to promulgate a new law, which would still be illegal because it would be ex post facto.

That was not an acceptable answer. The question was sent back to the Legal Department, and this time it was impressed upon the lawyers that "the execution would take place regardless of the legality." The Kempeitai, they were told, would just fix the records "to look as if the flyers had resisted capture." The head of the Legal Department, Ayao Oyama, could not let that happen and instructed his lawyers to dig deeper. Perhaps there was something in the Hague Conventions?

The problem with the Hague Conventions was that they dealt with ground warfare, not air warfare. There had been an attempt to supplement the Hague Conventions with rules for air warfare back in the 1920s, but the very failure of that attempt meant that the rules for air warfare remained something of an open question.

It took some work, but the lawyers in the Legal Department finally came back with an answer and a detailed report explaining how captured airmen could, under certain circumstances, be prosecuted even in the absence of an existing Japanese law. If it could be shown that the Raiders had deliberately attacked civilians and indiscriminately bombed civilian areas, they could be considered war criminals under international law. Any punishment that followed, including execution, would be legal.

In an article published the following year, the diplomat, scholar, and regular adviser to the Japanese government on questions of international law, Junpei Shinobu, relayed the substance of the Legal Department's analysis. The "generous treatment" Japan had afforded to "prisoners who have either surrendered or been captured in the course of a series of decisive engagements," he argued, was due to the fact that they had "committed no offence." The same was not true, however, for those who "deliberately

carried out attacks on non-combatants and non-military objects in pref-
erence to undertaking attacks which are obligatory on the prosecution of
war." Such prisoners were not entitled to be treated as prisoners of war but
instead fell into a legal black hole, where "they can be punished for their
evil-doing, and such a punishment is justified."

This legal analysis not only offered a way to satisfy Sugiyama's desire
to punish the Americans, it also made it impossible for Foreign Minister
Togo to oppose. Togo was the one, after all, who was always advocating
for international law. Here, Japan would be enforcing it. As Shinobu explained, it was not merely Japan's right to prosecute the Doolittle Raiders,
it was its duty.

*   *   *

Masahiko Takeshita, a lieutenant colonel in the War Ministry's Military
Affairs Bureau (who would ultimately attempt a coup on August 15, 1945,
to prevent Emperor Hirohito from surrendering), made sure that the Legal
Department's report was distributed to the top commanders across the
Army. At nearly the same time, the findings of the Kempeitai's secret investigation into the raid began to spread. On May 26, the Kempeitai slipped a
copy of the results of its investigation to Sugiyama, which confirmed what
he had been saying all along.

Along with surveys of the damage around Japan, the report collected
transcripts of the interrogations of each of the captured Doolittle Raiders.
Their admissions were damning.

Robert Hite, the copilot on the plane that attacked Nagoya, had reportedly said, "I was resigned to the fate that a certain amount of damage
to residential areas and injuries to civilians would be inevitable. On the
other hand, I also thought that this was a good opportunity to carry out
so-called guerrilla type air raids." The phrase "guerrilla type air raid" was
the very phrase that had been in circulation in the Japanese press and had
even appeared, verbatim, in an editorial in Japan's *Photo Weekly Magazine*
the week after the raid.

"Did you do any strafing while getting away from Nagoya?" Hite had
been asked.

"I haven't revealed any information on this point," Hite had confessed,
"but the truth is that about five to six minutes after leaving the city we saw

in the distance what looked like an elementary school with many children at play. The pilot steadily dropped altitude and ordered the gunmen to their stations. When the plane was at an oblique angle, the skipper gave firing orders, and bursts of machine-gun fire sprayed the ground."

William Farrow, the pilot of Hite's plane, had reportedly told interrogators that he was not sure what he had hit because "at the time the Japanese antiaircraft guns were especially active, and since our only thought was to drop our bombs quickly and make a hurry—for safety, I believe it is natural that some damage was inflicted on residences, and some civilians may have been killed." He had also confirmed what Hite had said about the school: "I do not quite remember the place—there was a place which looked like a school, with many people there. As a parting shot, with a feeling of 'damn these Japs,' I made a power dive and carried out some strafing. There was absolutely no defensive fire from below."

Harold Spatz, the gunner on Farrow's plane, had come off as particularly cavalier. He had supposedly been asked, "What do you think of the fact that your plane bombed innocent civilians?"

Spatz had replied, "If the objective was to demoralize the general populace even if the bombing was directed at residential areas, etc. then personally I do not care as to how we did it."

"After the bombing of Nagoya, did you not actually carry out strafing?"

"I aimed at the children in the schoolyard and fired only one burst before we headed out to sea," Spatz had confessed. "My feelings at that time were 'damn the Japs,' I want to give them a burst of fire."

Dean Hallmark, whose target had been steel mills in Tokyo, also echoed the fear that Japanese antiaircraft fire had instilled in him. "Since antiaircraft fire was rather active," he was reported as saying, "and we were quite apprehensive about the arrival of Japanese fighter planes, our sole concern was to unload our bombs and make a hasty escape."

"From your technical experience, what did you honestly think of the bombing methods used on that day?" he had then been asked.

"In all probability there was a considerable amount of indiscriminate bombing."

Sugiyama let Tojo know that he approved of the course of action suggested by the Legal Department's analysis. Tojo then instructed Oyama to draft a directive for the use of military commissions. Enemy aircrews "whose actions did not violate international law were to be treated as ordinary prisoners of war. Those suspected of violating international law were to be subject to trial." If the trial "proved that the suspects were guilty of a wartime major offense, they were to be punished in accordance with the martial law." The procedures of the military commission, Tojo added, should be the same as the procedures applied to Japanese soldiers.

In June, the War Ministry formally issued a directive entitled "Measures Concerning Plane Crash Survivors." It instructed the Kempeitai to investigate anyone who had survived an enemy plane crash. If the investigation showed evidence of war crimes, the prisoners would be tried under the Wartime Law for Military Commissions, which the Army had issued in 1922.

The directive, as written, said that all such trials had to be conducted in Tokyo, but in the Doolittle Raiders case, the decision was made to get them out of the capital. The case remained controversial and no one in the War Ministry wanted their fingerprints on it. So, the Raiders were sent back to Shanghai to stand trial, and by the end of July, all the plans were in place. Then, in mid-August, the Army formally issued the Enemy Airmen's Law of 1942.

*   *   *

The verdict and death sentences against the Doolittle Raiders reached Tokyo the first week in September. No one was surprised that they had all been found guilty, but the cabinet was again divided over what to do. Japan's fortunes in the broader war had changed since the spring. The Pacific offensive had come to a standstill, and Japan's future looked bleak. While the tactical significance of the Doolittle Raid had been trivial, it prompted a series of disastrous changes in Japan's strategy in the summer of 1942, not the least the ill-conceived and ultimately ruinous Battle of Midway. More air raids now seemed certain.

Tojo told Bodine that it was the Battle of the Coral Sea, which had been fought a few weeks after the Doolittle Raid, that had been, for him, the turning point in the war. "There is one thing you must realize and understand," he explained. "To be defeated or beaten is one of the most hideous things that could happen to Japanese military officers."

Back in the autumn of 1942, when the verdicts came down, Sugiyama personally visited Tojo to make his case for why all the Raiders should be executed as sentenced. He went alone, and Tojo had been struck by the gesture, since Sugiyama always surrounded himself with an entourage.

As far as Sugiyama was concerned, the Doolittle Raiders had been convicted of atrocities, the murder of innocent children. Japanese soldiers were regularly put to death for far less serious crimes. What message would it send to the Americans if their pilots could attack the homeland and murder children in schools with impunity? Death for all of them was the only just punishment.

Tojo opposed carrying out the executions. Doing so would give the Americans valuable propaganda, and, who knew, the Raiders could be more useful alive as bargaining chips. So Tojo again persuaded Sugiyama on a compromise: What if the pilots and the one who admitted gunning down the schoolboy were executed and the rest were given life sentences as an expression of the emperor's mercy?

Late in the morning of October 3, 1942, Tojo took the compromise to Emperor Hirohito. The emperor agreed, and the final decision was then relayed to the 13th Army in Shanghai, where Sadamu Shimomura had just taken command.

*   *   *

Tojo readily admitted, looking back from 1946, after all the firebombs and atomic bombs that had been dropped, "the tragic spectacle of this country today makes this first raid look like a very small thing, but it was a great shock to the people at the time." The popular appetite for revenge was extraordinary. Even after the Raiders' executions were made public, newspapers editorials demanded more. One went so far as to propose that "all enemy aviators who fall in our hands, after defacing this blessed land of ours, should be beheaded without discrimination."

Tojo could not confirm what Bodine had been told about Sawada sending a cable to Tokyo asking for the lives of the Raiders to be spared. He also could not confirm that that was why Sawada had been relieved of his command just before the order to carry out the executions had been issued. But it was in his character to do something like that. "General Sawada had one weakness," Tojo said. "In my opinion he had a soft heart and was not the ruthless and forceful commander like General Yamashita."

It was surprising to hear Yamashita described this way. The Tiger of

Malaya had garnered a surprising amount of public sympathy for a Japanese general, in no small part because his lawyers had played up the fact that he had been one of Tojo's major opponents within the Japanese Army. To many American lawyers, Yamashita had come to embody all of their qualms over MacArthur's taking revenge on his former adversaries through summary trials.

Tojo, though, knew who Yamashita really was. They were the same age and had known each other for their entire careers. A protégé of General Sadao Araki, Yamashita was a charismatic fascist who had fostered the notion of Japan as an imperial power. He was one of the biggest militarists, if not the biggest, in the entire Army.

The irony was that he was probably innocent of what had occurred during the Battle of Manila; the Navy had been responsible for those atrocities, and Tojo explained to Bodine that the Army and the Navy were "extremely jealous and suspicious of one another." The Navy would never have listened to Yamashita's orders to do anything, not least to retreat.

But Yamashita's career was a trail of blood, and in the main, he was indifferent as to whose blood wet the ground beneath his feet. In his famous march down Malaya to Singapore, his men had killed hospital patients, prisoners, and, after the British capitulation, as many as five thousand Chinese civilians. Yamashita had even helped orchestrate a coup attempt in 1936 that had so destabilized Japan's civilian government that the country's lurch toward militarism had become all but inevitable. The bitter irony of it all was that MacArthur had convicted a guilty man of the wrong crime. And in the process, he had made Yamashita—of all people—a martyr to the rule of law and human decency.

Sawada was different, Tojo insisted. "He had no legal responsibility in relation to the sentences passed by this court." Whatever Sawada might say in terms of trying to absolve his codefendants of responsibility, there was no responsibility for him to assume.

"He is a very good soldier and an outstanding officer," Tojo said. "He would never disobey an order, and therefore he was compelled to follow my order and its dictates." Sawada and all the rest had been just the middlemen.

At bottom, Tojo thought everyone involved behaved rightly. The Raiders had committed atrocities. Tokyo had seen to it that they were punished in accordance with international law. And they had been. No one had done anything wrong.

EIGHTEEN

Bullshit. After all this work and with only a week left to prepare, Bodine was confronted by the prospect of having to build their case on bullshit. Sure, if Sawada had tried to stop the executions of Hallmark, Farrow, and Spatz, they might be able to spare him the death penalty and maybe even get him acquitted on a few of the charges. But when it came to Wako, Okada, and Tatsuta, the only line they were getting was that the Doolittle Raiders had been justly prosecuted for committing atrocities. Bullshit.

Japanese propaganda had made claims of American atrocities before anyone knew any of the facts. That was clear enough from the earliest Japanese broadcasts, made less than an hour after the attack, which had lamented the Raiders' craven targeting of "nonmilitary objectives" with hysterics befitting a radio melodrama.

Perhaps there had been some collateral damage. Among the Kempeitai records Bodine and Fellows had gotten from the old War Ministry was a damage report that had separated out examples of "inhumane attacking" and damage to nonmilitary targets, even schools. But it had been an air raid. Collateral damage, even of the tragic kind, was inevitable. That did not make the Doolittle Raiders war criminals. Japan had bombed plenty of cities in China and caused at least as much damage. War crimes had to be intentional. Why would the Raiders have gone out of their way, when they were low on fuel to begin with, to deliberately attack schoolchildren? American airmen just did not do that, not least the Doolittle Raiders.

In the movie *The Purple Heart*, the Japanese fabricated the same line about the fictional Doolittle Raiders. Upon hearing a witness claim that they had indiscriminately attacked civilians, the fictional Dean Hallmark jumped to his feet to object. "This man is a liar! Sure, we told him we hit our targets, but they weren't hospitals, temples, or schools. They were oil storage centers, airports, and shipyards. That's what we hit, and that's what we told him!"

It was clear that in real life, the Japanese party line had become that the Doolittle Raiders had been engaging in "guerrilla-type air raids" because they were too cowardly and dastardly to fight like real men. The failure of the Japanese Army to defend the homeland was therefore understandable, if not excusable. After all, who could have expected such inhumanity, especially from a country that prattled on so often about human rights and the law of war? And when the Japanese Army had needed to tie a bow on it all, they had tortured the Raiders into confessing, and tortured them so crudely that the Raiders aped party-line phrases such as "guerrilla-type air raids," so that the Japanese Army could launder their bullshit through a show trial based on fabricated evidence.

* * *

Fellows, however, was less certain. He had been working with Sawada's old friend Taosa Kubota to retrace the Raiders' steps in Japan and had ultimately tracked down an older Japanese officer who fit the description of Well-Well, the Japanese lawyer who had interrogated the Doolittle Raiders in Tokyo and had gotten them to all sign confessions. Well-Well's real name was Takaaki Taguchi, and he had no compunction about admitting his involvement. "I acted as interpreter during examinations by military experts concerning the military operation of the raid," he said.

Fellows wanted to know kind of questions the airmen had been asked.

"The instruments they carried, their speed, distance flown, and technical matters," Taguchi said. "I do not believe that any of the Doolittle Raiders were questioned through me on their having bombed schools or killing civilians." As far as Taguchi was concerned, the "fliers were cooperative in the course of the questioning and answered questions fully, telling what they knew about the raid."

What about torture? The Kempeitai certainly had a reputation for it. Fellows asked him whether the Raiders had been abused.

"Such treatment was not necessary as the fliers talked very freely," Taguchi claimed. Though he could not vouch for what had happened when he was not in the room, "I became friendly with several. None of them bore any outward signs of mistreatment or torture." He even remembered that when they had been departing Tokyo, "they shook hands with me and did not appear to be worried, although they did appear to have resigned themselves to whatever might become of them."

Taguchi's impression was corroborated by another officer named Tsune Namoto, who spoke English and admitted to having interrogated William Farrow's crew in Tokyo. Namoto denied that any of the Raiders had been mistreated, let alone tortured, and he remembered that one of the junior crew members on Farrow's plane—it would have been either Jacob De-Shazer or Harold Spatz—had admitted to strafing some nonmilitary objectives in Nagoya.

Fellows made a note that Namoto's claim had been corroborated by the Kempeitai's damage report. It also fit with what he had been told by some of the witnesses to the raid.

Fellows had interviewed a schoolteacher from the suburbs of Nagoya the day before, who claimed that an American plane had approached from the direction of the city and, as it grew near, had lowered its altitude and opened fire. It had been so close that the teacher thought the plane was going to crash into the school. Thankfully no one had been hurt, but it had just came out of nowhere. There was no explaining it.

Fellows got a similar story from an elementary school teacher in the suburban Shinagawa neighborhood of Tokyo. The planes had flown overhead around noon, he said, and one of them, which had been flying only a few hundred feet in the air, had dropped a bomb right next to the school. The blast had shattered all the windows, and fragments from the bomb had flown into the school. No one had been killed, but a few people had been injured. It was inexplicable. It was just a neighborhood school in a residential area. There was nothing military or industrial nearby, save for a cigarette factory.

Then there was Fuyo Hayakawa. She had come to Tokyo from her fishing village on the southern coast of the Ise Bay, the opposite side from Nagoya. Though only fifty-six years old, she looked ancient and had a scar across the wrinkles of her left cheek. Hayakawa claimed that she had been walking along the beach gathering shells with her neighbors when they had heard a low drone coming from the direction of Nagoya. When she had turned to look, she saw a fat green plane coming in very low over the water. It emitted a flapping sound as it passed over head, and the sand and water had jumped up in little spurts. Before she had known precisely why, she had felt some stings, one on her thigh and the other biting into her cheek.

Fellows asked Hayakawa to describe the plane.

She couldn't. She hadn't seen it clearly. She had no way of knowing whether or not it was an American plane.

Fellows asked her if there were airfields nearby or some other military installation. Perhaps there were large factories?

No, Hayakawa said. It was just a small village by the beach. There was nothing around. She didn't know why, but the plane had shot all over the beach and the village.

Fellows had Kubota write up her memories in a short statement and read it to her. When she agreed to it, Fellows asked her to sign, but she didn't know what he meant. She did not know how to write her name. So Fellows had her put her thumbprint underneath.

*　　*　　*

Bodine remained skeptical about all of these accusations that Fellows was uncovering. So much had happened in the war, and all the witnesses knew what the right answers were if they wanted to help their countrymen in Shanghai. They all knew what the propaganda was, and Kubota was Sawada's best friend. Wasn't it at least possible that he was curating the evidence? These were just uncorroborated stories.

That was, of course, not wholly true. Jacob DeShazer had admitted to indiscriminately strafing around Nagoya in a statement to American investigators who had come to see him at Walter Reed back in September. Robert Hite had apparently goaded DeShazer into giving some fishing boats a little heat as they had flown over Ise Bay, and DeShazer had opened up with his .30-caliber as the *Bat Out of Hell* buzzed overhead. It was certainly possible he had hit that old woman.

Bodine, though, thought about it like a pilot. Ammunition is heavy, and the Raiders would have wanted to lower their weight so that they would have more fuel to get to China. Who knew what they could see from the air? Every Japanese boat in the water had played a part for the Navy. It had been a little picket boat, after all, that had spotted the USS *Hornet* and alerted the Japanese to the Raiders' initial approach.

Bodine decided to join Fellows during the interview of some more teachers, this time from Tsurumaki National School, located in a residential suburb southwest of Tokyo. The teachers all came as a group to be interviewed at the Philippine Embassy.

Like the witnesses Fellows had previously interviewed, the teachers all claimed that on the day of the raid, American airplanes had flown overhead and attacked their school. The planes had dropped incendiary bombs that, in the teachers' description, had "opened up like umbrellas and came down like leaflets."

Still skeptical, Bodine asked how they had known the plane was American.

The teachers said they could tell from the symbols on the wings. The Japanese planes had bright red dots. The American planes had stars.

Bodine knew that that proved nothing. Thousands of American planes had flown over Tokyo by March 1946. It was widely known how they were painted and so he decided to contrive a little lie detector test on the fly. He drew two circles on a piece of paper, each with a star at the center, with one of the stars drawn on top of a narrow, horizontal rectangle. Both drawings were "roundels," or wing markings, from Army Air Forces planes.

"Which of the two following insignia did you see?" he asked.

The teachers all pointed to the one without the rectangle. As Bodine knew, the rectangle had been added only in June 1943, after the Doolittle Raid but more than a year before the next American bombers had flown over Tokyo. In short, the teachers had guessed right.

Bodine pressed them on whether the firebombing of their school might have been just accidental collateral damage. "Are there any factories in the vicinity of the school?"

"No. There are only a hospital, stores, and homes," one of the teachers said. "Tsurumaki National School did not burn, but the hospital, stores and homes in that vicinity burned."

*   *   *

Before leaving Japan, Bodine and Fellows made their way out to Mizumoto Elementary School in the Katsushika district. The Mizumoto

School had played an outsized role in the Japanese mythology of the Doolittle Raid.

More than an hour's drive north, Katsushika was a different kind of place than Tokyo city was. Whereas Tokyo's city dwellers were living off rations amid the ashes of their former homes, the people of Katsushika continued to work family farms and had remained as content and well fed during and after the war as they had always been. Though technically part of metropolitan Tokyo, it was far removed from, or at least far less touched by, the war. The big exception had been the Doolittle Raid.

The morning of the raid had been an ordinary one until an alarm sounded during first period. The teachers had quickly made their way into the faculty lounge, where the blackboard read, "8:30 a.m. a warning against possible enemy attack on the southern part of the Kanto Plain was issued."

Volunteers from the local civil defense team had quickly congregated at the school, parking their bicycles neatly in front of the school's gym. Mizumoto Elementary School was the most prominent building amidst the patchwork of family farms, and the organizers of the civil defense team had designated the school as the community's rallying point. With no more information to go on, two members of the civil defense team had decided to stay in the faculty lounge for the morning so that the school's telephone could be used to keep in touch with district headquarters if necessary. But nothing happened. The rest of the morning had passed without incident.

It was Saturday, so the first and second graders had been sent home before lunchtime. The older students were scheduled to be dismissed at 2:00 p.m., right after fourth period. On Saturdays, fourth period was usually something lighter, such as gym, farming lessons for the boys and sewing lessons for the girls, or an extra recess. Saturdays were lower key, and on this particular Saturday, the principal had taken the day off, as had about a third of the teachers.

It was a clear day, which was welcome in cherry blossom season. Chiaki Nishikawa, one of the teachers who had come in to work that day, talked it over with the rest of the faculty, and they decided to let the students go home a little early. Instead of 2:00 p.m., they gathered the students in the yard closer to 1:30 p.m. and announced that school was out to all the eager children who already had their caps donned and book bags slung in the hope of getting home a little early.

As the children scattered to their homes, Nishikawa and the rest of the teachers made their way back to the faculty lounge to finish up odds and ends. They were chatting about nothing worth remembering when they heard the school's groundskeeper shouting. "Teachers, air raid!"

Everyone fell silent. In the distance, they could hear the drone of the air raid siren.

Nishikawa put down the bit of paperwork she had been doing, but no one panicked. There was no need to. They had gone through the drill that morning. Everyone prepared to take their assigned posts, and the fire brigade got to work running its protocols. It was just a siren.

Everything went according to plan until the sound of the siren started being punctuated by antiaircraft fire. The men of the civil defense team quickly proved themselves useless as one especially brave man started frantically shouting, as if he were on fire, "Enemy airplanes are coming!"

Nishikawa took charge. The students were still walking home. Under the rules, teachers were not to leave the school until the air raid siren had been turned off, but the children were out in the open. Nishikawa ordered all those who could keep their wits about them to run out and round up the children, get them somewhere safe.

Nishikawa made her way into the yard as the students in their caps and book bags rushed past her back into the school. Those further down the road ducked into houses or ditches. Nishikawa was still not convinced that this was anything more than a drill until, to the south, she saw a plane flying low across the horizon, followed by the sound of a deep explosion. "Yes," she thought, "that was an enemy plane."

The antiaircraft fire continued, but the little gray puffs were as pathetic as they looked. Whatever the guns were shooting at, they were not getting anywhere near the plane that had just dropped the bomb.

Nishikawa stared at the little plane on the horizon until it passed out of view. She scanned the sky impatiently, looking for the Japanese fighters she was sure were chasing after it. Certainly some Japanese fighters would be in close pursuit. But the sky stayed clear, blue, and empty.

It seemed to be all over, but as Nishikawa turned to make her way back into the school, she heard another drone, another plane, this time coming from the north. Perhaps the Japanese Air Force was finally arriving?

But as she stared at the little black dot growing larger against the sky, she couldn't help but think that it was flying strangely low. As it got closer, it seemed as if it was barreling directly toward her. And as it got closer still, she could see the pilot in his leather flying helmet, which to her looked like a little green bonnet.

The plane's twin engines growled overhead. There was something mesmerizing about it. It was such a heavy machine. It was so close. It was like being on the platform as a train roared by. And as the big fat heavy plane dusted over her, the machine gun in its nose opened up onto the school with a metallic *flap-flap-flap*.

Nishikawa dived reflexively into the bushes and stayed hidden there until the dull buzz of the plane's engines faded out toward the south. Shaken, she got up and was walking back into the school when another teacher ran up to her, ashen faced. "A student has been injured!"

Nishikawa ran through the hallway and found the body of a thirteen-year-old boy in a pool of blood. His cap and book bag were still on. Yukitero Furusawa, another teacher at the school, was trying to revive the boy. But he wasn't moving.

The boy had apparently been in farming class during fourth period and had left a little later than the rest of the students because he wanted to clean the farm tools extra well. He had been only about a hundred feet from the school's gate when he would have seen the grown-ups scrambling toward him, yelling "Air raid! Air raid!"

The boy had rushed back into the school, and Furusawa ushered him along with the other remaining students into a classroom on the second floor. He had told them to take cover, and they all ducked under their desks just as they had been taught. But then a bullet cut a perfectly round hole through a window, sending them all scrambling into the hallway. At first Furusawa thought that the boy had simply stumbled in the confusion and paid almost no attention to him. But then, when he went back into the hallway, he saw that the boy was still on the floor.

Nishikawa rummaged through the boy's book bag and found his notebook. The term had just begun, so the notebook was nearly empty, but his name had been written on the front page: Minosuke Ishide.

Nishikawa shouted "Minosuke!" into the boy's face, but he gave no sign of recognition. She and three other teachers picked him up, and dribbled a trail of blood down the hallway as they had carried him to the nurse's office. They laid him out on a table, and Nishikawa pulled away at his clothes in search of where he had been hit. There it was, a small hole in his belly, just below the waist.

Nishikawa wadded up a bandage to plug the hole as she tried to figure out what to do. The nearest hospital was twenty-five miles away. The school had once had a nurse, but she had quit months earlier and the district had never replaced her. Nishikawa telephoned the local doctor, who sometimes came to the school, but no one answered.

Nishikawa ordered a member of the civil defense team to hurry to the boy's house to tell his family, who somehow got to the school in what seemed like only a few minutes. The boy's mother wailed his name, and the boy's father furiously shouted at Nishikawa, "Why didn't you send him home earlier! Before the attack!"

There was no sign that the doctor was on his way, so they lifted the boy onto a stretcher and Nishikawa told the civil defense team to rush him to the Mitsubishi paper factory. It was only a few miles away and had a clinic for the workers. The boy was no longer breathing and had no pulse, and by the time they got him to the clinic at the paper factory, it was too late.

The Japanese press clamored for every lurid detail of the boy's death. The school's principal did not mention that he had taken the day off but told the press, "I feel very sorry for the family of the victim, Ishide." To further brandish his patriotism, he said, "There is no way to show indignation against the enemy who committed this awful act of attacking innocent children. We can only swear to devote our efforts to the one objective of annihilating the Americans and the British."

Asahi Shimbun ran the story of Minosuke Ishide the day after the Doolittle Raid under the headline "Evil Enemy Strafes Schoolyard." The article left no details unreported, describing the bomber's diving to the ground before firing off a dozen rounds into the school. "At 2:00 p.m. that day he breathed his last in the arms of his teachers." It was an act, *Asahi* wrote, that was bereft of "human morality" and "has roused the indignation of all."

The next day, the boy's parents held a memorial service at their home, which became a venue not just for local mourning but for national outrage. Newspapers covered the memorial service, and a gunned-down child became the personification of American barbarism.

Under the headline "Bitter Funeral Service for Student," *Asahi* described the tragic funeral of the boy "who fell victim to inhumane strafing by enemy aircraft on the afternoon of the 18th."

The boy's tombstone was etched with six characters 悲運銃撃善士 ("A blessed Buddha, who was tragically shot") and became a pilgrimage site every April 18 throughout the rest of the war, when newspapers would run photos of children paying their respects to mark the anniversary. On the first such anniversary, a classmate of Minosuke Ishide wrote an essay describing the plane flying overhead as he dived into a hedge in fear. Over the course of the year, the child's fear had blossomed into rage, so that now he imagined, "Had I a machine gun, I would have shot it down."

* * *

Furusawa, the teacher who had first found the boy, painfully described the day to Bodine and Fellows with all the excruciating detail he could muster. He drew them a detailed map of the school grounds and the path of the plane and handed them the pane of glass from the second-floor classroom, which had a perfectly round hole in it.

Despite the man's evident grief, Bodine remained skeptical. What proof did they have that this hole had been made by an American plane? And even if it had been an American plane, what proof was there that this hole had been made during the Doolittle Raid?

Furusawa led them to a hole in the wall of the classroom. There was still a bullet embedded in it. Bodine and Fellows yanked the board loose and wrenched out the slug inside. Furusawa also gave them two other bullets that had been recovered from the schoolyard after the raid was over.

Bodine could tell right away that they were from a .30-caliber machine gun. It was the same .30-caliber ammunition that the Army Air Forces had phased out in the summer of 1942, and the only time an American plane had flown over this part of Japan before then had been on April 18, 1942.

Hadn't Chase Nielsen's plane, the *Green Hornet*, flown over northern Tokyo? The *Green Hornet* wasn't the only one, but it had been in the area. Nielsen had always insisted that they had never fired their guns. He had always said that the allegations that they had killed a child were impossible because his plane's gun had jammed during testing over the Pacific. But that was the main .50-caliber heavy gun. He had never said anything about the .30-caliber gun that William Dieter could have been firing from the bombardier's seat. That gun wasn't very loud, and Nielsen was back in the navigator's compartment. With all the engine noise inside the cockpit, Nielsen might not even have been able to hear if Dieter had fired off a few rounds.

When Bodine and Fellows went outside, they could see that Mizumoto Elementary School stood alone. With its surrounding playground, it looked just like any elementary school in rural America. There was no mistaking it, and in every direction, there were farm fields. The nearest building was a small workshop a mile away.

The Doolittle Raiders were unimpeachable American heroes. Bodine admired them as much as anyone else did. They had turned the tide of the war by risking everything on a seemingly impossible mission. Seven men had died in the effort. Four had allegedly been murdered by Bodine and Fellow's Japanese clients. President Roosevelt, whose death a year earlier had vaulted him into American sainthood, had declared that the United States would hold anyone who had participated in the Raiders' trial and execution "personally and officially responsible for these diabolical crimes." Now, with only a week left before trial, Bodine and Fellows stood in the middle of Japanese farmland with a troubling answer to a taboo question: Were the Doolittle Raiders actually guilty?

THE TRIAL

* * *

NINETEEN

Chase Nielsen got himself good and cleaned up. He gave his face a fresh shave and combed his thick black hair over from a part above his right ear. He pulled his black socks over where the scars still marked his shins, tucked his khaki shirt smartly into his matching trousers, and stepped into his highly polished black Oxford shoes. He tied his khaki tie in a half Windsor knot, making sure to tuck its tails between his second and third shirt buttons. He pulled his green wool officer's jacket over his shoulders, pinched its three brass buttons closed, and fastened his brass-buckled waist belt just below where his ribs fanned out from his breastbone.

Nielsen had returned to Shanghai for one reason that January, despite its having been the place of some of his worst memories: he was there to tell his story. He had told it many times, but not yet so many times that he had forgotten it. He was there to speak for Dean Hallmark, William Farrow, Harold Spatz, and Robert Meder, whom the Japanese had murdered, and for Robert Hite, George Barr, and Jacob DeShazer, whose souls were still struggling to make it out alive.

It was a Monday morning, March 18, 1946. Things were supposed to have gotten under way the previous week, but Bodine and Fellows's trip to Japan had lasted longer than expected and the presiding judge, Edwin McReynolds, had granted them the weekend to prepare. The crowd, the reporters, the two dozen lawyers, the interpreters, and the courtroom staff all grew quiet when one of the MPs called for attention and, with the same formality with which they had entered before, the military commission judges, now numbering five, took their seats at the bench. The stern-faced McReynolds positioned himself at the center and began at 9:00 a.m. sharp: "The Commission is in session."

John Hendren took the podium to deliver his opening statement. "Gentlemen, the provable facts in the case of United States versus Shigeru Sawada and others will show," Hendren began before diverting into a dry timeline of events that Nielsen had both heard about and explained an uncountable number of times.

Hendren offered no gory details, no embellishments. His timeline had all the emotional resonance of a telegraph machine, and, seeming to recognize as much, he concluded by saying "This gentlemen, is briefly the evidence that will be offered. I have not gone into detail at this time but that will be the evidence that will be offered in detail as to the treatment these men received." That morning, it would be up to Nielsen to offer that evidence and to tell the world the definitive story of the Doolittle Raiders.

* * *

Robert Dwyer knew that the opening statement in any trial is bound by strict rules: no argument, just the facts. Still, they were there to do something big. This wasn't an ordinary trial.

Dwyer could have made an opening statement that chilled the blood. When Hendren had blandly said, "the evidence that will be offered in detail as to the treatment the Raiders received," he could just as easily have said, "The evidence will show that Japanese soldiers in Shanghai, the area under Shigeru Sawada's command, gouged Nielsen between the fingers with pencils right down into his nerves. The evidence will show that Japanese soldiers in Shanghai, the area under Shigeru Sawada's command, used a bamboo pole to wrench his knee joints apart. The evidence will show that they did not stop there and that the same Japanese soldiers in Shanghai, the area under Shigeru Sawada's command, subjected Chase Nielsen and the rest of the Doolittle Raiders to other forms of 'special treatment' that you or I would call torture." Those would still have been just facts, but they would have let the world know what this case was really all about.

Dwyer might have done the opening statement differently, but he was happy to be where he was. He was at the prosecution table. He had worked hard to get there. If he pulled this off, not only would he send Sawada and the rest to the gallows but he—Robert Dwyer, the son of E. J. Dwyer of Rochester, New York—would have set a precedent for treating the perversion of justice as a war crime under international law.

Dwyer was unsure if McReynolds and the rest of the military commission judges would accept this new legal theory. Command responsibility had survived by dint of only two votes on the US Supreme Court. Dwyer would need to prove that this was the right case to set that precedent. They would need to show that the Japanese had used false and fraudulent evidence to sentence the Doolittle Raiders to death on false and fraudulent charges. They would have to convince McReynolds and the rest of the judges that murder was still murder, even if the murder weapon was paperwork.

McReynolds had given Dwyer every reason to be optimistic that he was on their side. McReynolds had been an Army aviator for decades and was the protégé of Robert Olds, a founding member of the so-called Bomber Mafia, a small but influential group of Air Corps Tactical School instructors who preached the gospel of strategic bomb-the-bastards-until-they-submit airpower. Olds had even handpicked McReynolds to join him for a landmark stunt flight on which then-Lieutenant Curtis LeMay had been the navigator. Disciples of the Bomber Mafia, such as McReynolds and LeMay, had all been taught to revere the movement's messiah, Brigadier General William "Billy" Mitchell, who had predicted war with Japan as early as 1925 and whose name had christened the B-25B bombers that Doolittle had used in his famous raid.

At the arraignment the month before, McReynolds had dismissed all of the defense's legal motions with barely a second thought and made it clear that he was there to help the prosecution as much as he could. Less was known about the other four military commission judges, but two of them, Colonel Richard Wise and Colonel Joseph Murphy, were also from the Army Air Forces, meaning that McReynolds would have a lot of sway over them. The other two were just as likely to fall into line; Colonel John Gamber had been an ordinance officer during the war and Lieutenant Colonel C. R. Berry, as the junior officer, could be expected to follow the lead of the others.

Dwyer's confidence was also buoyed by the fact that Joseph Keenan, dressed in his trademark bow tie, was sitting to his right at the prosecution table. Keenan was not going to stay for the whole trial, but as the top war crimes prosecutor in Tokyo, his sitting at the table for the trial's opening days made it clear to the world, not least to McReynolds and the rest of the judges, that Dwyer had all the weight of General Douglas MacArthur behind him.

When Keenan had arrived the previous week, he held a press conference with Dwyer and Hendren at his side to give his full-throated support to their controversial new legal theory. The Japanese could be tried as war criminals for perverting justice, Keenan had said, because they had created an ex post facto law and tried the Doolittle Raiders before a kangaroo court. It had been, Keenan insisted, "an attempt to terrorize and prevent our men from carrying out perfectly lawful acts. It was a vicious type of terrorism."

While in Shanghai, Keenan treated Dwyer as a protégé. When Keenan was invited for a goodwill audience with Madame Chiang Kai-shek on behalf of MacArthur, he took Dwyer along as part of his entourage. It was easy for Dwyer to imagine his seat next to Keenan there in Shanghai naturally leading to a seat at his side during the Tokyo Trial.

Keenan remained at odds with his staff of international prosecutors back in Tokyo, who sought to undermine him by leaking that they had no idea when he planned to return from China. During their press conference, reporters made a point of pressing Keenan on why he was spending his time watching the Doolittle Trial instead of finally bringing Hideki Tojo up on charges.

Keenan assured the press that he had "twenty top-bracket" indictments ready to go, and, to the further surprise of his staff back in Tokyo, he announced that the final list of charges would be revealed two weeks later, on April 1. The fact that he was in Shanghai simply showed how "vitally interested" he was in the Doolittle Trial. "It affects very high-ranking Japs."

Asked why those "high-ranking Japs"—namely, Sadamu Shimomura—were not in Shanghai on trial themselves, Hendren took over. "We like to refer to this as the 'first Doolittle Trial,'" he told them. "There quite likely will be other Japs tried later on the basis of this trial record."

Keenan picked up the point. "We don't want people to think just the lower levels are being punished," he told the assembled reporters. "We are going to make a thorough search and see how high we can attach the

responsibility of this barbarous treatment of the American prisoners of war."
Keenan was confident that Sawada, Wako, Okada, and Tatsuta would soon
send a message from the gallows. "There couldn't be a case more aggravating."

* * *

"Does the defense desire to make an opening statement at this time?"

Edmund Bodine rose to his feet. "The defense does not wish to make
an opening statement," Bodine replied and sat back down.

Bodine wanted to get through this trial without making a fool of himself. He had never done this before, and he did not have General Douglas
MacArthur's viceroy next to him. Instead, he had Charles Fellows, who
despite his baby face, seemed eager for a fight no matter what the risks to
his military career might be.

Also next to Bodine at the counsel table were his three Japanese cocounsel, whom McReynolds and the rest of the military commission judges
could barely tell apart from the defendants. The newest member of the
team, Shinji Somiya, was a law professor back in Tokyo and just spent two
months in the South Pacific, where the Australians had tried ninety-one
Japanese prison guards for mistreating prisoners of war on the island of
Ambon. Somiya had led an all-Japanese defense team and had succeeded
in persuading the Australians to acquit more than half of the soldiers. Only
a handful of the Japanese guards, the worst of the worst, had ultimately
been sentenced to death. Here in Shanghai, Somiya had reassured Sawada
and the rest that the Japanese and American lawyers defending them would
combine their strengths, overcome their weaknesses, and give all four defendants a real chance at making it out alive.

Though Bodine had to appreciate Somiya's optimism, McReynolds
had given them no reason to hope that this trial would end any differently
than Yamashita's had.

Sure, Bodine had seen the bullet holes in the school walls and could
trace the .30-caliber bullets to the nose gun of one of the B-25Bs that Jimmy
Doolittle had led over Japan. Based on the flight paths, it was possible—
even likely—that those .30-caliber bullets had come from the nose gun of
the *Green Hornet*, the plane on which Chase Nielsen had been the navigator. But he could not very well stand up in court and say that the Doolittle
Raiders, Chase Nielsen among them, had gunned down schoolchildren.

Perhaps they could soften Sawada's image, perhaps they could shift blame effectively to people like Shimomura, but the grisly fate that awaited Sawada, Wako, Okada, and Tatsuta seemed clear, and it looked more and more inevitable the longer Hendren questioned his first witness.

* * *

"Please state your name and residence."

"Chase Jay Nielsen," Hendren's witness replied in his soft southwestern accent. "On temporary duty in the China theater."

Hendren asked Nielsen to describe the Doolittle Raid. "Who briefed you on the targets?" he asked.

"General Doolittle," Nielsen replied, confirming, as if there had been any doubt, his anointed status as one of the handpicked Doolittle Raiders.

Hendren then led Nielsen through all the details that he had promised in his opening statement. Nielsen recounted the planning of the Doolittle Raid, how the pilots had drawn cards to see who would get to bomb the Imperial Palace, and how Doolittle had put a stop to the fun and games. "He told us definitely to leave the Imperial Palace alone, to bomb our objectives and nothing else."

"Did you observe the bombs drop?" Hendren asked.

"Well," Nielsen replied, "while we were in our bank, turning to get out of the fire, and I saw our first three bombs explode right in the southern end of the steel mill."

"Did you observe where the last bomb dropped?"

"Yes, sir, I did," Nielsen said. "Our last bomb was our incendiary and we scattered it all down through the steel mill area."

"On that flight did your plane bomb or strafe any churches?" Hendren asked.

"No, sir, we did not."

"On that flight did your plane bomb or strafe any hospitals?"

"No, sir, it did not."

"On that flight did your plane bomber strafe any children?"

"No, sir, we did not."

Nielsen's answers grew increasingly indignant as he got into a rhythm. Hendren then asked Nielsen to recount the getaway to China, their capture, and the torture he had suffered in the Shanghai airport, and Nielsen made a point of saying with pride "I merely gave them my name, rank and serial number."

"And then what happened?"

"Well," Nielsen replied, "when I wouldn't tell them anything, they would kick me and slap me."

"Who slapped you? Was it military personnel?"

"I imagine they were. They had on uniforms."

Bodine broke in to make his first objection of the trial. Nielsen should not be testifying about "imaginary" people and places, he said.

"Well, we can clear that up," Hendren said dismissively before McReynolds could say anything. He turned back to Nielsen. "Do you *know* whether they were military personnel?"

"I know they were military personnel." Nielsen insisted. "They were wearing Army uniforms and insignia and I think they belong to the 13th Expeditionary Army in China."

As soon as the words "I think" came out of Nielsen's mouth, Bodine objected again.

McReynolds made clear that he did not find Bodine's objections amusing. "The objection of the defenses is denied," McReynolds said, "for the reason that the commission will consider the weight of the evidence as given, whether it is a fact, or his imagination or belief."

"Captain Nielsen," Hendren continued, "would you stand out in front of the bench and show the commission any scars that you have on your leg from the kicking?"

"I certainly will." Nielsen raised his left pant leg and rolled down his sock. Everyone in the courtroom leaned in to see the pink scars still across his shins. "I was given several different types of torture," he said as he pulled his sock back up.

"During this treatment did you answer the questions?" Hendren asked.

"All I gave them was my name, rank and serial number," Nielsen said again.

"What other physical treatment was administered to you at that time?"

"Well, I was given what they call the water cure."

"Explain to the commission what that was?"

"Well, I was put on my back on the floor with my arms and legs stretched out, one guard holding each limb. The towel was wrapped around my face and water was poured on until I was almost unconscious from strangulation, then they would let up until I get my breath, then it starts over again."

"What was your sensation when they were pouring water on the towel, what did you physically feel?"

"Well, I felt more or less like I was drowning, just gasping between life and death."

"During the administration of his treatment did you answer the questions?"

"No," Nielsen said, letting his pride border on bravado. "I did not."

Hendren asked Nielsen to describe having his knees wrenched apart by a bamboo pole, and Nielsen got down from the stand and squatted down to give a sense of the pressure the pole had put on his joints as the Japanese soldiers stomped away at his thighs.

"During this time did the Japanese keep on questioning you?" Hendren asked.

"Yes, they did." Nielsen replied.

"What answers did you give them to the questions?"

"I told them I had given them all the information I had—my name, rank and serial number." Nielsen then described the mock execution in which he had been spared only because they had said, "We are knights of the Bushido of the Order of the Rising Sun; we don't execute at sundown; we execute at sunrise."

Hendren walked Nielsen through his questioning in Tokyo, and Nielsen described being slapped around while tied to a chair, locked away in solitary confinement, and questioned so often that he never got any sleep. That had gone on, he explained, for eighteen days.

"What answers did you give to the questions?" Hendren asked.

"All I gave them," Nielsen repeated, "was my name, rank and serial number."

"At the conclusion of the eighteen days of questioning did you sign any papers?"

"Yes, sir," Nielsen admitted, "we all signed papers."

"What papers did you sign and what did they consist of?"

"Well, they were written in Japanese but they were interpreted." Nielsen explained that he had been told that the papers gave "a small sketch of our life's history—where we went to school, where we had Army training" and the fact that his plane had "bombed steel mills in the northeast area of Tokyo at the edge of a bay."

Nielsen recounted being shipped back to Shanghai, first to Bridge House and then on to Jiangwan Military Prison. Hendren asked him about his trial there in August 1942. "Do you recognize any person in this room," he asked, "as having been at the court-martial hearing?"

"Yes, sir, I do." Nielsen replied.

"Would you please point out to the commission that person or persons that are in this court?"

Nielsen glared as he pointed each man out. "Wako, the second one in the civilian clothes, and Okada in uniform."

"Were you afforded a defense counsel at the hearing?" Hendren asked.

"No, sir, we were not," Nielsen replied.

"Did any witnesses go before the tribunal while you were in the court-room?"

"There were no witnesses."

"Were you ever served any charges or advised of the charges against you?"

"No, sir, we were not."

"Were the proceedings interpreted to you in English?"

"Nothing was interpreted in English."

"How long did this hearing last?"

"From twenty minutes to a half hour."

Nielsen then described the fate of Robert Meder, who had died of "insufficient food, malnutrition, lack of medical care, dysentery and beri-beri" as well as the fates of Dean Hallmark, William Farrow, and Harold Spatz. They had been executed by the Japanese 13th Army on October 15, 1942.

"Do you know," Hendren asked, "who was commanding general of the Japanese 13th Expeditionary Army in China?"

"Yes, sir, I do," Nielsen said. "At the time it was Lieutenant General Sawada."

"Is Lieutenant General Sawada in this courtroom?"

"Yes, sir."

"Will you point him out to the commission please?"

"The man on this end and with glasses on," Nielsen answered confidently.

It went on like that all day Monday, and Nielsen never lost his stride. When evening approached, Hendren asked for a recess and Nielsen got his first taste of the press coverage.

It was everything Nielsen could have hoped for. In nearly every English-language newspaper, he was the star of the show telling his story. The Shanghai *Stars and Stripes* featured his testimony on its front page with the headline "Doolittle Flier Tells of Deaths." The papers ran photos of Nielsen in the witness chair with Hendren positioned stiffly at his side. Another newspaper featured a large photo of him posing with Bodine and Kumashiro as he lifted his pant leg to reveal his scars to the world.

* * *

Hendren's questioning continued through most of Tuesday morning and Bodine readied himself to cross-examine Nielsen. It was a daunting task. All that morning, McReynolds continued to give the same response to every objection he and Fellows could muster: "Overruled." But they had both been making notes. Could the trial in 1942 really have only been twenty to thirty minutes long? How had Nielsen picked out Wako and Okada? How had he picked out Sawada? Bodine jotted down a question to ask on cross-examination: "Is not most of your testimony based on what you have been told by the prosecution and others?"

Hendren concluded his questioning of Nielsen with selections from Dwyer's stack of photographs. As Hendren held each photo up, he asked Nielsen to name the people he recognized. Each showed one of the captured Doolittle Raiders still in their prime.

"I recognize Lieutenant Barr."

"Spatz and Sergeant DeShazer."

"Barr and Lieutenant Farrow."

"Lieutenant Hite."

Hendren then ceded the floor, and Bodine stepped up to the podium to cross-examine a witness for the first time in his life. To avoid his saying anything foolish, Bodine, Fellows, and Elizaveta had written out a script. Four typewritten pages in all, it methodically went through the key facts and presented them as questions for Nielsen. Next to particularly important facts, Fellows made sure to include references to the evidence file just in case Nielsen said something surprising.

Bodine had three goals. The first was not to embarrass himself.

The second was to show that neither Sawada, Wako, Okada, nor Tatsuta had directly been involved in any of the torture that Nielsen and the rest of the Raiders had suffered. It was the Kempeitai, the prison guards in Nanking, and the high command in Tokyo that had been to blame for everything.

The third was to get Nielsen to admit that there had been at least some damage to nonmilitary targets during the Doolittle Raid. Bodine did not need to call Nielsen a liar and a war criminal. He only needed him to admit that there had been some accidental damage. If they could show that the Doolittle Raiders had not been 100 percent accurate, either because they had been pumping with combat adrenaline or because bombing over a dense urban area is difficult, that would open the door to arguing that the charges the Japanese had levied against them had not been entirely "false and fraudulent."

Fellows wanted to go further, proposing the question "Had a Japanese plane strafed schools and children in Hyrum, Utah, would you agree the pilot should be treated as a war criminal?" But Bodine was not going to ask that question.

When the three of them had been writing out the script, they had had every reason to believe that this much should be possible. Back in December, some war crimes investigators had visited Nielsen in Utah to do a detailed interview in preparation for his trip to Shanghai. Bodine and Fellows had been given a transcript of that interview and had noticed that when Ham Young's investigators had asked Nielsen where Hallmark had dropped their incendiary bombs, Nielsen had said, "residential areas."

Bodine knew enough about munitions to know that incendiaries were basically just clusters of fireballs that scattered as soon as they left the belly of a plane. There was no way of accurately dropping incendiary bombs, and no one seriously doubted what Doolittle had meant when he had told his men to drop those incendiaries "where they would do the most good."

But Nielsen's testimony the day before had given Bodine reason to worry. His ears had perked up when Hendren had asked Nielsen an almost identical question and Nielsen had claimed to have dropped his incendiary bombs on a "steel mill area" rather than a "residential area." Which was true? Was Nielsen confused? Was he misremembering? Was he lying?

It wasn't the first time Bodine had noticed inconsistencies in Nielsen's testimony. The most sensitive involved his testimony about torture.

Nielsen's vivid descriptions, particularly of the waterboarding and the mock execution, seemed off. Nielsen had been telling his story for months, but the first time these particularly gruesome details had emerged had been when he wrote "Saga of Living Death." None of those details had been mentioned to Ham Young when he had questioned Nielsen back in Chongqing the previous August.

Young had squarely asked not only Nielsen but also Hite and DeShazer to confirm who had been subjected to the waterboard, and they had all said that only Dean Hallmark, George Barr, and Robert Meder had been singled out for that particularly notorious cruelty. Maybe Nielsen hadn't been ready to talk about it. Maybe Young had made a mistake in his notes. Whatever the truth, the litany of the horrors Nielsen suffered seemed to grow more gruesome with each retelling. As Nielsen had recounted them again on the witness stand, Bodine had jotted down a note on his legal pad: "Never mentioned in August statement the treatment."

Bodine had no desire to publicly call Chase Nielsen, Doolittle Raider, a liar. He was sensitive to all that Nielsen suffered and continued to suffer. And the longer Bodine thought about it, the more doubts he had about doing anything with this particular note.

It was not as if the things Nielsen had described never happened. With the exception of the mock execution, every horror Nielsen detailed had provably happened to at least one of the captured Doolittle Raiders. It was simply a question of whether every one of these horrors had happened to Nielsen personally. The worst that could be said was that Nielsen was recounting the experiences of his now missing or dead buddies as his own for dramatic effect.

Bodine could not very well call the Kempeitai's torturers to testify that they had tortured Nielsen *this* way but not *that* way. It was unthinkable. So Bodine scratched out his note. When he took his place at the lawyers' podium he decided it was best to stick to his script.

* * *

Dwyer looked on from the prosecution table as Bodine, the seducer of his beloved Sweater Girl, clumsily ambled his way through his first cross-examination. Dwyer understood as well as anyone else that cross-examination can be the most difficult thing a lawyer does. It is like leading a complicated dance, requiring equal measures of preparation and flexibility, a keen sense of listening, and a willingness to improvise. The cross-examiner must ensure that his or her dance partner steps in exactly the right place at exactly the right time without realizing that the foot never had a choice to step anywhere else.

What Dwyer saw, though, was Bodine reading from a script, desperately clutching his prepared questions as tightly as a baby squeezes its parents' fingers as it learns to walk.

"Isn't it a fact," Bodine asked Nielsen accusingly, "that prior to the raid on Tokyo you all—all of you fliers hated the Japs?"

"Yes, sir," Nielsen replied. "I don't think we had any more love for them than you did."

"Therefore," Bodine continued, "you would have very much liked to have killed some Japs on this raid, wouldn't you?"

"Certainly," Nielsen agreed.

"You considered, therefore, all the Japanese enemies, didn't you?"

"That is right," Nielsen snorted back. "They were. I haven't changed my mind yet."

"Then had you been ordered to, would you have strafed Japs whether they were soldiers or civilians?" Bodine said, trying to trap him.

"Through the training I have had in the Army," Nielsen said confidently, his chest of decorations glinting at Bodine, "when I go into war it is nothing but military installations and as far as innocent people are concerned, that is out. We want the military installations."

"Weren't you told to strafe and drop your incendiary bombs where they would 'do the most good,'" Bodine stammered, "in the congested areas?"

"We were told," Nielsen replied indignantly, "to use our machine guns for defense against enemy aircraft because we didn't carry too many rounds of ammunition. Told to drop our incendiary bombs where they would do the most good over some congested area like aircraft factories or oilfields."

"What was the caliber of the gun in the nose?"

"Thirty caliber," Nielsen said.

"Are you sure that none of the guns on the plane—on your plane—were fired while you were over Japan?"

"I'm absolutely sure."

"Isn't it possible that from where you were in the navigator's compartment that you couldn't hear anyway if the foldable gun in the nose fired?"

"Have you ridden in a B-25B with the nose gun?" Nielsen asked sarcastically.

"I have," Bodine shot back.

"They are quite easy to hear," Nielsen said, though for the first time slightly less sure of himself.

"I don't think so," Bodine retorted.

Dwyer was as puzzled as everyone else as Bodine's cross-examination devolved into an awkward and embarrassing argument with Nielsen over aviation acoustics. The interpreter ultimately had to interrupt them, confusedly asking "What is the answer to that question?"

"I'm waiting for the answer," Bodine said.

"Well, I definitely know they were not fired," Nielsen insisted.

At one point, Bodine floundered through a set piece that had been clearly written into his script. "In which prison do you consider it you received the worst treatment?" Bodine asked him.

"In the Bridge House," Nielsen replied.

"In which prison did you receive the next worst treatment?" Bodine continued

"While we were at Tokyo."

"The next worse treatment?"

Nielsen then caught Bodine up short with the reply "Jiangwan."

That still left Nanking and Fengtai, which everyone, including Nielsen, knew were much worse than Jiangwan. Meder had died in Nanking, and Barr had nearly died in Fengtai. But Nielsen saw where Bodine was going, just as everyone else in the courtroom did. Bodine had a line he was waiting to deliver, and Nielsen could see him clumsily double-check his script (which said in parentheses, "only if he says Jiangwan was the least worst") before awkwardly running with his set piece anyway.

"Therefore," Bodine asked, "would you say that you received the best treatment in Jiangwan Prison?"

"Not of our entire stay over here, no," Nielsen replied glibly.

"Of the three prisons, Bridge House, Tokyo, Jiangwan," Bodine asked, scrambling to recover, "would you say you received the best treatment of those three in Jiangwan?"

"Yes, I'd say we did," Nielsen conceded smugly as he watched Bodine grow more and more flustered.

From Dwyer's vantage point, only a few feet to Bodine's right and only a few more feet across from Nielsen, Bodine's cross-examination could not have gone any better for the prosecution. Nielsen was confident, consistent, and just about the most sterling example of martial credibility anyone had ever seen. Nearly an hour went by before Dwyer even felt the urge to object, and McReynolds reliably sustained that objection without a second thought, throwing Bodine a few more steps off the beat.

* * *

As the day wore on, Nielsen had more and more difficulty concealing his annoyance at Bodine's aimless badgering, though he was facing it all down with ease. But then something changed.

Nielsen looked on in respectful, if slightly contemptuous, silence as Bodine took a moment to look over his notes.

"Weren't you told to drop your incendiary bombs on the congested *residential* section?" Bodine asked, going off his script.

"We had a congested military installation to drop our bombs on," Nielsen insisted confidently. "We were directed to drop our bombs in the steel mill area, which we did."

"Then you deny," Bodine asked, "that you were told to drop the incendiary bombs in the congested residential areas?"

"I deny it," Nielsen snorted. "Yes."

"Didn't you say in a previous statement," Bodine prodded him, "that you had dropped your incendiary bomb in a congested residential area?" Bodine suddenly looked less flustered.

"What I said"—Nielsen hesitated—"as congested as Tokyo is, there was a residential area right up against the steel mill and when you drop an incendiary cluster it spreads, you just can't help it."

Bodine held up a typewritten copy of Nielsen's statement from back in December. "Didn't you make a statement to Carl L. Sebey, Special Investigator, in Utah on December 7, 1945, as follows: 'We dropped our incendiary clusters in a congested residential area.'"

"What I meant by that statement is—"

Bodine cut him off sharply. "I didn't ask what you meant."

"The witness is entitled to explain an answer," Dwyer broke in.

"The witness will answer first," McReynolds said, placating Dwyer's flash of put-on umbrage, "then explain."

"Yes, I made the statement," Nielsen replied, flustered for the first time that day.

"What I meant by that statement," Nielsen explained, "is that the bomb was dropped in the congested district, and, as I stated before, Tokyo's pretty well congested and residential districts are built right up against military objectives and industrial plants and if any of those bombs went into the residential district, that is the way it happened."

"Then, Captain," Bodine asked coolly, "why did you tell Carl L. Sebey that?"

"He was undoubtedly told that," Nielsen admitted. "I didn't write the statement up. I made the statement."

"You signed such a statement, didn't you?" Bodine pressed him.

"Yes," Nielsen admitted, "I did."

As Nielsen began to struggle with the details, the tension in the courtroom began to grow the way ice makes a wispy shuddering sound as it begins to break underfoot.

"If the Court please," Hendren interjected, coming to the rescue, "the prosecution would like to object to that line of questioning."

Bodine had failed to have the transcript of Nielsen's December statement admitted into evidence. That sent Hendren, Bodine, and McReynolds into a circular discussion about whether Nielsen's statement to Carl Sebey, Special Investigator, could even be admitted into evidence under the military commission's rules, and the confusion ultimately led Bodine to ask for a fifteen-minute recess to consult with Fellows.

Those fifteen minutes, as Bodine learned the rules of procedure, gave Nielsen time to collect himself and fix the details of his story in his mind. Bodine then returned to the podium. "Captain," he asked Nielsen, "did you sign a statement in the presence of Carl L. Sebey, Special Investigator, in Hyrum, Utah?"

"Yes," Nielsen admitted, "I signed a statement taken by Mr. Sebey."

"Is this a copy of that statement?" Bodine asked as he handed Nielsen a copy.

Nielsen took a moment to leaf through the forty-three pages of transcript. It was all there. He had signed it. It was even notarized. But he was uncertain about what it all said. He had told his story so many times that he actually was beginning to forget. But those were his words.

"Yes, sir," Nielsen conceded, "that is a copy of the statement."

Bodine then turned back to McReynolds with a flourish of awkward legal jargon: "If it please the Commission, then, I offer this statement in evidence as Defense Exhibit 'A.'"

Hendren tried to object again, but McReynolds was tired of the technicalities. "The Commission will accept the statement as evidence in the record."

*　*　*

For the first time that day, Bodine was in control. His competitive instinct to win had kicked in the way it always had on the gridiron. So he looked back over his notes instead of his script.

Bodine had jotted down a note the day before as Nielsen had testified about the Japanese documents he had signed while being held in Tokyo. On the witness stand, Nielsen had said he had signed them because the Japanese lawyer, Well-Well, had told him that the documents were just some benign "sketch of his life history." Since his arrival in Shanghai, Nielsen had been emphatic that he had never confessed to anything; that he had never given up any information beyond his name, rank, and serial number. But Bodine remembered something else from Nielsen's December statement. Young's war crimes investigators had asked Nielsen if Well-Well had told him that the Japanese documents were a confession.

Now at the podium, Bodine recited Nielsen's answer back to him. "He explained it only after I signed it. He told me then that it was a confession to the crime of bombing school buildings and strafing Japanese civilians. I laughed at him then and told him that he knew that it was not true. He made no answer to my statement."

Bodine then looked up from his papers and turned his competitor's stare onto Nielsen. Was this his statement from December?

"I never did make a statement like that," Nielsen erupted, "because I knew nothing about the fact that we were even sentenced for bombing schools and strafing schoolchildren until we were in Nanking."

"I ask you again," Bodine pressed him, "did you sign this statement?"

"Yes, I signed that statement." But, Nielsen protested, "I'm sure that statement was never made to Mr. Sebey."

"I don't think you understand me, captain," Bodine said with a sharp stiff arm. "The question was asked to you at this time and you gave this answer." Bodine read Nielsen's statement back to him again. "Now I ask you, did you make this statement or do you deny making this statement?"

"I deny making the statement." With every utterance of the word "statement," Nielsen floundered more.

"May I interrupt the defense counsel for the moment?" Lieutenant Colonel Berry, the most junior of the judges, stepped in to try to help Nielsen. "It seems there is something peculiar to the word 'statement.' When you say statement I think the witness does not know which statement you refer to."

Bodine turned back to Nielsen. "In *this* statement that you signed at Utah in the presence of Carl L. Sebey, you are asked the question by Sebey: 'Did Well-Well explain the contents of this paper?'"

Nielsen stayed silent.

"That is the paper that you signed in Tokyo," Bodine continued, making sure he was clear. "And you made this answer to him—to Sebey at Utah: 'He explained it only after I had signed it. He told me then that it was a confession to the crime of bombing school buildings and strafing Japanese civilians. I laughed at him and then told him that he knew that it was not true. He made no answer to my statement.'

"Now I ask you," Bodine said, "did you give this answer to Sebey?"

"I don't deny signing the paper in Tokyo." Nielsen pointed to the paper Bodine was holding. "I don't deny signing that paper there but I *do* deny giving that answer to that question."

Another of the military judges, Colonel Murphy, broke in from the bench to offer relief. "As I understand it, this is a copy of a document produced in Utah last fall which incorporates a translation of a statement signed by the witness in Tokyo in 1942, is that correct?"

"No, sir," Bodine corrected him. "This is the 'Testimony of Captain Nielsen in the Matter of the Capture and Subsequent Imprisonment of

Captain Nielsen.' It was given to Carl L. Sebey, SIC, at Hyrum, Utah, on December 7, 1945."

Bodine had caught Nielsen in a lie or at least a severe lapse of memory. Nielsen continued to insist that he had not given the answer, that Sebey must have misunderstood him, that he had not signed a confession in Tokyo, but his protests became increasingly and awkwardly unbelievable.

Bodine then thought again about the unthinkable note that he had crossed out. This confession to Well-Well had no doubt been the product of torture, but Nielsen had repeatedly claimed, both in his statements to the press and on the stand the day before, that he had never broken under torture. To admit that he had signed a confession would mean that one of two things was true: either Nielsen was a war criminal, or he could be made to talk. Nielsen was unwilling to admit either, so Bodine pressed him for the truth.

"What," Bodine asked, "were the questions you were asked in Shanghai right after your capture?"

"Where I came from; if I was American army personnel, and what I was doing in this portion of China," Nielsen replied.

"What questions did they ask of you in Tokyo?"

"Well, similar questions."

"Did you consider all these questions they asked, did you consider them of great military importance?"

"I didn't consider any of them of military importance."

"Do you mean to tell the commission," Bodine asked in mock disbelief, "that you took all this punishment rather than tell these unimportant questions?"

"I mean to say that," Nielsen stumbled out, "I took the punishment to avoid answering those questions to avoid answering more questions that would've followed."

What about the moment he had signed the confession for Well-Well in Tokyo? Bodine asked. "Were you being tortured then?"

"No, I was not being tortured," Nielsen admitted.

"How is it then, captain," Bodine pressed him, "that you signed this document in Tokyo when you had taken so much worse treatment and refused to give any information before?"

"I signed the document," Nielsen protested, "to avoid getting the treatment I'd been getting, because I was subject to the same thing."

Bodine could see that Nielsen was struggling. He was holding on tight, but the stress of being on the witness stand, of rifling through his memories and trying to distinguish what was true and what was just a story, was causing him to unravel.

Bodine confronted a choice: he could back off and release the pressure on his brother in arms, or he could dig his cleats into the turf and drive his shoulder into Nielsen's solar plexus.

"Do you expect me to believe, then, that all this trouble was to obtain a statement of no importance from you?" Bodine asked, digging in. "Isn't it more reasonable to believe it was a full confession?"

"It may be," Nielsen barked back. "It can be most anything!"

And there it was. Nielsen had admitted to having broken under torture. Though he still refused to admit that he had knowingly signed a confession, all of his denials, all his prior flashes of "name, rank, and serial number" bravado suddenly rang hollow. It was not something Bodine could say or needed to say, but for a moment, Nielsen looked like someone who had forgotten what the truth was.

*　　*　　*

The tension in the silences between the questions and answers had reached a breaking point. Nielsen had grown to hate Bodine as he watched him again look away from his script and back down into his notes.

"You stated yesterday, captain, that Lieutenant General Sawada was the commanding general of the 13th Army," Bodine said. "How did you know this?"

"This has been decided through investigation by Major Dwyer and I since I came back over here," Nielsen replied.

"Then all your testimony regarding General Sawada," Bodine continued, "is based on what the prosecution has told you and what you have seen with them, is that true?"

"My testimony against General Sawada is based on this fact," Nielsen snapped. "That he was in command of the 13th Japanese Army here and responsible for the execution of my three buddies!"

It was an honest answer but a foolish one. Nielsen was exhausted. He had been on the stand for two days, enduring Bodine's questioning for hours, as every inconsistency in his story, every inconsistency in everything he had ever said, was brought into the unfair and unforgiving light of the world's attention. Nielsen resented it, and he resented Bodine.

Bodine had only one more question, but first he asked to have Nielsen's December statement to Carl Sebey read into the record in its entirety. McReynolds agreed.

The insult of it, the frustration of it, welled up furiously, but Nielsen had to sit quietly on the witness stand as all of the contradictions leaped out. Once the rereading was done, Bodine asked Nielsen if that was, in fact, the statement he had made back in December.

"Yes, sir." Nielsen admitted curtly.

Bodine turned to McReynolds and, like a real lawyer, a real lawyer used to the routines and trite phrases of the profession, said, "That is all."

* * *

For Nielsen, it was a relief to see Hendren get back up to the podium. He was there to help, to wrap Nielsen in the American flag, and to remind everyone that he was a Doolittle Raider. "Captain Nielsen," Hendren asked, "are you the sole surviving member of your plane which bombed Tokyo in April 1942?"

"I'm the only one of my crew left from the raid," Nielsen said ruefully.

"So, Captain Nielsen, you are the only living person who knows what happened on that raid?"

"Yes, I'm the only one."

"Captain Nielsen, on that raid, did that plane in which you were riding, bomb or strafe anything but military objects in its raid over Tokyo or over Japan?"

"We bombed nothing but military installations," Nielsen said defiantly.

"That is all." Hendren went to sit down, but before Nielsen could get up from the witness stand, McReynolds unexpectedly interrupted him. The judges had some questions, and they were all about his good-for-nothing December statement.

"Prior to signing the statement on 27 December," Colonel Gamber asked Nielsen, "did you carefully read it over?"

"Mr. Sebey took the statements from me in shorthand," Nielsen told him. "He returned to Fort Douglas, typed them up, and sent the statement up for me to sign and have notarized and I had talked so much about this bomb raid I didn't care to read it over anymore. I signed it in front of a notary and that was the size of it."

Lieutenant Colonel Berry then asked about the inconsistencies Bodine had drawn out between his testimony and his December statement. "Do you wish me to read the answer to you again?" Berry asked.

"No, sir." Nielsen chuckled. "I think I know what it is." But he could take no comfort in Berry's reaction.

"Well," Berry said, brooking no humor, "I believe I'll reread the answer so you will know what it is." He then did so, focusing especially on where Nielsen had admitted to signing a "confession to the crime of bombing school buildings and strafing Japanese civilians."

It was excruciating to hear that line again and again, but Nielsen stuck defiantly to his denials even after Colonel Murphy tried to give him an opportunity to confess a little confusion.

"Your position then," Colonel Murphy asked, "is that neither this conversation about bombing of schools and hospitals, women and children, took place with Well-Well. Not only did it not take place with Well-Well, but that it did not take place either in Salt Lake City with Sebey with respect to what you told Well-Well when Well-Well asked you."

"Yes sir," Nielsen insisted.

McReynolds looked from side to side. "There appear to be no more questions," McReynolds said. "The witness is excused."

TWENTY

As Nielsen stepped down from the witness stand, Dwyer knew he had a problem. His perfect witness had tried to be too perfect. He had gotten caught, and Bodine, the pilot who hadn't even finished law school, had been the one to catch him. It had been as unexpected as it was consequential.

If McReynolds and the rest of the judges now believed that Nielsen had, in fact, signed a confession, that would undermine Dwyer's whole theory of their case. True, he and Hendren could still argue that the confessions had been extorted under torture, but that would require them to agree that Nielsen had been lying or misremembering. If he could not be trusted about one thing, how could anything else he had said be trusted? Could he even be trusted when it came to his allegations of torture?

Dwyer needed another of the Doolittle Raiders to testify, to corroborate the key facts that would make or break his case, if they were to persuade McReynolds and the rest of the judges that Sawada and his gang deserved the gallows for the torture and murder of the Doolittle Raiders. They needed George Barr.

* * *

After Nielsen, Hite, and DeShazer had left Beijing, none of them had heard from Barr again, and it seemed obvious why. When Ray Nichols had called the OSS medic over to inspect Barr's marionette of a body, the signs of life he had shown could be easily written off as medical technicalities. His pulse was easy to miss, and had Barr been anyone else, the odds were that he would have been assigned to the black end of the triage spectrum, where the only things military medicine had to offer were enough syrettes of morphine to make him good with the inevitable. But Barr was not anyone else. He was a Doolittle Raider.

Barr awoke a few weeks after the Raiders' rescue by the OSS, alone in Beijing, to see a Chinese nurse hooking a tube to the needle that was already in his arm. "It will give you strength," the man had said to him in English. "And you will soon be well again."

For Barr, it was a relief to be alive, but he was suspicious. Barr could never tell the Chinese apart from the Japanese, and it was unclear what kind of gunk they were putting into his veins. At least two of the bags that had been hung above him were blood, but there was no telling what was in the others.

The last clear memories Barr had were from early August. He remembered sweltering alone on the floor of his cell in Fengtai, wondering how long it would be before he would die as Meder had in Nanking Prison. He had watched Meder wither away until that day in early December 1943.

Barr had been helping to deliver the food. The day's ration for each man was portioned onto a little metal plate, and Barr's job had been to walk down the corridor, delivering the plates to the cells like a waiter on a train. That was when he had found Meder dead in his cell. No good had come from it. The only thing that had changed after Meder's death was that Nanking Prison had switched from metal plates to plastic bowls.

Meder's ashes had been put into a glass jar that was placed in a cardboard box that was tied with a string. That box had then been put into Meder's cell, which was right across the hall from Barr's. It was a strange kind of mausoleum, seemingly intended to remind them all that this prison was to be their crypt. Barr had made it his mission in life to keep track of Meder's ashes and had kept his vigil the entire time they were in Nanking, but when they were all transferred to Fengtai, the ashes had gone missing.

Barr had asked anyone who would listen whether Meder had been brought with them, but no one had ever given him an answer. Lying limp in the early August heat, bathing in a pool of sweat on the floor of his cell in Fengtai, Barr knew that it was only a matter of time before he would find himself namelessly filed away inside a glass jar and placed in a cardboard box tied with a string.

The next thing Barr knew, though, he was in a Chinese hospital with Canadian and British roommates. They spoke English and seemed nice enough, and all of them seemed to be relishing the end of the war. It was magic.

Barr had no memory of the war having ended. There were just fever dreams, like the one in which he was in Heaven with Robert Hite, who cheered him on with his syrupy Texas drawl, "Come on, George, wake up! It's all over now. We're free!" But there was nothing real he could hold on to.

Everyone tried to convince Barr that the war was over—that the Americans had developed the atomic bomb and forced Japan to surrender unconditionally—but it just didn't ring true. If the war was over, where were the other Doolittle Raiders? Why was there gunfire in the distance? Why was he stuck in this room?

Lying on his back day after day, Barr had never felt so alone. Even the years in solitary confinement had felt safer. He had known what the bastards were up to. Now he did not know what to believe. The American doctor, the Canadian and British roommates, were they all stooges? The voice in his head, as it assembled his paranoid doubts, spoke with greater and greater confidence as it explained that this was all part of some new Japanese conspiracy to torment him.

In the middle of September, Barr was flown on a stretcher to the US Army hospital in Kunming but the change in scenery did little to help. As convincing as a massive US Army base might seem to be, Barr's conspiracy theory simply grew in its grandeur. The big giveaway was how the supposedly "American" nurses would check on him by peering through the window on the door of his room with the exact same sinister glare as the Japanese had. And so Barr retreated into silence. He was not going to say anything to incriminate himself any further. He remembered the straitjacket. He remembered the waterboard. He knew what those people were capable of.

Making matters worse, who Barr was and how he had gotten to Kunming had been lost in the bureaucratic paper machine along the way. To the medical staff in Kunming, Barr was just "Case No. 269." His attending physicians reasonably assumed that his ramblings about the Doolittle Raid were delusions; he was not their first patient with wild fantasies of wartime glory and torture at the hands of the Japanese. Anyone who had seen the movie *The Purple Heart* could have told the same stories.

Barr had awakened into a world where no one around him believed the one thing that he knew for certain was true. The Doolittle Raid was the greatest thing he had ever done in his life. He had celebrated his twenty-fifth birthday a week into the voyage on the *Hornet* and would never forget having breakfast in the mess hall when he had gotten the call that it was time to go, rushing up to the deck with his camera, some candy bars, and a carton of cigarettes. He had packed for adventure like a little boy running away with the circus. He knew who he was. He knew what had happened. And if all these so-called doctors and nurses didn't believe him, it was just natural for him not to believe them and their tall tales about atomic bombs and unconditional surrender.

As the weeks went by, Barr's physical strength returned. Still, maintaining the coherence of his paranoid delusions proved mentally exhausting, and he assumed that his difficulty in keeping his thoughts together was the effect of some pernicious Oriental poison. He started refusing food, medication, and treatment of any kind. When he did talk, it was to tell the nursing staff that he knew what they were up to or to tell them where they could shove the so-called thermometer. One night, he woke up screaming, and when he jumped out of bed, orderlies rushed in. It took three men to restrain him as he gritted his teeth and made what the nurse recorded in Case No. 269's chart as "animal-like sounds with occasional threats to his 'torturers.'"

In early October, Case No. 269 was slated for return to the United States. Barr strolled out onto the tarmac to the C-47 that was supposedly there to return him home, and he looked out to the horizon. It was a broad view of the sky that he had not seen in more than three years. The beauty of its openness filled his chest like a cool breath. It overwhelmed him. He was free. At long last, he was free. He wasn't tied to anything. No one was holding his arms. It was just him and that great big open sky. And so, before anyone could be the wiser, he made a break for it.

Barr bolted down the tarmac. The further he got, the firmer his conviction was that he would never be trapped like an animal again. He would run off the edge of the world if he had to. He ran and ran until everything stopped with a blunt black thud.

Barr awoke inside the tight confines of a C-47. He was on his back again. When he tried to sit up, the sheet pulled him back down tightly. He tried to uncross his arms, but he couldn't. The Japanese had put him back into the straitjacket.

Barr was ultimately admitted into a hospital in San Francisco with no identification or records. The orderlies perfunctorily led him to a room by himself and offered him some new pajamas.

Left alone, Barr paced about, unsure of what would happen next or what he was supposed to do. No one told him to do or not do anything. He was just there in his small hospital room with nothing but life ahead of him.

Then Barr noticed a small pocketknife on the nightstand. He immediately understood what the Japanese were up to. They wanted to see if they had finally made him into an animal. Had he learned to be helpless? Would he just stay in his cage? Or would he claim his dignity the traditional way by committing seppuku?

Barr unfolded the blade, held it before him, and stabbed himself in the chest. It stung, but the blade was too small and dull to do more than draw a little blood. Nevertheless, he had done it. He had passed the test. He was still a man, and he wasn't going to let himself be played by any more Japanese games. If all that was ahead of him was life in this small room, he was not about to just mill about in his new pajamas.

Barr scrambled for another solution. The window was open, but he was on the second floor, only high enough to break an ankle. He then saw a small electric space heater in the room across the hall. When the coast was clear, he snatched it and fashioned its cord into a noose around his neck. He pulled up a chair, knotted the cord to the overhead light, and kicked his feet free. His body jolted as the cord pulled into his neck. His feet seemed to be having second thoughts because they were reaching for the chair, but the rest of him just swung and dangled. Then, as he was making himself good with the inevitable, sparks started to shower him. Before he could make sense of it, he was on the floor in a heap of glass.

Barr's failed suicide attempt landed him in a padded room in the high-security mental ward. His attending physician noted in his chart that he "was supposed to be one of the original Doolittle fliers" but that this must have been an error; he was just another "disturbed mental." He was tied again into a straitjacket and put onto the next train to Schick General Hospital in Clinton, Iowa. As the train rolled across the great American plains, Barr looked out his window at the vast barrenness of what he was sure was China.

Barr would have probably stayed just another anonymous mental case had it not been for Charles and Eleanor Townes, a childless couple in New York, who had made a charity case of Barr when he was just another orphan boy in Brooklyn. Barr had sent them a short note from his hospital bed back in September 1945, telling them how he had made it through the war. But when no further word had come, Eleanor Townes had reached out to Jimmy Doolittle, who had promised her that he would do everything he could to help her jigger the Army bureaucracy that had swallowed their boy up whole.

In the middle of November, Townes tracked Barr down to Schick General's maximum-security mental ward. Doolittle paid Barr a personal visit right around Thanksgiving.

Doolittle bounded into the visiting room of Schick General, all eyes upon him and his trademark ebullience. He threw his hand into Barr's as if it were nothing. "Hi, George!" he said, beaming. "It's good to see you. How are you?"

Barr's eyes filled with tears. For weeks, nothing had convinced anyone of who Barr really was and nothing had convinced Barr of where he really was. It could all be explained away. But Jimmy Doolittle's broad grin could not be. It was the first time Barr knew he was home.

* * *

Back in the Shanghai courtroom, Dwyer had a flash of genius. Barr was still thousands of miles away and would never, could never, come back to this place. In a court-martial, indeed in any other American trial, Barr would have been out of reach. But this was a military commission.

Dwyer called Hendren to the stand, and Hendren explained how after discovering that Barr was alive, they had immediately sent a special agent to his hospital room in Clinton, Iowa, to get his story. Dwyer pulled out the transcript of that interview, gave copies to each of the judges, and placed his own on the podium in front of him. Dwyer then announced that he would reveal to the world the dramatic story of George Barr.

Dwyer had spent months building this case from behind the scenes.

Now he was in the spotlight. As he steadied himself for his first big moment of the trial, all eyes on him, he was abruptly interrupted by Colonel Murphy, who was leafing through his copy of Barr's statement.

"Has this been declassified?" Murphy asked.

"I don't know whether that has been declassified or not," Dwyer replied anxiously, "but I know there has been a precedent set, particularly in the case of *United States v. Yamashita*, where documents classified as high secret were read into the record."

"Read to non-military personnel?"

"Read in open court," Dwyer assured him. "I can state for the record that I was present when that occurred."

Barr's statement was more than fifty pages long, and Lieutenant Colonel Berry, undoubtedly just as exhausted as everyone else by Nielsen's two days of testimony, stopped Dwyer just as he prepared to hold forth again.

"You have offered the statement or whatever it is as an exhibit," Berry said. "Can you save time by failing to read it into the record and supplying each member of the Commission a copy of it?"

Dwyer persisted, even though Berry was probably justified in his request. Dwyer gave the excuse that the court reporters needed him to read it aloud. Of course, Dwyer could have just given them a copy, but there were news reporters to think about, too. He could not simply hand them a fifty-one-page document conspicuously marked CLASSIFIED on every page. Dwyer also knew that the drama of Barr's experiences would be lost not just on the press but on the judges if it was simply left in black and white. The only way to convey it effectively was to read it aloud word by agonizing word.

McReynolds allowed it, and so, for the remainder of the day and the whole of the next morning, Dwyer played the part of George Barr, describing with bracing specificity and total credibility the torture he had experienced at the hands of the Japanese.

Barr's description of the waterboard, in particular, was chilling. It had happened the day after the raid, when he and the rest of the crew of the *Bat Out of Hell* had been flown from Nanchang to the Japanese headquarters in Nanking. Up until that point, the Japanese had been more interested in snapping pictures of them than anything else, and Barr had been happy to oblige. He had even smiled for the camera.

Things had changed when they had gotten to Nanking. The questioning had been impatient and incessant. For a while, Barr had kept his mouth shut, sticking to his name, rank, and serial number as he had been trained to do. He was blindfolded and cuffed to a chair and took a fair bit of punishment as they all took swings at him. But before he knew it, the bastards had wrestled him to the ground and snaked a rag over his face, leaving his nose open, and started pouring water in.

Barr had tried to hold his breath as the water spattered on his face, but eventually a few bubbles had started to escape and the water wriggled into any gap and crevice in his sinuses where air might have been hiding. Every fitful effort to snort the water out had opened up new opportunities for it to leach in more deeply. Barr had tried to twist his face away from the spout to defeat their technique, to get the water out and let the air back in, but he couldn't. He had been pinned to the floor by stiff, indifferent hands, and so, from his sinuses, the water had slithered to the back of his throat and then into his lungs, where it had put the panic of death into him. The stiff hands had held firm as the water seeped into Barr's chest, but just as he had begun to make himself good with the inevitable, the officer in charge had given the signal to stop.

Flipped onto his side, Barr had vomited the water out of his lungs in heaves, until he could cough. He had coughed until he could catch a breath, and once it looked as if he was about to return to his senses, the officer in charge had given the signal to do it again. On had gone the rag, then the spatter, then the bubbling into the sinuses, then the slither into the throat and lungs, and then the weight of the water as it pushed the life out of him from the inside. It had gone like that, round and round, until Barr was willing to elaborate beyond his name, rank, and serial number.

"The water was going down into my lungs," Barr said, trying to explain why his training on keeping his mouth shut had failed. "It just stopped your breathing."

*　*　*

Dwyer reached the end of his testimony on behalf of George Barr, Doolittle Raider, close to lunchtime. In the final pages of his dramatic reading, Dwyer conveyed a loss that was even more tragic than the horror of the waterboard.

"When did you first hear of the death of Lieutenant Dean E Hallmark, Lieutenant William G Farrow, and Sergeant Harold A. Spatz?" Barr had been asked.

"We never did learn of their death, just their disappearance," he had replied. "We never knew what really happened to them."

"When did you find out for the first time what happened to them?"

"Well, I haven't given up hope yet."

There it was. Even in December 1945, three months after the ashes of Hallmark, Farrow, and Spatz had turned up in mismarked urns at International Funeral Directors in Shanghai, Barr had remained in a mix of ignorance and denial. He was a Rip Van Winkle who had become lost to the world not in sleep but in agony. The Army had failed him once when it had lost him in the shuffle as just another mental case of the postwar demobilization. Now, at this trial, it could make amends. George Barr was a Doolittle Raider. It was the Army's chance to give him the justice he deserved.

TWENTY-ONE

The trial continued for the next six days, and Dwyer methodically presented the finer points of the prosecution's case. Like the story of George Barr, the crucial pieces of evidence were not testimony from witnesses but written statements and documents.

The rules of evidence had been changed to allow witnesses to submit written statements rather than testify in person. As a strictly legal matter, that made Dwyer's case easier to prove. Instead of forcing Jimmy Doolittle to fly all the way to Shanghai to be cross-examined on what he had meant when he told his men to drop their incendiary bombs where they would "do the most good," Dwyer could simply do his best Jimmy Doolittle impression and read aloud Doolittle's sworn statement that "any damage to civilians or civilian property was an unfortunate circumstance incident to the military operations, and not premeditated."

There was a downside, though: there would be no photographs of Doolittle and Dwyer standing shoulder to shoulder. The trial also got boring as each document was painstakingly read aloud for the court reporters and simultaneously translated into Japanese. One of the things that had made Yamashita's trial so sensational was the long parade of witnesses, Filipinos mostly, who had recounted the horrors that had been inflicted upon them during the Battle of Manila. The Doolittle Trial, on the other hand, increasingly had all the courtroom drama of a dictation exercise, and Hendren began fretting as the press coverage started to fall off the front page of even the local Shanghai papers.

Dwyer was building to a big finish, one that was certain to recapture the public's imagination and rekindle the fading wartime spirit, but in the six days it took him to get there, things were getting tedious. And to make matters worse, he was running into unexpected problems.

* * *

Moritada Kumashiro could not have been prouder of himself as Dwyer faltered and fumbled. Kumashiro thought Dwyer was a bully. Ryuhei Okada was a gentle, philosophical soul, and Kumashiro could see the stress was wearing on him.

Being there made Kumashiro feel like a good friend, and he enjoyed the opportunity to play at being a lawyer, just like in the movies. Most of the witnesses Dwyer and Hendren called to testify were Japanese, and Bodine was happy to leave the cross-examinations to his Japanese colleagues. Working through translators had been wearying for everyone. It always seemed as if something was being lost between the languages, and Kumashiro felt he had risen to the occasion by getting important facts out of Dwyer's witnesses, such as that the 11th Army, not Sawada's 13th Army, had been in control of Nanchang, where Farrow's crew had been captured; that the Kempeitai had been under its own chain of command altogether; and that Jacob DeShazer had admitted to firing his gun indiscriminately around Ise Bay.

Kumashiro was also justly satisfied with himself as he watched Dwyer grow more and more livid with frustration. Without Tadahiro Hayama as a witness, Dwyer had no one to testify about what had been in the missing Japanese case file. Hayama had told Dwyer that he had seen cable traffic directly between Sawada and Tokyo orchestrating the executions of the Doolittle Raiders. He had painted Sawada as the kind of mastermind that everyone in America wanted to see hanged by the neck until dead. It had been one of Dwyer's big breakthroughs in the case.

Now, all Dwyer could do was read aloud from a thirteen-page statement that the Doolittle Raiders' prosecutor, Itsuro Hata, had written from his hospital bed in Tokyo before dying of stomach ulcers the previous January. Yes, it put the blame squarely on Sawada for allowing the trial and execution to be directed from Tokyo, but it did not paint him as anything like the mastermind Hayama had described.

Hata, alive or dead, was also anything but a credible witness. Before Hayama had told Dwyer about the missing case file that directly implicated Sawada, everyone had believed that the closest thing to a mastermind in the case of the Doolittle Raiders was "the prosecutor." It was the prosecutor who had given Tatsuta all of his orders and instructions. It was the prosecutor who had taken the blank pieces of paper that at least some of the Raiders had signed. It was the prosecutor who had told Tatsuta he could loot Dean Hallmark's bomber jacket. Hata's motive to pass the blame to anyone but himself was obvious.

Dwyer blamed Hayama's presence at the defense table for why he was now struggling, and it was not just the missing case file. The previous November, Dwyer had interviewed a dozen soldiers from the 13th Army and they had assured Dwyer that Tatsuta not only had supervised the executions of Hallmark, Farrow, and Spatz, but had also given the order to fire. Even Shoshin Ito, the head of the 13th Army's Legal Department, had said as much to Hendren back in Tokyo.

As a legal matter, it was an insignificant point. Who cared whether Tatsuta had said the word "Fire"? He had seen to it that Hallmark, Farrow, and Spatz were tied to crosses and had bull's-eyes painted on their foreheads. Dwyer, though, wanted to put the proverbial gun in Tatsuta's hand. He wanted a clear picture in the judge's minds of the fatal word "Fire" coming out of Tatsuta's mustachioed lips. He assumed that his witnesses from the 13th Army would put it there, but when they finally got onto the stand, Dwyer's clear picture suddenly became blurry.

"Do you remember who gave the command to fire?" Dwyer would ask, expecting to hear Tatsuta's name, only to be met with some variation on "I do not remember" or, even worse, the claim that "As a civilian attached to the Army, I'm afraid that he had no power to directly order military personnel that comprised firing squad." That, in turn, put Dwyer into the awkward position of having to challenge the credibility of his own witnesses and accusing them of changing their stories.

"I think the defense will have to object," Fellows said in his aw-shucks kind of way, "to the prosecution's attempt to impeach his own witness."

Dwyer was not one to control his temper, so he didn't. "In the first place," he thundered, "the witness is obviously a hostile witness. There can be no doubt about that. This man tied one of the fliers to the cross. He is a member of the same outfit. Previously he tied one of those fliers to the cross."

"The defense objection is overruled," McReynolds said predictably.

Dwyer accused Hayama of intimidating his witnesses and sought to drive the point home by asking one particularly recalcitrant witness, a Japanese warrant officer who had come down from Jiangwan, to point Hayama out in the courtroom.

"Do you know Lieutenant Hayama?" Dwyer demanded.

"I do," the warrant officer replied.

"Do you see him in the court room?"

"He is."

"Point him out," Dwyer barked out as an order, rather than a question.

The warrant officer silently complied.

"For the record, the witness points to Lieutenant Hayama," Dwyer said disdainfully, "one of the defense counsel."

In his frustration, Dwyer took the stand himself and had Hendren question him about the questions and answers he had gotten from the now recalcitrant witnesses a few months earlier.

Bodine took the chance to object, just as Dwyer had done when Bodine had been struggling to cross-examine Nielsen. "Are they trying to impeach their own witnesses?" Bodine asked. "If they have any further questions to ask, the witnesses are here."

Hendren acknowledged that it was an odd thing to do but said, "I think it is proper for the record and it is evidence that has probative value before the commission."

"Objection overruled," McReynolds said. "Proceed."

Exchanges like these left Kumashiro feeling that his cultivation of Hayama had contributed more to the defense than Shinji Somiya had—and that gave him tremendous pleasure.

Somiya and Kumashiro had disliked each other almost instantly, despite the fact that they had very similar backgrounds. Like Kumashiro, Somiya had been an idealist in the early days of the war and had gone to Manila as an adviser to the Japanese government in the hope of making the Philippines self-sustaining, just as Kumashiro had sought to do for the Chinese in Shanghai. And like Kumashiro, Somiya had grown frustrated by the Japanese Army's greater interest in extracting the natural resources from Japan's new protectorates than modernizing them.

But Somiya had become an easy nemesis, even easier, in some ways, than Dwyer. It was not simply that he threatened Kumashiro's pride of place on the defense team, it was that Somiya could not help but remind everyone how educated he was. He tended to cross his arms and tilt his massive head back when he spoke, which, because he was so short, was the only way he could look down his nose at Kumashiro. He also tended to put so much gravel into his voice that it sounded as though speaking to someone so uneducated caused him pain.

But Kumashiro knew his business. He knew people. And he knew that keeping Hayama off the stand and at the defense table did more for their case than the Geneva Conventions, the US Constitution, and the volumes in every law school library in the world combined. In this courtroom battle, Kumashiro thought, "having Hayama as an ally was worth one million soldiers."

* * *

The previous week had been bruising for Dwyer, but he wasn't finished yet. The story of a violent crime is a story about pain, and a good prosecutor can channel that pain into the courtroom, can recall the victim's pain for those sitting in the relative comfort of a jury box or on the judge's bench, and can persuade everyone who is listening to feel that pain as if it were a memory of their own.

Dwyer began his finale by calling the director of International Funeral Directors in Shanghai, who identified four wooden boxes, each smaller than a hatbox and draped with a small American flag. The funeral director recounted how the three urns had been brought to him in October 1942 by soldiers from the 13th Army, who had instructed him to register them under fake names. But, Dwyer had him explain, they had real names now:

"From Smith to Hallmark"
"Gande to Farrow"
"Brister to Spatz"

Dwyer then handed him the flag-draped box containing the ashes of Robert Meder and neatly assembled all four flag-draped boxes on the judge's bench. Dwyer solemnly picked one up into his two hands as a photographer snapped a flattering shot of him in profile.

"The prosecution," Dwyer said, "now offers in evidence as Exhibit 'C,' the ashes of Lieutenant Dean E. Hallmark, Lieutenant William Glover Farrow, Sergeant Harold A. Spatz and Lieutenant Robert J. Meder."

The stage was now set for Dwyer's last witness, Colonel George Armstrong, the Army's top surgeon for the China Theater. With twenty-one years of experience as a physician, Armstrong was impressive and utterly credible.

Dwyer read Armstrong a long biographical history of Robert Meder and described in clinical detail the inadequate diet he had endured at Bridge House and throughout his years of captivity by the Japanese. In December 1943, Meder's weight had fallen from 175 pounds to 110 pounds, and when he had died, Dwyer explained, "he suffered from swelling of the ankles and knees and from dysentery, beriberi and general physical debility," adding "that his general diet throughout this period consisted of rice, soup and fish, about six ounces a meal, three times a day."

"Now," Dwyer concluded, "Colonel Armstrong, assuming these facts to be true, can you state, in light of your medical experience, with reasonable certainty whether or not the flow of circumstances herein described, which began with his imprisonment and court-martial, was a proximate cause of the death of Lieutenant Meder?"

"If the court please," Fellows interjected with an I-don't-know-where-to-begin impatience, "the defense has many objections to such a question being asked."

McReynolds stopped him. "Let us get this translated first."

Everyone waited as the translator plodded through Dwyer's lengthy chronology and the particulars of Meder's diet while in the Japanese prison. When the translator finished, Dwyer defended his question. "The witness can answer whether or not he can state on the facts or not."

"This particular hypothetical question has many controversial issues of fact," Fellows insisted, "including several facts which I'm sure the record definitely shows not to be true."

Dwyer, however, was ready and gave no ground. "The evidence on each and every point stated in the hypothetical question has been offered," he said confidently. "Whether it is believed by the commission or not is something of course that neither defense counsel nor prosecution know."

Dwyer then used Fellows's objection as an opportunity to reiterate the most damning facts leading to Meder's death.

"The commission," McReynolds said, overruling Fellows, "will hear the answer and the commission will consider all the assumptions as pointed out to it by the prosecution, and will weigh the answer."

"My answer is 'Yes,'" Armstrong replied crisply. "My opinion is that the individual in your question died from beriberi, as the symptoms that you have described are that of an advanced stage of which we call chronic beriberi. Chronic beriberi is due to lack of certain elements in the diet, principally a vitamin deficiency."

"Would you say, Colonel," Dwyer continued, "that the facts assumed in the hypothetical question were generally the proximate cause of the death of Lieutenant Meder?"

"Your dietary history alone would be sufficient," Armstrong said, "the others being contributory only."

As Dwyer sat down, Fellows approached the podium. It was clear that Dwyer had gotten under his skin. "Colonel," he asked sarcastically, "in the original hypothetical question, let us further suppose that this hypothetical Lieutenant Meder had been injured by a plane crash. Would that have contributed to his death?"

Dwyer jumped to his feet. "We object to Lieutenant Meder being referred to as a hypothetical," he said solemnly. "He is a very real person."

Fellows pressed on, trying to take a page out of John Hendren's playbook. In Hendren's famous mercy killing case, he had won by suggesting that something other than the two slugs of lead from his client's pistol had killed the poor sergeant as he had burned to death in a flaming heap of wreckage. "Is it not true, Colonel," Fellows asked, "that different men's systems demand different diets?"

"That is true."

"What may be sufficient for the diet of one man may be entirely insufficient for the diet of another?"

"That is true."

"Isn't it therefore very difficult on the hypothetical question given by Major Dwyer to give an accurate opinion?"

"With the time element involved," Armstrong began, "with the diet over that period described, and the symptoms described, the diagnosis is unquestionable and the death undoubtedly the result of cardiac failure which we know he had because of the swelling of the legs which was described in this case."

Fellows sat down, silent and embarrassed. Instead of stumping his witness, his questioning had made the image of Meder suffering from beriberi all the more vivid in everyone's mind.

"Colonel," Colonel Murphy chimed in from the bench as if to drive the point home, "what are the generally recognizable symptoms of early and advanced beriberi?"

"In adults," Armstrong explained, "beriberi symptoms are painful muscles, loss of appetite, loss of weight, painful sensation in the extremities, nausea and from the beginning diarrhea. In an advanced case the individual gets to a place he is unable to look at food needed. He has a persistent, almost constant, diarrhea, pain of the muscles and inability to stand. He gets a swelling of the feet and ankles and into the legs, which sometimes goes up to the abdomen so that in an advanced case you might have an increase in weight rather than a loss. All of this finally affects the heart." With that Armstrong stepped down.

Dwyer then pulled out copies of the last letters that Hallmark, Farrow, and Spatz had written home the night before they were put to death. They had given the letters to Caesar dos Remedios, who had passed them along to Tatsuta, who had given them to Yasuo Karakawa, the Chief of Staff for the 13th Army, who in turn had forwarded them to Heitaro Kimura, the Vice Minister of War in Tokyo, with a note reading "I hereby send you for reference copies of last papers of three American aviators who air attacked the mainland."

Translations of the letters had been made into Japanese for intelligence purposes and been filed away in the War Ministry's records. Those translations had been forgotten until SCAP in Tokyo had turned them up while sifting through imperial Japan's paperwork and translated them back into English. Now Dwyer read them for the world in open court.

Harold Spatz had written a short letter to his brother, Robert Jr. All he could write was "I will say my last goodbye to you and take care of yourself and may God bless you." He had then written a letter to his father that ran on for a few more sentences. Most of it was a bequest of the belongings he had left behind in Lebo, Kansas: "My personal property consists of my clothes, and that is all I know of that I have of any value. If I have inherited anything since I became of age I will it to you and I want you to know that I love you and may God bless you." He closed his letter by saying "I want you to know that I died fighting for my country like a soldier."

William Farrow had taken the moment to reflect spiritually. When he had started training to become a pilot back in 1940, he had written himself a plan that he had given the title "My Future."

"My aim is decided—I'm going into some branch of aviation," he had written. "I have only to apply myself daily toward this end to achieve it." He had listed his ten weaknesses and the ten things he would need to do to develop himself. Some were obvious, such as staying in shape, researching aviation, and doing well in school. But others were matters of the Christian faith that had seeped into him back in South Carolina: "Stay close to God—do his will and commandments. He is my friend and protector. Believe in him—trust in his ways—not to my own confused understanding of the universe."

Confronting his own death, Farrow had thought of "Thanatopsis" by William Cullen Bryant, whose closing stanza recalls how life on earth is fleeting:

> So live, that when thy summons comes to join
> The innumerable caravan, which moves
> To that mysterious realm, where each shall take
> His chamber in the silent halls of death,
> Thou go not, like the quarry-slave at night,
> Scourged to his dungeon, but, sustained and soothed
> By an unfaltering trust, approach thy grave,
> Like one who wraps the drapery of his couch
> About him, and lies down to pleasant dreams.

Reflecting on what might happen the next day, he had written that his greatest regret was that he would never become a missionary. "I've built my house upon a rock," he wrote in a letter to his Aunt Marge. "You have always been an inspiration to me—you, Pee-wee, and aunt Mary. I'm thankful for having known and loved you all." He then wrote another letter to console his mother. "Please carry on for me—don't let this get you down," he asked her. "Just rely on God to make everything right, and I will see you again hereafter."

Farrow had written his final words to Lib. He had been sure he was going to marry Lib once the war was done. He had dreamed about their future home together and the fireplace they would have, just like the one at her parents' house. He had missed the songs she played on her guitar, her excitement when he had taken her up in an airplane, and the walks through the backwoods in the springtime, when the brush was redolent with fresh growth. He told her that she was "the only girl that would have meant the completion of my life. I have visualized the kind of life being married to you would have meant to me, and to both of us, and I know we would have found complete happiness. It's a pity we were born in this day and age. At least we had part of that happiness." He had closed simply, saying "Goodbye, and may God be with you."

Dean Hallmark had thought he was finally going to a prisoner of war camp, where he had been looking forward to getting some good beefsteak in his Red Cross packages. He had fought his way back from death. He had survived a plane crash. He had survived the waterboard. He had survived Bridge House. When he had been taken into his cell in Jiangwan that particular day, his head had been filled by thoughts of the future and he had set on the idea of being a commercial pilot, maybe even for Pan Am, jetting all over the world, looking sharp in his captain's uniform. Then Remedios had given him the news.

"I hardly know what to say," he had written to his family back in Texas. "They have just told me that I'm liable to execution. I can hardly believe it. I'm at a complete loss for words." He had thought of his girlfriend, Pauline, and about how it was football season, and how the entire state of Texas would be watching the games and eating some good food.

Hallmark had made sure to give a little of the "top hat," which Remedios had encouraged him to write about how good his treatment had been. It was a bitter humiliation, but he knew he had to look out for his men. He was the pilot. He was the leader. If writing a bit of bullshit "top hat" spared them what he had gone through, then he was happy to do it.

Facing death after all he had endured still overwhelmed him, though. Why had they nursed him back to health only to execute him? "It still seems that I am in a dream and can't believe what is happening," he wrote.

"I wish the court would reconsider and have a heart for us to understand that we have people at home that love us and we them and that we like to see them again and live in peace."

Dwyer and Hendren wanted one more statement read into the record: the words of the late President Franklin D. Roosevelt delivered on April 21, 1943, in which he personally promised the nation that "the American Government will hold personally and officially responsible for these diabolical crimes all of those officers of the Japanese Government who have participated therein and will in due course bring those officers to justice."

* * *

Later that afternoon, Dwyer led everyone on a tour of Jiangwan. The group arrived at four in the afternoon, two hours before sunset. Hayama and Nielsen conducted a joint tour of the prison and execution grounds, with Nielsen leading everyone through the cell block and describing what life had been like in there.

Everyone could see how cramped and dismal the cells had been. They also saw scratchings that George Barr had made into the floor, hoping to remind the future that he had once been alive:

LT. G. BARR, USAAC.
24TH BOMB. SQDN.
COLUMBIA, S.C., USA
TOOK OFF FROM AC HORNET 4/17/42
BOMBED NAGOYA JAPAN
FLEW 17 HOURS TO CHINA
NO GAS. JUMPED
CAPTURED 4/18/42

The tour group then went next door to the Noboru Unit's L-shaped courtroom. It was a plain room with a wood floor measuring about thirty by sixty feet. It had no obvious evidentiary value, but it offered a sense of place. Standing in the courtroom, everyone could project themselves back in time. Nakajo, Okada, and Wako would have been sitting in judgment over there. The Doolittle Raiders would have stood here, with Hallmark's stretcher somewhere over there. It was testimony by apparition.

To complete the tour, the group shuffled over to the old Chinese cemetery. Hayama led them to the spot, just in front of the ruins of an old Chinese temple, where the executions had taken place. Dwyer had Remedios and two Japanese soldiers kneel on the ground about ten feet apart from each other. They put their arms out as if tied to crosses, each man filling the approximate amount of space that Hallmark, Farrow, and Spatz had filled back in 1942.

Dwyer had been building up to this moment for weeks. He was doing something unprecedented. It was not simply a whodunit; it was a war crimes trial. It was a case about justice and the law and the war and what the world would be like from here on out. The day before, the UN Security Council had met for the first time, and coverage of that event was in all the papers the morning of their trip to Jiangwan. The *New York Times* played up the grandiosity of the moment: "The Old World that twice in a generation summoned the United States on the field of battle came to the New World yesterday in search of peace." That was what this trial was about. That was what this moment was about. Dwyer had been summoned to this field of battle and through justice would lead the way to peace.

This group had spent weeks trying to imagine what had happened in this place three and a half years earlier. By closing the prosecution's case with a visit to the scene of the crime, Dwyer wanted to prove that all the evidence, all the testimony, all the legal arguments, all the documents read aloud to the court reporters and then translated into Japanese, all of it was not about something mythical. Something had actually happened to real men in this place on a date in time. The presentation of a good legal case, like the presentation of a good play, is all about the ending. And whatever troubles Dwyer had stumbled over, he had made sure that no one would forget how his play had ended.

Now, in late March 1946, a little after four in the afternoon, it was later in the day than it had been on October 15, 1942, but because of the season, the sun would have been about as low in the sky. It was also probably a bit chillier than it had been three and a half years earlier, and there would have been freshly fallen autumn leaves amid the matted grass and errant golf balls that had escaped from the links still abutting the old Chinese cemetery. But those subtle variations did nothing to loosen the collective lump in everyone's throat.

For three small-town American boys such as Hallmark, Farrow, and Spatz, the moment would have been dreamlike in its unreality. In 1942, the closest Allied forces were thousands of miles and years away from returning to this place. The three of them could not have been farther from home as they looked out at the dozens of strange Japanese faces gawking at them, having all gathered together for one reason: to watch them die.

Even after they were tied to the crosses, the blindfolds were draped around their eyes, and the black dots were painted on their foreheads, there had still been a few moments left to be lived. They would have heard the sound of the rifles being readied only a few paces in front of them. They would have heard a man yelling military commands in a language they did not understand but whose meaning was clear: "Ready. Aim. Fire." Even if the thought never had time to form into words, they had still had time to anxiously wonder "Is this it?"

The reenactment was less evidence in a trial than it was a memorial. Whoever was responsible, whatever the politics, whatever this all meant for history, this spot was where three young men had died. And with that, the prosecution rested its case.

TWENTY-TWO

Edmund Bodine needed more time. The trial had started on Monday, March 18, which meant that he and Fellows had had only a weekend to collect their thoughts after returning from Japan. The prosecution had rested its case the following Tuesday afternoon, and now Bodine was due to make the defense's opening statement at 9:00 a.m. on Saturday.

The raw from-the-belly power of Dwyer's restaging of the Doolittle Raiders' executions had made everything about the defense's case seem flimsy, but there was no hiding. It was only halftime. Bodine had to go out there again. Wednesday, then Thursday, then Friday. The crush of everything pounded like a headache.

Moritada Kumashiro and Shinji Somiya continued to bicker incessantly. Somiya complained about Kumashiro's cross-examinations because rather than making simple, helpful points in a way that could build up to something meaningful, Kumashiro acted as though he were a lawyer in a movie. He badgered witnesses about small points, whose relevance was impossible to guess, and asked seemingly every question as if he were ready to shout "Ah-ha!" as soon as the answer was given. Somiya, for his part, had a better command of the courtroom, but he could also be tediously pedantic in the way that only a law professor can be. Bodine had brought both men onto the case to make it easier for him, Fellows, and Elizaveta to focus on getting ready for the trial. Mediating their egoes took away time that he needed to get ready for Saturday.

Bodine was also worried about Elizaveta, whose restlessness to get married could no longer be ignored. The world was changing fast. The Chinese Civil War was escalating all around them, and the same shifting alliances that had led Winston Churchill to make his "Iron Curtain" speech earlier that month had prompted the Soviet government to offer amnesty to exiled White Russians. Elizaveta's mother and brother had just gotten their new Russian passports and were planning to return. Elizaveta had waited, assuming that she would soon need to apply for a US passport, but the longer she waited, the more likely it was that the troika would be separated and she would be left stateless and alone in Shanghai.

Never one to accept circumstances beyond her control, Elizaveta had given Bodine an ultimatum: If they weren't married by April 6, a week to the day after he was supposed to give the defense's opening statement, she would return to Russia with her mother.

Bodine needed more time, if only to collect his thoughts. His whole reason for staying in Shanghai, for taking on this thankless case, for risking whatever was left of his career as a pilot, was threatening to vanish behind the Iron Curtain.

On Friday, less than twenty-four hours before he was supposed to stand in the well of Ham Young's makeshift courtroom on the sixth floor of the Ward Road Jail and give the defense's opening statement, he pled with McReynolds for more time to prepare.

McReynolds granted the request. Bodine would not have to make the defense's opening statement that Saturday. He could have until Monday morning, no more.

* * *

Bodine wrote out a draft of his opening statement that raised twelve points. That number alone was a sign of the problems he and the rest of the team continued to have in coming up with a coherent defense. It was a truism, or perhaps a superstition, of the legal profession that every argument has three points. It was an old religious idea, common to the Jesuits and taught at schools such as Bodine's alma mater, Georgetown: *Omne trium perfectum*—"Everything perfect comes in threes." And Bodine's draft of the opening statement was far from perfect.

Running little more than a page, it began by emphasizing that Sawada had known nothing about the trial and in any event had had no power to change the sentence. All of the defendants, including Wako, Okada, and Tatsuta, had just been cogs in a machine being run from Tokyo. They had never tortured anyone. They had just done what they had been told to do and had had no reason to know that what they were doing was wrong. Then, toward the end of the draft, Bodine smuggled in a meek little sentence that said there was at least some evidence that "the charges against the Doolittle fliers before the Japanese tribunal were not false and fraudulent and that the fliers did actually bomb indiscriminately and did strafe schools, causing the death of civilians and schoolchildren."

Bodine gave his draft to Fellows, who immediately saw that it needed a lot of work. Bodine had begun his draft by saying "We will prove that . . ." For one thing, it was not the defense's job to "prove" anything. That was the prosecution's job. For another, an opening statement was not allowed to be an argument; Bodine was allowed to say only what "the evidence will show." These were technical points, but the last thing Fellows wanted was for Bodine to draw an objection right out of the gate. Dwyer and Hendren had both gotten Bodine hung up on the niceties of trial procedure at crucial moments in Nielsen's cross-examination, and it was not hard to imagine the big, sly Irish grin on Dwyer's face if he saw an opportunity to haze the neophyte at the podium yet again. So Fellows penciled in the correct way to begin: "The evidence of the defense will show . . ."

Fellows continued through the draft, making a few notes here and there, but the small things were not the problem. By the time he had read through to the end, the overall story Bodine told left him cold. Sure, all the necessary bits were there, but from the first sentence to the last, it just seemed so . . . defensive. Bodine was arguing on the prosecution's turf.

Fellows wrote a new introduction and showed it Bodine. "The evidence for the defense in this case will show," he began and then itemized three points:

a. That during the now famous raid on Tokyo on 18 April 1942, schools and civilians were bombed and strafed by the Raiders;

b. That pursuant to the capture of some of the Raiders, the heads of the Japanese government met and determined that the raid was in violation of the Laws of War

and that these fliers were guilty both because they participated in the raid and that in fact the fliers confessed
to having bombed and strafed innocent civilians;

c. That at all times while under the custody of these accused they were treated in strict conformity to Japanese
Laws and instructions of the Japanese government.

Fellows gave the draft back to Bodine to look over. There it was in three
pungent points. It started the right way and followed the rule of three. But
could Bodine really say all of that in open court? Did it have to be him? It
was not as if the Japanese had been all that innocent to begin with.

Fellows was unwilling to be timid. Dwyer and Hendren had made the
case about the Doolittle Raid, and with senior Army Air Forces officers
sitting as judges, avenging the young airmen lost in the Air Forces' most
celebrated mission was not hard to sell. If the prosecution had built its case
on a legend, the defense needed to make the case about the truth, wherever
it led. They would have to put cracks into the mystique of the Doolittle
Raid. If they could get McReynolds and the rest of the judges to harbor
even small doubts about what had actually happened on April 18, 1942,
they might just well create enough doubt about the guilt of the four men
whose lives were now in their hands.

As defense lawyers, they had to be brave enough to fight for the truth.
That was their duty. And if they were going to go down this road, Bodine had to be the one to lead the way. Kumashiro and Somiya certainly
couldn't do it; it would just be written off as Japanese propaganda. Fellows
couldn't do it, either. It would be seen as the same kind of tricks Frank Reel
had pulled in Yamashita's case all over again. The question in everyone's
mind would be why Bodine hadn't done it. Bodine was a pilot, just like
McReynolds, just like Nielsen. If anyone was going to speak an unspeak-
able truth, it should be him.

But how could they even prove it? Bodine had tried to get Nielsen to
admit that at least some of the raid had been directed at residential areas,
but Nielsen had not budged. The photos Bodine had taken at Mizumoto
Elementary School had not turned out, meaning that to prove their case,
Bodine and Fellows would have to personally testify about what they had
seen in Japan. Bodine would have to be sworn in as a witness in a US Army

courtroom and vouch for Imperial Japan's most slanderous propaganda. It would be an act of career-ending heresy, all to help four men who were not free of guilt to begin with.

*   *   *

Bodine wrestled with what to do. Real lawyers got practice putting aside what other people thought of them for representing the worst of the worst. Real lawyers even learned to make it a point of professional pride. John Adams, the coauthor of the Declaration of Independence and the second president of the United States, had taken the case of the British soldiers charged with the Boston Massacre. He had put all his rhetorical skills to work for some of the most hated men in America and won a full acquittal. More than 150 years later, Adams was still a hero to lawyers everywhere, but Bodine, as if he needed reminding, was not a lawyer. He had no practice being hated by proxy. Yet it weighed on him that these four men had trusted him with their lives.

Fifteen years earlier, Bodine had found himself in their situation. It was Columbus Day 1930, and Bodine had driven up to Boston to see the Fordham/Boston College game with Billy Shea and Joey Watral, two of his buddies from Xavier. Fordham was a football powerhouse back then and an easy favorite for three good Catholic boys enjoying a day off from New York's premiere Jesuit high school. Fordham would soon recruit Jim Crowley, one of Notre Dame's storied "Four Horseman," as head coach and give a full ride to a small but pugnacious Brooklyn boy by the name of Vince Lombardi.

The game itself was a slog. It was an Indian summer day, and the heat got up into the nineties. Boston College's defense proved tougher than expected, and though they never got close to their own end zone, they played rough and forced Fordham to give away at least five good touchdown chances. At one point, Fordham's quarterback took an arm to the face and got his nose broken while returning a punt down the field. It was only in the fourth quarter that Fordham made the press all the way down to the ten-yard line, and even then, the only points Fordham could get on the board were from an easy field goal. Fordham won 3–0.

Bodine and his buddies had to get back to New York for school the next day, so they crowded onto the bench seat of Alma Bodine's Ford coupe around 9:00 p.m. Bodine did the driving, even though he did not have a driver's license, and he figured that if he drove down the old Boston Post Road through the night, they could get into New York City in time for school the next morning.

Around 5:15 a.m., Bodine was still a few hours from New York and approaching the town of Norwalk, Connecticut. There were no streetlights along the highway, and the car's headlights were getting dimmer as the battery ran low. The hot day and long, low-lit night made it hard for Bodine to see the road under his sagging eyelids. He had been following a Plymouth whose taillights gave him a point of focus to keep him in his lane, but then the Plymouth stopped short.

Bodine was going a solid forty miles an hour and swerved into the open left lane. Suddenly, out of the darkness came the flutter-flash of something heavy into his left headlight, followed by a hard *crack-fwop-thump-flop* into the teeth of the Ford coupe's steel grille. It was a sound with a weight Bodine could feel.

Bodine floored the gas as broken glass tinkled down onto the pavement and as the voice of a man yelling "Stop!" quickly grew fainter behind him. He kept up speed for a full minute, making it a half mile further down the old Boston Post Road and saying nothing to his two buddies. Then Billy Shea, who was riding in the passenger's seat, told Bodine they had to stop. Bodine's left headlight was broken, and the impact into the grille was causing engine trouble.

In the rearview mirror, the lights of the Plymouth started closing in behind them. Bodine saw a service station under a sign that read LYON'S GARAGE. It was closed that early in the morning, but he turned the car off and coasted into its driveway. Bodine and Shea scrambled out of the side doors, but by the time they were on their feet, the Plymouth had caught up with them and turned broadside to block the driveway.

A man hopped off the Plymouth's running board before it even came to a complete stop. He was round bodied and round headed and had no neck to speak of. He was visibly delirious with rage, and he had a pistol. "Don't try to get away," he yelled as he pointed the barrel at Bodine, "or I will blow you through!"

The man with the pistol, it turned out, was Officer Paul McGrath. He and his partner, Frank Stratton, had pulled over a stolen car and had been in the process of taking it back from two AWOL marines when Stratton had walked out onto the highway with his flashlight to stop traffic.

The driver of the Plymouth had seen Stratton's signal to stop, but Bodine had not. In his haste to swerve around the Plymouth, he had bashed his left headlight and then the grille of Alma Bodine's Ford coupe into Stratton's body, dragging him almost seventy feet, fracturing his skull, tearing his scalp from forehead to ear, breaking more than a dozen of his bones, and leaving him to die on the pavement, which had peeled the skin from his face, hands, and legs by the time his body came to rest.

In his fury, McGrath shouted questions that were impossible to answer: Why hadn't Bodine stopped? Hadn't he heard McGrath yelling at him? Hadn't he seen Stratton in the road? Did he know he had hit a police officer?

All Billy Shea could say was that they were "terribly sorry." Bodine stuttered that his lights weren't working and began to weep. "I didn't see him."

Bodine was arrested and his parents had to post $2,000 for bail; Billy and Joey had to each put up $500. Bodine's parents also sent up a lawyer from New York and hired a local lawyer, John Dwyer (no relation to Bodine's future adversary), who had been practicing law for fifteen years and was working toward getting appointed as a judge in Norwalk.

Two days after the crash, the Norwalk coroner held an inquest. Everyone who had been near the scene testified that Bodine had been responsible, including the two AWOL marines whose arrest had started it all. McGrath claimed that Bodine had turned off his headlights as part of a ploy to get away, making a point of saying that he had tested the headlights in the driveway of Lyons' Garage and found them to be in perfect working condition, except for the one that had been broken on the body of Sergeant Frank Stratton. The coroner concluded that Bodine had been "criminally careless and responsible for the death of the deceased."

Stratton's death made the papers from Boston to New York in no small part because it turned out that Stratton was the cousin of the celebrity dwarf General Tom Thumb from P. T. Barnum's circus. A father of six and grandfather of six more, the sixty-four-year-old Stratton was the oldest officer in the Norwalk Police Department. With a face that had yielded in time to the kindliness that every once-hard man's gaze reclines into as he approaches his retirement years, he was warmly remembered for all the times he could be seen jutting his belly forward with the pride of having lived a man's life as he played crossing guard at intersection of West Washington and Franklin Streets for the students of Franklin Junior High. At his funeral, Stratton's casket was marched solemnly through the streets of Norwalk in a parade crowded with locals, politicians, and police from all the nearby counties. Truckloads of flowers were heaped onto his grave site in Riverside Cemetery.

Bodine was charged with manslaughter and driving without a license. He faced at least a year in prison, but over the next nine months, John Dwyer, Bodine's local lawyer, went to work to negotiate his case down with the Norwalk prosecutor's office.

As bad as things were, the coroner's report had offered some glimmers of hope. All the witnesses said it had been dark, very dark, too dark to see Sergeant Frank Stratton standing in the road. Though Bodine had been driving relatively fast, 30 to 40 miles per hour, that was a typical highway speed at the time. Both Billy Shea and Joey Watral said that Bodine's brakes had not been working well and that they had not known they had hit someone until Officer McGrath had told them. Billy Shea said that he had thought they had just sideswiped a car.

The most incriminating piece of evidence was Officer McGrath's claim that Bodine had fled the scene and turned his lights off to avoid being followed, but even that allegation was not airtight. The driver of the Plymouth that had chased Bodine down could not remember seeing Bodine turn his lights off before he pulled off the road, and McGrath had been surfing on the Plymouth's running board with the wind blowing in his eyes and adrenaline pumping through his brain. There was no telling what he had really seen.

Then there was Bodine's age. At the police station, Bodine had said he was eighteen. In 1930, someone had to be at least sixteen years old to be prosecuted for any crime in Connecticut, but there was a movement under way to raise the age to eighteen. And it turned out that Bodine's mother, Alma, was not so sure her boy was a man just yet.

Good Catholic mother that she was, Alma Bodine had had nine children over the course of little more than a decade. Giving birth to five girls and four boys in such a short period of time, only half of whom had survived into adulthood, had caused one pregnancy to flow into the next.

She could be very sloppy with paperwork, and she seemed to remember Bodine being born in 1914, not 1912, meaning he was at most sixteen. She was sure she had given birth to a little boy sometime in October 1914. Maybe that was her Edmund? Bodine might very well be fifteen. And if he was fifteen, he would be too young to be prosecuted. The case would have to be dismissed. Did the Norwalk prosecutor's office really want to bank its whole case on what Alma Bodine would say when asked for the birthday of her baby boy?

The Norwalk prosecutors agreed to cut Bodine a deal, a quiet deal that stayed out of the papers. Bodine agreed to a *nolle prosequi*, a Connecticut procedure that everyone called a "nollie," under which the prosecutor agreed to hold off prosecuting for thirteen months. If Bodine stayed out of trouble for a year and a month, the nollie would automatically turn into a dismissal of all the charges and Bodine's record would be sealed.

Bodine's local lawyer had taken a risk in even agreeing to be his lawyer. Bodine was a prep school boy from New York City who had killed a cop and fled the scene. Twisting the arm of the local prosecutor to let him off with a nollie was great for Bodine but a terrible political strategy if John Dwyer ever wanted to snag a judicial appointment from the governor of Connecticut. But he did it. Bodine was his client. He had agreed to take the case. And it was his duty, moral as much as professional, to put Bodine's life ahead of his own aspirations. He had to choose justice for his client, no matter how hated that would make him.

Stratton's wife later sued Bodine's parents for her husband's lost wages, and Bodine missed the spring semester as his future was being negotiated. But the nollie gave him a chance to graduate from Xavier and then Georgetown, to make the varsity football team that fall, to be his high school class president, to be a pitchman for Ford, and to travel the world as a pilot in the US Army Air Forces.

Bodine would say that not a day went by when he didn't think about what he had done, and in his years of Catholic schooling, he regularly encountered the writings of St. Thomas Aquinas, who said that justice is inevitable; the only question is how it is served: "A man is either punished against his will or makes amends of his own accord."

Consciously or not, Bodine always found himself drawn to choices that bore the mark of penance for the life of Sergeant Frank Stratton. He had been drawn to becoming a police officer after college, an odd job for a wealthy young man who had just graduated from Georgetown. He had been drawn to Fordham Law School despite his lack of academic chops to see him all the way through. And when looking for ways to stay in Shanghai with his beloved Lailia, he had been drawn to the way that now asked him to choose justice on behalf of four men who were hated by everyone he admired or aspired to be like.

TWENTY-THREE

Monday morning, after McReynolds finished the perfunctory introductions and called the trial to order, Bodine stood at the podium. "May it please the Commission," he began. "The evidence for the defense in this case will show to the Commission the background of this case." Bodine was hesitating, stalling by stuffing a few extraneous words in before the point he did not want to get to. But then he steeled himself: "And will show that during the now famous raid on Tokyo on April 18, 1942, schools and civilians were bombed—"

John Hendren jumped to his feet. "If it please the Commission," he cried, "the prosecution objects!"

A moment lapsed as Hendren searched for a reason for his objection. It was clear that Hendren knew he did not like what he was hearing. It was so, so . . . objectionable. But he had to come up with a reason, an actual legal reason why it could not be uttered in court.

Lacking anything concrete, Hendren went with "relevance." It was the vaguest of the evidentiary objections. It was a plea for the judge to say that some truth does not matter. It was a demand that the judge see the world one way and not any other. "It is irrelevant to the issue before this Commission," Hendren breathlessly insisted, beaming reasonableness from the sculpted angle of his jaw down the sharp pleats of his pants to the highly buffed polish of his shoes, "and is highly objectionable."

Hendren had stopped Bodine cold, but then Fellows jumped in. "If it please the Commission," Fellows said, "the theory of the defense is that we can establish a *corpus delicti* for the Japanese court, to show that schools were bombed and strafed, civilians were strafed and killed. Thereafter we intend to show that confessions were made by these fliers. That certainly is probative evidence for this court to consider in trying to pass judgment on another court."

Hendren interrupted him: "They were all individual of each other and therefore you can impose no liability on Lieutenant Hallmark or Lieutenant Farrow for what these other planes might have done."

McReynolds cut them both off. "Subject to objection by any member of the commission," he announced, "the prosecution's objection is overruled."

It was a stunning moment. It was not exactly the first time McReynolds had overruled an objection in favor of Bodine and Fellows, but it certainly seemed that way. McReynolds had just given them permission to mount a defense of four Japanese soldiers by arguing that some of the Second World War's most celebrated heroes had committed atrocities. Dwyer and Hendren's strategy from the start had been to put the Doolittle Raiders' trial on trial. Now Bodine and Fellows were putting the Doolittle Raiders themselves on trial.

"I will continue," Bodine said picking up from where Hendren had interrupted him, "that pursuant to the capture of these Raiders, we will prove that the heads of the Japanese government met and determined that the raid was in violation of the laws of war and that the fliers were guilty."

Bodine continued through the rest of his opening, defending each of the defendants based upon his lack of individual responsibility. As a parting shot, he added that the Doolittle Raiders had been "proven guilty of indiscriminate bombing and killing of civilians and schoolchildren and therefore denied the rights of prisoners of war and *rightfully* treated as war criminals."

Bodine then took the stand so Fellows could question him about what they had seen on their trip to Mizumoto Elementary School. Fellows picked up a pane of glass off the defense table and approached his witness. "I will hand you an object," Fellows announced, "and ask you to state what this is, if you know."

"One of the schoolteachers gave me this pane of glass," Bodine explained, "when I was there and said that—"

"Just a moment," Dwyer cut in, deciding to take charge after Hendren's feckless plea of relevance. "I object to the following remarks as to what the schoolteacher said." It was hearsay. Unlike an objection for relevance, hearsay was a bona fide legal objection about the rules. A witness could not just testify about what he had heard someone say (hence, hear-say). He had to testify only about what he personally knew to be true.

But this was a military commission. Dwyer knew full well that the ordinary rules of evidence, even something as old as the hearsay rule, didn't apply. "Objection overruled," McReynolds said. "You may proceed."

Bodine explained that it was the "pane of glass that the bullet came through that entered the body of one of the students."

Fellows then had Bodine authenticate a map that the teachers had drawn of the path the plane had taken over the school four years earlier.

Dwyer got up again. "Prior to renewing our objection to the admissibility of this Exhibit, we would like to ask Colonel Bodine one or two questions." Dwyer sensed McReynolds' skepticism but assured him that he was not simply trying to make Bodine more uncomfortable than he clearly already was sitting in the witness stand.

"We say again," Dwyer insisted, "that the court-martial which tried these fliers; that the men who constituted the court and the man who proved its action, are the focal points in this case and the evidence, or so-called evidence, which they seek to bring in and granted degree of admissibility of this trial—and to bring that in in 1946 when it wasn't considered by anybody in 1942, and have no bearing on the guilt or innocence of these men as to what they did in 1942."

As soon as Dwyer finished saying his piece, McReynolds shot him down again: "Objection overruled."

Fellows returned to his questioning of Bodine: "I will hand you an object that has been marked Exhibit A and ask you to state what it is, if you know."

"They are two bullets," Bodine replied, "that were handed to me by the schoolteacher."

"That is the Mizumoto school?" Fellows asked.

"Yes."

"I hand you what has been marked for identification as defense Exhibit B, and ask you to state what it is, if you know."

"This is a piece of board from the school building which I helped rip out from the wall and it is behind this piece of wood that I picked up the two parts of the bullet embedded in the 2 x 4."

"Is this from the Mizumoto primary school?" Fellows asked.

"It is," Bodine replied.

Dwyer interjected again, this time demanding to cross-examine Bodine before he said another word about what had or had not been inside the two-by-four that he had pulled from the Mizumoto Elementary School. This time, McReynolds agreed.

"Colonel Bodine," Dwyer asked as he approached the podium, "are you a ballistics expert?"

"I'm not," Bodine admitted.

"Can you state what kind or type bullet, if it was a bullet," Dwyer said skeptically, "that made the hole in this Exhibit B that you have testified to?"

"I cannot," Bodine admitted.

"Do you know what these pieces of metal are," Dwyer asked, doing little to temper his sarcasm, "that you call Exhibit A?"

"They appear to me," Bodine replied, "to be parts to a thirty caliber bullet."

"Now just what makes you say that?" Dwyer asked.

"From my experience in the Army," Bodine (the pilot) replied, "experience with thirty caliber and fifty caliber bullets."

"Objection overruled," McReynolds (the pilot) said to Dwyer (the lawyer). "The evidence will be considered whatever its value."

Fellows then asked if Bodine had taken any photos of the bullet holes.

"I did take a number of pictures of the bullet holes, yes."

"What was the result?"

"It was a bad day, and they didn't turn out."

"To that," Dwyer chortled, "the prosecution has no objection." The laughter the remark provoked gave Dwyer a quick moment in which to reassert control over the courtroom.

Fellows returned to asking Bodine about the pictures he had tried to take after the two of them had walked outside Mizumoto Elementary School. "Taking these pictures, did you look over the countryside?"

"I did."

"What was in the neighborhood of the school?"

"On the west side," Bodine said ruefully, "as far as I could see were rice paddy fields; on the north side there were rice paddy fields and there was a small building that appeared to be a small factory about a mile and a half from the school building; on the south there is nothing but paddy fields and on the east nothing but paddy fields."

"Are you in the American Army?" Fellows asked.

"Yes, I am."

"Did you see anything that you would regard as a military target anywhere in the proximity of that school?"

"I did not," Bodine replied.

"I object to the question," Dwyer interrupted, "and ask that it be stricken from the record." Dwyer was no longer in a joking mood. "The question is improper and there is no qualification of the witness as an expert. In the second place, the conditions existing in 1946 are in no way shown to be anything like conditions that may have existed in 1942, and a question such as that calls for the opinion of the witness is not a proper question."

This time, McReynolds agreed and sustained the objection. Still, the point had been made, and for the rest of the day, Bodine and Fellows took turns reading aloud the statements of schoolteachers, peasant farmers, and other "non-military targets," in the stilted jargon of the law of war, about what they had witnessed throughout Japan on April 18, 1942.

Though *The Stars and Stripes* did not cover it, the local Shanghai papers could not resist the day's sensational testimony. The Mizumoto Elementary School, they wrote, was in the middle of nowhere, implying what only Bodine and Fellows had dared to say out loud.

* * *

The most conspicuous absence from Bodine's opening statement was something he had learned, or thought he had learned, about Sawada. During his and Fellows's trip to Tokyo, Yasuo Karakawa, Sawada's former chief of staff in the 13th Army, had told Bodine and Fellows that Sawada had tried to stop the Doolittle Raiders' executions. Karakawa distinctly remembered Sawada going so far as to send a cable directly to Tokyo in a failed effort to spare the Doolittle Raiders' lives. Karakawa not only disputed that Sawada had been the mastermind, he painted Sawada as a hero.

The problem was that Sawada denied it. Sawada insisted that he had never sent cables directly to Tokyo. That wasn't the chain of command. The closest he had gotten to getting personally involved was an informal conversation he had had with General Shunroku Hata. As the commander of the China Expeditionary Army, Hata had been Sawada's direct superior, and Sawada had been obliged to report to him regularly on the activities of the 13th Army. In late September 1942, Sawada had been in Nanking to brief Hata on that summer's operations, and he recounted what he had known about the Doolittle Raiders' case, which was not that much.

Sawada had learned about the 13th Army's responsibility for the Doolittle Raiders only after he had returned to Shanghai from the front lines on September 17, 1942. Colonel Shoshin Ito, the head of the 13th Army's Legal Department, had briefed him on how Tokyo had sent the Doolittle Raiders to Shanghai to be tried with "justice and strictness." Ito had handed Sawada a copy of the Noboru Unit judgment, assuring him that it was being handled like any other court proceeding. All the usual formalities had been followed and so Sawada had stamped his chop on it.

Sawada had made his trip to Nanking a few days after getting the briefing from Ito and had relayed all of what he had learned to General Hata. Hata, Sawada had discovered, was already aware of everything about the Doolittle Raiders. Colonel Ito had sent the case file to Nanking while Sawada was still at the front, and Hata's people had forwarded it to Tokyo.

"I'm awaiting the orders from Tokyo," Hata had explained, "and I cannot do anything about this." Once Tokyo approved the sentences, Hata had promised to issue the appropriate orders to Shanghai quickly so that the matter could be resolved.

"I feel sorry for them, for the fliers," Sawada had said to Hata. They were just boys serving their country. To Sawada, the death sentences had seemed too severe. "Will you do something about it?" Sawada had known he was taking a bit of a risk voicing his concern, but he was pleasantly surprised when Hata agreed with him.

"I feel the same way," Hata had said, "but since the orders are to wait for the approval of Tokyo, we have to wait." It was out of their hands.

That was the extent of Sawada's involvement in the case. There had been no heroic cables to Tokyo, as Karakawa had claimed.

* * *

For Bodine's purposes, Sawada's conversation with Hata was better than nothing, and he made a point of putting the story before McReynolds and the rest of the military commission judges in the hopes of casting Sawada in a more sympathetic, if not heroic, light.

Doing so was essential. Bodine and Fellows knew that their defense could not be left to rise or fall on the single argument that Sawada and the rest were innocent because the sainted Doolittle Raiders had been guilty. Sure, they had evidence—compelling evidence that they had revealed to the world—but the reporters covering the trial had been reluctant to let any of it go to print. And if reporters were spooked into circumspection, there was no way that McReynolds and the rest of the judges would be any more eager to follow the evidence to its logical conclusion.

Over the course of the next few days, Bodine and Fellows mustered as much evidence as they could to show that Sawada had just been in the middle of everything. He was not, like Yamashita, at the top. He was no mastermind.

To prove their case, Bodine convinced Major General Masatoshi Miyano, General Hata's former chief of staff, to come to Shanghai to testify about how circuitous the Japanese military bureaucracy in China had been back in 1942 and how nothing Sawada had done made him responsible, morally or legally.

"What is a chop?" Bodine asked Miyano on the witness stand.

"The chop," Miyano explained, "is something which verifies that the person had seen the document."

"The person had *seen* the document?" Bodine clarified.

"There are times when it is a verification that he had seen it," Miyano confirmed, "and also times when he puts his chop on it to verify his agreement or sanction."

In other words, in the bureaucratic minutiae of the Imperial Japanese Army, Sawada's "chop" did not constitute an order or imply that Sawada could have done anything more than he had done, and Miyano was confident that there was nothing else Sawada could have done. When General Hajime Sugiyama, the Chief of Staff of the Imperial Army, had sent his personal emissary to Nanking with a dossier of evidence that had included the Doolittle Raiders' confessions to having committed atrocities against Japanese civilians, the death sentences had become inevitable. Everyone understood that. Not even General Hata could have done anything different.

Bodine's script of questions for Miyano put ample bureaucratic distance between Sawada and the center of the action, but Miyano's testimony was complicated to the point of tedious. After spending an entire morning having Miyano laboriously tie together the Japanese Army's competing chains of command, Bodine lost the momentum.

Dwyer and Hendren seized the opportunity to make things simple again: the 13th Army had tried the Doolittle Raiders for violating an ex post facto law based upon evidence tainted by torture. No one could dispute that, Hendren reminded everyone. "At the time of the trial of the Doolittle fliers," he then asked, "was General Sawada the commanding general of the 13th Army?"

"Yes," Miyano replied, slashing through every fiber of the who-reported-to-whom Gordian knot that Bodine had tied together.

The simple fact that Bodine could not deny was that Sawada had been in command. If McReynolds and the rest concluded that the trial and execution of the Doolittle Raiders had been a war crime, then the Yamashita precedent made him responsible. It did not matter that he had been away at the front lines any more than it mattered that Yamashita had fled into the mountains. In the absence of a real mastermind, Sawada was the ultimate repository of culpability for anything that had happened under his command.

Thankfully for Sawada, Bodine and Fellows had found another witness, whom Dwyer and Hendren had somehow missed. If there was any man who was, in fact, most responsible, it was this man. He had masterminded the plot to try the Doolittle Raiders before a show trial, to convict them with evidence corrupted by torture, and to execute them all as war criminals. It had not been his idea, but he had built his professional career on making others' ideas into a well-executed reality. And he had just flown in from Tokyo to testify.

TWENTY-FOUR

Shoshin Ito made the short drive from the Jiangwan Airfield to the 13th Army's headquarters and settled into the officer's quarters that had been readied for his arrival. He had not been to the place in more than two years, but it all still looked the same. Back then, he had been a mere colonel, heading up the 13th Army's Legal Department. Now he was a major general.

Given what he was expected to say on the stand, there was no good reason he should not have been sitting next to Sawada, Wako, Okada, and Tatsuta in the courtroom. But with the trial already well under way, he could be confident about his personal security. He had spent hours talking to John Hendren back in Tokyo. Hendren had been very interested in Sawada and even more interested in Ito's old friend Sadamu Shimomura. Hendren, though, had never expressed the slightest interest in him. Ito had mastered the art of being boring, which always led everyone to assume he was innocuous.

If Ito was ever going to be charged for his role in the Doolittle Raiders' torture, trial, and executions, he knew, he would have been arrested already. Shimomura had technically been arrested back in February, but people in the know, not the least Shimomura himself, knew that the arrest had been a political sham. It had been MacArthur's way of placating the reporters after Dwyer had leaked Shimomura's name to the press. Behind the scenes, the responsible individuals in the interim Japanese government, with whom MacArthur worked every day to realize his vision of a democratic Japan, had lobbied to let Shimomura stay under house arrest instead of being sent to Sugamo. But MacArthur knew that leaving Shimomura in Sugamo while the Doolittle Trial played itself out protected him and anyone else from being sent to Shanghai against their will.

The threat of war crimes prosecutions had loomed over Ito since the war's end, but the Doolittle Raiders case was not his paramount concern. Ito was confident that back in 1942, he had done all the paperwork in the Doolittle Raiders case as completely as any trial paperwork could be done. It was a prominent case; Ito had known that from the moment he saw the cover memorandum on the case file, personally signed by Vice Minister of War Heitaro Kimura. It might as well have been signed by Tojo himself. Ito knew what Tokyo wanted, and he had ascended to the rank of major general in the Japanese Army by making sure his superiors always had the necessary paperwork to get what they wanted.

Now in his midfifties, Ito had grown up in a small village outside of Nagoya. He had sought to cut his own path to respectability by studying law at Kyoto Imperial University, but, as he lacked family connections, his best option was to work as a lawyer for the Legal Department of the War Ministry. He quickly discovered, however, that lawyers in the Japanese Army had very little authority or prestige. Culturally, they were viewed by most soldiers like monks in a whorehouse. "The legal section is the scum of the Army" was the prevailing attitude toward Japanese military lawyers. For a status-conscious man in a status-conscious organization, Ito had lamented the fact that military lawyers were not even treated as soldiers until April 1942 and were not given the status of full military officers until 1943.

Ito had climbed his way up the chain of command from the scum to the third highest rank an army officer could earn, and he had done so by being pedantic to the point of boring. His superiors did not follow all, or even most, of what he said. But that was his virtue; it made him sound like a chemist explaining the principles of combustion to an artillery officer who wanted a big explosion. Ito's paperwork made sure the higher-ups could do anything they wanted to do and that when they did it, everything was on the right—or at least defensible—side of the law.

That was not always an easy thing to do. It took precision and patience, and those were uncommon traits in the Army. When Ito first got the case file on the Doolittle Raiders back in July 1942, he could see right away that the file was a bit thin. It had been brought to him by Major Izumi Ogata from the Kempeitai's Shanghai office, the man responsible for running Bridge House's dungeon. Ogata was impatient to wash his hands of the Doolittle Raiders, who had been his unhappy responsibility for more than a month. Even though there were only eight of them, they took up an entire cell by themselves, and they attracted too much attention.

Like everyone else on April 18, 1942, Ito knew most of what he did about the Doolittle Raid from the media. But a few days after it hit the news, the 13th Army received its own internal report from the field, saying that Sawada's men had captured three Americans south of Ningbo. When the news got out, the 13th Army's spokesman told the Shanghai press corps that the Americans were being sent to Tokyo to face justice for having "machine-gunned innocent children" and "intentionally dropped incendiary bombs on a hospital."

Ito did not think much more about the Doolittle Raiders until Ogata came to his office. "The airmen," Ogata explained, "are to be tried by a military tribunal," and Tokyo headquarters had ordered that it be done by the 13th Army in Shanghai. Ogata wanted it to be done as quickly as possible.

At first, that made no sense to Ito. The Army had a law to prosecute war criminals in China. He had supervised several such trials at Jiangwan. But that law did not provide for jurisdiction in this kind of case. The Doolittle Raiders, whatever they had done, had not committed any crimes in China.

Ito then saw among the documents Ogata had given him a notice from Sugiyama's deputy explaining the plan for the "forthcoming execution of punishment against the crew of the American air-raiding planes" and a draft of a new law that lawyers in the War Ministry had written. It did not single out the Doolittle Raiders by name, but it did not have to. It authorized the Army to conduct military commissions and to impose the death penalty against any foreign airman who committed "outrageous and inhuman acts ignoring humanity."

Ito saw several problems with the whole scheme that only a lawyer could solve. The first was the proposed new law itself: it was an ex post facto law. But perhaps this law was not really a new law. What if it was simply a codification of the existing customs of international law? Certainly, attacking civilians and terrorizing them with airplanes violated the customary laws of war. So long as it was clear in the Noboru Unit's judgment that the Doolittle Raiders were being convicted of violating the customs of international law, Ito figured, this new law would appear sufficiently legal.

The other problem—and from Ito's perspective the bigger one—was with the evidence. The only evidence in the case file was a stack of confessions that the Doolittle Raiders had given to the Kempeitai. Ito knew right away that they would not be enough, particularly in a high-profile case. What if the Raiders denied having made the confessions? Everything would fall apart.

Ito explained all this to Ogata: "There would be nothing to prove it." To make the case, he would need the *corpus delicti*. "Get in touch with Tokyo Headquarters," he told Ogata, and ask them "to prepare the report of the damages concerning the indiscriminate bombings of civilians together with those damage reports." Ito explained that he wanted official reports with "such information as damages and losses sustained in the bombing and strafing."

Ogata had made the request, but the Tokyo Kempeitai had been slow in acting on it. That meant that Ogata had remained stuck taking care of the Doolittle Raiders in Bridge House throughout July and into August. He soon made a habit of going to Jiangwan to hassle Major Itsuro Hata, Ito's assistant in the Legal Department, nagging him to have the 13th Army take the Doolittle Raiders off his hands.

Ito resisted Ogata's pestering. The only reason to transfer the Doolittle Raiders to Jiangwan would be for trial, and if they were transferred for trial before all the evidence to try them was in place, how would that look? Ogata needed to be patient. Ito knew what he was doing. No one could say that anything was done improperly if they got the paperwork right. In the meantime, why not have the Kempeitai question the Doolittle Raiders again to confirm the confessions they had given in Tokyo? That would help thicken the case file for trial.

Ogata had his men question some of the Doolittle Raiders up on Bridge House's fifth floor, and he was pleased to report that, after only three hours of interrogation, "They admitted everything."

Ito never learned the reason for the delay that had so frustrated the impatient and imprecise Ogata. Various theories surfaced later. One, which was claimed without any evidence by lawyers defending General Shunroku Hata against war crimes charges of his own, was that Hata had formally protested the plan to try the Doolittle Raiders and that Hata's protest had forced the lawyers in Tokyo to reconsider the idea for a few weeks. Another, and more plausible, explanation was that the lawyers in Tokyo had paused the plan to try the Doolittle Raiders at the end of July 1942 because of events that were unfolding at the very same time in the United States.

* * *

In the afterglow of his by then famous raid, Jimmy Doolittle had gone on a tour of the nation's air bases. On Sunday, June 14, 1942, he visited Mitchell Field on Long Island, where he had done his "blind flying" stunt fifteen years earlier. He was there to convince the public that the Doolittle magic would rub off on those responsible for defending Long Island's nearly three hundred miles of coastline.

Doolittle did not know it at the time, but just after midnight the day before, a Nazi submarine had, in fact, surfaced off the coast of Long Island, depositing four Nazi saboteurs on the beach. A Coast Guard coxswain had stumbled upon them as they had come ashore, but, armed with only a flashlight, he had accepted a $260 bribe from the group's ringleader in exchange for a promise to keep silent.

The run-in with the coxswain apparently spooked the group's ringleader, and within a few days, he and one of his confederates turned themselves in to the FBI. In short order, the remaining saboteurs were arrested, along with a second team of Nazi saboteurs, who had landed a few days later in Florida. Fearing embarrassment over how close the saboteurs had come to carrying out their plans, President Roosevelt was persuaded to resurrect the use of military commissions in the United States for the first time in forty years. They offered the possibility of trying the saboteurs in secret and all but ensured sentences of death for them all.

The secret trial of the Nazi saboteurs before a military commission got under way in July 1942, just as Japan's War Ministry was finalizing the preparations for the trial of the Doolittle Raiders. But the team of US Army lawyers who had been assigned to defend the saboteurs were appalled by how un-American the trial turned out to be. They publicly petitioned the US Supreme Court to intervene and declare the trial unlawful.

The case of the Nazi saboteurs became an international media sensation and raised the possibility that the Supreme Court might hold that military commissions were illegal. Such a decision would, at the very least, complicate the ability of other countries to conduct war crimes trials of their own, including, as it happened, Japan's plans to prosecute the Doolittle Raiders.

On July 31, however, the Supreme Court issued a short summary opinion called a *per curiam*. "RULING UNANIMOUS," read the headline, "Supreme Bench Backs President's Power over Invader Saboteurs." The military commission quickly found all eight Nazis guilty and sentenced them to death, and on August 8, 1942, the White House announced that six of the saboteurs had died in the electric chair. Roosevelt, in an act of mercy, had commuted the sentence of the two Nazis who had turned themselves in to thirty years at hard labor.

The Supreme Court would not issue its formal legal opinion in the case until October 1942; it was an opinion that would form the basis of its decision in the Yamashita case three years later. But the international attention the case garnered in August 1942 gave the Axis powers a unique opportunity to condemn the United States for hypocrisy and barbarism. Italian radio covered the news of the execution, saying "Roosevelt's blood purge continues," and the Japanese press condemned the Supreme Court for ratifying "President Roosevelt's exceptional powers" and illegitimately expanding the authority of military tribunals. In Germany, the Foreign Office spokesman promised reprisals. When they came, the spokesman continued, the Americans would have no room to criticize.

It was only a few days after the Roosevelt administration executed the Nazi saboteurs that Ito found himself again interrupted by Izumi Ogata. Ogata handed Ito the final version of the Enemy Airmen's Law and an order from General Hata directing the 13th Army to try the Doolittle Raiders without delay. Sugiyama let it be known that he wanted them executed as soon as possible.

*　*　*

The crew of the *Green Hornet*, the sixth plane off the USS *Hornet*, 1942. From left to right: Lieutenant Chase Nielsen, Lieutenant Dean Hallmark, Sergeant Donald Fitzmaurice, Lieutenant Robert Meder, Corporal William Dieter.

The crew of the *Bat Out of Hell*, the sixteenth plane off the USS *Hornet*, 1942. From left to right: Lieutenant George Barr, Lieutenant William Farrow, Sergeant Harold Spatz, Lieutenant Robert Hite, Corporal Jacob DeShazer.

3

President Franklin Roosevelt awarding James Doolittle the Congressional Medal of Honor, 1942.

4

Jacob DeShazer, Robert Hite, and Chase Nielsen following their arrival in Washington, DC, on September 4, 1945.

5

Japanese Army photograph of Robert Hite being marched from an airplane following his capture by the Japanese, 1942.

6

Japanese Army photograph of the crew of the *Bat Out of Hell* in Nanchang, 1942. From left to right: William Farrow, Jacob DeShazer, George Barr, Harold Spatz, Robert Hite.

7

Chase Nielsen, John Hendren, Robert Dwyer, 1946.

8

Robert Dwyer returning to Shanghai's Ward Road Jail from Tokyo, 1946. From left to right: Shigeru Sawada, Robert Dwyer, Yusei Wako, unknown military police officer in trademark "snowdrop" helmet.

9

Sotojiro Tatsuta posing for newspaper photographs in Ward Road Jail, 1946.

Robert Dwyer, Elizaveta Snigursky, and Edmund Bodine standing outside Ward Road Jail, 1946.

Elizaveta Snigursky standing in front of a C-47 "Gooney Bird" with Edmund Bodine in the cockpit, 1946.

12

Elizaveta Snigursky and Charles Fellows in Broadway Mansions, 1946.

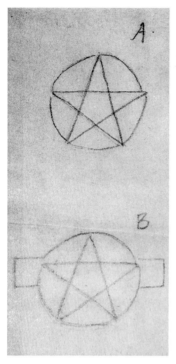

Edmund Bodine's drawings of Army Air Force roundels from 1942 and 1945 to test the credibility of the teachers from Tsurumaki National School, 1946.

13

14

Hideki Tojo and Edmund Bodine in Sugamo Prison, 1946.

15

The four defendants in the case of *United States v. Sawada, et al.* seated in the courtroom, 1946. From left to right: Sotojiro Tatsuta, Ryuhei Okada, Yusei Wako, Shigeru Sawada.

Robert Dwyer, Joseph Keenan, and John Hendren at the prosecution table during the trial of *United States v. Sawada, et al.* (Elizaveta Snigursky is visible over Hendren's left shoulder, sitting behind the bar), 1946.

Chase Nielsen being questioned by John Hendren during the trial of *United States v. Sawada, et al.*, 1946.

Old Chinese cemetery where Dean Hallmark, William Farrow, and Harold Spatz were executed with three wooden crosses planted as part of the prosecution's reenactment, 1946.

The reading of the verdict in the case of *United States v. Sawada, et al.*, 1946. From left to right at the counsel tables: Robert Dwyer, John Hendren, Moritada Kumashiro, Shinji Somiya, Tadahiro Hayamao. From left to right in the well: Edmund Bodine, Shigeru Sawada, Yusei Wako, Ryuhei Okada, Sotojiro Tatsuta, Charles Fellows.

Ito was confident, even after Shigeru Sawada had been arrested, that he had gotten the paperwork in the Doolittle Raiders case right. The final version of the Enemy Airmen's Law had been significantly improved for appearance's sake, redefining the description of the crimes as "violations of wartime international law." That made it no more an ex post facto law than the law the Americans had used to try the Nazi saboteurs.

Ito also had resisted the urge to treat the case as anything special. He had been tempted to appear before the tribunal in person as the prosecutor, since doing so would put his name in front of the higher-ups in Tokyo, maybe even Emperor Hirohito. But he did the sensible thing and left it to his assistant, Major Itsuro Hata, since that was Hata's usual responsibility.

Every case, whether a military commission or a court-martial, was heard by three judges, and Ito always personally assigned one of them, a lawyer, from the Legal Department. That judge, in turn, would select two others from a pool of thirty officers stationed elsewhere in the 13th Army, who were, in essence, on the list for jury duty.

Ito assigned Yusei Wako to act as the Legal Department's judge. Wako had arrived only in May 1942 and had not yet been with the 13th Army when the Doolittle Raiders had been captured. On paper, Wako could never be accused of having had personal knowledge of the case. Ito told Wako to select two more judges from the usual pool without any fanfare.

Wako, for his part, actually did a good job in selecting the other judges. Toyama Nakajo was a lieutenant colonel and the highest-ranking judge on the list. Ryuhei Okada had had experience with Americans from his day job in the Special Services Section and had sat as a judge in the trial of some other Americans back in June. Wako announced their selection in the barracks newsletter, as was usual, and made no mention of the fact that it was for the case of the infamous Doolittle Raiders.

* * *

By the time Ito returned to Shanghai in March 1946, though, he had reason to regret having given Wako any role in the Doolittle Raiders case. Wako could do some things right, but he could also be very unpredictable. The slightest bit of stress caused him to lose control of himself, and Ito was forced to have him committed to the hospital for twenty days in November

1943. Wako was the first officer in the 13th Army ever to be committed for mental health issues, and because a diagnosis of insanity would haunt him for the rest of his life, Ito saw to it that Wako's medical paperwork simply said "slight respiratory disease" and "nervous prostration."

For a combination of reasons, some paternal and others perhaps more self-interested, Ito saw to it that Wako was transferred along with him in early 1944 to the Legal Department of Japan's Western District Army. Located in Fukuoka, the Western District Army was responsible for Kyushu, Japan's large southwestern island, where Nagasaki is located.

Sadamu Shimomura had been promoted to be the commander of the Western District Army, and Shimomura tapped Ito to head its legal department. Ito, in turn, tapped Wako as his legal assistant, and once in Fukuoka, Wako was put in charge of the Western District Army's brig, a position not unlike the one Sotojiro Tatsuta held at Jiangwan. The brig was small, its responsibilities were light, and Wako seemed placated by the status of being in charge of something.

Things in Fukuoka had been fine for a year, but then Shimomura was promoted again and his replacement was a procurement bureaucrat, who had very little experience commanding an actual army. Morale collapsed, and the usual turf wars and resentments within the chain of command flowered into outright dysfunction.

It did not help that the war had turned decidedly against Japan by early 1945 or that Curtis LeMay was laying flaming waste to the country's urban map. After the fall of Okinawa in June 1945, no one doubted that the invasion of Kyushu was imminent. The Western District Army would be the only line of defense between the invading Allies and the Japanese mainland. It was only a matter of time.

The stress made Wako even more erratic and abusive. He was apt to pick fistfights with subordinates and then threaten them with court-martial if they struck him back. And putting him in charge of the brig increasingly turned out to have been a mistake. When he had been given the job the year before, the prisoners had been delinquent Japanese soldiers, but throughout 1945, the crews of Curtis LeMay's B-29s were being captured on Kyushu and brought to Fukuoka.

Initially, it was Army policy to send captured enemy airmen to Tokyo for prosecution under the Enemy Airmen's Law, but LeMay's strikes on

Japan's transit network made that increasingly impracticable. After the second firebombing of Tokyo on May 18, 1945, in which the Imperial Palace was damaged, the political situation in Tokyo had changed dramatically.

Lawyers within the War Ministry now argued that instead of trying captured Americans under the Enemy Airmen's Law, they should just be summarily executed. Summary execution, the lawyers argued, was a legitimate act of reprisal for the indiscriminate destruction of civilian homes, hospitals, and schools by LeMay's B-29s. Great Britain had adopted a similar policy during the First World War and subjected German submarine crews to reprisals for the U-boats' notorious practice of indiscriminately torpedoing any Allied vessel found in the Atlantic. The proposed change in Army policy, however, was opposed by influential factions within the cabinet, who argued that it was contrary to international law, and so a compromise was reached.

Ito was shown a cable marked TOP SECRET with instructions to burn after reading. The cable said that the Kempeitai was implementing a new policy approved by the cabinet. Enemy airmen were no longer to be transported to Tokyo for detention and "disposition" under the Enemy Airmen's Law. Instead, each headquarters would determine the "disposition" of the airmen as appropriate.

Ito could see the deliberate ambiguity right away. In Japanese, the word for "disposition" (処理, pronounced "shori") can mean "disposal," which implied that the airmen were to be summarily executed. But it can also just mean "disposition," which implied that local headquarters could carry out trials under the Enemy Airmen's Act if captured American airmen were suspected of committing war crimes.

The Western District Army already had at least eight American airmen in Wako's brig. The head of the Intelligence Section, Yoshinao Sato, read the cable the way it was undoubtedly intended to be read, taking it as permission to summarily execute them all. Sato had gotten whatever intelligence his men could extract from them. He was now ready to dispose of them, and Wako was happy to oblige.

Ito intervened, though. There were records of the men being held by the Western District Army. They could not just disappear without a trace. But, Ito said, he had reviewed the file and found evidence that at least four of them had participated in indiscriminate bombing. He had assigned their cases to one of his best lieutenants to prepare the cases for trial under the Enemy Airmen's Law. They could be executed, but only after the paperwork was in order.

Sato agreed to go along with Ito's effort to be precise with the paperwork. But then, after the sun went down on June 19, 1945, Fukuoka came up as the next target of Curtis LeMay's B-29s. In a single night, a quarter of Fukuoka was destroyed. Thousands of men, women, and children were burned to death.

Ito spent the night in an air raid shelter and went out to survey the damage the next morning. His office was still smoldering, and he ordered some enlisted men to salvage whatever files they could from the fire and move them into Wako's brig. The brig was brick, so it, and its American inmates, had withstood the firebombing reasonably well.

Ito spent the morning seeing what was left of the city. He returned to headquarters in the early afternoon and learned that while he had been out, Wako had dug a pit. Sato had given Wako permission to behead the eight Americans, who had survived the firebombing in his brig.

Ito rushed to the execution ground, but only three of the Americans were still alive. Five lay headless in a pit that had grown muddy from the blood draining out of their neck stumps. One head was still tethered to its body by a flap of skin, the sword not having come down hard enough to cut cleanly through. Wako, Ito learned, had killed the man along with one of the other awkward bodies in the pit.

Ito considered ordering them all to stop. He was a general, after all, but he doubted that his order would be obeyed. Sato was clearly in charge and in no mood to entertain further arguments about the meaning of the word "disposition."

Ito stood by as Wako handed his sword to a young lieutenant whose mother had been killed the night before and simply looked on as the young lieutenant chopped his revenge through the neck of the sixth American, then the seventh, then the eighth.

As he watched the blindfolded heads roll off their clumsy bodies and into Wako's pit, Ito's mind turned to paperwork. Ito had sent cables to Tokyo identifying the men. There was a paper trail that led from this pit of mutilated corpses right back to him.

Sato offered a solution to Ito's paperwork problem in the form of a forged damage report that said the Americans had all been killed in the firebombing. Sato planned to send the report to Tokyo under the general's name; all Ito had to do was send a copy to the Legal Department in Tokyo under his own name so that everything matched.

Ito looked over the forged report. It said that sixteen Americans had died in the firebombing, yet only eight had been dumped into Wako's pit. Why the difference?

There were doctors at Kyushu Imperial University, Sato explained, who needed test subjects for some medical experiments. Sato had been detaining another eight Americans, who were no longer of any intelligence value, and so he had sent them. They had gotten rid of what was left of the bodies, but the paperwork was all a mess, and so Sato figured this was a good opportunity to clean up the books all at once.

Ito signed his name to the forged documents and sent them to Tokyo. But he knew that it was only a matter of time before witnesses came forward or the beheaded bodies were dug up from Wako's pit. Ito would be called to account for why the paperwork, with his name on it, did not match up. The whole affair had been bloody, sloppy revenge.

Ito had not made that mistake in the case of the Doolittle Raiders. There he had been in control, and he had done things precisely and with patience. And his name was on none of the paperwork.

* * *

Bodine suspected that Ito's testimony could be big. Back in February, Fellows had found Wako babbling and distraught. That was not unusual. Wako regularly suffered from hallucinations that prevented him from sleeping. A recurring one had led him to demand a trial before Roosevelt, whom he insisted would return to Earth after the Battle of Armageddon. Wako claimed to have learned that prophecy after hearing President Roosevelt's voice on a shortwave radio broadcast in December 1942.

This time, though, Wako had been distraught about something that made some sense. "We all do not understand," he complained, "why Colonel Ito is not brought to trial." After all, Wako said, "he handled everything in place of the commander." Wako was distraught because he was being made a scapegoat for everything that Ito had orchestrated at the behest of Tokyo. "General Sawada was only a puppet," Wako insisted. "Everything was decided in Nanking and Colonel Ito handled everything. The four of us, we are only small people and have no say."

Given the source, it was hard to know how seriously to take what Wako was saying. And the first time Bodine and Fellows had a chance to meet Ito in person, it was hardly obvious that he would be willing to testify that he had, in fact, handled everything.

During some downtime in the midst of the trial, Bodine and the rest of the defense team went up to Jiangwan to see Ito. He had given them the impression of wanting to be helpful, in particular to Sawada, who, he confirmed, had been away during the summer of 1942 and had learned about the whole Doolittle Raider affair only after he had returned to Shanghai in September. But to Bodine's dismay, Ito insisted on answering seemingly every question with a pedantic recitation on the minute structure of Japanese bureaucracy.

"Sawada did not have any control whatsoever, did he?" Bodine asked, trying to keep things simple.

"As far as this case is concerned, General Sawada had no definite control not only to change the decision of the court, but even the case was not done by his discretion but by the order." Ito then continued that, in an ordinary case, "the commander has the right to change the sentence, but as far as this case is concerned the commander has no right at all."

"I would lay emphasis on that," Bodine told him, wading through the thicket of words to the conclusion.

On some points, Ito could be helpfully clear. "I just wonder, out of curiosity," Bodine said to Kumashiro, who was translating, "if the court had acquitted these men or General Ito refused to try them, what would happen?"

"I was under the control of the 13th Army," Ito said matter-of-factly, "subject to instructions from the Nanking headquarters, and I would be charged with disobedience."

"Be very forceful on that point to the court," Bodine instructed him before turning to the evidence at the trial. "If the judges," Bodine asked, referring to Wako and Okada, "found out that the evidence was taken under torture by the Kempeitai, would the Kempeitai officers be arrested?"

Ito looked confused. Hayama interjected to try to clarify. "Was your experience that at the time the case was arrived at by torture by the Kempeitai, because the prosecutor will ask you a question," he explained.

"When I was approached by the Shanghai Kempeitai together with the investigations of the Tokyo Kempeitai," Ito said, "I never thought it was made under torture."

"In your experience, out of your own experience," Hayama asked, "were investigation reports of the Tokyo Kempeitai obtained by torture?"

"No," Ito replied.

"Tell him to stick to that strongly," Bodine told Kumashiro, no doubt delighted by Ito's ability to give a succinct answer at long last. But when Bodine asked who had made the decision to try the Doolittle Raiders in the first place, Ito returned to his long and elliptical answers. Kumashiro digested what he said as best he could and then turned back to Bodine. "He thinks that the case originated in Tokyo, not Nanking headquarters."

"Did he think," Bodine pressed him, "that it was up to Sawada to have the actual approval of the findings of the court or up to Hata or Tokyo?"

"It originated from Tokyo," Ito said before digressing again into subtle distinctions.

Ito's testimony was not something that lent itself to being scripted. Even when asked simple yes-or-no questions, Ito offered a multitude of details. With all but a few exceptions, he never came right out and said what Bodine wanted to hear. And at no point did he admit that he, Shoshin Ito, had masterminded the trial and execution of the Doolittle Raiders.

When it finally came time to call Ito to the stand, Bodine had Fellows do the questioning. Fellows had a way of asking seemingly innocent questions that slowly but surely led to all the facts coming to light. If Fellows could get Ito to describe everything that had happened in the summer of 1942 step-by-step, it could be the biggest moment of the whole case.

Ito would never have to dramatically declare "I was the mastermind" on the stand. If Fellows was at his best, the conclusion would present itself automatically. The only risk was that Fellows could get frustrated when things weren't going his way, and when he got frustrated, he could get sarcastic. It was not a good look for a baby-faced captain to have in front of some old Army colonels.

It was Wednesday morning, the third day of the defense's case, and Ito took the stand to be sworn in. Fellows was ready. But just as he was about to ask Ito his first question, to walk him through the summer of 1942, step-by-step, Dwyer interrupted.

TWENTY-FIVE

"The prosecution has a preliminary statement to make with reference to this witness," Dwyer announced.

Dwyer had never met Ito before; all he knew for sure was that Hendren liked him. During Hendren's visit to Tokyo, Ito had come off as serious, knowledgeable, and a voice of reasonableness. He had given Hendren a stack of paperwork on the Doolittle case, and nowhere was Ito's name even mentioned, let alone implicated. Best of all, Ito had gone out of his way to be helpful in Hendren's ill-fated pursuit of Sadamu Shimomura. Had they not been thwarted in dragging Shimomura to Shanghai for trial, Hendren would have almost certainly asked Ito to come to Shanghai as a witness for the prosecution.

But Dwyer had his doubts. Chief among them was that Ito was there for the defense. There was also something Tatsuta had said back in February, right before the charges were announced. Dwyer had been badgering Tatsuta, again trying to get him to confess to having made the Doolittle Raiders sign blank pieces of paper in order to forge their signatures on confessions. Tatsuta remained unwilling to admit as much, but for the first time, he had mentioned Ito's name.

"Did Colonel Ito have anything to do with the court-martial trial of the fliers?" Dwyer had asked.

"Yes," Tatsuta had said, "he had plenty to do with it. Before the order comes down from Lieutenant General Sawada, Colonel Ito makes arrangements and goes and tells Lieutenant General Sawada what is to be done by this one and by that one. Actually, the order comes from Colonel Ito."

"On the order of Lieutenant General Sawada?"

"Yes." Tatsuta had replied.

"Was he in the court on the day of the trial?"

"Yes."

"What did you see Colonel Ito do in the courtroom?"

"Well," Tatsuta had tried to remember, "I was there for ten minutes. Colonel Ito was only listening to the court proceedings." But then he had claimed to remember that Ito had personally taken the death sentence to General Sawada for approval.

"Do you remember the date?"

"If you check over the records there is everything," Tatsuta had said, trying to get Dwyer to see Ito's significance. "The time and date is all written down."

"The records were burned!" Dwyer had snapped at him.

Dwyer had heard Ito's name once or twice before, but his name hadn't been on any of the paperwork Dwyer had so painstakingly reviewed that fall. It hadn't been on the Noboru Unit judgment, which had been Dwyer's key for determining who had participated in the Doolittle Raiders' show trial and execution, and Tatsuta had never named him before. Tatsuta had just talked about the "prosecutor," who Dwyer had just assumed was Major Itsuro Hata, the prosecutor listed on the Noboru Unit judgment.

At the time, Dwyer had put what Tatsuta was saying out of his mind—the man had every reason to deflect blame with the charges on the way—and having just returned in humiliation from Tokyo, Dwyer could do nothing with the information even if he wanted to. The trial had been scheduled to start in less than two weeks. Even assuming that Dwyer was able to investigate Ito and draft more charges against him in that short amount of time, Ito, like Shimomura, was in Tokyo. He would need a warrant to arrest him and probably the personal approval of MacArthur. There was no indication that Young would support such a request after the drama with Shimomura. Even raising the possibility risked complicating the case he and Hendren had already built against Sawada.

Now, however, Ito had come to Shanghai as a witness for the defense. Unsure of why Ito was there or what he would say, Dwyer bluffed.

"This witness," Dwyer explained, "is not entitled to the protection of the 24th Article of War nor the Fifth Amendment of the Constitution guaranteeing the privileged against testifying against himself." There was accordingly a need, he continued, "to advise this witness that in the event he is ever tried before a military commission of the United States Army, any statement he may here make may be used against him."

Dwyer knew there would be no second Doolittle Trial, but he wanted Ito to at least think that if blame did not fall on Sawada, Wako, Okada, and Tatsuta, it could very well fall on him.

Fellows, for his part, saw through what Dwyer was doing. "If the court please," Fellows protested, "I think the prosecution is trying to intimidate the witness at this time; we strenuously object to this!"

Without a second thought, McReynolds batted Fellows away, overruled his objection, and turned to Dwyer. "The commission desires to know the status of the witness at the present time regarding the possibility of being a prisoner, retired status, or what is his status?"

"That we can't answer," Dwyer said mischievously, "and that is the reason why we state it is in the realm of possibility."

"If the commission please," Fellows interrupted, "I know the witness is not a prisoner."

"As to his future status," Dwyer replied, "I don't think anybody can advise the commission on that."

"Under the circumstances," McReynolds agreed, "the commission feels that the witness should be advised of his rights."

"The witness has been advised of his rights by the reading of that statement I think," Fellows snarked.

Dwyer trained his predator's gaze onto Ito. "General Ito," Dwyer asked, "do you understand what has been said up to now in this courtroom about you?"

"I do," Ito replied.

"You are advised that any statement you may make here may be used against you." Satisfied with himself, Dwyer turned to Fellows. "You may examine the witness."

"The defense counsel for the accused and each of the accused," Fellows erupted, "asks the Commission to declare this a mistrial for the reason that an attempt has been made to intimidate this witness prior to his testimony."

"May it please the commission," Dwyer said insouciantly, "defense counsel is putting words into the mouth of the prosecution." Dwyer was happy to have a fight—delighted, really, to have broken through Fellows's wall of boyish good humor. "We have said nothing. We don't wish to have anyone infer, including this witness, that he will be charged." Dwyer then defended his warning to Ito on the grounds of the rules. Paragraph 16, subparagraph E, allowed all testimony in the military commission to be used in future cases. The prosecution was just doing the right thing, Dwyer explained, so that Ito knew the risks he was taking by testifying.

Fellows looked as though he needed a cigarette as he flailed and tried to fight back against Dwyer's mastery of the technicalities, but McReynolds cut him off.

"The motion requested by the defense for mistrial is denied," McReynolds snapped. "Proceed."

*　　*　　*

Dwyer's bluff initially had its desired effect on both Fellows and Ito. As Fellows tried to walk Ito through the events of 1942, Ito answered each question slowly and cautiously. But Fellows gradually regained his poise and, through hours of patient questioning, got Ito to describe the summer of 1942 step-by-step from his vantage point as the head of the 13th Army's Legal Department. Ito never declared, "I am the mastermind!" The inference, though, became increasingly inescapable as he recounted how the Doolittle Raiders had come back to Shanghai and been kept in Bridge House until their trial.

As Ito described it, the trial had been on the morning of August 28, 1942. The now dead Colonel Toyama Nakajo had been the presiding judge and called the commission to order at 10:00 a.m. The eight Doolittle Raiders had stood about thirty feet away from the judges' bench, and each had been asked for his name, nationality, rank, and other biographical details.

Major Itsuro Hata, as Ito's representative for the prosecution, had then read the charges Ito had approved aloud in Japanese: On April 18, one American plane had flown over Tokyo, indiscriminately bombing and strafing schools and civilian areas. The other had flown over Nagoya, also indiscriminately bombing and strafing schools and civilians, including fishermen on the beach. As Hata had read through the charges, Ito explained, the interpreter relayed to the Doolittle Raiders all of what was going on.

Wako, as the Legal Department's representative on the judge's bench, had asked the important questions and had the Doolittle Raiders confirm the details of the confessions they had given to the Kempeitai. Each question, Ito explained, had been relayed by the interpreter to the Doolittle Raiders, who in turn, had all confirmed that the confessions were real.

Wako had then put the central question to the eight Doolittle Raiders: Was it true that they had bombed indiscriminately and gunned down children in schoolyards? Ito was sure that the question had been translated accurately based upon the Doolittle Raiders' reactions. The crew of William Farrow's plane had admitted to firing over Nagoya, though the crew of Dean Hallmark's plane denied ever using their machine gun at all.

Wako had challenged Hallmark's crew on their denials. "You had incendiary bombs and you bombed out many objects," he had said. "Since you had incendiary bombs didn't you intend to bomb heavily populated areas?"

Hallmark had not been responsive but the two men still on their feet, Chase Nielsen and Robert Meder, had admitted as much, though both continued to deny strafing schoolchildren with their machine guns.

But Wako then reminded them of their confessions to the Kempeitai. In those confessions, they had admitted to strafing civilians. Those were their signatures on the confessions, weren't they?

The translator again appeared to have relayed the question to Nielsen and Meder, but this time there had been no response. The two men had just stood there. For everyone in the courtroom back in August 1942, that silence spoke volumes. When confronted with their own signed statements confessing to atrocities, the Doolittle Raiders had not denied the charges.

Hata had then made his closing remarks. He reiterated the evidence collected by the Kempeitai, including how the damage reports had corroborated the Raiders' confessions. The evidence of guilt, Hata had insisted, was clear. "In view of the new military law," he concluded, "I request that the penalty be the death sentence."

Nakajo had adjourned the trial around noon, and Ito received the

Noboru Unit judgment a little while later. All eight of the Doolittle Raiders had been found guilty as charged and, accordingly, sentenced to death. As Ito had expected, the judges based their verdict on the Raiders' confessions and the damage report from the Kempeitai.

Fellows presented Ito with a copy of the Kempeitai's investigation file, which Fellows and Bodine had gotten from Sawada's old friends back in Tokyo. In that file, Fellows explained, were the confessions the Doolittle Raiders had signed for the Kempeitai back in 1942. He asked Ito to confirm that they were the confessions that Wako had relied upon during the trial. Ito confirmed that they were.

"Were the confessions signed by the fliers?" Fellows asked.

"Yes," Ito replied.

McReynolds took copies of the confessions and admitted them into evidence. It took a minute, but Dwyer realized that they needed to object and nudged Hendren into action.

"If the Commission please, the prosecution objects to these exhibits being presented to the Commission," Hendren said. "We do not wish to argue with the Commission, but their use could not be of a reliable nature before this Commission and they have no probative value." The objection was a mush of words, reasonably stated but lacking any legal rationale.

"I would like to add a further statement," Dwyer interjected, trying to assist. "There is no evidence here as to any official who took the document down or had it in his custody, nor is there any official here to authenticate the document." There was no way of knowing, in other words, if the purported confessions were forgeries.

"If the Commission please," Fellows replied, reveling in the opportunity to throw his own mastery of the technicalities back at Dwyer, "paragraph 16, subparagraph 5 of the Rules and Regulations Governing the Trial of War Criminals, provides that a copy of any document is admissible as evidence."

"This is a copy of a copy," Dwyer protested.

"The Commission is aware of the rules," McReynolds retorted. "Defense Transcript Exhibit No. 14 is received in evidence."

By the time Fellows was done, Dwyer could see that his whole case was in mortal danger. Ito clearly bore more responsibility for the Doolittle Raiders' trial and execution than anyone. And Ito's claim that the Doolittle

Raiders had confessed at their trial in August 1942 contradicted Dwyer and Hendren's central contention that Wako and Okada had knowingly accepted false and fraudulent evidence to convict them on false and fraudulent charges. There was only man who could stop the bleeding.

* * *

Chase Nielsen was getting ready to board a plane to leave Shanghai. His orders were due to expire, everyone having assumed back in December that the trial would be over by now. He could probably have had them extended, but he had been in Shanghai for three months by that point and there were personal things he needed to do back in Utah. He had also gotten whatever closure he was likely to get.

Nielsen had been allowed to tell his story to the world and to history, even if Bodine had tripped him up a little bit on some of the details. And Nielsen had also seeen to it that the bodies of Fitz and Dieter, the gunner and bombardier on the *Green Hornet*, had made their way home.

Being back in Shanghai, Nielsen had worked with the Army's grave investigators to retrace his steps and to locate them. When Nielsen returned to the little village of Juexi, the locals still remembered the night the Americans had crashed into the ocean. The house of the mayor, Shimiao Yang, who had sheltered Nielsen, Dean Hallmark, and Robert Meder was still there, but Yang himself was not. There were stories in the village of a massacre done in retaliation for the help Juexi had given the Raiders. Yang had supposedly had been shot.

It had not been difficult for Nielsen to find the hill where they had buried Fitz and Dieter four years earlier. The coffins they had packed with sawdust had been left undisturbed, but once they were dug up, there was not much left inside. All that was really discernable amid the sawdust was the two men's flying jackets. The leather had rotted some in the seaside humidity, but their nameplates were still legible: D E FITZMAURICE and W J DIETER. There was still enough of them there to be sent home for a proper Catholic burial.

With the ashes of Hallmark, Farrow, Spatz, and Meder now recovered, Nielsen could take solace in the fact that all of the Doolittle Raiders, everyone with whom he had shared that special bond, would make it home. But before he could make his own way home, he got a message from John Hendren: he was needed back in court immediately.

Nielsen rushed back to Ward Road Jail's sixth-floor courtroom and entered to see Dwyer slowly asking Shoshin Ito a series of inane questions in an effort to stall for time until Nielsen was found. Hendren, seeing Nielsen come in, stood up.

"May it please the commission," Hendren interrupted, "we would like to call Captain Nielsen at this time."

As Ito rose to give Nielsen his seat, Colonel Murphy stopped him. "May I ask one question of this witness?" Colonel Murphy asked, leafing through the copies of the Doolittle Raiders' alleged confessions to the Kempeitai. "These confessions," Murphy asked, "purported confessions which were written in Japanese and presented at the trial in Shanghai, were they read in English to the accused at the trial?"

"Yes," Ito replied with atypical brevity.

With that Ito stepped down, and Nielsen took his place. Nielsen then listened as Hendren read through excerpts of confessions that he and the other Doolittle Raiders had supposedly given to the Kempeitai back in Tokyo. After each statement, Hendren asked Nielsen to confirm or deny the authenticity of what was being read, and one after the other, Nielsen gave emphatic denials:

"That answer was not given."

"No, I never did."

"I never did. As a matter of fact, Lieutenant Hallmark was pretty proud of the job we had done because we had bombed our target."

"I never did hear him say anything about strafing or shooting anything."

"No sir, I never did."

Hendren then finished by having Nielsen answer the question that Colonel Murphy had just asked Ito before he stepped down: "Captain Nielsen, were any of these questions and answers read in court at the time you were tried on 28 August 1942?"

"No, sir," Nielsen answered, confidently speaking not just for himself but for all of the Doolittle Raiders.

Nielsen tried to suppress his bitterness as he watched Bodine take his place behind the podium. There was no script in Bodine's hands this time.

"When you were examined in Tokyo," Bodine asked, "were you examined singly or in group?"

"We were examined singly," Nielsen replied.

"Then you don't know, of your own knowledge, what the answers were of the other pilots, then, do you?"

"I base my opinion," Nielsen snarled, "on what they told me when we were all together after we came to Shanghai."

"You don't—I will ask you again," Bodine said, "you don't know all the answers they gave to their interrogation in Tokyo, do you?"

"No, sir," Nielsen replied contemptuously. "That I don't know."

With that, Bodine was done with him. Hendren was done with him. And Nielsen was done with the trial. It was already after five, so McReynolds broke for the day. Everyone was set to return for more testimony from Shoshin Ito the next morning. Nielsen, though, would not be there. He would be leaving Shanghai for good. He would be going home.

*　*　*

The next morning, Ito was back on the stand. Dwyer had spent the night working through his notes as the early symptoms of a cold began to set in between his ears. He came into court ready for a fight, but he knew that cross-examining Ito was going to be difficult. Ito was happy to incriminate himself. That meant that Dwyer could not trap him. The only viable strategy was to make Sawada and anyone else connected with Ito look as villainous and corrupt as he was.

"Did you ever hear of the Geneva Prisoner of War Convention?" Dwyer asked.

"I don't remember clearly," Ito replied, "but I have read of it."

"You know that on February 4, 1942, the Japanese government agreed with the United States government to abide by the terms of the Geneva Convention?"

"I read it once, but I don't remember now."

Dwyer then walked Ito through the treaty article by article, and Ito admitted that the Doolittle Raiders had not been given the rights it afforded as prisoners of war. They had been denied access to the Red Cross. They had been held in solitary confinement. They had been tortured and ultimately killed or left to die of neglect. Ito did not, and could not, deny any of it.

Dwyer then cut to the heart of the case. The so-called trial Ito had orchestrated in August 1942 hadn't really been a trial at all. Tokyo had sent the case file to Shanghai because it had known that Ito would ensure that the Doolittle Raiders were sentenced to death. Dwyer waned Ito to admit, right there on the witness stand, that Wako and Sawada and Okada and Tatsuta had been in on it.

"Was Wako in your office as a legal officer?" Dwyer asked.

"Yes," Ito confirmed, "he was."

"You talked this over with Wako, this trial, didn't you?" Dwyer pressed him.

"About what?" Ito replied, confused by the question.

"Withdraw the question." Dwyer stopped for a second to rephrase. "Did you talk to Wako about these papers that came from Tokyo?"

"Wako read it before I did," Ito admitted.

"Wako read it before you did?" The answer was stunning even to Dwyer. Wako, the judge in the case, had read the case file along with all the cables from Tokyo that ordered the Doolittle Raiders to be executed?

"Yes," Ito confirmed.

"General Ito," Dwyer said, turning to the others involved, "did General Sawada have the power as commanding general of the 13th Army to change the decision of the military tribunal?"

"Yes," Ito replied.

"He could revoke the decision of the tribunal, couldn't he?"

"Yes."

"He could reduce the penalty, couldn't he?"

"Yes."

"He could order a new trial, couldn't he?"

"Yes."

"Did General Sawada take any action on that record?"

"He just read the report," Ito said, agreeing that Sawada had never objected to anything that Ito had done, "that is all."

"General Ito," Dwyer then asked, "did Wako object to being on this court—this military tribunal?"

"He did not object," Ito replied.

"Did Okada object to serving on the military tribunal?"

"He did not."

"It was an honor to serve, wasn't it?"

"I imagine they all thought so."

With a few well-phrased questions in the right order, Dwyer had gotten Ito to make everyone else look almost as culpable as he was. They were not as villainous, perhaps. But they had willingly embraced a system that had abandoned international law and left a vacuum in which the cruelest could thrive. Sawada could have done something and hadn't. Wako knew that this so-called trial had only one acceptable outcome. And everyone involved was happy—no, "honored"—to do his part to achieve the outcome that Ito had engineered.

Painting them all as Ito's accomplices cut both ways, though. Ito was not on trial, and although being associated with him made them all look more culpable than the angels, they all looked far less culpable than Ito, who had somehow slipped between the raindrops. Even the Shanghai *Stars and Stripes*, whose coverage had reliably supported Dwyer and Hendren throughout the trial, saw trouble. "Ito's evidence," its reporter had to admit, "damaged the prosecution case for the second straight day."

Ito—not Sawada, Wako, Okada, or Tatsuta—had ordered Izumi Ogata, the head of the Kempeitai, to keep the Doolittle Raiders in Bridge House. That meant that the waterboarding of Dean Hallmark and Robert Meder had been done at *his* behest. Ito had directed Wako to conduct the trial using the evidence *he* had prepared, confessions and all. Ito had briefed Sawada on what *he* had done while Sawada had been at the front. Ito had signed Sawada's name to the Noboru Unit judgment, which *he* had sent up to the chain of command and on to Tokyo. How had Dwyer and Hendren missed all of that?

Dwyer could take some solace from the fact that Shoshin Ito was a master of paperwork. His name had never appeared on any of the documents Dwyer had compiled that fall. The witnesses Dwyer had interviewed in Shanghai had barely mentioned him, at least by name. No one had ever given Dwyer any reason to believe Ito was significant until Tatsuta had started trying to throw blame Ito's way the day before the charges were announced.

But Hendren: How had he been so blind? He had spent days with Ito in Tokyo and spoken to several other high-ranking officers who knew Ito better than anyone else did. Yet Hendren had never thought that Ito's eagerness to help in the hunt for Shimomura was suspicious. He had not done the hard work of putting the case together that Dwyer had. Hendren simply had not known enough to see how the pieces that were right in front of him fit together, and he had become so blinded by the glorious vision of being the man who sent Shimomura to the gallows that he could not see that Ito had something to hide.

By the time Ito stepped down from the witness stand, it was as clear to Dwyer as it was to everyone that Ito was the "prosecutor." He had made sure that Tokyo got exactly what it wanted. He had "participated." He was the mastermind. But none of that mattered as he walked out of the courtroom, out the gates of Ward Road Jail, and out to the car that would drive him to the northern suburbs of Shanghai, where he would soon board a flight back to Tokyo as a free man.

TWENTY-SIX

As the trial entered its final week, all that was left was for Sawada, Wako, Okada, and Tatsuta to testify. Bodine knew that putting them on the stand posed risks, risks that ordinary criminal defendants rarely take. But these were not ordinary criminal defendants. Taking the stand was the only chance these four defeated enemy soldiers had to be anything more than four disgraced Japs in the eyes of McReynolds and the rest of the judges. It was their only chance to be seen as human beings.

Wako, for his part, resisted Bodine and Fellows' strenuous efforts to achieve even that modest goal. Bodine had let Fellows do the questioning and Fellows strained to humanize Wako. But try as Fellows might, Wako did his best to appear like some oracular demon. Seeing Fellows struggling, Dwyer took the opportunity to pepper Fellows with objections to throw him off even more, and McReynolds was so uninterested in trying to figure out what Wako had to say that he sustained each one.

At one point, during one of Wako's rambling answers, the court interpreter threw up his hands. "He is speaking of some other angle," the interpreter complained. "He is not answering the question."

Fellows tried to rephrase his question, which drew an objection. Without a second thought, McReynolds said, "Objection sustained. Proceed."

"If the court please," Fellows said, somewhat stunned to be so briskly shut down, "before proceeding—"

"Objection sustained," McReynolds said, cutting Fellows off curtly. "Proceed."

Bodine tried to come to Fellows' defense. "The court has to hear the reasons of the defense counsel," he protested.

"The commission," McReynolds scolded Bodine, "decided to sustain the objection."

Fellows ended by asking simple biographical questions whose sole purpose was giving Wako a chance to humanize himself: "How old are you?" "Are you married or single?" "Is your wife alive?" "Do you have any children?" But Wako answered each with stream-of-consciousness expeditions through the cataracts and eddies of his mind.

"Captain Wako," Fellows finally said, exasperated, "is there any statement that you want to make to the court concerning the trial of the Doolittle fliers? Do you wish to make a statement?" It was like telling a poorly trained dog to sit for the sixth time.

Wako started rambling through answers to questions that Fellows had asked him earlier that morning in no particular order. Then, pertinent to nothing, he said, "General Shimomura issued the order of execution."

The interpreter, already struggling to keep up, again pleaded exhaustion. "I cannot understand what he says here."

Fellows interrupted, "Ask him to repeat that part of the answer."

"Lieutenant General Shimomura issued the order of execution," Wako continued. "His chop was square. His chop was one centimeter square. The order was addressed to Colonel Ito from General Shimomura." Wako seemed to be trying to say something that was very important, at least in his own mind.

"Captain Wako, you have been accused before this court of having failed to afford a fair trial to certain American fliers." Fellows tried one last time. "Is there anything further you want to say? Do you understand that statement?"

Wako nodded "Yes" but then sat silently for an awkward moment as if he was waiting for something.

"Do you want to say anything else to the court?"

"No," Wako answered matter-of-factly.

*   *   *

If Wako was impossible to humanize, Tatsuta was all too human. When Bodine asked Tatsuta to describe his feelings about the execution of Hallmark, Farrow, and Spatz, Tatsuta was full of remorse.

"I do not know what relation I had with you in the previous life," Tatsuta recounted saying to them, "but we have been living together under the same roof. And on this day you are going to be executed, but I feel sorry for you. My sympathies are with you. Men must die sooner or later. Your lives were very short but your names will remain everlastingly." He then claimed that Farrow had said, "Thank you very much for all the trouble you have taken while we were in your confinement, but please tell the folks at home that we died very bravely."

"Christ was born and died on the cross," Tatsuta recalled replying, "and you on your part must die on the cross but when you are executed—when you die on the cross you will be honored as God's and I told them to pray and then made a sign which resembled the sign of the cross in the parade. I told them you will soon be bound to the crosses and when this is done it is a fact that it is a form that man's faith and cross will be united. Therefore, have faith. They then said—they smiled and said they understood very well."

It was the same abased performance that Tatsuta had put on for the reporters during his confrontation with Nielsen back in January. But despite its melodrama, Bodine could tell that there was something surprisingly affecting about it.

Ordinarily, as people testified, the courtroom was a din of rustling papers, shifting chairs, spectators coming in and going out, side whispers, or Dwyer getting ready to make an objection. But as Tatsuta recounted the final moments of Dean Hallmark, William Farrow, and Harold Spatz, the room was silent. The reporters hung on his every word and the only cracks in the quiet were light sniffs and muffled gasps as some struggled to hold back tears.

* * *

Dwyer, for his part, found Tatsuta's lamentations hard to take. Did Tatsuta feel these swells of remorse when he was looting Hallmark's bomber jacket? In a brief cross-examination, he flipped Tatsuta's invocation of the crucifixion against him, painting Tatsuta as the Roman soldier scourging the condemned Jesus on the march to Golgotha.

"Why did you say like 'Christ'?" Dwyer pressed him. "Why did that come to your mind?"

"Because those three were about to die on the cross," Tatsuta replied, "and I wanted to ease their mind."

"Do you know the story of Christ on the cross?"

"I do not know the story, but I know the ceremony."

"Isn't it a fact," Dwyer thundered back at him, "that the Doolittle Raiders got about the same kind of treatment as Christ did?"

"I do not know," Tatsuta said lamely, somehow earning even more sympathy under Dwyer's badgering.

* * *

Okada testified over three days, during which Fellows asked the same humanizing questions about whether he was married and had children and Dwyer could see that Okada came off as genuinely humble and sincere. He looked like what he was and had always aspired to be: a philosopher. Fellows succeeded in making Okada seem like a photo negative of Shoshin Ito. Ito had connived behind the scenes to reach a foregone conclusion. Okada described struggling with the evidence in an effort to be fair.

The public proceedings in the Doolittle Raiders' trial, Okada explained, had lasted the morning of August 28, 1942, but his deliberations with Wako and Toyama Nakajo had continued long after the courtroom had closed. They had read through all the evidence and weighed it against the testimony from the courtroom.

Only Wako had had his mind made up from the beginning. Nakajo had been troubled by the lack of evidence showing that these particular Doolittle Raiders were the ones who had gunned down the schoolchildren in Mizumoto Elementary School. There had been thirteen planes over Tokyo that day. How could they know who had fired the fatal shots?

Wako had tried to allay Nakajo's concerns with legal arguments. Precisely who did what was irrelevant, Wako had explained. The Doolittle Raiders were coconspirators like the robbers of a bank. They had undertaken the action together, as a group. They were all therefore equally responsible for what the group had done. They had all pulled the trigger in spirit, if not in reality.

Nakajo had been unsatisfied by Wako's legalisms. This was not a bank robbery. This was a war. These were soldiers. Everything they had done was done as a group. Would Wako be responsible if Okada committed a crime? It made no sense. Nakajo had wanted to see real evidence that the men he was judging for their lives were personally guilty of atrocities.

For Okada, Wako's legal arguments had been less persuasive than the fact that the Doolittle Raiders had dropped incendiary bombs. Those kinds of bombs, in Okada's opinion, showed indifference to the civilians whose homes they had burned. The Doolittle Raiders had all known what they were doing when they showered Japan with fireballs.

The pieces of evidence that ultimately mattered the most to everyone, Okada explained, had been the confessions. The confessions taken by the Kempeitai were very detailed. Each man had signed one, they had been corroborated by the Kempeitai's damage reports, and none of them denied signing when Wako had given them the opportunity to do so in open court. Under the Enemy Airmen's Law, the Doolittle Raiders' signatures on those confessions were as good as signatures on their own death warrants.

Fellows then asked Okada the key question: "Captain Okada, did you believe at the end of the testimony that the fliers were guilty?"

"Yes," Okada replied earnestly.

"Did you believe that sincerely and honestly? Did you?"

"Yes."

It was then Dwyer's turn. His cold was festering, and it was beginning to show, but his cross-examination started well enough. If Fellows was going to build his defense around Okada's sincere belief in the Doolittle Raiders' guilt, Dwyer was going to show that Okada knew, or at least should have known, that he was part of a sham.

"Do you know what is meant by a fair trial?" Dwyer asked him.

"I don't know," Okada replied, "what is the definition from the standpoint of law."

"A trial like this?" Dwyer said as he grandly gestured around the courtroom. "A trial like the trial you are in now."

"This might be another form of a fair trial," Okada suggested.

"Do you remember Lieutenant Hallmark in that courtroom on August 28?" Dwyer then asked.

"Yes," Okada answered warily.

"Was he lying down?"

"Yes," Okada admitted.

"As a matter of fact," Dwyer barked, "he couldn't stand, could he!"

"The other fliers stood up and walked forward individually and spoke,"

Okada said, trying to explain. Hallmark did not stand, but "sat up and spoke when his turn came."

"Did you give Lieutenant Hallmark a fair trial?" Dwyer demanded.

"I believe I did," Okada replied. "As I answered previously, I felt sorry for him."

"You felt so sorry for him you voted the death penalty, didn't you?"

"I didn't think of such a thing."

"Did you ask him whether he was married?" Dwyer asked sarcastically, turning Fellows's efforts to humanize the Japanese against them.

"I don't remember."

"Did you ask him whether he had any children?"

"I don't remember."

"Did any one of these eight fliers have a defense counsel?"

"No," Okada admitted, "they did not have."

"Was everything interpreted just the same as it is being interpreted in this trial?"

"Yes."

"I am asking you," Dwyer said making sure he was being clear, "whether anything was translated from Japanese into English?"

"Of course, it was interpreted," Okada insisted.

"Do you know Captain Nielsen?" Dwyer asked, as if the question were a clear retort to Okada's insistence that there had, in fact, been an interpreter.

"Yes."

"Did you hear Captain Nielsen say that nothing was translated into English?"

"Nielsen, I think, said that," Okada replied, "but there is no doubt as to the Japanese having been interpreted into English."

Dwyer wanted to pit Okada's credibility against Nielsen's and the rest of the Doolittle Raiders'. However philosophical Okada looked, however sincere, Dwyer was going to force McReynolds and the rest of the judges to decide who they were going to believe. Were they really going to take the word of these Japanese war criminals over the word of the Doolittle Raiders?

Dwyer was making progress, but then McReynolds called the Sunday recess at noon on Saturday. Bodine had requested an early break for personal reasons, stopping Dwyer only halfway through his cross-examination.

That meant Dwyer would have to pick up where he left off on Monday morning.

When the trial reconvened, Dwyer's cold had enjoyed an extra day and a half to swirl and swell inside his head. All things considered, though, the session began productively.

Dwyer walked Okada through all the evidence that Bodine and Fellows had gathered in Japan as part of their broader effort to put the Doolittle Raiders on trial, reminding him of all the statements from schoolteachers and hospital workers, who had recounted their horror as the Raiders had savagely bombed and strafed from overhead.

"You remember all of these statements being read, don't you?" Dwyer asked Okada innocuously.

"I believe I heard all," Okada answered.

"When did you first see these statements?"

"These statements?"

"Yes, the statements contained in these defense exhibits?"

"I heard them in this court."

"Is that the first time you ever heard any statements of any kind from these people?" Dwyer asked.

"Yes," Okada replied. The answer did not seem particularly controversial. Bodine and Fellows had gotten the statements during their trip to Tokyo. But that was Dwyer's point.

"These statements were not submitted to your military tribunal in the Doolittle case," Dwyer said, closing Okada in his trap, "were they?"

"No," Okada admitted, "never."

"Nor were any statements of these people submitted to the tribunal in the Doolittle case, were they?"

"No."

"The Tokyo Kempeitai investigation," Dwyer said contemptuously, "you relied on that in making your decision, didn't you?"

"Yes."

"Did you know who in the Kempeitai office prepared that?"

"I do not know."

"Did you ask him any questions about that investigation? Did you ask the Kempeitai officer who prepared the investigation any questions?"

"No, I did not."

"So, you accepted the statement of a man whom you never saw in that trial, is that right?"

"No, that is not the meaning," Okada said backpedaling. "I heard from Major Hata that these statements had been already verified by the prosecutors of the Kempeitai and also that somebody else in the Kempeitai had already verified by the prosecutor or someone else in the Kempeitai." The more Okada tried to explain himself, though, the worse it got. He had taken evidence from an organization known to use torture at face value, an organization that he knew and had admitted to knowing had used torture, and had to now explain himself.

Dwyer then went in for his big finish. "You told this commission you were a professor of ethics," he said. "How long were you a professor of ethics?"

"About twelve or thirteen years."

"Do you know what a dictionary is?"

"Yes?" Okada said, sensing that he was about to be tricked again.

"I'm going to read you the definition of ethics as given by Webster," Dwyer then said, "and ask you if that is your idea of ethics."

Okada looked puzzled. Was Dwyer really going to read the definition of the word "ethics" from Webster's dictionary aloud in court?

Sure enough, he did. "Webster says 'ethics is the science of moral duty, broadly, the science of ideal human character.' And his other definition is 'moral principles, quality or practice.'" Dwyer was strangely satisfied with himself as looked up from the dictionary and at Okada. "Do you agree with that definition?"

"That is a general meaning," Okada answered cautiously. Then a partial smile cracked on his face at the absurdity of the situation. "That is rather abstract, but that is the meaning."

The courtroom burst into laughter, and Dwyer was caught flatfooted. It had seemed so profound as he imagined it in his mucus-glutted mind that weekend. He believed he would be, through the haze of his occluded sinuses, making a serious point, a profound point, about natural law and justice: Okada fancied himself a philosopher, but he had been content to oblige a legal system that had sent young men to their deaths based on an unjust ex post facto law and evidence fabricated through torture. The laughter drew Dwyer into a rage.

"You think that is pretty abstract, do you?" Dwyer shouted back.

"Yes," Okada responded coolly, confident that he was not the only one who thought Dwyer was being ridiculous.

"Isn't there anything," Dwyer bellowed, "concrete about humanity or human character?"

"If the court please," Fellows interjected. "I think the prosecutor is getting away from the clear facts of this case and has gone off into an argument between himself and the witness."

"There is no argument," Dwyer snapped.

Between his sniffles, he realized he had lost control of the courtroom, of himself. No one was following him into the philosophical forest of natural law and ethics. His flailing was undermining everything else he had accomplished. He needed to get the courtroom back on his side, so he swallowed his pride along with the bolus of snot and made a joke of his failed attempt at moral profundity.

"What philosophy did you study and teach?" Dwyer asked. But before Okada could answer, Dwyer cracked his big Irish grin and added, "Was it German?"

"Mostly German," Okada admitted.

The courtroom again erupted in laughter, this time on Dwyer's side, and he took that as his cue to sit down. "No further questions."

* * *

Bodine knew a lot about Sawada by that point, and he knew there was a lot to like. Sawada was not the stock-character villain that Bodine had been led to expect when he had first gotten mixed up in the case. The way Sawada carried himself and his military career defied every stereotype of the Japanese imperial general. When Sawada took the stand and was asked his religion for the purposes of swearing him in, he spoke with such calm and modesty that his reply seemed obvious: "Buddhism."

Bodine had been frustrated, though, by the old man's inscrutability. The things that made Sawada sympathetic, even likable, to an American pilot like Bodine were the very things that Sawada seemed most embarrassed about. Sawada was not one of Japan's chauvinists. He had traveled throughout the West during his career. He had adopted a counterinsurgency strategy in China, governing his occupation forces by the principle of "construction" instead of bone-grinding brutality. His son had even gotten a degree in Western philosophy before being swept up by the Army during the war. But none of these were things that Sawada wanted to talk to Bodine or Fellows about, let alone testify about on the stand before the world.

As far as Sawada was concerned, Japan had lost the war and he had been fired. Try as Bodine might to persuade him otherwise, Sawada stubbornly put his reputation as a Japanese imperial general ahead of any effort to save him from the gallows. Even after Shoshin Ito had all but confessed to being the mastermind that Dwyer and Hendren had tried to make Sawada out to be, Sawada insisted that he, as the commanding general, was nevertheless responsible for anything Ito had done.

Even Shinji Somiya, with all of his experience and stature, could not persuade Sawada how foolish his stubbornness was. "Accepting the punishment on behalf of the country," Somiya insisted, "is neither an honor nor a benefit to anyone." All it did was make it more likely that Sawada would be sent to the gallows, and the more defiant Sawada was, the more likely it was that Wako, Okada, and Tatsuta, as his subordinates for whom he was responsible, would be forced to stand next to him with nooses around their necks too.

On the stand, Bodine walked Sawada methodically through his involvement in the Doolittle Raiders case. Sawada admitted that his personal involvement had not been significant, but he was unwilling to let his men take the blame. He refused to admit that they had done anything wrong, Shoshin Ito included. The only thing Sawada was adamant about was not being blamed for what the Kempeitai had done. The Kempeitai had not been his responsibility. He was happy to suffer whatever consequences the Americans thought necessary for everything his men had done. But not the Kempeitai.

"Is there anything, General," Bodine asked by way of somewhat frustrated conclusion, "that you want to tell this Commission at this time in regard to the charges against you or in regard to anything in regard to the Doolittle Trial?" Sawada did not need to gnash his teeth and rend his garments the way Tatsuta had. All he needed to do was acknowledge some regret for wrongdoing. All Bodine needed was some sign of remorse.

"Yes, I have." Sawada replied. "The trial of the Doolittle fliers was ordered by Tokyo and it was not tried under my order. The regulations used for the trial was established by Tokyo also. Concerning their treatment, it also was ordered by Tokyo."

Sawada had begun well, but then it became clear that he had no intention of prostrating himself. He was not going to admit that he or anyone else in Japan had done anything wrong to the Doolittle Raiders, who as far as Sawada was concerned, had murdered a little boy in school. "The trial was conducted in a fair way under those regulations," he continued. "Everything done by them was fair under the laws and regulations. I regret now that I could not conduct this case myself."

As soon as Bodine sat down, Hendren took full advantage of Sawada's defiance. Bodine had emphasized all the ways that Sawada had not been in control: because of directions from Tokyo, because his subordinates had done things without telling him, because he had not been in control of the Kempeitai. Sawada had chaffed at each admission. He was a commanding general of the Imperial Japanese Army. Any suggestion that he had not been in full control of everything that had happened within his area of command was a suggestion that he was soft. It was an insult to his competence, to his very identity, and Hendren saw the opening.

"Did you know how prisoners were treated at Bridge House by the Kempeitai?" Hendren asked.

"I didn't know anything about what was going on there," Sawada protested, though not with particular credibility.

"These boys were prisoners of your Army at that time," Hendren pressed him, "right?"

"As soon as the Kempeitai took them over," Sawada explained, "my responsibility—there isn't any of my responsibility at all."

"You heard Captain Nielsen testify about being given the water treatment out there," Hendren pressed him, "didn't you?"

"I heard him say that he received it from the Kempeitai."

"Did you ever hear of anyone else around there having the water treatment given to them before this trial?"

"I never heard of it."

"You didn't make any inquiries around Shanghai did you," Hendren said mockingly, "while you were the Big General here?"

"There was no detailed instructions," Sawada explained with bravado, "because I ordered my subordinates to treat prisoners of war fairly and I knew that they followed my instructions."

"The treatment of the prisoners was carried out under your command responsibility, wasn't it?" Hendren demanded. The wording of the question was subtle. Hendren was being deliberate in using the phrase "command responsibility" from Yamashita's case. He was asking Sawada if he was guilty. He was asking if Sawada was willing to follow Yamashita to the gallows on behalf of the defeated Empire of Japan.

"Yes," Sawada replied with no hesitation.

"And when General Ito—anything General Ito did, he did at your command or under your command responsibility," Hendren insisted, "didn't he?"

"Because Ito acted for me," Sawada said coolly, "whatever he has done is my responsibility."

"And whatever Wako and Okada did is your responsibility, isn't it?"

"Whatever any subordinates have done is my responsibility."

"Then you are responsible for whatever happened to those boys, weren't you?"

"Yes," Sawada said, steely-eyed, "I have the responsibility of the Army."

Hendren sat down, justly satisfied with himself, and Bodine got back up and tried to minimize the damage.

Sawada had admitted—no, insisted—that he was guilty, and Bodine needed to get Sawada to clarify that when he said that he had been "responsible," he meant solely as a function of being in command; he had not been "personally responsible."

But Sawada would have none of Bodine's efforts to minimize him. He was happy to assign blame to the Kempeitai when it belonged there, but he was not going to let Wako, Okada, and Tatsuta or even Shoshin Ito be responsible for him. Privately, he would admit to being disturbed by what his men had done, by what a sham the trial had been. He blamed himself for rubber stamping it and especially for not supervising Ito more strictly. But he would never publicly let any of them take responsibility. "As their superior officer," he insisted, "I am responsible for their acts."

Then Bodine got an idea. Sawada would not let any responsibility go below him in the chain of command. But what about up?

"Isn't it true," Bodine asked him, "that General Hata was the one who referred the Doolittle fliers to be tried in Shanghai?"

"Yes, sir," Sawada conceded, "that is true."

General Shunroku Hata, of course, was not in the courtroom, and that gave Bodine the chance to remind everyone who else was not in the courtroom and who bore just as much "command responsibility" as Sawada did.

"General," Bodine asked, "did you know that the United States commanding general of China requested that General Shimomura be brought to China as one of the accused in this trial?"

"May it please the commission," Hendren leapt to his feet. "I object to the question!"

Whatever warm self-satisfaction Hendren had earned in his cross-examination of Sawada turned cold. "I don't know whether he is telling him that the commanding general of the China Theater asked for it or whether he is asking the question. And even if the commanding general of the American Army sent a message for Shimomura that wouldn't prove or disprove any issue in this case."

"I'll withdraw the question," Bodine conceded. But simply having asked the question was sufficient, and Sawada stepped down.

* * *

With all the testimony now taken, the defense's case was complete. It was just before 4:00 p.m. on Tuesday, April 9, 1946. The only thing left was the closing arguments, and McReynolds had agreed to give both sides an extra day to prepare. Everyone started packing up for the day as Hendren recited the formalities that must be said when the taking of evidence is over.

"Does the Commission desire any testimony brought on behalf of the Commission?" he asked perfunctorily.

"Yes, there is," McReynolds said, stopping everyone in place. He then looked over at Lieutenant Colonel Berry, the most junior officer on the bench.

"I would like," Berry said, "General Sawada to take the stand, please."

Bodine was caught up short along with everyone else. What had been left unsaid? Why hadn't Berry asked any questions earlier? Berry had shown few signs of sympathy toward Bodine, let alone Sawada, during the trial; he had even interrupted Bodine's cross-examination of Chase Nielsen in order to help Nielsen regain his footing. But a request from a judge is a request from a judge. So Sawada got up, returned to the witness chair, and was reminded that he was still under oath.

"General Sawada," Berry asked, "at any time after you returned from the front to Shanghai on or about 17 September 1942, did you send, or direct to be sent, a personal message from you to Tokyo, any telegraphic message to Tokyo?" The question came seemingly out of nowhere.

"I could not directly communicate with Tokyo," Sawada replied, as if the answer were self-evident. "Therefore, I did not do it."

The reason Berry was asking, he explained, was that he had been reading over trial exhibits and noticed that among the documents the defense had submitted, there was a statement signed by Sawada's former chief of staff, Yasuo Karakawa.

"Now, in that statement," Berry said, "General Karakawa alleges that you sent a telegram to Tokyo and he quotes one of the alleged phrases in that telegram. What do you have to say to that?"

"I brought this matter up before the Supreme Commander of Nanking," Sawada said, referring to his conversation with General Hata four years earlier. "Karakawa may be mistaken about this and may have taken it for Tokyo authority."

"What do you mean by that part of your answer which says, 'may have taken it for Tokyo authority'?" Berry asked.

"I talked about this matter to the Supreme Commander of Nanking and Karakawa on his part thought that I sent a telegram to Tokyo and he must have been misunderstood—he must have made a mistake."

"You did *not* send a telegram to Tokyo?" Berry asked, seeming to go out of his way to give Sawada yet another chance to help himself.

"That is the truth," Sawada replied.

With that, the testimony was over. As the courtroom cleared out, Bodine could see Shinji Somiya yelling at Sawada. "You fool!" he scolded him. "You could have avoided punishment if only you had agreed with what Karakawa had testified." It was bewildering to Somiya that Sawada could be so dense, so simple. But Sawada just shrugged it off.

TWENTY-SEVEN

How do you tell a man that he will be killed tomorrow? The easiest way, at least on the conscience of the person delivering the news, is to say that "death is what justice requires." In more primitive times, divine justice was revealed through the verdict of some ordeal, be it trial by fire or trial by combat. The barest reason for death that could be given to Shigeru Sawada, Yusei Wako, Ryuhei Okada, and Sotojiro Tatsuta was that they were defeated enemies. They were despised individually for their participation in the deaths of four American heroes, and their four deaths were what the victor's justice required in return.

But this was not victor's justice, or at least it was not meant to be. This was an American trial. For Dwyer, it was about ethics. He did not need a dictionary to know what that meant. He had taken an oath to uphold the US Constitution first when he had joined the bar and then again after he had been drafted into the Army. And the principle the Constitution held most dear was the rule of law.

Sure, Dwyer's counterparts in Manila had, under the thumb of Douglas MacArthur, taken shortcuts in sending Yamashita to the gallows. The trial of the Nazi saboteurs had also been a black mark that most people chalked up to the anxiety that had pervaded the country in the first year of the war. But Dwyer had worked himself weary to ensure that the trial of Sawada was not just a "judicial lynching." He had made mistakes, no doubt, and he was not immune to the seductions of glory. But as he walked into court, his head throbbing from his still pitiless cold, he was there to deliver justice.

The trial's closing arguments lasted two days and were a dogfight of pros and cons for sentencing Sawada, Wako, Okada, and Tatsuta to death. There were points and counterpoints from every conceivable perspective on what the Doolittle Raid, the trial of Sawada, and the war itself meant to history. Even the three Japanese lawyers got to take their turns at the podium.

Kumashiro predictably laid it on thick, thanking the United States for teaching Japan what a fair trial was all about as his country ventured into a new era of democracy and justice. "This lofty ideal and incessant courage of the United States are well appreciated with hearty respect, for which we are second to none to cooperate with you," he said. "I earnestly hope for the Commission, not only for the honour of the American Nation but also for the equity of the human being, the fair and prudent judgment be given."

Shinji Somiya and Tadahiro Hayama took a different tack. Both men sought to show the judges, to show the world, how deft and skillful real Japanese lawyers were. Shoshin Ito, they seemed to say under every breath, was an aberration. He was not one of them.

Somiya had written a well-researched and well-presented legal argument that proceeded methodically through all of the essential issues in the case and the governing international law. It was an argument that Dwyer could have pulled off the shelf of the Harvard Law School Library.

Hayama, too, had written out a scholarly argument that he asked Fellows to read aloud for everyone to hear. Fellows, for his part, happily obliged, though the exercise grew ludicrous every time he encountered one of Hayama's gaudy flourishes of erudition, not least his insistence on leaving every quote in its original language, be it German or Latin.

Hayama closed with a quote from the nineteenth-century German political theorist Ferdinand Johann Gottlieb Lassalle. Fellows dutifully, albeit awkwardly, gnawed through the words amid the furrowed brows of US Army officers, who had a very different reaction to the sound of the German language than Hayama did in 1946: "Das Anbrechen einer neuen Zeit besteht immer nur in dem erlangten Bewusstsein über das, was die bisher vorhandene Wirklichkeit an sich gewesen ist." ("The new period begins just when we are conscious of what it is that heretofore existed.") However awkward, the sentiment behind Hayama's sesquipedalian super-fluities was sincere and captured both why he had helped Dwyer build his case against his countrymen the previous autumn and why he had turned coat to join the defense team that winter.

The reporters still covering the trial were duly impressed, no doubt in part because of Hayama's readiness to condemn Japanese militarism and to call the "incident" in China "a flagrant crime against Chinese." When Dwyer and Hendren were asked for their reaction to this, the official position of the prosecution was that everyone had been treated to "a masterpiece of international law."

Dwyer planned to speak last, which was good because Hendren's closing argument was as dull as his opening statement had been, only longer. Hendren had wrapped himself in his self-confident sense of reasonableness and argued, largely by insisting, that death sentences were the only reasonable response to what the Japanese had done to the Doolittle Raiders. He spoke with a deliberate cadence that was patient yet firm, earnest yet put on, and above all else, a labor to sit through by the time he passed the one-hour mark.

Hendren read from the charges and described the wrongdoing of the Japanese as self-evident. The only true victims in this case had been the Doolittle Raiders. It was not hard to convince any American, let alone the seasoned Army colonels sitting behind the bench, that any harm done to the Doolittle Raiders had been wrong and that any wrong done to them had been a wrong against all of the United States that deserved nothing less than death on the gallows.

For Hendren, the conditions at Sotojiro Tatsuta's brig spoke for themselves. How could an American boy be held like that? "You saw the cells," he said with a flash of disgust. "I would call them no more than dog kennels." Tatsuta had been responsible for that, just as he had been responsible for murdering the Doolittle Raiders in cold blood when he got the execution order from Itsuro Hata. "He could have said to Hata, 'I don't want to carry out these orders. I love these boys,'" Hendren argued. "But what did he do? He gathered up his henchmen and went out to the cemetery; he erected the crosses; he had the coffins built; he has admitted all."

"The defense will try to contend," he continued, that the Doolittle Raiders "violated the rules of warfare in the bombing of Japan. Well, gentlemen, if they did, then every American pilot and every crew that went over Japan are equally guilty." Even if some civilian areas had been bombed during the Doolittle Raid, Hendren insisted with a bit of awkwardness, "I think you'll agree it was a very light bombing of civilians." But, he reminded everyone, the Doolittle Raid had been an "authorized mission." He said the phrase repeatedly as a mantra against any accusation that the Raiders could possibly have stepped over any line. Sure, there might have been some collateral damage. But as part of an "authorized mission" against military objectives, "that is bound to happen."

"They had dropped their bombs leaving the scene of the raid. We know they were low on gas and were trying to conserve every drop. Yet, they tell us that one punched another and said, 'there is a schoolhouse, let's go down and give it a good strafing.' They could see the children playing. Now we know that American boys don't do that," Hendren insisted.

Dwyer could see as well as anyone else that his Caesar's wife routine touched the right nerve. As the starched and pressed embodiment of middle American reasonableness, Hendren was forcing the court to decide who they were really going to believe. Anything other than a conviction and death sentence would implicitly find the Doolittle Raiders guilty. Was that something US military officers were really willing to do in 1946?

* * *

Bodine was the first to step to the podium for the defense. Though it was only a few catty-corner steps from his seat at the defense table to the podium, he had gone a long way by the time he stood there.

Bodine had come to Shanghai with the rest of the Army that autumn justly feeling that he was on the winning side. Opportunity extended to every horizon, but he had taken a job no one else wanted because he was, at bottom, a boy in love with a girl.

The previous Saturday, April 6, 1942, as Dwyer had been cross-examining Okada, Bodine had persuaded McReynolds to call the Sunday recess early because that was the day Elizaveta's ultimatum expired. He had made arrangements for them to elope that afternoon with a party afterward at Broadway Mansions and had arrived at Christ the King Church in the

French Concession just in time. He had been decked out in his Eisenhower jacket, and everyone had been there waiting for him: Father O'Connell; Bodine's best man, Cullen "Cab" Brannon; Elizaveta's maid of honor, Minnela Silva, the Portuguese concierge at Broadway Mansions. The only one not there was Elizaveta. And no one had known where she was.

Bodine had waited with good humor, but then, after a few nervous minutes turned into an awkward hour, Father O'Connell's keen sense for pastoral care had led him to open the whiskey early. As they drank, Father O'Connell had done his best to console this newly lost member of his flock. "Well, it's the smartest thing she would ever do," Father O'Connell had ribbed him as he poured another. "She's too good for you, Ed."

It was then that Elizaveta had burst into the church, hair windblown, dress shit spattered, and face furious. It turned out that while Bodine and Father O'Connell had been swallowing enough whiskey to throw their legal competence to conduct a marriage into doubt, Elizaveta had been stranded at Broadway Mansions. Her car had never arrived, and, frantic, she had called a jeep from the Army car pool. That meant that to get to Christ the King, she had had to bounce her way in an open-topped jeep through the feculent streets of Shanghai in her white wedding dress as the oleander woven into her hair scattered and tangled in the wind.

But she had made it, she was beautiful, and her Russian fury melted into a jolly glow as the organist chimed in with Wagner's "Bridal Chorus" from *Lohengrin*, her cue to walk down the aisle of the mostly empty church, dressed in her somewhat white dress and tangled oleander, to her Edmund, who was waiting for her in his Eisenhower jacket. Father O'Connell and Cab Brannon stood on either side of Bodine in case his whiskey buzz gave him any trouble staying upright, and Father O'Connell walked them through their vows as the two of them found themselves starting a family with a person and in a place they could never have imagined.

Now, having been a husband for almost a week, Bodine stood at the podium before McReynolds and the rest of the judges to make his closing statement, and Elizaveta was in her usual place behind the bar with the rest of the wives. Bodine was well pressed in his airman's uniform, though not as well pressed as Hendren was. The words he spoke were also not as polished or lawyerly. Bodine was not eloquent, but he was sincere. And he had the credibility that only a pilot in his situation could have.

Whatever anxieties Bodine had over the future of his career in the Army now came second to his earnest insistence on what he now knew to be true. He had met the schoolteachers who had cowered as American planes had strafed overhead. He had pulled the .30-caliber bullets from the wall of the room where a little boy had been shot through the belly almost exactly four years earlier. He had reminded McReynolds that Nielsen himself had admitted to dropping incendiary bombs on "congested residential areas" before he had tried to backpedal on the stand. How could charges be "false and fraudulent" when they were true?

Shigeru Sawada was no Yamashita. Sawada deserved to live his life into old age. "The prosecutor in this trial has in no way established any proof whatsoever by which they can show that General Sawada *knowingly and willfully* constituted the military tribunal to try the Doolittle Raiders." Those two words, "knowingly" and "willfully," were the essence of the crime. Even if the charges had been false and fraudulent, there was no evidence that Sawada had ever known he had done anything wrong or corrupt.

There were people, Bodine pointed out, who had been corrupt. If the Army was genuinely interested in punishing those most responsible for the Doolittle Raiders' ordeal, where was General Shunroku Hata? Where was General Sadamu Shimomura? Where was General Shoshin Ito? Where was anyone from the Kempeitai? Sawada might have said he was "responsible," but McReynolds and everyone else knew the truth. "These are the men," Bodine insisted, "*directly* responsible." And what kind of justice would demand that Sawada be hanged by the neck until dead while all those other men were allowed to live full lives?

Bodine then turned the closing of the defense's case over to Fellows, who took his turn at the podium as the living embodiment of the apple-cheeked earnestness that had swelled inside the American soul the moment peace was declared the previous August.

"I came into this case with some eagerness and some joyful expectations," Fellows began. "I envisioned myself getting a trip to Tokyo, getting out of the office for a while, picking up some new courtroom experience, something new, but after reading the statements that the prosecution had, after talking to these accused, after getting into my head the idea in the background of this case, I lost most of my anticipation and became, in fact, very humble, and approached this case with a great degree of humility. I realized I was representing not only these four accused, their families and their friends, but also to some extent the Japanese judicial system. I also represented the one thing that we blame these Japanese for not giving the American fliers—I represent the defense."

"I, along with Colonel Bodine," Fellows continued, "represent what we say the American judicial system has that the Japanese did not have. I realize that the result of this case does set a precedent for future cases for years to come, that at some time in the future an American officer may be on trial on the precedent set as a result of this case. The precedent of this case is setting an example whereby that officer may be tried. I therefore defended these accused as I would want to be defended. I'm not satisfied with the results of my work, not satisfied with what I've done, but I've tried and I'm still trying."

Even if McReynolds and the other judges believed everything Chase Nielsen had said, even if they accepted that the Doolittle Raiders had never done anything that could justly be thought of as war crimes, even if Hallmark, Farrow, and Spatz had been executed on the basis of false and fraudulent evidence, these four Japanese men had not been responsible for that fraud. There was only one person who had known that what he was doing was wrong. "That is Colonel Ito," Fellows said. "The only person who could have ascertained by the facts of this case that these orders constituted a wrong to these fliers was Colonel Ito. Only he could've ascertained that innocent persons were being put to trial and were treated as criminals."

The legal issues in the case were complicated. Fellows acknowledged as much, and he argued the technicalities as deftly as anyone could. But, he pointed out, McReynolds and the rest of the judges were not alone in struggling with them. An Australian war crimes tribunal had, just two weeks earlier, ruled that a Japanese commander was not responsible for the results of an unfair trial, so long as he had no reason to know it was unfair. Unless Sawada, Wako, Okada, and Tatsuta had shared in Shoshin Ito's desire to pervert justice, they could not be justly considered war criminals. To Fellows, the Australian Army had shown that the law of war was not the law of the jungle. Justice for war crimes did not need to be victor's justice. International law could be applied as real law.

* * *

Dwyer strutted to the podium to perform his closing argument as if it were the grand finale of an opera. He was there to hold forth for McReynolds and the rest of the world and to propound the definitive history of the Doolittle Raid and what it meant for mankind.

"About four years ago," he began, "sixteen planes took off from the aircraft carrier *Hornet*." Dwyer's voice was raspy from his cold, but point by point, he proceeded to describe the Doolittle Raiders' saga in simple, direct terms. "Of these facts," he said, "there is no dispute.

"Four men have died, three by musketry and one by malnutrition. Now the question is, is anybody responsible for that? Was it something for which there is justification, or should somebody be brought before this court of justice and be tried for their acts? And that is what we have done in this case."

The war, for Dwyer, continued in this courtroom. He proceeded methodically, damningly, through each of the defendants' actions during the August 1942 and the *direct* responsibility each man bore for having perverted justice. "I suppose I have coasted around court rooms as much as the average fellow who has practiced say twelve or fourteen years and in all my life I've never seen, and I doubt whether I have read, of any trial which was quite the mockery of justice that this one was."

This trial, here in 1946, Dwyer reminded everyone, had lasted seventeen days. The Doolittle Raiders' supposed trial had lasted maybe an hour. "I say it is physically impossible; I say it is mathematically impossible; I say it is metaphysically impossible to try defendants on the charges of having taken off from an aircraft carrier, bombed Tokyo, flying to China, what happened on the raids in Tokyo and Nagoya, read the charges, translate everything and they even say they let the defendants take the stand and explain their own story. This commission knows, and anyone who reads this record knows, that is a boldfaced lie."

This trial, in 1946, was the precedent. That trial, in 1942, had been nothing more than the paperwork for murder.

"They did no more than to give a mockery to justice!" Dwyer bellowed, twisting his face into a kabuki expression of disbelief. "Believe me, I say that you will find virtually no where, even in the German law upon which the Japanese law is based, will you find any precedent for such a trial is this."

All of them attempted to pass blame to "Tokyo," it was all Tokyo's doing. "Tokyo is the third largest city in the world," Dwyer said, "nobody's name is mentioned as to what they mean by Tokyo." The law was not about philosophical first principles, dictionary definitions, or political abstractions. It was not about German philosophers. It was not a machine, and lawyers were not the mere parts of a mechanism. It was about people.

"I say no system can exist except as it is put in operation and its principles are put into effect by human beings. Systems and ways of living have no life in textbooks, but they have life when translated into human action, and you have seen it translated by the men who sit here to be judges of this tribunal. Without the Sawadas and the Okadas and the Wakos and the Tatsutas that system could never exist and those who put its tenets into power and effect, they are as evil as the system which they carry out."

* * *

The verdict was set to be announced Monday, April 15, 1946. That morning, Bodine made his way to the defense team's office, which was down the hall from the courtroom in Ward Road Jail. He was running typically late as he got word that the announcement of the verdict had been delayed until early afternoon.

"The judges are still deliberating," Bodine said as he walked into the office where Fellows, Kumashiro, Hayama, and Somiya were waiting. "I don't think court will convene until 1300. We should probably have lunch."

In relatively short order, Bodine had sandwiches and coffee delivered. As they shared the conviviality of what was likely to be their last meal together, Bodine made a point of complementing the Japanese on how well they had all done. They had done all they could. There was nothing to regret.

Word arrived that court would be called to order at 1:30 p.m. They were not yet finished eating, but nothing kills the appetite like a verdict, so they made their way down the hall and filed into the courtroom, which was soon as packed as it had been the first day of trial. Even General Wedemeyer made an appearance as photographers set up stage lights that seemed especially glaring. Sawada, Wako, Okada, and Tatsuta were soon led into the courtroom and sat stiffly in their simple wooden chairs, waiting with everyone else.

At 2:00 p.m., the courtroom was called to order. McReynolds led the rest of the judges in their usual procession to their respective places behind the bench. All were seated.

McReynolds read from papers in front of him and began by noting that the offenses charged "resulted largely from obedience to the laws and instructions of the government and their military superiors." The defendants had "exercised no initiative to any marked degree." He then noted that those who bore the most responsibility, such as those responsible for creating the ex post facto Enemy Airmen's Law, were not before the commission.

"The circumstances set forth above do not entirely absolved the accused from guilt," McReynolds continued. "However, they do compel unusually strong mitigating considerations, applicable to each accused in various degrees." McReynolds then turned to each of the defendants.

First, Sawada. The commission recognized that he had been absent at the front and had learned about the trial weeks after there was anything he could do about it. McReynolds also noted that he "did make oral protest to his immediate superior, the commanding general of the Japanese Imperial Expeditionary Forces in China to the effect that in his opinion the sentences were too severe." That said, the commission found that Sawada had been negligent in not personally investigating how the Doolittle Raiders were being treated and in taking Shoshin Ito's representations at face value.

McReynolds then turned toward Wako. As the only lawyer, he bore special responsibility. He had accepted evidence from the Kempeitai in Tokyo. Yet despite the fact that he had been "legally trained, he accepted the evidence without question and tried to judge the prisoners on this evidence which was false and fraudulent."

Okada, McReynolds explained, was different. He did not have legal training and had only been following orders. However, he did have freedom of conscience and the right to decide the case before him as his conscience directed. Yet he had gone along with Wako in finding the Doolittle Raiders guilty of crimes that, McReynolds repeated, were based on false and fradulent evidence.

Finally, Tatsuta. He had failed to treat the Doolittle Raiders as prisoners of war, which he had been required to do because they had committed no crimes. However, he had also been following the instructions of his superiors. There was also no evidence that he had mistreated anyone, other than to deny them the rights and privileges that they should have been given as prisoners of war.

McReynolds then addressed the four men directly. "The accused will stand before the Commission." They got up from their wooden chairs and stood stiffly in the well of the courtroom. Though unbidden, Bodine and Fellows got up too and stood next to them.

McReynolds looked down at the papers in front of him. "The Commission in closed session, all members being present, upon secret written ballot, two-thirds of the members at the time the vote was taken concurring in each finding, finds as follows:

"You, Shigeru Sawada," McReynolds sternly recited. ". . . Guilty, except the words 'knowingly and willfully,' and 'by court-martial,' of the excepted words not guilty."

"And you, Yusei Wako . . . Guilty."

"And you, Ryuhei Okada . . . Guilty."

"And you, Sotojiro Tatsuta . . ." Guilty on all charges except for the words "deliberate" and "without justification" and other elements of the charges that had been at the core of Dwyer and Hendren's case, including "did specifically order and command certain Japanese soldiers to fire."

It was a puzzling verdict. The commission had found all of the defendants guilty, but in the cases of Sawada and Tatsuta, it had removed the essential elements of the crimes charged. The commission had found them guilty but not of *being* guilty. What did all this mean?

"The Commission," McReynolds stated, "in closed session, all members present, upon secret written ballot, two-thirds of the members at the time the vote was taken concurring, sentences each of the accused as follows:"

SAWADA: Five years at hard labor.
WAKO: Nine years at hard labor.
OKADA: Five years at hard labor.
TATSUTA: Five years at hard labor.

As McReynolds read the sentences aloud, what had been a funereal silence only seconds before broke into a din of gasps and disbelief. Looking over at the prosecution table, Bodine could see Dwyer and Hendren struggling to keep the shock and disappointment from registering on their faces.

McReynolds called the room to attention and then asked simply, "Is there anything else?"

Hendren stood, doing his best to keep his mask of professionalism. "Does the defense have anything?" he asked. "We have nothing further."

Bodine was dumbstruck. "On behalf of the Japanese counsel," Kumashiro chimed in amid the confusion, "I would like to express my hearty thanks to this commission to the fair and sympathetic verdict in the case."

McReynolds nodded. "The commission adjourns to be reconvened at my order."

With that, it was over. The courtroom became a crowded din and McReynolds came down from the bench to shake hands with all the lawyers. When he reached the defense table, he said, "I appreciate you all for working so long and hard on this. I've never experienced such an emotional trial." And to Somiya's bewilderment, whose unyielding formality befit a lawyer of his stature back in Japan, Dwyer and Hendren also came over to shake hands and offer him as genuine a smile as each could muster. It was as if the ninth inning had just ended and it was time for the players to give each other a hearty "Good game."

* * *

The verdict hit Chase Nielsen hard. He was back in Utah, and there was something cruel about the fact that something in which he had invested so much of his heart and soul was being treated as though it were just the news of the day.

In a letter to William Dieter's mother, letting her know that her son's remains were on their way home, Nielsen apologized that the trial had been a disappointment: "I'm sorry Justice could not see fit to even its sides for the mothers and families of the three executed. I feel I've done all in my power, and I feel I've lost, but justice will be meted out someday yet. With prayers for your comfort I remain Capt. C. Jay Nielsen."

Nielsen wrote to Dean Hallmark's family in Texas, "I thought if I went back to Shanghai to testify it would help but it looks as though I've been made a fool of." The managing editor of the *Philadelphia Daily News* also reached out to Hallmark's family, offering "We will be glad to print any criticism you wish to make." Hallmark's mother responded furiously. "In my estimation," she said, "the representatives of our country have fallen down in avenging the murder of our son. I am amazed at the light sentence given the murders. We have heard from people all over the nation and they feel the same. . . . This won't ever be forgotten."

Hallmark's mother was joined by William Farrow's mother, who told reporters that the Japanese "deserve the death penalty. Nothing the Americans could do to them would be equal to what they did to my son and the other fliers."

Only Harold Spatz's father, phlegmatic Kansan that he was, took the news in stride. "I think the sentences were pretty stiff," he told reporters. "It is all a part of war, we must take it as it comes. Nothing can be done to bring Harold back."

The *Los Angeles Times* ran a scathing editorial lamenting that "at this rate, nobody in Japan but Tojo can be held deserving of the supreme penalty." The lack of any death sentences reignited the public's discontent with MacArthur's decision to spare Emperor Hirohito. Farrow's mother went so far as to say that she looked forward to Tojo being prosecuted and executed for his role in her son's death but was disappointed because "Emperor Hirohito was in higher command than Tojo and I think the records of this trial also should be used in judgment against Hirohito. If it is proved that Hirohito had delivered the execution orders to Tojo then he should be given the death penalty."

Congressman Francis Walter, a member of the US House Judiciary Committee, introduced a resolution to investigate the handling of the case. "What the Japanese officers admitted in their trial is murder in every State in the Union," he told reporters, "Some of us cannot understand the light sentence given in the military courts." Letters to President Truman and General Eisenhower demanded that the trial be redone so that death sentences could be imposed. The battle, it seemed, was not over.

* * *

As the man responsible for war crimes prosecutions in China, getting answers, satisfying answers, for the higher-ups fell to Ham Young.

Within a week after the verdict was announced, Hendren had gotten his ticket home and Somiya had returned to Japan to serve as defense counsel in the Tokyo Trial, which had just begun. Tying up the Doolittle Trial's loose ends therefore fell to Dwyer for the prosecution and Bodine, Fellows, and Kumashiro for the defense.

Young called a meeting in his office and also invited Colonel McReynolds to figure out what should be done. Young explained that he was under orders to make a recommendation to Wedemeyer about whether the trial should be redone and if more severe sentences could be imposed. That recommendation would be passed along to the Secretary of War in Washington.

McReynolds was crystal clear: he opposed any retrial. He and his fellow judges had tried the case over three weeks. They had heard dozens of witnesses. Dwyer had done a great job; so had Hendren. But the evidence was the evidence, and justice was justice. As one of the original apostles of the Bomber Mafia, McReynolds stood by their verdict and their sentence.

Ham Young did not want a retrial, either, if only because it would clearly violate the rule against double jeopardy. A man cannot be put on trial for the same crime twice. It was a principle of law recognized not only in the US Constitution but around the world. How ironic it would be if the United States abandoned a judicial guarantee deemed indispensable by all civilized people in a case whose very allegation was that the Japanese had conducted an unfair trial.

But there were strong political forces at work. The thirst for revenge not only threatened a few military careers, it could jeopardize the whole effort to have war crimes trials at all.

* * *

That August, Young and his staff finalized a forty-page, single-spaced report on the Doolittle Raiders trial that painstakingly went through all the law and evidence. The key question, as Young framed it, was whether the trial had been conducted legally. If it had been, there could be no retrial without violating double jeopardy.

Young started with the charges: Had the charges been legally sound? Had denying the Doolittle Raiders a fair trial and executing them been a violation of the law of war? "Here the test is international law," Young wrote, "not the national law, civil or military of any one nation, not the law of the United States nor Japan, but the law of nations."

Young conceded that the charges were "not the usual type of war criminal acts that have been the issues and other trials to date. Indeed, it is believed that this case constitutes a precedent in this regard." But being a precedent-setting case did not mean that the charges had not been violations of the law of war.

It was true that the Japanese had been entitled to try their enemies for violating international law, but they had had to conduct an actual trial, not a show trial. As Young explained, "It is axiomatic that certain minimum safeguards must be guaranteed a defendant in any hearing which would justify its being termed a 'trial.' While a sovereign state is free to adopt any law it sees fit, however anachronistic and barbarous its enactment may be, nevertheless, civilized nations are not obligated, either in law or in morals, to be bound by such barbarism."

Young singled out the Enemy Airmen's Law, which had been created for the express purpose of punishing the Doolittle Raiders. "It was *ex post facto* terroristic in concept and was enacted primarily to permit a pseudo-legal sentence of death for the Doolittle Raiders."

Procedurally, the trial in 1942 had betrayed all of the corrupt barbarism of the law it had ostensibly been enforcing—worst of all, the evidence the Japanese had used to convict the Doolittle Raiders was tainted by torture.

"The untrustworthiness of any admissions or confessions made under torture would clearly vitiate a conviction based thereon," Young concluded. The fact that the Doolittle Raiders might have reaffirmed those confessions during that trial did not clean those confessions. At the time, the Doolittle Raiders remained in the hands of the same people who had tortured them. The fact that neither Wako nor Okada had gone "behind them to ascertain the circumstances under which they were obtained, would itself indicate unfairness and criminality on the part of the accused Japanese."

Therefore, Young wrote confidently, the verdicts of guilty had been justified, and he recommended that Colonel Shoshin Ito, General Shunroku Hata, and General Sadamu Shimomura also be tried for their "unlawful acts in this case."

Young then turned to the sentences. "The Commission," he wrote, "by awarding such extremely lenient and inadequate penalties committed a serious error of judgment." But, he insisted, there could not be, nor should there be, any effort to change those sentences now that they had been rendered. The case, he explained, "involved the illegal performance of judicial functions under the law of war by the accused, and with few recorded precedents available, the commission membership no doubt was particularly conscious of its own obligations in this regard." Regardless, he concluded, "if an error in judgment was made, then contrary to the Japanese ideas of justice and humanity, the commission favored the accused with all the benefits thereof."

It had been a year since Ham Young had first learned the stories of Chase Nielsen, Robert Hite, and Jacob DeShazer that day in Chongqing. The Tokyo Trial was now well under way. The Nuremberg Trial was wrapping up. The Cold War had replaced World War II on the front pages of the newspapers. Chiang Kai-shek had violently reignited the Chinese Civil War after months of US-mediated negotiations with Mao Zedong had fallen apart. And as Young delivered his memo to General Wedemeyer, Billy Mitchell, the American messiah of strategic bombing, whose name christened Jimmy Doolittle's B-25Bs back in 1942, was posthumously awarded a Congressional Medal of Honor.

With his report on the Doolittle Trial now complete, Young advised Wedemeyer to approve the verdicts and the sentences imposed against Shigeru Sawada, Yusei Wako, Ryuhei Okada, and Sotojiro Tatsuta. He could tell the War Department with a clear conscience that doing so was what justice required.

AFTERWORD

In Japan, the Doolittle Raid is still remembered for the schoolchildren who were killed. In 1999, a children's book was published commemorating the death of Minosuke Ishide at Mizumoto Elementary School. The school itself has a memorial to him on the wall of an old classroom that has since been converted into a local library and museum.

The book, entitled *Akichan*, tells the story of a little girl named Narumi who sees the ghost of a small boy wearing the military-style uniform worn by schoolchildren in the 1940s. When the boy calls out to her "Akichan," the childhood name of her grandmother, Narumi tells her grandmother that she saw a ghost. The ghost, the grandmother explains, is Minosuke Ishide. "The black plane targeted Ishide," she tells Narumi, who befriends the ghost and learns the importance of connecting the past to the future.

In 2003, researchers affiliated with Japan's Self-Defense Force published a detailed study of the Doolittle Raid. Endeavoring to consolidate all the known documents from Japan's archives as well as scholarship from the United States, the researchers concluded that the attack on Mizumoto Elementary School had been carried out not by Dean Hallmark and Chase Nielsen's plane but by the third plane that had taken off from the *Hornet* that morning. The civilian damage the researchers attributed to Hallmark's plane included the firebombing of three homes in Yokohama and the strafing of another home in which an infant was killed.

None of that information was available at either trial, either the Japanese trial in 1942 or the American trial in 1946, but that did not stop both from attempting to make definitive verdicts about history. Both trials sought to connect the past to the future and were intended to be judgments about the future's past more than they were about the individual guilt of any of the men involved.

The Japanese trial sought to establish a judgment of the Doolittle Raiders' culpability as war criminals that has been preserved to this day in the Japanese historical memory. The American trial sought to delegitimize that judgment as "false and fraudulent" and made way in the American historical memory for the Doolittle Raiders to become an uncomplicated fixture of twentieth-century American folklore.

Dozens of books, TV shows, and movies have told the story of the Doolittle Raid in heroic terms, and there are at least two extraordinary websites brimming with biographies, photographs, personal histories, commemorative artwork, and discussion forums. When I interviewed Richard E. Cole, Doolittle's copilot, he was surprised that anyone would want to go to the trouble of writing yet another book about it.

* * *

Chase Nielsen never came around to the idea that the result of the Doolittle Trial was what justice required, but it gave him the closure he needed to let go of the bitterness that had so consumed him in the first half of 1946. Soon after his return to Utah, his mother introduced him to a pretty young lady named Cleo, who worked with her at the Ogden Depot. On July 17, 1946, Chase and Cleo were married at the Latter-Day Saints Temple in Logan. They raised three children and Nielsen forwent Arlington National Cemetery to remain buried next to her at the Hyrum City Cemetery in Utah.

In 1966, Nielsen had the opportunity to expand "Saga of Living Death" into the book *Four Came Home*. Coauthored by Carroll V. Glines, the personal biographer of Jimmy Doolittle, Nielsen, Hite, DeShazer, and Barr offered the story of their captivity as a tale of hope and solidarity for young Americans who were then finding themselves in enemy hands in Vietnam. The North Vietnamese had followed the dubious lead of Imperial Japan and declared that captured American airmen were not entitled to be prisoners of war because they were unlawful combatants.

Nielsen wrote very little about the trial in which he had played so central a role, but *Four Came Home* was sanguine that the trial had honored the memories of Hallmark, Farrow, Spatz, and Meder as well as anything could because those men had fought "to preserve the American way of life based on a system of law, which recognized the dignity and the rights of all men. These four brave, young men had paid the ultimate price to help preserve that system."

Nielsen also had the pleasure of living out the rest of his life as one of the Doolittle Raiders, enjoying the glow of a modest but earnestly heroic celebrity. The Raiders' annual reunions, which Nielsen regularly attended, grew over time from rowdy gatherings of young men, who shared a miraculously heroic moment together, to full-fledged World War II festivals attended by thousands of autograph seekers, history buffs, and picnickers. The last was in April 2013, just outside Elgin Field in Florida, where Jimmy Doolittle had trained them for their mission seventy-one years earlier. At the time, four were still alive, including Robert Hite, who was too ill to attend but would go on to live two more years in the care of his family.

Among the four Doolittle Raiders that Ray Nichols and his OSS team rescued from Fengtai, the only one who did not live into his nineties was George Barr, who died in 1967 of a heart attack. After Barr's wife, three daughters, and son were initially denied full survivors' death benefits, Jimmy Doolittle again fought with the Army bureaucracy until Barr's death was ruled to be service connected. Ray Nichols, for his part, translated the skills he learned in the OSS into a position with the International Cooperation Administration, the forerunner of USAID, and died under mysterious circumstances in 1956 while on mission in Vietnam.

*　*　*

Shigeru Sawada, Yusei Wako, Ryuhei Okada, and Sotojiro Tatsuta were transferred to Sugamo Prison on September 21, 1946. When they arrived, Sadamu Shimomura was still detained there. SCAP was struggling to figure out a way of releasing him without drawing public attention. It would take until following spring. Shimomura was given the alias "Shigeru Sakamoto" and told to lie low in Tatayama, a small town outside Tokyo. MacArthur directed that Shimomura's release "be given no publicity" and the reporters in Tokyo agreed to keep quiet.

Sawada ultimately testified before the Tokyo Tribunal in 1947, where Joseph Keenan made good on his promise to include charges against

Shunroku Hata and Hideki Tojo for their roles in the Doolittle Raiders' saga as part of the Tokyo Trial. Hata was convicted for a variety of war crimes he and his men had committed in China and sentenced to life imprisonment. Tojo was sent to the gallows on December 23, 1948, where he was hanged by the neck until dead.

The Indian judge on the Tokyo Tribunal, Radhabinod Pal, dissented. He thought that Japan's Enemy Airmen's Law was no more ex post facto than the charter establishing the Tokyo Tribunal was and that the Doolittle Raiders had committed war crimes by bombing indiscriminately. Some legal historians have criticized Pal for being shallow in his analysis, at least with respect to Tojo, who acted against his own conscience to appease militarists such as Chief of Staff Hajime Sugiyama. Tojo, more than anyone else, knew that he was using the formalities of a trial not to decide the truth but to legitimize revenge with evidence corrupted by torture.

In 1949, while still serving his sentence, Sawada petitioned to have Okada and Tatsuta released. By that time, another military commission in Yokohama had sentenced some other Japanese soldiers for similarly participating in the unfair trial under the Enemy Airmen's Law. The junior officer and warden in that case had been required to serve less than three years, in comparison to the five-year sentences imposed on Okada and Tatsuta. Sawada, Okada, and Tatsuta were all released on January 9, 1950.

Yusei Wako was released with the last of the Japanese war criminals on December 29, 1958, and he had been lucky to survive that long. Two years after the Doolittle Trial, Wako, along with Shoshin Ito and Yoshinao Sato, the intelligence chief from the Western District Army, were tried for their involvement in the execution of the American prisoners in Fukuoka. Wako and Sato had been sentenced to death. Shoshin Ito had received ten years at hard labor for forging the paperwork to cover up the murders.

While awaiting his death sentence, Wako received support in his pursuit of clemency from Jacob DeShazer, who by that time had returned to Japan as a missionary. DeShazer wrote a letter opposing Wako's execution. "It is certainly not an act for our leading Christian nation to do. By executing criminals, we are putting ourselves, in the eyes of God and the other nations of the world, on the same cruel level as the butchering Nazi and Japanese governments." Japan, he wrote, should be given the opportunity to democratize and Christianize. "Wako was once an enemy who had some obscure job of punishing his enemies, myself, and some of my friends, but for the above reasons I now earnestly forgive him and will strive to love. I petition you for his sake."

Sawada lived into his early nineties, old enough to see his son become one of Japan's preeminent professors of Western philosophy. Sawada's military diaries were posthumously published in 1982 and avoided discussing the Doolittle Raiders or his war crimes trial. But in private, he always admired Edmund Bodine and Charles Fellows for what they had done for him. Before he said his final good-byes, he gave each of them two antique samurai swords. The fact that he had given each man two swords was significant under the Bushido, or samurai code of chivalry. The essence of the Bushido was a strict distinction between the soldier and the civilian, with the samurai devoting themselves to principles of loyalty, self-sacrifice, and excellence. As one of its tenets, a samurai was always required to carry two swords to distinguish himself.

*   *   *

Fellows passed his swords down to his son, Robert, upon returning to hearth and home in Oklahoma. Nothing brought Fellows greater joy than family life, perhaps other than golf, which he played with Robert rain or shine from the moment the boy could hold a club. The sport suited him as he went to work as the in-house counsel for a series of oil companies, where he never had to try a case again. Fellows's wife, Evie, always pushed for them to travel the world together, but Fellows liked being home. It was not until after he died of lung cancer in 1979 that Evie made her own trip to Shanghai to see its *chao nao* for herself.

*   *   *

Bodine stayed in China with the Army until the summer of 1948, when it became clear that Mao Zedong's victory over Chiang Kai-shek was only a matter of time. Bodine's decision to stay in China that long, not to mention his marriage, had come as a tremendous shock to Alma and the rest of the Bodine clan back in Douglaston, Long Island.

Just before he and Elizaveta had eloped, Bodine had sent Alma a telegram US Army rate that read, GETTING MARRIED SATURDAY, APRIL 6, WISH YOU WERE HERE. LOVE LT. COL. E. J. BODINE. To make amends for the surprise, he wrote a long letter home on the anniversary of his father's death, which included a letter Elizaveta had written to introduce herself.

Alma, normally one to respond to her son the same day she received his letters, took nearly three months to write back. "It has taken all this time for me to make up my mind to write, as you certainly know by now, because I was shocked at your marriage," she wrote. "You have certainly forgotten your duty to your folks."

As she was wont to do, Alma served up an ample helping of maternal guilt: "It seems to me that you have forgotten that you still have a mother and was greatly insulted when you had forgotten Mother's Day and Father's Day, but the folks at home didn't forget. There are a great many things I sit and think of in the past but you are too far away to write you. I'm very embittered by your attitude and as I may never see you again probably the least said the better."

Alma nevertheless dutifully accepted her new daughter-in-law, despite her suspicion that every Russian was a communist, and asked for her dress and shoe sizes. She closed her letter by noting "I have been very sick and had two spells. I thought it was the end. The doctor worked over me for thirty-five minutes before he brought me to. But I don't suppose you are interested so I won't go into details. I guess I have written all the news. Mother."

Upon receiving his mother's bitter response, Bodine knew he had to mend her feelings. Thankfully, he had just the balm. Perhaps it was the afterglow of his victory, but within a few weeks after their marriage, Elizaveta was pregnant with their first child, whom they would call Edmund Bodine, Jr. Bodine sent his mother another letter and included a picture of himself with Elizaveta to show how happy they were.

When the letter arrived in Douglaston, Long Island, Alma put aside her grudge. Bodine's niece had just gotten back from a trip to the Statue of Liberty, and when she saw Elizaveta in the picture, she said, "That's Liberty." For Alma, the name stuck. Calling her son's new Russian wife "Liberty" seemed to make her feel better about the arrangement. That afternoon, she wrote the longest and most joyful letter she had sent her son in some time, adding that she hoped "Liberty will be over the nausea period. I went through that nine times and know what it is."

Alma included $500 in money orders along with a note: "Do not lose it in gambling." Her joy helped her accept the distance that had grown between them. "When you left home five years ago to go to Alabama you certainly left for good, which shocks me as I always thought you would stick to me and you would be the one that would close my eyes in death," she wrote to him. "But I was wrong. You couldn't be further away if we were in different worlds. But I guess I can take it. Will close. Mother."

Bodine had undoubtedly gone to a different world from that of the comfortable, conservative Republican Bodine clan of Douglaston, Long Island. The world was changing all around him, and he was in the thick of it. By the summer of 1946, Ham Young had already assigned him as the chief defense counsel on two more interesting cases, (though Bodine would not ultimately get his law degree until 1951, from the Thomas Goode Jones School of Law in Montgomery, Alabama).

One case involved a German spy ring that had continued to operate in China after Germany surrendered. Bodine was now having to deal with the spies' ringleader, a Nazi named Ludwig Ehrhardt, whose real name was Lothar Eisentrager.

Bodine would ultimately enlist the help of Frank Reel, Yamashita's lawyer, who took the Eisentrager case all the way up to the Supreme Court. Reel lost again in an opinion written by Justice Robert H. Jackson, who had returned to his seat on the Court after securing twelve death sentences as the lead prosecutor of the Nuremberg Trial.

The other case involved the trial and execution of an Air Force major named David Henry Houck, who had been shot down over Hong Kong on January 15, 1945. The Japanese had tried and executed him under the Enemy Airmen's Law for strafing a Chinese fishing boat.

The facts were better for the Japanese involved than they had been in the Doolittle case, but after the public outcry over the leniency shown to Sawada, Bodine knew it was going to be a tough job. To help him, he persuaded Moritada Kumashiro to stay a little longer in Shanghai, though the Japan Town that Kumashiro loved had largely withered away into the *chao nao*.

To make the reunion complete, Dwyer prosecuted the case. This time, Dwyer got two death sentences, though both were later commuted to life imprisonment.

* * *

Before Hendren left Shanghai for Missouri, he wrote a letter to Joseph Keenan in Tokyo that began by noting his happiness that they had established "the principle that a judge is criminally responsible for affording an unfair hearing to any accused." Nevertheless, Hendren was bitter about the leniency of the sentences and blamed them on the reluctance of the older guard in the Army to accept the theory of command responsibility. The Army, he wrote, has always "been a great outfit to 'pass the buck' and never admit failures or responsibilities and you cannot expect regular army officers to look favorably upon a series of cases that hold them strictly accountable not only for their acts but for the acts of men serving under them."

Looking forward to Keenan's preparation of the Tokyo Trial, Hendren recommended keeping war crimes trials focused on "brutal atrocities of a physical nature" and to get "a good public relations man and to keep the public interest up in your cases. As far as I can see now the public does not give a damn any more about war crimes." He also put in a good word for Dwyer, who was still hoping to join Keenan for the Tokyo Trial, and pitched himself for a job in Washington, DC, once Keenan got back.

Hendren started his own law firm back in Missouri later that year and in 1948 became the Chairman of the Missouri Democratic State Committee, helping native son Harry S. Truman win reelection as President. Asked for his thoughts on the fifth anniversary of the Doolittle Raid, he could think of only one man: Sadamu Shimomura. "He was never tried so far as I know," Hendren lamented.

* * *

The job for Dwyer as a prosecutor on the Tokyo Trial never materialized, but he remained committed to the Doolittle Raiders and the pursuit of justice against Japanese war criminals. In September 1946, Dwyer made a special trip out to Jiangwan to round up William Farrow's personal effects to send to his mother. Dwyer's father had died that June, and he knew how the little artifacts of a loved one's life—a jacket, a notebook, a wallet, a ring of keys—sometimes had the power to tear a little hole through death's thick wall. Dwyer boxed up what he could find and sent it along with a letter of consolation. He made sure that Farrow's mother knew he was doing everything he could to honor her son's memory, even if she thought he had fallen short at the Doolittle Trial.

Dwyer took the trial's mixed results in stride and was awarded the Bronze Star for his efforts just a month before his father's death. Back in Rochester for the funeral, Dwyer also discovered that he had earned considerable local celebrity in his own right as an international war crimes prosecutor. He was happy to sit for interviews in which he held forth not just about the Doolittle Trial but also about the current state of Asia-Pacific politics.

When he returned to Shanghai later in the summer of 1946, Dwyer even went to visit Shigeru Sawada in prison before he was shipped off to Sugamo. Given their earlier exchanges, Dwyer's visit caught Sawada by surprise, but Dwyer made it clear that he did not hold a grudge. The war was over, their war was over, and Dwyer sought to make the deep peace that is possible only between former adversaries. Dwyer even handed Sawada a gift of chocolates.

Sawada respected the "manliness" of Dwyer's gesture and was impressed by how beautifully Dwyer had wrapped his gift. One of the subtler aspects of Japanese traditional culture is *tsutsumi*, or the art of gift wrapping. In a culture that prizes feigned diffidence, the actual gift communicates far less than the time and beauty invested in wrapping it. An unwrapped gift is crass, even insulting. It is too direct. Dwyer, as a human being, was an unwrapped gift. But with an elegantly wrapped box of chocolates and a few kind words, he let Sawada know that he knew how to package a message.

Dwyer remained in Shanghai through the fall and winter and counted Bodine and Elizaveta among his best friends, even as the demands of child rearing dampened their ability to enjoy the nightlife as much as they all had the year before. Then, on March 19, 1947, a year to the day after his first big moment in the Doolittle Trial, his dramatic reading of the words of George Barr, Dwyer drank himself to death. The official cause was acute uremia, and there were rumors that he had been poisoned, but those close to him remembered seeing him at dinner that night launching into an aggressive bender.

Bodine was a pallbearer at Dwyer's funeral at Christ the King Church in Shanghai, and when his body was returned to Rochester, more than a hundred mourners paid their respects. His hometown paper lamented the loss of one of its great American sons, who had just been selected, it turned out, to work directly for General Douglas MacArthur in Tokyo.

* * *

The memory of the Doolittle Trial has faded under the shadow of the Nuremberg and Tokyo Trials, but Dwyer and Hendren's achievement has had a lasting legacy. In the 1949 Geneva Conventions, American negotiators insisted on closing every legal black hole that the overclever Japanese lawyers had exploited to justify their mistreatment of the Doolittle Raiders.

Ever since then, anyone captured in battle has been and continues to be presumed to be a prisoner of war and can be denied that status only after a regularly constituted tribunal finds otherwise. The Conventions forbid torture and mistreatment under all circumstances. Solitary confinement is banned unless necessary to protect from disease. And the Conventions specify the elements of a fair trial, including the rights to have counsel of choice, to call and question witnesses, to prepare and present a defense, to know the evidence against you, and to have quality translations of the charges, evidence, and proceedings. Ex post facto laws are banned, and enemy nationals cannot be segregated into separate and unequal tribunals. The Conventions make the denial of a fair and regular trial in itself a "grave breach," which is the most serious class of war crime known in international law.

In a special provision, known as Common Article 3, minimum rules are set forth that apply under all circumstances of armed conflict, even if someone is not entitled to be treated as a prisoner of war. Common Article 3 prohibits "murder of all kinds, mutilation, cruel treatment and torture" as well as "outrages upon personal dignity, in particular humiliating and degrading treatment." And whereas Dwyer and Hendren were forced to rely upon international law's principles and its logic, Common Article 3 forbids injustice in black and white. "The passing of sentences and the carrying out of executions without previous judgment pronounced by a regularly constituted court, affording all the judicial guarantees which are recognized as indispensable by civilized peoples," the Conventions decree, "are and shall remain prohibited at any time and in any place whatsoever."

AUTHOR'S NOTE

As a professor and practitioner of war crimes law for the past fifteen years, I began this project intending to write a more traditional scholarly examination of the case of *United States v. Sawada, et al.* and the lessons it has for contemporary international and national security law. However, so many extraordinary aspects of the story revealed themselves to me over the course of my research that I felt compelled to write it as a work of narrative nonfiction in the hope that a nonspecialist audience might enjoy it and find it all as enlightening as I did.

That, in turn, created its own challenges, not the least learning how to write less like a lawyer and more like a human being and, at the same time, staying meticulous with the scholarship so that the final work would be both credible and useful to specialists in the fields of history, military studies, and law. All told, therefore, writing this book probably took twice as long as it would have had I just committed to one purpose or the other.

In trying to achieve both aims at once, I had to make a few choices about the presentation of the material that are atypical for works of scholarship and so I will describe them as best as I can below.

* * *

Spelling and Vocabulary. To facilitate readability and to avoid confusion, I have used modern vocabulary and spellings in my descriptions. This mattered most for proper nouns, where I used the pinyin "Chongqing" for "Chunking" and "Beijing" for "Peking," as well as "Taiwan" for "Formosa."

I have also used the Western style of writing full proper names, such that given names precede family names, even though the opposite is typical usage in most Asian languages. And I have avoided the use of diacritics when writing in pinyin or romaji, since they are more likely to cause confusion than clarity for the nonspecialist reader.

The major exception to all of these usage choices is Generalissimo Chiang Kai-shek, the leader of the Kuomintang. He remains a well-known public figure, but the trend in modern scholarship of using the pinyin "Jiǎng Jièshí" has not entered the mainstream. I have therefore retained the period spelling and traditional Asian word order of his name, since that is how he remains most commonly known to an English-language audience.

*   *   *

Quotations. There are numerous quotations throughout the book, which have all been taken verbatim from the primary sources in which they appear. Quotations drawn from foreign language sources have been translated into English either by me or (more often) by my very able research assistants, who were all native speakers of the languages they translated.

There are approximately twenty quotations in which I have made nonsubstantive edits to the verbatim wording in order to avoid confusion or facilitate readability—for example, by ensuring verb agreement or cutting garbled crosstalk from transcriptions. Rather than make these edits conspicuous in the text with editing marks, which could have made the quotations less readable to nonspecialist readers, I have included the full text of the unedited verbatim quotations in the references whenever a particular quote in the text has been edited in this way.

I have made three blanket exceptions to this practice for the purposes of clarity and consistency. The first is the use of military rank abbreviations. Because ranks are abbreviated inconsistently by the transcriptionists from whom most of the quotes are taken, I have edited any quotation that used such abbreviations and spelled out the rank. The second is that I have used the pinyin spelling "Jiangwan" for the Shanghai suburb that was spelled "Kiangwan" in the period written about, including within the half dozen quotations in which the period spelling appeared. The third aimed to deal with the fact that the Kempeitai is identified by various descriptors in the transcripts and reports from which I have quoted, including the "military police," the "gendarmerie," and the "gendarmes." I have therefore replaced all of these alternative descriptors with "Kempeitai" in quotations.

Quotations of spoken words are drawn from audio recordings, stenographic transcripts, firsthand accounts, and, with respect to certain events surrounding the romantic relationship between Edmund Bodine and Elizaveta Snigursky, interviews I conducted with their children in which particular quotes were treated as set pieces of their family's oral history. There is obviously some danger in presenting quotes from these latter two sources as accurate records of speech, due to faulty memory or hearing, the human tendency to paraphrase, and other methodological reasons.

I contemplated using the sometimes-deployed technique of italicizing quotations that are not taken from stenographic transcriptions. However, I ultimately decided against doing so for two reasons. The first was that I find the technique visually distracting and it would be confusing for anyone who had not seen the technique used before or not bothered to flip back to this page to find out what was going on with the random italics. The second and overriding reason is that as a litigator, I have reviewed thousands upon thousands of pages of stenographic transcriptions of interviews and court proceedings. That experience has taught me that these purportedly verbatim transcripts are consistently replete with errors of all kinds, big and small, to form and content, due to the inherent limitations of stenography. The age of the transcripts relied upon in this book is also a cause for concern, given that shorthand was the typical stenographic method at the time, and many of the interactions recorded in these purportedly verbatim transcripts are riven with layers of translation issues.

Affording the quotations drawn from stenographic transcripts a privileged position, therefore, risked overstating their relative veracity to the same extent that italicizing or otherwise off-setting quotations from firsthand accounts and the Bodines' oral history risked understating their relative veracity. In other words, with the exception of the few audio recordings cited, all of the sources from which quotations of speech are drawn can only be treated as evidence of that speech, not as definitive repositories of it. I have therefore treated quotations of speech as ordinary quotations in the text, excluded many potentially interesting and illuminating quotations where I had doubts about their credibility as to form or content, and rigorously cited the sources from which any quote is drawn, noting where there is a meaningful conflict between sources, so that the reader can always judge for themselves.

*   *   *

References. There are approximately 1,700 notes and references supporting the text of this book, which have all been prepared in the trailing-phrase endnote style. I have sought to support potentially contentious factual claims with multiple primary sources, and where a particular fact depends upon inferences that are unstated in the text, I have endeavored to explain the basis of those inferences as clearly as possible in the notes. Likewise, when sources conflict on a key point, I have noted the conflict in the references.

One practice worth flagging is how I have gone about citing to the trial transcript of *United States v. Sawada.* Because a significant portion of the book is dedicated to recounting this trial, I thought it would be both needlessly burdensome and uselessly redundant to attribute every quote to its given page number in the transcript. The citations in the references therefore generally mark the first page of the series of pages underlying what is recounted in the text (in legal writing, we would mark this practice by writing "*et seq.*"). Given that the transcript is now publicly available in searchable form on the International Criminal Court's website (see below), those who want to identify the particular page from which a quote is taken can readily do so.

Finally, to further reduce the length of the citations while still making them transparent and easy to use for specialists and researchers, I have employed the following abbreviations to refer to the most frequently used archives, collections, and document repositories:

Bodine Papers: The personal papers of Edmund J. Bodine, Hernando Beach, Florida.

CBI Records: Records of U.S. Army Forces in the China-Burma-India Theaters of Operations, Record Group 493, National Archives at College Park, Maryland.

China War Crimes File: China War Crimes File, Entry 180, Records of the Office of the Judge Advocate General (Army), Record Group 153, National Archives at College Park, Maryland.

Doolittle Papers: The James H. Doolittle Papers, History of Aviation Collection, Special Collections Department, McDermott Library, The University of Texas at Dallas.

Doolittle Raiders Papers: Doolittle Tokyo Raider Association Papers, History of Aviation Collection, Special Collections Department, McDermott Library, The University of Texas at Dallas.

Fairfield Files: Fairfield County, Coroner Records 1883–1979, Fiscal Services Office, Connecticut State Library.

FDR Library: Franklin D. Roosevelt Presidential Library and Museum Archives, Hyde Park, New York.

Glines Papers: C. V. Glines, Jr. Papers, History of Aviation Collection, Special Collections Department, Eugene McDermott Library, The University of Texas at Dallas.

Intelligence Dossiers: Records of the Investigative Records, Repository, Intelligence and Investigative Dossiers—Personal Name File 1939—1976, Entry # A1 134-B, Office of the Assistant Chief of Staff, Records of the Army Staff, Record Group 319, National Archives at College Park, Maryland.

IMTFE Transcript: R. John Pritchard and Sonia Magbanua Zaide, eds., *The Tokyo War Crimes Trial: Complete Transcript of the Proceedings of the International Military Tribunal for the Far East* (Garland, 1981). The full transcript is also now available online at the International Criminal Court's Legal Tools Database https://www.legal-tools.org/.

Allied Occupation Records: Records of Allied Operational and Occupation Headquarters, World War II, Record Group 331, National Archives College Park, Maryland.

OSS Washington/Pacific Field Station Files: Office of Strategic Services Washington/Pacific Coast/Field Station Files, Entry #UD 140, Records of the Office of Strategic Services, Record Group 226, National Archives College Park, Maryland.

OSS Field Station Files: Field Station Files, Entry A1 154, Records of the Office of Strategic Services, Record Group 226, National Archives College Park, Maryland.

POW Records: Records of the Prisoner of War Information Bureau, Records of the Office of the Provost Marshall General, Record Group 389, National Archives at College Park, Maryland.

Sawada Record: *United States v. Sawada, et al.*, Box 1728, Records of the Supreme Commander for the Allied Powers, Legal Section, Prosecution Division, Records of Allied Operational and Occupation Headquarters, World War II, Record Group 331, National Archives at College Park, Maryland.

Sawada Trial Transcript: *United States v. Shigeru Sawada, et al.*, Proceedings Before Military Commission Convened by Order of the Commanding General, United States Forces, China Theater, at Shanghai, China, Record of Trial, Box 1728, Records of the Supreme Commander for the Allied Powers, Legal Section, Prosecution Division, Records of Allied Operational and Occupation Headquarters, World War II, Record Group 331, National Archives at College Park, Maryland. The full transcript is also now available online at the International Criminal Court's Legal Tools Database https://www.legal-tools.org/.

SCAP Prosecution Records: Records of the Supreme Commander for the Allied Powers, Legal Section, Prosecution Division, Records of Allied Operational and Occupation Headquarters, World War II, Record Group 331, National Archives at College Park, Maryland.

War Crimes Case Files: Case Files, Entry 144, War Crimes Branch, Records of the Office of the Judge Advocate General (Army), Record Group 153, National Archives at College Park, Maryland.

Yasukuni Archives: 靖國偕行文庫（図書館）[Yasukuni Shrine Library], Tokyo, Japan.

ACKNOWLEDGMENTS

This book was the product of years of effort by dozens of people, who demonstrated such remarkable dedication and talent that this book makes me look far smarter than I am.

First among many equals are my agent, Rachel Vogel, who helped me conceive this book, and my editors, Thomas LeBien, who brought this book to life; Jofi Ferrari-Adler, who kept it alive; and Julianna Haubner, who made it something that people will hopefully enjoy reading despite my best efforts to thwart her at every turn. I likewise owe a debt of gratitude to Jonathan Karp for taking a risk on this project and sticking by it for all the right reasons, as well as to Simon & Schuster's team of crack copy editors, who caught everything that was wrong or dumb in my writing.

Just as indispensable were my research assistants, Rina Fujii, Kei Watanabe, Katharina Groth, Peiyao Sun, Scott Johnston, Randy Asherbranner, and, last but certainly not least, Kei Kato; thanks to Curtis Milhaupt, Kentaro Matsubara, and Shelly Habel, who introduced me to many of these extraordinary people.

I am grateful to Charles "Pop-Pop" Paradis; Phyllis Eastburn; David Glaizer; Philip Sundel; Samuel Morison; Justin Swick; Brigadier General John Baker, USMC; Captain Brian Mizer, USN; Major Brett Robinson, USAF; Adam Thurschwell; Katherine Newell; Nancy Hollander; Cherise Pilger; Kristina Hon; Weike Wang; and Vika Nazganova for helping me understand this story as well as the times, cultures, and places that were all very new to me.

I am also grateful to all of those who gave me their time for personal interviews, which were essential to making this story come alive. Some prefer to remain anonymous, but others whom I can happily name include Richard Cole, Fred Borch, John Disosway, Tom Vetter, Terry Nielsen, Robert Fellows, Katie Fellows, Haruo Somiya, Koichi Ikeda, Shigeo Komatsu, Charles Kuzma, Elizabeth Bodine, and Natalie Bodine, the latter two of whom I am especially grateful to for allowing me to rummage through their family's extraordinary archive of documents and their continued willingness to assist me over many years.

Similarly, I could not have done this project without the dozens of librarians, museum curators, archivists, and court clerks who helped me find what I needed along the way, and the extraordinary scholarship of James Gray, James M. Scott, C. V. Glines, and Weiyong Zheng, who all generously offered both their insights and the wealth of their research.

And, of course, nothing would have been possible without the support of my family, who never stopped asking me, "Are you still working on that book?"

NOTES

THE MURDER

3   *gotten off the phone*: Sotojiro Tatsuta, interview by Evelyn Knecht, February 10, 1947, p. 1, Box 719, *Intelligence Dossiers*; Sotojiro Tatsuta, interview by Edmund Bodine and Charles Fellows, February 21, 1946, p. 4, Bodine Papers.

3   *Tatsuta gathered*: Walter G. Rundle, "Jap Describes Execution of 3 Doolittle Fliers," United Press, January 18, 1946.

3   *A skinny man*: Walter G. Rundle, "Jap Describes Execution of 3 Doolittle Fliers," United Press, January 18, 1946.

4   *translator at his side*: Caesar Luis DosRemedios, Statement, September 19, 1945, p. 2, Prosecution Exhibit 26, Sawada Record.

4   *Farrow*: Factsheet, "Airplane 60-22168," undated, Box 40, Glines Papers.

4   *Tatsuta had been told*: Tatsuta Sotojiro, interview by Robert Dwyer, November 16, 1945, p. 1, Box 40, Glines Papers.

4   *remind Tatsuta*: Sawada Trial Transcript, 466 (Testimony of Sotojiro Tatsuta).

4   *his oldest son*: Tatsuta Sotojiro, interview by Robert Dwyer, November 16, 1945, p. 6, Box 40, Glines Papers.

4   *"something might happen"*: Sawada Trial Transcript, 465 (Testimony of Sotojiro Tatsuta).

4   *take the chance*: Walter G. Rundle, "Jap Describes Execution of 3 Doolittle Fliers," United Press, January 18, 1946

4   *told the guards*: Sawada Trial Transcript, 465 (Testimony of Sotojiro Tatsuta).

4   *Tatsuta's translator*: Caesar Luis DosRemedios, Statement, September 19, 1945, pp. 2–3, Prosecution Exhibit 26, Sawada Record. Remedios claims in his statement that he did not know the Raiders were being executed, but merely surmised this fact from the circumstances. However, this is contradicted by his own description of what he told the Raiders, their reactions, and the fact that they gave him their personal belongings on the night before they were executed. It is also highly implausible that Remedios would not have known of their executions due to the wide publicity given to the executions in the Shanghai press at tht time, his close

proximity to all the relevant actors, and the statements from every other member of Tatsuta's staff that describe the executions as widely known and extremely significant at the time. Remedios's denial on this point, therefore, when speaking to Jason Bailey in 1945 appears motivated by concern over his own legal exposure for his role in the Raiders' captivity and executions. Remedios's conflict of interest was noted by Edmund Bodine in his trial notes and was briefly developed on the record during the Doolittle Trial in 1946. Sawada Trial Transcript, 147.

4   *not much*: Army Advisory Group, Nanking China, Cable, April 3, 1945, War Crimes Files, Incoming and Outgoing Radios, Box 14, China War Crimes Files.

5   *"make use of them"*: Caesar Luis DosRemedios, Statement. September 19, 1945, p. 4, Box 40, Glines Papers ("Lt. Farrow handed these to me stating that some day I might make use of them").

5   *Noboru Unit*: The full code name of the 13th Army was the "Noboru 7330 Unit." I have used its colloquially shortened form, "Noboru Unit," throughout.

5   *links next door*: Irene Kuhn, "Tea and Ashes," in Overseas Press Club of America, eds., *Deadline Delayed* (New York: E. P. Dutton, 1947), 268, 272.

5   *Japanese military tradition*: Helen Craig, Full Translation of Statements by Colonel Tomomori and Lieutenant General Inada and accompanying documents, August 13, 1947, p. 8, Box 1081, War Crimes Case Files.

5   *three wooden crosses*: Jason Bailey, "Interrogation of Mayama Shigeji," September 28, 1945, p. 1, Box 40, Glines Papers.

5   *small table*: Tatsuta Sotojiro, interview by Robert Dwyer, November 16, 1945, pp. 3–4, Box 40, Glines Papers.

5   *the official witness*: Tatsuta Sotojiro, interview by Robert Dwyer, November 16, 1945, p. 3, Box 40, Glines Papers.

5   *historic moment*: Yasuo Karakawa, interview by John Hendren, January 5, 1946, p. 5, Box 40, Glines Papers.

5   *early evening*: Itsuro Hata, "Particulars Relating to the Punishment of the American Airman Who Raided the Japanese Homeland on 18 April 1942," translation by Allied Translator and Interpret Section, United States Army Forces, Pacific, Doc. 1870, October 1945, "Inclosure [*sic*] No. 8, Record of Execution," p. 11, Prosecution Exhibit 25, Sawada Record.

5   *"physically sound"*: Itsuro Hata, "Particulars Relating to the Punishment of the American Airman Who Raided the Japanese Homeland on 18 April 1942," translation by Allied Translator and Interpret Section, United States Army Forces, Pacific, Doc. 1870, October 1945, "Inclosure [*sic*] No. 8, Record of Execution," p. 11, Prosecution Exhibit 25, Sawada Record.

5   *"Hata read"*: Sawada Trial Transcript, 473 (Testimony of Sotojiro Tatsuta).

5   *firing squad*: Itsuro Hata, "Particulars Relating to the Punishment of the American Airman who Raided the Japanese Homeland on 18 April 1942," Translation by Allied Translator and Interpret Section, United States Army Forces, Pacific, Doc. 1870, October 1945, "Inclosure [*sic*] No. 8, Record of Execution," p. 11, Prosecution Exhibit 25, Sawada Record.

5   *one bullet*: Jason Bailey, "Interrogation of Mayama Shigeji," September 28, 1945, p. 1, Box 40, Glines Papers.

5   *Tatsuta and his men*: Tatsuta Sotojiro, interview by Robert Dwyer, November 16, 1945, p. 3, Box 40, Glines Papers.

5   *commander of the firing squad*: Sawada Trial Transcript, 174 (Testimony of Yoneda Isamu).

6   *pulse was gone*: Tatsuta Sotojiro, interview by Robert Dwyer, November 16, 1945, p. 3, Box 40, Glines Papers.

6   *final salute*: Sawada Trial Transcript, 151 (Testimony of Shigeji Mayama).

6   *cart the coffins*: Tatsuta Sotojiro, interview by Robert Dwyer, November 16, 1945, p. 4, Box 40, Glines Papers.

6   *ordered the clerk*: Sawada Trial Transcript, 478 (Testimony of Sotojiro Tatsuta).

6   *have it tailored*: Caesar Luis DosRemedios, Statement, September 19, 1945, p. 3, Box 40, Glines Papers.

6   *life imprisonment*: Chase Nielsen, statement taken by Stacey Grayson, undated (September 7, 1945), p. 3, Bodine Files.

7   *kept them in solitary*: Tatsuta Sotojiro, interview by Robert Dwyer, November 16, 1945, p. 6, Box 40, Glines Papers.

7   *the cells*: Irene Kuhn, "Tea and Ashes," in Overseas Press Club of America, eds., *Deadline Delayed* (New York: Dutton, 1947), 268, 274.

CHAPTER ONE

11   *Nielsen joined*: Utah State Archives and Records Service, Salt Lake City, Utah, Military Service Cards, ca. 1898–1975, Department of Administrative Services, Division of Archives and Records Service, Series 85268, Reel 92; Chase Jay Nielsen, Resume, April 16, 1963, Series II, Box 5, Doolittle Raiders Papers.

11   *head for numbers*: Terry Nielsen, personal interview, August 19, 2015.

11   *swarthy complexion*: "Hyrum Boy Flew with Doolittle," *Cache American*, May 22, 1942, 1; "Utah Pilot Aids in Raid on Japanese," *Daily Herald*, May 20, 1942, 1; "Logan Social Events Reported," *Deseret News*, December 20, 1941.

11   *"Volunteers"*: George Barr, interview by W. L. Brown and Chester I. Lappen, December 30, 1945, p. 2, Prosecution Transcript Exhibit 21, Sawada Record.

12   *family man*: According to Robert Hite, the only man to turn down the request did so because he had a pregnant wife. James Curtis Hasdorff, *United States Air Force Oral History Program: Interview of Lt. Col. Robert L. Hite* (USAF Historical Research Center, 1982), 31–32.

12   *broke the news*: Ray J. Nelson, "Lt. Nielsen Keeps Word That I'll Be Coming Back," *Ogden Standard-Examiner*, August 24, 1945, 3A.

12   *stationed at Eglin*: For histories of the crews and training regimen, see James M. Scott, *Target Tokyo* (New York: Norton, 2015), 85–97; C. V. Glines, *The Doolittle Raid* (New York: Orion Books, 1988), 25–35; James Merrill, *Target Tokyo* (Chicago: Rand McNally, 1964), 26–35; Duane Schultz, *The Doolittle Raid* (New York: St. Martin's Press, 1988), 59–77; James H. "Jimmy" Doolittle, *I Could Never Be So Lucky Again* (New York: Bantam, 1991), 226–31.

12   *Army Air Service*: Doolittle, *I Could Never Be So Lucky Again*, 36–43.

12   *mortality rate*: War Department, *Annual Reports, 1918*, vol. 1 (U.S. Government Printing Office, 1919), 54–56

12   *air traffic tickets*: Department of Commerce, Aeronautics Branch, Notice of Violation of Air Commerce Regulations by Owner or Person in Command of Aircraft Involving Incurrence of Penalty, October 8, 1930, Series I, Box 2, Doolittle Papers.

12   *doctorate*: James H. Doolittle, "Wind Gradient and Velocity" (PhD diss., Massachusetts Institute of Technology, 1925).

12   *developed*: Doolittle, *I Could Never Be So Lucky Again*, 119–24

12   *fly blind*: "Blind Plane Flies 15 Miles and Lands; Fog Peril Overcome," *New York Times*, September 25, 1929, 1; Doolittle, *I Could Never Be So Lucky Again*, 139–40.

13   *war began to loom*: Doolittle, *I Could Never Be So Lucky Again*, 198–210.

13   *Special Aviation Project No. 1*: Henry Arnold, Memorandum for the President, January 28, 1942, Series I, Safe File, Box 2, Franklin D. Roosevelt, Papers as President: The President's Secretary's File, 1933–1945, FDR Library; William Ellis, "Mid-Continent Airlines and the B-25B Special Project," September 4, 1988, pp. 1–2, Box 37, Glines Papers.

13   *Arnold asked Doolittle*: Doolittle, *I Could Never Be So Lucky Again*, 212.

13   *Doolittle's solution*: J. H. Doolittle to Henry Arnold, "B-25B Special Project," undated, reproduced at https://perma.cc/DA7C-L7Y2, also reproduced at Carroll V. Glines, *Doolittle's Tokyo Raiders* (New York: Van Nostrand Reinhold, 1981), 37–41. The initial idea for launching a bombing raid on Japan from an aircraft carrier came from Navy submarine captain Francis Low, who had coincidentally been doing an inspection of the newly built USS *Hornet* in Norfolk, Virginia. While in Norfolk, he saw a runway on which a carrier deck had been painted to train Army bombers. Watching them take off and land gave him the idea that Army bombers could take off from a carrier, an idea that he passed up his chain of command until it reached the head of the Army Air Forces, Henry "Hap" Arnold, who asked Doolittle whether it was possible. Scott, *Target Tokyo*, 29–31; Carroll V. Glines, *Doolittle's Tokyo Raiders* (New York: Van Nostrand Reinhold, 1981), 11–19

13   *landing strip in China*: Henry Arnold, Memorandum for the President, January 28, 1942, Series I, Safe File, Box 2, Franklin D. Roosevelt, Papers as President: The President's Secretary's File, 1933–1945, FDR Library.

13   *the only way*: Jimmy Doolittle, "My Raid Over Tokyo, April 1942," August 14, 1965, pp. 2–4, Series IV, Box 4, Doolittle Papers.

13   *replace every unnecessary ounce*: William Ellis, "Mid-Continent Airlines and the B-25B Special Project," September 4, 1988, Box 37, Glines Papers.

13   *Doolittle's volunteers trained*: James Doolittle, "Report on the Aerial Bombing of Japan," June 5, 1942, p. 10, Box 36, Glines Papers; Henry L. Miller, "Temporary additional duty assignment, report on," May 7, 1942, Box 39, Glines Papers; Richard Cole, Remarks, undated, pp. 3–5, Series II, Box 1, Doolittle Raiders Papers; W. B. Courtney, "Through Hell and High Brass: The Story of Jimmy Doolittle," *Colliers*, December 11, 1948, p. 82.

13   *Doolittle kept drilling*: Charles Greening, "The First Joint Action," December 21, 1948, pp. 10–12, Box 37, Glines Papers; James Doolittle, "Report on the Aerial Bombing of Japan," June 5, 1942, pp. 3–6, Box 36, Glines Papers.

13   *led his men*: James Doolittle, "Report on the Aerial Bombing of Japan," June 5, 1942, p. 12, Box 36, Glines Papers; Doolittle, *I Could Never Be So Lucky Again*, 231.

13   *sixth plane*: Glines, *The Doolittle Raid*, 93.

13   *played football*: Roland Scott, "Remembering a Fallen Hero, Close Friend," *Auburn Alumnews* 17, no. 7 (1987): 9

14   *Meder*: *Fourteenth Census of the United States*, 1920, Cleveland Ward 2, Cuyahoga, Ohio, Enumeration District 13, Records of the Bureau of the Census, Record Group 29, National Archives and Records Administration.

14   *seem as urbane*: Chase Nielsen Oral History, undated audio, Series II, Box 5, Doolittle Raiders Papers.

14   *"Dieter"*: *Fourteenth Census of the United States,* 1920, Vail, Crawford, Iowa, Enumeration District 89, Records of the Bureau of the Census, Record Group 29, National Archives and Records Administration.

14   *Fitzmaurice*: Tim to Todd Joyce, February 8, 2011, Series II, Box 2, Doolittle Raiders Papers.

14   *good Catholic boys*: Earl L. Dieter to Jesse and May (Farrow), September 6, 1945, Series II, Box 2, Doolittle Raiders Papers.

14   *boarded*: William Halsey, "Report of Action, April 18, 1942, with notable events prior and subsequent thereto," April 28, 1942, p. 1, Box 1038, Records of the Chief of Naval Operations, Record Group 38, National Archives, College Park.

14   *flyboy's nonchalance*: *The Reminiscences of Captain Stephen Jurika*, vol 1, pp. 173–74, Box 7, Stephen Jurika Papers, Collection # 80035, Hoover Institution Archives, Stanford University.

14   *disembarked*: William Halsey, "Report of Action, April 18, 1942, with notable events prior and subsequent thereto," April 28, 1942, p. 3, Box 1038, Records of the Chief of Naval Operations, Record Group 38, National Archives, College Park.

14   *less than pleased*: *The Reminiscences of Captain Stephen Jurika*, vol 1., p. 174, Box 7, Stephen Jurika Papers, Collection # 80035, Hoover Institution Archives, Stanford University.

14   *loudspeaker broke in*: Richard Cole, Remarks, undated, p. 5, Series II, Box 1, Doolittle Raiders Papers.

14   *scheduled his raid*: James Doolittle, "Report on the Aerial Bombing of Japan," June 5, 1942, pp. 13–14, Box 36, Glines Papers.

14   *Stephen Jurika*: *The Reminiscences of Captain Stephen Jurika*, vol. 1, p. 185, Box 7, Stephen Jurika Papers, Collection # 80035, Hoover Institution Archives, Stanford University.

14   *handed out the targets*: Charles Greening, "The First Joint Action," December 21, 1948, pp. 18–19, Box 37, Glines Papers.

15   *off limits*: James H. Doolittle, interview by Carl Olson, December 27, 1945, p. 1, Sawada Record.

15   *contemplated bombing*: Jimmy Doolittle, "My Raid Over Tokyo, April 1942" August 14, 1965, p. 6, Series IV, Box 4, Doolittle Papers.

15   *target maps*: Sawada Trial Transcript, 61 (Testimony of Chase Nielsen).

15   *low-level bombing*: James H. Doolittle, interview by Carl Olson, December 27, 1945, p. 2, Sawada Record.

15   *To help*: James H. Doolittle, interview by Carl Olson, December 27, 1945, p. 1, Sawada Record.

15   *"The Diet Building"*: *The Reminiscences of Captain Stephen Jurika*, vol. 1, p. 459, Box 7, Stephen Jurika Papers, Collection # 80035, Hoover Institution Archives, Stanford University.

15   *"You don't"*: *The Reminiscences of Captain Stephen Jurika*, vol. 1, p. 459, Box 7, Stephen Jurika Papers, Collection # 80035, Hoover Institution Archives, Stanford University ("You didn't have to estimate, you didn't have to use a stopwatch. You had these major physical points to look at.").

15   *"Fly over these"*: *The Reminiscences of Captain Stephen Jurika*, vol. 1, pp. 458–59,

Box 7, Stephen Jurika Papers, Collection # 80035, Hoover Institution Archives, Stanford University ("You then pass over a river and the next big complex that you see, with chimneys belching yellow smoke, to lay your eggs.).

15 *supposedly set up*: Joseph McNary, Memorandum for the President, "First Special Bombing Mission (China)," April 16, 1942, Series I, Safe File, Box 2, Franklin D. Roosevelt, Papers as President: The President's Secretary's File, 1933–1945, FDR Library; J. H. Doolittle to Henry Arnold, "B25B Special Project," undated, reproduced at https://perma.cc/DA7C-L7Y2.

15 *special radio frequency*: Joseph Stilwell to Adjutant General, War Department, Cable, April 16, 1942, Box 158, Henry Harley Arnold Papers, 1903–1989, Library of Congress; Henry Arnold to Joseph Stillwell, Cable, April 6, 1942, "Draft Submitted to Col. Sam Marshall for his story on Tokyo Raid," undated, p. 3, Box 40, Glines Papers. Some of the message traffic concerning the planning and aftermath of the Doolittle Raid is reproduced in a document titled, "Draft Submitted to Col. Sam Marshall for his story on Tokyo Raid." This document was probably produced in 1943 for Colonel S. L. A. Marshall, who served in the Historical Branch, G-2, WDGS, from August 1, 1943, to November 15, 1944, and produced the first study of the Doolittle Raid, titled "The Great Tokyo Raid," Box 40, S. L. A. Marshall Papers, 1900–1979, MS 186, C.L. Sonnichsen Special Collections Department, The University of Texas at El Paso Library.

15 *"If captured"*: The Reminiscences of Captain Stephen Jurika, vol 1., p. 473, Box 7, Stephen Jurika Papers, Collection # 80035, Hoover Institution Archives, Stanford University ("If they were captured dropping bombs on Japan, the chances of their survival would be awfully slim, very, very, slim.").

16 *tips for staying alive*: The Reminiscences of Captain Stephen Jurika, vol. 1, pp. 176, 191, Box 7, Stephen Jurika Papers, Collection # 80035, Hoover Institution Archives, Stanford University.

16 *a letter*: "Tokyo Raiders Believed Held Jap Prisoners," *Ogden Standard Examiner*, October 24, 1942, 1.

16 *he assured her*: Ray J. Nelson, "Lt. Nielsen Keeps Word That I'll Be Coming Back," *Ogden Standard-Examiner*, August 24, 1945, 3A.

16 *radar contact*: William Halsey, "Report of Action, April 18, 1942, with notable events prior and subsequent thereto," April 28, 1942, p. 6, Box 1038, Records of the Chief of Naval Operations, Record Group 38, National Archives, College Park.

16 *seven hundred nautical miles*: Jimmy Doolittle, "My Raid Over Tokyo, April 1942" August 14, 1965, pp. 15, Series IV, Box 4, Doolittle Papers.

16 *order to launch*: The Reminiscences of Captain Stephen Jurika, vol. 1, p. 184, Box 7, Stephen Jurika Papers, Collection # 80035, Hoover Institution Archives, Stanford University.

16 *sea was rough*: William Halsey, "Report of Action, April 18, 1942, with notable events prior and subsequent thereto," April 28, 1942, p. 5, Box 1038, Records of the Chief of Naval Operations, Record Group 38, National Archives, College Park.

16 *took the lead*: Deck Log, Aircraft Carrier Hornet (CV-8), April 18, 1942, Logbooks of U.S. Navy Ships, Entry 11, Records of the Bureau of Naval Personnel, Record Group 24, National Archives College Park; William Halsey, "Report of Action, April 18, 1942, with notable events prior and subsequent thereto," April 28, 1942, p. 3, Box 1038, Records of the Chief of Naval Operations, Record Group 38, National Archives College Park.

16   Green Hornet's *turn*: Sawada Trial Transcript, 44 (Testimony of Chase Nielsen).

16   *northern approach*: Sawada Trial Transcript, 45–49 (Testimony of Chase Nielsen).

16   *Hallmark led them*: Chase Nielsen, Robert Hite, and Jacob DeShazer, "Saga of Living Death," p. 3, Series II, Box 5, Doolittle Raiders Papers.

17   *weather turned*: Sawada Trial Transcript, 49 (Testimony of Chase Nielsen).

17   *made the call*: C. V. Glines, *Four Came Home* (Missoula, MT: Pictorial Histories, 1995), 31 (firsthand account of Chase Nielsen).

17   *early dark*: Chase Nielsen, Robert Hite, and Jacob DeShazer, "Saga of Living Death," p. 3, Series II, Box 5, Doolittle Raiders Papers.

17   *engines started kicking*: Sawada Trial Transcript, 49 (Testimony of Chase Nielsen).

17   *smacked his head*: Chase Nielsen, Robert Hite, and Jacob DeShazer, "Saga of Living Death," p. 3, Series II, Box 5, Doolittle Raiders Papers.

17   *saw Fitz*: Glines, *Four Came Home*, 32 (firsthand account of Chase Nielsen).

17   *crushed him*: Earl L. Dieter to Jesse and May (Farrow), September 6, 1945, Series II, Box 2, Doolittle Raiders Papers.

18   *ripped the cord*: Spencer Moosa, "Doolittle Raiders Tell Experiences," Associated Press, August 25, 1945 (recounting Nielsen's description of the crash); Glines, *Four Came Home*, 32 (firsthand account of Chase Nielsen).

18   *bobbed to the surface*: Sawada Trial Transcript, 50 (Testimony of Chase Nielsen).

18   *came ashore*: 民国31年4月20日爵溪乡公所多长杨世森呈文查本 [Shimiao Yang, Report from Mayor of Juexi Town, April 20, 1942], Xiangshan County Archives.

18   *proper funeral*: Chase Nielsen to Mrs. Dieter, September 18, 1945, Series II, Box 2, Doolittle Raiders Papers.

18   *interpreter greeted*: Chase Nielsen, Robert Hite, and Jacob DeShazer, "Saga of Living Death," p. 6, Series II, Box 5, Doolittle Raiders Papers.

CHAPTER TWO

19   *kept its promise*: Chase Nielsen, Robert Hite, and Jacob DeShazer, "Saga of Living Death," p. 7, Series II, Box 5, Doolittle Raiders Papers.

19   *in Shanghai*: Sawada Trial Transcript, 51 (Testimony of Chase Nielsen).

20   *kick to the shin*: Edward Young, Memorandum, "Treatment of Captured Doolittle Fliers, Tokyo Raid, 18 April 1942," August 27, 1945, p. 7, Box 3, China War Crimes Files. The widespread use of this torture technique is documented in Allied Translator and Interpreter Section, "Japanese Methods of Prisoner of War Interrogation," Research Report No. 134, June 1, 1946, p. 3, Box 1624, Records of the SCAP Legal Section, Administrative Division, Entry 1237, Allied Occupation Records.

20   *"You understand"*: Chase Nielsen, Robert Hite, and Jacob DeShazer, "Saga of Living Death," p. 7, Series II, Box 5, Doolittle Raiders Papers.

20   *bamboo pole*: Edward Young, Memorandum, "Treatment of Captured Doolittle Fliers, Tokyo Raid, 18 April 1942," August 27, 1945, p. 7, Box 3, China War Crimes Files.

20   *his kneecaps*: Chase Nielsen, Robert Hite, Jacob DeShazer, "Saga of Living Death," pp. 10–11, Series II, Box 5, Doolittle Raiders Papers.

20   *pencils*: Edward Young, Memorandum, "Treatment of Captured Doolittle Fliers, Tokyo Raid, 18 April 1942," August 27, 1945, p. 7, Box 3, China War Crimes Files.

20 *pain radiating*: Chase Nielsen, Robert Hite, and Jacob DeShazer, "Saga of Living Death," pp. 11–12, Series II, Box 5, Doolittle Raiders Papers.

20 *"hanging by his hands"*: Edward Young, Memorandum, "Treatment of Captured Doolittle Fliers, Tokyo Raid, 18 April 1942," August 27, 1945, p. 7, Box 3, China War Crimes Files.

20 *door opened*: Chase Nielsen, Robert Hite, and Jacob DeShazer, "Saga of Living Death," pp. 15–16, Series II, Box 5, Doolittle Raiders Papers.

20 *thumbs-up*: Chase Nielsen, Robert Hite, and Jacob DeShazer, "Saga of Living Death," p. 16, Series II, Box 5, Doolittle Raiders Papers.

21 *two months*: Sawada Trial Transcript, 58–63 (Testimony of Chase Nielsen).

21 *main interrogator*: Chase Nielsen, Robert Hite, and Jacob DeShazer, "Saga of Living Death," p. 19, Series II, Box 5, Doolittle Raiders Papers.

21 *the crew*: Factsheet, "Airplane 60-22168," undated, Box 40, Glines Papers.

21 *freak of nature*: Chase Nielsen Oral History, undated audio, Series II, Box 5, Doolittle Raiders Papers.

21 *all together*: George Barr, interview by W. L. Brown and Chester I. Lappen, December 30, 1945, p. 20, Prosecution Transcript Exhibit 21, Sawada Record.

21 *first time*: Chase Nielsen, Robert Hite, and Jacob DeShazer, "Saga of Living Death," pp. 19–20, Series II, Box 5, Doolittle Raiders Papers.

21 *Bridge House*: Izumi Ogata, interview by Alf Watson, January 15, 1946, p. 1, Bodine Papers.

21 *dungeon*: James L. Norwood and Emily L. Shek, *Prisoner of War Camps in Areas Other Than the Four Principal Islands of Japan*, American Prisoner of War Information Bureau, Liaison and Research Branch, July 31, 1946, pp. 1–3, POW Records; Greg Leck, *Captives of Empire: The Japanese Internment of Allied Civilians in China (1941–1945)* ([Bangor, PA]: Shandy Press, 2007), 105.

22 *incessant electric lights*: W. H. Hudspeth, August 28, 1945, Box 67, OSS Washington/Pacific Field Station Files.

22 *Cell 5*: Shun Wong, interview by Robert Dwyer, December 18, 1945, p. 1, Box 40, Glines Papers.

22 *already packed*: Sawada Trial Transcript, 63 (Testimony of Chase Nielsen).

22 *were packed*: Henry Pringle, *Bridge House Survivor: Experiences of a Civilian Prisoner-of-War in Shanghai & Beijing* (Chicago: Earnshaw Books, 2010), 6–10; Leck, *Captives of Empire*, 105; Statement of Kenneth William Johnstone, August 30, 1945, Box 57, OSS Washington/Pacific Field Station Files; Statement re arrest of Supt. J.A. McFarlane, undated, Box 57, OSS Washington/Pacific Field Station Files; Statement of Philip William Giovannini, August 30, 1945, Box 57, OSS Washington/Pacific Field Station Files; Statement of Howard Watson Roda, August 31, 1945, Box 57, OSS Washington/Pacific Field Station Files.

22 *cell to themselves*: George Barr, interview by W. L. Brown and Chester I. Lappen, December 30, 1945, p. 22, Prosecution Transcript Exhibit 21, Sawada Record; Ernest LeRoy Healey, October 6, 1945, Box 4, China War Crimes Files.

22 *playing guard duty*: Chase Nielsen, Robert Hite, and Jacob DeShazer, "Saga of Living Death," p. 22, Series II, Box 5, Doolittle Raiders Papers.

22 *made out of wood*: James Edgar, Bridge House Report by Dr. James Edgar, undated, Box 57, OSS Washington/Pacific Field Station Files; Statement of W. N. Dickson, August 31, 1945, Box 57, OSS Washington/Pacific Field Station Files; Statement of W. H. Hudspeth, August 28, 1945, Box 57, OSS Washington/Pacific Field

Station Files; Report to the American Rescue Party by Roger Pierard on his detention by the Japanese Gendarmery in Shanghai, August 31, 1945, Box 57, OSS Washington/Pacific Field Station Files; Statement by Sephra Gaston Briggs, August 30, 1945, Box 57, OSS Washington/Pacific Field Station Files; Edwin Arthur Thompson, "Events Leading to My Detention and Incidents Occurring during This Period from 7 October, 1942 to transfer to Haiphong Road Camp on 18 January, 1943," August 31, 1945, Box 57, OSS Washington/Pacific Field Station Files; Statement of Eric Davies, August 30, 1945, Box 57, OSS Washington/Pacific Field Station Files.

22 *humidity caused*: Affidavit of H. G. W. Woodhead, July 25, 1946, China War Crimes Files.

22 *grown swollen*: Robert Hite and Jacob DeShazer, Statement, September 7, 1945, p. 2, Prosecution Exhibit 22, Sawada Record.

22 *its guards*: Pringle, *Bridge House Survivor*, 6–10; Statement of Kenneth William Johnstone, August 30, 1945, Box 57, OSS Washington/Pacific Field Station Files; Statement re arrest of Supt. J. A. McFarlane, undated, Box 57, OSS Washington/Pacific Field Station Files.

22 *chopping a chunk*: Robert Hite and Jacob DeShazer, Statement, September 7, 1945, p. 2, Prosecution Exhibit 22, Sawada Record.

22 *were taken up*: The sources leave some uncertainty about this point. The following sources taken together, however, strongly support the conclusion. A Chinese prisoner in an adjacent cell in Bridge House reported seeing two or three of the Raiders taken away for waterboarding. Shun Wong, interview by Robert Dwyer, December 18, 1945, p. 2, Box 40, Glines Papers. This additional interrogation at Bridge House was admitted to by the Kempeitai. Izumi Ogata, interview by Alf Watson, January 15, 1946, pp. 1–2, Bodine Papers. Finally, when interrogated by Edward Young soon after their liberation, the Raiders reported that Hallmark, Meder, and Barr had been waterboarded. Edward Young, Memorandum, "Treatment of Captured Doolittle Fliers, Tokyo Raid, 18 April 1942," August 27, 1945, p. 5, Box 3, China War Crimes Files. Barr later described being waterboarded once in Nanking, but never after that. George Barr, interview by W. L. Brown and Chester I. Lappen, December 30, 1945, p. 12, Prosecution Transcript Exhibit 21, Sawada Record. While Nielsen later claims to have been waterboarded, he describes this as occurring at the airport in Shanghai soon after his capture, not during the period in Bridge House. Chase Nielsen, interview by Stacey Grayson, September 7, 1945, p. 1, Bodine Files. The most reasonable inference, therefore, is that Hallmark and Meder were subjected to waterboarding in Bridge House.

22 *infamous fifth floor*: Leck, *Captives of Empire*, 105.

22 *torture-enhanced*: Pringle, *Bridge House Survivor*, 6–10.

22 *came back limp*: Shun Wong, interview by Robert Dwyer, December 18, 1945, p. 2, Box 40, Glines Papers.

22 *the starvation*: Pringle, *Bridge House Survivor*, 11–12; James Edgar, Bridge House Report by Dr. James Edgar, undated, Box 57, OSS Washington/Pacific Field Station Files; Statement of W. N. Dickson, August 31, 1945, Box 57, OSS Washington/Pacific Field Station Files; Statement of Eric Davies, August 30, 1945, Box 57, OSS Washington/Pacific Field Station Files.

23 *guards could be bribed*: C. V. Glines, *Four Came Home* (Missoula, MT: Pictorial Histories, 1995), 74.

23   *obsessed by thoughts*: Tah Lung Chung, interview by Robert Dwyer, January 8, 1946, p. 2, Box 40, Glines Papers.

23   *dinners he would be having*: Dean Hallmark to Mother, Dad, and Sis, October 1942, Box 11, China War Crimes Files.

23   *slab of beefsteak*: Glines, *Four Came Home*, 75 (firsthand account of Robert Hite).

23   *apple cider*: George Barr, interview by W. L. Brown and Chester I. Lappen, December 30, 1945, pp. 27–28, Prosecution Transcript Exhibit 21, Sawada Record.

23   *vegetable soup*: Alexander John Sterelny, interview by Robert Dwyer, January 5, 1946, p. 2, Box 40, Glines Papers; Alexandra J. Hindrava, interview by Robert Dwyer, November 24, 1945, p. 3, Box 40, Glines Papers.

23   *playing games*: Chase Nielsen, Oral History, undated audio, Series II, Box 5, Doolittle Raiders Papers.

23   *mealtime game*: Charles Hoyt Watson, *DeShazer: The Doolittle Raider Turned Missionary* (Winona Lake, IN: Light & Life, 1952), 76.

23   *scratched their names*: Statement of Arthur Vincent Toovey Dean, undated, Box 57, OSS Washington/Pacific Field Station Files.

23   *compare notes*: Robert Hite and Jacob DeShazer, Statement, September 7, 1945, p. 1, Prosecution Exhibit 22, Sawada Record.

24   *water pump*: Henry Forsythe Pringle, Statement, August 28, 1945, Box 57, OSS Washington/Pacific Field Station Files; Lewis Sherman Bishop, interview by Thomas Watt, August 7, 1945, p. 2, Box 40, Glines Papers; James Edgar, Bridge House Report by Dr. James Edgar, undated, Box 57, OSS Washington/Pacific Field Station Files.

24   *fourth-floor bathtub*: Chase Nielsen, Oral History, undated audio, Series II, Box 5, Doolittle Raiders Papers.

24   *open truck*: Chase Nielsen, Robert Hite, and Jacob DeShazer, "Saga of Living Death," p. 22, Series II, Box 5, Doolittle Raiders Papers.

24   *hour's drive*: James L. Norwood and Emily L. Shek, *Prisoner of War Camps in Areas Other Than the Four Principal Islands of Japan*, American Prisoner of War Information Bureau, Liaison and Research Branch, July 31, 1946, p. 13, POW Records.

24   *truly pleasant*: Chase Nielsen, Robert Hite, and Jacob DeShazer, "Saga of Living Death," p. 22, Series II, Box 5, Doolittle Raiders Papers. The most detailed description of Jiangwan and the 13th Army Headquarters in this period comes from Irene Kuhn, "Tea and Ashes," in Overseas Press Club of America, eds., *Deadline Delayed* (New York: E. P. Dutton, 1947), 268–72; see also James L. Norwood and Emily L. Shek, *Prisoner of War Camps in Areas Other Than the Four Principal Islands of Japan*, American Prisoner of War Information Bureau, Liaison and Research Branch, July 31, 1946, 13, POW Records. The 13th Army had requisitioned Jiangwan's "Civic Center" as its headquarters, a complex built in the early 1930s as part of an urban revitalization project initiated by Wang Jingwei's unity government, which consisted of four landmark buildings that were initially dedicated to being a library, a museum, a stadium, and a massive city hall, which had a pagoda tile roof in the Chinese neoclassical style. Jeffrey S. Cody, Nancy S. Steinhardt, and Tony Atkin, eds., *Chinese Architecture and the Beaux-Arts* (Honolulu: University of Hawaii Press, 2011), 177, 186; Christian Henriot, *Shanghai 1927–1937: Municipal Power, Locality, and Modernization* (Berkeley: University of California Press, 1993), 177–81; Chiang Kai-shek had converted it into his most fortified defensive position in Shanghai at the outset of the Sino-Japanese War, but by the fall of 1937,

the Japanese Army overran it in the midst of a torrential rainstorm, and established it as Japan's principal garrison in the area. "Japan's Army Pushes Ahead: Attacks Chinese Second Line Northwest of Shanghai, Seizes Kiangwan," Associated Press, September 14, 1937.

24 *except for Dean Hallmark*: George Barr, interview by W. L. Brown and Chester I. Lappen, December 30, 1945, pp. 27–28, Prosecution Transcript Exhibit 21, Sawada Record.

24 *weight had dropped*: Chase Nielsen, Robert Hite, and Jacob DeShazer, "Saga of Living Death," p. 22, Series II, Box 5, Doolittle Raiders Papers.

24 *crowded L-shaped*: Caesar Luis DosRemedios, Statement, September 19, 1945, p. 3, Box 40, Glines Papers.

24 *seven or eight Japanese officers*: Edward Young, Memorandum, "Treatment of Captured Doolittle Fliers, Tokyo Raid, 18 April 1942," August 27, 1945, p. 5, Box 3, China War Crimes Files.

24 *talked back and forth*: Sawada Trial Transcript, 65–66 (Testimony of Chase Nielsen).

24 *an interpreter*: George Barr, interview by W. L. Brown and Chester I. Lappen, December 30, 1945, p. 29, Prosecution Transcript Exhibit 21, Sawada Record.

24 *oddly dressed*: Chase Nielsen, interview by Carl Sebey, December 7, 1945, pp. 6–7, Bodine Files.

25 *Barr almost collapsed*: Sawada Trial Transcript, 66 (Testimony of Chase Nielsen).

25 *spoke at them*: Edward Young, Memorandum, "Treatment of Captured Doolittle Fliers, Tokyo Raid, 18 April 1942," August 27, 1945, p. 5, Box 3, China War Crimes Files.

25 *Nielsen complied*: Sawada Trial Transcript, 66 (Testimony of Chase Nielsen).

25 *pose for pictures*: Sawada Trial Transcript, 95 (Testimony of Chase Nielsen).

25 *Jiangwan's brig*: Sawada Trial Transcript, 67 (Testimony of Chase Nielsen).

25 *a kennel*: Sawada Trial Transcript, 493 (Statement of John Hendren).

25 *The cells*: Irene Kuhn, "Tea and Ashes," in Overseas Press Club of America, eds., *Deadline Delayed*, 268, 274.

25 *guard led them*: Rikisaburo Komatsu, interview by Robert Dwyer, November 20, 1945, pp. 2–3, Box 40, Glines Papers.

25 *middle of October*: Chase Nielsen, Robert Hite, and Jacob DeShazer, "Saga of Living Death," p. 27, Series II, Box 5, Doolittle Raiders Papers.

25 *rumors*: Chase Nielsen, interview by Carl Sebey, December 7, 1945, p. 7, Bodine Files.

25 *"For bombing"*: Chase Nielsen, Robert Hite, and Jacob DeShazer, "Saga of Living Death," p. 28, Series II, Box 5, Doolittle Raiders Papers. This quotation is drawn from Nielsen's memory. It has been repeated with slight variations, such as "through the kindness of His Majesty, the Emperor, we had been spared to life imprisonment with special treatment." Chase Nielsen, Affidavit, undated (September 7, 1945), p. 2, Bodine Files. In *Four Came Home*, it is recounted as "but, through the graciousness of His Majesty, the Emperor, your sentences are hereby commuted to life imprisonment . . . with special treatment." *Four Came Home*, 91 (firsthand account of Chase Nielsen).

25 *live together*: Tatsuta Sotojiro, interview by Robert Dwyer, November 16, 1945, p. 6, Box 40, Glines Papers.

26 *prison in Nanking*: Edward Young, Memorandum, "Treatment of Captured Doolittle Fliers, Tokyo Raid, 18 April 1942," August 27, 1945, p. 6, Box 3, China War Crimes Files.

26   *one of the guards*: Chase Nielsen, Robert Hite, and Jacob DeShazer, "Saga of Living Death," p. 29, Series II, Box 5, Doolittle Raiders Papers.

26   *located in the northeast*: Edward Young, Memorandum, "Treatment of Captured Doolittle Fliers, Tokyo Raid, 18 April 1942," August 27, 1945, p. 6, Box 3, China War Crimes Files.

26   *some food*: Statement of W. S. Cunningham, August 28, 1945, China War Crimes Files.

26   *Three times a day*: Edward Young, Memorandum, "Treatment of Captured Doolittle Fliers, Tokyo Raid, 18 April 1942," August 27, 1945, p. 6, Box 3, China War Crimes Files.

26   *"tin cup news"*: Chase Nielsen, Robert Hite, and Jacob DeShazer, "Saga of Living Death," p. 34, Series II, Box 5, Doolittle Raiders Papers.

26   *the guards*: Chase Nielsen, Oral History, undated audio, Series II, Box 5, Doolittle Raiders Papers.

26   *Meder was*: Chase Nielsen, Robert Hite, and Jacob DeShazer, "Saga of Living Death," p. 34, Series II, Box 5, Doolittle Raiders Papers.

27   *something wasn't right*: Robert Hite and Jacob DeShazer, Statement, September 7, 1945, p. 3, Prosecution Exhibit 22, Sawada Record.

27   *increasingly hard*: Chase Nielsen, Affidavit, undated (September 7, 1945), p. 3, Box 40, Glines Papers.

27   *keep down food*: Soshi Yasuharu, Medical Report on Second Lieutenant Robert J. Meder, December 1, 1943, Box 2179, POW Records.

27   *as he wasted away*: George Barr, interview by W. L. Brown and Chester I. Lappen, December 30, 1945, pp. 35–36, Prosecution Transcript Exhibit 21, Sawada Record.

27   *Meder was motionless*: Soshi Yasuharu, Medical Report on Second Lieutenant Robert J. Meder, December 1, 1943, Box 2179, POW Records.

27   *final respects*: Robert Hite and Jacob DeShazer, Statement, September 7, 1945, p. 3, Prosecution Exhibit 22, Sawada Record.

27   *he found Meder*: James Curtis Hasdorff, *United States Air Force Oral History Program: Interview of Lt. Col. Robert L. Hite* (USAF Historical Research Center, 1982), 79.

27   *brimmed with heroes*: For a discussion of the spiritual significance of suffering in the LDS church, see Harold B. Lee, *Teachings of the Presidents of the Church* (Salt Lake City: The Church of Jesus Christ of Latter-day Saints, 2000), 206–15.

27   *been imprisoned*: *The Doctrine and Covenants of the Church of Jesus Christ of Latter-day Saints* (Salt Lake City: The Church of Jesus Christ of Latter-day Saints, 1981), §121.

28   *He added*: Terry Nielsen, personal interview, August 19, 2015.

28   *His biggest project*: Glines, *Four Came Home*, 99.

28   *youngest of six*: Fifteenth Census of the United States, 1930, Benson, Cache, Utah, Enumeration District 0002, Records of the Bureau of the Census, Record Group 29, National Archives and Records Administration.

28   *middle of six*: Sixteenth Census of the United States, 1940, Utah, Enumeration District 3-11, Records of the Bureau of the Census, Record Group 29, National Archives and Records Administration.

28   *imagined every detail*: Glines, *Four Came Home*, 99.

28   *packed into a train*: Chase Nielsen, Robert Hite, and Jacob DeShazer, "Saga of Living Death," p. 38, Series II, Box 5, Doolittle Raiders Papers.

29   *Fengtai Prison Camp*: James L. Norwood and Emily L. Shek, *Prisoner of War Camps*

in Areas Other Than the Four Principal Islands of Japan, American Prisoner of War Information Bureau, Liaison and Research Branch, July 31, 1946, pp. 10–12, POW Records; Henry Pringle, *Bridge House Survivor*, 93.

29   *not the worst*: Edward Young, Memorandum, "Treatment of Captured Doolittle Fliers, Tokyo Raid, 18 April 1942," August 27, 1945, p. 7, Box 3, China War Crimes Files.

29   *no electric lights*: Office of Strategic Services Report A-62488, "Prison #1047, in which Doolittle Raiders were Confined," October 3, 1945, China War Crimes Files.

29   *smaller and sparer*: Memorandum, North China 1407 Prison Camp, August 1945, Box 57, Washington/Pacific Coast/Field Station Files.

29   *until the evening*: The following account of Nielsen's experience of liberation is taken from Chase Nielsen Oral History, undated audio, Series II, Box 5, Doolittle Raiders Papers, which is substantively similar to the account provided in Chase Nielsen, Robert Hite, Jacob DeShazer, "Saga of Living Death," pp. 39–41, Series II, Box 5, Doolittle Raiders Papers.

30   *"Well, son"*: Chase Nielsen Oral History, undated audio, Series II, Box 5, Doolittle Raiders Papers.

CHAPTER THREE

31   *The assignment*: Office of Strategic Services, Operation Magpie, August 13, 1945, Box 218, *OSS Field Station Files*.

31   *Wisconsin National Guard*: *Official National Guard Register for 1943* (G.P.O., 1943), 869.

31   *being destroyed*: Japan's War Minister had issued orders that summer to destroy all documents, particularly those relating to prisoners of war. Sadamu Shimomura, interview by Ralph Jones, May 25, 1946, p. 2, Box 1732, SCAP Legal Section Investigation Division, Investigation Reports 1945–49, Allied Occupation Records.

31   *Operation Magpie*: Office of Strategic Services, Operation Magpie, August 13, 1945, Box 218, OSS Field Station Files; F. G. Jarman to C. V. Glines, April 19, 1965, Box 40, Glines Papers; Richard Hamada to C. V. Glines, undated, Box 40, Glines Papers.

31   *All they knew*: F. G. Jarman to C. V. Glines, April 19, 1965, Box 40, Glines Papers; Richard Hamada to C. V. Glines, undated, Box 40, Glines Papers.

31   *loaded his team*: Office of Strategic Services, Air Drop Manifest, Mission: Magpie, August 13, 1945, Box 218, Field Station Files; Kevin Richter and Ray Nichols, Informal Report on Magpie Mission, undated, Box 56, OSS Washington/Pacific Field Station Files; Hawaii Nisei Project, Center for Oral History, "Dick Hamada," https://perma.cc/GME3-GU42.

31   *leaflets proclaimed*: Copy of leaflet dropped on China by the Office of Strategic Services provided by Richard Hamada to C. V. Glines, undated, Box 40, Glines Papers.

31   *only one*: Richard Hamada to C. V. Glines, undated, Box 40, Glines Papers.

31   *Born in Hawaii*: Dick Hamada, "Japanese-American Soldier for the Office of Strategic Services (OSS)," Honna Doolittle Hoppes, ed., *Just Doing My Job* (Santa Monica, CA: Santa Monica Press, 2009), 309–11

31   *first Japanese Americans*: T. M. Kobayashi, Memorandum Historical Information, October 20, 1945, Box 2108, General Records of the Adjutant General's Office 1911–62, Records of the Adjutant General's Office, Record Group 407, National Archives, College Park.

32   *join the OSS*: Hamada, "Japanese-American Soldier for the Office of Strategic Services (OSS)," 313–16.

32   *more afraid of the tigers*: Hawaii Nisei Project, Center for Oral History, "Dick Hamada," https://perma.cc/GME3-GU42.

32   *slashed the wrapper*: F. G. Jarman to C. V. Glines, April 19, 1965, Box 40, Glines Papers; Richard Hamada to C.V. Glines, undated, Box 40, Glines Papers.

32   *do any good*: Kevin Richter and Ray Nichols, "Informal Report on Magpie Mission," undated, Box 56, OSS Washington/Pacific Field Station Files.

32   *jump light flashed*: Richard Hamada to C. V. Glines, undated, Box 40, Glines Papers.

32   *quarter after five*: Kevin Richter and Ray Nichols, Informal Report on Magpie Mission, undated, Box 56, OSS Washington/Pacific Field Station Files.

32   *feeling of isolation*: F. G. Jarman to C. V. Glines, April 19, 1965, Box 40, Glines Papers.

32   *armed with*: Office of Strategic Services, Operation Magpie, August 13, 1945, Box 218, Field Station Files; Richard Hamada, Copy of Letter from General Wedemeyer, Box 40, Glines Papers.

32   *some pops*: Kevin Richter and Ray Nichols, Informal Report on Magpie Mission, undated, Box 56, OSS Washington/Pacific Field Station Files; F. G. Jarman to C. V. Glines, April 19, 1965, Box 40, Glines Papers.

32   *bullets buzzed past*: F. G. Jarman to C. V. Glines, April 19, 1965, Box 40, Glines Papers.

33   *Japanese lieutenant*: Richard Hamada to C. V. Glines, undated, Box 40, Glines Papers.

33   *crumpled leaflet*: Hawaii Nisei Project, Center for Oral History, "Dick Hamada," https://perma.cc/GME3-GU42.

33   *Each American*: Richard Hamada to C. V. Glines, undated, Box 40, Glines Papers.

33   *diffuse the situation*: Richard Hamada to C. V. Glines, undated, Box 40, Glines Papers.

33   *pulled up*: Kevin Richter and Ray Nichols, Informal Report on Magpie Mission, undated, Box 56, OSS Washington/Pacific Field Station Files.

34   *Takahashi*: In OSS cables, Takahashi's name is spelled in various ways, such as "Talahashi." Office of Strategic Services, Cable, August 19, 1945, Box 281, OSS Field Station Files.

34   *collecting their supplies*: Richard Hamada to C. V. Glines, undated, Box 40, Glines Papers.

34   *Takahashi arrived*: Kevin Richter and Ray Nichols, Informal Report on Magpie Mission, undated, pp. 1–2, Box 56, OSS Washington/Pacific Field Station Files.

34   *be patient*: Office of Strategic Services, Cable, August 18, 1945, Box 218, OSS Field Station Files; Office of Strategic Services, Cable, August 17, 1945, Box 218, OSS Field Station Files.

34   *Takahashi suggested*: Richard Hamada to C. V. Glines, undated, Box 40, Glines Papers.

34   *gave the impression*: Office of Strategic Services, Cable, August 20, 1945, Box 8, OSS Field Station Files.

34   *a dangerous thing*: Richard Hamada to C. V. Glines, undated, Box 40, Glines Papers.

34   *"extreme danger"*: F. G. Jarman to C. V. Glines, April 19, 1965, Box 40, Glines Papers.

34   *lead with his letter*: Kevin Richter and Ray Nichols, Informal Report on Magpie Mission, undated, Box 56, OSS Washington/Pacific Field Station Files.

34   *Nichols made clear*: F. G. Jarman to C. V. Glines, April 19, 1965, Box 40, Glines Papers.

34   *invited Nichols*: Kevin Richter and Ray Nichols, Informal Report on Magpie Mission, undated, p. 2, Box 56, OSS Washington/Pacific Field Station Files.

35   *a better letter*: Copy of pass issued to Richard Hamada by Japanese Force, Box 40, Glines Papers; F. G. Jarman to C. V. Glines, April 19, 1965, Box 40, Glines Papers.

35   *Grand Hôtel des Wagons-Lits*: Office of Strategic Services, Cable Takahashi to Wedemeyer, August 20, 1945, Box 218, OSS Field Station Files; Office of Strategic Services, Cable, August 17, 1945, Box 218, OSS Field Station Files; Office of Strategic Services, Cable, August 18, 1945, Box 8, OSS Field Station Files.

35   *brand-new hotel*: Henry Pringle, *Bridge House Survivor: Experiences of a Civilian Prisoner-of-War in Shanghai & Beijing* (Chicago: Earnshaw Books, 2010), 93.

35   *dangerous to wander*: Kevin Richter and Ray Nichols, Informal Report on Magpie Mission, undated, p. 3, OSS Washington/Pacific Field Station.

35   *personal bodyguards*: Kevin Richter and Ray Nichols, Informal Report on Magpie Mission, undated, pp. 3–4, OSS Washington/Pacific Field Station Files; Richard Hamada to C. V. Glines, undated, Box 40, Glines Papers.

35   *continuing their advance*: Ray Nichols to Albert Wedemeyer, Cable, August 20, 1945, Box 608, Records of the Special Staff, Adjutant General, CBI Records; Office of Strategic Services, Cable, August 22, 1945, Box 8, OSS Field Station Files; Office of Strategic Services, Cable, August 20, 1945, Box 8, OSS Field Station Files.

35   *Atrocities were rampant*: Mark Ealey, "An August Storm: the Soviet-Japan Endgame in the Pacific War," *Asia-Pacific Journal* 4, no. 2 (2006); Office of Strategic Services, Cable, August 28, 1945, Box 218, OSS Field Station Files; Office of Strategic Services, Cable, September 3, 1945, Box 8, OSS Field Station Files.

35   *slave labor*: Office of Strategic Services, "General info on Ta Hu Shan dist. Liaoning Prov," October 24, 1945, Box 44, Shanghai Intelligence Files, Records of the Office of Strategic Services, Record Group 226, National Archives, College Park.

35   *sent a cable*: Goku Takahashi, Memorandum to Chiang Kai-Shek and General Wedemeyer, undated, Box 40, Glines Papers.

35   *Within three days*: Office of Strategic Services, Cable, August 17, 1945, Box 218, OSS Field Station Files.

35   *negotiated the release*: Auchincloss, "The Men of the Magpipe Mission," undated, Box 187, OSS Field Station Files; Office of Strategic Services, Cable, August 28, 1945, Box 218, OSS Field Station Files.

35   *provided rooms*: F. G. Jarman to C. V. Glines, April 19, 1965, Box 40, Glines Papers.

35   *success*: Auchincloss, "The Men of the Magpipe Mission," undated, Box 187, OSS Field Station Files.

35   *first group*: Pringle, *Bridge House Survivor*, 93.

36   *a rumor*: Kevin Richter and Ray Nichols, Informal Report on Magpie Mission, undated, p. 6, Box 56, OSS Washington/Pacific Field Station Files.

36   *Nichols confronted*: Statement of Richard P. Adams, February 18, 1946, Box 3, China War Crimes Files.

36   *got into his face*: Pringle, *Bridge House Survivor*, 93.

36   *brought out*: Chase Nielsen Oral History, undated audio, Series II, Box 5, Doolittle Raiders Papers.

36   *dramatically emaciated*: Robert Hite and Jacob DeShazer, Statement, September 7, 1945, p. 4, Prosecution Exhibit 22, Sawada Record. For a vivid physical description, see Spencer Moosa, "Doolittle Raiders Tell Experiences," Associated Press, August 25, 1945. For a photo taken upon their arrival in Chongqing, see Carroll V. Glines, *Doolittle's Tokyo Raiders* (New York: Van Nostrand Reinhold, 1981), 372.

36   *sweat rash*: James Curtis Hasdorff, *United States Air Force Oral History Program: Interview of Lt. Col. Robert L. Hite* (USAF Historical Research Center, 1982), 95.

36   *"off his rocker"*: Chase Nielsen Oral History, undated audio, Series II, Box 5, Doolittle Raiders Papers.

36   *Nichols had found*: Office of Strategic Services, Cable, August 21, 1945, Box 8, OSS Field Station Files.

36   *banner headlines*: "Japanese Execute Our Airmen; U.S. Will Punish All Responsible," *New York Times*, April 22, 1943, 1.

36   *open letter*: Henry Arnold to All Personnel of the Army Air Forces, April 21, 1943, Box 40, Glines Papers.

36   *reliable reports*: C. D. Smith, Report on Japanese Prison Camps, March 5, 1945, pp. 11–12, China War Crimes Files.

37   *newest honored guests*: Office of Strategic Services, Cable, August 21, 1945, Box 8, OSS Field Station Files; Office of Strategic Services, Cable, August 23, 1945, Box 218, OSS Field Station Files; Chase Nielsen Oral History, undated audio, Series II, Box 5, Doolittle Raiders Papers.

37   *next three days*: Chase Nielsen, Robert Hite, and Jacob DeShazer, "Saga of Living Death," p. 41, Series II, Box 5, Doolittle Raiders Papers.

37   *eating themselves fat*: Charles Hoyt Watson, *DeShazer: The Doolittle Raider Turned Missionary* (Winona Lake, IN: Light & Life 1952), 125–127; Chase Nielsen Oral History, undated audio, Series II, Box 5, Doolittle Raiders Papers.

37   *Nichols wanted to know*: Kevin Richter and Ray Nichols, Informal Report on Magpie Mission, undated, p. 6, Box 56, OSS Washington/Pacific Field Station Files.

37   *George Barr*: Office of Strategic Services, Cable, August 29, 1945, Box 218, OSS Field Station Files; Pringle, *Bridge House Survivor*, 93.

37   *His feet*: James M. Scott, *Target Tokyo* (New York: Norton, 2015), 457.

37   *the team's medic*: Office of Strategic Services, Cable, August 29, 1945, Box 218, OSS Field Station Files; F. G. Jarman to C. V. Glines, April 19, 1965, Box 40, Glines Papers; Office of Strategic Services, Cable (requesting special provisions and air transport), August 26, 1945, Box 218, OSS Field Station Files.

CHAPTER FOUR

38   *airfield outside Beijing*: Kevin Richter and Ray Nichols, Informal Report on Magpie Mission, undated, p. 8, Box 56, OSS Washington/Pacific Field Station Files; Office of Strategic Services, Cable, August 23, 1945, Box 218, OSS Field Station Files; Office of Strategic Services, Cable, August 24, 1945, Box 8, OSS Field Station Files.

38   *unsafe to move*: Office of Strategic Services, Cable, August 24, 1945, Box 218, OSS Field Station Files.

38   *going home*: F. G. Jarman to C. V. Glines, April 19, 1965, Box 40, Glines Papers.

38   *Seven Dragons Airport*: "Doolittle Fliers in Chunking," United Press, August 25, 1945.

38   *a telegram*: "Jay Nielsen Arrives in China; Enroute Home," Cache American, August 28, 1946, 1.

38   *The news*: The text of Thora Ricks's original telegram has not been recovered. Ricks, however, was reported to have used this phrase when asked about the news of Chase Nielsen's recovery. "Ogdenite's Mate, Lt. C.J. Nielsen, Freed from Nips," *Ogden Standard-Examiner*, August 23, 1945, 1.

38   *hero's welcome*: "Three Doolittle Raiders Headed Back for U.S.," Associated Press, August 23, 1945.

39   *some advice*: "Three Doolittle Raiders Headed Back for U.S.," Associated Press, August 23, 1945.

39   *gone sore*: Oral History, undated audio, Series II, Box 5, Doolittle Raiders Papers.

39   *hard to say anything*: 2nd. Lt. Kelly Cahalan, "Doolittle Raiders," Ogden ALC Public Affairs, 2000.

39   *he collapsed*: "Three Doolittle Raiders Headed Back for U.S.," Associated Press, August 23, 1945.

39   *next morning*: "Three Doolittle Raiders Headed Back for U.S.," Associated Press, August 23, 1945.

39   *Kublai Khan*: Among educated Japanese, this story is traditionally not taken too seriously and is generally thought of as a legend. However, recent archeological studies suggest that it may be largely true. James Delgado, *Khubilai Khan's Lost Fleet: History's Greatest Naval Disaster* (New York: Random House, 2009). And regardless of its truth, its key relevance to Japanese politics at the time was the widespread belief that it was true.

40   *divinely ordained*: Shinichi Fujii, *The Essentials of Japanese Constitutional Law* (Yuhikaku, 1940), 406, 423.

40   *in Hyde Park*: White House Usher's Diary, April 18, 1942, Franklin D. Roosevelt, Papers as President: The President's Personal File, FDR Library.

40   *Mum was the word*: Henry Arnold to C. V. Glines, April 25, 1949, Box 41, Glines Papers.

40   *the headline*: "Washington Hails Report of Bombing," *New York Times*, April 19, 1942, 38.

40   *The news*: "Nippon Reports Capital, 3 Other Cities Raided, Fires Set in War Factory Areas," Associated Press, April 18, 1942 (relaying Japanese broadcasts); "Japan Reports Tokyo, Yokohama Bombed by 'Enemy Planes' in Daylight; Claims 9; Big Raids over France; Leahy is Recalled," *New York Times*, April 18, 1942, 1.

40   *multipage spread*: "The News of the Week in Review," *New York Times*, April 19, 1942, §4, 1–2.

40   *German broadcasts*: "Plane Carrier Loss Report Mere Rumor," Associated Press, April 18, 1942.

40   *media analysts*: Kirke L. Simpson, "Raiding Nation Supplies Puzzle on Tokyo Bombing Base, Report," *Wide World War Analyst*, April 19, 1942; "Were Planes Land Based? Aero Expert Speculates," *International News Service*, April 19, 1942.

41   *vehemently denied*: "Soviet Denies Use of Territory," Associated Press, April 22, 1942.

41   *secret air bases*: "Washington Silent on Assault, Nips Unable to Trace Warcraft's Route," Associated Press, April 19, 1942.

41 *first press conference*: Usher's Log, April 21, 1942, Franklin D. Roosevelt, Papers as President: The President's Personal File, FDR Library.

41 *questions came*: Press Conference #820, April 21, 1942, pp. 6–8, Press Conferences of President Franklin D. Roosevelt, 1933–1945, FDR Library.

41 "*Well, you know*": Press Conference #820, April 21, 1942, p. 6, Press Conferences of President Franklin D. Roosevelt, 1933–1945, FDR Library ("Well, the only thing I can think of is—on that—you know occasionally I have a few people in to dinner, and generally in the middle of dinner some—I know she isn't—it isn't an individual, it's just a generic term—some 'sweet young thing' says, 'Mr. President, couldn't you tell us about so and so?'").

42 *his fireside chat*: Franklin D. Roosevelt, "Fireside Chat 21: On Sacrifice," April 28, 1942, in Samuel Rosenman, ed., *The Public Papers and Addresses of Franklin D. Roosevelt*, vol. 11 (New York: Russell & Russell, 1969).

42 *first word*: Joseph Stilwell to Adjutant General, War Department, Cable, April 25, 1942, Box 158, Henry Harley Arnold Papers, 1903–1989, Library of Congress.

43 *Unbeknownst to Doolittle*: There is a myth, apparently believed by Doolittle himself, that the landing strip in Quzhou failed to appear because the putative radio operator died in a plane crash on the way. For example, see James Doolittle, "My Raid Over Tokyo, April 1942," August 14, 1965, p. 24, Series IV, Box 4, Doolittle Papers. This appears to have been a story contrived after the fact to avoid the embarrassment of Chiang Kai-shek. The cable traffic shows that when Joseph Stilwell first informed Chiang that Americans would need to land at the airfield in Quzhou, Chiang gave his approval but then changed his mind after learning that the planes were due to continue on to India in support of the British, whose century of occupation in China was a regular point of Chinese nationalist resentment. Under the Lend-Lease Program, the British already had a habit of filching the best American equipment even after Stillwell had promised it to Chiang. Maochun Yu, *The Dragon's War: Allied Operations and the Fate of China 1937–1947* (Annapolis, MD: Naval Institute Press, 2006), 164–65. Stilwell therefore relented and assured Chiang that he could keep the planes but impressed upon Chiang that the United States needed his full cooperation. Chiang, however, refused to allow the use of airfields in Quzhou and demanded that the operation be pushed back until May. George Marshall, the U.S. Army's chief of staff, who shared Stilwell's disdain for Chiang, personally replied the following day. The mission, Marshall informed him, was "so imminent that it is impossible to recall." The bombers would be stopping in Quzhou only to refuel and their arrival there "should be immediately anticipated and all arrangements perfected." George Marshall to Joseph Stillwell and Clayton Bissell, War Dept. No. 449, April 12, 1942; Series I, Safe File, Box 2, Franklin D. Roosevelt, Papers as President: The President's Secretary's File, 1933–1945, FDR Library; Clayton Bissell to Chiang Kai-shek, "Special Projects," April 15, 1942, Box 612, Records of the Special Staff, Adjutant General, CBI Records. But in the days before the Raid, Chiang never agreed to the use of Quzhou and made no preparations for its use. Clayton Bissell to Chiang Kai-shek, "First Special Air Project," April 19, 1942, Box 612, Records of the Special Staff, Adjutant General, CBI Records; Clayton Bissell to Chiang Kai-shek, "Clarification of Situation," April 18, 1942, Box 612, Records of the Special Staff, Adjutant General, CBI Records; Joseph Stilwell to George Marshall, Cable, April 16, 1942, "Draft Submitted to Col. Sam Marshall for his story on Tokyo Raid," undated, p. 7, Box 40, Glines

Papers; Joseph McNary, Memorandum for the President, "First Special Bombing Mission (China)," April 16, 1942, Series I, Safe File, Box 2, Franklin D. Roosevelt, Papers as President: The President's Secretary's File, 1933–1945, FDR Library. One of Chiang's concerns was that Quzhou would be targeted by the Japanese in retaliation, which turned out to be true. Quzhou became a prime target after it was learned that it was the Raiders' destination and local Chinese were forced by the Imperial forces to manually destroy its airfield, which was rock-solid concrete and pressed clay, making the digging of ditches by hand backbreaking labor. Extensive documentation of this is on display at the Quzhou Museum in Zhejiang, China.

43   *Doolittle for promotion*: Department of Defense, Office of Public Information, Press Branch, "Lieutenant General James J. Doolittle, USAFR," January 1955, p. 3, Series I, Box 1, Doolittle Papers.

43   *cave in Quzhou*: Jimmy Doolittle, "My Raid Over Tokyo, April 1942," August 14, 1965, pp. 28–29, Series IV, Box 4, Doolittle Papers. This cave remains largely undisturbed. On a personal visit, there were still traces of their time in the cave, including etchings into the walls. According to locals, the cave is now a popular spot for teenagers who want to evade adult supervision.

43   *Leland D. Faktor*: James Doolittle, "Report on the Aerial Bombing of Japan," June 5, 1942, pp. 22–23, Box 36, Glines Papers.

43   *captured the crew*: Clayton Bissell to Chiang Kai-shek, "First Special Project Prisoners," May 2, 1942, Box 612, Records of the Special Staff, Adjutant General, CBI Records; Joseph Stilwell to Adjutant General, War Department, Cable, May 4, 1942, Box 158, Henry Harley Arnold Papers, 1903–1989, Library of Congress.

43   *another intelligence report*: Joseph Stilwell to Adjutant General, War Department, Cable, May 18, 1942, Box 158, Henry Harley Arnold Papers, 1903–1989, Library of Congress.

43   *last names*: Joseph Stilwell to Adjutant General, War Department, Cable, May 20, 1942, Box 158, Henry Harley Arnold Papers, 1903–1989, Library of Congress.

43   *a rumor*: James Doolittle, "Report on the Aerial Bombing of Japan," June 5, 1942, p. 24, Box 36, Glines Papers.

43   *work back channels*: Clayton Bissell to Chiang Kai-shek, "First Special Project Prisoners," May 2, 1942, Box 612, Records of the Special Staff, Adjutant General, CBI Records; James Doolittle, "Report on the Aerial Bombing of Japan," June 5, 1942, p. 30, Box 36, Glines Papers; Joseph Stillwell to Henry Arnold, Cable, May 4, 1942, "Draft Submitted to Col. Sam Marshall for his story on Tokyo Raid," undated, p. 8, Box 40, Glines Papers.

43   *front page*: W. H. Lawrence, "Airman Decorated" *New York Times*, May 20, 1942, 1.

43   *Red Skelton*: Hedda Hopper, "Looking at Hollywood," *Chicago Tribune*, June 15, 1942, 17.

44   *Warner Bros.*: "H-wood Story Opportunists Pounce on Every New War Break," *Variety*, June 10, 1942.

44   *James Hilton*: "Author of Shangri-La Just Misses Doolittle, The Shangri-La Flier," *Variety*, June 17, 1942.

44   *Distinguished Service Cross*: "Honor Roll," *Air Forces News Letter* 25, no. 4 (June 1942): 7; War Department, General Order 49, October 1, 1942.

44   *biographies*: "Tokyo Raiders Decorated," United Press, June 27, 1942.

44   *father beamed*: "Utah Man Listed with Bomb Crew," *Daily Herald* (Provo, Utah), May 20, 1942, A1.

44 *from Utah*: "Utah Takes Pride in Flier's Achievement," *Salt Lake Tribune*, May 22, 1942, 10.

44 *publicly claimed*: "9 Yank Flyers Missing After Raid on Tokyo," International News Service, October 20, 1942.

44 *confidential letter*: J. H. Doolittle to Floyd Nielson, May 22, 1942, Series II, Box 5, Doolittle Raiders Papers.

44 *stayed bedridden*: "Hyrum," *Cache American*, October 9, 1942, 4.

44 *Japanese radio broadcasts*: "Hyrum Flier Reported Captured," *Cache American*, October 27, 1942, 1; "Admit Three More; War Dept. Lists Missing Tokyo Airmen," United Press, October 24, 1942; "9 Yank Fliers Missing After Raid on Tokyo," International News Service, October 20, 1942.

44 *defended itself*: "Tokyo Raiders Believed Held Jap Prisoners," *Ogden Standard-Examiner*, October 24, 1942, 1.

44 *the news*: Ray J. Nelson, "Lt. Nielsen Keeps Word That I'll Be Coming Back," *Ogden Standard-Examiner*, August 24, 1945, 3A.

44 *press release announcing*: Sidney Mashbir, Allied Translator and Interpreter Section, South West Pacific Area, Research Report No. 72: Japanese Violations of the Laws of War, April 29, 1944, p. 78, Box 10, China War Crimes Files; "見よ・米機のこの非道", 朝日新聞, 昭和17年10月20日 ["Look at the Atrocity of the American Planes," *Asahi Shimbun*, October 20, 1942].

45 *Utah's governor*: Herbert Maw to Mr. and Mrs. Floyd Nielsen, November 10, 1942, Series II, Box 5, Doolittle Raiders Papers.

45 *full-dress ceremony*: "Utahn, Captive of Japs, Is Rewarded," *Ogden Standard-Examiner*, November 11, 1942, 8-A.

45 *All hope*: "Japs Execute U.S. Fliers Taken in Doolittle Raid," United Press, April 21, 1943; "Hyrum Resident Feared Victim of Jap Cruelty," *Salt Lake Tribune*, April 22, 1943, 8.

45 *first heard the news*: "Army Depot Grieves with Wife of Tokyo Attacker," *Ogden Standard-Examiner*, April 23, 1943, 13.

45 *strangers chatted*: "Utah Mother of Tokyo Bomber Hopeful Her Son Still Alive," *Ogden Standard-Examiner*, April 22, 1943, 1.

45 *thinly veiled obituaries*: Frank Francis, "News and Views," *Ogden Standard-Examiner*, April 22, 1943, 1.

45 *Newspapers around the country*: "Wife and Parents of Captive," *Chicago Tribune*, April 23, 1943, 6; "Army Depot Grieves with Wife of Tokyo Attacker," *Ogden Standard-Examiner*, April 23, 1943, 13; "Mother, Wife, Still Hope for Flier," *Deseret News*, April 22, 1943, 14.

45 *refused to believe*: "Some Parents Hold Hope for Tokyo Raid Prisoners," Associated Press, April 22, 1943; "Utah Mother of Tokyo Bomber Hopeful Her Son Still Alive," United Press, April 22, 1943.

45 *named a B-25*: "Bomber Named after Utah Flyer," *Cache American*, June 11, 1943, 1.

45 *courtroom drama*: The Purple Heart (20th Century Fox, 1944).

47 *played in Ogden*: "Ogden Now Showing," *Ogden Standard-Examiner*, June 19, 1944, 9.

47 *Thora gushed*: Ray J. Nelson, "Lt. Nielsen Keeps Word That I'll Be Coming Back," *Ogden Standard-Examiner*, August 24, 1945, 3A.

47 *assembled press corps*: "Three Doolittle Raiders Headed Back for U.S.," Associated Press, August 23, 1945.

47   *sense of humor*: Spencer Moosa, "Doolittle Raiders Tell Experiences," Associated Press, August 25, 1945.

48   *boasted scornfully*: "Three Doolittle Bombers Describe Treatment in Japan," Associated Press, August 26, 1945.

48   *Nielsen got emotional*: Spencer Moosa, "Doolittle Raiders Tell Experiences," Associated Press, August 25, 1945.

48   *could not answer*: "Three Doolittle Bombers Describe Treatment in Japan," Associated Press, August 26, 1945.

CHAPTER FIVE

49   *revenge*: C. V. Glines, *Four Came Home* (Missoula, MT: Pictorial Histories, 1995), 72.

49   *hands on a gun*: Chase Nielsen, Robert Hite, and Jacob DeShazer, "Saga of Living Death," p. 13, Series II, Box 5, Doolittle Raiders Papers.

49   *George Barr*: Chase Nielsen Oral History, undated audio, Series II, Box 5, Doolittle Raiders Papers.

49   *grown up in Wisconsin*: Fred Borch, personal interview, August 25, 2015; Fred L. Borch, "From West Point to Michigan to China: The Remarkable Career of Edward Hamilton Young (1897–1987)," *Army Lawyer*, December 2012; "Edward Hamilton Young," *Assembly* 49, no. 1 (September 1990): 154–55.

49   *new military law school*: The Judge Advocate General's Legal Center and School, *The Army Lawyer: A History of the Judge Advocate General's Corps, 1775–1975* (G.P.O, 1975), 186–89.

50   *onto the faculty*: Edward H. Young, "The Judge Advocate General's School," *Judge Advocate Journal* 1, no. 1 (June 1944): 18–24; Izner B. Wyatt, "The Army's School for iIs Lawyers," *American Bar Association Journal* 29, no. 3 (March 1943): 135; "Judge Advocate School Housed in Quad," *Michigan Alumnus*, October 10, 1942, 21.

50   *top lawyer*: "Col. Young Moved from Campus to Overseas Post," *Ann Arbor News*, December 20, 1944; "Col. Young Leaves Ann Arbor for New Post," *Michigan Daily*, December 21, 1944; Fred L. Borch, "From West Point to Michigan to China: The Remarkable Career of Edward Hamilton Young (1897–1987)," *Army Lawyer*, December 2012.

50   *describe Chiang*: Barbara Tuchman, *Stilwell and the American Experience in China, 1911–1945* (London: Macmillan, 1971), 371.

50   *official textbook*: Edward H. Young, *Constitutional Powers and Limitations* (West Point, 1941).

50   *Legion of Merit* "Honored: Legion of Merit Is Awarded to Col. E.H. Young," *Michigan Daily*, April 1, 1945.

50   *honorary doctorate*: "Edward Hamilton Young," *Assembly* 49, no. 1 (1990): 154–55.

50   *After being bombed*: Edna Tow, "The Great Bombing of Chongqing and the Anti-Japanese War," in Mark Peattie, Edward Drea, and Hans van de Ven, eds., *The Battle for China: Essays on the Military History of the Sino-Japanese War of 1937–1945* (Stanford, CA: Stanford University Press, 2011), 256–82.

50   *tediously political city*: For a superb cultural history of the wartime relationship between the United States military and the Kuomintang, see Zach Sicmcha Fredman,

"From Allies to Occupiers: Living with the U.S. Military in Wartime China, 1941–1945," (PhD diss., Boston University, 2016).

50 *endless negotiations*: Barbara Tuchman, *Stilwell and the American Experience in China, 1911–1945*, 641–78; Lyman P. Van Slyke, ed., *The China White Paper, August 1949* (Stanford, CA: Stanford University Press, 1967), 61–71. For a contrarian view, see Hans van de Ven, "Stillwell in the Stocks: The Chinese Nationalists and the Allied Powers in the Second World War," *Asian Affairs* 34, no. 3 (2003): 245–59.

50 *China Theater's War Crimes Office*: Edwin O. Shaw, "Establishment of War Crimes Branch Offices," February 7, 1945, Box 13, China War Crimes Files; Edward H. Young to Theater Judge Advocate, Headquarters U.S. Forces, India Burma Theater, "War Crimes," April 25, 1945, Box 12, China War Crimes Files.

50 *War Department's War Crimes Office*: *Legal Work of the War Department, 1 July 1940–31 March 1945: A History of the Judge Advocate General's Department*, Army Service Forces, Office of the Judge Advocate General (G.P.O., 1946), 12–14.

51 *diplomatic inquiries*: The Secretary of State to the Minister in Switzerland (Harrison), October 23, 1942, in E.R. Perkins, ed., *Foreign Relations of the United States: Diplomatic Papers, 1942, General; The British Commonwealth; the Far East*, vol. 1 (G.P.O., 1960), Doc. 710; The Secretary of State to the Minister in Switzerland (Harrison), November 12, 1942, in E. R. Perkins, ed., *Foreign Relations of the United States: Diplomatic Papers, 1942, General; The British Commonwealth; the Far East*, vol. 1 (G.P.O., 1960), Doc. 714.

51 *formal communiqué*: 在京瑞西国公使宛往翰, 昭和18年2月17日, 空襲参加米国飛行士処罰関係文書, 国立公文書館アジア歴史資料センター [Letter to Swiss Envoy in Tokyo, "Materials Regarding Punishment of American Air Crews Participating Air Raid," February 17, 1943, Japan Center for Asian Historical Records], National Archives of Japan; Minister in Switzerland (Harrison) to the Secretary of State, February 23, 1943, in E. R. Perkins, ed., *Foreign Relations of the United States: Diplomatic Papers, 1943, The British Commonwealth. Eastern Europe, the Far East*, vol. 3 (G.P.O., 1963), Doc. 828.

51 *give the names*: Minister in Switzerland (Harrison) to the Secretary of State, March 24, 1943, in E. R. Perkins, ed., *Foreign Relations of the United States: Diplomatic Papers, 1943, The British Commonwealth. Eastern Europe, the Far East*, vol. 3 (G.P.O., 1963), Doc. 848.

51 *diplomatic protest*: The Secretary of State to the Minister in Switzerland (Harrison), April 12, 1943, in E. R. Perkins, ed., *Foreign Relations of the United States: Diplomatic Papers, 1943, The British Commonwealth. Eastern Europe, the Far East*, vol. 3 (G.P.O., 1963), Doc. 710.

51 *every epithet possible*: "The Japs Have Sealed Their Own Doom," *Idaho Standard*, April 28, 1943.

51 *Congressmen called*: "America Is Determined to Blot Out Nips, Says President," Associated Press, April 22, 1943, 1.

51 *publicly denounced*: "America Is Determined to Blot Out Nips, Says President," Associated Press, April 22, 1943, 1.

52 *reviewed the script*: Script Review: The Purple Heart, October 15, 1943, Box 3418, Records of the Los Angeles Branch Office, Records of the Office of War Information, Record Group 208, National Archives at College Park.

52 *assured the public*: Statement by the President, "Japanese Trial and Execution of

American Aviators," April 21, 1943, *Department of State Bulletin* 8, no. 200 (April 24, 1943): 337.

52   *academic interest*: See, e.g., Hans Kelsen, *Peace Through Law* (Chapel Hill: University of North Carolina Press, 1944).

52   *trial of some Nazi saboteurs*: *Ex parte Quirin*, 317 U.S. 1 (1942).

52   *increasingly possible*: Office of Strategic Services, James Donovan, General Counsel Memorandum, War Crimes Information Memo #1, April 12, 1945, Box 8, OSS Field Station Files; Office of Strategic Services, Paul Eckel, Letter to Chief, SI, OSS, China Theater, May 8, 1945, Box 8, OSS Field Station Files; Paul L. E. Helliwell, Memorandum from Japan-China Section FESI, OSS, Washington to Chief SI, OSS, CT, dated May 9, 1945, June 11, 1945, Box 8, OSS Field Station Files.

52   *cataloging Japanese war crimes*: Sidney Mashbir, Allied Translator and Interpreter Section, South West Pacific Area, Research Report No. 72: Japanese Violations of the Laws of War, April 29, 1944, Box 10, China War Crimes Files.

52   *Potsdam Declaration*: Proclamation by the Heads of Governments, United States, China, and the United Kingdom, done at Potsdam, July 27, 1945, ¶10, in Richardson Dougall, ed., *Foreign Relations of the United States: Diplomatic Papers, the Conference of Berlin (the Potsdam Conference)*, 1945, vol. 2 (G.P.O., 1960), Doc. 1382.

52   *massive lists*: United Nations War Crimes Commission, Far Eastern and Pacific Sub-Commission, "List of War Criminals and Material Witnesses (Japanese)," September 1945, Box 8, OSS Field Station Files; United Nations War Crimes Commission, Far Eastern and Pacific Sub-Commission, "First List of War Criminals Holding Key Positions (Japanese)," September 1945, Box 8, OSS Field Station Files.

52   *public education*: Willis West to Psychological Warfare Office, "War Crimes," August 8, 1945, Box 12, China War Crimes Files.

52   *formulated a plan*: Edward Young, Memorandum, "Report of Activities of War Crimes Branch Office, China Theater," August 27, 1945, ¶¶ 26–30, Box 11, China War Crimes Files; Willis West, Memorandum "War Crimes," August 1, 1945, Box 8, OSS Field Station Files.

53   *first big opportunity*: Office of Strategic Services, Cable, August 24, 1945, Box 218, OSS Field Station Files; Office of Strategic Services, Cable, August 23, 1945, Box 218, OSS Field Station Files.

53   *Young and his staff*: Edward Young, Memorandum, "Treatment of Captured Doolittle Fliers, Tokyo Raid, 18 April 1942," August 27, 1945, Box 3, China War Crimes Files.

53   *everything was vibrating*: William Halsey, "Report of Action, April 18, 1942, with notable events prior and subsequent thereto," April 28, 1942, p. 5, Box 1038, Records of the Chief of Naval Operations, Record Group 38, National Archives, College Park.

53   *image in his mind*: James Curtis Hasdorff, *United States Air Force Oral History Program: Interview of Lt. Col. Robert L. Hite* (USAF Historical Research Center, 1982), 44; George Barr, "Destination: Forty Months of Hell," in Carroll V. Glines, ed., *Doolittle's Tokyo Raiders* (New York: Van Nostrand Reinhold, 1981), 307.

53   *no air defense*: Robert Hite, "Biographical Sketch," undated, Series II, Box 3, Doolittle Raiders Papers.

53   *a few shots*: Robert Hite, Questionnaire, undated, p. 4, Box 40, Glines Papers.

53   *radio silence*: George Barr, "Destination: Forty Months of Hell," in Glines, ed., *Doolittle's Tokyo Raiders*, 309.

53   *over Nanchang*: Glines, *Four Came Home*, 47.

53   *only light*: George Barr, interview by W. L. Brown and Chester I. Lappen, December 30, 1945, p. 7, Prosecution Transcript Exhibit 21, Sawada Record.

53   *thought to himself*: James Curtis Hasdorff, *United States Air Force Oral History Program: Interview of Lt. Col. Robert L. Hite* (USAF Historical Research Center, 1982), 53; Robert Hite, Questionnaire, undated, p. 7, Box 40, Glines Papers.

53   *comfort himself*: Doug Clarke, "Doolittle Raiders: Shangri-La," *Fort Worth Star Telegram*, April 18, 1982, 1.

54   *The next morning*: James Curtis Hasdorff, *United States Air Force Oral History Program: Interview of Lt. Col. Robert L. Hite* (USAF Historical Research Center, 1982), 53–55.

54   *"coolie hut"*: Robert Hite, Biographical Sketch, undated, pp. 3–4, Series II, Box 3, Doolittle Raiders Papers.

54   *galled him*: James Curtis Hasdorff, *United States Air Force Oral History Program: Interview of Lt. Col. Robert L. Hite* (USAF Historical Research Center, 1982), 55.

54   *DeShazer was picked up*: Edward Young, Memorandum, "Treatment of Captured Doolittle Fliers, Tokyo Raid, 18 April 1942," August 27, 1945, p. 2, Box 3, China War Crimes Files.

54   *rounded up*: Sawada Trial Transcript, 115–17 (Testimony of Tatsuo Kumano).

54   *atmosphere in Nanchang*: George Barr, interview by W. L. Brown and Chester I. Lappen, December 30, 1945, pp. 8–9, Prosecution Transcript Exhibit 21, Sawada Record.

54   *DeShazer admitted*: Sawada Trial Transcript, 120 (Testimony of Tatsuo Kumano).

54   *the next day*: Chase Nielsen, Robert Hite, and Jacob DeShazer, "Saga of Living Death," pp. 26–27, Series II, Box 5, Doolittle Raiders Papers. The Doolittle Raiders did not know where they were taken, but based upon the diary of Shunroku Hata, they were taken to Nanking. 畑俊六(著), 伊藤隆/照沼康孝(編), 続・現代史資料 (4) 陸軍 畑俊六日誌 (みすず書房, 1983年) [Shunroku Hata, *More Contemporary History Materials (4) Army—Diary of Shunroku Hata*, ed. Takashi Ito and Yasutaka Terunuma (Misuzu Shobo, 1983)], 346–347.

54   *questions came impatiently*: George Barr, interview by W. L. Brown and Chester I. Lappen, December 30, 1945, p. 13, Prosecution Transcript Exhibit 21, Sawada Record.

54   *What is a "hornet"*: Edward Young, Memorandum, "Treatment of Captured Doolittle Fliers, Tokyo Raid, 18 April 1942," August 27, 1945, p. 2, Box 3, China War Crimes Files.

54   *Hite was slapped around*: Edward Young, Memorandum, "Treatment of Captured Doolittle Fliers, Tokyo Raid, 18 April 1942," August 27, 1945, p. 7, Box 3, China War Crimes Files.

54   *worst of the abuse*: Charles Hoyt Watson, *DeShazer: The Doolittle Raider Turned Missionary* (Winona Lake, IN: Light & Life 1952), 55.

54   *waterboard him*: George Barr, interview by W. L. Brown and Chester I. Lappen, December 30, 1945, pp. 12–13, Prosecution Transcript Exhibit 21, Sawada Record.

54   *died back in Nanking*: Office of Strategic Services, Cable, August 26, 1945, Box 218, OSS Field Station Files.

54 *DeShazer said*: Edward Young, Memorandum, "Treatment of Captured Doolittle Fliers, Tokyo Raid, 18 April 1942," August 27, 1945, p. 1, Box 3, China War Crimes Files.

55 *mention of a trial*: Edward Young, Memorandum, "Treatment of Captured Doolittle Fliers, Tokyo Raid, 18 April 1942," August 27, 1945, pp. 5–6, Box 3, China War Crimes Files.

55 *a little booklet*: Edward Young, Memorandum, "Treatment of Captured Doolittle Fliers, Tokyo Raid, 18 April 1942," August 27, 1945, p. 4, Box 3, China War Crimes Files.

55 *Nielsen remembered*: Sawada Trial Testimony, 61–62 (Testimony of Chase Nielsen).

55 *sequestered away*: Edward Young, Memorandum, "Treatment of Captured Doolittle Fliers, Tokyo Raid, 18 April 1942," August 27, 1945, p. 5, Box 3, China War Crimes Files.

55 *October 15, 1942*: Chase Nielsen, Robert Hite, and Jacob DeShazer, "Saga of Living Death," pp. 22–26, Series II, Box 5, Doolittle Raiders Papers; Sawada Trial Transcript, 98 (Testimony of Chase Nielsen).

55 *the night before*: Sawada Trial Transcript, 31–32 (Testimony of Chase Nielsen); Caesar Luis DosRemedios, Statement. September 19, 1945, p. 3, Box 40, Glines Papers.

55 *seen them again*: Edward Young, Memorandum, "Treatment of Captured Doolittle Fliers, Tokyo Raid, 18 April 1942," August 27, 1945, p. 5, Box 3, China War Crimes Files.

55 *Pressed for names*: Edward Young, Memorandum, "Treatment of Captured Doolittle Fliers, Tokyo Raid, 18 April 1942," August 27, 1945, p. 5, Box 3, China War Crimes Files.

56 *"Big Bad Wolf"*: C. D. Smith, Report on Japanese Prison Camps, March 5, 1945, p. 5, China War Crimes Files.

56 *good for information*: Chase Nielsen, interview by Carl Sebey, December 7, 1945, p. 5, Bodine Files.

56 *mistreatment*: Edward Young, Memorandum, "Treatment of Captured Doolittle Fliers, Tokyo Raid, 18 April 1942," August 27, 1945, p. 8, Box 3, China War Crimes Files.

56 *worst in Tokyo*: Edward Young, Memorandum, "Treatment of Captured Doolittle Fliers, Tokyo Raid, 18 April 1942," August 27, 1945, p. 3, Box 3, China War Crimes Files.

56 *a belt*: George Barr, interview by W. L. Brown and Chester I. Lappen, December 30, 1945, p. 16, Prosecution Transcript Exhibit 21, Sawada Record.

56 *bamboo stick*: Robert Hite and Jacob DeShazer, Statement, September 7, 1945, p. 1, Prosecution Exhibit 22, Sawada Record.

56 *Nielsen lifted*: Edward Young, Memorandum, "Treatment of Captured Doolittle Fliers, Tokyo Raid, 18 April 1942," August 27, 1945, p. 7, Box 3, China War Crimes Files.

57 *isolation and neglect*: Edward Young, Memorandum, "Treatment of Captured Doolittle Fliers, Tokyo Raid, 18 April 1942," August 27, 1945, pp. 6–7, Box 3, China War Crimes Files.

57 *asked for details*: The use of this straitjacketing in Nanking is independently corroborated by Statement of Charles Allen Stewart, August 29, 1945, Box 4, China War Crimes Files. The following account of its use on George Barr is taken from

George Barr, "Tokyo Raid Hero Tells of Torture," *Sunday Mirror*, May 5, 1945, 2, 18; Chase Nielsen, Robert Hite, and Jacob DeShazer, "Saga of Living Death," pp. 29–32, Series II, Box 5, Doolittle Raiders Papers; Glines, *Four Came Home*, 105–6 (firsthand account of George Barr).

57 *no one was sure*: Office of Strategic Services, Cable (directing that Barr be evacuated to Kunming as soon as possible), August 28, 1945, Box 218, OSS Field Station Files; Office of Strategic Services, Cable (expressing concern over Barr's condition), August 30, 1945, Box 218, OSS Field Station Files.

CHAPTER SIX

61 *a few dozen*: Jeremiah J. O'Connor Memorandum to Theater Prison Officer through Theater Provost Marshall, December 10, 1945, Box 12, China War Crimes Files.

61 *served under Young*: Henry W. Clune, "Seen and Heard," *Rochester Democrat & Chronicle*, July 29, 1944, 21; "Robert T. Dwyer Wins Rank of Captaincy," *Rochester Democrat & Chronicle*, June 24, 1944, 8.

61 *graduate of Harvard*: "Harvard Undergrads Entertained by Club," *Rochester Democrat & Chronicle*, January 2, 1928, 15.

61 *legal office*: John Hendren to the Judge Advocate General, Washington 25, "Prosecution of War Criminals in the Case of 2nd Lt. Dean Edward Hallmark, 95th Squadron, 17th Bomber Group, USAAF, 2d Lt William Glover Farrow, 34th Squadron, 17th Bomber Group, USAAF and Sgt Harold A. Spatz, 34th Squadron, 17th Bomber Group, USAAF, an 15 October 1942," November 19, 1945, p. 1, Box 12, China War Crimes Files.

61 *New York Republicans*: "Many Surprises Mark Republican Slate with Younger Party Elements Given Call," *Rochester Democrat & Chronicle*, August 16, 1934, 1–2.

61 *from Missouri*: "Leaders of Young Democrats," *St. Louis Star & Times*, February 17, 1938, 3.

61 *always dressed impeccably*: Tom Vetter, personal interview, February 2, 2015.

61 *shared office space*: "Assignment of Office Space and Billeting, Headquarters USF CT in Shanghai," September 28, 1945, Box 651, China/theater/Special Staff/Interpreter Affairs Section, Entry UD-UP 300, Subject Files 1944-1946, CBI Records; John Hersey, "Letter from Shanghai," *New Yorker*, January 24, 1946, 86.

62 *relocated his headquarters*: Theater HQ in Shanghai, *Shanghai Stars & Stripes*, October 17, 1945, 8.

62 *colonial enclaves*: Harriet Sergeant, *Shanghai* (London: Trafalgar Square, 1991), 2.

62 *Broadway Mansions*: Peter Hibbard, *The Bund Shanghai* (Hong Kong: Airphoto International, 2007), 27.

62 *dining room*: Hibbard, *The Bund Shanghai*, 271.

62 *officers' club*: Natalie and Elizabeth Bodine, personal interview, December 17, 2014.

62 *"Sweater Girl"*: Natalie and Elizabeth Bodine, personal interview, December 17, 2014.

62 *"Petrushkas"*: Alfred Emile Cornebise, *The Shanghai Stars and Stripes: Witness to the Transition to Peace, 1945–1946* (Jefferson, NC: MacFarland, 2010), 77.

62 *sex trade*: Christian Henriot, *Prostitution and Sexuality in Shanghai: A Social History,*

1849–1949, trans. Noël Castelino (Cambridge: Cambridge University Press, 2001), 101

62 *catch an American*: Liliane Willens, *Stateless in Shanghai* (Hong Kong: Earnshaw Books, 2010), 178.

62 *"Three Little Girls"*: Franc Schor, "Three Little Girls," *Shanghai Stars & Stripes*, October 13, 1945, 8.

63 *hit song*: Cornebise, *The Shanghai Stars and Stripes*, 77.

63 *always deflected*: Natalie and Elizabeth Bodine, personal interview, December 17, 2014.

63 *guidebooks advertised*: Peter Hibbard, *All About Shanghai and Environs* (1935; reprint, Hong Kong: Earnshaw Books, 2008), 83.

63 *exotic and erotic*: Hibbard, *All About Shanghai and Environs*, 45.

63 *Red Rose*: Marcia Reynders Ristaino, *Port of Last Resort: The Diaspora Communities of Shanghai* (Stanford, CA: Stanford University Press, 2002), 89.

63 *geisha houses*: Henriot, *Prostitution and Sexuality in Shanghai*, 84.

63 *"jeep girls"*: Ristaino, *Port of Last Resort*, 243.

63 *"pheasants"*: Gail Hershatter, "The Heirarchy of Shanghai Prostitution, 1870–1949," *Modern China* 15, no. 4 (1989).

63 *"taxi dancer"*: Andrew David Field, *Shanghai's Dancing World: Cabaret Culture and Urban Politics 1919–1954* (Hong Kong: Chinese University Press, 2010), 197; Henriot, *Prostitution and Sexuality in Shanghai*, 108.

63 *Joseph Stillwell*: Graham Earnshaw, *Tales of Old Shanghai* (Hong Kong: Earnshaw Books, 2012), 42.

63 *Everyone knew*: Richard Cushing, "GIs in Shanghai Wallow in Luxury," Associated Press, November 4, 1945.

63 *bespoke American flags*: Willens, *Stateless in Shanghai*, 178.

64 *he was drafted*: "The Draft," *Rochester Democrat & Chronicle*, August 23, 1942, 25.

64 *by running*: "Dwyer Disappointed," *Rochester Democrat & Chronicle*, November 7, 1934, 16; "Complete Republican Ticket," *Rochester Democrat & Chronicle*, August 16, 1934.

64 *eligible bachelors*: Arch Merrill, "The Bachelor Brigade," *Rochester Democrat & Chronicle*, November 24, 1940, 68.

64 *weather observer*: "2d of Law Firm Goes into Army," *Rochester Democrat & Chronicle*, January 15, 1943, 16.

64 *JAG School*: "Robert T. Dwyer Wins Rank of Captaincy," *Rochester Democrat & Chronicle*, June 24, 1945, 8.

65 *pretty mundane*: John Hendren to Commanding General, Fourteenth Air Force, et al., November 1, 1945, Box 1, Correspondence 1942–1945, Entry# A1 1059, Records of the Office of the Judge Advocate General (Army), Record Group 153, National Archives, College Park.

65 *Young wanted to know*: John Hendren to Theater Judge Advocate, USF CT, Shanghai, China, "Prosecution of War Criminals in the Case of the Death of Lt Glover Farrell, 2d Lt Dean A. Hallmark, and Sgt Harold A. Spatz, Doolittle Fliers, Executed about 15 October 1942," November 09, 1945, Box 12, China War Crimes Files.

65 *The file*: J. S. Bailey to Edward H. Young, September 24, 1945, Box 12, China War Crimes Files.

65 *assistant attorney general*: "Fined for Failure to Turn Over Sales Tax Records," *St.*

Louis Post-Dispatch, June 4, 1936, 17; "Two on Bond Accused of Sales Tax Evasion," *St. Louis Post-Dispatch*, November 10, 1936, 24; "Indict Firm on Eight Sales Tax Complaints," *Daily Capital News*, November 10, 1936, 4.

66 *New Deal Democrat*: "Leaders of Young Democrats," *St. Louis Star & Times*, February 17, 1938, 3.

66 *mostly in Washington*: "Society," *Jefferson City Post-Tribune*, April 27, 1943, 3.

66 *beauty pageant*: "Pretty Missouri Delegate in Race for Beauty Title," Associated Press, June 24, 1936.

66 *society pages*: "Democratic Women Received at Mansion," *Jefferson City Post-Tribune*, October 18, 1942, 3.

66 *international news*: Clyde A. Farnsworth, "Officer Cleared in Mercy Shooting of Yank Trapped in Burning Plane," Associated Press, March 2, 1945.

67 *a bit thin*: John Hendren to the Judge Advocate General, Washington 25, "Prosecution of War Criminals in the Case of 2nd Lt. Dean Edward Hallmark, 95th Squadron, 17th Bomber Group, USAAF, 2d Lt William Glover Farrow, 34th Squadron, 17th Bomber Group, USAAF and Sgt Harold A. Spatz, 34th Squadron, 17th Bomber Group, USAAF, an 15 October 1942," November 19, 1945, Box 12, China War Crimes Files.

68 *sent to Shanghai*: Jason Bailey to Colonel Edward H. Young, September 12, 1945, Box 12, China War Crimes Files.

68 *part of a G-man*: Irene Kuhn, "Tea and Ashes," in Overseas Press Club of America, eds., *Deadline Delayed* (New York: E. P. Dutton, 1947), 269.

68 *American presence*: Willens, *Stateless in Shanghai*, 178.

68 *Shanghai YMCA*: Jason Bailey to Colonel Edward H. Young, September 12, 1945, Box 12, China War Crimes Files.

68 *lend him a jeep*: Jason Bailey to Colonel Edward H. Young, September 17, 1945, Box 12, China War Crimes Files.

68 *biggest find*: Jason Bailey, "Interrogation of Mayama Shigeji," September 28, 1945, p. 1, Box 40, Glines Papers.

68 *In its storeroom*: Masayoshi Koga, interview by Robert Dwyer, November 20, 1945, p. 1, Box 40, Glines Papers.

68 *three urns*: Julian Hartt, "How Doolittle Fliers Executed Told," International News Service, September 29, 1946.

68 *the same date*: Masayoshi Koga, interview by Robert Dwyer, November 20, 1945, p. 1, Box 40, Glines Papers; "Fliers' Ashes Feature Trial," United Press, March 23, 1946.

68 *other major discovery*: 登第七三三〇部隊軍律会議，判決文，昭和17年8月28日，BC級(アメリカ裁判関係)上海裁判・第4号事件 [Noboru 7330 Unit Military Commission, Judgment, August 28, 1942, BC Class (Regarding American Trials) Shanghai Trial—Case No. 4], National Archives of Japan.

68 *follow-up report*: Soshi Yasuharu, Medical Report on Second Lieutenant Robert J. Meder, December 1, 1943, Box 2179, POW Records.

69 *Hayama had come forward*: 羽山忠弘，ある戦犯事件弁護の思い出，大東法学第18号179頁 (1991年) (1991Âπ¥) [Tadahiro Hayama, "Recollection of Defending a War Trial Case," 18 *Daito Hogaku* 179 (1991)], 193.

69 *cabled back*: Army Advisory Group, Nanking China, Cable, undated (approx. September 24, 1945), War Crimes Files, Incoming and Outgoing Radios 21 April 1945 to 6 March 1946, Box 14, China War Crimes Files.

69 *call a press conference*: Army Advisory Group, Nanking China, Cable, September 26, 1945, War Crimes Files, Incoming and Outgoing Radios 21 April 1945 to 6 March 1946, Box 14, China War Crimes Files.

69 *gathered the press*: Irene Kuhn, "Tea and Ashes," in Overseas Press Club of America, eds., *Deadline Delayed*, 269.

70 *outlined their case*: John Hendren to Theater Judge Advocate, USF CT, Shanghai, China, "Prosecution of War Criminals in the Case of the Death of Lt Glover Farrell, 2d Lt Dean A. Hallmark, and Sgt Harold A. Spatz, Doolittle Fliers, Executed about 15 October 1942, November 09, 1945," Box 12, China War Crimes Files.

71 *closed the memo*: John Hendren to Chief of Staff, United States Forces, China Theater, APO (Thru: The Theater Judge Advocate, USF CT, APO 879), "Prosecution of War Criminals Responsible for the Trial and Execution of Second Lieutenant William Glover Farrell, Second Lieutenant Dean A. Hallmark and Sergeant Harold A. Spatz, Doolittle Fliers, Executed About 15 October 1942, November 13, 1945," Box 12, China War Crimes Files.

71 *top priority order*: Albert Wedemeyer, "Prosecution of War Criminals," November 11, 1945, Box 12, China War Crimes Files.

CHAPTER SEVEN

72 *Ham Young announced*: "China Trials Start Soon," *Shanghai Stars & Stripes*, November 30, 1945, 8.

72 *territory around Shanghai*: "Communist Claims Army of 400,000 Near Shanghai," *Shanghai Stars & Stripes*, October 10, 1945, 1.

72 *dozen photographs*: Photographs of Doolittle Fliers, Prosecution Exhibit B, Sawada Record.

73 *Roosevelt had promised*: Statement by the President, "Japanese Trial and Execution of American Aviators," April 21, 1943, *Department of State Bulletin* 8, no. 200 (April 24, 1943): 33.

73 *record of execution*: Itsuro Hata, "Particulars Relating to the Punishment of the American Airman who Raided the Japanese Homeland on 18 April 1942," translation by Allied Translator and Interpret Section, United States Army Forces, Pacific, Doc. 1870, October 1945, "Inclosure [*sic*] No. 8, Record of Execution," p. 11, Prosecution Exhibit 25, Sawada Record.

73 *interview with Ham Young*: Edward Young, Memorandum, "Treatment of Captured Doolittle Fliers, Tokyo Raid, 18 April 1942," August 27, 1945, p. 5, Box 3, China War Crimes Files.

73 *located Remedios*: Caesar Luis DosRemedios, Statement, September 19, 1945, p. 4, 6, Prosecution Exhibit 26, Sawada Record.

73 *Ward Road Jail*: James L. Norwood and Emily L. Shek, *Prisoner of War Camps in Areas Other Than the Four Principal Islands of Japan*, American Prisoner of War Information Bureau, Liaison and Research Branch, July 31, 1946, pp. 7–9, POW Records.

74 *persuaded the Chinese*: Edward Young to Jeremiah O'Connor, "War Crimes," May 1, 1946, p. 2, Box 12, China War Crimes Files.

74 *Remedios had lived*: Caesar Luis DosRemedios, Statement, Document 14, September 19, 1945, p.1, China War Crimes Files.

74 *treated the Macanese*: Liliane Willens, *Stateless in Shanghai* (Hong Kong: Earnshaw Books, 2010), 51.

74 *Retreating and unremarkable*: George Barr, interview by W. L. Brown and Chester I. Lappen, December 30, 1945, pp. 33, Prosecution Transcript Exhibit 21, Sawada Record.

74 *his own imprisonment*: Caesar Luis DosRemedios, Statement, Document 14, September 19, 1945, p. 1, China War Crimes Files.

74 *passed through*: First Floor Plan of Ward Road Gaol, Shanghai, October 6, 1944, Box 5, China War Crimes Files.

74 *first major interview*: Tatsuta Sotojiro, interview by Robert Dwyer, November 16, 1945, Box 40, Glines Papers.

76 *"Lieutenant General Sawada"*: Tatsuta Sotojiro, interview by Robert Dwyer, November 16, 1945, p. 3, Box 40, Glines Papers.

76 *been a farmer*: Yasuo Tatsuta to Robert C. Mikesh, February 1965, Box 40, Glines Papers.

77 *The presiding judges*: *Trial of the Major War Criminals before the International Military Tribunal, Nuremberg: 14 November 1945–1 October 1946* ("Blue Series"), vol. 2 (International Military Tribunal, Nuremberg, 1947), 30.

77 *New York Times*: Kathleen McLaughlin, "Allies Open Trial of 20 Top Germans for Crimes of War," *New York Times*, November 21, 1945, 1.

77 *records were burnt*: Masayoshi Koga, interview by Robert Dwyer, November 20, 1945, p. 1, Box 40, Glines Papers.

77 *Dwyer asked one guard*: Shoso Takeguchi, interview by Robert Dwyer, November 20, 1945, p. 2, Box 40, Glines Papers.

77 *fifteen meters*: Sheigeji Mayama, interview by Robert Dwyer, November 20, 1945, p. 2, Box 40, Glines Papers.

77 *twenty*: Minezaki Yutaka, interview by Robert Dwyer, November 20, 1945, p 2, Box 40, Glines Papers.

77 *fifty*: Isamu Yoneda, interview by Robert Dwyer, November 20, 1945, p. 2, Box 40, Glines Papers.

77 *early morning*: Sheigeji Mayama, interview by Robert Dwyer, December 17, 1945, p. 4, Box 40, Glines Papers.

77 *lunchtime*: Tomoichi Yoneya, interview by Robert Dwyer, November 20, 1945, p. 1, Box 40, Glines Papers.

77 *sundown*: Sawada Trial Transcript, 472 (Testimony of Sotojiro Tatsuta); Itsuro Hata, "Particulars Relating to the Punishment of the American Airman who Raided the Japanese Homeland on 18 April 1942," translation by Allied Translator and Interpret Section, United States Army Forces, Pacific, Doc. 1870, October 1945, "Inclosure [*sic*] No. 8, Record of Execution," p. 11, Prosecution Exhibit 25, Sawada Record.

77 *five minutes*: Tatsuta Sotojiro, interview by Robert Dwyer, November 16, 1945, p. 3, Box 40, Glines Papers.

77 *for ten*: Tomoichi Yoneya, interview by Robert Dwyer, November 20, 1945, p. 2, Box 40, Glines Papers.

78 *order to fire*: Isamu Yoneda, interview by Robert Dwyer, November 20, 1945, p. 1, Box 40, Glines Papers; Sheigeji Mayama, interview by Robert Dwyer, November 20, 1945, p. 3, Box 40, Glines Papers; Tomoichi Yoneya, interview by Robert Dwyer, November 20, 1945, p. 2, Box 40, Glines Papers.

78 *"Do you remember"*: Yoneya Tomoichi, interview by Robert Dwyer, November 20, 1945, p. 1, Box 40, Glines Papers.

78   *"looked alike"*: Sheigeji Mayama, interview by Robert Dwyer, November 20, 1945, p. 1, Box 40, Glines Papers.

78   *given Jason Bailey*: Jason Bailey, cable, undated (September 1945), War Crimes Files, Incoming and Outgoing Radios 21 April 1945 to 6 March 1946, Box 14, China War Crimes Files.

78   *Fearing that innocent people*: 羽山忠弘, ある戦犯事件弁護の思い出, 大東法学第18号179頁 (1991年) [Tadahiro Hayama, "Recollection of Defending a War Trial Case," 18 *Daito Hogaku* 179 (1991)], 193.

78   *the photos labeled*: Tadahiro Hayama, interview by Robert Dwyer, November 20, 1945, p. 3, Box 40, Glines Papers.

78   *every Japanese newspaper*: "American Pilots Confess Wanton Attack on Tokyo School, Hospital Civilians," *Shanghai Times*, October 22, 1942, 1; "見よ・米機のこの非道", 朝日新聞, 昭和17年10月20日 ["Look at the Atrocity of the American Planes," *Asahi Shimbun*, October 20, 1942].

79   *they confessed*: "American Pilots Confess Wanton Attack on Tokyo School, Hospital Civilians," *Shanghai Times*, October 22, 1942, 1.

79   *did not know anyone*: Tadahiro Hayama, interview by Robert Dwyer, November 20, 1945, p. 2, Box 40, Glines Papers.

79   *He was from*: 神代護忠, 上海支店時代の思い出 (1994年) [Moritada Kumashiro, "Recollection of the Days at Shanghai Branch," Manuscript (1994)], p. 127, Call No. GK77-G2, National Diet Library.

79   *had been drafted*: 羽山忠弘, ある戦犯事件弁護の思い出, 大東法学第18号179頁 (1991年) [Tadahiro Hayama, "Recollection of Defending a War Trial Case," 18 *Daito Hogaku* 179 (1991)], 182.

79   *professional curiosity*: Tadahiro Hayama, interview by Robert Dwyer, November 20, 1945, p. 1, Box 40, Glines Papers.

80   *Bailey had asked*: General Headquarters, United States Army Forces, Pacific, Military Intelligence Section, General Staff Doc. 1274, September 30, 1945, p. 1, Box. 1357, Army-Intelligence Document File, Records of the Army Staff, Record Group 319, National Archives, College Park; Army Advisory Group, Nanking China, cable, September 28, 1945, War Crimes Files, Incoming and Outgoing Radios 21 April 1945 to 6 March 1946, Box 14, China War Crimes Files.

80   *international news*: "Jap Killer Arrested," United Press, October 16, 1945.

80   *major still had it*: Tadahiro Hayama, interview by Robert Dwyer, November 20, 1945, pp. 2–3, Box 40, Glines Papers.

80   *"Where is the case file"*: Tadahiro Hayama, interview by Robert Dwyer, November 20, 1945, p. 2, Box 40, Glines Papers ("Where are the records now do you know?").

CHAPTER EIGHT

81   *Airmen trained*: Major Muir S. Fairchild, "National Economic Structure," April 5, 1939, in Phil Haun, ed., *Lectures of the Air Corps Tactical School and American Strategic Bombing in World War II* (Lexington: University of Kentucky Press, 2019).

81   *Roosevelt appealed*: Franklin D. Roosevelt, "An Appeal to Great Britain, France, Italy, Germany, and Poland to Refrain from Air Bombing of Civilians," September 1, 1939, in Gerhard Peters and John T. Woolley, eds., The American Presidency Project, https://perma.cc/5XEH-FCGC.

81   *military doctrine*: Kenneth P. Werrell, *Blankets of Fire: US Bombers over Japan during World War II* (Washington, DC: Smithsonian, 1996), 15.

81   *sternly instructed*: James Doolittle, "Report on the Aerial Bombing of Japan," June 5, 1942, p. 15, Box 36, Glines Papers.

81   *diplomatic protest*: Department of State, "United States Communication of April 12, 1943 to the Japanese Government," April 12, 1943, *Department of State Bulletin* 8, no. 200 (April 24, 1943): 337–39.

81   *end the war*: Werrell, *Blankets of Fire*, 157.

82   *Chemists at Harvard*: Robert M. Neer, *Napalm: An American Biography* (Cambridge, MA: Belknap, 2013), 23–33.

82   *never a believer*: Curtis LeMay, *Mission with LeMay* (Garden City, NY: Doubleday, 1965), 349–53; *The Fog of War: Eleven Lessons from the Life of Robert S. McNamara* (Sony Pictures Classics 2003).

82   *"goop bombs"*: Peter Edson, "Washington Notebook," Newspaper Enterprise Association, March 17, 1945.

82   *"block burners"*: Barrett Tillman, *Whirlwind: The Air War Against Japan, 1942–1945* (New York: Simon & Schuster, 2010), 139.

82   *On March 9*: Werrell, *Blankets of Fire*, 160–207. For other quality histories on the firebombing of Japan, see Daniel Ellsberg, *The Doomsday Machine: Confessions of a Nuclear War Planner* (New York: Bloomsbury, 2017); Barrett Tillman, *Whirlwind: The Air War Against Japan, 1942–1945* (New York: Simon & Schuster, 2010); Robert Pape, *Bombing to Win: Air Power and Coercion in War* (Ithaca, NY: Cornell University Press, 1996); John Dower, *War Without Mercy: Race and Power in the Pacific War* (New York: Pantheon, 1986); and Haywood Hansell, *The Strategic Air War Against Germany and Japan* (Washington, DC: U.S. Air Force, 1986).

82   *urban map*: One way to understand the firebombing of Japan is to say that it followed the logic of the map. Thousands of maps and aerial photographs were printed and marked up to show population density, strategic value, and the inflammability of Japan's population centers square mile by square mile. After each mission, new maps would be produced blacking out what targets had been destroyed to both show progress and future targets. David Fedman and Cary Karacas, "A Cartographic Fade to Black: Mapping the Destruction of Urban Japan During World War II," *Journal of Historical Geography* 38 (2012): 320.

82   *warning leaflets*: XXI Air Force, *Air Intelligence Report* 1, no. 22, August 4, 1945, USB-10, Roll, 4, Security-Classified Intelligence Library 1932–1947, Entry 46, Records of the U.S. Strategic Bombing Survey, Record Group 243, National Archives, College Park. LeMay was persuaded to drop the leaflets because the warnings would both heighten chaos on the ground and placate Americans who were troubled by his apparent embrace of "terror bombing." Concerns over terror bombing arose soon after the first firebombing of Tokyo and the Air Force released a public statement stating, "There has been no change in the basic policy of the USAAF, which still confines its bombing efforts to attack on military objectives." Peter Edson, "Washington Notebook," Newspaper Enterprise Association, March 17, 1945.

82   *following two weeks*: Leaflet, undated, Miscellaneous Historical Document File, No. 258, Harry S. Truman Library.

82   *Soviets invaded Manchuria*: For detailed histories of the Soviet invasion of China and its significance, see Richard Frank, *Downfall: The End of the Imperial Japanese*

Empire (New York: Penguin, 2001), 276–290, 322–49; John Toland, *The Rising Sun: The Decline and Fall of the Japanese Empire* (1970; reprint, New York: Modern Library, 2003), 806–8; David Glantz, "August Storm: The Soviet 1945 Strategic Offensive in Manchuria," *Leavenworth Papers*, no. 7 (February 1983).

82   *sixty-two square miles*: André Sorensen, *The Making of Urban Japan: Cities and Planning from Edo to the Twenty-First Century* (London: Routledge, 2004), 162.

82   *100-square-foot bungalows*: Ishida Yorifusa, "Japanese Cities and Planning in the Reconstruction Period: 1945–1955," in Carola Hein, Jeffrey Diefendorf, and Ishida Yorifusa, eds., *Rebuilding Urban Japan After 1945* (London: Palgrave Macmillan, 2003), 24.

83   *"Little America"*: John Dower, *Embracing Defeat: Japan in the Wake of World War II* (New York: Norton, 1999), 47, 206–11.

83   *under the command*: R. K. Sutherland, "Office of the Supreme Commander for the Allied Powers," Directive No. 2, September 3, 1945, Box 2219, SCAP General Orders October 1945–November 1947, Allied Occupation Records.; *MacArthur in Japan: The Occupation: Military Phase*, vol. 1 (1950; reprint, Washington, DC: U.S. Army Center for Military History, 1994), 71–82.

83   *the wizard's palace*: For cultural/political histories of SCAP in Tokyo, see Stephen Mansfield, *Tokyo: A Cultural History* (Oxford University Press, 2009), 200–16; Eiji Takemae, *Inside GHQ: The Allied Occupation of Japan and Its Legacy*, Robert Ricketts and Sebastian Swann, trans. (New York: Continuum, 2002); Michael Molasky, *The American Occupation of Japan and Okinawa: Literature and Memory* (London: Routledge, 1999); John Dower, *Embracing Defeat: Japan in the Wake of World War II* (New York: Norton, 1999); Michael Schaller, *The American Occupation of Japan: The Origins of the Cold War in Asia* (New York: Oxford University Press, 1985).

83   *Dwyer made his way*: Robert Dwyer, Memo to Edward Young, Report of Observations Made at Headquarters, Supreme Commander, Allied Forces Pacific, Tokyo and Rear Echelon at Manila, Philippine Islands, 1945, p. 1, Box 12, China War Crimes Files.

83   *SCAP's Legal Section*: R. K. Sutherland, "Legal Section," General Order No. 21, December 9, 1945, Box 2219, SCAP General Orders October 1945–November 1947, Allied Occupation Records; Robert Dwyer, Memo to Edward Young, "Report of Observations Made at Headquarters, Supreme Commander, Allied Forces Pacific, Tokyo and Rear Echelon at Manila, Philippine Islands," undated, p. 1, Box 12, China War Crimes Files.

83   *remake postwar Japan*: John Dower, *Embracing Defeat: Japan in the Wake of World War II* (New York: Norton, 1999), 69.

83   *Dwyer's former colleagues*: Robert Dwyer, Memo to Edward Young, Report of Observations Made at Headquarters, Supreme Commander, Allied Forces Pacific, Tokyo and Rear Echelon at Manila, Philippine Islands, 1945, Box 12, China War Crimes Files.

83   *Truman had just appointed*: R. K. Sutherland, "International Prosecution Section," General Order No. 20, December 8, 1945, Box 2219, SCAP General Orders October 1945–November 1947, Allied Occupation Records.

83   *Every component*: Robert Dwyer, Memo to Edward Young, "Report of Observations Made at Headquarters, Supreme Commander, Allied Forces Pacific, Tokyo and Rear Echelon at Manila, Philippine Islands," 1945, p. 1, Box 12, China War Crimes Files.

84   *Some cables*: Sawada Trial Transcript, 232–33 (Testimony of John Hendren).

84   *Before returning*: Robert Dwyer, Memo to Edward Young, "Report of Observations Made at Headquarters, Supreme Commander, Allied Forces Pacific, Tokyo and Rear Echelon at Manila, Philippine Islands," undated, p. 1, Box 12, China War Crimes Files.

84   *a girlfriend derby*: "It's Derby Day in Shanghai," *Shanghai Stars & Stripes (China Bowl Supplement)*, December 1, 1945.

85   *scars of war*: The scale of the destruction in Manila can be appreciated from more than two hundred photographs publicly posted by the Philippine government. Presidential Museum and Library of the Philippines, "Battle of Manila 1945," Flickr photo album, https://flic.kr/s/aHsk7KPdAb.

85   *greatest humiliation*: A secret intelligence report on the public's morale, prepared the week before the Doolittle Raid, concluded that "the final, long-delayed American relinquishment of Bataan Peninsula to the Japanese invaders came as a climax to a week of almost unbelievably bad news." The report was concerned that in "most of the newspapers there seemed little tendency to equivocate about the gravity of these reverses. The headlines were black and unhappy." Bureau of Intelligence, Office of Facts and Figures, Survey of Intelligence Materials, No. 19, April 15, 1942, Box 155, President's Secretary's File, Office of War Information: Survey of Intelligence: Apr. 1942, FDR Library.

85   *Yamashita had been*: The best histories of the Malaya/Singapore campaign are James M. Scott, *Rampage: MacArthur, Yamashita, and the Battle of Manila* (New York: Norton, 2018), 36–44; Allan A. Ryan, *Yamashita's Ghost: War Crimes, MacArthur's Justice, and Command Accountability* (Lawrence, KS: University Press of Kansas, 2012), 12–30; Richard Lael, *The Yamashita Precedent: War Crimes & Command Responsibility* (Wilmington, DE: Rowman & Littlefield, 1982), 5–38; John Toland, *The Rising Sun: The Decline and Fall of the Japanese Empire* (1970; reprint, New York: Modern Library, 2003), 270–77.

86   *found his position*: Frank A Reel, *The Case of General Yamashita* (Chicago: University of Chicago Press, 1949), 63–106; Scott, *Rampage*, 46–54.

86   *In his diary*: "Notebook-diary presumably belonging to a member of Akatsuki 16709 Force, covering period 31 July 44–21 Feb 45," Extracts, Item 13, reproduced in *United States v. Tomoyuki Yamashita*, Trial Exhibits, Box 143, War Crimes Branch, General Administrative Records, Records of the Office of the Judge Advocate General (Army), Record Group 153, National Archives, College Park.

86   *Yamashita retreated*: For the most comprehensive historical accounts of the Battle of Manila, see James M. Scott, *Rampage: MacArthur, Yamashita, and the Battle of Manila* (New York: Norton, 2018); Richard Lael, *The Yamashita Precedent: War Crimes & Command Responsibility* (Wilmington, DE: Rowman & Littlefield, 1982), 5–38.

86   *Yamashita waited*: Allan A. Ryan, *Yamashita's Ghost: War Crimes, MacArthur's Justice, and Command Accountability* (Lawrence, KS: University Press of Kansas, 2012), xxiii.

86   *make an example*: B. M. Fitch, Memorandum to Commanding General, United States Army Forces, Western Pacific, "Trial of General Tomoyuki Yamashita," September 24, 1945, reproduced in *United States v. Tomoyuki Yamashita*, Trial Transcript, p. 67, Box 127, War Crimes Branch, General Administrative Records, Records of the Office of the Judge Advocate General (Army), Record Group 153, National Archives, College Park.

86   *chronicle of horrors*: Lael, *The Yamashita Precedent*, 60–76.

86   *end of the world*: Frank A. Reel, *The Case of General Yamashita* (Chicago: University of Chicago Press, 1949), 103.

87   *firsthand look*: Army Advisory Group, Nanking China, Cable, November 19, 1945, "War Crimes Files, Incoming and Outgoing Radios 21 April 1945 to 6 March 1946," Box 14, China War Crimes Files.

87   *The morning after his arrival*: Robert Dwyer, Memo to Edward Young, "Report of Observations Made at Headquarters, Supreme Commander, Allied Forces Pacific, Tokyo and Rear Echelon at Manila, Philippine Islands," undated pp. 2–3, Box 12, China War Crimes Files.

87   *"desk generals"*: Reel, *The Case of General Yamashita*, 40.

87   *those weren't the rules*: "Trial of War Criminals by Military Commission, Shanghai China," February 1946, pp. 21–23, Box 12, China War Crimes Files.

87   *one rule of evidence*: Robert Dwyer to Edward H. Young, "Conference at Manila with respect to War Criminal Prosecutions," undated, pp. 1–2, Box 12, China War Crimes Files; Myron C. Cramer Memorandum to the Assistant Secretary of War, "Trial of War Criminals, October 9, 1944, p. 2, China War Crimes Files; T. H. Green Memorandum for the Chief, Civil Affairs Division, Office of the Chief of Staff, W.D.G.S, "Trial of War Criminals," October 30, 1943, Box 12, pp. 5–6, China War Crimes Files; Commander in Chief of the Army and Navy, "Appointment of a Military Commission," July 2, 1942, 7 Fed. Reg. 5103.

88   *gone to Harvard*: Robert Dwyer, Memo to Edward Young, "Report of Observations Made at Headquarters, Supreme Commander, Allied Forces Pacific, Tokyo and Rear Echelon at Manila, Philippine Islands," undated, pp. 2–3, Box 12, China War Crimes Files.

88   *directed a skit*: "Graduation Skit of 6th Officer Candidate Class," July 10, 1944, *Scrapbook 1943–46*, The Judge Advocate's General School, University of Michigan Ann Arbor, Michigan, vol. 2, 25–26.

88   *Reel was relentless*: Reel, *The Case of General Yamashita*, 119.

88   *filed a lawsuit*: Yamashita v. Styer, Supreme Court of the Commonwealth of the Philippines, 42 Off.Gaz. 664 (November 27, 1945).

88   *ridiculous chase*: Reel, *The Case of General Yamashita*, 187.

88   *dismissed the case*: Yamashita v. Styer, Supreme Court of the Commonwealth of the Philippines, 42 Off.Gaz. 664 (November 28, 1945).

88   *Reel was trying*: "Yamashita Asks to Be Tried by Supreme Court," Associated Press, December 3, 1945.

88   *lawyers to a minimum*: Robert Dwyer to Edward H. Young, "Conference at Manila with Respect to War Criminal Prosecutions," undated, p. 2, Box 12, China War Crimes Files.

89   *got his chance*: Robert Dwyer, Memo to Edward Young, "Report of Observations Made at Headquarters, Supreme Commander, Allied Forces Pacific, Tokyo and Rear Echelon at Manila, Philippine Islands," undated, pp. 2–3, Box 12, China War Crimes Files.

89   *ballroom of Mansion House*: Lael, *The Yamashita Precedent*, 60–76.

89   *Military police*: Robert Dwyer, Memo to Edward Young, "Report of Observations Made at Headquarters, Supreme Commander, Allied Forces Pacific, Tokyo and Rear Echelon at Manila, Philippine Islands," undated, pp. 2–3, Box 12, China War Crimes Files.

89   *production values*: Reel, *The Case of General Yamashita*, 27.

89   *Dwyer counted*: Robert Dwyer, Memo to Edward Young, "Report of Observations Made at Headquarters, Supreme Commander, Allied Forces Pacific, Tokyo and Rear Echelon at Manila, Philippine Islands," undated, p. 3, Box 12, China War Crimes Files.

89   *Dwyer knew many*: Robert Dwyer to Edward H. Young, "Conference at Manila with Respect to War Criminal Prosecutions," undated, p. 9, Box 12, China War Crimes Files.

89   *Dwyer even recognized*: Robert Dwyer, Memo to Edward Young, "Report of Observations Made at Headquarters, Supreme Commander, Allied Forces Pacific, Tokyo and Rear Echelon at Manila, Philippine Islands," undated, p. 3, Box 12, China War Crimes Files.

90   *"earnest oriental"*: Reel, *The Case of General Yamashita*, 14.

90   *called the room*: Robert Dwyer to Edward H. Young, "Conference at Manila with Respect to War Criminal Prosecutions," undated, p. 4, Box 12, China War Crimes Files.

90   *not actually a lawyer*: Reel, *The Case of General Yamashita*, 40.

90   *Yamashita himself was big*: Reel, *The Case of General Yamashita*, 56.

90   *patient dispassion*: "Yamashita Trial, Manila, Philippine Islands," Film Recording, Records of the Office of the Chief Signal Officer, 1860–1985, Record Group 111, National Archives, College Park.

90   *the links*: Scott, *Rampage*, 53–54, 343–45; Reel, *The Case of General Yamashita*, 102.

90   *Benjamin Harrison*: State v. Harrison, 107 N.J.L. 213, 152 A. 867 (Sup. Ct. 1931).

91   *prosecutors had figured*: Application of Yamashita, Case Nos. 61, 672, Brief for the Respondent in Opposition (U.S., January 7, 1946), 54.

91   *the major world powers*: Hague Convention (IV) Respecting the Laws and Customs of War on Land and Its Annex: Regulations Concerning the Laws and Customs of War on Land, October 18, 1907, 1 Bevans 631.

91   *command responsibility*: "Trial of War Criminals by Military Commission, Shanghai China," February 1946, pp. 17–19, Box 12, China War Crimes Files.

92   *older military cases*: General Order No. 264, Headquarters, Division of the Philippines, September 9, 1901, General Orders of the U.S. Commander in the Philippines, Records of United States Army Overseas Operations and Commands, 1898–1942, Record Group 395, National Archives, College Park.

92   *smacked of victor's justice*: A. Frank Reel, "Even his Enemy," *Ohio State Bar Association Report* 19, no. 10 (1946), 166–68; In re Yamashita, 327 U.S. 1, 35–40 (1946) (Murphy, J., dissenting). ("The only conclusion I can draw is that the charge made against the petitioner is clearly without precedent in international law or in the annals of recorded military history. This is not to say that enemy commanders may escape punishment for clear and unlawful failures to prevent atrocities. But that punishment should be based upon charges fairly drawn in light of established rules of international law and recognized concepts of justice.")

92   *not a rule*: John H. Hendren to Joseph Keenan, April 16, 1946, Box 1, Joseph Berry Keenan Papers 1942–1947, Harvard Law School Library; Ryan, *Yamashita's Ghost*, 319–24.

92   *"It is absurd"*: United States v. Tomoyuki Yamashita, Trial Transcript, p. 4061, Boxes 127–143, War Crimes Branch, General Administrative Records, Records of the

Office of the Judge Advocate General (Army), Record Group 153, National Archives, College Park.

92   *then concluded*: *United States v. Tomoyuki Yamashita*, Trial Transcript, p. 4063, Boxes 127–143, War Crimes Branch, General Administrative Records, Records of the Office of the Judge Advocate General (Army), Record Group 153, National Archives, College Park.

92   *was unfazed*: Reel, *The Case of General Yamashita*, 147.

CHAPTER NINE

93   *It was bitter cold*: "Cold Unusual, Not in this City," *Shanghai Stars & Stripes*, January 19, 1945, 1

93   *arrest warrant*: Shiro Inoue, interview by John Hendren, January 2, 1945, p. 1, Box 40, Glines Papers.

94   *looking for people*: Alexandra J. Hindrava, interview by Robert Dwyer, November 24, 1945, Box 40, Glines Papers; Alexander John Sterelny, interview by Robert Dwyer, January 5, 1946, Box 40, Glines Papers; B. P. Yung, interview by Robert Dwyer, November 22, 1945, Box 40, Glines Papers.

94   *Alexander Hindrava*: Alexandra J. Hindrava, interview by Robert Dwyer, November 24, 1945, Box 40, Glines Papers.

94   *everyone had been happy*: Alexander John Sterelny, interview by Robert Dwyer, January 5, 1946, p. 1–2, Box 40, Glines Papers; Edwin Arthur Thompson, "Events Leading to My Detention and Incidents Occurring during this Period from 7 October, 1942 to transfer to Haiphong Road Camp on 18 January, 1943," August 31, 1945, Box 57, OSS Washington/Pacific Field Station Files.

94   *Hindrava's own experiences*: Alexandra J. Hindrava, interview by Robert Dwyer, November 24, 1945, pp. 3–4, Box 40, Glines Papers.

96   *Supreme Court issued*: *Application of Yamashita*, 326 U.S. 693 (1945).

96   *Young told reporters*: "Crimes Trial Put Off Here," *Shanghai Stars & Stripes*, December 19, 1945, 8.

96   *putting a moratorium*: Army Advisory Group, Nanking China, cable, December 27, 1945, War Crimes Files, Incoming and Outgoing Radios 21 April 1945 to 6 March 1946, Box 14, China War Crimes Files; Copy of Radio (Restricted Priority) to Wedemeyer and Terry for Action, December 27, 1945, Box 12, China War Crimes Files; Willis West to Theater Judge Advocate, General Headquarters, United States Army Forces, Pacific, Advance Echelon, Tokyo, Japan, "State Department Correspondence," December 27, 1945, Box 12, China War Crimes Files.

96   *"Japs to Face"*: "Japs to Face Brilliant Prosecutor," *North-China News*, February 21, 1946.

96   *thick dossier*: Army Advisory Group, Nanking China, cable, January 14, 1946, War Crimes Files, Incoming and Outgoing Radios 21 April 1945 to 6 March 1946, Box 14, China War Crimes Files.

96   *nothing to offer*: Shiro Inoue, interview by John Hendren, January 2, 1945, p. 1, Box 40, Glines Papers.

97   *started off well*: Shigeru Sawada, interview by John Hendren, January 2, 1945, p. 3, Box 40, Glines Papers.

99   *to Yasuo Karakawa*: Yasuo Karakawa, interview by John Hendren, January 5, 1945, pp. 3–5, Box 40, Glines Papers.

99 *to Shoshin Ito*: Shoshin Ito, interview by John Hendren, January 6–7, 1946, pp. 3–4, Bodine Papers.

99 *head its legal department*: Shoshin Ito, interview by R. N. Tait, October 28, 1946–November 18, 1946, p. 3, Box 1081, War Crimes Case Files.

99 "*Who was*": Shoshin Ito, interview by John Hendren, January 6–7, 1946, p. 3, Bodine Papers.

100 *Sadamu Shimomura*: Sadamu Shimomura, interview by Ralph Jones, May 25, 1946, p. 1, Box 1732, SCAP Legal Section Investigation Division, Investigation Reports 1945–49, Allied Occupation Records.

100 *just disbanded*: MacArthur in Japan: The Occupation: Military Phase, vol. 1 (1950; reprint, Washington, DC: U.S. Army Center for Military History, 1994), 126.

100 *taken into custody*: John Hendren to Edward H. Young, "Apprehension of Lieutenant General Sadamu Shimomura," undated, pp. 1–2, Box 12, China War Crimes Files.

100 *made his case*: John Hendren, "Trial of Japanese Responsible for the Execution of the Doolittle Fliers in Shanghai, China, October 1942—Request for authority to place on trial Lt. Gen. Shimomura," January 3, 1946, p. 2, Box 719, Intelligence Dossiers.

101 *The Kempeitai*: Imperial Ordinance No. 337, November 29, 1898, Doc. 1334 (Exhibit 3350), International Military Tribunal for the Far East, Special Collections, Columbia University Law Library; War Department Technical Manual TM-E 30-480, *Handbook on Japanese Military Forces* (War Department, 1944), 84–85; "Kempei—The Japanese Military Police," War Department, Military Intelligence Division, *Bulletin* 3, no. 10 (1945): 22–25.

101 *Swiss consul*: Report of the Swiss Consul in Shanghai, September 29, 1942, Box 89, Records of the Special War Problems Division, Subject Files, Department of State Central Files, Record Group 59, National Archives, College Park.

101 *even the Japanese*: Greg Leck, *Captives of Empire: The Japanese Internment of Allied Civilians in China (1941–1945)* ([Bangor, PA]: Shandy Press, 2007), 109.

CHAPTER TEN

102 *John Hendren stood*: "New Doolittle Arrest," *Shanghai Stars & Stripes*, January 21, 1946, 2.

103 *hometown paper*: "Hero Reunited with Family," *Ogden Standard-Examiner*, September 12, 1945.

103 *George Barr*: George Barr, interview by W. L. Brown and Chester I. Lappen, December 30, 1945, Prosecution Transcript Exhibit 21, Sawada Record.

103 "*We're all rejoicing*": "Ogdenite's Mate, Lt. C. J. Nielsen, Freed from Nips," *Ogden Standard-Examiner*, August 23, 1945, 1.

103 *everything irritating*: James M. Scott, *Target Tokyo* (New York: Norton, 2015), 463.

103 *Those feelings confused*: James Curtis Hasdorff, *United States Air Force Oral History Program: Interview of Lt. Col. Robert L. Hite* (USAF Historical Research Center, 1982), 101–2.

103 *all too common*: Craig Haney, "Mental Health Issues in Long-Term Solitary and 'Supermax' Confinement," *Crime & Delinquency* 42 (2003); Stuart Grassian, "Psychiatric Effects of Solitary Confinement," *Journal of Law & Policy* 22 (2006); Patricia B. Sutker et al., "Cognitive Deficits and Psychopathology Among Former

Prisoners of War and Combat Veterans of the Korean Conflict," *American Journal of Psychiatry* 148 (1991).

104 *religious epiphany*: C. V. Glines, *Four Came Home* (Missoula, MT: Pictorial Histories, 1995), 107–9 (firsthand account of Jacob DeShazer).

104 *studying to be a minister*: Donald Goldstein and Carol Aiko DeShazer Nixon, *Return of the Raider: A Doolittle Raider's Story of War & Forgiveness* (Lake Mary, FL: Creation House, 2010), 83–87.

104 *happy to oblige*: Army Advisory Group, Nanking China, cable, December 15, 1945, War Crimes Files, Incoming and Outgoing Radios 21 April 1945 to 6 March 1946, Box 14, China War Crimes Files.

104 *"When Washington asked"*: "Doolittle Survivors Want Japs Punished," *North-China Daily*, January 19, 1946, 1.

104 *newest celebrity*: "Doolittle Raider Returns," *Shanghai Stars & Stripes*, January 19, 1946, 1.

104 *an army town*: John Hersey, "Letter from Shanghai," *New Yorker*, January 24, 1946, 82.

104 *locals dressed*: "Yank about China," *Shanghai Stars & Stripes*, December 13, 1945, 4.

105 *Hendren naturally*: "Doolittle Survivor Tells Tale," *China Press*, January 19, 1945, 2.

105 *The Foreign Correspondents' Club*: Peter Hibbard, *The Bund Shanghai* (Hong Kong: Airphoto International, 2007), 271.

105 *southwestern accent*: "Doolittle Raider Returns," *Shanghai Stars & Stripes*, January 19, 1946, 1.

105 *natural storyteller*: "Doolittle Survivor Tells Tale," *China Press*, January 19, 1945, 2.

105 *Walter Reed General Hospital*: Chase Nielsen, interview by Stacey Grayson, September 7, 1945, Box 40, Glines Papers.

105 *Nielsen remembered*: Edward Young, Memorandum, "Treatment of Captured Doolittle Fliers, Tokyo Raid, 18 April 1942," August 27, 1945, pp. 2–3, Box 3, China War Crimes Files.

105 *international celebrity*: Ted Lawson, *Thirty Seconds Over Tokyo* (New York: Penguin, 1943).

105 *Lawson wrote*: Ted Lawson, "Thirty Seconds Over Tokyo," *Colliers*, May 22, 1943, pp. 11–15 et seq.

105 *dedicated to*: Lawson, *Thirty Seconds Over Tokyo*, dedication.

106 *"most stirring story"*: W. I. White, "First Blow at Japan's Heart; A Pilot's Own Story of His Part in the Doolittle Raid on Tokyo," *New York Times Book Review*, July 11, 1943, 1.

106 *MGM released*: *Thirty Seconds Over Tokyo* (Metro-Goldwin-Mayer 1944).

106 *rave reviews*: Bosley Crowther, "'Thirty Seconds Over Tokyo,' a Faithful Mirror of Capt. Ted Lawson's Book, With Van Johnson, Tracy, at Capitol," *New York Times*, November 16, 1944, 19.

106 *write his own story*: Chase Nielsen, Robert Hite, and Jacob DeShazer, "Saga of Living Death," Series II, Box 5, Doolittle Raiders Papers.

106 *Waterboarding*: Sensational stories were printed throughout the war and post-war period emphasizing Japan's use of waterboarding. See Selwyn Pepper, "Accuser Quotes Jap General on Killing Filipinos," *St. Louis Post-Dispatch*, November 4, 1945, 12; "Unpredictable Japs Are Friendly at Times, then Brutal, says Former Luzon Prisoner," *Press & Sun-Bulletin*, May 17, 1945, 5; "Transport Brings 4145 Here; Women Recount Jap Brutality," *News-Pilot*, May 3, 1945, 1; "Ex-Prisoners

Review Horrors of Canbanatuan," *Oakland Tribune*, 13; "Doctors Learn of Japs' 'Water Cure,'" United Press, May 9, 1944; "Water 'Cure' Given by Japs," Associated Press, February 2, 1944; "Gripsholm Passenger Calls Japs 'Beasts' During Visit Here," *Lake Geneva Regional News*, September 24, 1942; W. L. Clark, "As We See It," *Windsor Star*, September 11, 1942, 2; "Grew Reveals Jap Barbarities,'" Associated Press, August 31, 1942; Neal O'Hara, syndicated column, McNaught Syndicate, August 6, 1942; Edwin Koons, "Life as a Jap Prisoner," Associated Press, July 25, 1942; Relman Morin, "Here's How the Japs Gave the 'Water Cure' to U.S. Missionary," Associated Press, July 23, 1942. Waterboarding quickly entered the cultural vocabulary as something of a morbid joke. War bonds advertisements at the end of the war quipped, "The boys coming back from Europe and Okinawa probably won't lope up to you breathlessly and dangle a medal around your neck for buying War Bonds, but you can bet your bottom Jap yen they won't give you the water cure either." Fred Allen, "How Smart People and Jack Benny Latch on to their Money," syndicated war bonds advertisement (1945). There were numerous syndicated cartoons that used waterboarding as a punch line. See, e.g., "The Water Cure," *Oaky Doaks* (May 1945); "The Water Cure for 'Tigger Tim,'" *Room and Board* (September 1944); "The Water Cure," *Little Orphan Annie* (July 1944); Monte Barret and Russell Ross, "The Water Cure," *Jane Arden* (July 1943); Chic Young, "Water Cure for a Drip!" *Blondie* (June 1943); Roy Crane, "The Wrong Answers," *Wash Tubbs* (October 1942). Purveyors of folk medicine even began to claim that it may have some perverse therapeutic value. See, e.g., Ralph Morton, "Water Cure Cures," Associated Press, July 6, 1945; "Barret Plans Some Use of 'Water Cure,'" *Daily Press*, November 26, 1943.

106 *demonstrated at public*: Robert T. Bellaire, "1,451 Jap Gripsholm Rails, Sing 'America' as Ship Docks," United Press, August 26, 1942.

106 *Nielsen recounted*: Chase Nielsen, Robert Hite, and Jacob DeShazer, "Saga of Living Death," p. 9, Series II, Box 5, Doolittle Raiders Papers.

107 *"Well, well, well"*: Chase Nielsen, Robert Hite, and Jacob DeShazer, "Saga of Living Death," pp. 13–15, Series II, Box 5, Doolittle Raiders Papers.

107 *paid $2,250*: Charles Hoyt Watson, *DeShazer: The Doolittle Raider Turned Missionary* (Winona Lake, IN: Light & Life 1952), 130.

107 *No book deal*: Chase Nielsen to C. V. Glines, June 4, 1962, Series II, Box 5, Doolittle Raiders Papers.

107 *Nielsen's every word*: "Doolittle Raider Returns," *Shanghai Stars & Stripes*, January 19, 1946, 1.

107 *"We bombed military"*: "New Doolittle Arrest," *Shanghai Stars & Stripes*, January 21, 1946, 2.

107 *had unsuccessfuly lobbied*: William H. Newton to Public Relations Officer, undated, Box 12, China War Crimes Files.

107 *Now Hendren invited*: "Jap Warden Faces Man He Guarded," *China Press*, January 20, 1946, 3.

107 *the best Japanese*: George K. T. Wang, "Captain Who Led Firing Squad Talks," *Shanghai Herald*, January 19, 1946, 1.

108 *Another asked Tatsuta*: "Capt. Sotojiro Tatsuta Bows to Capt. Chase J. Nielsen (Photo)," Associated Press, January 1946.

108 *Asked if he recognized*: Jane Cochran, "Flier Finds His Vengeance Complete After Four years," International News Service, January 31, 1946.

108 *"poked his face"*: "The Japanese Version of How They Avenged the Doolittle Attack on Tokyo," *New York Times*, January 30, 1946, 3.

108 *"You are dying"*: "New Doolittle Arrest," *Shanghai Stars & Stripes*, January 21, 1946, 2.

108 New York Times: "The Japanese Version of How They Avenged the Doolittle Attack on Tokyo," *New York Times*, January 30, 1946, 3.

108 *The following Saturday*: Sotojiro Tatsuta, interview by Robert Dwyer, January 26, 1946, Bodine Papers.

108 *Nielsen was adamant*: Chase Nielsen, interview by Stacey Grayson, September 7, 1945, p. 1, Box 40, Glines Papers.

109 *Tatsuta explained away*: Sotojiro Tatsuta, interview by Robert Dwyer, November 16, 1945, p. 5, Bodine Papers.

109 *"When was it"*: Sotojiro Tatsuta, interview by Robert Dwyer, January 26, 1946, p. 1, Bodine Papers.

111 *They had admitted*: Edward Young, Memorandum, "Treatment of Captured Doolittle Fliers, Tokyo Raid, 18 April 1942," August 27, 1945, p. 5, Box 3, China War Crimes Files.

112 *Noboru Unit judgment*: 登第七三三〇部隊軍律会議, 判決文, 昭和17年8月28日, BC級(アメリカ裁判関係)上海裁判・第4号事件 [Noboru 7330 Unit Military Commission, Judgment, August 28, 1942, BC Class (Regarding American Trials) Shanghai Trial—Case No. 4], National Archives of Japan.

113 *promulgated until*: 支那派遣軍軍令第4号・敵航空機搭乗員処罰ニ関スル軍律, 昭和17年8月13日, BC級(アメリカ裁判関係)上海裁判・第4号事件 [China Expeditionary Army Military Code No. 4—Military Code on the Punishment of Enemy Air Crews, August 13, 1942, BC Class (Regarding American Trials) Shanghai Trial—Case No. 4], National Archives of Japan.

113 *every civilized legal system*: For a history of the ex post facto concept that was current at the time, see Jerome Hall, "Nulla Poena Sine Lege," *Yale Law Journal* 47, no. 2 (1937): 165–93.

113 *Japanese criminal code*: Penal Code, Act. No. 45 of 1907, article 6, trans. J. E. de Becker, *The Criminal Code of Japan* (Kelly & Walsh, 1907).

114 *framing innocent people*: For then-contemporary sources on the law governing wrongful prosecution, see Francis B. Sayre, "Criminal Conspiracy," *Harvard Law Review* 35 (1922): 393–427; Percy Henry Winfield, *The History of Conspiracy and Abuse of Legal Procedure* (Cambridge: Cambridge University Press, 1921); James Wallace Bryan, *The Development of the English Law of Conspiracy* (Baltimore: Johns Hopkins University Press, 1909).

114 *allowed people to sue*: See, e.g., *Sharpe v. Johnston*, 76 Mo. 660 (1882).

114 *Hata was already*: Sawada Trial Transcript, 190–91 (Testimony of John Hendren).

114 *Hendren had interviewed*: Yusei Wako, interview by John Hendren, January 2, 1945, Box 40, Glines Papers.

114 *detainee in Sugamo*: Yusei Wako, interview by Robert Tait, August 25, 1947–September 5, 1947, p. 1, Box 1081, War Crimes Case Files.

114 *"Did you get"*: Yusei Wako, interview by John Hendren, January 2, 1945, p. 2, Box 40, Glines Papers.

115 *Alexander Hindrava*: Alexandra J. Hindrava, interview by Robert Dwyer, November 24, 1945, p. 4, Box 40, Glines Papers.

115 *same thing had happened*: Caesar Luis DosRemedios, Statement, September 19, 1945, p. 1, Prosecution Exhibit 26, Sawada Record.

115 *Dwyer's quick temper*: 神代護忠，上海支店時代の思い出 (1994年 [Moritada Kumashiro, "Recollection of the Days at Shanghai Branch," Manuscript (1994)], p. 227, Call No. GK77-G2, National Diet Library (describing Dwyer's temper when discussing the Raiders' trial during his closing argument).

115 *SCAP had searched*: John Hendren to Theater Judge Advocate, USF CT, Shanghai, China, "Prosecution of War Criminals in the Case of the Death of Lt Glover Farrell, 2d Lt Dean A. Hallmark, and Sgt Harold A. Spatz, Doolittle Fliers, Executed about 15 October 1942," November 9, 1945, Box 12, China War Crimes Files.

115 *no one by the name*: Army Advisory Group, Nanking China, Cable, January 20, 1946, War Crimes Files, Incoming and Outgoing Radios 21 April 1945 to 6 March 1946, Box 14, China War Crimes Files.

115 *"The Japanese population"*: *MacArthur in Japan: The Occupation: Military Phase*, vol. 1 (1950; reprint, Washington, DC: U.S. Army Center for Military History, 1994), 170.

115 *hiding in plain sight*: The large Japanese population and Shanghai gave many war crimes suspects easy cover. At the end of November, Army investigators had arrested Tohoru Miki in Shanghai. Miki had been a notorious torturer, responsible for as many as two hundred American dead. His record of service in the Japanese Army read like an itinerary through some of the most notorious sites of Japanese brutality: the Bataan Death March, the Hoten Prison Camp. Investigators scoured Korea, China, and Japan for him over the course of four months. Then, it turned out, he was just living a quiet life in Japan Town. He had moved there in 1944 with his wife to take up a job after being discharged from the Army. "Japanese Torture Suspect Tabbed," Associated Press, November 30, 1945; Review of the Record of Trial by a Military Commission of Miki Toru, First Lieutenant (now Captain), Imperial Japanese Army, May 15, 1946, China War Crimes Files.

CHAPTER ELEVEN

116 *Frustrated by SCAP*: Robert Dwyer, "Report of Incident Concerning Apprehension of Capt. Okada Ryuhei," January 25, 1946, p. 1, Box 11, China War Crimes Files.

116 *enlisted the Japanese*: Office of Strategic Services, "Retention of Japanese Technicians," February 12, 1946, Box 44, Shanghai Intelligence Files, Entry #182, Records of the Office of Strategic Services, Record Group 226, National Archives, College Park; *MacArthur in Japan*, 191 (commenting on Chiang Kai-shek's retention of 70,000 Japanese "technicians" well into 1947); Donald G. Gillin and Charles Etter, "Staying On: Japanese Soldiers and Civilians in China, 1945–1949," *Journal of Asian Studies* 42, no. 3 (1983): 497–518. Chinese Communist newspapers frequently highlighted the fact that Chiang Kai-Shek's army was heavily populated by "Japanese occupation troops." Office of Strategic Services, "Translation of Chinese Communist Newspaper," January 12, 1946, Box 44, Shanghai Intelligence Files, Entry #182, Records of the Office of Strategic Services, Record Group 226, National Archives, College Park; Office of Strategic Services, "Translation of Chinese Communist Newspaper," January 21, 1946, Box 44, Shanghai Intelligence Files, Entry #182, Records of the Office of Strategic Services, Record Group 226, National Archives, College Park.

116   *Like every other American*: Telegram from the Secretary of State to the Embassy in China (February 7, 1946) in *Foreign Relations of the United States, 1946,* vol. 10, *The Far East: China,* ed. Ralph Goodwin et al. (Washington, DC: U.S. Government Printing Office, 1972), Doc. 605 ("retention [of] Japs including 'technicians' in China [is] highly undesirable and [is] inconsistent with US policy of elimination Jap influence from China").

116   *Dwyer found it*: Robert Dwyer, "Report of Incident Concerning Apprehension of Capt. Okada Ryuhei," January 25, 1946, p. 1, Box 11, China War Crimes Files.

116   *Dwyer's feelings of unease*: Robert Dwyer, "Report of Incident Concerning Apprehension of Capt. Okada Ryuhei," January 25, 1946, p. 1, Box 11, China War Crimes Files.

117   *Dwyer rushed to catch*: Robert Dwyer, "Report of Incident Concerning Apprehension of Capt. Okada Ryuhei," January 25, 1946, p. 1, Box 11, China War Crimes Files.

118   *Chiang Kai-shek was touchy*: Edward Young, "Arrest of Jap Suspects," undated, Box 11, China War Crimes Files.

118   *Wu had left*: Robert Dwyer, "Report of Incident Concerning Apprehension of Capt. Okada Ryuhei," January 25, 1946, p. 1, Box 11, China War Crimes Files.

118   *knew what a pain*: Edward Young to Jeremiah O'Connor, "War Crimes," May 1, 1946, Box 12, China War Crimes Files.

118   *deliberately avoided*: Edward Young, "Arrest of Jap Suspects," undated, Box 11, China War Crimes Files.

118   *Dwyer therefore decided*: Robert Dwyer, "Report of Incident Concerning Apprehension of Capt. Okada Ryuhei," January 25, 1946, p. 1, Box 11, China War Crimes Files.

118   *It was well past dark*: Robert Dwyer, "Report of Incident Concerning Apprehension of Capt. Okada Ryuhei," January 25, 1946, pp. 2–3, Box 11, China War Crimes Files.

119   "*He only recognizes*": Robert Dwyer, "Report of Incident Concerning Apprehension of Capt. Okada Ryuhei," January 25, 1946, pp. 2, Box 11, China War Crimes Files. ("He only recognized the authority of the Chinese.")

121   *kept at him*: Robert Dwyer, "Report of Incident Concerning Apprehension of Capt. Okada Ryuhei," January 25, 1946, p. 3, Box 11, China War Crimes Files.

121   *One of the first questions*: Ryuhei Okada, interview by Robert Dwyer, January 24, 1946, p. 1, Bodine Files.

122   *was increasingly worried*: 神代護忠, 上海支店時代の思い出 (1994年) [Moritada Kumashiro, "Recollection of the Days at Shanghai Branch," Manuscript (1994)], pp. 113–14, Call No. GK77-G2, National Diet Library.

122   *Japanese interrogation manuals*: Allied Translator and Interpreter Section, "Japanese Methods of Prisoner of War Interrogation," Research Report No. 134, June 1, 1946, p. 3, Box 1624, Records of the SCAP Legal Section, Administrative Division, Entry 1237, Allied Occupation Records.

122   *A secret memorandum*: "Fundamental Rules for Interrogating War Prisoners, Operation Officer's Guide (Part I)," June 14, 1945, *Materials on the Trial of Former Servicemen of the Japanese Army Charged with Manufacturing and Employing Bacteriological Weapons* (Moscow: Foreign Languages Publishing House, 1950), 173–74.

123   *reformed its legal system*: Par Kristoffer Cassel, *Grounds of Judgment: Extraterritoriality*

and *Imperial Power in Nineteenth-Century China and Japan* (Oxford: Oxford University Press, 2012), 150.

123 *torture was routine*: Paul Heng-Chao Ch'en, *The Formation of the Early Meiji Legal Order: The Japanese Code of 1871 and Its Chinese Foundation* (Oxford: Oxford University Press, 1981), 64–71; Harou Abe, "Self-Incrimination—Japan and the United States," *Journal of Criminal Law, Criminology and Political Science* 46, no. 5 (1956): 613–31.

123 *abolished all state-sanctioned torture*: Reforms to the laws of torture in Japan, beginning in the early 1870s, were incremental. First, torture was prohibited against women who were either pregnant or had recently given birth. Then, torture was forbidden against the clergy, the elderly, and the disabled. Then, the means of torture were regulated. The infamous "abacus board," a striated wooden plank on which a prisoner was forced to kneel as large stone weights were placed upon his thighs, became only permissible for serious crimes or as a last resort when a simple beating with an "interrogation stick" proved insufficient. A perverse consequence of these early regulations was to actually increase the use of torture. So long as an interrogator stayed within the bounds of the law, he was free to do as he would. The limits imposed by regulation, in other words, became a clear line that could be gone up to with impunity. But as the decade progressed, elite opinion grew to oppose the use of torture categorically. In 1874, the liberal Japanese legal scholar Mamichi Tsuda wrote a series of celebrated essays on the abolition of torture in which he leveraged the popular desire to end the "unequal treaties." "If we do not abolish torture," he wrote "we cannot eventually ride forth side by side with the various countries of Europe and America. If we do not abolish torture, we cannot conclude equal treaties with them. If we do not abolish torture, we cannot place under our laws the Europeans and Americans settled in our country." Likewise, the French legal scholar Gustave Émile Boissonade de Fontarabie, whom Japan's new government had hired as an advisor to modernize Japan's legal system, publicly argued that torture was a barbaric practice that was contrary to the modernity Japan was seeking, to the presumption of innocence, to human dignity, and to obtaining reliable evidence. In 1876, Japan's new parliament repealed the requirement that criminals confess and further limited the use of torture by requiring a warrant from a judge and express prior authorization from the Ministry of Justice. The effect of this law was immediate and dramatic. Between 1877 and 1879, no applications for torture warrants were sought. This of course did not mean that torture was not still being used behind closed doors. But the taboo had been established leading to the full abolition in the following years. For a detailed discussion of the abolition of torture in Japan, see Paul Heng-Chao Ch'en, *The Formation of the Early Meiji Legal Order: The Japanese Code of 1871 and Its Chinese Foundation* (Oxford: Oxford University Press, 1981); Par Kristoffer Cassel, *Grounds of Judgment: Extraterritoriality and Imperial Power in Nineteenth-Century China and Japan* (Oxford: Oxford University Press, 2012); Haruo Abe, "Criminal Justice in Japan: Its Historical Background and Modern Problems," *American Bar Association Journal* 47, no. 6 (1961): 555–59; Harou Abe, "Self-Incrimination—Japan and the United States," *Journal of Criminal Law, Criminology and Political Science* 46, no. 5 (1956): 613–31.

123 *conventional wisdom*: Sidney Mashbir, Allied Translator and Interpreter Section, South West Pacific Area, "Research Report No. 72: Japanese Violations of the Laws of War," April 29, 1944, pp. 89–96, Box 10, China War Crimes Files.

CHAPTER TWELVE

125 *getting into Tokyo*: Robert Dwyer to Edward H. Young, "Report of Mission to Tokyo for Apprehension of Licutenant General Sadamu Shimomura," undated, p. 2, Box 12, China War Crimes Files.

125 *Hendren had submitted*: John Hendren to Edward H. Young, "Apprehension of Lieutenant General Sadamu Shimomura," undated, pp. 2–3, Box 12, China War Crimes Files.

125 *fired off a cable*: Cable CG China to CINCAFPAC, January 11, 1946, Box 719, Intelligence Dossiers.

125 *sent its response*: Army Advisory Group, Nanking China, Incoming Cable, January 20, 1946, War Crimes Files, Incoming and Outgoing Radios 21 April 1945 to 6 March 1946, Box 14, China War Crimes Files.

126 *another cable arrived*: Cable from CINCAFPAC ADV to CG China, January 22, 1946, War Crimes Files, Incoming and Outgoing Radios 21 April 1945 to 6 March 1946, Box 14, China War Crimes Files.

126 *shot back a cable*: Army Advisory Group, Nanking China, Outgoing Cable, January 22, 1946, War Crimes Files, Incoming and Outgoing Radios 21 April 1945 to 6 March 1946, Box 14, China War Crimes Files.

126 *"It is impracticable"*: Cable from CINCAFPAC ADV to CG China, January 16, 1946, Box 719, Intelligence Dossiers. This is a carbon copy of the cable that is on file and may be a draft. The carbon copy is dated January 16, 1946. However, in a contemporaneous memorandum, John Hendren claims that this cable was not received until January 26, 1946. John Hendren to Edward H. Young, "Apprehension of Lieutenant General Sadamu Shimomura," undated, p. 2, Box 12, China War Crimes Files. There are no other cables on that date that fit his description. There therefore may have been a delay both in the sending and receiving of this cable.

126 *took the cable*: John Hendren to Edward H. Young, "Apprehension of Lieutenant General Sadamu Shimomura," undated, p. 3, Box 12, China War Crimes Files.

127 *Dwyer got to work*: Robert Dwyer to Edward H. Young, "Report of Mission to Tokyo for Apprehension of Lieutenant General Sadamu Shimomura," undated, p. 2, Box 12, China War Crimes Files.

129 *absolving the emperor*: John Dower, *Embracing Defeat: Japan in the Wake of World War II* (New York: Norton, 1999), 324.

129 *Priorities were shifting*: Robert Dwyer to Edward H. Young, "Report of Mission to Tokyo for Apprehension of Lieutenant General Sadamu Shimomura," undated, p. 3, Box 12, China War Crimes Files.

129 *personal praise of MacArthur*: Douglas MacArthur, "Demobilization of Japanese Armed Forces," October 16, 1945, *Political Reorientation of Japan, September 1945 to September 1948: Report*, vol. 2 (G.P.O, 1949), Appx. F, 7.

129 *"flat conflict of interest"*: Robert Dwyer to Edward H. Young, "Report of Mission to Tokyo for Apprehension of Lieutenant General Sadamu Shimomura," undated, p. 3, Box 12, China War Crimes Files ("raised a flat conflict of interest between war crimes and occupation").

129 *formal memorandum*: Robert Dwyer to Edward H. Young, "Report of Mission to Tokyo for Apprehension of Lieutenant General Sadamu Shimomura," undated, pp. 3–4, Box 12, China War Crimes Files.

129 *Dwyer explained*: Robert Dwyer to Chief of Staff, General Headquarters, Supreme

Commander for the Allied Powers, APO 500, "Apprehension of Lt. Gen. Shimomura," January 31, 1946, Box 12, China War Crimes Files.

130 *He then told Dwyer*: Robert Dwyer to Edward H. Young, "Report of Mission to Tokyo for Apprehension of Lieutenant General Sadamu Shimomura," undated, pp. 3–4, Box 12, China War Crimes Files.

130 *he pointed out*: Robert Dwyer to Edward H. Young, "Report of Mission to Tokyo for Apprehension of Lieutenant General Sadamu Shimomura," undated, p. 6, Box 12, China War Crimes Files. ("When dealing with important Japanese, it was not good policy to accept their services in the occupation program and then proceed to hang them for war crimes.")

130 *Was it true*: Robert Dwyer to Edward H. Young, "Report of Mission to Tokyo for Apprehension of Lieutenant General Sadamu Shimomura," undated, p. 5, Box 12, China War Crimes Files.

131 *That night*: Robert Dwyer to Edward H. Young, "Report of Mission to Tokyo for Apprehension of Lieutenant General Sadamu Shimomura," undated, p. 6, Box 12, China War Crimes Files.

131 *result of a dispute*: Yuma Totani, *The Tokyo War Crimes Trial: The Pursuit of Justice in the Wake of World War II* (Cambridge, MA: Harvard University Press, 2008), 18, 29.

131 *put Keenan in charge*: "MacArthur Loses: Special Trial Awaits," United Press, March 25, 1945; "Recommended Tojo Trial Oct 7," Associated Press, November 25, 1945.

131 *Keenan was*: Totani, *The Tokyo War Crimes Trial*, 34.

131 *These war crimes*: Neil Boister and Robert Cryer, *The Tokyo International Tribunal: A Reappraisal* (Oxford: Oxford University Press, 2008), 272.

131 *brought in*: "Keenan's Crack FBI Man Prefers Nips to Mobsters," United Press, February 28, 1946.

132 *appreciate the pressures*: Totani, *The Tokyo War Crimes Trial*, 18, 29.

132 *headed back*: Robert Dwyer to Edward H. Young, "Report of Mission to Tokyo for Apprehension of Lieutenant General Sadamu Shimomura," undated, p. 6, Box 12, China War Crimes Files.

132 *Young called Hendren*: John Hendren to Edward H. Young, "Apprehension of Lieutenant General Sadamu Shimomura," undated, p. 3, Box 12, China War Crimes Files.

133 *Hata had died*: Army Advisory Group, Nanking China, cable, January 29, 1946, War Crimes Files, Incoming and Outgoing Radios 21 April 1945 to 6 March 1946, Box 14, China War Crimes Files.

133 *forgotten to mention*: Harold Fair, Death of Major Itsuro Hata, wanted in connection with execution of Doolittle Flyers, February 8, 1946, Box 11, China War Crimes Files.

133 *cable lamented*: Army Advisory Group, Nanking China, cable, January 31, 1946, War Crimes Files, Incoming and Outgoing Radios 21 April 1945 to 6 March 1946, Box 14, China War Crimes Files.

133 *Hendren protested*: John Hendren to Edward H. Young, "Apprehension of Lieutenant General Sadamu Shimomura," undated, p. 2, Box 12, China War Crimes Files.

133 *regular flights*: Robert Dwyer to Edward H. Young, "Report of Mission to Tokyo for Apprehension of Lieutenant General Sadamu Shimomura," undated, p. 4, Box 12, China War Crimes Files.

134 *photographers snapped*: Robert Dwyer returning to Shanghai's Ward Road Jail from Tokyo, 1946, Bodine Files.

134 *stories that ran*: "2 Defendants Die Before Atrocity Trial," *China Press*, February 5, 1946, 6.

134 *story headlined*: "Arrest of Shimomura Is Ordered," *Shanghai Herald*, February 7, 1946, 1.

134 *issued orders*: John B. Cooley, "Release of Shimomura Sadamu from Internment," February 12, 1947, Box 719, Intelligence Dossiers.

134 *issued its decision*: In re Yamashita, 327 U.S. 1 (1946).

135 *softer light*: Allan A. Ryan, *Yamashita's Ghost: War Crimes, MacArthur's Justice, and Command Accountability* (Lawrence, KS: University Press of Kansas, 2012), 9.

135 *any less politicized*: Richard Lael, *The Yamashita Precedent: War Crimes & Command Responsibility* (Wilmington, DE: Rowman & Littlefield, 1982), 89.

135 *confront Shigeru Sawada*: Sawada Shigeru, interview by Robert Dwyer, February 12, 1946, Bodine Papers.

135 *"As the prosecutor"*: 沢田茂(供述), 井上忠男(調査), 昭和38年9月20日, 井上忠男戦争裁判資料 [Shigeru Sawada, interview by Tadao Inoue, September 20, 1963, p. 7, Tadao Inoue War Tribunal File], Yasukuni Archives.

135 *asked him flat out*: Sawada Shigeru, interview by Robert Dwyer, February 12, 1946, p. 1, Bodine Papers.

136 *Sotojiro Tatsuta*: Yusei Wako, interview by Robert Dwyer, February 12, 1946, Bodine Files.

136 *the honor went*: Sotojiro Tatsuta, interview by Robert Dwyer, February 12, 1946, Bodine Files; *United States v. Shigeru Sawada*, Charge and Specifications, February 1, 1946, Sawada Record.

137 *promotion to major*: "Robert T. Dwyer Named as Major," *Rochester Democrat & Chronicle*, February 12, 1946, 15.

CHAPTER THIRTEEN

141 *Snigursky went by*: Marriage Record, Edmund Bodine and Elizaveta Sadovsky, undated, Bodine Papers.

141 *She had been born*: E. W. Sutherland, Permission to Marry, February 26, 1946, Bodine Papers.

141 *To the erotically*: Natalie Bodine, personal interview, December 17, 2014; Miscellaneous Love Notes, undated, Bodine Papers.

141 *Elizaveta had put*: Natalie and Elizabeth Bodine, personal interview, December 17, 2014.

141 *The Americans were*: Natalie Bodine, personal interview, December 17, 2014.

142 *She wanted a man*: Natalie and Elizabeth Bodine, personal interview, December 17, 2014.

142 *accepted a dance*: U.S. Army, Report of Proceedings of Board of Inquiry in the Case of Lt Col Edmund Bodine, 3481A, USAF, 23–24 February 1954, p. 113 (Testimony of Edmund Bodine), Bodine Papers.

142 *it was no surprise*: Edmund Bodine, "Personal History Statement," July 25, 1946, p. 4, Exhibit 5, U.S. Army, Report of Proceedings of Board of Inquiry in the Case of Lt Col Edmund Bodine, 3481A, USAF, 23–24 February 1954, Bodine Papers.

142 *He was known*: John Davey, *Rivers of Consciousness: 1913–1978*, vol. 1, *The Lives*

and Times of Edward D. Cuffe, Gentleman (Jayde Design, 2013), 213; Alma Bodine to Edmund Bodine, August 2, 1946, Bodine Papers.

142   *Bodine was a redhead*: Natalie and Elizabeth Bodine, personal interview, December 17, 2014.

143   *she had gone out*: U.S. Army, Report of Proceedings of Board of Inquiry in the Case of Lt Col Edmund Bodine, 3481A, USAF, 23–24 February 1954, p. 66 (Testimony of Cullen Brannon), Bodine Papers.

143   *But then the questions*: Natalie and Elizabeth Bodine, personal interview, December 17, 2014.

143   *Elizaveta normally*: Natalie Bodine, personal correspondence, July 7, 2016.

144   *Bodine's father*: Natalie and Elizabeth Bodine, personal interview, December 18, 2014.

144   *"Time on My Hands"*: Vincent Youmans, Harold Adamson, and Mack Gordon, "Time on My Hands" (1930).

144   *As they danced*: Natalie and Elizabeth Bodine, personal interview, December 17, 2014.

145   *Bodine enjoyed*: Broadway Mansions Christmas Menu, December 25, 1945, Bodine Papers.

145   *He had been deployed*: Individual Flight Record: Edmund Bodine, U.S. Army, Official Military Personnel Files (OMPF), National Personnel Records Center, National Archives at St. Louis; Aubry Moore, Report, August 27, 1945, Records of the 68th Composite Wing, Air Force Historical Research Agency; Edmund Bodine, "Application for Commission in the Regular Army," January 25, 1946, p. 2, Exhibit 5, U.S. Army, Report of Proceedings of Board of Inquiry in the Case of Lt Col Edmund Bodine, 3481A, USAF, 23–24 February 1954, Bodine Papers.

145   *a gambling habit*: Natalie Bodine, personal interview, December 17, 2014.

145   *Xavier*: *Xavier* 12, no. 4 (January 1933), Xavier High School Archives, New York, NY.

146   *Georgetown*: Edmund J. Bodine, Georgetown University Transcript, June 6, 1937, Bodine Papers.

146   *various jobs*: Edmund Bodine, "Personal History Statement," July 25, 1946, p. 4, Exhibit 5, U.S. Army, Report of Proceedings of Board of Inquiry in the Case of Lt Col Edmund Bodine, 3481A, USAF, 23–24 February 1954, Bodine Papers.

146   *At twenty-seven*: AR 615-160 § 13.01, July 20, 1938; Bruce Ashcroft, "We Wanted Wings: A History of the Aviation Cadet Program" (HQ AETC Office of History and Research, 2005), 16.

146   *still eligible*: Edmund Bodine, "Application for Commission in the Regular Army," January 25, 1946, p. 2, Exhibit 5, U.S. Army, Report of Proceedings of Board of Inquiry in the Case of Lt Col Edmund Bodine, 3481A, USAF, 23–24 February 1954, Bodine Papers.

146   *widely called*: Terry M. Love, *L-Birds: American Combat Liaison Aircraft of World War II* (New Brighton, MN: Flying Books International, 2001), 36.

146   *L-Birds had*: Love, *L-Birds*, 34.

146   *L-Birds were deployed*: Jim Gray, "USAAF Liaison Squardons of WWII," *L-5 Newsletter*, no. 25 (2014): 5–12; William T. Y'Blood, "Any Place, Any Time, Anywhere: The 1st Air Commando Group in World War II," *Air Power History* 48, no. 2 (2001): 4–15; Love, *L-Birds*, 67–71.

146   *It weighed*: War Department, Technical Manual, TM 9-206, "Browning Machine Gun, Cal. .30, M1919A6," September 1, 1943, 4.

146   *bounced around*: Joseph Stilwell to Adjutant General, War Department, cable, May 23, 1942, Box 158, Henry Harley Arnold Papers, 1903–1989, Library of Congress.

146   *was innaccurate*: Charles Greening, "The First Joint Action," December 21, 1948, pp. 3–4, Box 37, Glines Papers.

146   *phased it out*: Gordon L. Rottman, *Browning .30-Caliber Machine Guns* (Oxford: Osprey, 2014), 31.

146   *steel beasts*: War Department, Technical Manual, TM 9-227, "20-MM Automatic Gun M1 and 20-MM Aircraft Automatic Gun AN-M2," June 1, 1943, 7.

146   *maximum load*: T.O. No. 01-135DA-1, Pilots Flight Operating Instructions, Army Model L-2, L-2A, L-2B, and L-2M Airplanes, January 20, 1944, p. 5; "Stinson L-5 Sentinel," March Field Air Museum, http://www.marchfield.org/l5.htm.

146   *"air commandos"*: Love, *L-Birds*, 67.

147   *distinguished himself*: Edmund Bodine, Officer Military Record, undated, Bodine Papers; Edmund Bodine, Officer's, Warrant Officer's and Flight Officer's Qualification Record, undated, Bodine Papers; Edmund Bodine, "Efficiency Report," July 25, 1945, Exhibit 3, U.S. Army, Report of Proceedings of Board of Inquiry in the Case of Lt Col Edmund Bodine, 3481A, USAF, 23–24 February 1954, Bodine Papers.

147   *As a major*: James Gray, Personal Correspondence, February 28, 2019.

147   *choice assignments*: Edmund Bodine, Flight Log, Bodine Papers; Individual Flight Record: Edmund Bodine, U.S. Army, Official Military Personnel Files (OMPF), National Personnel Records Center, National Archives at St. Louis; Aubry Moore, Report, August 27, 1945, Records of the 68th Composite Wing, Air Force Historical Research Agency; Edmund Bodine, Officer Military Record, undated, Bodine Papers.

147   *into the Plans Office*: Edmund Bodine, "Application for Commission in the Regular Army," January 25, 1946, p. 2, Exhibit 4, U.S. Army, Report of Proceedings of Board of Inquiry in the Case of Lt Col Edmund Bodine, 3481A, USAF, 23–24 February 1954, Bodine Papers.

147   *The only flying*: Edmund Bodine, Flight Log, Bodine Papers.

147   *Hundreds of men*: Alfred Emile Cornebise, *The Shanghai Stars and Stripes: Witness to the Transition to Peace, 1945–1946* (Jefferson, NC: MacFarland, 2010), 80–94.

147   *a long-wished-for return*: In January 1946, American soldiers in Shanghai (and across the world) demonstrated to pressure the government to hasten their demobilization. John C. Sparrow, *History of Personnel Demobilization in the United States Army*, Department of the Army Pamphlet No. 20-210 (Department of the Army, 1952), 163–69.

147   *"Young needed people"*: Edward Young to the Judge Advocate General, Washington, D.C., Memorandum, November 20, 1945, Box 13, China War Crimes Files; Jeremiah J. O'Connor, Memorandum to Theater Fiscal Director, December 17, 1945, Box 12, Box 12, China War Crimes Files. Young had anticipated the trials would begin in mid-December, but politics in Washington had slowed things down. Young had protested, cabling back to Washington, "It is urgent that definite instructions concerning five war crimes cases now pending trial be sent here as delay is hampering prosecution." But no permission was forthcoming and the men available to actually conduct these trials were rapidly dwindling down to precious few who remained willing to pass up the opportunity to return home. Army

Advisory Group, Nanking China, cable, January 3, 1946, War Crimes Files, Incoming and Outgoing Radios 21 April 1945 to 6 March 1946, Box 14, China War Crimes Files; COMGEN CHINA to COMGENIB info Fenn and Bacon, cable, November 10, 1945, Box 1, Correspondence 1942–1945, Entry# A1 1059, Records of the Office of the Judge Advocate General (Army), Record Group 153, National Archives, College Park.

147 *The exploits of:* Army Advisory Group, Nanking, China, cable, February 1946, War Crimes Files, Incoming and Outgoing Radios 21 April 1945 to 6 March 1946, Box 14, China War Crimes Files.

147 *a little night school:* Fordham Law School Bulletin, 1938–39; *Fordham Law School Bulletin*, 1939–40; *Fordham Law School Bulletin*, 1940–41.

147 *dropped out:* Bodine evidently was required to repeat his second year of law school and did not pass. It is unclear whether he withdrew voluntarily. See Statement of Reasons, January 18, 1954, p. 1, Exhibit 5, U.S. Army, Report of Proceedings of Board of Inquiry in the Case of Lt Col Edmund Bodine, 3481A, USAF, 23–24 February 1954, Bodine Papers.

147 *his Army records:* Edmund John Bodine, Application for Federal Recognition as a National Guard Officer and for Appointment in the National Guard of the United States, September 30, 1940, U.S. Army, Report of Proceedings of Board of Inquiry in the Case of Lt Col Edmund Bodine, 3481A, USAF, 23–24 February 1954, Exhibit 4, Bodine Files.

147 *Young's deputy:* Edward Cuffe to Natalie Bodine, January 26, 1997, Bodine Files.

147 *happy to vouch:* Jeremiah J. O'Connor, Affidavit, undated, Respondent Exhibit 12, U.S. Army, Report of Proceedings of Board of Inquiry in the Case of Lt Col Edmund Bodine, 3481A, USAF, 23-24 February 1954, Bodine Files.

148 *penchant for chain-smoking:* Robert Fellows, personal interview, April 23, 2013.

148 *The first time:* Natalie and Elizabeth Bodine, personal interview, December 17, 2014.

149 *Vichy France:* Christine Cornet, "La fin d'un pari: Le retour de la concession française à la Chine," *Le Paris de l'Orient. Présence française à Shanghai, 1849–1946* (Musée Albert Kahn, 2002), 86-94.

149 *had the scent:* Harriet Sergeant, *Shanghai* (London: Trafalgar Square, 1991), 36.

149 *colonial subjects:* Jean-Claude Manso, "La Compagnie français de tramways et d'élairage electriques de Shanghai (1906—1953)," *Le Paris de l'Orient. Présence française à Shanghai, 1849–1946* (Musée Albert Kahn, 2002), 135–43.

149 *had to switch:* Marcia Reynders Ristaino, *Port of Last Resort: The Diaspora Communities of Shanghai* (Stanford, CA: Stanford University Press, 2002), 19; Liliane Willens, *Stateless in Shanghai* (Hong Kong: Earnshaw Books, 2010), 40.

149 *uncanny Paris:* François Ged, "Architecture et urbanisme," *Le Paris de l'Orient. Présence française à Shanghai, 1849–1946* (Musée Albert Kahn, 2002), 120–33.

149 *the painted signs:* Sergeant, *Shanghai*, 36; Willens, *Stateless in Shanghai*, 157.

149 *"Little Moscow":* For excellent historical analysis of the Russians' cultural place in early-twentieth-century Shanghai, see Ristaino, *Port of Last Resort*, 81; E. H. Anstice, "Shanghai's White Russians," *Contemporary Review* 151 (1937): 215.

149 *Bodine climbed:* Natalie and Elizabeth Bodine, personal interview, December 17, 2014.

150 *Pasha had married:* U.S. Army, Report of Proceedings of Board of Inquiry in the Case of Lt Col Edmund Bodine, 3481A, USAF, 23–24 February 1954, pp. 20–31 (Testimony of Elizabeth Bodine), Bodine Papers.

150 *Ukrainian gangs*: Willens, *Stateless in Shanghai*, 91.

150 *returned them alive*: Sergeant, *Shanghai*, 51.

150 *unbreakable* troika: Natalie Bodine, personal interview, December 17, 2014.

150 *the Chinese cook*: Natalie and Elizabeth Bodine, personal interview, December 17, 2014.

CHAPTER FOURTEEN

152 *"able to take advantage"*: Letter to the Editor: "Tojo's Trial," *Shanghai Stars & Stripes*, January 17, 1946, 4.

152 *"The Doolittle Raiders Murderers"*: «суд над убийцами летчиков ген. Дулиттла,» Новости Дня [literally, "Trial of Murderers of Gen. Doolittle Airmen," *News of the Day*], March 18, 1946, 1.

153 *On one occasion*: Natalie Bodine, personal correspondence, July 4, 2016.

153 *in Shanghai leading*: "Inspection Teams Fly Over China," Associated Press, January 21, 1946.

153 *During the war*: John Andrew Prime, "World War II Rescue Captured in Chinese Book," *Times* (Sheveport, Louisiana), December 30, 2007, 13A; John Pomfret, "Rediscovering the Ties That Bind," *Washington Post*, June 13, 1998.

153 *Only thirty-five*: General Gabriel P. Disosway, Air Force, Official Biography, February 1, 1966, https://perma.cc/Q83V-GU67.

153 *wry sense of humor*: John Disosway, personal interview, March 25, 2019.

153 *But the only question*: Natalie and Elizabeth Bodine, personal interview, December 17, 2014; Natalie Bodine, personal correspondence, July 4, 2016.

153 *"grasshoppers"*: Terry M. Love, *L-Birds: American Combat Liaison Aircraft of World War II* (New Brighton, MN: Flying Books International, 2001), 36.

153 *dinner plans*: Edward Cuffe to Natalie Bodine, January 26, 1997, Bodine Files.

154 *Nielsen was holding*: John Davey, *Rivers of Consciousness: 1913–1978*, vol. 1, *The Lives and Times of Edward D. Cuffe, Gentleman* (Jayde Design, 2013), 216.

154 *loved him*: *Nielsen v. Nielsen*, Case No. 45-cv-6434, Complaint (District Court, First Judicial District, Utah, December 10, 1945).

154 *She had met*: Terry Nielsen, personal interview, November 25, 2019.

154 *only joint asset*: *Nielsen v. Nielsen*, Case No. 45-cv-6434, Decree (District Court, First Judicial District, Utah, December 24, 1945).

154 *Nielsen had enlisted*: Utah State Archives and Records Service, Salt Lake City, Utah, Military Service Cards, ca. 1898–1975, Creating Agency: Department of Administrative Services, Division of Archives and Records Service, Series 85268, Reel 92; Chase Jay Nielsen, Resume, April 16, 1963, Series II, Box 5, Doolittle Raiders Papers.

154 *Fellows was a lawyer*: Robert Fellows, personal interview, April 23, 2013.

156 *To be a war crimes trial*: *In re Yamashita*, 327 U.S. 1, 7 (1946); *Ex parte Quirin*, 317 U.S. 1, 28 (1942).

156 *What had Sawada*: Sawada Trial Transcript, 22–25 (Statement of Charles Fellows).

156 *How could a prison warden*: Sawada Trial Transcript, 236–37 (Statement of Charles Fellows).

156 *How could that*: Sawada Trial Transcript, 29–31 (Statement of Charles Fellows); Sawada Trial Transcript, 238–41 (Statement of Charles Fellows).

156 *Fellows also turned*: Edward Huggins, *United States v. Kaburagi, et al.*, Brief in Support of Special Plea, February 14, 1946, Bodine Files.

157   *The Chinese were*: "Trial of China's No. 1 Puppet Opens in Soochow," United Press, April 5, 1946.

157   *The trials were*: "China Quislings Wait Trial in Gloomy Ward Road Jail," *Shanghai Stars & Stripes*, January 28, 1946, 5.

157   *It was precisely*: In fact, the Supreme Court took up the argument four years later (and ruled against it) in *Johnson v. Eisentrager*, 339 U.S. 763 (1950).

157   *"Would you rather"*: Shigeru Sawada, interview by Edmund Bodine, February 14, 1946, p. 4, Bodine Files. ("Would you rather be tried by the Americans or by the Chinese? If you wish we will transfer you to the Chinese.")

157   *Back in 1930*: *State v. Bodine*, Case No. 30-cr-SEALED (Conn., October 15, 1930).

158   *He had asked*: Natalie and Elizabeth Bodine, personal interview, December 17, 2014.

158   *Valentine's Day*: Shigeru Sawada, interview by Edmund Bodine, February 14, 1946, Bodine Files.

158   *Born in Kochi*: 沢田茂(著), 森松俊夫(編), 参謀次長沢田茂回想録 (芙蓉書房, 1982年) [Shigeru Sawada, *Memoir of Deputy Chief of Staff Shigeru Sawada*, ed. Toshio Morimatsu (Fuyo Shobo, 1982)], 9.

158   *He took command*: "Translation of Diary of General Shigeru Sawada," undated (1946), p. 1, Box 11, China War Crimes Files.

159   *retired to civilian life*: 沢田茂(著), 森松俊夫(編), 参謀次長沢田茂回想録 (芙蓉書房, 1982年) [Shigeru Sawada, *Memoir of Deputy Chief of Staff Shigeru Sawada*, ed. Toshio Morimatsu (Fuyo Shobo, 1982)], 326.

159   *Sawada did not*: Robert Mikesh, Summary of interview by Shigeru Sawada, February 2, 1965, p. 9, Box 40, Glines Papers.

159   *find a Japanese lawyer*: "Request from Lieutenant General Sawada," undated, Bodine Files.

159   *lengthy defense*: Shigeru Sawada, interview by Edmund Bodine, February 14, 1946, p. 1, Bodine Files.

160   *That was when*: Robert Mikesh, summary of interview by Shigeru Sawada, February 2, 1965, p. 4, Box 40, Glines Papers.

160   *Bodine stopped him*: Shigeru Sawada, interview by Edmund Bodine, February 14, 1946, p. 1, Bodine Files.

160   *Sawada seemed to get*: "Request from Lieutenant General Sawada," undated, Bodine Files.

160   *In the days after*: 畑俊六(著), 伊藤隆/照沼康孝(編), 続・現代史資料 (4) 陸軍 畑俊六日誌 (みすず書房, 1983年) [Shunroku Hata, *More Contemporary History Materials (4) Army—Diary of Shunroku Hata*, ed. Takashi Ito and Yasutaka Terunuma (Misuzu Shobo, 1983)], 347.

160   *Sawada had relayed*: "Translation of Diary of General Shigeru Sawada," undated (1946), p. 1, Box 11, China War Crimes Files; Robert Mikesh, Summary of Interview of Shigeru Sawada, February 2, 1965, p. 2, Box 40, Glines Papers.

160   *About a week*: 畑俊六(著), 伊藤隆/照沼康孝(編), 続・現代史資料 (4) 陸軍 畑俊六日誌 (みすず書房, 1983年) [Shunroku Hata, *More Contemporary History Materials (4) Army—Diary of Shunroku Hata*, ed. Takashi Ito and Yasutaka Terunuma (Misuzu Shobo, 1983)], 347–48.

161   *"We cannot allow"*: Chief of Staff for the Expeditionary Force in China to Assistant Minister of War, cable, April 25, 1942, Doc. 629 (Exhibit 3370), International

Military Tribunal for the Far East, Special Collections, Columbia University Law Library ("As we cannot allow American air force, after inhumanely blind-bombing at the time of air raids of the Mainland, to escape to the Chinese continent seeking the base or hoping to strive for their safety by becoming prisoners of war, we want positively to destroy such enemies and as such actions contain espionage elements also we wish to make a statement to the effect that we intend to punish such actions with severity to be grave offenses of war. But it may have some relations to international laws and provisions, we wish to have the prompt opinions from the Center as regards to this matter.").

161   *Sawada had departed*: "Statement of Lieutenant General Sawada," undated, Bodine Files.

161   *destroy every Chinese airfield*: 畑俊六(著), 伊藤隆/照沼康孝(編), 続・現代史資料 (4) 陸軍 畑俊六日誌 (みすず書房, 1983年) [Shunroku Hata, *More Contemporary History Materials (4) Army—Diary of Shunroku Hata*, ed. Takashi Ito and Yasutaka Terunuma (Misuzu Shobo, 1983)], 352.

161   *The rampage*: John Cox to Jeremiah J. O'Connor, "Materials Relative to the Rescue of the Doolittle Fliers by the Chinese on the Chekiang Coast, 18 April 1942," May 23, 1946, Box 11, China War Crimes Files. James Scott has done some of the most detailed historical analysis of this attack; see James M. Scott, *Target Tokyo* (New York: Norton, 2015), 385; James M. Scott, "The Untold Story of the Vengeful Japanese Attack After the Doolittle Raid," *Smithsonian Magazine*, April 15, 2015.

161   *There were reports*: Yasua Karakawa, interview by John Hendren, January 5, 1945, p. 6, Box 40, Glines Papers.

161   *It was the largest*: "Translation of Diary of General Shigeru Sawada," undated (1946), p. 1, Box 11, China War Crimes Files.

161   *Complicating matters*: Sawada Trial Transcript, 279 (Testimony of Masatoshi Miyano).

161   *"When I first came back"*: Shigeru Sawada, interview by Edmund Bodine, February 14, 1946, p. 1, Bodine Files.

161   *"I am responsible"*: Robert Mikesh, summary of interview by Shigeru Sawada, February 2, 1965, p. 6, Box 40, Glines Papers.

161   *"I don't care"*: 沢田茂(供述), 井上忠男(調査), 昭和38年9月20日, 井上忠男戦争裁判資料 [Shigeru Sawada, interview by Tadao Inoue, September 20, 1963, Tadao Inoue War Tribunal File, Yasukuni Archives].

162   *One had even attempted*: Natalie and Elizabeth Bodine, personal interview, December 17, 2014.

162   *Tradition-minded Japanese*: For a discussion of the concept, see Ruth Benedict, *The Chrysanthemum and the Sword: Patterns of Japanese Culture* (Houghton Mifflin, 1946). Shinji Somiya also noted the American's confusion over the Japanese understanding of the concept of "responsibility." 上海米機搭乗員所罰ニ対スル戦犯事件－宗宮弁護士報告, 空襲軍律研究資料その1 ["Shanghai War Crimes Trial Regarding the Punishment of American Air Crews—Attorney Somiya's Report,"] undated, pp. 82–83, Materials Regarding Military Discipline for Air Raids—Part 1, Yasukuni Archives.

162   *Fellows went back*: Shigeru Sawada, interview by Charles Fellows, February 15, 1946, Bodine Papers.

162   *News was about to break*: Ray T. Maddocks, "Trial of Japanese War Criminals," February 18, 1946, Bodine Papers.

CHAPTER FIFTEEN

163   *On February 27, 1946*: Sawada Trial Transcript, 1.

163   *To attend*: Willis West to the Theater Engineer, "Court-room Facilities," January 8, 1946, Box 12, China War Crimes Files.

163   *The air was*: Jim Becker, " 'Beast of the East' and his Guilty Pals," *Shanghai Stars & Stripes,* Magazine Supplement, March 9, 1946, 4.

163   *packed with spectators*: 神代護忠，上海支店時代の思い出（1994年）[Moritada Kumashiro, "Recollection of the Days at Shanghai Branch," Manuscript (1994)], p. 137, Call No. GK77-G2, National Diet Library.

164   *the sentiments ranged from*: Jim Becker, " 'Beast of the East' and his Guilty Pals," 4.

164   *the four defendants wore*: Jim Becker, " 'Not Guilty,' Doolittle Japs Shout; Trial Date Set," *Shanghai Stars & Stripes*, February 28, 1946, 2.

164   *They sat stiffly*: 神代護忠，上海支店時代の思い出（1994年）[Moritada Kumashiro, "Recollection of the Days at Shanghai Branch," Manuscript (1994)], p. 137, Call No. GK77-G2, National Diet Library.

164   *the trapdoor*: "Yamashita Hanged for War Crimes," Associated Press, February 23, 1946.

164   *Sawada had known*: 沢田茂(著)，森松俊夫(編)，参謀次長沢田茂回想録（芙蓉書房，1982年）[Shigeru Sawada, *Memoir of Deputy Chief of-Staff Shigeru Sawada*, ed. Toshio Morimatsu (Fuyo Shobo, 1982)], 25.

164   *"The soldier"*: Douglas MacArthur, *Reminiscences* (New York: McGraw-Hill, 1964), 295–96.

165   *white armband*: "Jap Underground Flourishing in Shanghai," *Shanghai Stars & Stripes*, December 11, 1945, 5.

165   *it was a neighborhood*: Greg Leck, *Captives of Empire: The Japanese Internment of Allied Civilians in China (1941–1945)* (Bangor, PA: Shandy Press, 2007), 28.

165   *movie theaters*: 神代護忠，上海支店時代の思い出（1994年）[Moritada Kumashiro, "Recollection of the Days at Shanghai Branch," Manuscript (1994)], pp. 230–31, Call No. GK77-G2, National Diet Library; Liu Jianhui, *Demon Capital Shanghai: The "Modern" Experience of Japanese Intellectuals,* trans. Joshua Fogel (Portland, ME: Merwin Asia, 2012), 134.

165   *moved to Shanghai*: 神代護忠，上海支店時代の思い出（1994年）[Moritada Kumashiro, "Recollection of the Days at Shanghai Branch," Manuscript (1994)], pp. 230–31, Call No. GK77-G2, National Diet Library.

165   *"Greater East Asia Co-Prosperity Sphere"*: For a discussion and resources, see Jeremy Yellen, *The Greater East Asia Co-Prosperity Sphere: When Total Empire met Total War* (Ithaca, NY: Cornell University Press, 2019); John Dower, *War Without Mercy: Race and Power in the Pacific* (New York: Pantheon, 1987), 262–92; Joyce Lebra, ed., *Japan's Greater East Asia Co-prosperity Sphere in World War II: Selected Readings and Documents* (Oxford: Oxford University Press, 1975); Eri Hotta, *Pan-Asianism and Japan's War 1931–1945* (London: Palgrave Macmillan, 2007), 199–223.

165   *Japanese idealists*: Parks M. Coble, "Japan's New Order and the Shanghai Capitalists," in David P. Barrett and Larry N. Shyu, eds., *Chinese Collaboration with Japan, 1932–1945* (Stanford, CA: Stanford University Press, 2001), 140.

165   *Kumashirio was one*: 神代護忠，上海支店時代の思い出（1994年）[Moritada Kumashiro, "Recollection of the Days at Shanghai Branch," Manuscript (1994)], p. 99, Call No. GK77-G2, National Diet Library.

165 *"Japanese Officer Wanted"*: "Japanese Officer Wanted by USAF Is Caught in Camp," *Shanghai Herald*, January 26, 1946, 2.

166 *Could it be*: 神代護忠, 上海支店時代の思い出 (1994年) [Moritada Kumashiro, "Recollection of the Days at Shanghai Branch," Manuscript (1994)], pp. 101–2, Call No. GK77-G2, National Diet Library.

166 *Okada was*: 岡田舜平, 二つの戦犯裁判 (光人社, 2009年) [Shumpei Okada, Two War Trials (Kojinsha, 2009)], 65.

166 *Before being drafted*: 岡田舜平, 二つの戦犯裁判 (光人社, 2009年) [Shumpei Okada, Two War Trials (Kojinsha, 2009)], 46–47.

166 *made the most*: T. Suckane et al., "Petition to the American Military Commission," March 3, 1946, Defense Exhibit 18, Sawada Record.

166 *Kumashiro had not seen*: 神代護忠, 上海支店時代の思い出 (1994年) [Moritada Kumashiro, "Recollection of the Days at Shanghai Branch," Manuscript (1994)], pp. 102–3, Call No. GK77-G2, National Diet Library.

167 *Ward Road Jail*: James L. Norwood and Emily L. Shek, *Prisoner of War Camps in Areas Other Than the Four Principal Islands of Japan*, American Prisoner of War Information Bureau, Liaison and Research Branch, July 31, 1946, pp. 7–9, POW Records.

167 *Kumashiro worried*: 神代護忠, 上海支店時代の思い出 (1994年) [Moritada Kumashiro, "Recollection of the Days at Shanghai Branch," Manuscript (1994)], p. 110, Call No. GK77-G2, National Diet Library.

167 *the singular symbol*: It is difficult to overstate the role the jeep played in defining the American presence in Shanghai; see John Hersey, "Letter from Shanghai," *New Yorker*, January 24, 1946, 82; Marcia Reynders Ristaino, *Port of Last Resort: The Diaspora Communities of Shanghai* (Stanford, CA: Stanford University Press, 2002), 243; Letter to the Editor: "Safe Driving," *Shanghai Stars & Stripes*, November 10, 1945, 4; "Yank About China," *Shanghai Stars & Stripes*, December 11, 1945, 4.

167 *Fellows tried*: 神代護忠, 上海支店時代の思い出 (1994年) [Moritada Kumashiro, "Recollection of the Days at Shanghai Branch," Manuscript (1994)], p. 110, Call No. GK77-G2, National Diet Library.

167 *The only time*: Robert Fellows, personal interview, April 23, 2013.

167 *"I want to get"*: 神代護忠, 上海支店時代の思い出 (1994年) [Moritada Kumashiro, "Recollection of the Days at Shanghai Branch," Manuscript (1994)], p. 110, Call No. GK77-G2, National Diet Library.

168 *Okada, though*: 神代護忠, 上海支店時代の思い出 (1994年) [Moritada Kumashiro, "Recollection of the Days at Shanghai Branch," Manuscript (1994)], pp. 113–14, Call No. GK77-G2, National Diet Library.

169 *From then on*: 神代護忠, 上海支店時代の思い出 (1994年) [Moritada Kumashiro, "Recollection of the Days at Shanghai Branch," Manuscript (1994)], p. 126, Call No. GK77-G2, National Diet Library.

169 *Hayama had helped*: Tadahiro Hayama, interview by Robert Dwyer, November 20, 1945, Box 40, Glines Papers.

169 *He didn't want*: 羽山忠弘, ある戦犯事件弁護の思い出, 大東法学第18号179頁 (1991年) [Tadahiro Hayama, "Recollection of Defending a War Trial Case," 18 *Daito Hogaku* 179 (1991)], 193.

169 *Kumashiro liked*: 神代護忠, 上海支店時代の思い出 (1994年) [Moritada Kumashiro, "Recollection of the Days at Shanghai Branch," Manuscript (1994)], p. 127, Call No. GK77-G2, National Diet Library.

169 *Hayama had mixed feelings*: 羽山忠弘，ある戦犯事件弁護の思い出，大東法学第18号179頁 (1991年) [Tadahiro Hayama, "Recollection of Defending a War Trial Case," 18 *Daito Hogaku* 179 (1991)], 188–89.

169 *fiercely guarded independence*: *Constitution of the Empire of Japan*, trans. Ito Miyoji (November 28, 1890), art. 58.

169 *When Tojo publicly attacked*: Takaaki Hattori, "The Legal Profession in Japan: Its Historical Development and Present State," in Arthur Taylor von Mehren, ed., *Law in Japan: The Legal Order in a Changing Society* (Cambridge, MA: Harvard University Press, 1963), 122.

169 *Fairness in trials*: Marquis Hirobumi Ito, *Commentaries on the Constitution of the Empire of Japan*, trans. Baron Miyoji Ito (Chu-o Daigaku, 1906), 115.

169 *What kind of murder trial*: 羽山忠弘，ある戦犯事件弁護の思い出，大東法学第18号179頁 (1991年) [Tadahiro Hayama, "Recollection of Defending a War Trial Case," 18 *Daito Hogaku* 179 (1991)], 189.

169 *Kumashiro welcomed*: 神代護忠，上海支店時代の思い出 (1994年) [Moritada Kumashiro, "Recollection of the Days at Shanghai Branch," Manuscript (1994)], p. 127, Call No. GK77-G2, National Diet Library.

170 *Joining Kumashiro*: Sawada Trial Transcript, 507–14 (Statement of Tadahiro Hayama).

170 *Elizaveta was made*: Courtroom photograph, February 27, 1946, Bodine Papers.

170 *where Kiyoko*: 神代護忠，上海支店時代の思い出 (私家版, 1994年) [Moritada Kumashiro, Recollection of the Days at Shanghai Branch (privately published, 1994)], p. 136.

170 *At 10:00 a.m.*: Sawada Trial Transcript, 1; *United States v. Sawada et al.*, Procedure on Arraignment, undated, p. 1, Bodine Files.

170 *There was a script*: *United States v. Sawada et al.*, Procedure on Arraignment, undated, p. 1, Bodine Files.

171 *Fellows thought*: 神代護忠，上海支店時代の思い出 (私家版, 1994年) [Moritada Kumashiro, Recollection of the Days at Shanghai Branch (privately published, 1994)], p. 136.

171 *Elizaveta agreed*: Natalie Bodine, personal interview, January 1, 2020.

171 *Bodine was always*: Among the Bodine Papers is a copy of James Truslow Adams, *The Epic of America* (Boston: Little, Brown, 1931), which Bodine gave to Elizaveta the week after the trial was over and inscribed with the note "May the contents of this book inspire in you the same feeling I have for my country. Edmund."

171 *Everything had proceeded*: Sawada Trial Transcript, 2–3.

172 *This routine formality*: George Thomas Foster, "Letters of Doolittle Fliers Before Execution Revealed," NBC, February 27, 1946.

172 *Everything was going*: Sawada Trial Transcript, 10.

172 *Kumashirio and Hayama*: 神代護忠，上海支店時代の思い出 (1994年) [Moritada Kumashiro, "Recollection of the Days at Shanghai Branch," Manuscript (1994)], p. 136, Call No. GK77-G2, National Diet Library.

172 *"If the court"*: Sawada Trial Transcript, 10.

173 *"Subject to objection"*: Sawada Trial Transcript, 12, 18.

173 *All four stood*: Sawada Trial Transcript, 32.

173 *The gesture*: Jim Becker, "'Not Guilty,' Doolittle Japs Shout; Trial Date Set," *Shanghai Stars & Stripes*, February 28, 1946, 2.

CHAPTER SIXTEEN

174   *Elizaveta went*: Elizaveta Bodine, handwritten diary/letter, March 1946, Bodine Papers.

174   *Elizaveta's knowledge*: Liu Jianhui, *Demon Capital Shanghai: The "Modern" Experience of Japanese Intellectuals*, trans. Joshua Fogel (Portland, ME: Merwin Asia, 2012), 134.

174   *visiting Japanese students*: Natalie Bodine, personal interview, December 17, 2014.

174   *Elizaveta's disappointment*: Elizaveta Bodine, handwritten diary/letter, March 1946, Bodine Papers.

174   *fit of jealousy*: Natalie and Elizabeth Bodine, personal interview, December 17, 2014.

175   *love notes*: Miscellaneous Love Notes, undated, Bodine Papers.

175   *favorite French perfume*: Natalie and Elizabeth Bodine, personal interview, December 17, 2014.

175   *front-page article*: "Geishas for Tokyo's GIs," *Shanghai Stars & Stripes*, January 1, 1946.

175   *MacArthur had*: John Dower, *Embracing Defeat: Japan in the Wake of World War II* (New York: Norton, 1999), 129; Yuki Tanaka, *Japan's Comfort Women: Sexual Slavery and Prostitution During World War II and the U.S. Occupation* (New York: Routledge, 2002), 146; Sarah Kovner, *Occupying Power: Sex Workers and Servicemen in Postwar Japan* (Stanford: Stanford University Press, 2012), 19–30.

175   *"panpan girls"*: Alvin Grauer, *So I Went to Japan: The Delights, Despairs, and Minor Perils Experience by Allied Personnel Stationed in Postwar Japan* (Tokyo: Nippon Times, 1946), 34; Kovner, *Occupying Power*, 75–84.

175   *"Panglish"*: Dower, *Embracing Defeat*, 132–37.

175   *"I've promised many"*: "Wife Deal Shocks Japan," *Shanghai Stars & Stripes*, January 10, 1946, 1.

175   *All Elizaveta could think*: Elizaveta Bodine, handwritten diary/letter, March 1946, Bodine Papers.

176   *The Army had*: E. W. Sutherland, Permission to Marry, February 26, 1946, Bodine Papers.

176   *not a US citizen*: U.S. Army, Report of Proceedings of Board of Inquiry in the Case of Lt Col Edmund Bodine, 3481A, USAF, 23–24 February 1954, p. 98 (Testimony of Edmund Bodine), Bodine Papers.

176   *Bodine had passed*: Edmund Bodine to Commanding General, Rear Echelon, Hq. U.S. Forces, China Theater, Permission to Marry, January 27, 1946, Bodine Papers.

176   *beamed back*: Alma Bodine to Edmund Bodine, February 15, 1946, Bodine Papers.

176   *She always signed*: Alma Bodine to Edmund Bodine, July 21, 1946, Bodine Papers.

176   *"What a terrible name"*: Alma Bodine to Edmund Bodine, February 15, 1946, Bodine Papers.

176   *Byron had*: Alma Bodine to Edmund Bodine, July 10, 1946, Bodine Papers.

176   *Alma adored*: Alma Bodine to Edmund Bodine, July 14, 1946, Bodine Papers.

176   *"The French girl"*: Alma Bodine to Edmund Bodine, July 10, 1946, Bodine Papers.

177   *She went out*: Elizaveta Bodine, handwritten diary/letter, March 1946, Bodine Papers.

177   *The two weeks*: Lindesay Parrott, "Japanese Disavow All War in New Constitution Draft," *New York Times*, March 7, 1946, 1.

177   *A model*: Constitution of Japan (DRAFT), February 12, 1946, Constitution File No. 1, Document No. 12, Alfred Hussey Papers, National Diet Library.

178   *The authors of*: The most comprehensive English language histories and document collections on the drafting of the Japanese Constitution are Dale M. Hellegers, *We the Japanese People: World War II and the Origins of the Japanese Constitution* (Stanford, CA: Stanford University Press, 2002); Kyoko Inoue, *MacArthur's Japanese Constitution: A Linguistic and Cultural Study of Its Making* (Chicago: University of Chicago Press, 1991); Ray Moore and Donald Robinson, eds., *The Japanese Constitution: A Documentary History of Its Framing and Adoption* (Princeton University Press, 1998); Supreme Commander for Allied Powers, Government Section, *Political Reorientation of Japan, September 1945 to September 1948* (G.P.O., 1949). The National Diet Library has also created a richly resourced website, which is available at https://www.ndl.go.jp/constitution/e/library/library.html.

178   *dutifully checked in*: Tokyo to Headquarters, United States Forces China Theater, Shanghai, China, cable, February 21, 1946, Bodine Files.

178   *Keenan was contemplating*: Army Advisory Group, Nanking China, cable, February 25, 1946, War Crimes Files, Incoming and Outgoing Radios 21 April 1945 to 6 March 1946, Box 14, China War Crimes Files.

178   *Bodine and Fellows's arrival*: "4 Ex-Jap Officers Plead Innocent," Associated Press, February 27, 1946.

178   *all the troublemaking*: Donal Sullivan, "Cambridge Lawyer Describes Yamashita Trial Incidents," *Boston Globe,* February 21, 1946, 4.

178   *Keenan had been forced*: "Keenan Ired at Dissenting U.S. Supreme Judges," Associated Press, February 13, 1946.

178   *Their main reason*: "Request from Lieutenant General Sawada," undated, Bodine Files.

178   *The scale*: Charles Kuzma, personal interview, April 3, 2016. There are numerous other accounts from Americans entering Tokyo that reflect upon the stunning scale of destruction. One particularly notable one was given by Chase Nielsen, who reported seeing comparable destruction in Tokyo and Nagasaki as he flew over both cities on his way back to Shanghai in January 1946. "Tokyo Raider Plans Leave Before New Assignment," *Ogden Standard-Examiner,* April 19, 1946.

179   *Roosevelt had wanted*: Franklin Roosevelt to Claire Chennault, March 15, 1944, Series I, Safe File, Box 1, Franklin D. Roosevelt, Papers as President: The President's Secretary's File, 1933–1945, FDR Library.

179   *micro huts*: Supreme Commander for the Allied Powers, *Summation of non-military activities in Japan*, No. 6 (March 1946), §1(6).

179   *distribute blankets*: Supreme Commander for the Allied Powers, *Summation of non-military activities in Japan*, No. 6 (March 1946), §1(3).

179   *although the famine*: Supreme Commander for the Allied Powers, *Summation of non-military activities in Japan*, No. 6 (March 1946), §1(52).

179   *so scarce that*: Supreme Commander for the Allied Powers, *Summation of non-military activities in Japan*, No. 7 (April 1946), §1(57).

179   *Yet somehow*: John W. Bennett et al., "Doing Photography and Social Research in the Allied Occupation of Japan, 1948–1951: A Personal and Professional Memoir" (2003), manuscript, Ohio State University Library.

179   *That all suited Fellows*: Robert Fellows, personal interview, April 23, 2013; Natalie Bodine, personal interview, January 1, 2020.

179 *In the Ginza*: Jesus Solis, *Japan's Black Market: Yakuza, SCAP, and the Culture of the Yami'ichi* (M.A. diss., University of Colorado, 2012), 13.

180 *had come to despise*: "Chinese Students Protest Soviets Holding Manchuria," International News Service, February 26, 1946; "Chinese Protest Foreign Business," Associated Press, January 27, 1946; "Chinese Stage Protest March," Associated Press, January 25, 1946; "U.S. Sailors Beaten by Chinese During Unemployment Protest," Associated Press, January 22, 1946; "Chinese Protest American Soldiers," Associated Press, January 14, 1946.

180 *The friendliest locals*: "Yank about China," *Shanghai Stars & Stripes*, December 7, 1945, 4.

180 *At Tokyo's Imperial Hotel*: "Formula for Victory," *Shanghai Stars & Stripes*, November 8, 1945, 4.

180 *When Fellows forgot*: Robert Fellows, personal interview, April 23, 2013.

180 *Fellows wanted*: 神代護忠，上海支店時代の思い出 (1994年) [Moritada Kumashiro, "Recollection of the Days at Shanghai Branch," Manuscript (1994)], p. 110, Call No. GK77-G2, National Diet Library.

180 *Kubota was*: "Request from Lieutenant General Sawada," undated, Bodine Files.

180 *The retired governor*: 歴代知事編纂会(編)，新編日本の歴代知事 (歴代知事編纂会, 1991年) [The Successive Governors Compilation Committee, ed., *New Edition: The Successive Governors of Japan*, 1991)], 481; 秦郁彦(編)，日本官僚制総合事典1868–2000 (東京大学出版会, 2001年) [Ikuhiko Hata, ed., *The Complete Encyclopedia of Japanese Bureaucracy 1868–2000* (Tokyo: University of Tokyo Press, 2001], 227.

180 *top lawyer*: Ayao Oyama, Deposition, September 30, 1937, Doc. 2675 (Exhibit 3354), International Military Tribunal for the Far East, Special Collections, Columbia University Law Library.

180 *coordinated with*: Army Advisory Group, Nanking China, cable, March 2, 1946, War Crimes Files, Incoming and Outgoing Radios 21 April 1945 to 6 March 1946, Box 14, China War Crimes Files.

180 *send Shinji Somiya*: 岡田舜平，二つの戦犯裁判 (光人社, 2009年) [Shumpei Okada, *Two War Trials* (Kojinsha, 2009)], 192.

180 *Kempeitai's file*: Sawada Trial Transcript, 259 (Testimony of Charles Fellows).

181 *Sawada had given*: "Request from Lieutenant General Sawada," undated, Bodine Files.

181 *To placate the press*: Memorandum for Record, "Apprehension of Lt. General Shimomura," February 6, 1946, Box 719, Intelligence Dossiers.

181 *Wiry and energetic*: W. T. Ryder, "Who's Who—Shimomura," undated, Box 719, Intelligence Dossiers.

181 *Shimomura liked*: Sadamu Shimomura, Statement, March 8, 1946, Defense Exhibit 10, Sawada Record.

181 *the loudest advocates*: Ben-Ami Shillony, *Politics and Culture in Wartime Japan* (Oxford: Oxford University Press, 1981), 41.

181 *Shimomura had*: Sadamu Shimomura, Statement, March 8, 1946, Defense Exhibit 10, Sawada Record.

182 *Kubota said*: Taosa Kubota, Statement, March 9, 1946, Defense Exhibit 17, Sawada Record.

182 *He had spent time*: Sawada Trial Transcript, 437 (Testimony of Shigeru Sawada).

182 *Had Sawada been born*: Taosa Kubota, Statement, March 9, 1946, Defense Exhibit 17, Sawada Record.

182 *said the same thing*: Issuo Karakawa, "Circumstances Relating to Lt General Sawada," March 7, 1946, Defense Exhibit 15, Sawada Record.

182 *Sawada instructed*: Hisashi Kisaki, Testimony of Kisaki Hisashi Concerning Lt. Gen. Sawada, March 14, 1946, p. 1, Defense Exhibit 16, Sawada Record.

183 *When the time*: Greg Leck, *Captives of Empire*, 55.

183 *When the sun*: Wen-Hsin Yeh, *Shanghai Splendor: Economic Sentiments and the Making of Modern China, 1843–1949* (Berkeley: University of California Press, 2008), 157; B. V. A. Röling and C. F. Rüter, eds., *The Tokyo Judgment—The International Military Tribunal for the Far East (IMTFE), 29 April 1946–12 November 1948* (Amsterdam: APA-University Press 1977), 378.

183 *Businesses had*: Hisashi Kisaki, Testimony of Kisaki Hisashi Concerning Lt. Gen. Sawada, March 14, 1946, p. 1, Defense Exhibit 16, Sawada Record.

183 *Sawada notified*: Leck, *Captives of Empire*, 73.

183 *models of collaboration*: Graham Earnshaw, *Tales of Old Shanghai* (Hong Kong: Earnshaw Books, 2012), 117. In May 1942, Britain's commander in chief in India telegrammed the War Office in London that Shanghai was full of "British subjects, many of military age, living more or less normal lives, although good prospects exist if effort made. Reports also indicate some continue serve in police and the municipal administration. The fact that extremely few British civilians have so far escaped is significant in view of these reports. Her prestige will be still further lowered if British subjects continue serve the puppet Municipal Council and if British firms continue to operate by agreement with Japanese as appears to be the case."

183 *As Karakawa explained*: Issuo Karakawa, "Circumstances Relating to Lt General Sawada," March 7, 1946, Defense Exhibit 15, Sawada Record.

183 *Sawada understood*: Hisashi Kisaki, Testimony of Kisaki Hisashi Concerning Lt. Gen. Sawada, March 14, 1946, p. 2, Defense Exhibit 16, Sawada Record.

183 *issued a general order*: Hisashi Kisaki, Testimony of Kisaki Hisashi Concerning Lt. Gen. Sawada, March 14, 1946, pp. 1–2, Defense Exhibit 16, Sawada Record.

184 *Those who fought*: Shunroku Hata, Statement, March 7, 1946, p. 2, Defense Exhibit 9, Sawada Record.

184 *Sawada had scolded*: Shigeru Sawada, Statement, undated, Bodine Files.

184 *sent a telegram*: Issuo Karakawa, "Circumstances Relating to Lt General Sawada," March 7, 1946, Defense Exhibit 15, Sawada Record.

184 *Sugiyama had sent*: Hajime Sugiyama to Shunroku Hata, cable, October 10, 1942, Doc. 1027-B (Exhibit 3130), International Military Tribunal for the Far East, Special Collections, Columbia University Law Library.

184 *Sugiyama had directed*: "Measures for the Disposition of the American Airmen Who Raided the Homeland," October 10, 1942, Doc. 1027-C (Exhibit 3131), International Military Tribunal for the Far East, Special Collections, Columbia University Law Library.

184 *"Are you there contending"*: Sawada Trial Transcript, 27–28.

185 *Per the chain of command*: Sawada Trial Transcript, 329 (Testimony of Masatoshi Miyano); Shigeru Sawada, interview by Evelyn Knecht, February 7, 1947, p. 2, Box 719, Intelligence Dossiers.

185 *The rules of evidence*: Paul Caraway, "Regulation Governing the Trial of War Criminals," January 21, 1946, pp. 3–4, Box 13, China War Crimes Files.

186 *Dwyer was planning*: James H. Doolittle, interview by Carl E. Olson, December 27, 1945, Prosecution Exhibit 23, Sawada Record.

186 *Karakawa agreed*: Issuo Karakawa, "Circumstances Relating to Lt General Sawada," March 7, 1946, Bodine Files.

CHAPTER SEVENTEEN

187 *shot himself*: John Toland, *The Rising Sun: The Decline and Fall of the Japanese Empire* (1970; reprint, New York: Modern Library, 2003), 873.

188 *personal permission*: John Davey, *Rivers of Consciousness: 1913–1978*, vol. 1, *The Lives and Times of Edward D. Cuffe, Gentleman* (Jayde Design, 2013), 216.

188 *For whatever his reasons*: Photograph of Edmund Bodine and Hideki Tojo, Sugamo Prison, March 1946, Bodine Papers.

188 *Roosevelt had remained*: Franklin D. Roosevelt, "Fireside Chat 25: On the Fall of Mussolini," July 28, 1943, in Samuel Rosenman, ed., *The Public Papers and Addresses of Franklin D. Roosevelt*, vol. 12 (New York: Russell & Russell, 1969).

188 *the latter being*: Neil Boister and Robert Cryer, *The Tokyo International Tribunal: A Reappraisal* (Oxford: Oxford University Press, 2008), 18.

188 *"JAPS EXECUTE DOOLITTLE"*: Peter Garrison, "Jimmy Doolittle," *Flying Magazine* 115, no. 10 (October 1988): 75–82.

188 *Bodine hulked*: George Jones, "His Suicide Foiled; Japanese Warlord Attempts Suicide," *New York Times*, September 12, 1945, 1.

189 *"I would not like"*: Toland, *The Rising Sun*, 870–73.

189 *led his countrymen*: John Dower, *Embracing Defeat: Japan in the Wake of World War II* (New York: Norton, 1999), 492.

189 *Tojo returned*: Edmund Bodine, handwritten notes on Tojo Interview, undated, Bodine Papers.

189 *At the end of 1939*: B. V. A. Röling and C. F. Rüter, Eds., *The Tokyo Judgment—The International Military Tribunal for the Far East (IMTFE), 29 April 1946–12 November 1948* (Amsterdam: APA-University Press 1977), 386.

189 *pushing Tojo's name*: 沢田茂(著), 森松俊夫(編), 参謀次長沢田茂回想録 (芙蓉書房, 1982年) [Shigeru Sawada, *Memoir of Deputy Chief of-Staff Shigeru Sawada*, ed. Toshio Morimatsu (Fuyo Shobo, 1982)], 63.

189 *Tojo told Bodine*: Sawada Trial Transcript, 272 (Testimony of Edmund Bodine).

189 *"what are you doing"*: Edmund Bodine, handwritten notes on Tojo Interview, undated, Bodine Papers.

190 *unprecedented power*: Ben-Ami Shillony, *Politics and Culture in Wartime Japan* (Oxford: Oxford University Press, 1981), 10–11, 62.

190 *Complicating matters*: Shinichi Fujii, *The Essentials of Japanese Constitutional Law* (Yuhikaku, 1940), 88; George Beckmann, *The Making of the Meiji Constitution: The Oligarchs and the Constitutional Development of Japan, 1868–1891* (Westport, CT: Greenwood Press, 1975), 65.

190 *fraught consensus*: For an excellent English-language history of politics of Japan in this period, *see* Eri Hota, *1941: Countdown to Infamy* (New York: Knopf, 2013).

190 *relayed a warning*: 宇垣纏, 戦藻録 (原書房, 1968) [Matome Ugaki, Record of War (Hara Shobo, 1968)], 107.

190 *sent the alert*: Chiaki Nishikawa, Firsthand Account of the Attack on the Mizumoto School, 東京大空襲・戦災誌第2巻 (東京空襲を記録する会, 1973年) [*The Great Tokyo Air Raids—Records of War Damages*, vol. 2 (Association for Recording Tokyo Air Raids, 1973)], 25.

190   *written two haikus*: 宇垣纒, 戦藻録 (原書房, 1968) [Matome Ugaki, *Record of War* (Hara Shobo, 1968)], 107.

190   *"Yamabuki petals"*: In the *hanakotoba* (花言葉), or Japanese language of flowers, yamabuki are the flowers given to celebrate newborns and generally represent good luck.

190   *Everyone knew it*: 軍事史学会(編), 大本営陸軍部戦争指導班機密戦争日誌・上 (錦正社, 1998年) [The Military History Sociery of Japan, *Confidential War Diary of the War Maneuver Unit*, Army Section, Imperial General Headquarters, vol. 1 (Kinseisha, 1998)], 239.

191   *the Army's lookouts*: 坂本和房,『2機の飛行機』東京大空襲・戦災誌第2巻 (東京空襲を記録する会, 1973年) [Kazufusa Sakamoto, "Airplane with Two Tail Units," *The Great Tokyo Air Raids—Records of War Damages*, vol. 2 (Association for Recording Tokyo Air Raids, 1973)], 41.

191   *The Army's fighter aircraft*: The United States Strategic Bombing Survey (Pacific), Report No. 62, *Japanese Air Power*, Military Analysis Division (July 1946), 9–10.

191   *When the artillerymen*: 東久邇稔彦, 一皇族の戦争日記 (日本週報社, 1957年) [Naruhiko Higashikuni, *The War Diary of a Member of the Royal Family* (Nihonshuhosha, 1957)], 106–7.

191   *to wonder*: 曽根脩輔『初の東京空襲』東京大空襲・戦災誌第2巻 (東京空襲を記録する会, 1973年) [*The Great Tokyo Air Raids—Records of War Damages*, vol. 2 (Shunsuke Sone, "First Tokyo Air Raid," Association for Recording Tokyo Air Raids, 1973)]; 羽山忠弘, ある戦犯事件弁護の思い出, 大東法学第18号179頁 (1991年) [Tadahiro Hayama, "Recollection of Defending a War Trial Case," 18 *Daito Hogaku* 179 (1991), 185].

191   *Mrs. Aoki*: 北川博,『火爆弾を捕まえた主婦の物語』東京大空襲・戦災誌第2巻 (東京空襲を記録する会, 1973年) [Hiroshi Kitagawa, "A Tale of the Housewife Who Captured the Firebomb," *The Great Tokyo Air Raids—Records of War Damages*, vol. 2 (Association for Recording Tokyo Air Raids, 1973)], 31.

191   *come to blows*: 東久邇稔彦, 一皇族の戦争日記 (日本週報社, 1957年) [Naruhiko Higashikuni, *The War Diary of a Member of the Royal Family* (Nihonshuhosha, 1957)], 104.

191   *Higashikuni had been*: Shillony, *Politics and Culture in Wartime Japan*, 58.

192   *"There is no country"*: 敵の空襲企図全く失敗に帰す", 写真週報, 昭和17年4月 29日 ["Plan of the Enemy Air Raid Ends in Complete Failure," *Photo Weekly Magazine*, April 29, 1942], pp. 12–13.

192   *Konoe had been*: Hotta, *Japan 1941*, 208–14; Toland, *The Rising Sun*, 105–20.

192   *The Japanese are*: 東久邇稔彦, 一皇族の戦争日記 (日本週報社, 1957年) [Naruhiko Higashikuni, *The War Diary of a Member of the Royal Family* (Nihonshuhosha, 1957)], 106.

192   *A large fleet*: Deck Log, Aircraft Carrier Hornet (CV-8), April 18, 1942, Logbooks of U.S. Navy Ships, Entry 11, Records of the Bureau of Naval Personnel, Record Group 24, National Archives, College Park.

192   *In Osaka*: 菅谷すみ,『血の死』東京大空襲・戦災誌第2巻 (東京空襲を記録する 会, 1973年) Sumi Sugaya, "Death in Blood," *The Great Tokyo Air Raids—Records of War Damages*, vol. 2 (Association for Recording Tokyo Air Raids, 1973)], 33–34.

193   *The Tokyo suburbs*: 東久邇稔彦, 一皇族の戦争日記 (日本週報社, 1957年) [Naruhiko Higashikuni, *The War Diary of a Member of the Royal Family* (Nihonshuhosha, 1957)], 104.

193 *a schoolyard*: "空襲にあたって・ヨイコドモの手記", 朝日新聞, 昭和18年4月19日 ["On the Air Raid—Good Boys' Notes," *Asahi Shimbun*, April 19, 1943].

193 *telephone company employee*: 中西敬三郎『後ろの穴』東京大空襲・戦災誌第2巻 (東京空襲を記録する会, 1973年) Keizaburo Nakanishi, "Hole in the Back," *The Great Tokyo Air Raids—Records of War Damages*, vol. 2 (Association for Recording Tokyo Air Raids, 1973)].

193 *an old woman*: 第一復員省法務局調, 昭和17年4月18日空襲時ニ於ケル被害 [The Damage by the Air-Raiding Attack of April 18th, 1942, Investigated by Legal Bureau of First Ministry of Demobilization], Bodine Files.

193 *An article*: 『敵の空襲企図全く失敗に帰す』写真週報, 昭和17年4月29日 ["Plan of the Enemy Air Raid Ends in Complete Failure," *Photo Weekly Magazine*, April 29, 1942], pp. 12–13.

193 *day of the parliamentary elections*: Ben-Ami Shillony, *Politics and Culture in Wartime Japan* (Oxford: Oxford University Press, 1981), 26.

193 *excitement was palpable*: 軍事史学会(編), 大本営陸軍部戦争指導班機密戦争日誌・上 (錦正社, 1998年) [The Military History Society of Japan, ed., Confidential War Diary of the War Maneuver Unit, Army Section, Imperial General Headquarters, vol. 1 (Kinseisha, 1998)], 241.

193 *Sugiyama wanted*: Hideki Tojo, Interrogation, March 29, 1946, pp. 1–4, Doc. 4183 (Exhibit 1984), International Military Tribunal for the Far East, Special Collections, Columbia University Law Library; *IMTFE Transcript*, 29,047-29,049 (Testimony of Ryukichi Tanaka); 宗宮真司『上海米機搭乗員所罰ニ対スル戦犯事件 – 宗宮弁護士報告』日付不詳, 空襲軍律研究資料その1 [Shinji Somiya, "Shanghai War Crimes Trial Regarding the Punishment of American Air Crews—Attorney Somiya's Report," undated, p. 66, Materials Regarding Military Discipline for Air Raids, Part 1], Yasukuni Archives. When questioned on the witness stand, however, Tojo denied that Sugiyama wanted the Raiders executed without a trial. *IMTFE Transcript*, 36,490.

193 *Togo had been adamant*: *IMTFE Transcript*, 35,768-35,772 (Testimony of Shigenori Togo).

194 *privately chastised*: *IMTFE Transcript*, 36,490-36,491 (Testimony of Hideki Tojo).

194 *Emperor Hirohito had been*: 軍事史学会, 大本営陸軍部戦争指導班機密戦争日誌・上 (錦正社, 1998年) [The Military History Society of Japan, *Confidential War Diary of the War Maneuver Unit, Army Section, Imperial General Headquarters*, vol. 1 (Kinseisha, 1998)], 244.

194 *first countries to sign*: D. Schindler and J. Toman, eds., *The Laws of Armed Conflicts* (Boston: Martinus Nijhoff, 1988), 341–64.

194 *Japan's militarists*: For a discussion of the reasons Japan failed to ratify the 1929 Geneva Convention, see B.V.A. Röling and C.F. Rüter, Eds., *The Tokyo Judgment—The International Military Tribunal for the Far East (IMTFE), 29 April 1946–12 November 1948* (Amsterdam: APA-University Press, 1977), 422; Neil Boister and Robert Cryer, *The Tokyo International Tribunal: A Reappraisal* (Oxford: Oxford University Press, 2008), 195.

194 *In light of*: Reply from Vice Minister of War to Vice Minister of Foreign Affairs, January 23, 1942, "Record of Conference in War Ministry, May 6, 1942, regarding decision not to apply the Geneva Convention and orders issued in consequence thereof," Doc. 1465A (Exhibit 1958), International Military Tribunal for the Far East, Special Collections, Columbia University Law Library.

195   *agreed to a compromise*: IMTFE *Transcript*, 35,768–35,770 (Testimony of Shigenori Togo); *IMTFE Transcript*, 36,414–36,417 (Testimony of Hideki Tojo).

195   *"It would be safe"*: Reply from Vice Minister of War to Vice Minister of Foreign Affairs, January 23, 1942, "Record of Conference in War Ministry, May 6, 1942, regarding decision not to apply the Geneva Convention and orders issued in consequence thereof," Doc. 1465A (Exhibit 1958), International Military Tribunal for the Far East, Special Collections, Columbia University Law Library.

195   *a diplomatic communiqué*: 東郷外務大臣発在京瑞西国公使宛書翰, 昭和17年1月29日, 茶園義雄(編), BC級戦犯米軍上海等裁判資料 (不二出版, 1989年) [Letter from Foreign Minister Togo to Swiss Envoy in Tokyo, January 29, 1942, in Yoshio Chaen, ed., *Materials Regarding BC Class War Criminals American Army Shanghai Trial* (Fuji Shuppan, 1989)], 49; The Chargé in Switzerland (Huddle) to the Secretary of State, February 4, 1942, in E. R. Perkins, ed., *Foreign Relations of the United States: Diplomatic Papers, 1942, General; The British Commonwealth; the Far East*, vol. 1 (G.P.O., 1960), Doc. 680.

195   *come from lawyers*: IMTFE *Transcript*, 35,769 (Testimony of Shigenori Togo).

195   *Togo understood*: IMTFE *Transcript*, 35,770 (Testimony of Shigenori Togo).

195   *under no obligation*: IMTFE *Transcript*, 14,665–14,668 (Testimony of Heitaro Kimura).

195   *The capture of*: IMTFE *Transcript*, 29,041–29,054 (Testimony of Ryukichi Tanaka).

195   *In the weeks after the raid*: 軍事史学会, 大本営陸軍部戦争指導班機密戦争日誌・上 (錦正社, 1998年) [The Military History Society of Japan, *Confidential War Diary of the War Maneuver Unit, Army Section, Imperial General Headquarters*, vol. 1 (Kinseisha, 1998)], 241.

195   *explore all the options*: 軍事史学会, 大本営陸軍部戦争指導班機密戦争日誌・上 (錦正社, 1998年) [The Military History Society of Japan, *Confidential War Diary of the War Maneuver Unit, Army Section, Imperial General Headquarters*, vol. 1 (Kinseisha, 1998)], 244, 248.

195   *Tojo directed*: Tsune Nemoto, Statement, March 19, 1946, Defense Exhibit 7, Sawada Record.

196   *set to work*: Genzaburo Oki, Statement, June 6, 1946, Box 1732, SCAP Legal Section Investigation Division, Investigation Reports 1945-49, Allied Occupation Records.

196   *an attempt to supplement*: Rules Concerning the Control of Wireless Telegraphy in Time of War and Air Warfare. Drafted by a Commission of Jurists at the Hague, December 1922–February 1923, reprinted in 32 *American Journal of International Law (Supplement)* 12 (1938). For a discussion, see Röling and Rüter, Eds., *The Tokyo Judgment*, 1023–25; James W. Garner, "Proposed Rules for the Regulation of Aerial Warfare," 18 *American Journal of International Law* 56 (1924).

196   *with an answer*: 軍事史学会, 大本営陸軍部戦争指導班機密戦争日誌・上 (錦正社, 1998年) [The Military History Society of Japan, *Confidential War Diary of the War Maneuver Unit, Army Section, Imperial General Headquarters*, vol. 1 (Kinseisha, 1998)], 260.

196   *Any punishment*: "China Expeditionary Force Order No. 4, Military Law Concerning the Punishment of Enemy Airmen Interpretation of Article II," undated, General Headquarters, Supreme Commander for the Allied Powers, Military Intelligence Section General Staff, Allied Translator and Interpreter Section, Doc. No. 6789, Bodine Files. This legal analysis, which was sent to the 13th Army, described

the Enemy Airman's Law as simply implementing Article 22 of the Hague Conventions. Article 22 limited in general terms the "choice of methods to be employed against an enemy." While Article 22 did not specify those forbidden methods precisely, the lawyers in the War Ministry concluded that "from a common sense point of view, it clarifies such acts are contrary to human decency and it can be said that this article prohibits any and all such actions and measures of warfare absolutely inexcusable in the prosecution of war." Article II of the Enemy Airmen's Law, which had formed the basis of the Doolittle Raiders' convictions, was therefore simply a codification and clarification of this general principle of international law applied to aerial warfare and punished "individuals who in flagrant disregard of human decency commit atrocities."

196   *In an article*: Jumpei Shinobu, "Punishment to War Prisoners," *Contemporary Japan: A Review of East Asiatic Affairs* 12, no. 6 (1943): 688–92

197   *not merely Japan's right*: Shinobu, "Punishment to War Prisoners," 692.

197   *report was distributed*: 軍事史学会, 大本営陸軍部戦争指導班機密戦争日誌・上 (錦正社, 1998年) [The Military History Society of Japan, *Confidential War Diary of the War Maneuver Unit, Army Section, Imperial General Headquarters*, vol. 1 (Kinseisha, 1998)], 260.

197   *the findings*: 木戸幸一, 木戸幸一日記下巻 (東京大学出版会, 1966年) [Koichi Kido, *Koichi Kido Diary*, vol. 2 (University of Tokyo Press, 1966)], 963.

197   *slipped a copy*: 帝国本土ヲ空襲セル米機搭乗者調状況ニ関スル件報告「通牒」, 昭和17年5月26日, BC級(アメリカ裁判関係)上海裁判・第4号事件, ["Notification: Report Regarding the Status of Interrogation of the American Air Crews," May 26, 1942, BC Class (Regarding American Trials) Shanghai Trial, Case No. 4], National Archives of Japan.

197   *Their admissions*: Akihito Nakamura to Hajime Sugiyama, "Gendarmerie 3, Special Secret Service Report No. 352," May 26, 1942, Allied Translator and Interpreter Section Doc. No. 6789, Bodine Files.

197   *The phrase*: "敵機来襲と国民の覚悟", 週報, 昭和17年4月22日 ["Enemy Plain Attack and People's Readiness," *Photo Weekly Magazine*, April 22, 1942], pp. 2–4.

197   "*Did you do*": Akihito Nakamura to Hajime Sugiyama, "Gendarmerie 3, Special Secret Service Report No. 352," May 26, 1942, Allied Translator and Interpreter Section Doc. No. 6789, p. 2, Bodine Files.

198   *Sugiyama let*: U.S. Army, Record of Trial, *United States v. Kajuro Aihara, et al*, p. 813 (Testimony of Riukichi Tanaka), Box 1645, Records of the SCAP Legal Section, Prosecution Division, Entry 1321, Allied Occupation Records.

198   *Tojo then instructed*: Fumio Oyama, Affidavit, September 30, 1947, Doc. 347 (Exhibit 2560), International Military Tribunal for the Far East, Special Collections, Columbia University Law Library.

199   *formally issued*: Heitaro Kimura, cable, "Military Secret Order No. 2190," July 28, 1942, Doc. 1681 (Exhibit 1992), International Military Tribunal for the Far East, Special Collections, Columbia University Law Library.

199   *The case remained*: IMTFE Transcript, 29,054-29,055 (Testimony of Ryukichi Tanaka).

199   *Raiders were sent*: SINTIC 2809, "File, from Japanese Maj Gen Ito, relating to trial of American airmen by court-martial," Box 11, China War Crimes Files.

199   *formally issued*: 支那派遣軍軍令第4号・敵航空機搭乗員処罰ニ関スル軍律, 昭和17年8月13日, BC級(アメリカ裁判関係)上海裁判・第4号事件 [China

Expeditionary Army Military Code No. 4—Military Code on the Punishment of Enemy Air Crews, August 13, 1942, BC Class (Regarding American Trials) Shanghai Trial, Case No. 4], National Archives of Japan.

199 *The verdict*: Sawada Trial Transcript, 327 (Testimony of Masatoshi Miyano).

199 *prompted a series*: By 1943, the strategic success of the Doolittle Raid in halting offensive operations throughout Asia, including initiatives to invade the Soviet Union and Australia, were evident. George Atcheson to the Secretary of State, "Report on April 18, 1942 Air Raid on Japan by American Air Force," August 9, 1943, Box 2215, Military Intelligence Division Regional File 1922-44, Japan, Records of the War Department General and Special Staffs, Record Group 165, National Archives, College Park. The authors of the U.S. Strategic Bombing Survey concluded that the desire to prevent more Doolittle Raids placed an irrational premium on destroying the U.S. carrier fleet. This led the Japanese Navy to launch a hastily conceived assault on the U.S. fleet at Midway, which resulted in the routing of the loss of four aircraft carriers. Japan also overcompensated on homeland defense. Prior to the Raid, Japan enjoyed air superiority for a radius of 3,000 miles around the mainland. The Doolittle Raid made the Army overcautious in the deployment of its airpower. It bulked up Japan's air defenses, reserving three brigades and five fighter units solely for homeland defense. This left the Army and Navy underprotected in the field and effectively ceded air superiority in the Pacific to the United States. In the Battle for the Solomon Islands, for example, the Japanese Navy repeatedly requested air support, but was denied despite the enormous overcapacity of idle air power on the mainland. US Strategic Bombing Survey Group, U.S. Strategic Bombing Survey (Pacific War), *Summary Report* (July 1, 1946), 3–6; The United States Strategic Bombing Survey (Pacific), Report No. 62, *Japanese Air Power* (July 1946), 9–10.

199 *More air raids*: 東久邇稔彦, 一皇族の戦争日記 (日本週報社, 1957年) [Naruhiko Higashikuni, [Naruhiko Higashikuni, *The War Diary of a Member of the Royal Family* (Nihonshuhosha, 1957)], 112.

199 *Tojo told Bodine*: Edmund Bodine, handwritten notes on Tojo Interview, undated, Bodine Papers.

199 *when the verdicts*: Hideki Tojo, Interrogation, March 29, 1946, pp. 1–4, Doc. 4183 (Exhibit 1984), International Military Tribunal for the Far East, Special Collections, Columbia University Law Library.

200 *Sugiyama was concerned*: 畑俊六(著), 伊藤隆/照沼康孝(編), 続・現代史資料 (4) 陸軍 畑俊六日誌 (みすず書房, 1983年) [Shunroku Hata, *More Contemporary History Materials (4) Army—Diary of Shunroku Hata*, ed. Takashi Ito and Yasutaka Terunuma (Misuzu Shobo, 1983)], 375–376; Hideki Tojo, Interrogation, March 29, 1946, pp. 1–4, Doc. 4183 (Exhibit 1984), International Military Tribunal for the Far East, Special Collections, Columbia University Law Library.

200 *persuaded Sugiyama*: Hideki Tojo, Interrogation, March 29, 1946, pp. 1–4, Doc. 4183 (Exhibit 1984), International Military Tribunal for the Far East, Special Collections, Columbia University Law Library.

200 *Tojo took*: 木戸幸一, 木戸幸一日記下巻 (東京大学出版会, 1966年) [Koichi Kido, *Koichi Kido Diary*, vol. 2 (University of Tokyo Press, 1966)], 963; Stephen Large, *Emperor Hirohito and Showa Japan: A Political Biography* (New York: Routledge, 1992), 254 n.5.

200 *The emperor agreed*: Hajime Sugiyama to Shunroku Hata, cable, October 10, 1942,

Doc. 1027-B (Exhibit 3130), International Military Tribunal for the Far East, Special Collections, Columbia University Law Library.

200 *Tojo readily admitted*: Hideki Tojo, Interrogation, March 29, 1946, pp. 1–4, Doc. 4183 (Exhibit 1984), International Military Tribunal for the Far East, Special Collections, Columbia University Law Library.

200 *One went so far*: The Minister in Switzerland (Harrison) to the Secretary of State, November 5, 1942 (quoting an October 21, 1942 article appearing in *Nichi Nichi*), in E. R. Perkins, ed., *Foreign Relations of the United States: Diplomatic Papers, 1942, General; The British Commonwealth; the Far East*, vol. 1 (Washington, DC: U.S. Government Printing Office, 1960), Doc. 711.

200 *"In my opinion"*: Edmund Bodine, handwritten notes on Tojo Interview, undated, Bodine Papers.

201 *public sympathy*: James Marlow, "Yamashita Case Raises Problems," Associated Press, February 5, 1946; James D. White, "Interpreting the News," Associated Press, February 8, 1946; "Jap Comment on Yamashita Varies," International News Service, February 9, 1946; Donald Sullivan, "Cambridge Lawyer Describes Yamashita Trial Incidents," *Boston Globe*, February 21, 1946, 4; "Yamashita, One of Japan's Ablest Leaders," *Harrisburg Telegraph*, February 23, 1946, 9.

201 *played up the fact*: "Yamashita Opposed Tojo War Crimes Court Told," United Press, November 27, 1945.

201 *To many American*: Osmond K. Fraenkel, "War, Civil Liberties and the Supreme Court 1941 to 1946," *Yale Law Journal* 55 (1946): 730–32; A. Frank Reel, "Even his Enemy," *Ohio State Bar Association Report* 19, no. 10 (1946).

201 *Yamashita really was*: Ben-Ami Shillony, *Revolt in Japan: The Young Officers and the February 26, 1936 Incident* (Princeton, NJ: Princeton University Press, 2015), 19, 31, 37.

201 *The Navy would*: Edmund Bodine, handwritten notes on Tojo Interview, undated, Bodine Papers.

201 *In his famous march*: Allan A. Ryan, *Yamashita's Ghost: War Crimes, MacArthur's Justice, and Command Accountability* (Lawrence, KS: University Press of Kansas, 2012), 16, 24.

201 *Yamashita had*: Shillony, *Revolt in Japan*, 149, 195, 211.

201 *"He had no legal"*: Hideki Tojo, Affidavit, March 13, 1946, Defense Exhibit 8, Sawada Record.

201 *"He would never"*: Edmund Bodine, handwritten notes on Tojo Interview, undated, Bodine Papers.

CHAPTER EIGHTEEN

202 *radio broadcasts*: Deck Log, Aircraft Carrier *Hornet* (CV-8), April 18, 1942, Logbooks of U.S. Navy Ships, Entry 11, Records of the Bureau of Naval Personnel, Record Group 24, National Archives, College Park.

202 *damage report*: 第一復員省法務局調, 昭和17年4月18日空襲時ニ於ケル被害 ["The Damage by the Air-Raiding Attack of April 18th, 1942," Investigated by Legal Bureau of First Ministry of Demobilization], Bodine Files.

202 *In the movie*: *The Purple Heart* (20th Century Fox, 1944); a transcript of the film, evidently derived from closed captioning, is available at https://perma.cc/375L-CL2W.

203   *fit the description*: Takaaki Taguchi, Statement, March 12, 1946, Bodine Files.

204   *Taguchi's impression*: Tsune Nemoto, Written Statement, March 13, 1949, Defense
       Exhibit 7, Sawada Record.

204   *Fellows made a note*: Tsune Nemoto, Written Statement, March 13, 1949, Bodine
       Files.

204   *Fellows had interviewed*: Goichiro Takahashi, Statement, March 12, 1946, Defense
       Exhibit 1, Sawada Record.

204   *a similar story*: Nobuyossi Nagasawa, Statement, March 14, 1946, Defense Exhibit
       2, Sawada Record.

204   *Fuyo Hayakawa*: 第一復員省法務局調, 昭和17年4月18日空襲時ニ於ケル被害
       ["The Damage by the Air-Raiding Attack of April 18th, 1942," Investigated by
       Legal Bureau of First Ministry of Demobilization], Bodine Files.

205   *Fellows asked Hayakawa*: Fuyo Mayakawa, Statement, March 11, 1946, Bodine
       Files.

205   *at Walter Reed*: Robert Hite and Jacob DeShazer, Statement, September 7, 1945, p.
       1, Prosecution Exhibit 22, Sawada Record.

205   *Hite had apparently*: Robert Hite, Questionnaire, undated, p. 5, Box 40, Glines
       Papers.

205   *Ammunition is heavy*: Edward Cuffe, Private Correspondence, January 26, 1997,
       Bodine Papers.

206   *Bodine decided to join*: Hitoshi Hiraoka, Naohiko Tsuda, and Shoei Kukubu, inter-
       view by Edmund Bodine, March 13, 1946, Defense Exhibit 4, Sawada Record.

207   *the people of Katsushika*: Supreme Commander for the Allied Powers, *Summation of
       non-military activities in Japan*, No. 7 (April 1946), §1(57).

207   *The big exception*: Yukoteru Furusawa and Namio Okumura, Affidavit, March 11,
       1946, Bodine Files.

207   *The morning of*: Chiaki Nishikawa, First-hand Account of the Attack on the Mi-
       zumoto School, 東京大空襲・戦災誌第2巻 (東京空襲を記録する会, 1973年)
       [*The Great Tokyo Air Raids—Records of War Damages*, vol. 2 (Association for Re-
       cording Tokyo Air Raids, 1973)], 25–29.

209   *Yukitero Furusawa*: Yukoteru Furusawa and Namio Okumura, Affidavit, March 11,
       1946, Bodine Files.

209   *from the school's gate*: Chiaki Nishikawa, First-hand Account of the Attack on the
       Mizumoto School, 東京大空襲・戦災誌第2巻 (東京空襲を記録する会, 1973
       年) [*The Great Tokyo Air Raids—Records of War Damages*, vol. 2 (Association for
       Recording Tokyo Air Raids, 1973)], 25–29.

209   *The boy had rushed*: Yukoteru Furusawa and Namio Okumura, Affidavit, March
       11, 1946, Bodine Files.

209   *Nishikawa rummaged*: Chiaki Nishikawa, First-hand Account of the Attack on the
       Mizumoto School, 東京大空襲・戦災誌第2巻 (東京空襲を記録する会, 1973
       年) [*The Great Tokyo Air Raids—Records of War Damages*, vol. 2 (Association for
       Recording Tokyo Air Raids, 1973)], 25–29.

210   *There it was*: Tetsuzo Terakado, "Investigation Report of Unnatural Death," April
       18, 1942, Bodine Papers.

210   *Nishikawa wadded*: 第14回 少国民の殉職 ["Martyrdom of Children, No. 14"]
       https://perma.cc/298D-XG4B (relaying firsthand accounts).

210   *Nishikawa telephoned*: Chiaki Nishikawa, First-hand Account of the Attack on the
       Mizumoto School, 東京大空襲・戦災誌第2巻 (東京空襲を記録する会, 1973

年) [*The Great Tokyo Air Raids—Records of War Damages*, vol. 2 (Association for Recording Tokyo Air Raids, 1973)], 25–29

210　*The boy was*: Tetsuzo Terakado, "Investigation Report of Unnatural Death," April 18, 1942, Bodine Papers.

210　*"I feel very sorry"*: "鬼畜の敵、校庭を掃射", 朝日新聞, 昭和17年4月19日 ["Evil Enemy Strafe School Yard," *Asahi Shimbun*, April 19, 1942].

210　*At 2:00 p.m.*: "鬼畜の敵、校庭を掃射", 朝日新聞, 昭和17年4月19日 ["Evil Enemy Strafe School Yard," *Asahi Shimbun*, April 19, 1942].

210　*It was an act*: "敵機は燃え、墜ち、退散", 朝日新聞, 昭和17年4月19日 ["Enemy Planes Burned, Fell, and Retreated," *Asahi Shimbun*, April 19, 1942].

210　*The next day*: "恨み深し、学童告別式", 朝日新聞, 昭和17年4月20日 ["Bitter Funeral Service for Student," *Asahi Shimbun*, April 20, 1942].

211　*The boy's tombstone*: 総務省, 一般戦災死没者の追悼, 石出巳之助之墓 [Ministry of Internal Affairs and Communications, Memorial to the War Dead, Tomb of Minosuke Ishide], https://perma.cc/R8SG-HY3Q.

211　*pilgrimage site*: 第14回 少国民の殉職 ["Martyrdom of Children, No. 14"] https://perma.cc/298D-XG4B (relaying firsthand accounts).

211　*"Had I a machine gun"*: "空襲にあたって・ヨイコドモの手記", 朝日新聞, 昭和18年4月19日 ["On the Air Raid—Good Boys' Notes," *Asahi Shimbun*, April 19, 1943].

211　*painfully described*: Yukoteru Furusawa and Namio Okumura, Affidavit of School Teachers, March 11, 1946, Bodine Papers.

211　*pane of glass*: Sawada Trial Transcript, 263 (Testimony of Edmund Bodine).

211　*Bodine could tell*: Sawada Trial Transcript, 266.

211　*same .30-caliber ammunition*: Gordon L. Rottman, *Browning .30-Caliber Machine Guns* (Oxford: Osprey, 2014), 31.

211　*Nielsen had always*: Chase Nielsen, interview by Stacey Grayson, September 7, 1945, p. 2, Box 40, Glines Papers.

212　*looked just like*: Sawada Trial Transcript, 268 (Testimony of Edmund Bodine).

212　*The nearest building*: Yukoteru Furusawa and Namio Okumura, Affidavit of School Teachers, March 11, 1946, Bodine Papers.

CHAPTER NINETEEN

215　*Nielsen had returned*: "Doolittle Survivors Want Japs Punished," *North-China Daily*, January 19, 1946, 1.

215　*It was a Monday*: Sawada Trial Transcript, 34.

215　*Things were supposed*: *United States v. Shigeru Sawada, et al.*, Adjournment of Proceedings, March 10, 1946; *United States v. Shigeru Sawada, et al.*, Adjournment of Proceedings, March 13, 1946, both reproduced at pp. 33–34 of the Sawada Trial Transcript.

216　*The stern-faced*: Sawada Trial Transcript, 34.

216　*John Hendren took*: Sawada Trial Transcript, 36–37.

216　*"the evidence"*: Sawada Trial Transcript, 36.

217　*McReynolds had been*: Arthur H. Wagner and Leon Braxton, *Birth of a Legend: The Bomber Mafia* (Bloomington, IN: Trafford, 2012), 63–66, 215.

217　*Olds had even*: "Former Wright Field Officer Aids in Record Military Hop," *Dayton Herald*, January 10, 1938, 11.

217   *"William "Billy" Mitchell"*: William Mitchell, *Winged Defense* (New York: Putnam, 1925); Donald Miller, *Masters of the Air: America's Bomber Boys Who Fought the Air War Against Nazi Germany* (New York: Simon & Schuster, 2006), 38–46; Robert T. Finney, *History of the Air Corps Tactical School, 1920–1940*, USAF Historical Study 100 (Air Force History and Museums Program, 1955/1998), 56–62; Walter J. Boyne, "The Tactical School," *Air Force Magazine* 9 (2003), 80–83.

217   *Less was known*: For a list of the judges and their military occupational specialties, see Ray T. Maddocks, Military Commission Order, February 18, 1946, Sawada Record.

217   *Dwyer's confidence*: "Chief Counsel Attends Doolittle Trial," *Shanghai Evening Post*, March 28, 1946.

218   *When Keenan had arrived*: "Keenan Arrives Here, Sees Newsmen at Trial," *North China Daily News*, March 18, 1946.

218   *The Japanese could*: "Keenan Will Study Trial Testimony Here," *North China Daily News*, March 17, 1946.

218   *"an attempt to terrorize"*: "Twenty Top Bracket Jap War Criminals," *North China Daily News*, March 19, 1946.

218   *When Keenan was invited*: Joseph Keenan, Memorandum, "interview by Madame Chiang Kai-shek, Shanghai China," March 28, 1946, Box 2, Joseph Berry Keenan Papers 1942-1947, Harvard Law School Library.

218   *Keenan remained*: Yuma Totani, *The Tokyo War Crimes Trial: The Pursuit of Justice in the Wake of World War II* (Cambridge, MA: Harvard University Press, 2008), 34.

218   *Keenan assured*: "Twenty Top Bracket Jap War Criminals," *North China Daily News*, March 19, 1946.

218   *Asked why*: "Keenan Will Study Trial Testimony Here," *North China Daily News*, March 17, 1946.

218   *Keenan picked*: "Twenty Top Bracket Jap War Criminals," *North China Daily News*, March 19, 1946.

219   *"Does the defense"*: Sawada Trial Transcript, 36.

219   *The newest member*: 宗宮信次、戦犯は国際法上の先例とすべきか、日本法学第23号第5号 (1957年) [Shinji Somiya, "Should War Criminals Be International Law Precedents?," 18 *Nihon Hogaku* 5 (1957)], pp. 607–8.

219   *Here in Shanghai*: Shinji Somiya, "The Account of Legal Proceedings of Court for War Criminal Suspects," p. 36, trans. Kazuo Yoshioka, MLMSS 2207, Williams Papers, Mitchell Library, Sydney; 上海米機搭乗員所罰ニ対スル戦犯事件 – 宗宮弁護士報告、空襲軍律研究資料その1 ["Shanghai War Crimes Trial Regarding the Punishment of American Air Crews—Attorney Somiya's Report,"] undated, p. 89, Materials Regarding Military Discipline for Air Raids—Part 1, Yasukuni Archives.

220   *"Please state"*: Sawada Trial Transcript, 39.

220   *southwestern accent*: Jim Becker, "Doolittle Flier Tells of Deaths," *Shanghai Stars & Stripes*, March 19, 1946, 1.

220   *"He told us"*: Sawada Trial Transcript, 42.

220   *"Did you observe"*: Sawada Trial Transcript, 46.

220   *"On that flight"*: Sawada Trial Transcript, 48.

221   *"I merely gave"*: Sawada Trial Transcript, 51.

221   *Bodine broke in*: Sawada Trial Transcript, 51–52.

221   *"I certainly will"*: Sawada Trial Transcript, 55.

222   *Nielsen got down*: Sawada Trial Transcript, 56.

222   *Hendren walked Nielsen*: Sawada Trial Transcript, 60–61.

223   *Nielsen recounted*: Sawada Trial Transcript, 65–67.

223   *Nielsen then described*: Sawada Trial Transcript, 73–74.

223   *Nielsen had learned*: Sawada Trial Transcript, 75.

224   *In nearly every*: "Execution of Doolittle's Men Told at Trial of Jap Officers," *Chicago Tribune*, March 19, 1946, 9; "4 on Trial for Doolittle Killings," United Press, March 18, 1946; Richard Cushing, "4 Japs on Trial Accused of Killing Doolittle Men," Associated Press, March 18, 1946.

224   *The* Shanghai Stars & Stripes: Jim Becker, "Doolittle Flier Tells of Deaths," *Shanghai Stars & Stripes*, March 19, 1946, 1.

224   *Another newspaper*: "Chief Counsel Attends Doolittle Trial," *Shanghai Evening Post & Mercury*, March 20, 1946.

224   *Hendren's questioning*: Sawada Trial Transcript, 73–77.

224   *"Is not most"*: Edmund Bodine, *United States v. Sawada*, Handwritten Trial Notes March–April 1946, Bodine Papers.

224   *Hendren concluded*: Sawada Trial Transcript, 76–77.

224   *written out a script*: Edmund Bodine, *United States v. Sawada*, Draft Questions for Cross-examination of Chase J. Nielsen, March 1946, Bodine Papers.

225   *When the three*: Chase Nielsen, interview by Carl Sebey, December 7, 1945, Bodine Files.

225   *given a transcript*: Edmund Bodine, *United States v. Sawada*, Handwritten Trial Notes March–April 1946, Bodine Papers.

225   *There was no way*: Chase Nielsen, interview by Carl Sebey, December 7, 1945, p. 2, Bodine Files.

225   *Hendren had asked*: Sawada Trial Transcript, 48.

226   *Nielsen's vivid*: Sawada and Somiya also expressed skepticism about Nielsen's claims of torture. Robert Mikesh, Summary of interview by Shigeru Sawada, February 2, 1965, p. 7, Box 40, Glines Papers; 宗宮真司『上海米機搭乗員所罰ニ対スル戦犯事件 – 宗宮弁護士報告』日付不詳，空襲軍律研究資料その1 [Shinji Somiya, "Shanghai War Crimes Trial Regarding the Punishment of American Air Crews—Attorney Somiya's Report," undated, pp. 84–85, Materials Regarding Military Discipline for Air Raids—Part 1], Yasukuni Archives.

226   *Nielsen had been*: Chase Nielsen, Robert Hite, and Jacob DeShazer, "Saga of Living Death," pp. 7–15, Series II, Box 5, Doolittle Raiders Papers.

226   *None of those details*: Edward Young, Memorandum, "Treatment of Captured Doolittle Fliers, Tokyo Raid, 18 April 1942," August 27, 1945, p. 7, Box 3, China War Crimes Files.

226   *"Never mentioned"*: Edmund Bodine, *United States v. Sawada*, Handwritten Trial Notes March–April 1946, Bodine Papers.

226   *He was sensitive*: John Davey, *Rivers of Consciousness: 1913–1978*, vol. 1, *The Lives and Times of Edward D. Cuffe, Gentleman* (Jayde Design, 2013), 213.

226   *Bodine scratched*: Edmund Bodine, *United States v. Sawada*, Handwritten Trial Notes March–April 1946, Bodine Papers.

226   *He took his place*: Sawada Trial Transcript, 77.

227   *"Isn't it a fact"*: Sawada Trial Transcript, 77–78.

227   *"What was the caliber"*: Sawada Trial Transcript, 79–80.

228   *"In which prison"*: Sawada Trial Transcript, 89–90.

228 *double-check his script*: Edmund Bodine, *United States v. Sawada*, Draft Questions for Cross-examination of Chase J. Nielsen, March 1946, Bodine Papers.

228 *"would you say"*: Sawada Trial Transcript, 90.

229 *Nearly an hour*: Sawada Trial Transcript, 81.

229 *"Weren't you told"*: Sawada Trial Transcript, 80.

229 *"Didn't you say"*: Sawada Trial Transcript, 80.

229 *"We dropped our"*: Sawada Trial Transcript, 82 ("Didn't you make a statement to Carl L. Sebey, SIC, in Utah on December 7, 1945, as follows: 'We dropped our incendiary clusters in a congested residential area?'").

230 *Hendren interjected*: Sawada Trial Transcript, 83.

230 *Those fifteen minutes*: Sawada Trial Transcript, 84.

231 *He had jotted*: Edmund Bodine, *United States v. Sawada*, Handwritten Trial Notes March–April 1946, Bodine Papers.

231 *On the witness stand*: Sawada Trial Transcript, 61.

231 *Young's war crimes*: Chase Nielsen, interview by Carl Sebey, December 7, 1945, p. 7, Bodine Files.

231 *"He explained"*: Sawada Trial Transcript, 86.

231 *"I never did"*: Sawada Trial Transcript, 86.

233 *"What," Bodine asked*: Sawada Trial Transcript, 91.

234 *"You stated yesterday"*: Sawada Trial Transcript, 93.

235 *For Nielsen*: Sawada Trial Transcript, 104.

CHAPTER TWENTY

238 *he had sent*: George Barr, interview by W. L. Brown and Chester I. Lappen, December 30, 1945, Prosecution Transcript Exhibit 21, Sawada Record.

238 *Barr awoke*: Office of Strategic Services, cable, September 3, 1945, Box 218, OSS Field Station Files.

238 *see a Chinese nurse*: C. V. Glines, *Four Came Home* (Missoula, MT: Pictorial Histories, 1995), 136.

238 *Barr could never*: Glines, *Four Came Home*, 139 (firsthand account of George Barr). In truth, Barr was being given heavy doses of vitamin B and plasma. Office of Strategic Services, cable, August 29, 1945, Box 218, OSS Field Station Files; Office of Strategic Services, cable, August 29, 1945, Box 8, OSS Field Station Files.

238 *At least two*: James M. Scott, *Target Tokyo* (New York: Norton, 2015), 457.

238 *He had watched*: George Barr, interview by W. L. Brown and Chester I. Lappen, December 30, 1945, pp. 35–36, Prosecution Transcript Exhibit 21, Sawada Record.

239 *The next thing*: Glines, *Four Came Home*, 136.

239 *Lying on his back*: George Barr, "Nightmares Still Plague Hero of Tokyo Bombing," *Daily Mirror*, May 6, 1946, 10; Glines, *Four Came Home*, 139 (firsthand account of George Barr).

239 *In the middle*: Office of Strategic Services, cable, September 11, 1945, Box 187, OSS Field Station Files.

239 *Barr's conspiracy theory*: George Barr, "Nightmares Still Plague Hero of Tokyo Bombing," *Daily Mirror*, May 6, 1946, 10.

239 *The big giveaway*: Glines, *Four Came Home*, 140 (firsthand account of George Barr).

240 *To the medical staff"*: Glines, *Four Came Home*, 140 (quote from medical file).

240 *He had celebrated*: Factsheet, "Airplane 60-22168," undated, Box 40, Glines Papers.

240 *would never forget*: George Barr, "Destination: Forty Months of Hell," in Carroll V. Glines, ed., *Doolittle's Tokyo Raiders* (New York: Van Nostrand Reinhold, 1981), 305.

240 *rushing up to the deck*: George Barr, Questionnaire, undated, p. 2, Box 40, Glines Papers.

240 *As the weeks*: George Barr, "Nightmares Still Plague Hero of Tokyo Bombing," *Daily Mirror*, May 6, 1946, 10.

241 *Barr bolted*: Glines, *Four Came Home*, 144–45.

241 *Barr was ultimately*: Glines, *Four Came Home*, 147.

242 *Barr would have*: Glines, *Four Came Home*, 152–53.

242 *Eleanor Townes had*: Glines, *Four Came Home*, 153.

242 *Doolittle paid Barr*: Glines, *Four Came Home*, 154.

242 *Dwyer called Hendren*: Sawada Trial Transcript, 107.

243 *"Has this been"*: Sawada Trial Transcript, 107 ("Have they been declassified?").

243 *"Can you save"*: Sawada Trial Transcript, 108.

243 *Barr's description*: George Barr, interview by W. L. Brown and Chester I. Lappen, December 30, 1945, p. 12, Prosecution Transcript Exhibit 21, Sawada Record.

243 *Up until that point*: Tatsuo Kumano, interview by Robert Dwyer, November 21, 1945, pp. 1–5, Box 40, Glines Papers.

243 *Things had changed*: George Barr, interview by W. L. Brown and Chester I. Lappen, December 30, 1945, p. 12, Prosecution Transcript Exhibit 21, Sawada Record.

244 *"The water was going"*: George Barr, interview by W. L. Brown and Chester I. Lappen, December 30, 1945, p. 12, Prosecution Transcript Exhibit 21, Sawada Record.

244 *In the final pages*: George Barr, interview by W. L. Brown and Chester I. Lappen, December 30, 1945, p. 32, Prosecution Transcript Exhibit 21, Sawada Record.

CHAPTER TWENTY-ONE

246 *The rules of evidence*: Report: Trial of War Criminals by Military Commission, Shanghai, China, February 1946, pp. 13–14, Box 12, China War Crimes Files.

246 *his best Jimmy Doolittle*: Sawada Trial Transcript, 130.

247 *press coverage began*: John H. Hendren to Joseph Keenan, April 16, 1946, Box 1, Joseph Berry Keenan Papers 1942–1947, Harvard Law School Library.

247 *Kumashiro thought*: 神代護忠, 上海支店時代の思い出 (1994年) [Moritada Kumashiro, "Recollection of the Days at Shanghai Branch," Manuscript (1994)], pp. 174–76, Call No. GK77-G2, National Diet Library.

247 *Kumashiro could see*: 神代護忠, 上海支店時代の思い出 (1994年) [Moritada Kumashiro, "Recollection of the Days at Shanghai Branch," Manuscript (1994)], p. 170, Call No. GK77-G2, National Diet Library.

247 *Bodine was happy*: Sawada Trial Transcript, 112–24 (Testimony of Tatsuo Michael Kumano), 147–71 (Testimony of Shieji Mayama), 141–76 (Testimony of Yoneda Isamu), 176–82 (Testimony of Yoneya Tomoichi), 182–85 (Testimony of Yutaka Minozaki), 198–204 (Testimony of Suzuki Kuichi).

247 *Kumashiro felt*: 神代護忠, 上海支店時代の思い出 (1994年) [Moritada Kumashiro, "Recollection of the Days at Shanghai Branch," Manuscript (1994)], p. 144, Call No. GK77-G2, National Diet Library.

247 *getting important facts*: Sawada Trial Transcript, 120–22 (Testimony of Tatsuo Michael Kumano).

247   *Now all Dwyer*: Sawada Trial Transcript, 190–91.

247   *Yes, it put*: Itsuro Hata, "Particulars Relating to the Punishment of the American Airman Who Raided the Japanese Homeland on 18 April 1942," translation by Allied Translator and Interpret Section, United States Army Forces, Pacific, Doc. 1870, October 1945, pp. 3–4, Prosecution Exhibit 25, Sawada Record.

248   *they had assured*: Isamu Yoneda, interview by Robert Dwyer, November 20, 1945, p. 1, Box 40, Glines Papers; Sheigeji Mayama, interview by Robert Dwyer, November 20, 1945, p. 3, Box 40, Glines Papers; Tomoichi Yoneya, interview by Robert Dwyer, November 20, 1945, p. 2, Box 40, Glines Papers.

248   *Even Shoshin Ito*: Shoshin Ito, interview by John Hendren, January 6–7, 1946, p. 3, Bodine Papers.

248   "*Do you remember*": Sawada Trial Transcript, 151.

248   "*As a civilian*": Sawada Trial Transcript, 154 (Testimony of Shigeji Mayama).

249   "*I think the defense*": Sawada Trial Transcript, 186.

249   "*Do you see*": Sawada Trial Transcript, 148.

249   *In his frustration*: Sawada Trial Transcript, 185.

249   *Exchanges like these*: 神代護忠, 上海支店時代の思い出 (1994年) [Moritada Kumashiro, "Recollection of the Days at Shanghai Branch," Manuscript (1994)], p. 216, Call No. GK77-G2, National Diet Library.

249   *Like Kumashiro*: 盛田良治, 日本占領期フィリピンの現地調査, 人文学報第79号163頁 (1997年) [Yoshiharu Morita, "Field Research of the Philippines Islands During the Japanese Occupation," 79 *Jimbun Gakuho* 163 (1997)].

250   *Somiya had grown*: Koichi Ikeda, personal interview, April 21, 2015.

250   *He tended to cross*: Shigeo Komatsu, personal interview, May 12, 2015.

250   *was so short*: Harou Somiya, personal interview, April 21, 2015.

250   *In this courtroom battle*: 神代護忠, 上海支店時代の思い出 (1994年) [Moritada Kumashiro, "Recollection of the Days at Shanghai Branch," Manuscript (1994)], p. 127, Call No. GK77-G2, National Diet Library.

250   *Dwyer began his finale*: Sawada Trial Transcript, 207–10.

251   *Dwyer solemnly picked*: "Fliers' Ashes Feature Trial," United Press, March 23, 1946.

251   "*now offers in evidence*": Sawada Trial Transcript, 209.

251   *With twenty-one years*: Sawada Trial Transcript, 220.

252   "*Is it not true*": Sawada Trial Transcript, 225 ("Is it not further true, Colonel, that different men's systems demand different diets?").

253   *Dwyer then pulled*: Sawada Trial Transcript, 232–33.

253   *They had given*: Caesar Luis DosRemedios, Statement, September 19, 1945, p. 2, Prosecution Exhibit 26, Sawada Record.

253   "*I hereby send*": Sawada Trial Transcript, 233 (Testimony of John Hendren).

253   *Those translations*: Army Advisory Group, Nanking China, cable, March 7, 1946, War Crimes Files, Incoming and Outgoing Radios 21 April 1945 to 6 March 1946, Box 14, China War Crimes Files.

253   *Harold Spatz had*: Harold Spatz to Robert Spatz, Jr., October 1942, Box 11, China War Crimes Files.

253   *He had then written*: Harold Spatz to Robert Spatz, October 1942, Box 11, China War Crimes Files.

254   *William Farrow had taken*: David Lawrence, "Today in Washington," *New York Evening Post*, October 22, 1942.

254   *Confronting his own death*: William Farrow to Jesse Farrow, October 1942, Box 11, China War Crimes Files.

254   *"So live"*: *Poems by William Cullen Bryant: Classic American Poetry of the Romantic Era* (Adansonia, 2018), 16.

254   *"I've built my house"*: William Farrow to Margaret Stem, October 1942, Box 11, China War Crimes Files.

254   *"Please carry on"*: William Farrow to Jesse Farrow, October 1942, Box 11, China War Crimes Files.

255   *Farrow had written*: William Farrow to Elizabeth Sims, October 1942, Box 11, China War Crimes Files.

255   *Dean Hallmark had*: Dean Hallmark unaddressed letter, October 14, 1942, Box 11, China War Crimes Files.

255   *looking forward*: Ling Chung, interview by Robert Dwyer, January 8, 1946, p. 2, Box 40, Glines Papers.

255   *When he had been*: Dean Hallmark to Mother, Dad, and Sis, October 1942, Box 11, China War Crimes Files.

255   *"They have just"*: Dean Hallmark to Mother, Dad, and Sis, October 1942, Box 11, China War Crimes Files.

255   *football season*: Dean Hallmark to Mother, Dad, and Sister, October 1942, Box 11, China War Crimes Files.

256   *"I wish the court"*: Dean Hallmark to Mother, Dad, and Sis, October 1942, Box 11, China War Crimes Files.

256   *"the American Government"*: Sawada Trial Transcript, 230.

256   *Later that afternoon*: Sawada Trial Transcript, 244.

256   *They also saw*: 羽山忠弘, ある戦犯事件弁護の思い出, 大東法学第18号179頁 (1991年) [Tadahiro Hayama, "Recollection of Defending a War Trial Case," 18 *Daito Hogaku* 179 (1991)], 193.

256   *scratchings that George Barr*: Irene Kuhn, "Tea and Ashes," in Overseas Press Club of America, eds., *Deadline Delayed* (New York: Dutton, 1947), 268, 274.

256   *a plain room*: Yusei Wako, interview by John Hendren, January 2, 1946, p. 1, Box 40, Glines Papers.

256   *To complete the tour*: Sawada Trial Transcript, 244.

257   *"The Old World"*: James Reston, "Council in Session," *New York Times*, March 26, 1945, 1.

258   *Once a photographer*: Photo of Execution Reenactment, March 1946, Bodine Papers.

CHAPTER TWENTY-TWO

259   *Somiya complained*: 宗宮真司『上海米機搭乗員所罰ニ対スル戦犯事件 – 宗宮弁護士報告』日付不詳, 空襲軍律研究資料その1 [Shinji Somiya, "Shanghai War Crimes Trial Regarding the Punishment of American Air Crews—Attorney Somiya's Report," undated, p. 79, Materials Regarding Military Discipline for Air Raids—Part 1], Yasukuni Archives.

260   *to offer amnesty*: U.S. Army, Report of Proceedings of Board of Inquiry in the Case of Lt Col Edmund Bodine, 3481A, USAF, 23–24 February 1954, pp. 25–56 (Testimony of Elizabeth Bodine), Bodine Family Archives.

260   *the more likely*: Before the modern international law governing refugees, statelessness was especially dangerous because such individuals were at the mercy of whichever government controlled the places in which they found themselves. For more on the legal plight of the White Russian refugees in China at this time, see Anatol M. Kotenev, "The Status of the Russian Emigrants in China," *American Journal of International Law* 28, no. 3 (July 1934).

260   *Never one to accept*: Natalie and Elizabeth Bodine, personal interview, December 17, 2014.

260   *McReynolds granted*: *United States v. Sawada, et al.*, Adjournment of Proceedings, March 29, 1946, Bodine Papers.

260   *Bodine wrote out*: Edmund Bodine, *United States v. Sawada*, Draft Opening Statement, March 1946, Bodine Papers.

262   *The photos*: Sawada Trial Transcript, 268 (Testimony of Edmund Bodine).

263   *John Adams*: For then-contemporary discussions of John Adams and his role in the Boston Massacre Case, see Samuel Willard, *Great Americans of History: John Adams* (H. G. Campbell, 1903), 117–18; Colonel Robert McCormick, "The Boston Massacre," *Chicago Tribune*, March 2, 1947, 20; "Trends of the Times," Syndicated Feature, January 1946. ("John Adams, American patriot, defended in court the legal rights of the British soldiers prosecuted for the Boston Massacre. Did that make John Adams a defender of the Boston Massacre? If you answer yes, you fail in your American intelligence test.")

263   *had no practice*: Natalie Bodine, personal interview, January 1, 2020.

263   *Bodine had driven*: "Sergeant Frank Stratton Is Killed; Driver Arrested Fleeing from Scene," *Norwalk Hour*, October 14, 1930, 1.

263   *Fordham would soon*: For a history of college football in this period, see David Maraniss, *When Pride Still Mattered: A Life of Vince Lombardi* (New York: Simon & Schuster, 1999).

263   *The game itself*: "Fisher's Nose Broken in Game with Eagles," *Boston Globe*, October 14, 1930, 14; "Goal from Field Enables Fordham Eleven to Edge Out Boston College, 3 to 0," *Hartford Courant*, October 14, 1930, 15.

263   *Alma Bodine's Ford*: Coroner's Report, "Case of Death of Frank Stratton, Town Norwalk, October 14th 1930," Fairfield County, Coroner Records 1883–1979, vol. 58, p. 572, Fairfield Files.

263   *around 9:00 p.m.*: Inquiry re Death of Frank Stratton, p. 50 (Testimony of Edmund Bodine), October 16, 1930, Fairfield Files.

264   *Around 5:15 a.m.*: Coroner's Report, "Case of Death of Frank Stratton, Town Norwalk, October 14th 1930," Fairfield County, Coroner Records 1883–1979, vol. 58, p. 572, Fairfield Files.

264   *There were no streetlights*: Inquiry re Death of Frank Stratton, p. 20 (Testimony of Michael M. Hall), October 16, 1930, Fairfield Files.

264   *He had been following*: Inquiry re Death of Frank Stratton, p. 17 (Testimony of Frank Rich), October 16, 1930, Fairfield Files.

264   *Bodine was going*: Inquiry re Death of Frank Stratton, p. 27 (Testimony of Theodore R. Houck), October 16, 1930, Fairfield Files.

264   *swerved into*: Inquiry re Death of Frank Stratton, p. 49 (Testimony of Edmund Bodine), October 16, 1930, Fairfield Files.

264   *It was a sound*: Inquiry re Death of Frank Stratton, pp. 35–36 (Testimony of Joseph John Watral), October 16, 1930, Fairfield Files.

264 *Bodine floored*: Inquiry re Death of Frank Stratton, pp. 4–5, 9–10 (Testimony of Paul McGrath), October 16, 1930, Fairfield Files.

264 *Then Billy Shea*: Inquiry re Death of Frank Stratton, p. 41 (Testimony of William Stephen Shea), October 16, 1930, Fairfield Files.

264 *Bodine's left headlight*: Inquiry re Death of Frank Stratton, p. 37 (Testimony of Joseph John Watral), October 16, 1930, Fairfield Files.

264 *Bodine saw*: Inquiry re Death of Frank Stratton, p. 13 (copy of police report written by Paul McGrath, October 14, 1930), October 16, 1930, Fairfield Files.

264 *Bodine and Shea scrambled*: Inquiry re Death of Frank Stratton, p. 27 (Testimony of Theodore R. Houck), October 16, 1930, Fairfield Files.

264 *He was round bodied*: "Gets His Man" *Norwalk Hour*, October 14, 1930, 1.

264 *"Don't try"*: Inquiry re Death of Frank Stratton, p. 39 (Testimony of Joseph John Watral), October 16, 1930, Fairfield Files.

264 *The man with the pistol*: Inquiry re Death of Frank Stratton, pp. 1–4 (Testimony of Paul McGrath), October 16, 1930, Fairfield Files.

264 *The driver*: Inquiry re Death of Frank Stratton, p. 25 (Testimony of Theodore R. Houck), October 16, 1930, Fairfield Files.

265 *he had bashed*: Inquiry re Death of Frank Stratton, p. 4 (Testimony of Paul Mc-Grath), October 16, 1930, Fairfield Files.

265 *fracturing his skull*: Medical Examiner's Report, "Case of Death of Frank Stratton, Town Norwalk, October 14th 1930," Fairfield County, Coroner Records 1883–1979, vol. 58, p. 571, Fairfield Files.

265 *McGrath shouted*: Inquiry re Death of Frank Stratton, pp. 6–7 (Testimony of Paul McGrath), October 16, 1930, Fairfield Files; Inquiry re Death of Frank Stratton, pp. 33–34 (Testimony of John L. Mooshian), October 16, 1930, Fairfield Files.

265 *All Billy Shea*: Inquiry re Death of Frank Stratton, pp. 11–12 (Testimony of Paul McGrath), October 16, 1930, Fairfield Files.

265 *Bodine stuttered*: Inquiry re Death of Frank Stratton, pp. 7–8 (Testimony of Paul McGrath), October 16, 1930, Fairfield Files.

265 *"I didn't see"*: Inquiry re Death of Frank Stratton, p. 31 (Testimony of John L. Mooshian), October 16, 1930, Fairfield Files.

265 *Bodine was arrested*: Inquiry re Death of Frank Stratton, p. 13 (copy of Police Report written by Paul McGrath, October 14,1930), October 16, 1930, Fairfield Files.

265 *his parents had*: "Sergeant Frank Stratton Is Killed; Driver Arrested Fleeing from Scene," *Norwalk Hour*, October 14, 1930, 1.

265 *had been practicing*: "Fifty Are Taking Bar Examinations," *Hartford Courant*, December 31, 1915, 5.

265 *was working toward*: "Judicial Resolutions," *Hartford Courant*, January 25, 1933, 9.

265 *Two days after*: Inquiry re Death of Frank Stratton, October 16, 1930, Fairfield Files; "Driver Refuses to Give Testimony," *Norwalk Hour*, October 17, 1930, 1–2.

265 *McGrath claimed*: Inquiry re Death of Frank Stratton, pp. 7–8 (Testimony of Paul McGrath), October 16, 1930, Fairfield Files.

265 *The coroner concluded*: Coroner's Report, "Case of Death of Frank Stratton, Town Norwalk, October 14th 1930," *Fairfield County, Coroner Records 1883–1979*, vol. 58, p. 574, Fairfield Files.

265 *Statton's death made*: "Long Island Man Held as Driver Who Killed Policeman in Norwalk," *Hartford Courant*, October 15, 1930; "Man Held in Death of Norwalk Officer," *Boston Globe*, October 15, 1930; "Hit-Run Autoist Kills Cousin of Circus

Celebrity," *New York Daily News*, October 15, 1930; "Cousin of Tom Thumb Killed," *Boston Globe*, October 14, 1930.

265 *A father of six*: "Sergeant Frank Stratton Is Killed; Driver Arrested Fleeing from Scene," *Norwalk Hour*, October 14, 1930, 1.

266 *At his funeral*: "Honor Sergeant Stratton in Final Glowing Tribute," *Norwalk Hour*, October 17, 1930.

266 *Bodine was charged*: State v. Bodine, Case No. 30-cr-SEALED (Conn., October 15, 1930).

266 *Both Billy Shea*: Inquiry re Death of Frank Stratton, pp. 32–39 (Testimony of Joseph John Watral), October 16, 1930, Fairfield Files; Inquiry re Death of Frank Stratton, pp. 41–43 (Testimony of William Stephen Shea), October 16, 1930, Fairfield Files.

266 *Billy Shea said*: Inquiry re Death of Frank Stratton, p. 44 (Testimony of William Stephen Shea), October 16, 1930, Fairfield Files.

266 *The driver of the Plymouth*: Inquiry re Death of Frank Stratton, pp. 27–28 (Testimony of William Stephen Shea), October 16, 1930, Fairfield Files.

266 *At the police stations*: Inquiry re Death of Frank Stratton, p. 49 (Testimony of Edmund Bodine), October 16, 1930, Fairfield Files.

266 *In 1930*: An Act Concerning Juvenile Courts, Pub.Acts 1921, c. 336 (Connecticut).

266 *a movement under way*: Juvenile Courts, Cumulative Supplement to General Statutes, January Sessions 1931, 1933, and 1935, State of Connecticut, c. 95 (1935).

266 *Giving birth to*: Alma Bodine, Affidavit, February 10, 1954, U.S. Army, Report of Proceedings of Board of Inquiry in the Case of Lt Col Edmund Bodine, 3481A, USAF, 23–24 February 1954, Respondent Exhibit 10, Bodine Papers.

266 *She was sure*: Certificate #53163, New York, New York, Birth Index, 1910–1965 [database online], Lehi, UT, USA: Ancestry.com, 2017.

267 *The Norwalk prosecutors*: Background source, personal interview, 2019.

267 *Stratton's wife*: Stratton v. Bodine, Case No. 31-cv-37041 (Fairfield Superior Court, 1931); "Cona. Company Sued for $50,000," *Hartford Courant*, October 29, 1931, 3.

267 *Bodine missed*: Mary Kinahan-Ockay (Xavier High School Archivist), personal correspondence, May 2019.

267 *class president*: The Xavier 12, No. 4 (January 1933), Xavier High School Archives, New York, NY.

267 *Bodine would say*: Natalie Bodine, personal correspondence, May 20, 2019.

267 *"A man is either"*: Thomas Aquinas, *Summa Theologica*, III.85.3.

CHAPTER TWENTY-THREE

269 *Monday morning*: Sawada Trial Transcript, 245.

270 *Bodine then took the stand*: Sawada Trial Transcript, 256.

271 *Dwyer knew*: "Trial of War Criminals by Military Commission, Shanghai China," February 1946, pp. 11–12, Box 12, China War Crimes Files.

272 *"Is this from"*: Sawada Trial Transcript, 266.

273 *Bodine and Fellows took*: Sawada Trial Transcript, 247–62.

273 *Mizumoto Elementary School*: "Teachers Testify for Defense at Doolittle Hearing," *North China Daily News*, April 1, 1946.

273 *Yasuo Karakawa*: Issuo Karakawa, "Circumstances Relating to Lt General Sawada," March 7, 1946, Defense Exhibit 15, Sawada Record.

274 *The problem was*: Sawada Trial Transcript, 448 (Testimony of Shigeru Sawada).

274 *The closest he had*: Sawada Trial Transcript, 432 (Testimony of Shigeru Sawada).

274 *Colonel Shoshin Ito*: "Translation of Diary of General Shigeru Sawada," undated (1946), p. 2, Box 11, China War Crimes Files.

274 *All the usual*: Sawada Trial Transcript, 346–47 (Testimony of Shoshin Ito).

274 *Sawada had stamped*: Sawada Trial Transcript, 433 (Testimony of Shigeru Sawada).

274 *Sawada had made*: Sawada Shigeru, interview by Robert Dwyer, February 12, 1946, p. 2, Bodine Papers.

274 *already aware*: Sawada Trial Transcript, 432 (Testimony of Shigeru Sawada).

274 *"I feel sorry"*: Sawada Trial Transcript, 448 (Testimony of Shigeru Sawada).

275 *For Bodine's purposes*: Sawada Trial Transcript, 432 (Testimony of Shigeru Sawada).

275 *To prove their case*: Sawada Trial Transcript, 284.

276 *Bodine's script*: Edmund Bodine, *United States v. Sawada*, Draft Questions for Masatoshi Miyano, March 1946, Bodine Papers.

276 *"At the time"*: Sawada Trial Transcript, 292.

CHAPTER TWENTY-FOUR

277 *He had spent hours*: Shoshin Ito, interview by John Hendren, January 6–7, 1946, Bodine Files.

277 *Shimomura had*: A month after the Doolittle Trial concluded, SCAP was discussing how to release Shimomura with minimal public attention. "Release of Suspected War Criminal," June 1, 1946, Box 719, Intelligence Dossiers.

277 *It had been MacArthur's*: Memorandum for Record, undated, Box 719, Intelligence Dossiers; C. A. Willoughby, Memorandum for the Chief of Staff, July 15, 1946, Box 719, Intelligence Dossiers.

277 *Behind the scenes*: Office of the Chief of Civil Intelligence, Memorandum for Record, February 8, 1946, Box 719, Intelligence Dossiers.

278 *But leaving Shimomura*: James M. Scott, *Target Tokyo* (New York: Norton, 2015), 472.

278 *Ito had known*: Shoshin Ito, interview by Edmund Bodine et al., March 24, 1946, p. 2, Bodine Files.

278 *Now in his midfifties*: H. C. Bishop, "Military and Biographical History of Ito, Shoshin," undated, Box 1081, War Crimes Case Files.

278 *"scum of the Army"*: Gunji Shimomitsu to Walton H. Walker, Petition, February 21, 1949, p. 2, Box 1079, War Crimes Case Files.

278 *treated as soldiers*: Shoshin Ito, interview by R. N. Tait, October 28, 1946–November 18, 1946, pp. 1–3, Box 1081, War Crimes Case Files.

278 *full military officers*: Gunji Shimomitsu to Walton H. Walker, Petition, February 21, 1949, p. 2, Box 1079, War Crimes Case Files.

278 *When Ito first got*: Itsuro Hata, "Particulars Relating to the Punishment of the American Airman Who Raided the Japanese Homeland on 18 April 1942," translation by Allied Translator and Interpret Section, United States Army Forces, Pacific, Doc. 1870, October 1945, p. 3, Prosecution Exhibit 25, Sawada Record; Shoshin Ito, interview by Edmund Bodine et al., March 24, 1946, p. 2, Bodine Files.

279 *brought to him*: Shoshin Ito, interview by R. N. Tait, October 28, 1946–November 18, 1946, pp. 9–11, Box 1081, War Crimes Case Files; Izumi Ogata, interview by Alf Watson, January 15, 1946, p. 1, Bodine Papers; Shoshin Ito, interview by Edmund Bodine et al., March 24, 1946, p. 1, Bodine Files.

279   *they took up*: Izumi Ogata, interview by Alf Watson, January 15, 1946, p. 3, Bodine Papers.

279   *Like everyone else*: Shoshin Ito, interview by John Hendren, January 6–7, 1946, p. 1, Bodine Files.

279   *the 13th Army received*: "Translation of Diary of General Shigeru Sawada," undated (1946), p. 1, Box 11, China War Crimes Files.

279   "*machine-gunned innocent children*": "Complete Failure of Air Raid on Nippon Stressed by Army Spokesman Here," *Shanghai Times*, April 22, 1942.

279   *Ito did not think*: Shoshin Ito, interview by Edmund Bodine et al., March 24, 1946, p. 1, Bodine Files.

279   "*The airmen*": Itsuro Hata, "Particulars Relating to the Punishment of the American Airman Who Raided the Japanese Homeland on 18 April 1942," translation by Allied Translator and Interpret Section, United States Army Forces, Pacific, Doc. 1870, October 1945, p. 3, Prosecution Exhibit 25, Sawada Record ("The airmen were to be tried by the military tribunal").

279   *At first*: Shoshin Ito, interview by Edmund Bodine et al., March 24, 1946, p. 1, Bodine Files.

279   *The Army had*: The Japanese had used military commissions in China since 1939 to try anyone who violated the military laws in China. Procedurally, these military commissions largely mirrored ordinary Japanese courts-martial with the important proviso that they were only required to do so "as much as possible." Toshizo Nishio, "Regulations Pertaining to the Judicial Decision by Martial Law of the Dispatched Army in China," October 1, 1939, Bodine Files. In the main, it was understood that these tribunals would be used to try Chinese spies and guerrillas, though in practice, this included any Chinese who opposed Japan's occupation. Japan's official position was that the war in China never actually rose to a state of "war." Instead, Japan insisted that the fighting in China was merely an "incident." Pursuant to various treaties, agreements, and concessions, Japan had the legal right to be in China. If its legal rights were compromised in some way, Japan claimed the right to use military force to protect its interests. Japan was not, therefore, at war with China. Instead, the Japanese Army was only suppressing hostile Chinese elements, whose attacks against Japanese soldiers were acts of criminality. The principal consequence of this was that Chinese fighters were not treated as prisoners of war. The Japanese claimed the right to attack Chinese forces at will, but if those same Chinese forces returned fire, they were acting as "guerrillas" and "bandits." For a discussion, *see* B. V. A. Röling and C.F. Rüter, Eds., *The Tokyo Judgment—The International Military Tribunal for the Far East (IMTFE), 29 April 1946–12 November 1948* (Amsterdam: APA-University Press 1977), 386.

279   *not committed any crimes*: Shoshin Ito, interview by Edmund Bodine et al., March 24, 1946, pp. 1, 6, Bodine Papers.

279   *among the documents*: Seimu Tanabe to Jun Atomiya, July 28, 1942, Doc. 1793 (Exhibit 1993), International Military Tribunal for the Far East, Special Collections, Columbia University Law Library.

279   *It authorized*: Deputy Chief of Staff, Notification by the Vice-Chief of the Army General Staff, General Staff Secret Document No. 383-1, July 28, 1942, Bodine Papers. Article II of the draft specified four crimes made triable by military commission: 1) bombing, strafing, or making other kinds of attacks "for the purpose of terrorizing and wounding or killing the ordinary populace," 2) bombing, strafing,

or carrying out attacks for the purpose of destroying civilian property; 3) bombing, strafing, or carrying out attacks against nonmilitary targets not otherwise collateral damage; and 4) perpetrating "outrageous and inhuman acts ignoring humanity."

279   *The first was*: Shoshin Ito, interview by Edmund Bodine et al., March 24, 1946, p. 2, Bodine Files.

279   *But perhaps this law*: Sawada Trial Transcript, 316 (Testimony of Shoshin Ito); Shoshin Ito, interview by R. N. Tait, October 28, 1946–November 18, 1946, p. 2, Box 1081, War Crimes Case Files; Itsuro Hata, "Particulars Relating to the Punishment of the American Airman Who Raided the Japanese Homeland on 18 April 1942," translation by Allied Translator and Interpret Section, United States Army Forces, Pacific, Doc. 1870, October 1945, pp. 4–5, Prosecution Exhibit 25, Sawada Record. The view that the Enemy Airmen's law was a mere codification of existing international law, and therefore not an ex post facto law, was widespread. *IMTFE Transcript*, 36,419-36,420 (Testimony of Hideki Tojo). ("This law is an assembly of the rules and customs of land warfare and of the draft regulations concerning aerial warfare, and was therefore not in the nature of a new set of regulations, but was rather a compilation of the principles of the law and regulations then existing in international practice."); "China Expeditionary Force Order No. 4, Military Law Concerning the Punishment of Enemy Airmen Interpretation of Article II," undated, General Headquarters, Supreme Commander for the Allied Powers, Military Intelligence Section General Staff, Allied Translator and Interpreter Section, Doc. No. 6789, Bodine Files.

280   *The other problem*: Shoshin Ito, interview by R. N. Tait, October 28, 1946–November 18, 1946, pp. 10–11, Box 1081, War Crimes Case Files; Itsuro Hata, "Particulars Relating to the Punishment of the American Airman Who Raided the Japanese Homeland on 18 April 1942," translation by Allied Translator and Interpret Section, United States Army Forces, Pacific, Doc. 1870, October 1945, p. 3, Prosecution Exhibit 25, Sawada Record.

280   *"Get in touch"*: Shoshin Ito, interview by Edmund Bodine et al., March 24, 1946, p. 2, Bodine Files.

280   *Ito explained*: Itsuro Hata, "Particulars Relating to the Punishment of the American Airman Who Raided the Japanese Homeland on 18 April 1942," translation by Allied Translator and Interpret Section, United States Army Forces, Pacific, Doc. 1870, October 1945, p. 3, Prosecution Exhibit 25, Sawada Record.

280   *Ogata had made*: Shoshin Ito, interview by R. N. Tait, October 28, 1946–November 18, 1946, p. 11, Box 1081, War Crimes Case Files.

280   *He soon made*: Izumi Ogata, interview by Alf Watson, January 15, 1946, pp. 1–3, Bodine Papers.

280   *In the meanitime*: Shoshin Ito, interview by R. N. Tait, October 28, 1946–November 18, 1946, p. 11, Box 1081, War Crimes Case Files.

280   *Ogata had his men*: Izumi Ogata, interview by Alf Watson, January 15, 1946, p. 2, Bodine Papers.

281   *Ito never*: Shoshin Ito, interview by R. N. Tait, October 28, 1946–November 18, 1946, p. 11, Box 1081, War Crimes Case Files.

281   *Various theories*: IMTFE Transcript, 29,043-29,044 (Testimony of Riukichi Tanaka).

281   *visited Mitchell Field*: "Flying Generals in Conference at Mitchell Field," *New York Times*, June 14, 1942, 5.

281   *Doolittle did not know*: For the history of the case of the Nazi Saboteurs, see Noah Feldman, *Scorpions: The Battles and Triumphs of FDR's Great Supreme Court Justices* (New York: Twelve, 2010), 215–25; David Alan Johnson, *Betrayal: The True Story of J. Edgar Hoover and the Nazi Saboteurs Captured during WWII* (New York: Hippocrene Books, 2007); Michael Dobbs, *Saboteurs: The Nazi Raid on America* (New York: Knopf, 2004); Eugene Rachlis, *They Came to Kill* (New York: Random House, 1961); George Dasch, *Eight Spies Against America* (New York: R. M. Mc-Bride, 1959).

281   *A Coast Guard coxswain*: Testimony of John C. Cullen, *United States v. Burger, et al.*, Military Commission to Try Persons Charged with Offenses Against the Law of War and the Articles of War, July 8, 1942 to July 31, 1942, p. 102, Box 17, Court-Martial Case Files, Entry 1009, Records of the Judge Advocate General, Record Group 153, National Archives, College Park.

281   *The run-in*: "Reminiscences of Kenneth Claiborne Royall: oral history, 1963," p. 41, Columbia University Oral History Collection.

281   *In short order*: Opening Statement of the Prosecution, *United States v. Burger, et al.*, Military Commission to Try Persons Charged with Offenses Against the Law of War and the Articles of War, July 8, 1942 to July 31, 1942, pp. 71–72, Box 17, Court-Martial Case Files, Entry 1009, Records of the Judge Advocate General, Record Group 153, National Archives, College Park.

281   *Fearing embarrassment*: Johnson, *Betrayal*, 148.

281   *The secret trial*: *United States v. Burger, et al.*, Military Commission to Try Persons Charged with Offenses Against the Law of War and the Articles of War, July 8, 1942 to July 31, 1942, Boxes 17–21, Court-Martial Case Files, Entry 1009, Records of the Judge Advocate General, Record Group 153, National Archives, College Park.

281   *But the team*: "Reminiscences of Kenneth Claiborne Royall: oral history, 1963," p. 34, Columbia University Oral History Collection.

282   *They publicly petitioned*: *Ex parte Quirin*, Case Nos. 1–7, Transcript of Oral Argument (U.S., July 29, 1942), 81.

282   *The case of*: Dobbs, *Saboteurs*, 238.

282   *"On July 31"*: *Ex parte Quirin*, 317 U.S. 1 (1947).

282   *"RULING UNANIMOUS"*: Lewis Wood, "Ruling Unanimous," *New York Times*, August 1, 1942.

282   *had commuted*: Dasch, *Eight Spies Against America*, 159.

282   *it was an opinon*: *In re Yamashita*, 327 U.S. 1, 7 (1946).

282   *"Roosevelt's blood purge"*: Rachlis, *They Came to Kill*, 289.

282   *Japanese press condemned*: "U.S.A. Supreme Court Rejects Saboteur Plea," *Shanghai Times*, August 2, 1942, 8.

282   *the Foreign Office spokesman*: Rachlis, *They Came to Kill*, 289.

282   *Ito found himself*: Shoshin Ito, interview by R. N. Tait, October 28, 1946–November 18, 1946, pp. 10–11, Box 1081, War Crimes Case Files.

282   *Sugiyama let it be known*: Seimu Tanabe to Jun Atomiya, July 28, 1942, Doc. 1793 (Exhibit 1993), International Military Tribunal for the Far East, Special Collections, Columbia University Law Library.

283   *Ito was confident*: Sawada Trial Transcript, 346–47 (Testimony of Shoshin Ito).

283   *The final version*: 支那派遣軍軍令第4号・敵航空機搭乗員処罰ニ関スル軍律, 昭和17年8月13日, BC級(アメリカ裁判関係)上海裁判・第4号事件 [China

Expeditionary Army Military Code No. 4—Military Code on the Punishment of Enemy Air Crews, August 13, 1942, BC Class (Regarding American Trials) Shanghai Trial, Case No. 4], National Archives of Japan.

283 *He had been tempted*: Sawada Trial Transcript, 322 (Testimony of Shoshin Ito); Shoshin Ito, interview by Edmund Bodine et al., March 24, 1946, p. 3, Bodine Files; Itsuro Hata, "Particulars Relating to the Punishment of the American Airman Who Raided the Japanese Homeland on 18 April 1942," translation by Allied Translator and Interpret Section, United States Army Forces, Pacific, Doc. 1870, October 1945, p. 3, Prosecution Exhibit 25, Sawada Record.

283 *Every case*: Shoshin Ito, interview by Edmund Bodine et al., March 27, 1946, p. 7, Bodine Files; Ryuhei Okada and Yusei Wako, interview by Charles Fellows, February 15, 1946, p. 1, Bodine Files; Sawada Trial Transcript, 320 (Testimony of Shoshin Ito).

283 *Wako had arrived*: Yusei Wako, interview by Robert Tait, August 25, 1947–September 5, 1947, p. 1, Box 1081, War Crimes Case Files.

283 *On paper*: Shoshin Ito, interview by R. N. Tait, October 28, 1946–November 18, 1946, p. 2, Box 1081, War Crimes Case Files.

283 *Toyama Nakajo*: Shoshin Ito, interview by Edmund Bodine et al., March 24, 1946, p. 3, Bodine Files.

283 *Ryuhei Okada*: Noboru 7330 Butai Special Court-Martial, June 29, 1942, U.S. Army Translation, September 30, 1945, China War Crimes Files.

283 *Wako announced*: Ryuhei Okada and Yusei Wako, interview by Charles Fellows, February 15, 1946, p. 1, Bodine Files.

284 *The slightest bit*: Proceedings of a Board of Officers in the Case of Yusei Wako, Convicted Japanese War Criminal, May 18, 1949, Box 1079, War Crimes Case Files.

284 *Ito was forced*: U.S. Army, Record of Trial, *United States v. Kajuro Aihara, et al*, p. 801 (Testimony of Yusei Wako), Box 1645, SCAP Legal Section, Prosecution Division, Entry 1321, Allied Occupation Records.

284 *Ito saw to it*: Shiro Okada to Walton H. Walker, "Petition," March 22, 1949, Box 1079, War Crimes Case Files.

284 *For a combination of reasons*: Yusei Wako, interview by Robert Tait, August 25, 1947–September 5, 1947, p. 1, Box 1081, War Crimes Case Files.

284 *Sadamu Shimomura*: Central Liaison Office, Tokyo Police File, "Shimomura Sadamu (General): Minister of War in the Higashikuni Cabinet, 17 August 1945–5 October 1945," p. 4, Box 719, Intelligence Dossiers.

284 *tapped Ito*: Shoshin Ito, interview by R. N. Tait, October 28, 1946–November 18, 1946, p. 3, Box 1081, War Crimes Case Files.

284 *tapped Wako*: H. C. Bishop, "Military and Biographical History of Wako Yusei," undated, Box 1081, War Crimes Case Files.

284 *Wako was put*: Yusei Wako, interview by Robert Tait, August 25, 1947–September 5, 1947, pp. 2–3, Box 1081, War Crimes Case Files.

284 *Things in Fukuoka*: Motoharu Shichida, Statement, January 3, 1949, pp. 2–3, Box 1079, War Crimes Case Files.

284 *After the fall*: Masazumi Inada, "Petition in Regard to the Aburayama Case," April 15, 1949, p. 2, Box 1079, War Crimes Case Files.

284 *He was apt*: Affidavit of Matsuzo Shimazaki, *United States v. Kajuro Aihara, et al.*, Prosecution Exhibit 192, pp. 17–18, Box 692, SCAP Legal Section, Prosecution Division, Entry 1321, Allied Occupation Records.

284   *the prisoners had been*: Yusei Wako, interview by Robert Tait, August 25, 1947–September 5, 1947, pp. 2–5, Box 1081, War Crimes Case Files.

284   *it was Army policy*: Shoshin Ito, interview by R. N. Tait, October 28, 1946–November 18, 1946, pp. 15–16, Box 1081, War Crimes Case Files.

285   *Lawyers within*: Statement of Riukichi Tanaka, *United States v. Kajuro Aihara, et al.*, Defense Exhibit H, pp. 1–2, Box 692, SCAP Legal Section, Prosecution Division, Entry 1321, Allied Occupation Records.

285   *Great Britain had*: Jun Hashimoto, "An Argument in Defense of Wako, A Defendant in the Tomomori Case," March 30, 1949, p. 6, Box 1079, War Crimes Case Files; *Reprisals Against Prisoners of War: Correspondence between The International Red Cross Committee and the British Government* (London: J. Causton & Sons, 1916); Brian A. Feltman, *The Stigma of Surrender* (Chapel Hill: University of North Carolina Press, 2015), 57–59.

285   *The proposed change*: Statement of Riukichi Tanaka, *United States v. Kajuro Aihara, et al.*, Defense Exhibit H, pp. 1–2, Box 692, SCAP Legal Section, Prosecution Division, Entry 1321, Allied Occupation Records.

285   *Ito was shown*: Statement of Takahashi Tanase, *United States v. Kajuro Aihara, et al.*, Defense Exhibit L, pp. 1–2, Box 692, SCAP Legal Section, Prosecution Division, Entry 1321, Allied Occupation Records; U.S. Army, Record of Trial, *United States v. Kajuro Aihara, et al.*, p. 335 (Testimony of Norifuma Takada), Box 1645, SCAP Legal Section, Prosecution Division, Entry 1321, Allied Occupation Records.

285   *each headquarters*: Allan Browne, Review of the Staff Judge Advocate, *United States v. Kajuro Aihara, et al.* (June 17, 1949), pp. 28–29, Box 1645, SCAP Legal Section, Prosecution Division, Entry 1321, Allied Occupation Records; Timothy Lang Francis, " 'To dispose of the Prisoners': The Japanese Executions of American Aircrew at Fukuoka, Japan, during 1945," *Pacific Historical Review* 66, no. 4 (November 1997): 469–501.

285   *at least eight American*: Yusei Wako, interview by Robert Tait, August 25, 1947–September 5, 1947, pp. 6–7, Box 1081, War Crimes Case Files.

285   *read the cable*: Shoshin Ito, interview by R. N. Tait, October 28, 1946–November 18, 1946, p. 17, Box 1081, War Crimes Case Files.

285   *Ito intervened*: Shoshin Ito, interview by R. N. Tait, October 28, 1946–November 18, 1946, p. 18, Box 1081, War Crimes Case Files.

286   *They could be*: Statement of Yoshinao Sato, Prosecution Exhibit 112, pp. 13–14, Box 1645, SCAP Legal Section, Prosecution Division, Entry 1321, Allied Occupation Records.

286   *Sato agreed*: U.S. Army, Record of Trial, *United States v. Kajuro Aihara, et al,* p. 659 (Testimony of Yoshinao Sato), Box 1645, SCAP Legal Section, Prosecution Division, Entry 1321, Allied Occupation Records; Yusei Wako, interview by Robert Tait, August 25, 1947–September 5, 1947, pp. 10–11, Box 1081, War Crimes Case Files.

286   *Thousands of men*: Wesley Craven and James Cate, *The Pacific: Matterhorn to Nagasaki. The Army Air Forces in World War II*, vol. 5 (Chicago: University of Chicago Press, 1953), 653–74.

286   *Ito spent the night*: Sadayoshi Murata, "Petition on Behalf of Shoshin Ito," February 10, 1949, p. 1, Box 1079, War Crimes Case Files.

286   *went out to survey*: Shoshin Ito, "Referential Materials for the Review of No 288 Case," March 25, 1949, p. 1, Box 1079, War Crimes Case Files.

286 *Ito spent the morning*: Shoshin Ito, interview by R. N. Tait, October 28, 1946–November 18, 1946, pp. 23–24, Box 1081, War Crimes Case Files.

286 *He returned*: Yusei Wako, interview by Robert Tait, August 25, 1947–September 5, 1947, p. 14, Box 1081, War Crimes Case Files.

286 *Ito rushed*: Shoshin Ito, interview by R. N. Tait, October 28, 1946–November 18, 1946, p. 21, Box 1081, War Crimes Case Files.

286 *One head was*: Yusei Wako, interview by Robert Tait, August 25, 1947–September 5, 1947, p. 15, Box 1081, War Crimes Case Files.

286 *Sato was clearly*: Shoshin Ito, interview by R. N. Tait, October 28, 1946–November 18, 1946, pp. 21–23, Box 1081, War Crimes Case Files.

286 *Ito stood by*: Kentaro Toji, interview by Robert Miller, December 29, 1947–January 2, 1948, pp. 2–6, Box 1737, SCAP Legal Section, Investigation Division, Investigation Reports 1945–49, Allied Occupation Records; Yusei Wako, interview by Robert Tait, August 25, 1947–September 5, 1947, p. 16, Box 1081, War Crimes Case Files.

286 *As he watched*: Shoshin Ito, interview by R. N. Tait, October 28, 1946–November 18, 1946, p. 36, Box 1081, War Crimes Case Files.

286 *Ito had sent cables*: Shoshin Ito, interview by R. N. Tait, October 28, 1946–November 18, 1946, p. 21, Box 1081, War Crimes Case Files.

286 *offered a solution*: U.S. Army, Record of Trial, *United States v. Kajuro Aihara, et al.*, pp. 680–81 (Testimony of Yoshinao Sato), Box 1645, SCAP Legal Section, Prosecution Division, Entry 1321, Allied Occupation Records.

287 *There were doctors*: Yoshinao Sato, interview by Norman Tracy, March 28, 1947, p. 2, Box 1737, SCAP Legal Section, Investigation Division, Investigation Reports 1945–49, Allied Occupation Records.

287 *clean up the books*: Shoshin Ito, interview by R. N. Tait, October 28, 1946–November 18, 1946, pp. 26–28, 36–37, Box 1081, War Crimes Case Files.

287 *Ito signed*: Opinion of the Board of Review in the Office of the Staff Judge Advocate *re Yokoyama, et al.*, February 6, 1950, p. 88, Box 1645, SCAP Legal Section, Prosecution Division, Entry 1321, Allied Occupation Records.

287 *Wako regularly suffered*: Sadayoshi Murata to Walton H. Walker, p. 2, February 24, 1949, Box 1079, War Crimes Case Files; Yonefusa Wako, written statement, March 21, 1946, Bodine Files.

287 *A recurring one*: U.S. Army, Record of Trial, *United States v. Kajuro Aihara, et al.*, p. 813 (Testimony of Yusei Wako), Box 1645, SCAP Legal Section, Prosecution Division, Entry 1321, Allied Occupation Records.

287 *"We all do not"*: Yusei Wako, interview by Edmund Bodine and Charles Fellows, February 18, 1946, p. 5, Bodine Files.

288 *During some downtime*: Shoshin Ito, interview by Edmund Bodine et al., March 24, 1946, Bodine Files; Shoshin Ito, interview by Edmund Bodine et al., March 27, 1946, Bodine Files.

288 *"Sawada did not"*: Shoshin Ito, interview by Edmund Bodine et al., March 27, 1946, p. 4, Bodine Files.

288 *"As far as this case"*: Shoshin Ito, interview by Edmund Bodine et al., March 27, 1946, pp. 3–4, Bodine Files ("As far as this case is concerned, commander Sawada had no definite control. . . .").

288 *"I just wonder"*: Shoshin Ito, interview by Edmund Bodine et al., March 27, 1946, p. 6, Bodine Files.

288   *If the judges*: Shoshin Ito, interview by Edmund Bodine et al., March 27, 1946, p. 8, Bodine Files. ("If the judges found out that the evidence was taken under torture by the Gendarmes? would Gendarmes be arrested?")

288   "*When I was approached*": Shoshin Ito, interview by Edmund Bodine et al., March 27, 1946, p. 8, Bodine Files.

289   "*In your experience*": Shoshin Ito, interview by Edmund Bodine et al., March 27, 1946, p. 8, Bodine Files.

289   *It was Wednesday*: Sawada Trial Transcript, 308.

CHAPTER TWENTY-FIVE

290   "*The prosecution has*": Sawada Trial Transcript, 309.

290   *Dwyer had never met*: Shoshin Ito, interview by John Hendren, January 6–7, 1946, Bodine Files.

290   *He had given Hendren*: SINTIC 2809, "File, from Japanese Maj Gen Ito, relating to trial of American airmen by court-martial," Box 11, China War Crimes Files.

290   *There was also something*: Tatsuta Sotojiro, interview by Robert Dwyer, February 12, 1946, pp. 1–2, Bodine Files.

292   "*This witness*": Sawada Trial Transcript, 309.

293   *Ito answered*: "Nip Places Doolittle Blame High," *Shanghai Stars & Stripes*, April 4, 1946, 2.

293   *The eight Doolittle Raiders*: Sawada Trial Transcript, 381.

293   *then read the charges*: Yusei Wako, interview by John Hendren, January 2, 1946, pp. 2–3, Box 40, Glines Papers.

294   *As Hata had read*: Sawada Trial Transcript, 326.

294   *the important questions*: Sawada Trial Transcript, 403 (Testimony of Ryuhei Okada).

294   *Each question*: Sawada Trial Transcript, 346–47.

294   *started to deny*: Ryuhei Okada and Yusei Wako, interview by Charles Fellows, February 15, 1946, p. 2, Bodine Files.

294   "*You had incendiary*": Sawada Trial Transcript, 403 (Testimony of Ryuhei Okada).

294   *The translator had*: Yusei Wako, interview by Edmund Bodine and Charles Fellows, February 18, 1946, p. 3, Bodine Files.

294   *his closing remarks*: Sawada Trial Transcript, 323.

295   *the judges had based*: Sawada Trial Transcript, 405 (Testimony of Ryuhei Okada).

295   "*Were the confessions*": Sawada Trial Transcript, 333.

296   *Chase Nielsen was*: Sawada Trial Transcript, 339.

296   *the bodies of*: Chase Nielsen to Mrs. Dieter, April 30, 1946, Series II, Box 2, Doolittle Raiders Papers.

296   *When Nielsen returned*: "Fliers' Bodies Exhumed by Grave Team," *Shanghai Stars & Stripes*, March 28, 1946, 2.

296   *Yang had supposedly*: 民国32年7月苏本善给第六区代行行政督察专员呈文 (Benshan Su, Report to Deputy Inspector of District Six, July 1943), Xiangshan County Archives.

296   *The coffins*: Chase Nielsen to Mrs. Dieter, April 30, 1946, Series II, Box 2, Doolittle Raiders Papers.

297   *Hendren, seeing Nielsen*: Sawada Trial Transcript, 339.

298   "*Then you don't*": Sawada Trial Transcript, 342.

298   *The next morning*: Sawada Trial Transcript, 345.

298   *Dwyer had spent*: Sawada Trial Transcript, 547 (Statement of Robert Dwyer).

298   *"Did you ever"*: Sawada Trial Transcript, 345.

299   *"Withdraw the question"*: Sawada Trial Transcript, 351.

300   *"Ito's evidence"*: "Nip Places Doolittle Blame High," *Shanghai Stars & Stripes*, April 4, 1946, 2.

301   *board a flight*: Request for Special Orders, April 17, 1946, Box 12, China War Crimes Files.

CHAPTER TWENTY-SIX

302   *modest goal*: Sawada Trial Transcript, 376–90.

302   *"He is speaking"*: Sawada Trial Transcript, 386.

304   *If Wako was*: Sawada Trial Transcript, 462-467. Note: the original sequence of testimony was Wako, Okada, Sawada, and then Tatsuta. I have addressed Tatsuta's testimony before Okada and Sawada's because of its stylistic and thematic contrast with Wako's testimony.

304   *"I do not know"*: Sawada Trial Transcript, 463.

304   *The reporters*: "He Was Kind to Doomed Fliers, Jap Warden Says," *North China Daily News*, April 9, 1946.

304   *The only cracks*: 神代護忠, 上海支店時代の思い出 (1994年) [Moritada Kumashiro, "Recollection of the Days at Shanghai Branch," Manuscript (1994)], p. 182, Call No. GK77-G2, National Diet Library.

304   *In a brief cross-examination*: Sawada Trial Transcript, 478.

305   *"Isn't it a fact"*: Sawada Trial Transcript, 478 ("Isn't it a fact, that these fliers got about the same kind of treatment as Christ did?").

305   *Okada testified over*: Sawada Trial Transcript, 401–6.

305   *The public proceedings*: Sawada Trial Transcript, 406–7; Ryuhei Okada and Yusei Wako, interview by Charles Fellows, February 15, 1946, p. 3, Bodine Files.

305   *Only Wako had*: 羽山忠弘, ある戦犯事件弁護の思い出, 大東法学第18号179頁(1991年) [Tadahiro Hayama, "Recollection of Defending a War Trial Case," 18 *Daito Hogaku* 179 (1991)], 190.

306   *For Okada*: Sawada Trial Transcript, 405.

306   *The Doolittle Raiders had*: Sawada Trial Transcript, 406; Ryuhei Okada and Yusei Wako, interview by Charles Fellows, February 15, 1946, p. 3, Bodine Files.

306   *The pieces of evidence*: Sawada Trial Transcript, 406; 神代護忠, 上海支店時代の思い出 (1994年) [Moritada Kumashiro, "Recollection of the Days at Shanghai Branch," Manuscript (1994)], p. 166, Call No. GK77-G2, National Diet Library.

306   *Fellows then asked*: Sawada Trial Transcript, 404.

306   *Dwyer's turn*: Sawada Trial Transcript, 407.

306   *His cold was*: Sawada Trial Transcript, 547 (Statement of Robert Dwyer).

306   *"Do you know"*: Sawada Trial Transcript, 408.

307   *"The other fliers"*: Sawada Trial Transcript, 410.

307   *McReynolds called*: Sawada Trial Transcript, 423.

308   *When the trial reconvened*: Sawada Trial Transcript, 547 (Statement of Robert Dwyer).

308   *All things considered*: Sawada Trial Transcript, 424.

309   *Dwyer then went*: Sawada Trial Transcript, 427.

309   *The courtroom burst*: 神代護忠, 上海支店時代の思い出 (1994年) [Moritada

Kumashiro, "Recollection of the Days at Shanghai Branch," Manuscript (1994)], p. 174, Call No. GK77-G2, National Diet Library.

310 *"You think that"*: Sawada Trial Transcript, 428.

310 *"Buddhism"*: Sawada Trial Transcript, 429.

310 *He had traveled*: Taosa Kubota, Statement, March 9, 1946, Defense Exhibit 17, Sawada Record; Sawada Trial Transcript, 437 (Testimony of Shigeru Sawada).

310 *He had adopted*: Hisashi Kisaki, Testimony of Kisaki Hisashi Concerning Lt. Gen. Sawada, March 14, 1946, pp. 1–2, Defense Exhibit 16, Sawada Record.

311 *His son had*: 沢田允茂, 昭和の一哲学者 戦争を生きぬいて (慶応大学出版, 2003年) [Yoshishinge Sawada, *Surviving the War as a Showa Philosopher* (Keio University Press, 2003)].

311 *As far as Sawada*: Robert Mikesh, Summary of Interview of Shigeru Sawada, February 2, 1965, p. 6, Box 40, Glines Papers.

311 *Accepting the punishment*: 宗宮真司『上海米機搭乗員所罰ニ対スル戦犯事件 – 宗宮弁護士報告』日付不詳, 空襲軍律研究資料その1 [Shinji Somiya, "Shanghai War Crimes Trial Regarding the Punishment of American Air Crews—Attorney Somiya's Report," undated, p. 84, Materials Regarding Military Discipline for Air Raids—Part 1], Yasukuni Archives.

311 *On the stand*: Sawada Trial Transcript, 429.

312 *"Yes, I have"*: Sawada Trial Transcript, 436.

312 *"Did you know how"*: Sawada Trial Transcript, 438.

313 *Privately, he would admit*: 沢田茂(供述), 井上忠男(調査), 昭和38年9月20日, 井上忠男戦争裁判資料 [Shigeru Sawada, interview by Tadao Inoue, September 20, 1963, pp. 15–19, Tadao Inoue War Tribunal File], Yasukuni Archives.

313 *"As their superior"*: Sawada Trial Transcript, 453.

314 *Everyone started packing*: Sawada Trial Transcript, 486.

315 *The reason Berry*: Issuo Karakawa, "Circumstances Relating to Lt General Sawada," March 7, 1946, Defense Exhibit 15, Sawada Record.

315 *"Now, in that statement"*: Sawada Trial Transcript, 487.

315 *But Sawada just shrugged*: 沢田茂(供述), 井上忠男(調査), 昭和38年9月20日, 井上忠男戦争裁判資料 [Shigeru Sawada, interview by Tadao Inoue, September 20, 1963, Tadao Inoue War Tribunal File], Yasukuni Archives; 宗宮真司『上海米機搭乗員所罰ニ対スル戦犯事件 – 宗宮弁護士報告』日付不詳, 空襲軍律研究資料その1 [Shinji Somiya, "Shanghai War Crimes Trial Regarding the Punishment of American Air Crews—Attorney Somiya's Report," undated, p. 83, Materials Regarding Military Discipline for Air Raids—Part 1], Yasukuni Archives.

CHAPTER TWENTY-SEVEN

317 *Kumashiro predictably*: Sawada Trial Transcript, 511.

317 *He was not*: Shinji Somiya, "The Account of Legal Proceedings of Court for War Criminal Suspects," p. 37, trans. Kazuo Yoshioka, MLMSS 2207, Williams Papers, Mitchell Library, Sydney.

317 *Somiya had written*: Sawada Trial Transcript, 524.

317 *Hayama, too*: Sawada Trial Transcript, 507.

317 *"Das Anbrechen einer"*: Ferdinand Lassalle, "System der erworbenen Rechte," *Gesammelte Reden und Schriften*, vol. 9 (Berlin: Cassirer, 1920), 31.

318 *The reporters still covering*: Sawada Trial Transcript, 510.

318   *"a masterpiece"*: "Death Penalty Asked for Japs Who Slew Airmen," Associated Press, April 11, 1946.

318   *Hendren had wrapped*: Sawada Trial Transcript, 489.

318   *He spoke with*: "Prosecutor Asks Death for Japs," *Shanghai Evening Post*, April 11, 1946.

318   *Hendren read*: Sawada Trial Transcript, 489–91.

318   *"He could have said"*: Sawada Trial Transcript, 494.

318   *"The defense will"*: Sawada Trial Transcript, 490.

319   *Bodine was the first*: Sawada Trial Transcript, 499.

319   *The previous Saturday*: Sawada Trial Transcript, 423.

319   *He had made arrangements*: Justin J. O'Connell to Edmund Bodine, June 13, 1946, Bodine Papers.

319   *had arrived*: Natalie and Elizabeth Bodine, personal interview, December 17, 2014.

320   *everyone had been there*: Marriage Record, April 6, 1946, Bodine Papers; Annotated Wedding Photographs, undated, Bodine Papers.

320   *The only one*: Natalie and Elizabeth Bodine, personal interview, December 17, 2014.

320   *organist chimed in*: Edmund Bodine, handwritten wedding instructions, April 1946, Bodine Papers.

320   *stood on either side*: Wedding photographs, April 6, 1946, Bodine Papers.

321   *Whatever anxieties*: Sawada Trial Transcript, 499–500.

321   *"The prosecutor in this trial"*: Sawada Trial Transcript, 501. ("The prosecutor in this trial has in no way established any proof whatsoever by which they can show that General Sawada *knowingly and willfully* constituted the military tribunal to try the Doolittle fliers.")

321   *Even if the charges*: Sawada Trial Transcript, 497.

321   *"These are the men"*: Sawada Trial Transcript, 502.

321   *Bodine then turned*: Sawada Trial Transcript, 515.

322   *"Only he could've"*: Sawada Trial Transcript, 516.

322   *An Australian war crimes*: *The Trial of Shinohara and Two Others*, Case No. 27, Vol. 5, Law Reports Trials of War Criminals (United Nations, 1950), 32.

322   *Unless Sawada*: Sawada Trial Transcript, 521–23.

323   *Dwyer strutted*: 神代護忠, 上海支店時代の思い出 (1994年) [Moritada Kumashiro, "Recollection of the Days at Shanghai Branch," Manuscript (1994)], p. 221, Call No. GK77-G2, National Diet Library.

323   *"About four years ago"*: Sawada Trial Transcript, 537.

323   *His voice*: Sawada Trial Transcript, 547 (Statement of Robert Dwyer).

323   *This trial*: Sawada Trial Transcript, 540.

323   *"They did no more"*: Sawada Trial Transcript, 542.

323   *twisting his face*: 神代護忠, 上海支店時代の思い出 (1994年) [Moritada Kumashiro, "Recollection of the Days at Shanghai Branch," Manuscript (1994)], p. 224, Call No. GK77-G2, National Diet Library.

323   *"Believe me"*: Sawada Trial Transcript, 543.

324   *All of them*: Sawada Trial Transcript, 540.

324   *"I say no system"*: Sawada Trial Transcript, 547.

324   *"The judges are"*: 神代護忠, 上海支店時代の思い出 (1994年) [Moritada Kumashiro, "Recollection of the Days at Shanghai Branch," Manuscript (1994)], pp. 231–32, Call No. GK77-G2, National Diet Library.

324 *Even General Wedemyer*: 宗宮真司『上海米機搭乗員所罰ニ対スル戦犯事件 –
宗宮弁護士報告』日付不詳, 空襲軍律研究資料その1 [Shinji Somiya, "Shang-
hai War Crimes Trial Regarding the Punishment of American Air Crews—Attorney
Somiya's Report," undated, p. 87, Materials Regarding Military Discipline for Air
Raids—Part 1], Yasukuni Archives.

324 *led into the courtroom*: 神代護忠, 上海支店時代の思い出 (1994年) [Moritada
Kumashiro, "Recollection of the Days at Shanghai Branch," Manuscript (1994)],
p. 232, Call No. GK77-G2, National Diet Library.

325 *At 2:00 p.m.*: Sawada Trial Transcript, 549.

326 *McReynolds then addressed*: Sawada Trial Transcript, 550.

326 *Though unbidden*: Photograph of the reading of the verdict in the case of *United
States v. Sawada, et al.*, April 15, 1946, Bodine Papers.

326 *McReynolds looked down*: Sawada Trial Transcript, 550.

326 *As McReynolds read*: 神代護忠, 上海支店時代の思い出 (1994年) [Moritada Kumashiro, "Recollection of the Days at Shanghai Branch," Manuscript (1994)], p.
234–235, Call No. GK77-G2, National Diet Library.

327 *McReynolds called*: Sawada Trial Transcript, 551.

327 *"I appreciate you"*: 神代護忠, 上海支店時代の思い出 (1994年) [Moritada Kumashiro, "Recollection of the Days at Shanghai Branch," Manuscript (1994)], p.
235, Call No. GK77-G2, National Diet Library.

327 *Somiya's bewilderment*: 宗宮真司『上海米機搭乗員所罰ニ対スル戦犯事件 – 宗
宮弁護士報告』日付不詳, 空襲軍律研究資料その1 [Shinji Somiya, "Shanghai
War Crimes Trial Regarding the Punishment of American Air Crews—Attorney
Somiya's Report," undated, p. 89, Materials Regarding Military Discipline for Air
Raids—Part 1], Yasukuni Archives.

327 *The verdict hit*: "Former POW Returns from Jap War Trials," *Salt Lake Tribune*,
April 19, 1946, 13; "Tokyo Raider Plans Leave Before New Assignment," Associated Press, April 19, 1946.

327 *"I'm sorry Justice"*: Chase Nielsen to Mrs. Dieter, April 30, 1946, Series II, Box 2,
Doolittle Raiders Papers.

327 *Nielsen wrote*: James M. Scott, *Target Tokyo* (New York: Norton, 2015), 470.

327 *"In my estimation"*: Scott, *Target Tokyo*, 469–70.

328 *deserve the death penalty*: "Families of Slain U.S. Fliers Differ on Verdict for Japs,"
Associated Press, April 16, 1946.

328 *"I think the sentences"*: "Families of Slain U.S. Fliers Differ on Verdict for Japs,"
Associated Press, April 16, 1946.

328 *The* Los Angeles Times: "Jap Sentences Are Inconsistent with Those for Nazis," *Los
Angeles Times*, April 1946.

328 *Emperor Hirohito was*: "Terms Given Killers of US Fliers Hit," Associated Press,
April 16, 1946.

328 *Congressman Francis Walter*: H. Res. 605, 92 Cong. Rec. 4026 (April 18, 1946).

328 *"What the Japanese"*: "Walter Asks Investigation of Jap's Light Sentences," Associated Press, April 18, 1946.

328 *Letters to President*: David Marcus to Commanding General, United States Army
Forces, China, "Resolutions of Tulsa Post No. 577, Veterans of Foreign Wars," June
11, 1946, Box 11, China War Crimes Files.

328 *Hendren had gotten*: John H. Hendren to Joseph Keenan, April 16, 1946, Box 1,
Joseph Berry Keenan Papers 1942–1947, Harvard Law School Library.

329 *Somiya had returned*: Request for Special Orders, April 17, 1946, Box 12, China War Crimes Files.

329 *Tying up*: 神代護忠，上海支店時代の思い出 (1994年) [Moritada Kumashiro, "Recollection of the Days at Shanghai Branch," Manuscript (1994)], pp. 231, Call No. GK77-G2, National Diet Library. Kumashiro states that only Bodine and Fellows remained, which suggests that Hayama returned to his duties in Jiangwan. This implication is supported by Hayama's own memoir, which does not mention this post-trial phase.

329 *Young called a meeting*: 神代護忠，上海支店時代の思い出 (1994年) [Moritada Kumashiro, "Recollection of the Days at Shanghai Branch," Manuscript (1994)], pp. 234, Call No. GK77-G2, National Diet Library.

329 *McReynolds stood by*: According to Sawada, Joseph Murphy visited him in Japan and talked to him about the judge's deliberations. None had favored a death sentence. They were originally going to sentence Sawada to twenty-five years but decided to reduce it given his age at the time, figuring that a lengthy sentence was likely to be the functional equivalent of a death sentence. 沢田茂(供述)，井上忠男(調査)，昭和38年9月20日，井上忠男戦争裁判資料 [Shigeru Sawada, interview by Tadao Inoue, p. 15, September 20, 1963, Tadao Inoue War Tribunal File], Yasukuni Archives.

329 *That August*: Edward Young, "Review of the Record of Trial by a Military Commission of Sawada, Shigeru, Lieutenant General, Imperial Japanese Army, *et al.*," August 1946, Box 11, China War Crimes Files.

329 *the test is international law*: Edward Young, "Review of the Record of Trial by a Military Commission of Sawada, Shigeru, Lieutenant General, Imperial Japanese Army, *et al.*," August 1946, p. 19, Box 11, China War Crimes Files.

330 "*It is axiomatic*": Edward Young, "Review of the Record of Trial by a Military Commission of Sawada, Shigeru, Lieutenant General, Imperial Japanese Army, *et al.*," August 1946, p. 20, Box 11, China War Crimes Files.

330 "*ex post facto terroristic*": Edward Young, "Review of the Record of Trial by a Military Commission of Sawada, Shigeru, Lieutenant General, Imperial Japanese Army, *et al.*," August 1946, p. 20, Box 11, China War Crimes Files ("*ex post facto* terroristic in concept and that it was enacted primarily to permit a pseudo-legal sentence of death for the 'Doolittle' fliers").

330 "*The untrustworthiness*": Edward Young, "Review of the Record of Trial by a Military Commission of Sawada, Shigeru, Lieutenant General, Imperial Japanese Army, *et al.*," August 1946, p. 23, Box 11, China War Crimes Files.

330 "*behind them*": Edward Young, "Review of the Record of Trial by a Military Commission of Sawada, Shigeru, Lieutenant General, Imperial Japanese Army, *et al.*," August 1946, p. 28, Box 11, China War Crimes Files.

330 *by awarding*: Edward Young, "Review of the Record of Trial by a Military Commission of Sawada, Shigeru, Lieutenant General, Imperial Japanese Army, *et al.*," August 1946, p. 32, Box 11, China War Crimes Files.

331 *if an error*: Edward Young, "Review of the Record of Trial by a Military Commission of Sawada, Shigeru, Lieutenant General, Imperial Japanese Army, *et al.*," August 1946, p. 33, Box 11, China War Crimes Files.

331 *The Nuremberg Trials: Trial of the Major War Criminals before the International Military Tribunal, Nuremberg: 14 November 1945–1 October 1946* ("Blue Series"), vol. 20 (International Military Tribunal, Nuremberg, 1947).

331   *the Chinese Civil War*: *The China White Paper, August 1949*, ed. Lyman P. Van Slyke (Stanford, CA: Stanford University Press, 1967), 170–217.

331   *Billy Mitchell*: 92 Cong. Rec. 10741 (August 8, 1946); H. Rept. 2625, 92 Cong. Rec. 9698; S. 881, 92 Cong. Rec. 10416.

AFTERWORD

333   *a children's book*: 石川久美子(文), 田代千津子(絵), アキちゃん、ふたり (光陽出版社, 1999年) [Kumiko Ishikawa, Chizuko Tashiro (Illustration), *Akichan: The Two of Us* (Koyo Shuppansha, 1999)].

333   *Endeavoring to consolidate*: 柴田武彦, 原勝洋, 日米全調査ドーリットル空襲秘録 (アリアドネ企画, 2003) [Takehiko Shibata and Katsuhiro Hara, *The Doolittle Raid: A Comprehensive Japan-US Survey* (Ariadne Kikaku, 2003)], 59–64.

333   *The civilian damage*: 柴田武彦, 原勝洋, 日米全調査ドーリットル空襲秘録 (アリアドネ企画, 2003) [Takehiko Shibata and Katsuhiro Hara, *The Doolittle Raid: A Comprehensive Japan-US Survey* (Ariadne Kikaku, 2003)], 73–77.

334   *two extraordinary websites*: https://childrenofthedoolittleraiders.com; http://www.doolittleraider.com/.

334   *When I interviewed*: Richard Cole, personal interview, August 20, 2014.

334   *gave him the closure*: James Curtis Hasdorff, *United States Air Force Oral History Program: Interview of Lt. Col. Robert L. Hite* (USAF Historical Research Center, 1982), 121.

334   *Soon after his return*: Terry Nielsen, personal interview, November 24, 2019.

334   *On July 17*: "Jay Nielsen Wedding," *South Cache Courier*, July 26, 1946, 1; "Hero of Tokyo Raid to Wed," *Ogden Standard-Examiner*, July 16, 1946, 1.

334   *remain buried*: "Cleo Rayona McCrary Nielsen," Find A Grave, https://perma.cc/3XQG-CSRX.

334   *In 1966*: C. V. Glines, *Four Came Home* (Missoula, MT: Pictorial Histories, 1995), ix.

334   *The North Vietnamese*: "Reply from the Government of the Democratic Republic of Vietnam," *International Review of the Red Cross*, No. 65, August 31, 1965, 527; Alexander Casella, "The Politics of Prisoners of War," *New York Times*, May 28, 1972, 9.

335   *they had fought*: Glines, *Four Came Home*, 132.

335   *After his wife*: Marcine Barr to J. H. Doolittle, February 5, 1968, Series IX, Box 3, Doolittle Papers; W. J. Driver to J. H. Doolittle, January 19, 1968, Series IX, Box 3, Doolittle Papers.

335   *on mission in Vietnam*: American Foreign Service, Report of the Death of an American Citizen (Ray Arthur Nichols), January 16, 1957, Box 1027, French Indochina A-Z, General Records of the Department of State, Record Group 59, National Archives, College Park; "U.S. Official Dies in Saigon," Associated Press, December 20, 1956.

335   *were transferred to Sugamo*: Army Advisory Group, "Residual Functions Involving War Crimes 30 June 1945 to May 1947," August 9, 1947, Box 13, China War Crimes Files.

335   *SCAP was struggling*: "Release of Suspected War Criminal," June 1, 1946, Box 719, Intelligence Dossiers.

335   *It would take until*: Okazaki to T. P. Davis, April 11, 1947, p. 2, Box 719, Intelligence Dossiers.

335 *be given no publicity*: John B. Cooley, "Release of Shimomura Sadamu from Internment," February 12, 1947, Box 719, Intelligence Dossiers.

335 *reporters in Tokyo agreed*: Bratton to Willoughby, "Release of Shimomura Sadamu," March 13, 1947, Box 719, Intelligence Dossiers.

335 *Sawada ultimately testified*: IMTFE Transcript, 26,847, *et seq.* (Testimony of Shigeru Sawada).

335 *Keenan made good*: Frank White, "Doolittle Fliers 'Didn't Have Chance,' Witness Testifies," Associated Press, September 4, 1947.

336 *Hata was convicted*: Judgment of the International Military Tribunal for the Far East, November 1948, p. 1,214, JAG Section, Law Branch, Army Library.

336 *Tojo was sent*: Lindesay Parrot, "Tojo and 6 Others Hanged by Allies as War Criminals," *New York Times*, December 23, 1948, 1.

336 *The Indian judge*: B. V. A. Röling and C. F. Rüter, eds., *The Tokyo Judgment—The International Military Tribunal for the Far East (IMTFE),* 29 April 1946–12 November 1948 (Amsterdam: APA-University Press 1977), 1023.

336 *Some legal historians*: Neil Boister and Robert Cryer, *The Tokyo International Tribunal: A Reappraisal* (Oxford: Oxford University Press, 2008), 195.

336 *In 1949*: Shigeru Sawada, "Petition for Okada, Matsumori, Hideo and Tatsuta, Sotojiro," May 5, 1949, Records of the Supreme Commander for the Allied Powers (SCAP), Box 1194, Records of the SCAP Legal Section, Administrative Division, Allied Occupation Records.

336 *The junior officer*: Robert Mikesh, Summary of Facts on Shigeru Sawada, Ryuhei Okada, Sotojiro Tatsuta, and Yusei Wako, undated, Box 40, Glines Papers.

336 *Yusei Wako was*: Robert Mikesh to C. V. Glines, April 13, 1965, Box 40, Glines Papers. Wako is reported to have confirmed that he spent twelve years in prison. However, archival documents suggest he may have bene released in 1956. James M. Scott, *Target Tokyo* (New York: Norton, 2015), 471.

336 *Two years after*: Allan Browne, Review of the Staff Judge Advocate, *United States v. Kajuro Aihara, et al.* (June 17, 1949), Box 1645, SCAP Prosecution Records.

336 *"It is certainly not"*: Jacob DeShazer to Walton H. Walker, May 21, 1949, Box 1079, War Crimes Case Files.

337 *Sawada's military diaries*: 沢田茂(著), 森松俊夫(編), 参謀次長沢田茂回想録 (芙蓉書房, 1982年) [Shigeru Sawada, *Memoir of Deputy Chief of-Staff Shigeru Sawada*, ed. Toshio Morimatsu (Fuyo Shobo, 1982)], 12–14.

337 *But in private*: 沢田茂(供述), 井上忠男(調査), 昭和38年9月20日, 井上忠男戦 争裁判資料 [Shigeru Sawada, interview by Tadao Inoue, September 20, 1963, Tadao Inoue War Tribunal File], Yasukuni Archives.

337 *Before he said*: Robert Fellows, personal interview, April 23, 2013.

337 *As one of its tenets*: A. H. McDonald, *Fact and Fiction in Japanese Imperialism* (London: Royal Institute for International Affairs, 1943), 4.

337 *Fellows passed*: Robert Fellows, personal interview, April 23, 2013.

337 *Nothing brought Fellows*: Katie Fellows, Reflections on Charles Fellows, May 20, 2013.

337 *Bodine stayed in China*: Edmund Bodine, Officer Military Record, undated, Bodine Papers; Edmund Bodine, Officer's, Warrant Officer's and Flight Officer's Qualification Record, undated, Bodine Papers.

337 *Bodine had sent*: Edmund Bodine, handwritten note to be cabled to Alma E Bodine, April 1946, Bodine Papers.

337   *To make amends*: Claire Lorraine to Edmund Bodine, May 5, 1946, Bodine Papers.

338   *to write back*: Alma Bodine to Edmund Bodine, June 21, 1946, Bodine Papers.

338   *He sent his mother*: Alma Bodine to Edmund Bodine, July 1, 1946, Bodine Papers.

339   *got his law degree*: Edmund Bodine, Florida Merit System, Application for Employment and Examination, August 14, 1964, Bodine Papers.

339   *One case involved*: *The Trial of Lothar Eisentrager and Others*, Case No. 84, Vol. 14, *Law Reports Trials of War Criminals* (United Nations, 1950), 8.

339   *Bodine would ultimately*: *Johnson v. Eisentrager*, 339 U.S. 763 (1950).

339   *The other case involved*: *The Trial of General Tanaka Hisakasu and Five Others*, Case No. 33, Vol. 5, *Law Reports Trials of War Criminals* (United Nations, 1950), 66.

339   *To help him*: 神代護忠、上海支店時代の思い出 (1994年) [Moritada Kumashiro, "Recollection of the Days at Shanghai Branch," Manuscript (1994)], pp. 239–42, Call No. GK77-G2, National Diet Library.

339   *To make the reunion*: Robert Dwyer to Edward H. Young, "Hong Kong Case— Execution of Major David Henry Hauck," April 29, 1946, Box 11, China War Crimes Files.

339   *This time*: *The Trial of General Tanaka Hisakasu and Five Others*, Case No. 33, Vol. 5, *Law Reports Trials of War Criminals* (United Nations, 1950), 70.

339   *Before Hendren left*: John H. Hendren to Joseph Keenan, April 16, 1946, Box 1, Joseph Berry Keenan Papers 1942–1947, Harvard Law School Library.

340   *Hendren started*: "John H. Hendren and Henry Andrae," *Daily Capital News*, December 6, 1946, 11.

340   *became the Chairman*: "Hendren Named Chairman," *St. Louis Globe-Democrat*, September 15, 1948.

340   *"He was never"*: "30 Who Took Part in First Tokyo Raid Hold Get-Together," *St. Louis Post-Dispatch*, April 19, 1947, 8.

340   *Dwyer's father*: "Death Claims E. J. Dwyer, 73," *Rochester Democrat & Chronicle*, June 17, 1946, 14.

340   *Dwyer boxed up*: Letter to Headquarters, American Graves Registration Service— China Zone, September 23, 1946, Box 11, China War Crimes Files.

341   *He was awarded*: "Maj. Robert T. Dwyer Given Bronze Star," *Rochester Democrat & Chronicle*, May 27, 1946, 16.

341   *He was happy*: "Hirohito May Be Ignored in War Trials," United Press, August 8, 1946; "Jap PWs 'Hard to Pin Down,' Says Prosecutor, Visiting Home," *Rochester Democrat & Chronicle*, July 9, 1946, 1.

341   *When he returned*: 沢田茂(供述)、井上忠男(調査)、昭和38年9月20日、井上忠男戦争裁判資料 [Shigeru Sawada, interview by Tadao Inoue, September 20, 1963, Tadao Inoue War Tribunal File], Yasukuni Archives.

341   *Sawada respected*: Robert Mikesh, Summary of Interview by Shigeru Sawada, February 2, 1965, p. 7, Box 40, Glines Papers.

341   *impressed by*: 沢田茂(供述)、井上忠男(調査)、昭和38年9月20日、井上忠男戦争裁判資料 (Shigeru Sawada, interview by Tadao Inoue, September 20, 1963, Tadao Inoue War Tribunal File), Yasukuni Archives.

341   *The official cause*: "War Crimes Officer Dies in Shanghai," United Press, March 20, 1947.

341   *there were rumors*: Natalie Bodine, personal interview, December 17, 2014.

341   *remembered seeing him*: John Davey, *Rivers of Consciousness: 1913–1978*, vol. 1, *The Lives and Times of Edward D. Cuffe, Gentleman* (Jayde Design, 2013), 213.

341   *Bodine was a pallbearer*: Dwyer Funeral Photos, May 21, 1947, Bodine Papers; "War Crimes Prosecutor Dies Here," *China Press*, May 20, 1947.

341   *returned to Rochester*: "Civic, Army Leaders Attend Dwyer Rites," *Rochester Democrat & Chronicle*, May 30, 1947, 25.

341   *His hometown paper*: "Bright Career Ends," *Rochester Democrat & Chronicle*, May 22, 1947, 9.

342   *Ever since then*: Geneva Convention Relative to the Treatment of Prisoners of War ("Third Geneva Convention"), August 12, 1949, 75 UNTS 135, arts. 4–5.

342   *The Conventions forbid*: Third Geneva Convention, arts. 3(a), 3(c), 17, 87, 130.

342   *Solitary confinement*: Third Geneva Convention, art. 21.

342   *The Conventions specify*: Third Geneva Convention, art. 96.

342   *Ex post facto laws*: Third Geneva Convention, art. 99; I.C.R.C., *Commentary: III Geneva Convention Relative to the Treatment of Prisoner of War* (I.C.R.C., 1960), 623. ("Nationals, friends, enemies, all should be subject to the same rules of procedure and judged by the same courts. There is therefore no question of setting up special tribunals to try war criminals of enemy nationality.")

342   *The Conventions make*: Third Geneva Convention, art. 130.

342   *forbids injustice*: Third Geneva Convention, art. 3(d).

PHOTO CREDITS

1. National Archives
2. National Archives
3. Associated Press
4. Associated Press
5. Bodine Family Archive
6. Bodine Family Archive
7. Nielsen Family Archive
8. Bodine Family Archive
9. Associated Press
10. Bodine Family Archive
11. Bodine Family Archive
12. Bodine Family Archive
13. Bodine Family Archive
14. Bodine Family Archive
15. Bodine Family Archive
16. Bodine Family Archive
17. Bodine Family Archive
18. Bodine Family Archive
19. Bodine Family Archive

INDEX

execution of three Raiders witnessed
by, 5
Hendren's request for transfer to Ward
Road Jail of, 125–26
as Raiders trial prosecutor, 69, 113,
114, 126, 283, 291, 293–94, 318
self-serving statement of, 247–48
in Tokyo hospital, 114, 126
Hata, Shunroku, 160, 276, 282, 290
in conversation with Sawada about
Raiders' death sentences, 274
Raiders trial and, 314
Tokyo Tribunal conviction of, 336
Young's recommendation for
prosecution of, 330
Hayakawa, Fuyo, 204–5
Hayama, Tadahiro, 69, 84, 93, 99
Doolittle Raid case file read by, 79–80,
95, 247
Dwyer's interview with, 78–80
as having mixed feelings about Raiders
trial, 169
on Raiders' signed confessions, 109
Sawada's request for executions
recalled by, 79–80, 111
Hayama, Tadahiro, as member of
Doolittle Trial defense team,
169–70, 248–49, 250
in closing arguments, 317–18
fair trial as goal of, 170
Japanese soldiers' identification of, 249
in tour of Jiangwan Prison, 256–57
Hendren, John, Jr., 70, 148, 177, 296, 328
arrest and transfer of Doolittle Trial
accused requested by, 125–26
arrest of Shimomura requested by,
100, 125–33, 301
background of, 65–66
Doolittle Trial verdict and, 340
in Fourteenth Air Force legal office,
61–62, 66
further Doolittle prosecutions
predicted by, 218
Ito interviewed by, 300–301
Ito's meeting with, 99–100, 277, 290
later career of, 340
memo to Young on prosecution
requirements from, 71

mercy killing acquittal won by, 66–67
on necessity of prosecuting
Shimomura, 100, 133, 301
ordered to proceed to trial without
Shimomura, 132–33
in press conference with Nielsen, 102,
105, 107
in search for Doolittle Raid case file,
96–97
in Sugamo Prison interrogation of
Sawada, 97–99
Wako interviewed by, 114–15
on war crimes charges against Sawada,
185
as Young's choice to prosecute
Doolittle case, 65
Hendren, John, Jr., in Doolittle Trial, 290
and Bodine's challenge to Disosway,
172
in closing arguments, 318–19
in cross-examination of Sawada,
312–13
Nielsen questioned by, 220–21, 235
Nielsen recalled to stand by, 297
in objection to admission of Raiders'
confessions as evidence, 295
in objection to Bodine's opening
statement, 269
in objection to "residential bombing"
questions, 230–31
opening statement of, 216
verdict and, 326–27
Hendren, Wilmoth, 66
Higashikuni, Prince Naruhiko, 190, 191
Hilton, James, 44
Hindrava, Alexander, 115
Bridge House torture of, 94–95
Hirohito, Emperor of Japan, 3, 14, 67,
68, 190, 191
compromise on Raiders' death
sentences approved by, 200
MacArthur's absolution of, 129, 132,
328
reprisals for Raiders' executions feared
by, 194
respect for international law urged by,
194, 195
surrender of, 82

ABOUT THE AUTHOR

Michel Paradis is a leading scholar and lawyer of international law and human rights. He has won high-profile cases in courts around the globe and worked for more than a decade with the US Department of Defense, Military Commissions Defense Organization, where he led many of the landmark court cases to arise out of Guantánamo Bay. He also holds the position of lecturer at Columbia Law School, where he teaches on the military, the Constitution, and the law of war. He has appeared on or written for NPR, MSNBC, the *New York Times, Washington Post, Wall Street Journal, Foreign Policy, Lawfare, America,* the *Intercept,* and the late *Weekly Standard.* He lives with his wife, daughters, and Yorkie in Manhattan.